fourth edition

An Integrated Language Perspective in the Elementary School

An Action Approach

CHRISTINE C. PAPPAS
University of Illinois at Chicago

BARBARA Z. KIEFER
Ohio State University

LINDA S. LEVSTIK
University of Kentucky

PEARSON
A and B

Boston • New York • San Francisco
Mexico City • Montreal • Toronto • London • Madrid • Munich • Paris
Hong Kong • Singapore • Tokyo • Cape Town • Sydney

Senior Series Editor: *Aurora Martínez Ramos*
Editorial Assistant: *Kevin Shannon*
Senior Marketing Manager: *Krista Groshong*
Editorial Production Administrator: *Annette Joseph*
Editorial Production Service: *Omegatype Typography, Inc.*
Composition and Manufacturing Buyer: *Andrew Turso*
Electronic Composition: *Omegatype Typography, Inc.*
Cover Administrator: *Joel Gendron*

For related titles and support materials, visit our online catalog at www.ablongman.com.

Between the time website information is gathered and then published, it is not unusual for some sites to have closed. Also, the transcription of URLs can result in typographical errors. The publisher would appreciate notification where these errors occur so that they may be corrected in subsequent editions.

Many of the designations used by manufacturers and sellers to distinguish their products are claimed as trademarks. Where those designations appear in this book, and Allyn and Bacon was aware of a trademark claim, the designations have been printed in initial or all caps.

Library of Congress Cataloging-in-Publication Data

Pappas, Christine.
    An integrated language perspective in the elementary school ; an action approach/
Christine C. Pappas, Barbara Z. Kiefer, Linda S. Levstik.—4th ed.
        p. cm.
    Includes bibliographical references and index.
    ISBN 0-205-39252-0 (alk. paper)
    1. English language—Study and teaching (Elementary) 2. Language arts
(Elementary)—Curricula. I. Kiefer, Barbara Zulandt II. Levstik, Linda S. III. Title.

LB1576.P257 2006
372.6–dc22

                                                                2005047622

Printed in the United States of America

10 9 8 7 6 5 4 3 2 1   10 09 08 07 06 05

Credits appear on page 438, which constitutes a continuation of the copyright page.

To our children, with love
Christina and Sara, Jon, Jennifer and Jeremy

Contents

6 Learning about Written Language   244

7 More How-To: Action Approaches in Integrated Language Classrooms   273

Guidelines for Teacher Inquiry 422

Acknowledgments

The authors would like to thank the reviewers of this edition:

    Diane Beals, University of Tulsa

    Carol Bowman, Ramapo College

    Debbie Doty, Northern Kentucky University

    Jacqueline Edmondson, Pennsylvania State University

    Lillian McEnery, University of Houston

    Randi Stanulis, Michigan State University

    Patricia Wheeler, Indiana State University

Their feedback was valuable in our journey in crafting this book.

Introduction

Teachers who work from an integrated language perspective *own*—with their students—their curriculum. Teachers plan and develop long-range study—called *thematic units*—so that their students have ample opportunities to use language for many meaningful purposes across the curriculum. In these classrooms, speaking, listening, reading, and writing are not separate subjects or ends in and of themselves, but tools that are used together for learning worthwhile and interesting multicultural content, ideas, and information. In the process, students learn both the content *and* the language. Activities and projects span the curriculum so that there is enough time for children to engage in systematic and reflective inquiry on a range of topics. As children use language to learn, their teachers collaborate, respond, facilitate, and support their efforts. These roles help teachers engage in their own inquiries into teaching and learning.

This fourth edition outlines our best and latest ideas about an integrated language perspective on teaching and learning in the elementary school, which now includes the middle school years through eighth grade. It is an action approach to implement theory and practice in educating students for a democratic, multicultural society. The thematic units that we depict in the book are informed by local, state, and national standards and guidelines, but they are also creative and reflect teachers' current classes of students. Only teachers who work with students on a day-by-day basis are able to develop curriculum that meets the needs of *all* children.

As teachers orchestrate and implement their curriculum through thematic units, they employ a range of routines, activities, or experiences that might be unfamiliar to you. Thus, beginning in this introductory chapter and throughout the book, any time we mention these routines, such as Sustained Silent Reading (SSR)*, Comparison Charts*, or Big Books*, we have marked them with an asterisk. You can find a more detailed explanation of these routines in Chapter 7, the how-to chapter. Another convention to note is that all of the titles of the thematic units we mention, discuss, or depict are in all CAPS for easy recognition.

To visualize what an integrated language perspective is like and to highlight some of the important themes of this fourth edition of the book, several scenarios are covered from two units (the first and last units covered in more detail in Chapter 4): a full-day kindergarten unit, WONDERING, and an eighth-grade unit called PERSPECTIVES.

1

Vignettes of Two Integrated Language Classrooms

Karla Jones's kindergarten

WONDERING thematic unit

WONDERING in Full-Day Kindergarten

Learning to Respond to Literature and the "What's Your Name?" Inquiry

Karla Jones, the kindergarten teacher, begins her first day of school helping children learn the major routines that will comprise each day (see Chapter 4 for details of her schedule), as well as briefly introducing the major topics that the children will be exploring for the first few months of school—names, going to school, the body, and so forth. She also launches the students' first inquiry about names, which is a means for them to get to know more about each other and for them to develop the community in which they will learn together this year. In addition, Karla believes that learning everyone's names will serve as an important resource for children learning about letters of the alphabet, phonemic awareness, and letter–sound relationships. This approach would make names salient for them, drawing the children's attention to these aspects of print to explore. Moreover, an important goal for this first day is to introduce the response journals they will use for the unit (and for the rest of the year).

Henkes (1991)

Making spaces for student voices is called interactive or dialogically oriented discourse.

She has the children gather around her as she reads *Chrysanthemum* by Kevin Henkes. This is her first read-aloud, so Karla wants children to know that they can offer their own ideas, comments, or questions as she reads books. "As I read, if you have something to bring up, let me know by raising your hand." As she reads the book, children bring up interesting comments about their own, their families', and friends' names. Sometimes several children may call out ideas simultaneously, which Karla affirms without noting that they had not raised their hands, because everyone seems to hear what each has said. Sometimes when more than one child speaks at the same time and their contributions overlap and may not be understood, Karla evokes the raising-your-hand "rule," pointing to three of the children, saying "one," "two," "three," so these students know that they will have an opportunity to share their ideas, but one at a time. Karla responds by accepting their initiations or sometimes asks for clarifications or expands on what a child has said. She also mentions that she is so glad that they are bringing up all of these good ideas because "we will be studying about everybody's names."

See Jones (2001) for a teacher who employed the one-two-three strategy to orchestrate student contributions.

At the end of the read-aloud, she has the children return to their desks. She and the helper of the day, Tyrone, pass out the Response Journals*. She tells the students, "I want you first to write your name—big—on the front. Your name is on your nameplate on your desk. Remember how everyone read his or her name before when we introduced each other." Karla spends a few minutes roving and helping various students in writing their names. Then she explains that this is a "response" journal—"it is a place for you to write and draw what you thought about the book we just read." She brings a large poster that lists possible ways for them to respond to the book: I liked . . . , I noticed . . . , I wonder . . . , I discovered . . . , I learned . . . , and so forth. Next to each phrase, she has a symbol (e.g., a heart next to "I liked," two eyes for "I noticed," a question mark for "I wonder") so that her emergent readers can begin to remember what each of these response possibilities represents. "So you can use any one of these to think about what you are going to say about the book. Or, if you have another idea that you want to write about and draw, that's fine, too. There is no right or wrong answer—we want to hear about *your* good ideas. You will use your kindergarten spelling, writing the best you can. And you will also draw what you thought was interesting or important in the book." As the children create their first response, Karla encourages children to think what they might say and draw. As they share with her what they might say, she encourages them to put down what letters make sense. As they draw, she has

Response Journals* provide opportunities for students to write about *and* draw their ideas about books.

Fisher (1995)

them explain how their picture relates to the book. Throughout, she takes notes on their efforts (even scribbles or strings of letters are okay at these early stages of writing), as she exclaims how interesting their ideas are, and how well their pictures depict those ideas.

Later in the day, she and the children have another read-aloud of the book *Nathaniel Talking* by Eloise Greenfield. Karla reads several of the poems in this book—"Nathaniel's Rap," "Making Friends," and "When I Misbehave." Afterward, Karla tells them about their name project. "We are going to do several inquiries about names." Latisha asks, "What's 'inquiries'?" Karla explains that the word *inquiry* is "finding out something, *wondering,* which we talked about in the morning. It is asking questions about something and trying to find some answers to them." As children seem to understand, Karla continues to tell them about their first inquiry. "The first one is for you to talk to your family about your name. You want to find out all about your name. Does it mean something? Are you named after another person? Do you have a nickname? How did you get your name and nickname? I have described this inquiry on a paper in an envelope for you to take home. I want you to remember to give it to your parents and ask them to read it and have a conversation about these questions about your name. Tomorrow, we will gather what everyone finds out and put it on a big chart." After answering any questions students have, Karla tells them that they can respond in their journals—write and draw—to any of the poems she read in the book.

Learning to Read Multimodally— Reading Text and Image

Karla's kindergarten is in an urban school, where many of the children have few books at home and have had few experiences of being read to as a regular practice. Karla, therefore, believes that she has to find ways to get children "hooked on books." One way she does this is to use lots of pop-up books, ones with which children can physically interact. Also, in using these books, Karla wants children to learn to attend to—to "read"—the pictures and illustrations in books, just as she had them write and draw to express and depict their ideas and meanings in their response journal. On this day, toward the end of the first week of the unit, during two morning read-aloud sessions, she quickly reads many pop-up books. She calls them "marathon" sessions, in which she quickly reads the texts, not asking for students' ideas this time, and not going into any depth on the various features of the pop-up books in the illustrations. "I'm not going over the pictures this time or giving you time to talk about the books the way we have before. That's because we are going to reread these books later on, and right now I want you to pay attention to and study how the person did the pictures—remember, we said that the person who did the pictures in a book is called the illustrator—and also who could be the author, the person who wrote the words of a book. In all of the books we will read this year, there will be the words to read and the pictures to read. To be a good reader—and writer—you need to learn both."

Karla has twenty-four students, so she has children pair up for twelve pairs of Buddy Reading*. She explains how they are to take turns reading each page, *carefully* exploring the illustrations, raising flaps, "feeling" the pictures, and pulling the tabs, which she has modeled during the read-alouds. She suggests that they go through the book several times because together each pair will share two important things they noticed as they read the pictures in their buddy-book—what the pairs thought were interesting, important, unusual, funny, and so forth. Karla gives each buddy pair two Post-it Notes to mark the two illustrations that the two buddies will share with the class. Students are excited to begin as she distributes the books. Although Karla has many more pop-up or flap books for students to examine and read during the unit, for this early experience, she has chosen a variety of some of the simpler ones—several books by David Carter (*Alpha Bugs, Feely Bugs, How Many Bugs in a Box*) and Eric Hill

Karla takes notes about student efforts as part of her ongoing assessment.

Greenfield (1988)

Finding out about students' names is a beginning inquiry in the unit.

Karla has marathon read-aloud sessions to quickly familiarize students about the message of the books and to model how to manipulate the pop-ups and flaps.

Literacy is a multimodal enterprise.

Carter (1994, 1995, 1988)

Hill (1980, 1994, 1996, 1998)

Cousins (1999); Demarest (2002); Augarde (2002); Pinto (2003); Capucilli (2003)

Students' responses to the pictures are shared with the class next to the Author's Chair*.

Students will create their own pop-up books.

Ed Tyson's Communication Arts and Social Studies block

PERSPECTIVES thematic unit

Hinton (1967); Philbrick (1993); Flake (1998); Anderson (1999)

The unit begins with responding to "outsiders" books via Literature Response Groups*.

A Sketchbook Journal* facilitates individual student response and small-group discussion.

Setting up response group "rules" is important for promoting rich discussions.

The *Freak the Mighty* group has its first response group meeting.

(*Where's Spot?*, *Spot Goes to School*, *Spot Sleeps Over*, *Spot Goes to the Farm*); and a book each by Lucy Cousins (*Where Is Maisy's Panda?*), Chris Demarest (*Here Come Our Firefighters!*), Steve Augarde (*Garage*), Sara Pinto (*The Alphabet Room*), and Alyssa Capucilli (*Biscuit Loves School*). As the buddies explore the books, Karla moves around the buddy pairs, noting their comments, asking what they are thinking about the illustrations, what they might choose to share later with the class, and what they might say about the two pages they have selected.

When all pairs are ready with their two pages with Post-it Notes, the buddies stand next to the Author's Chair* to present their findings of their reading of the illustrations. Because all of the children were familiar with all of the books due to the two marathon sessions, they ask questions or offer comments as well. After the whole-class sharing, children were very excited to read all of the books that the buddies read and shared. Karla will follow up with read-aloud sessions to reread the books, this time allowing for student comments. She will also emphasize during those times how the words in a book are connected to the pictures—sometimes the words tell certain ideas and the pictures tell different ideas, and sometimes the words and the pictures tell the same ideas but in different ways. She explains, "You want to read and wonder about *both* words and pictures." Toward the middle of next week, after all of the books are reread, Karla will ask all of the children to make their own two- to four-page pop-up books—or, as the children are already calling them, "flap books."

PERSPECTIVES in Eighth Grade

Responding to "Outsider" Literature

Ed Tyson teaches two sections of Communication Arts and Social Studies (as a block to two sets of students). He began the PERSPECTIVES unit with the topic of "outsiders." During the Communication Arts class, students are reading and responding to fictional literature from various authors—for example, *The Outsiders* by Hinton, *Freak the Mighty* by Philbrick, *The Skin I'm In* by Flake, and *Speak* by Anderson (see Chapter 4 for all of the options students had). Twice a week, on Tuesdays and Thursdays, students meet in Literature Response Groups* (sometimes called Book Clubs, Literature Study Groups, or Literature Circles) to discuss the books they have chosen to read. Each group (of three to four students) decides on when certain chapters are to be read, and each student prepares for these discussions by keeping a Sketchbook Journal*. Students note what stands out for them; they draw pictures or symbols that reflect powerful ideas or emotions; they create main Character Sociograms* to represent relationships with other characters; and so forth. (Ed had done a Focus Lesson* on the Sketchbook Journal* and on the possibilities of response, using copies of pages from these journals from previous students Ed has had.)

At the onset of the response groups, Ed and students worked on tentative "ground rules" for the group discussions, which they have put on a poster on the back wall. Ed told them he wanted them to have *real* conversations and to be respectful to each other so they could benefit from other points of view or perspectives. Ed emphasized the "perspectives" as a direct tie to the unit title and also set his expectations about student response for this unit and for the rest of the year. As he had the class brainstorm other "rules," students offered other ideas—"Don't hog the conversation," "Be ready to back up your ideas," "Don't feel that you have to have the right answer or response," "Questions are okay responses," "Encourage everybody in the group to have opportunities to talk," and "Be prepared for group!"

The *Freak the Mighty* group decided to read just two chapters for the first meeting (and then decide on how much to read for other meetings after they had a sense of the book). The book is about two boys, Max and Kevin, who both have unusual physical (and other) characteristics, and who become friends and partners so that together they were "Freak the Mighty." Josh begins the discussion with a question: "At the end of Chapter 2, do you really think that Max was sort of scared of Kevin?" Silky replies, "Oh, do you mean because Max says that 'that little dude really hates me. He *wants* me to die'?" Josh says, "Sort of," and then Jim and Whitney also bring in their own ideas. Both of them refer to earlier things that Max, the narrator of the story, talked about and how they had first met as preschoolers. Jim suggests that maybe even though Max was huge he was uncomfortable to do anything to young Kevin because he was on crutches and then braces, and Whitney notes that Max might have been sort of in awe of Kevin because he was doing all of these robot noises and telling Max he might have a laser cannon hidden inside his leg braces. The four seem to think that it could be seen either way. Silky thinks that they should follow this theme, maybe each doing some sociograms to track this aspect of Max and Kevin's relationship throughout the book.

Then all four shared their sketches—each had drawn Max or Kevin or both characters. Max was a big hulk of a guy (as Josh said), but "we don't really know much more about what he looks like." They all agreed, except that he didn't wear shoes that summer (and Josh, Jim, and Silky, who had drawn Max, had that feature in their pictures). Silky and Whitney depicted Kevin, showing him as small, with crutches, and having light-colored (blonde) hair.

Briefly, at the end of the group meeting, they decided to talk more about Max's grandparents, Grim and Gram, and Kevin's mother, "Fair Gwen of Air." All thought that these were strange names for grandparents (at least "Grim" for Max's granddad) and mother, and worthy of more attention. They decided to read four chapters for each meeting, which would also leave a separate meeting at the end to identify information that Ed wanted from each group to develop for a class Comparison Chart* on the outsider novels. Ed did not sit in this group's discussion today. He usually takes turns in visiting the groups, always sitting on the outside of them, taking notes, and not really participating unless students ask specifically for his response. Because it is the beginning of the year and literature response groups are new for some students in the class, Ed has asked them to rate each group's social processes (according to the poster rules the class had developed), and there is a whole-class debriefing on how groups did and what they need to work on next time. As has been his experience with small-group discussions, most groups do fine, but there are always a few groups that have "rough" patches that have to be ironed out in order to have rich and fruitful discussions.

Inquiry Projects in Outer Space

Ed's school is a departmentalized middle school that has grade-level pods where particular groups of students in a grade have the same teachers. This makes it possible for these teachers to get to know these students well and for them to be able to collaborate with each other regarding curricular topics in thematic units. For example, Maria Ruiz, the science teacher, has worked on an "Outer Space" subtopic for the PERSPECTIVES unit (see Chapter 4 for details of this and other subtopics that deal with the science curriculum).

The first week the class spent time identifying the various topics of inquiry that small groups of students will be exploring. They began with two whole-class sessions completing the first parts of a K-W-L Chart*. They brainstormed what students already knew about outer space, and what they wanted to know about it through their upcoming study. (What they will have learned will be noted on the chart at the end of the unit.) Through analyzing those items listed under the W column of the K-W-L Chart*, Maria and the class identified various areas of inquiry that small groups would work on in depth. Students' findings are to be reported in a classroom space museum that other students in the school will visit.

By the end of the first week, small groups are already busy with their individual study. During the Friday computer class, they used some relevant Internet sites that

Students share ideas that they might have noted down in print, as well as their sketches.

Maria Ruiz, the science teacher, is collaborating with Ed by having students explore the "Outer Space" topic.

The class began by identifying group topics of inquiry by first covering what they already knew and what they wanted to find out.

Internet websites, along with print-based books served as sources.

The Moon/Sun group will set up experiments, using ideas from two Gardner (1997a, 1997b) science project books.

may provide good resource material, and Maria and the librarian searched books that they could use and check out for study in and out of class. By the end of the next week, small groups were not only on their way in their inquiry, but also had some ideas about how they would report their findings in the museum. For example, the Moon/Sun group has planned a small pamphlet of information on its topic. This pamphlet will also describe various experiments to find out about the moon and sun, some of which they will set up in the museum. Another group called the "Zero G" group is studying how humans can adapt to life in space in the absence of gravity or weightlessness, which is one of the greatest challenges in space exploration. The members of this group, with the help from other classmates, have created interesting questions to examine: How does one live for months inside a small capsule in the company of only one or two others? How do astronauts eat and sleep when fresh food is unavailable and nights are only forty-five minutes long? How do they exercise and keep fit so muscular strength does not deteriorate? How do they go to the bathroom? This group has tentatively decided on a brochure that lists all of the various questions with short answers. They plan to illustrate each with their own sketches or by taking their own digital camera pictures in which group members "enact" various experiences—for example, Pedro pretends to shave and John is nearby with a small vacuum cleaner to catch the floating whiskers. They have already shown this particular picture to the class with great success during the weekly sharing time where groups report on the status of their inquiries to get feedback.

Several books are very helpful for the Zero G group inquiry—*Zero G*, *Escape from Earth*, and *NASA*.

Other groups are working on the planets (Planet group) and the Hubble telescope (Hubble group). Using ideas from *The Elements of Pop-Up: A Pop-Up Book for Aspiring Paper Engineers* and other resources, group members in the two groups are constructing third-dimensional models. (The math teacher, Ernie Kazminsky—students call him Mr. K—is developing a unit on ratios and beginning algebra to support the math students will need to create these models.) Another group is investigating the cosmic phenomena that are visible to the unaided eye—the great comets, meteor showers ("falling stars"), and total solar eclipses. Another topic has developed just this week that the class thinks should be examined as part of its study of outer space—namely, global warming—so three students from present four-member groups have volunteered to leave their groups to work on this topic. As Estelle explains, "It isn't really 'outer space' exactly, but it does have to do with the 'outer' atmosphere, so we think we need to study it." Because students from different groups had already come across some interesting information about global warming—which is why they thought it needed to be studied as a separate topic—they have all agreed to contribute all of their work and resources so far for this new group's endeavors. attempt

Carter & Diaz (1999)

Ernie Kazminsky, the math teacher, is also collaborating with Ed and Maria in the unit.

Pringle's book, *Global Warming*, was a salient resource in developing this topic of inquiry.

The teacher has an important role of facilitator in these group student inquiries. To that end, she has set up a Web-based blog so that she and students in the class can communicate with each other about the various group inquiries. As Maria explained, "We have limited class time to do all of the work you'll need to do for successful inquiries. And our weekly sharing meetings are just too short to cover everything that may come up, so we have to have other means to interact and know where we are, especially as we orchestrate our findings in setting up the museum. So we're going to use blogging to keep abreast of our work on your outer space explorations." She did a focus lesson on blogging after the class K-W-L graph organizer, showing how she posted their ideas, and then how they could extend the present "chart" and also further use the blogs during the unit. Blogging is a great tool for supporting such class investigation in many ways. For example, groups can provide weekly (or more frequent, if necessary) status reports on their inquiries for classmates and for Maria; Maria can use the blog to provide ongoing input, asking questions, providing extra information that might be useful for them; a group may ask for particular information or feedback on various tentative aspects or drafts of its ideas; a group may post information for another group that it came across in investigating its own area of study; and so

Maria is using a Web-based blog to support the "outer space" inquiries in the PERSPECTIVES unit.

Ferdig & Trammell (2004)

forth. Thus, blogs offer an integrated technical opportunity to monitor and support the inquiries of students in departmentalized classrooms where teachers see students approximately forty-five minutes a day. In fact, it was during the second week of student and teacher blogging that the possible topic of global warming emerged, which was finalized at a subsequent class meeting.

Summary

The preceding vignettes highlight the major five interrelated emphases in this edition.

Student-Directed Inquiry Is the Core of Children's Learning

We believe that *all* children—all humans—are active, constructive meaning makers. Children learn best when they are participating and engaging in the pursuit of essential questions and ideas about content connected to the world outside school. They are given opportunities to make choices about what and how to explore content; they collaborate with other students and the teacher in their study; and they are responsible for their own learning. This has always been a critical facet of the integrated language perspective, and we underscore it again in this edition. Inquiry projects provide students with authentic purposes for reading and writing a range of genres.

This is in contrast to the traditional, back-to-basics view, where children learn by passively practicing skills and facts from prepackaged materials.

A major reason for developing thematic units is to plan and organize curriculum as a blueprint for student-directed inquiry. Our emphasis in this edition on the essential questions and major concepts in the thematic units we talk about and illustrate in the book will make this feature of the perspective more evident.

Carroll (2004); Fried (2001)

Karla started her school year with the WONDERING thematic unit because she wanted to emphasize that learning is inquiry, even at kindergarten. Frequently, in more traditional classrooms, even older students are not used to engaging in inquiry or research. As a result, they lack skills in the inquiry process—how to choose topics, how to pose good questions, how to gather information or collect data from varied resources, how to organize and display this information, and so forth. However, both Karla and Ed (and his collaborating colleagues, Maria Ruiz and Ernie Kazminsky) use inquiry as the core of their curriculum. Thematic units enable many opportunities for these inquiries. Many are embedded in daily routines such as engaging in interactive, dialogically oriented read-alouds, writing and drawing in journals, meeting in response or inquiry groups, communicating with classmates and the teacher in blogs, and so forth. Inquiries allow for in-depth investigation, although they may constitute a number of interconnected smaller inquiries of shorter duration in the early grades, with longer ones in the upper-grade classrooms.

Lindfors (1999); Wells (1999)

Students Use a Range of Genres

Most human activities involve the use of language, and the nature of the language employed in these activities is determined on social grounds. This book reflects a social, functional view of language that considers two major questions: (1) How do people use language? Or what do people *do* with language? (2) How is language structured for use? We will use the term *text* to stress this functional role of language doing some job in some *context*. Based on contextual factors, language users make different linguistic choices, which in turn result in different wording patterns or different structures of text.

Eggins (1994)

A social, functional approach emphasizes how people use language and how language is structured for use.

Because there are recurring situations in the culture in which people interact and enact social activities, this contextual regularity gives rise to regularities in texts. These similar kinds, types, or classes of communicative events/texts are what is meant by

Kress (1993, 1999)

genres. That is, genres reflect patterns of textual and social regularity. By examining the nature and use of genres, we better understand what texts do and how they do it. And this understanding helps teachers see how best to create experiences in the classroom for students to use and learn the genres of our society.

Right in the beginning of the WONDERING unit, Karla read various genres. She read *Chrysanthemum*, a fantasy about a young mouse going to school, and poems from *Nathaniel's Talking*. The pop-up books represented a range of genres—alphabet books, counting books, fantasy stories, informational books on garages and firefighters, and so forth. In the PERSPECTIVES unit, students were reading and responding to "outsider" realistic fiction and using a range of information texts, including Internet websites.

We believe that children learn to read and write by engaging in a range of genres of high-quality children's literature and other media such as Internet websites. We think that although children's literature authors write *for* children, attempting to craft books that children will find interesting and exciting to read, these authors also use the typical linguistic patterns of adult genres and, therefore, better prepare students in literacy learning than do most textbooks, basals, or leveled books (which are contrived to teach only certain letter–sound features of words).

Literacy Is Multimodal

A big emphasis in this new edition is the multimodal nature of communication. The language mode is not the only way to express meanings. This mode is only one part of the broader communication landscape; others include the visual mode, the audio mode, the gestural mode, the spatial mode—and often communication consists of interrelated multimodal patterns of meaning. Language-based literacy is still necessary, but it is no longer sufficient for the kinds of literacy practices that already characterize and will continue to be developed in the future. Most books do not have just words; they also have pictures, graphs, charts, or photographs. Internet websites are comprised of various media. Karla had students paying attention to both the verbal and visual aspects of pop-up books; both Karla and Ed had students employing writing and illustrations in their response journals; Ed and Maria had students reading and writing verbal texts and also the various visual images that complemented them in the informational texts and the websites. Students were depicting their findings for the museum using a range of visual modes—photographs, three-dimensional displays, and so forth. Students need to develop mobility in meaning making among these modes of the communication landscape. This book provides many ways to create and assess multimodal curriculum and learning.

Classroom Instruction and Discourse Are Collaborative, Interactive, and Dialogically Oriented

Collaborative, interactive, dialogically oriented instruction and discourse are emphasized in this book. A certain teacher–student relationship, one where students engage in many opportunities to present and share their ideas, is explained and depicted. This is different from traditional classrooms where teachers control all of the classroom talk and topics of study. Dialogically oriented instruction and discourse are not all student centered—it is a joint venture in which both students and the teacher create knowledge together. Karla and Ed (in collaboration with Maria and Ernie) created units that allowed for many student-directed inquiries. Karla made sure that she had spaces for her kindergarteners' ideas in her read-alouds so she could respond to and build on their understandings. Ed provided literature response groups so his students could talk to each other about what they thought were significant in the "outsider" books. However, he monitored these group conversations so he could follow up on any misun-

[margin notes]

Genres, both oral and written, are classes of texts that recur because they do similar jobs in the world.

High-quality children's literature provides excellent examples of a range of genres to learn from.

Language is only one mode of a broader communication landscape.

Kress (2000, 2003); Unsworth (2001)

Students attended to both verbal and visual modes.

Burbules (2001)

Cazden (2001); Nystrand (1997); Wells (1999)

Dialogically oriented instruction and discourse constitute a joint teacher–student enterprise.

derstandings or had focus lessons to cover important points that students may have missed. Maria used blogs and weekly meetings to scaffold the group inquiries on outer space. And, as students became interested in the issue of global warming, it became an added topic of the curriculum. Thus, although teachers in integrated language classrooms develop thematic units to cover important essential curricular topics (and standards), the ways they implement the units permit mutual teacher–student dialogue. They treat students as apprentices.

Integrated Language Teachers Are Passionate, Collaborative, Reflective Teachers

Passionate teaching involves a love of ideas, mutual respect for students and their capabilities, and collaborative styles of teaching. There is no magic formula for teaching, but we believe that for it to be successful and meaningful in the learning and the lives of children, teachers must be ready to collaborate with the children in their classrooms. This is the only way that teachers can provide a multicultural education and develop culturally and linguistically responsive pedagogy. The purpose of this book is to try to help you be that kind of teacher.

Bartolome (1994); Fried (2001); Watson (2003); Willinsky (1990)

This notion of passion in teaching continues to be an important feature of the book. One of the major ways that teachers become passionate teachers is by taking risks, by being reflective about the teaching and learning in their classroom, school, and community. Passionate teachers are excited about content knowledge; they are challenged and captivated by how their students think about it and make connections of these content ideas in units to their life experiences. Thus, there are important parallels between teacher inquiry and student inquiry, and creating and implementing dialogically oriented instruction and discourse. Teacher research continues to be a topic throughout the book and in the "Guidelines for Teacher Inquiry" at the end of the book. We cover strategies and possibilities for both the already practicing teacher as well as the student teacher.

Teacher inquiry promotes and supports passionate teaching.

Reflective teachers raise questions about teaching–learning and study them in systematic ways, learning how to collect data as an integral part of their teaching. They develop ways of evaluating student learning in an ongoing manner; they create innovative performance-based assessment on how students apply what they have learned in their projects of inquiry. Karla collects data as her students write and draw in their journals; she takes notes as buddies decide which pages in the pop-up books to share. Ed sits outside the response groups to note issues or ideas group members are raising. Maria is making sense of the communication among her students as they explore the outer space topics. These teachers know about their learners in very in-depth ways, ways that cannot be captured via standardized tests. Thus, besides being better and passionate teachers, we believe that teacher researchers are better prepared to "speak out" about their students' learning *and* the issues in their profession.

Cochran-Smith & Lytle (1993); Hubbard & Power (2003)

An Overview of the Book

Descriptions of the book's chapters.

As its subtitle suggests, this book is an action approach that deals with the theory and practice of the integrated language perspective. The plan of the book is to provide you with the big picture in the first several chapters, and then in subsequent chapters to "go in close" by filling in more detailed, specific information. *Chapter 1* provides the theory and general principles of the integrated language perspective and introduces the concept of ideology and multimodal communication. *Chapter 2* describes the characteristics of the participants in the integrated language classroom—children and teachers—followed by the nature of classroom discourse that realizes a collaborative approach to teaching and learning. It also incorporates concepts of Developmental Discipline that we think are consistent with the perspective described in this book. *Chapter 3* shows how to plan thematic units. *Chapter 4* then demonstrates how to implement the units in the classroom and how to conduct teacher inquiry as an integral part of these thematic units. Nine prototypes in action at various grade levels and in various school settings are provided. *Chapter 5* goes into more detail about how to integrate language across various curricular areas—social studies, science, mathematics, and art and music. *Chapter 6* returns to the theory of the perspective introduced in Chapter 1, emphasizing important aspects of literacy. It provides a model of written genres, presents issues of ideology, explains more about the reading and writing processes, and includes more information about multimodal ideas as part of literacy. *Chapter 7* discusses in much greater detail many of the activities and routines mentioned in Chapters 3 and 4 (as well as in other chapters). *Chapter 8* covers a range of "kid-watching" procedures and techniques. *Chapter 9* deals with evaluation and accountability. *Chapter 10* provides suggestions for changing current programs in elementary schools along the integrated language perspective. Finally, *Guidelines for Teacher Inquiry* sets forth ideas for in-service and student teachers to *do* teacher research in fieldwork settings. Thus, these chapters are "integrated" in certain ways—Figure I.1 depicts how the major threads of ideas and themes in the various chapters and the Guidelines are interrelated in the book.

> **Explanations of the book's features**

In addition, four features have been incorporated to help you use this book more easily and effectively. The first feature is marginal notations, as you have already noted in reading this Introduction. Four types of notations are used throughout the book: (1) to cite the persons whose work and ideas we have drawn on in writing the book; (2) to refer to sources for possible further exploration of a topic, idea, or concept; (3) to highlight a specific concept, idea, or topic covered in the text; and (4) to provide a shorter definition or explanation of an important concept, idea, or topic discussed in the text.

> **figure I.1**
> **Interrelated Threads of This Book**

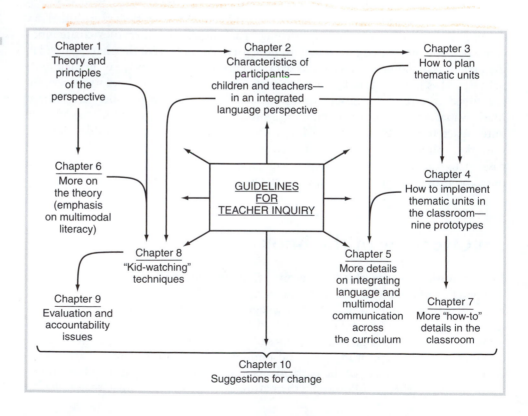

The second feature is a variety of activities that are found in Chapters 1, 2, and 6. Chapters 1 and 6 are heavy-duty theory chapters, and these activities are suggested to help you get a better understanding of the critical ideas about oral and written language that are discussed. Chapter 2 specifically covers the type of classroom discourse that is realized when teachers share power and authority with their students and take on a collaborative style of teaching. The activities offered in this chapter help you examine this crucial dimension of the integrated language perspective.

The third feature is the inclusion of bibliographic information for cited references. References are provided at the end of each chapter in two lists (when applicable): one provides the scholarly and professional works we have cited, listed alphabetically by author; the other gives the children's literature books we have mentioned, listed alphabetically by title.

The fourth feature is identifying routines, activities, or experiences that integrated language teachers employ in implementing their thematic units. These might be unfamiliar to you, thus, throughout the book, any time we mention these routines, such as Sustained Silent Reading (SSR)*, Comparison Charts*, Big Books*, or Literature Response Groups*, we have marked them with an asterisk. You can find a more detailed explanation of these routines in Chapter 7, the how-to chapter. Another convention to note is that all the titles of the thematic units we mention or discuss are in capital letters for easy recognition.

References

Bartolome, L. I. (1994). Beyond the methods fetish: Towards a humanizing pedagogy. *Harvard Educational Review, 64,* 173–194.

Burbules, N. (2001). The Web as a rhetorical place: In I. Synder (Ed.), *Silicon literacies: Communication, innovation and education in the electronic age* (pp. 75–84). New York: Routledge.

Carroll, P. S. (2004). *Integrated literacy instruction in the middle grades: Channeling young adolescents' spontaneous overflow of energy.* Boston: Pearson.

Cazden, C. B. (2001). *Classroom discourse: The language of teaching and learning.* Portsmouth, NH: Heinemann.

Cochran-Smith, M., & Lytle, S. (1993). *Inside/outside: Teacher research and knowledge.* New York: Teachers College Press.

Eggins, S. (1994). *An introduction to systemic functional linguistics.* London: Pinter.

Ferdig, R. E., & Trammell, K. D. (2004). Content delivery in the 'blogosphere.' *T.H.E Journal: Technological horizon in education, 31(7),* 12, 16–17, 20.

Fisher, B. (1995). *Thinking, and learning together: Curriculum and community in a primary classroom.* Portsmouth, NH: Heinemann.

Fried, R. L. (2001). *The passionate teacher: A practical guide.* Boston: Beacon Press.

Hubbard, R. S., & Power, B. M. (2003). *The art of classroom inquiry: A handbook for teacher-researchers.* Portsmouth, NH: Heinemann.

Jones, H. (2001). Creating safety zones in reading aloud to empower second graders as readers. In C. C. Pappas & L. B. Zecker (Eds.), *Teacher inquiries in literacy teaching-learning. Learning to collaborate in elementary urban classrooms* (pp. 113–124). Mahwah, NJ: Lawrence Erlbaum.

Kress, G. (1993). Genre as social process. In B. Cope & M. Kalantzis (Eds.), *The power of writing: A genre approach to writing* (pp. 22–37). London: Falmer Press.

Kress, G. (1999). Genre and the changing contexts for English language arts. *Language Arts, 76,* 461–469.

Kress, G. (2000). Multimodality. In B. Cope & M. Kalantzis (Eds.), *Multiliteracies: Literacy learning and the design of social futures* (pp. 182–202). London: Routledge.

Kress, G. (2003). *Literacy in the new media age.* London: Routledge.

Lindfors, J. W. (1999). *Children's inquiry: Using language to make sense of the world.* New York: Teachers College Press.

Nystrand, M. (1997). *Opening dialogue: Understanding the dynamics of language and learning in the English classroom.* New York: Teachers College Press.

Unsworth, L. (2001). *Teaching multiliteracies across the curriculum: Changing contexts of text and image in classroom practice.* Buckingham, England: Open University Press.

Watson, M. (2003). *Learning to trust: Transforming difficult elementary classrooms through Developmental Discipline.* San Francisco: Jossey-Bass.

Wells, G. (1999). *Dialogic inquiry: Toward a sociocultural practice and theory of education.* Cambridge: Cambridge University Press.

Willinsky, J. (1990). *The new literacy: Redefining reading and writing in the schools.* New York: Rutledge.

Children's Literature

The Alphabet Room by S. Pinto. Bloomsbury, 2003.

Alpha Bugs by D. A. Carter. Simon & Schuster, 1994.

Biscuit Loves School: Giant Lift-the-Flap by A. S. Capucilli. Illustrated by P. Schories. HarperCollins, 2003.

Chrysanthemum by K. Henkes. Mulberry Books, 1991.

The Elements of Pop-Up: A Pop-Up Book for Aspiring Paper Engineers by D. Carter and J. Diaz. Simon & Schuster, 1999.

Escape from Earth: Voyages through Time by P. Ackroyd. Dorling Kindersley, 2003.

Feely Bugs by D. A. Carter. Simon & Schuster, 1995.

Freak the Mighty by R. Philbrick. Scholastic, 1993.

Garage by S. Augarde. Charlesbridge, 2002.

Global Warming: The Threat of Earth's Changing Climate by L. Pringle. SeaStar Books, 2001.

Here Come Our Firefighters! by C. Demarest. Simon & Schuster, 2002.

How Many Bugs in a Box? by D. A. Carter. Simon & Schuster, 1988.

NASA by S. Tocci. Franklin Watts, 2003.

Nathaniel's Talking by E. Greenfield. Illustrated by J. S. Gilchrist. Black Butterfly Children's Books, 1988.

The Outsiders by S. E. Hinton. Viking, 1976.

Science Project Ideas about the Moon by R. Gardner. Enslow, 1997a.

Science Project Ideas about the Sun by R. Gardner. Enslow, 1997b.

The Skin I'm In by S. G. Flake. Hyperion Books for Children, 1998.

Speak by L. H. Anderson. Puffin Books, 1999.

Spot Goes to School by E. Hill. Puffin Books, 1994.

Spot Goes to the Farm by E. Hill. Puffin Books, 1998.

Spot Sleeps Over by E. Hill. Puffin Books, 1996.

Where Is Maisy's Panda? by L. Cousins. Candlewick Press, 1999.

Where's Spot? by E. Hill. G. P. Putnam, 1980.

Zero G: Life and Survival in Space by P. Bond. Cassell, 1999.

chapter

The Theory of the Integrated Language Perspective

The integrated language perspective is based on four major interrelated principles:

- Children are constructive learners. They are active meaning makers. They are continuously interpreting and making sense of their world based on what they have already learned, on what they have already constructed and reconstructed.

- Knowledge is in the minds of individuals. It is organized and constructed through social interaction. It is built-up mental representations that are based on our individual experiences and is constantly changing over our lives. Thus, it is always being modified; it is tentative and provisional. Knowledge is not a static, absolute, "out-there" object but a process of knowing or coming to know. Because we are social beings, our knowledge is always affected by our culture, existing social circumstances, the historical moment, and so forth.

- Language is a major system by which meanings are communicated and expressed in our social world. Because language is used for various purposes, our meanings are expressed in various ways, by various language patterns. Thus, language cannot be understood, interpreted, or evaluated unless it is related to the social contexts in which it is being used. Moreover, language and its patterns are learned through actual use, as part of human activity for various purposes in various social contexts.

- Although language is an important and prevalent mode to express meanings in communication, it is not the only mode. Oral and written language is part of a broader communication landscape that includes other modes of meaning—visual meanings, audio meanings, gestural meanings, and spatial meanings. Moreover, most of the time, communication consists of interrelated multimodal patterns of meaning. Learning these modes—and interrelations among them—is learned through social interaction and in participation in various social contexts of life.

In this chapter we examine these principles in more detail, and then extend and elaborate on them throughout the book. We begin by considering how children learn to use oral, or spoken, language.

Children are active, constructive learners.

Knowledge is organized and constructed by individual learners through social interaction.

Language is used for many social purposes that are expressed by many language patterns.

Language is part of a larger communication landscape that often interrelates with other modes of meaning.

How Do Children Learn Spoken Language?

Regardless of race, class, or family background, children learn their native language during infancy and the preschool years with ease and success. Without special tutoring or formal instruction they learn not only the structure of language but also how to use

13

it for numerous communicative purposes. They learn language within a natural environment of language use. An integrated language perspective applies to the classroom principles operating in early language acquisition. Therefore, the first question we must address is: What are the characteristics of a natural environment of language use? Infants, who initially do not know what a language is or what it is for, discover both by *interacting* with their immediate family and other members of their community. The medium of these interactions is *conversation*. Thus, our first step is to examine what goes on in our everyday face-to-face conversations.

What is the nature of conversation? How are conversations organized? Try to envision a normal conversation between two adults (a male and a female in this example). Consider the pattern of a typical conversation: First, the speaker expresses or translates the meaning of his experience, intentions, and ideas through a conventionally agreed-upon communication system so that these experiences, intentions, and ideas can then be shared with the listener, who is also an active meaning maker. The listener uses this coded message offered by the speaker and other cues provided in the situation to construct the meaning that she believes the speaker intended. She then signals in some way—by gesture or what she says next—that the meaning of the speaker's message has been understood. This exchange between a speaker and listener (who take turns as speaker and listener) is what linguists and psychologists call *intersubjectivity*. It means that I (the speaker) know that you (the listener) know what I mean, and you know that I know that you know. For any conversation to have any success at all, speakers and listeners have to be sure that they are talking about the same thing—referring to the same meanings. They also use *other modes of meaning* to make sense of what each is saying. They use gestures that participants might make or what seems to be reflected in their faces; they may use the stress or tone of certain words they utter. In addition, an integral part of these meanings that are being considered in this intersubjectivity are the values or *ideologies* that each participant expresses through language (and the other interrelated multimodal meanings).

Actually, this account of a typical conversation is too simplistic. It sounds as if the speaker's meanings are totally unknown to the listener until that speaker has completed his linguistic utterances during his turn in the conversation (and vice versa, for the listener's turn as speaker). In fact, at the very point of utterance, at the very beginning of a conversation, meanings are created for both participants. This is because, based on the situation or circumstances of the conversation, the listener usually has a good idea of what the speaker is going to say, the speaker can also predict what the listener will say next, and so forth. Most of these predictions are subconscious, operating below the level of awareness, and they account for most of what is understood in conversations. The ideologies the two members of the conversation may bring to the conversation are also subconscious, perhaps in this case because they are of a different gender and may see the topic from different perspectives.

This example also characterizes intersubjectivity in conversations as an all-or-nothing affair. That is not the case; rather, the intersubjectivity achieved by participants in conversations is always a matter of degree. We can all recall an extreme case, a conversation in which we felt that we and our conversational partner were not talking about the same thing at all. And sometimes it may be due to the fact that the other modes of meaning—the gestures or facial appearances—being communicated do not "match" with the linguistic content of the message. Nevertheless, most conversations are successful because most of the time intersubjectivity has been established.

Thus, an important aspect of a typical conversation is that it is a *collaborative* activity between participants who take turns offering, modifying, extending, and sustaining a meaning that is coconstructed by their joint efforts. In any conversation, participants must *negotiate* the meanings that are expressed. Again, it's done subconsciously—because each person has different ideas, experiences, and values. Also, each person has different purposes and expectations about what the conversation is to achieve. As with intersubjectivity, these processes of collaboration and negotiation are a matter of de-

---

Spoken language is learned within a natural environment of language use.

General organization of conversations

Intersubjectivity is understanding another's perspective so that meanings—including ideologies or values—can be shared.

Cope & Kalantzis (2000); Kress (2000, 2003)

Chouliarki & Fairclough (1999); Eggins (1994); Fairclough (1989, 1992); Lemke (1995); Luke (1996)

Bakhtin (1986); Hasan (1995)

Conversations require collaboration and negotiation.

gree. However, in most typical conversation interactions, each participant subconsciously makes constant adjustments to take account of the perspective of the other.

How do these ideas of intersubjectivity, collaboration, and negotiation function in learning spoken language? The following is a conversation between Mark, aged twenty-three months, and his mother (taken from Wells's longitudinal study of language development). This conversation occurred in the kitchen after breakfast while Mark's mother was involved in domestic tasks. Helen, Mark's nine-month-old sister, was also there, seated in her high chair. The conversation begins with Mark's discovery that when he looks into a mirror, he can see both himself and his mother. (See Figure 1.1.)

Even though Mark has limited linguistic resources—he uses one- or two-word utterances, and there is much repetition—it is clear that he is an active participant in a coherent conversation. His remarks are full of meaning and his mother is able to pick up that meaning and respond to it. They negotiate and collaborate to construct this meaning. Intersubjectivity occurs through his mother's responses in units 5 and 9 of Figure 1.1. It is lost later when she introduces a new topic (that Helen has fallen asleep) in units 17 and 18, but by unit 23, intersubjectivity has been achieved again. Now Mark can add information to his topic (*Jubs bread*) and his mother can take the meaning and reply with more information about the topic he has initiated. Note that Mark and his mother also use the stress of some of the words that Mark says—for example, Mark's utterances in units 1, 12, and 20. These are marked with a "v" to indicate that these were said to call or hold the attention of his mother. Moreover, it appears that both used his gaze (and perhaps also gestures) toward the mirror and the birds in the garden to accomplish the communication in the conversation.

Wells (1981)

Even very young children actively participate in conversations.

1	Mark: Mummy(v)		[Mark is looking in a
2	Mummy		mirror and
3		Mother: What?	sees reflection of
4	Mark: There, there Mark		himself and
5		Mother: Is that Mark?	his mother]
6	Mark: Mummy		
7		Mother: Mm	
8	Mark: Mummy		
9		Mother: Yes that's Mummy	
10	Mark: *		
11	Mummy		
12	Mummy(v)		
13		Mother: Mm	
14	Mark: There Mummy		
15	Mummy(v)		
16	There, Mark there		
17		Mother: Look at Helen	
18		She's going to sleep	
		(long pause)	
19	Mark: [e ə æ](=look at that)		[Mark can see
20	Birds Mummy(v)		birds in the
21		Mother: Mm	garden]
22	Mark: Jubs (=birds)		
23		Mother: What are they doing?	
24	Mark: Jubs bread		
25		Mother: Oh look	
26		They're eating the berries aren't they?	
27	Mark: Yeh		
28		Mother: That's their food	
29		They have berries for dinner	
30	Mark: Oh		

figure 1.1

Source: Wells, 1981, p. 102

Thus, this conversation between Mark and his mother is like an ordinary conversation. Turn-taking is well established, topics are sustained over turns, and both participants seem to understand each other's contributions. This successful interaction did not happen overnight. Its roots can be found in the time when Mark was a tiny baby.

Early Communication Developments

The past thirty years of research have indicated that intersubjectivity can be seen very early in infancy. Children have an innate ability to know another human being. Researchers have carefully studied the behavior of two-month-old babies and their mothers on videotape. They have been able to analyze how the babies move their whole bodies—how they move their mouths and faces, their hands and legs—along with those of the mothers' movements, and they have demonstrated that strong reciprocal, highly synchronized, interactional patterns exist between participants. The mother (or father, or another important caregiver) may talk to or smile at the young baby, who in turn may gurgle and move mouth and face (and other body parts) in such a way that researchers have termed the interaction a primitive conversation, or protoconversation. Thus, at the very beginning of life the infant's reciprocal behavior shows an ability to take account of another's perspective. These early interpersonal relations constitute a *primary intersubjectivity* and provide the initial communication framework by which children learn their language and how to make meaning in their culture.

The past several decades of research have shown that young babies also appear to know much more about the properties of objects than was earlier thought. Very young babies are endowed with an ability to hypothesize about how objects "work" in their world. At approximately six months, infants begin to interact with objects in a different way. As a result, a new kind of intersubjectivity is ushered in that influences language development in important ways. Before six months, a baby interacts with objects *or* humans but not with objects and people *simultaneously*. At this new stage, objects begin to be incorporated into the earlier, purely interpersonal intersubjectivity to form a new type of intersubjectivity called *secondary intersubjectivity*. As parent and baby interact with objects in everyday activities, the baby gains important understandings about action schemes involving objects. For example, the parent as an actor acts on an object such as a ball or cup, and the baby serves as recipient of this action. Then the roles of participants get reversed as the baby becomes the agent of the action on the ball (giving the ball back, for example), so that now the parent is the beneficiary of the action.

Another important aspect of language has its roots in this secondary intersubjectivity stage. Babies develop an understanding with their caregiver that they can share a focus on an object or person—a topic—that can then be commented on. That is, Baby, Mommy, or ball can serve as a topic about which something can be said: it can go or be up or pretty. Therefore, in the middle of the first year the young infant is already discovering two important universal features of language: that these basic relationships between agents (persons), actions, and objects can be encoded or expressed in language, and that an object in the world can serve as a *joint* topic, a focus that the baby can share *with* another person and that can subsequently be commented on. Much of what young children learn about the properties of objects is mediated by conversations about various everyday physical activities and is, therefore, largely constructed in social interaction.

The example of Mark's conversation shows how his present turn-taking, conversational exchanges with his mother have been supported by earlier reciprocity in routines of activity and vocalizations with another person. That is, Mark's language system has built on and extended these earlier understandings. His mother's showing that she values what he says in general, as well as the specific meanings he has expressed, is also present at the early beginnings of Mark's development of speech.

Mark also has clearly moved beyond what is called the *protolanguage* stage of language development that has been described by linguist Michael Halliday. Proto-

---

See Bates (1976) and Trevarthan (1979a, 1980) for more information on early infant communication.

Learning language and learning one's culture evolve out of early interpersonal communication.

Bower (1974, 1978); Kagan (1972); Stern (1985); Trevarthan (1979a, 1980); Trevarthan & Hubley (1978)

Trevarthan (1979a, 1979b, 1980); Trevarthan & Hubley (1978)

Secondary intersubjectivity

Bruner (1975a, 1975b, 1983, 1990)

Babies learn important universal properties of language through social interaction.

Halliday (1975, 1993)

language typically begins at the end of a child's first year or the beginning of the second year before conventional words, or vocabulary, and grammar develop. Protolanguage emerges when the child pairs certain sounds with certain meanings, or functions, in a regularized, systematic way. Mark's utterance in unit 19 of Figure 1.1 is a remnant of his protolanguage. That is, a particular set of sounds is used by Mark to mean "look at that." Babies can do things with language with such a system, although usually only immediate family members and caregivers can understand and interpret their communication efforts. One-year-olds, for example, can use their own sound-meaning constructions to give commands, get something, ask about something, or express a "we-ness" with another.

Protolanguage is a baby's system of regularized sound-meaning constructions.

Before adultlike grammar and vocabulary emerge, protolanguage provides a set of functions through which to communicate.

Back to Mark

Mark's language has developed from a protolanguage sound-meaning system to a rudimentary level of organization that relates meaning and sounds in a different and more complex way. Here are the beginnings of a *grammar,* a structural language system that allows him to mean two things at once. For example, Mark's *Jubs bread* (unit 24) enables him to express the meaning relationship of an agent, *Jubs* (his word for "birds"), and an object, *bread,* and at the same time express the pragmatic meaning of indicating this aspect of his experience (the birds and bread) to his mother.

Grammar: Language both classifies experience into categories and expresses that experience to others.

This primitive grammar will be gradually expanded and developed as Mark has more conversations about his everyday experiences. The next conversation (Figure 1.2) between Mark and his mother occurred two months later and gives us an idea of how children increase their mastery of the language system. Here Mark (now twenty-five months old) is looking out of the window. Earlier he had been watching a neighbor working in his garden and now the man has disappeared. Look how Mark has progressed in only two months! His utterances are longer and more complex (see units 11, 26, and 36 especially). He is a better respondent when his mother asks for information (units 17 and 22). Moreover, most of his talk deals with persons and events that are not present in the here and now but recalled or imagined. Here is evidence of Mark's developing understanding of a certain *script* in his culture: a knowledge of what typically happens at shops. A script, sometimes also called a *schema,* represents what Mark has generalized about the events that he has observed at the local shop and perhaps at others like it that he has visited. Mark's mother's behavior is critical in supporting this "story" about the shop. She provides a reasonable explanation for his question about where the man has gone. In units 9 and 10 Mark rejects it and provides in unit 11 an alternative—*gone to shop*—that is also expressed with a stressed tone to call his mother's attention. She checks this meaning in units 12 to 14 and then joins his game, again also giving him a message about how she values this kind of fun through language.

Wells (1981)

Nelson (1986); Swales (1990)

Scripts, or schemas, are generalized event knowledge.

Scripts specify obligatory and optional actors, actions, and props or objects relevant to particular goals and circumstances. Mark's mother helps him by suggesting the action of buying (unit 16) and then urges him to come up with different props. Mark tries out three actors as customers for the services obtained at the shop (the goal and circumstances of the script). First, the man (the disappearing neighbor), then his daddy, and finally Mark himself buy certain props. Mark tries out several props for the man to buy, but only Daddy and Mark buy sweets, obviously a favorite of Mark's.

These two conversations illustrate how children's participation in everyday conversations enables them to learn language *and* learn through language. In fact, these two types of learning are almost indistinguishable in the natural environment of language use. Notice how skillful the mother is in supporting this learning. She is "teaching" but not directing language lessons on sounds, words, or sentences, or lessons on birds or shops. She "leads from behind" by being "contingently responsive" to Mark's efforts. That is, she tracks and pays attention to what Mark is trying to express about what he already knows and what he is attempting to know. By addressing his meanings—which

Both learning language and learning through language are fostered in conversations.

Halliday (1975, 1982, 1993); Wells (1986, 1994)

figure 1.2

Source: Wells, 1981, p. 107

#	Mark	Mother	
1	Mark: Where man gone?		[Mark has seen
2	Where man gone?		a man work-
3		Mother: I don't know	ing in his
4		I expect he's gone	garden]
		inside because	
		it' s snowing	
5	Mark: Where man gone?		
6		Mother: In the house	
7	Mark: Uh?		
8		Mother: Into his house	
9	Mark: No		
10	No		
11	Gone to shop Mummy(v)		[The local shop
12		Mother: Gone where?	is close to
13	Mark: Gone shop		Mark's
			house]
14		Mother: To the shop?	
15	Mark: Yeh		
16		Mother: What's he going to buy?	
17	Mark: Er–biscuits		
18		Mother: Biscuits mm	
19	Mark: Uh?		
20		Mother: Mm	
21		What else?	
22	Mark: Er–meat		
23		Mother: Mm	
24	Mark: Meat		
25	Er–sweeties		
26	Buy a big bag sweets		
27		Mother: Buy sweets?	
28	Mark: Yeh		
29	M–er–man–buy		
	the man buy		
	sweets		
30		Mother: Will he?	
31	Mark: Yeh		
32	Daddy buy sweets		
33	Daddy buy sweets		
34		Mother: Why?	
35	Mark: Oh er–[ə] shop		
36	Mark: Mark do buy some–		
	sweet–sweeties		
37	Mark buy some–um–		
38	Mark buy some–um–		
39	I did		

include his values and beliefs—about the world, she expresses her values and helps Mark acquire a system of language structure to express or realize these meanings. Moreover, as noted earlier, Mark has acquired a system of multimodal meanings that interrelate with, and are part of, this linguistic system.

Bruner (1983); Kress (2000); Wells (1981, 1994); Wells & Chang-Wells (1992)

Spoken Communication

All language is communicated through texts.

People express meanings in both oral and written language through text. We do not speak or write isolated words or sentences. Instead, we speak and write through connected discourse or text. Individual words and sentences in a text can be understood only when they are related to other words, sentences, or the text as a whole. However, oral and written texts are different because they serve different purposes in our culture.

This section examines the nature of oral language texts so that they can be contrasted with written language texts and the reading and writing processes in a later section.

What Is a Text?

A text, either spoken or written, is a social exchange of meanings—a semantic unit. *A text is both a product and a process.* It is a product in that it is an output of a particular social interaction that can be recorded and studied. The two conversations between Mark and his mother in the preceding section were texts in this sense. In fact, every language example in this textbook is such a product (although no oral language texts could ever be duplicated exactly in print, of course).

It is the second sense of text that we want to emphasize, however. A text is also a process in that it represents a *continuous process of semantic choice* based on factors that are operating in a particular context of situation. For any context of situation, we can ask three general questions: (1) *What's happening?* What is the setting or subject matter? What are the topics being discussed? (2) *Who is taking part?* What is the personal relationship of the participants? (3) *What role is the language playing?* What do the participants expect their language to do for them in the situation? What is the purpose of the language being used?

On the basis of these three contextual factors, participants select certain wordings or expressions to relate their meanings. Consequently, Mark's and his mother's linguistic contributions were choices made because of particular factors operating in each conversational setting. And we couldn't have evaluated or even understood their wordings unless we also considered this situational information.

Language is a meaning potential or resource, and drawing on this resource, speakers make certain linguistic choices on the basis of what's going on in a situation. Different situations result in different linguistic choices, different wording patterns. For example, a college student's discussion of homework with a roommate in a dormitory would be different from this same student's conversation with a blind date while en route to a movie, which, in turn, would be different from the student's talk when meeting with the college dean over some academic issue. Our language varies depending on the context in which it is used. Language variation that exists in varying contexts is called *register*.

Typical Oral Language Registers

The participants' utterances in the following excerpts were all overheard at a place that is well known in our culture. Read through each numbered excerpt as though it were a clue, and see if you can guess where the language occurred:

1. *A:* How far do you want to go?   *B:* [Shrugs shoulders]

2. *A:* I want to sit in the first one.   *B:* Okay.

3. *A:* Right here.   *B:* Go ahead.

4. *A:* Ah, it's nice and cold in here.   *B:* Brrr! I'll say.

5. *A:* Did you forget your glasses?   *B:* Nah. [Pats glasses in shirt pocket]

6. *A:* Why are you sitting here?   *B:* 'Cause Joe is already sitting here.

7. *A:* Do I have a choice?   *B:* Sure.

8. *A:* Here's a seat.   *B:* Get in front.   *C:* Not too far.

A text is a social exchange of meaning.

Halliday (1996); Halliday & Hasan (1985); Halliday & Matthiessen (2004); Hasan (1995)

- A text represents a process of semantic choices.
- A text always relates to a context of situation.
- Context of situation: (1) What's happening? (2) Who is taking part? (3) What role is language playing?

Language is a resource used to express meanings to others.

Register is language variation.

Could you figure out where the texts were produced? Some people are puzzled until they read text 8. Many others continue to be perplexed, but then they all nod with understanding once the answer is given: a movie theater. All these excerpts, as you have probably already concluded, were gathered while people were finding their seats before the movie began. We can imagine the kind of language that would have been used in the lobby while people bought their tickets and refreshments. After the movie, the language would probably have been centered on the content of the movie. This language would be more difficult for us to predict because it would be so directly related to the specific movie being seen, but we could imagine what would most likely be discussed. For example, people would probably use evaluative language to report whether they liked the movie—their ideologies may be even very evident as they share or even debate about how they valued aspects of it. Perhaps they would also include in their conversations information about other movies of the same type or other movies made by the same actors, directors, and producers.

We want to make two important points about the language in the foregoing excerpts. First, the language is typical oral language that accompanies action—in this case, finding a seat at a movie during the summer (where there is air conditioning in the theater, hence, the remarks in text 4). Attention is focused only partially on what is said. Nonverbal gestures and other perceptual cues, such as specific objects present or the emphasis or tone of a participant's voice, contribute and support the meanings expressed in the actual situational setting. In conversations such as these, words fit the world. Short responses, such as *okay, sure,* and *go ahead,* as well as nonverbal gestures, such as shrugging one's shoulders, are typical in such contexts. Terms such as *the first one* and *here,* referring to a row, a seat, or the theater itself, that may have seemed ambiguous to you are easily interpreted by participants in the conversations.

The second point is that once you found out about the social situation, the language appeared to be familiar. This is because you already have a script, a schema, a mental representation about the events that typically occur at a movie theater. Along with this event knowledge, you also know about the kind of language (the type of linguistic register) that is likely to be used to express the meanings at a particular instance of this script. You can even predict or consider variations of this script. For example, if you have been to an opera or symphony concert, you know that open seating is unlikely. Tickets for particular seats must be purchased ahead of time, and an usher probably helps you find your seat. In contrast, seeing a rented movie on VCR equipment in your own home presents a related but very different variation of the going to the movies script.

During the preschool years, children acquire considerable event knowledge or scripts about a variety of familiar experiences (getting dressed scripts, baking cookies scripts, birthday party scripts, or going to restaurants scripts) and a range of oral language registers to express meanings in these contexts. Children learn to adjust their linguistic choices to meet the features of particular social contexts in their culture—the setting, the participants, and the specific task at hand. By the time children begin kindergarten they have remarkable oral *communicative competence;* they know how to use language appropriately in many social contexts. Moreover, they possess communicative competence in nonlinguistic modes—and how these modes might be interrelated with or integrated in linguistic messages. They are already expert "semioticians" in that they can "read" situations—that is, assign meanings to them—and act in suitable ways. They have also acquired a considerable vocabulary and internalized the fundamental aspects of grammar. In addition they have learned a lot about the "grammar" or patterns of other modes of communication.

Unfortunately, we do not always appreciate children's already developed control of language. If a child says very little (one- or two-word utterances) to our questions in the classroom, we frequently believe that the child has impoverished language skills. Teachers do not always consider that the child's short answers may actually be appro-

Margin notes

Spoken language usually accompanies action.

Halliday (1977, 1996); Hasan (1984a, 1996)

In typical oral language, words fit in the world.

Donaldson (1978); Lindfors (1999); Wells (1986)

Language is predictable.

Nelson (1986); Swales (1990)

Communicative competence is knowing how to use language appropriately on the basis of context.

Kress (1997); Newkirk (1989)

Children are adept semioticians—they have the social abilities to make sense of their culture.

Children's sparse language is rarely due to anything wrong with them but due instead to the particulars in the social setting.

priate in the social setting operating at that time. Nor are teachers always aware that in a particular context, children's language would reflect their distinctive "ways with words," which they have learned to assign meanings and use language competently in similar social circumstances in their communities.

Hasan, (1996); Heath (1983, 1996); McCollum (1991); Nieto (2000)

What are questions and answers like in everyday social contexts? Two examples follow. Example A illustrates a typical exchange between a parent and a teenager.

Example A

1. *Q:* Have you finished your homework?   *A:* Yes.
2. *Q:* Even your math?   *A:* Well, no.
3. *Q:* Cleaned up the kitchen?   *A:* No.
4. *Q:* When are you going to?   *A:* Soon.
5. *Q:* Promise?   *A:* Yes.

Except for question 1, all the questions in Example A are abbreviated, and all the answers are short. Yet you were able to understand the exchanges. These abbreviations are grammatically appropriate as well. They are what linguists call *elliptical constructions:* they presuppose or rely on other information already given. For example, in answer 1, it is understood that the *yes* is an affirmative response to the question about whether the teenager had finished the homework. The one-word response does not indicate the teenager's linguistic incompetence; instead, *yes* demonstrates that the teenager understood both the *content* and *form* of the question. In this context, *yes* is enough of an answer. The parent's questions 2 and 3 are also enough. *You* (the teenager) and *finished* in question 1 are meanings presumed in these questions; they need not be expressed again. The remaining questions and answers are likewise adequate.

Questions and answers in the real world are frequently short.

Now read through Example B, where all the presupposed understandings are included.

Example B

1. *Q:* Have you finished your homework?   *A:* Yes, I have finished my homework.
2. *Q:* Have you even finished your math?   *A:* Well, no. I haven't finished my math.
3. *Q:* Have you cleaned up the kitchen?   *A:* No. I haven't cleaned up the kitchen.
4. *Q:* When are you going to finish your homework and clean up the kitchen?   *A:* I am going to finish my homework and clean up the kitchen soon.
5. *Q:* Do you promise to finish your homework and clean up the kitchen soon?   *A:* I promise to finish my homework and clean up the kitchen soon.

Example B sounds unnatural because it is not typical of everyday conversations. This example, however, represents the kind of questions and answers that are promoted in many language textbooks and programs (especially for nonmainstream, culturally and linguistically different students). Teachers following the routines in these programs may ask children questions such as "How are you feeling?" or, pointing to a picture of a cat in a tree, "Where is the cat?" Answers such as "fine" or "in the tree" are not acceptable responses according to these programs. Instead, children are required to answer, "I am feeling fine," or "The cat is in the tree." They are admonished to say it in a "whole sentence," presumably because talking this way will teach them language skills. If they talked like this anywhere else, however, their speech would be considered odd.

Another feature of the questions in Example A is that they are genuine and authentic. The parent actually wants to know if the teenager has finished the homework and cleaned up the kitchen. Or perhaps, depending on the history between the parent

Questions and answers in the real world are authentic.

and teenager about homework and household duties, the parent is also attempting to remind the teenager about these responsibilities. Various family ideologies about the teenager's need to do household tasks and homework (as well as the teenager's resistance to them) may also be operating here, too. At any rate, very few questions in traditional classrooms are like those in Example A. Relying on questions from basal readers, language, social studies, and science textbooks, and so forth, teachers tend to look for answers that they themselves already know. These materials frequently list questions the teachers should ask as well as the "right answers" to these questions. In a story about a boy whose dog has run away, the teacher's manual of a basal reader may tell teachers to ask questions such as "What ran away?" "How did the boy feel?" "What was the color of the dog?" Next to these questions, the answers "the dog," "sad," and "black" may be found. Because teachers always ask the questions and because they already have the answers, children are always in a respondent position to provide answers that indicate the possession of certain information and vocabulary. In reading lessons and in the other lessons in other school subjects, children are given few opportunities to take an initiating role in asking their own questions. They are rarely asked about their own plans, thoughts, or feelings concerning their activities. (The descriptions and implications of traditional classroom talk versus alternative, more collaborative discourse, in which children do have opportunities to offer their own ideas, are covered in more detail in Chapter 2.)

Teachers obviously know about the nature of spoken language because they use language appropriately in a range of communicative contexts. However, their knowledge may be subconscious or tacit. Unless this tacit understanding becomes more of an explicit awareness on the part of the teachers, several things will happen. First, if they are not sensitive to various typical oral language registers or culturally different discourse styles, teachers will be confused about the "correctness" of children's spoken language. They will mistake appropriate children's language behavior as deficits. Second, without an understanding of how spoken texts are created and used, teachers will not be able to provide opportunities for children to employ a range of oral language registers in the classroom, nor will they be able to accommodate children's diverse "ways with words," the ways that children have learned to participate successfully in conversations in their communities. Finally, unless teachers recognize how spoken language differs from written language, teachers cannot support children in learning to use written language effectively. (Activity 1 at the end of this chapter can help you explore more about spoken language registers.)

See Activity 1.

Written Communication

As discussed in the previous section, we also communicate in written language through texts. Written texts are structured differently than typical spoken texts because we use them in our culture to serve different communicative functions. One of the most obvious differences between a spoken text and a written one is that a typical spoken text is constructed collaboratively by the participants in a conversation. In contrast, a reader's or writer's use of a written text is more of a solo enterprise. Readers and writers, usually unknown to each other, communicate across space and time. Consequently, written texts require a disembedded quality. Wordings must be organized in a different way and different language registers must be employed to accomplish this type of communication.

As will be noted in more detail later, even if a written text is usually used alone in a physical sense, a reader and writer can still "collaborate" with each other because each has internalized the conventions of language registers. Each has an idea of the kinds of interpretations that are likely, based on the ways the language patterns of the written text are expressed.

Written texts are different from spoken texts.

Halliday (1985, 1987, 1993, 1996); Nystrand & Wiemelt (1991); Smith (1982a, 1982b); Tannen (1985); Wells (1981, 1985, 1986, 1994); Wells & Chang-Wells (1992)

Written texts serve many various communicative functions.

Written texts are expressed by many various language registers.

Typical Written Language Registers

What are typical written language registers? How are they different from spoken texts? It is not the channel of communication alone—oral or written—that distinguishes written from spoken texts. Written phone messages can look like oral texts; oral presentations or lectures can be like written registers. Instead, it is the entire context in which the language is used and all factors (the setting, location, participants, and purpose) operating in that context that determine how particular language patterns are organized. Important differences between oral and written texts exist, but these differences do not represent a dichotomy based solely on whether a text is oral or written.

To clarify some of these differences, let's start by considering the following text. Can you interpret it?

You got a big *one* today.
It's got *lots*. *It*'s got *more* than *the other one*.
Can *I do it*?

The reason you are having trouble figuring out this text is that it is the beginning of a typical conversation. Although it was completely appropriate and understood in the context in which it was uttered, only information about the situation will enable you to decipher it.

Context

A six-year-old child is getting ready to dictate an original story, and a visiting teacher is preparing to take down the child's dictation. The story will be tape-recorded as it is being dictated, and this is a familiar routine for both participants. A new tape recorder has been brought to school today and is the focus of shared attention. The child is touching the buttons on the new recorder as she speaks the words above.

Now it is easy to figure out what the italicized words mean. *You* and *I* refer to the teacher and the child, the two participants in the conversation. The words *one* and *it* refer to the new tape recorder and *the other one* to the tape recorder that had been used in the past. *Lots* and *more* are easily understood as "lots of buttons" and "more buttons" (than the old tape recorder had). Finally, *do it* means "push the buttons."

The foregoing italicized words are *implicit* linguistic devices. They are called implicit because their interpretation must be found by reference to some other source. The question is: Where is that interpretative source? We have argued that a strong relationship exists between context and text structure, or the ways words are organized or patterned in texts. Thus, for any linguistic unit on which we want to focus, there are two environments: (1) the extralinguistic environment or actual situation (i.e., the context) related to the total text, and (2) the linguistic environment (i.e., the co-text), the actual language accompanying or surrounding that linguistic unit. Consequently, implicit devices could either be co-textual or purely contextual. In the foregoing conversation about the tape recorder, the source of interpretation for these implicit devices is contextual. The implicit devices are called *exophoric* because the source of their interpretation lies outside the co-text; they can be understood only through an examination of the immediate context of situation. Figure 1.3 depicts aspects of the situation that provide the interpretative sources for the exophoric implicit devices used in the conversation about the tape recorder. (Activity 2 will help you explore more about exophoric implicit wordings.)

The use of exophoric implicit wordings is typical in spoken language. Although the oral text example we have included is perhaps an extreme case with respect to its density of exophoric implicit wordings, it is a useful illustration to demonstrate that in conversations, words fit in the world. In written language, however, words create a world in that implicit and other types of wordings are chosen so that the text stands on its own. The typical written text creates its own context of situation, and the source

Implicit wordings

Halliday & Hasan (1976, 1985)

Two interpretative sources: situational environment, or context; and linguistic environment, or co-text.

Exophoric implicit devices point *outward* to the immediate situational context.

See Activity 2.

Wells (1986)

Words create a world in written language use.

figure **1.3**

You got a

big one

today. It's

got lots.

It's got more

than the

other one.

Can I do it?

Kress (2000, 2003)

of interpretation of implicit devices lies within the co-text, not the immediate sur-roundings in which a text is being used. (However, as will be argued in a later section in this chapter, such written linguistic texts do not exist by themselves. For example, texts in books, pamphlets, brochures, magazines, media and internet displays, and so forth, are often accompanied by other modes of the communication landscape—audio, visual, spatial, and gestural. Thus, although written texts rely on the wordings expressed in the co-text for interpretation more than oral texts do, these written mean-ings also interrelate—sometimes in significant ways—with patterns of meaning ex-pressed from nonlinguistic communication modes.)

We will discuss excerpts from two written texts to help you better understand these differences of language variation that characterize linguistic registers of written communication.

Two Examples of Written Texts

Wildsmith (1971)

Figure 1.4 contains the first six sentences of *The Owl and the Woodpecker,* a story writ-ten by Brian Wildsmith. Let's look first at how the author used implicit devices. In the first sentence *a Woodpecker* is introduced. This woodpecker then becomes the source with which to interpret subsequent implicit devices. The definite article *the* plus *Wood-pecker* are used (in sentences 2, 4, and 6) to refer back to the woodpecker. Other pro-nouns, *he, his, you, my,* and *I,* are also used to refer to the woodpecker and are thereby easily understood. The same kind of use of implicit devices is employed by Wildsmith with respect to the other main character and the woodpecker's tree. *An Owl* is pre-

figure 1.4
The Owl and the Woodpecker
Source: Wildsmith, 1971

sented in the third sentence and serves as the interpretative source to understand *the Owl* (in sentences 4 and 5) and *I* (in 5), and *there* (in 5) and *it* (in 6) through earlier mention of tree (in 2 and 6).

You can see that the implicit devices in this example of written language are very different from those we have seen in conversations. Rather than being exophoric, referring to items outside the text, these implicit devices in typical written language are *endophoric*. They refer to items inside the text for their interpretation. This doesn't mean that exophoric implicit wordings can be found only in spoken language and that endophoric implicit ones exist only in written language. Oral language also contains a lot of endophoric implicit wordings—for example, the elliptical constructions illustrated in the conversation about homework (page 21) were endophoric. Moreover, certain exophoric implicit wordings may also occur in written language, perhaps to refer to some visual aspect in an illustration, chart, graph, or diagram. It is a matter of degree: exophoric implicit wordings are typically found in spoken language because spoken language accompanies action; endophoric implicit wordings are usually present in written language because written language is used for more "disembedded" communication.

In written texts, the use of endophoric implicit wordings creates "threads" or "chains" of meaning. These threads or chains, illustrated for the woodpecker, owl, and the woodpecker's tree in Figure 1.4, run throughout the text. The chains help the text "hang together"; they contribute to the text's coherence. Because written texts, like stories, can be read at any time or place, they have to be more explicit than spoken text. Because written texts sustain continuous messages that do not rely *directly* on particular sets of circumstances for understanding them, implicit devices are usually used endophorically, and lexical, or content wordings—nouns, verbs, adjectives, and adverbs—are employed to a much larger extent. In addition, lexical items, or vocabulary, are frequently more formal and less colloquial. (Chapter 6 discusses these aspects of written language in more detail.)

The fact that typical written texts possess a disembedded quality and cannot be seen as having a direct relation between their message and the immediate surroundings in which they are being used does not mean they are not related to some context but that they are related to a context of our social system in a more complicated, indirect way. Written texts serve various purposes in our culture. Storybooks such as *The*

Halliday & Hasan (1976, 1985)

Endophoric implicit devices point *into* the text.

Endophoric implicit wordings form threads or identity chains within the text.

Pappas (1993); Hasan (1984b)

Chafe (1985); Chafe & Danielewicz (1987); Halliday (1985, 1987, 1996)

Written texts are also related to social contexts in our culture.

Bakhtin (1986); Halliday (1985, 1993, 1996); Halliday & Hasan (1985); Swales (1990)

Wildsmith (1974)

Information texts are expressed by different registers from stories.

Martin (1985, 1992); Martin & Peters (1985); Pappas (1991a, 1991b, 1993)

Classification chains, not identity chains

Owl and the Woodpecker create imaginative worlds and are used to entertain young children in our culture. Other written texts—for example, the information book *Squirrels*—also written by Wildsmith—play a different role in our culture. They attempt to explain and describe humans, animals, objects, places, and happenings in the world to young children. Variation in purpose and context in our culture means variation of language. Consequently, other registers and linguistic patterns are found in information books, as revealed by the first few sentences of *Squirrels* in Figure 1.5.

Consider the implicit pronoun devices first. *He* is used three times and *his* twice, all referring to *a squirrel* in the first sentence. Also, there is an *it* (in 5) that refers to *coat* (in 4). Thus, as in *The Owl and the Woodpecker*, the implicit devices used in *Squirrels* are endophoric. They refer to aspects of the co-text for their interpretation.

However, take another look at the *Squirrels* excerpt. Note that the threads or chains created are different in a subtle but important way. In *The Owl and the Woodpecker* the threads involved the same individual or animal (woodpecker and owl) or object (tree). In contrast, in *Squirrels* the threads depict a class of animals (squirrel) and object or part of a squirrel (coat). For example, if you trace the squirrel chain (illustrated with a single line) in Figure 1.5, you will discover that it does not refer to the same individual squirrel but to the same animal class, that is, all squirrels. This is why it is possible to include in this chain the plural form of the class, namely, *squirrels* in the last sentence. Thus, although Wildsmith used the same forms (*a woodpecker* and *a squirrel*) in the first sentence of each book, as well as the same implicit device *the* (plus *woodpecker* and *squirrel*) in both books, these forms are functioning quite differently in each book.

Most information books are similar to *Squirrels*. For example, they don't identify particular persons as characters and then follow their conflicts, motives, reactions, and

figure **1.5**

Squirrels

Source: Wildsmith, 1974

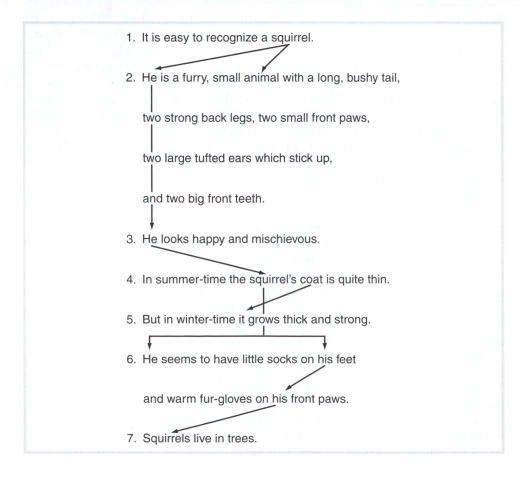

1. It is easy to recognize a squirrel.

2. He is a furry, small animal with a long, bushy tail,

   two strong back legs, two small front paws,

   two large tufted ears which stick up,

   and two big front teeth.

3. He looks happy and mischievous.

4. In summer-time the squirrel's coat is quite thin.

5. But in winter-time it grows thick and strong.

6. He seems to have little socks on his feet

   and warm fur-gloves on his front paws.

7. Squirrels live in trees.

exploits as stories do. Instead, information books make general statements about animals, objects, places, or people. Other linguistic features contribute to the general nature of information books that can be illustrated in *Squirrels*. Information books use the present tense; for example, *is, looks, seems to have.* (Storybooks are usually in the past tense, except in quoted dialogue.) Information books contain a lot of descriptive constructions (e.g., "[*a squirrel*] *is a furry, small animal . . .*"). (Of course, storybooks also contain descriptions but not nearly as many as information books.)

These are only some examples of the wording patterns found in information books. Again, just as teachers have a subconscious awareness of various types of spoken language registers, they also have a tacit understanding of various written language registers. They subconsciously know that meanings are expressed in imaginative, fictional narrative through wording patterns different from those expressed in nonfictional expository texts. However, unless these tacit understandings become more explicit, teachers will not be able to expose children to representative examples of the written genres used in our culture or to support children's efforts to read and write these genres on their own. (Activities 3 and 4 can help you explore more about differences between oral and written registers and about the differences between typical storybooks and information books.)

See Activities 3 and 4.

Examining Ideologies in the Two Written Texts

Different kinds of ideologies, values, perspectives, or biases are also expressed in different genres by various authors. Let's look at each of the Wildsmith books to examine the possibilities. In *The Owl and the Woodpecker,* the two main characters, the owl and the woodpecker, as well as all of the other animal characters, are male. The major conflict in the book involves how the woodpecker's pecking is keeping the owl awake all day. The owl becomes more and more irritable, causing strife in the forest. There is a meeting of the animals about this problem but no useful strategies come from it. It is only when a crisis of a great storm occurs and the woodpecker saves the owl's life by pecking next to his ear to wake him up that a solution to the problem gets developed.

So what perspectives might be examined here? First, the fact that all the characters are male is something that might be considered, as well as whether this maleness might have been seen by Wildsmith as necessary for creating the conflict in his story. That is, would the author have had to come up with a quite different conflict if his main characters had been female or if they had been of different genders? What "hidden" messages are given by the all-male cast, the failure of conflict resolution by the animals in the forest, or the characterization of the owl as a bully toward the smaller animals?

In the *Squirrels* book, Wildsmith also used masculine pronouns (*he, his, him*—instead of *it*) every time he referred to the singular form of the squirrel class. The only exception is the small section in which the female squirrel is mentioned and the birth of baby squirrels is covered. Can an informational book like this be giving a subtle message about gender? What is it? Also, do some of the vocabulary words in this book reflect the ideological claim that factual information about squirrels for young children should be written differently from factual writing about that topic for adults? That is, if the audience were adults, would a squirrel be described as "happy and mischievous" or as having "little socks on his feet"?

Our use of language is influenced by our values, or ideology, no matter what genres we are involved in. Sometimes the perspectives or biases embedded in language are easy to spot. However, most of the time these values are very subtle and unconscious and, therefore, hard to detect. Because the vocabulary and the grammatical patterns realized in texts (as well as the illustrations used in books) are integrally related to ideological issues, a critical stance has to be present in teaching reading and writing. However, for reasons that are themselves ideological, few of us have been educated to

All texts/genres reflect ideologies.

identify or examine ideology in texts. Instead, we have learned to read texts as kinds of "*natural* representations of reality," and we have never considered what values or biases we might be expressing when we write texts or use illustrations or other visual designs. Thus, understanding the ideological features of texts, other modes of the communication landscape, and other related issues of education is a major challenge for integrated language teachers who want to help their students develop this critical view in literacy learning.

It's a Multimodal World: The Communication Landscape

We have already noted that the language mode is not the only way to express meanings. We have said that there are others—namely, the visual mode, the audio mode, the gestural mode, the spatial mode—and often communication consists of interrelated multimodal patterns of meaning. Language-based literacy is still necessary, but it is no longer enough for the kinds of literacy practices that already characterize and will continue to be developed in the information age of the twenty-first century.

Most print-based written texts are multimodal. Both of the Wildsmith books that we have examined earlier—the story and the information book—included illustrations, which also depicted or represented meanings. For example, it was noted under the discussion of the ideologies of the two books that *The Owl and the Woodpecker* emphasized maleness and bulliness. Wildsmith also displayed this "bulliness" in his illustrations as well. He has a large owl with wings and feet talons or claws spread hovering over and swooping down towards small animals. The process of action (swooping down) is indicated by an "action line" or vector. In the *Squirrels* book, as already discussed, the language message begins by telling the various attributes of a squirrel (as a class). The picture structure on that page is considered to be a type of analytic process where a static squirrel is depicted with its characteristics—namely, having fuzziness, a long, bushy tail, two strong back legs, two small front paws, two large tufted ears, two big front teeth. Although the language message also notes that the squirrel "looks happy and mischievous," it is not apparent in the illustration. Nevertheless, it is clear to see that Wildsmith used different language and visual structures to express meanings in the two books/genres.

Newspapers, magazines, brochures, catalogs, and others are multimodal, consisting of written language and visual images or designs. Visual images—along with language texts—are also found in media and electronic communication. Thus, this multimodal communication landscape is diverse and is considered to be made of multiple literacies—hence, it is often called *multiliteracies*. As part of this multiliteracies emphasis, children's art (and other components of the arts) will be given emphasis in teaching and learning in this book. Art is not just a mode to express feelings and emotions, but it is also *cognitive* as well. It fosters in students flexible, creative strategies to depict meanings. Students learn *with* the arts, *through* the arts, and *about* the arts. Art fuses the imagination into the curriculum and underscores the inquiry approach in the integrated language perspective.

In the book, we may sometimes refer to the any of the possible various modes of the communication landscape involved in multiliteracies. However—besides the language mode—we give more attention to the visual mode. This is because in many contexts more and more visual images are given more space, and as a result, they have a significant role in communicating—with language—the essential message or information on a topic. As language is oriented to reporting/recording the actions and events of the world, visual images are oriented to displaying what the world is about. For this

Eggins (1994)

Exploring the ideological features of texts/images fosters a critical stance to literacy learning.

Kress (2002, 2003)

Kress & van Leeuwen (1996); Unsworth (2001)

"Multiliteracies" is used to emphasize the multimodal nature of texts.

Efland (2002); Goldberg (1997)

Kress (2003); Unsworth (2001)

reason, we have to rethink and expand our previous ideas about what constitutes the "context of situation." A multimodal text, which incorporates both language and images, involves *semantic choice of two kinds of meanings*. The reconfiguration of context for verbal–visual texts is as follows:

What is happening?

Ideational/representational patterns verbally and visually construct the ideas or content of the communication message—the nature of events, the objects and participants, and the circumstances in which they happen.

Who is taking part?

Interpersonal/interactive speakers/listeners, readers/writers, and viewers and what is viewed and has been constructed by illustrators.

What role is communication playing?

Textual/compositional meanings are concerned with how meanings are expressed by text and image—the relative emphasis or distribution of the information being expressed among elements of the text and image.

Under the "happening" question, *ideational patterns* stand for the content of the text and *representational patterns* consist of the meanings that are depicted or displayed by the image. Regarding the "who" question, *interpersonal relations* are those that occur between people and text and *interactive relations* consists of those that occur between viewers and the image. Finally, under the "communication-role" question, textual meanings have to do with text communication and compositional meanings involve communication through images. Because we focus on *both* text and images as being significant in literacy (or multiliteracies, as we have noted previously) processes and practices in this book, we will use *reader/viewer* and *writer/illustrator* for multimodal products having text and images. (More details of the preceding ideas are found in Chapter 6.)

Thus, the fact that literacy involves multimodal texts requires that we examine both modes in teaching and learning. As indicated earlier in the discussion about the different types of pictures in the two Wildsmith books, different genres employ visual structures, and the relationships between these images and the text are, therefore, different. Most nonfiction or informational texts include mostly photographs, diagrams, figures, and so forth, whereas fiction includes mostly illustrations. To account for multiliteracies, we need to attend to both, even at the early years of literacy learning, which is called emergent literacy.

Different genres employ different language patterns and different types of visual images.

Emergent Literacy

How do children learn how to use written texts? The research of the last few decades on early literacy has indicated that our previous belief that learning to read and write begins only when children are instructed in elementary school has to be questioned. Like talking and listening, the roots of reading and writing reach back into infancy. Early literacy begins when children encounter books and other written texts in their own social and cultural environments. Beginning understandings of written language are also learned within an environment of language use. Children learn that written texts, too, can be used to get things done. They learn what books and other written texts are, in what circumstances they are employed, and what is in reading and writing for them. This early awareness of the purpose of written language in the environment of their homes and communities is called *emergent literacy*.

Two major traditional assumptions are questioned in this new view of literacy. First, the mastery of oral language is no longer a prerequisite to the development of written language. Oral and written language develop simultaneously, each facilitating

Early literacy understandings are also learned within an environment of language use.

Goodman & Goodman (1979); Harste, Woodward, & Burke (1984); Holdaway (1979); Pontecorvo et al. (1996); Teale & Sulzby (1986); Sulzby & Teale (1991)

Emergent literacy

Schickedanz (1986); Sulzby (1996)

Written language develops along with oral language.

Literacy learning doesn't require special tutoring.

Reading to children is a crucial factor in fostering understanding of written language registers.

Cambourne (1981); Krashen (1993); Smith (1997); Wells (1985, 1986)

Literacy set

Holdaway (1979)

- Motivational factors focus on children wanting experiences with print.
- Linguistic factors concern children developing a familiarity with "book language."
- Operational factors have to do with children developing essential strategies for handling written language.
- Orthographic factors involve children learning the conventions of the medium of written language.

Kress (1997)

Hubbard (1989)

Holdaway's literacy set has to be expanded to include visual-image factors (as well as those pertaining to other modes of the communication landscape).

Halliday (1978)

Literacy is an extension of the potential of language to express meanings.

and supporting a child's understanding of the other. Second, literacy learning need not be tutored in specific ways. Instead of direct, formal instruction, children learn written language by interacting with adults or older children in reading and writing situations, by exploring print on their own, and by observing significant adults, especially their parents, actually using written language for their communicative ends. In other words, they learn literacy understandings similar to the way they learned their spoken language, that is, in the manner illustrated by Mark's oral language development. Thus, children's early, emergent efforts to read and write consist of their own inventions or approximations of adult written forms, just like those that Mark had constructed (e.g., *Jubs bread*) in developing his spoken language.

The term *emergent literacy* is used to emphasize the continuities and discontinuities in becoming literate, how young children develop early concepts and skills that precede and lead to conventional reading and writing. All children have acquired some of these understandings because our culture is a literate one. Individual children's knowledge about literacy, however, differs as a result of the manner and extent to which written language has been shared with them.

A major element contributing to young children's understanding of typical written registers and the ways they differ from typical spoken ones is adults' practice of reading storybooks and other types of written texts to children during the preschool years. Extensive and repetitive experiences with a range of favorite books enable young children to learn about these written registers. As a result, they develop a *literacy set*. Holdaway describes literacy set in terms of four factors: motivational, linguistic, operational, and orthographic. *Motivational* factors consist of children's seeking out, enjoying, and reenacting reading and writing events. *Linguistic* factors involve the ways in which children learn about the nature of written dialect or "book language"; for example, the ways they approximate the grammatical and lexical features of written texts as they "pretend read" a book that has been read to them. *Operational* factors relate to the imaginative, predictive, or self-correcting strategies that they develop for handling the disembedded qualities of written language. Finally, the *orthographic* factors pertain to children's early understandings of the conventions of print—directionality of written language, concepts of letters and words, the phonetic principle (that the spelling of words reflect letter–sound relationships).

Kress complements and adds other dimensions to early literacy learning. He, like Holdaway, stresses that our ideas of "cognition" involved in the paths to literacy needs to be broadened so that thought is not severed from pleasure, emotion, feeling, and affect. He also argues that because modes of communication—other than language—have become increasingly prominent, and even in many cases, dominant in the new media world, we need to consider how young children make meaning in these other modes as well. Visual images, in particular, are especially ever present, and young children use this mode found in books, magazines, Internet websites, TV advertisements, junk mail delivered at their homes, and so on—along with linguistic messages—to make sense of these texts. They also use both modes when they write and draw their meanings. And, in their drawings, as Hubbard has described, they contend with how to depict on paper (a two-dimensional object) entities and actions that occur in a third-dimensional world (e.g., how to show size, perspective, or movement). Young children's emergent forms— both linguistically and visually expressed—are creative, innovative precursors to adult conventions in these two modes. Thus, Holdaway's literacy set has to be expanded to include *visual-image factors* (and other modes of the communication landscape) as important dimensions in early literacy learning.

An integrated language perspective fosters and further builds on this initial literate behavior. Learning to read and write, *and* to use visual images, is seen as children's efforts to extend the potential or resource of various communication modes as new ways to understand and express meanings. All are tools of learning by which to communicate various purposes. Let's further examine this type of communication. How do readers and writers—and, as we note earlier, we'll add "viewers" and "illustrators"—employ multimodal texts in literacy practices? How do they manage this kind of social interaction?

Reader/Viewer–Writer/Illustrator Contract

We have noted how written texts have a disembedded quality because in written communication readers and writers are frequently unknown to each other and they are rarely communicating in the same place in time and space. However, that does not mean that readers and writers are not related or involved with each other. A writer must always keep the reader in view in composing or constructing a text; otherwise, the reader would never be able to interpret the writer's message. And the reader must constantly construct in reading what he or she believes to be the writer's message. Both readers and writers construct written texts; both are involved in problem-solving processes as they create meanings for some purpose. With any use of a written text, there is a reader–writer contract by which particular readers and writers achieve intersubjectivity in written communication.

As do speakers and listeners, writers (during the composing process) and readers (during the comprehension process) rely on their mental representation of the world to communicate. Researchers call these mental representations by different terms—*scripts, cognitive structures,* or *schemas.* In this book, although we may at times use any one of these terms, most of the time we use *schemas* to designate individual mental representations. The next section covers schemas in detail, but some general remarks about them are necessary now to clarify these reader–writer relationships.

Schemas are our individual organizations of what we know. They consist of what we know of our world—persons and personal relationships, the properties and features of objects, and the way language and other modes of communication work to express understandings and values. Our knowledge of conventions or registers of written language is crucial in a reader–writer contract, as shown in Figure 1.6. However, as can be seen, this figure also incorporates a "viewer" of images and "illustrator" (who can also be the writer/author or someone different from the writer) because visual images, photographs, or other designs are involved in many text productions. Thus, very frequently, the contract exists between a reader/viewer and a writer/illustrator one.

From a writer's side of the contract, a particular written text is the result of a writer's intentions to communicate meanings. If visual images are also incorporated, the illustrator will contribute meanings as well. Those meanings, drawn from the writer's and illustrator's schemas, are expressed through the conventions of written language and visual design. The text/design represents a blueprint, or a set of cues, that a reader/viewer uses to evoke the particular schemas needed to comprehend the writer/illustrator meanings. From the reader's/viewer's stance, expectations about what the conventions express or represent enable the reader/viewer to predict, according to his or her perceptions, what the writer/illustrator has communicated. Using

Written texts have a disembedded quality.

Cazden (1992); Wells (1985, 1986); Wells & Chang-Wells (1992)

Both reading and writing consist of the construction of texts.

Rosebery et al. (1989); Smith (1982b, 1997); Tierney & Pearson (1984); Unsworth (2001)

A reader–writer contract exists when written texts are used.

Schemas are our organized mental representations of our knowledge of the world.

Schemas include our people world, our object world, and our language world.

Karmiloff-Smith (1979)

A reader/viewer–writer/illustrator contract exists when multimodal written texts are used.

Unsworth (2001)

Writer's/illustrator's intentions

Reader's/viewer's expectations

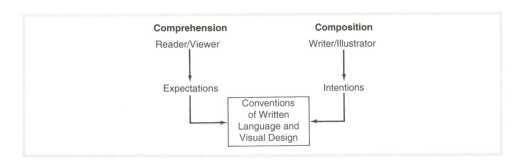

figure 1.6
Reader/Viewer–
Writer/Illustrator
Contract

Kress & van Leeuwen (1996); Rabinowitz (1987); Rosenblatt (1978); Smith (1997); Swales (1990); Unsworth (2001)

the cues provided by the writer/illustrator to spark the appropriate schemas, the reader/viewer constructs the perceived multimodal textual/design world the writer/illustrator has envisioned. Both readers/viewers and writers/illustrators bring meaning (based on their schemas) to such multimodal compositions.

Schemas: Our Mental Representations of Knowledge

Knowledge is constructed by individual learners.

Smith (1982a, 1982b, 1997); Wells (1986); Wells & Chang-Wells (1992)

Piaget (1926, 1969a, 1969b, 1975)

We are learning all the time. What we learn at any time is always based on what we already know. Knowledge of the world is not picked up by osmosis like a sponge but actively *constructed* by individual minds. It is a "theory of the world in the head" developed over a lifetime of experiences.

Jean Piaget, an influential proponent of this constructive view of learning and knowledge, described learning as a process of continuous modification of our schemas or cognitive structures in our mind. Through two simultaneous processes—assimilation and accommodation—children develop new information about the world to their schemas to adapt to their environment. *Assimilation* is the process by which knowledge is restructured by being integrated into existing schemas. In contrast, *accommodation* is the process by which knowledge is restructured by making modifications in existing schemas. In Piaget's theory, development is explained in terms of *global* knowledge restructuring. Children go through four broad, qualitatively different stages of development corresponding to age: sensorimotor stage (birth to two years), preoperational stage (two to seven years), concrete-operational stage (seven to eleven years), and formal-operational stage (beyond the eleventh year). Children's thinking processes are constrained and determined by what stage they are in. Children's logical processes are different from adults' in Piaget's view.

Piaget's theory of development is one of global knowledge restructuring.

Bruner (1986); Donaldson (1978); Dunn (1988); Lee & Smagorinsky (2000); Vygotsky (1962, 1978); Wells & Chang-Wells (1992); Wertsch (1985, 1989, 1991)

More recent research in both cognitive and developmental psychology has extended many Piagetian ideas about development, learning, and knowledge. Some aspects of his theory have been modified and reinterpreted. Whereas Piaget for the most part studied how children's schemas developed through interactions with objects in the physical world, more recent views emphasize how this knowledge is mediated and influenced through social interaction. As illustrated in earlier sections, children act on objects and play with toys on their own, but most of their activities with objects are immersed in a sea of conversation with others. Individual schemas constructed by individual learners are not developed in a void; schemas are influenced by social and cultural interactions and practices.

Current views emphasize the social aspects of acquiring knowledge.

Current views question Piaget's concept of egocentrism.

Another feature of Piaget's theory has also been challenged. Piaget characterized preschoolers' thought as *egocentric*. That is, young children are not able to take the point of view of another. However, this cannot be true, as noted when we discussed *intersubjectivity*. Through their reciprocal interactions with their parents, even two-month-olds demonstrate that they are sensitive to another's behavior. Babies are affected by the smile or other facial gestures and verbalizations of the adult, *and* their facial expressions, gurgles, and body movements affect the adult's movements, gestures, and articulations. Babies are already taking account of another person and adapting their behavior to respond. In fact, children could never learn language at all if they were as egocentric as Piaget suggested. Recall Mark and how hard he worked to achieve intersubjectivity with his mother—how he made sure that his mother understood what he was trying to tell her.

Finally, questions about Piaget's theory of how knowledge is reconstructed have been raised. In his view, restructuring of knowledge is global. Children in a particular stage of development apply the same kind of thinking processes no matter what the area or topic is. The procedures or routines that children employ in each stage are independent of the content of the knowledge they operate on because it is assumed that their schemas vary little across domains. Consequently, the process of learning is affected only slightly, or not at all, by the concepts contained in a learner's schemas in each domain. The procedures and routines used by children change only when they enter a new stage in which these general or global structures are modified.

In the more recent views of development, the area, topic, or conceptual domain that the learner is involved with or trying to figure out *is* significant. Properties or concepts in particular domains affect the thinking processes, routines, strategies, and procedures that children apply in their experiences. In this way, children's thinking and learning processes are similar to those of adults. Young children can learn things in particular domains much earlier in development than was previously thought *and* learning in those domains takes a much longer time during development than was previously realized. In this domain-specific knowledge restructuring view, inferences made by a learner at any time are based more on what and how concepts are structured and organized in particular domains, or specific content, than on the age of the learner. For example, if children have many experiences with clay—perhaps because their parents are potters, or they live and play where the ground is claylike, or they regularly play with leftover pie dough—then they may come to understand that a particular ball of clay is the same amount when it is rolled into a long "snake." In Piagetian terms, these children can conserve mass: They realize that the quantity of the clay is the same despite its transformation in shape. The reason these children can acquire these understandings at age four or five (instead of seven or eight, according to Piaget's theory) is that they have a schema in the particular domain of clay and its properties and transformations. In this view, children can be "experts" in a particular area in which adults may function as novices. How many five-year-old dinosaur experts do you know? How about eight-year-old *Star Wars* masters or space whizzes? Teenage computer hackers? These are all cases of children who have knowledge in a specific topic or domain, a domain that many adults may know little about.

In this book, certain important Piagetian notions are emphasized. Children are seen as active, constructive learners as they continuously generate and test hypotheses about aspects of their environment. Like Piaget, we stress the importance of cognitive conflict in children's development—that children learn when their theories are questioned. Conflict inducement leads to modification of their schemas.

However, we expand on these Piagetian views in two major ways. First, we emphasize the role of social interaction with others as an important source of cognitive conflict. Having to collaborate and cooperate with others about an area of interest promotes the restructuring of children's knowledge. With the assistance of others, children can go beyond their limits to solve problems through interaction. Second, we emphasize the importance of content or concepts in specific domains in development and learning. Traditional elementary schools frequently concentrate on basic skills, especially at the early grades, so that children can deal with content parceled out in later grades. An integrated language perspective, in contrast, insists that skills go hand in hand with content. Children comprehend and learn how to do things on the basis of their knowledge structures of specific content of particular topics, fields, or domains. Let's look further at how this domain-specific knowledge is organized and how it is developed.

The Organization of Schemas

Schemas are not random bits of information stored in any haphazard way. Instead, schemas are organized, coherent category systems consisting of three major components: (1) categories or concepts of knowledge; (2) features, attributes, characteristics, or rules for determining what constitutes a category or concept—that is, rules of category membership; and (3) a network of connections and interrelationships between

Carey (1985, 1988, 1991); Gelman & Baillargeon (1983); Keil (1984, 1991); Mandler (1983); Vosniadou & Brewer (1987)

Newer developmental theories emphasize knowledge restructuring in specific domains.

• Children are constructive learners.
• Children generate and test hypotheses.

Foreman & Kushner (1983)

Cognitive conflict leads to changes in children's schemas.

The importance of social interaction on knowledge restructuring

Bruner (1986); Lindfors (1999); Vygotsky (1978); Wells (1999); Wells & Chang-Wells (1992)

The importance of knowledge restructuring in specific domains

Schemas are organized.

categories or concepts, which includes how concepts are incorporated in social, cultural interactional procedures or routines. Thus, schemas can be conceived of as dynamic, always changing, structured mental representations of what we know. Each experience we have is interpreted in terms of the knowledge we have acquired, stored, and organized, and this knowledge is modified and reorganized (restructured) as a result of each experience.

Schemas as Semantic Maps of Domains

A good way to visualize schemas is to see them as *semantic maps*—that is, maps of concepts or meanings. Semantic maps are diagrams of what researchers think schemas in our minds are like. Although schemas or maps are related to each other in ways we do not quite understand, they are coherent units, or wholes, in different areas, or domains. Domains themselves are best seen as a continuum from general, broad fields, or areas of knowledge to more specific topics or concepts. For example, curricular areas or academic disciplines, such as biology or history, can be seen as illustrations of broad, general domains, whereas cats, dogs, and dinosaurs exemplify concepts at the specific end of the continuum. Similarly, mathematics, art, music, and language can be thought of as general symbolic domains. Then, within each of these general domains, more narrow domains can be considered, for example, geometry and algebra in mathematics, drawing and sculpture in art, symphonies and rock songs in music, stories and information books in written language, and so forth. Domain-specific knowledge restructuring can be conceived of as occurring at various levels of generality in development. However, it is distinguished from global knowledge restructuring in that schemas are not overarching structures developed in the same way over all domains. Children may be able to conserve a substance like clay but unable to conserve number. For example, they may not realize that there is the same number of beads in two rows when the beads in the shorter row are placed next to each other and the beads in the longer row are placed with spaces between them. Children who have played marbles with their parents and siblings may be able to conserve number but not substance. Some children may be already competent at reading stories when they begin school because their family has always read lots of stories to them; other children may enter school understanding many number concepts because their family has played a lot of board and card games requiring counting. Various communities offer different cultural "funds of knowledge" for their children to develop. In sum, knowledge structures are developed with more or less elaboration and differentiation in particular domains.

The Development of Schemas

How do people develop these domain-specific schemas? Children and adults alike learn by inventing new categories or concepts and by constructing and making new and different connections and relationships between these concepts. Although people have many similar experiences and, therefore, possess common knowledge, each individual has unique experiences and, therefore, develops unique schemas (unique categories, rules, and interrelationships).

To better understand how this development of a schema may occur, let's follow Sara as she learns about or constructs a schema in the domain of spiders. We begin our story when Sara is six or seven months old. Perhaps her first construction is the result of her observations of her parents' enactment of the cleaning the house script or schema. Sitting in her high chair, she notices how a spider, which has crawled out from a chair Mommy or Daddy has moved, is vacuumed up with all the other dirt that had accumulated since the last time the room was cleaned. Figure 1.7 is a semantic map depicting Sara's initial, rudimentary spider schema.

Nelson (1986); Rumelhart (1980); Smith (1982a, 1982b, 1997); Swales (1990)

Bromley et al. (1995); Daniels & Zemelman (2004); Wilhelm (2004)

Moll (1992)

Our knowledge is restructured as a result of our experience.

Semantic maps are diagrams depicting our concepts in domains.

Domains are areas of knowledge.

Schemas are developed in specific domains.

Schemas are unique and individualized.

The construction of a schema in the domain of spiders

Semantic map of Sara's initial spider schema

figure 1.7

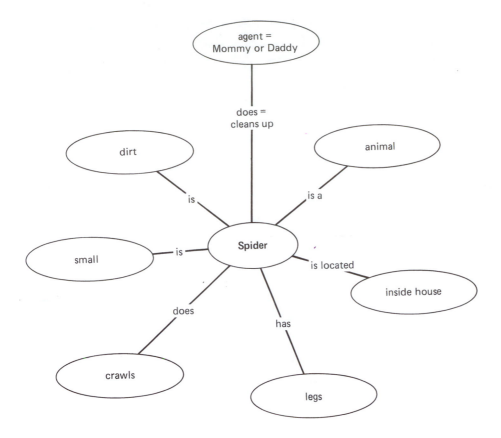

Because Sara has noted that the spider actively moves across the floor, she categorizes the creature as a type of animal. Also, both the action of "cleans up" and the agent (Mommy or Daddy) of that action are somehow part of her conception of spider. She develops certain characteristics of spider: that a spider has legs, crawls, and is small. She may also include a feature of "dirt" for the spider because the spider has been so much a part of the dirt that is usually cleaned up. Similarly, she develops the idea that the concept of spider can be found at a certain location, namely, "inside the house," because this is where the events of cleaning up the spider have occurred.

About two months later, Sara's parents begin to play the "itsy-bitsy spider went up the waterspout" game with her. Therefore, modifications in her spider schema evolve. Figure 1.8 is a semantic map showing this restructuring. She develops new connections to her spider concept. As a result of repeated instances of the itsy-bitsy spider family routine, her schema includes Sara and her parents, as agents, pretending to be a spider. In the game, fingers are like spider legs, so that idea is incorporated. Some idea that spiders may also possess fingers may be constructed in her schema as well. Another place that spiders can be found—in a waterspout—is added, although what a waterspout is Sara does not really understand. Similarly, she develops some preliminary notion that rain washes out spiders. Notice how a two-way mapping process that relates concepts and language is being evolved. Moreover, note the other communication modes that have been involved—the gestures the parents use as they told of the itsy-bitsy spider, all of the visual and spatial information she incorporated as to where spiders are to be found. Schemas provide clues to word meanings and other communication modes that people use, and others' word meanings and other modes embedded in everyday routines and conversations help modify one's own old schemas. This is a consistent pattern that continues throughout development.

Second semantic map of Sara's spider schema

figure 1.8

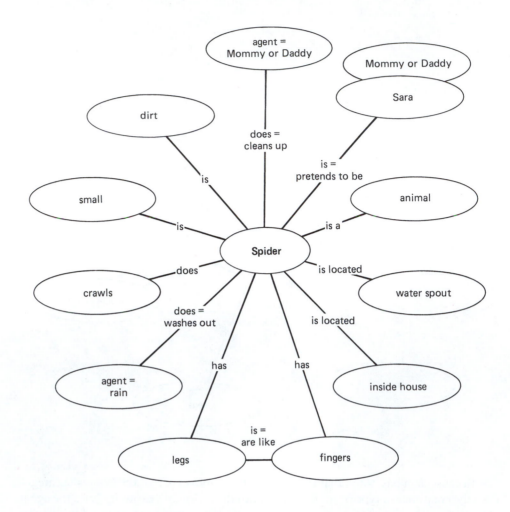

Third semantic map of Sara's spider schema

Fourth semantic map of Sara's spider schema

White (1952)

Fifth semantic map of Sara's spider schema

Gibbons (1993)

Over the years, Sara's spider schema becomes more and more elaborated, modified, reorganized, and restructured. Figures 1.9, 1.10, and 1.11 attempt to depict some of these changes. There isn't enough space to show all possible changes, so only the more salient ones are included.

As the semantic map in Figure 1.9 indicates, "spider," along with "fly," "ant," and "bee," has become part of a class of "bugs" in Sara's schema. The earlier dirt and fingers relationships have been dropped and new characteristics of spiders have been added—that they eat other bugs, lay eggs, and make webs. A new location connection—"outside"—has been incorporated and differentiated. Sara now understands that spiders can also be found outside in parks and gardens. She has also noted that people have varying degrees of liking for spiders.

As the result of hearing *Charlotte's Web* by E. B. White read aloud, and of later reading on her own, Sara's schema on spiders (Figure 1.10) again shows modification. Although *Charlotte's Web* is a fantasy, it provides useful information about spiders that induces Sara to elaborate on her "lays eggs" and "outside" connections. Of course, "make believe" connections (marked by asterisks) are also added—Charlotte, the spider in this delightful book, talks and spells words, thereby saving Wilbur the pig from slaughter.

Subsequently, Sara's spider becomes even more restructured (see Figure 1.11). As a result of a school project on spiders, the earlier "bugs" classification drops altogether, and Sara begins to differentiate between the class of "insects" and that of "arachnids," of which spiders are members. Using information books, such as *Spiders* by Gibbons, she learns that insects and arachnids have certain distinguishing features: insects have six legs and three body parts, whereas arachnids have eight legs and two body parts. As Sara

figure 1.9

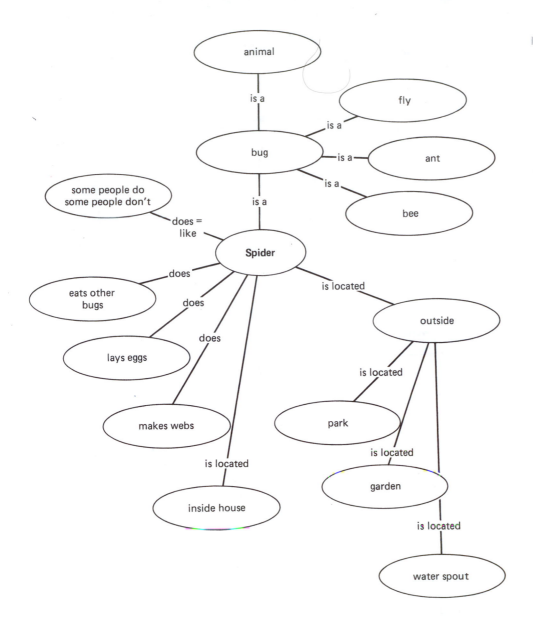

incorporates this distinction into her schema, she includes members of the insect class, noting that there are members of the arachnid class other than spiders. She also realizes that there are many kinds of spiders, including the largest tarantulas, as well as the poisonous black widow spiders. Sara has relied on the use of several information books in her study of spiders. However, an integral part of her inquiry has been an investigation of several African folktales that involve Anansi (or Ananse) the spider. As she read the Arkhurst "why" tales of how the spider got his "bald head" and "thin waist," these spider characteristics became included in her schemas. From other books—*Anansi the Spider* by McDermott and *Spider and the Sky God* and *Talk Talk: An Ashanti Legend,* both written by Deborah Chocolate—she relates how the spider Anansi has become an "African folk hero" having human qualities. He is a lovable "mischief maker" and "trickster," who can be shrewd in order to "triumph over larger foes."

Of course, our account of Sara's development of the spider schema is much too simplistic of how children actually construct and reconstruct their schemas. Networks of particular schemas overlap with and link to many other schemas, all of which are

Arkhurst (1964)
McDermott (1972);
Chocolate (1993a, 1993b)

figure **1.10**

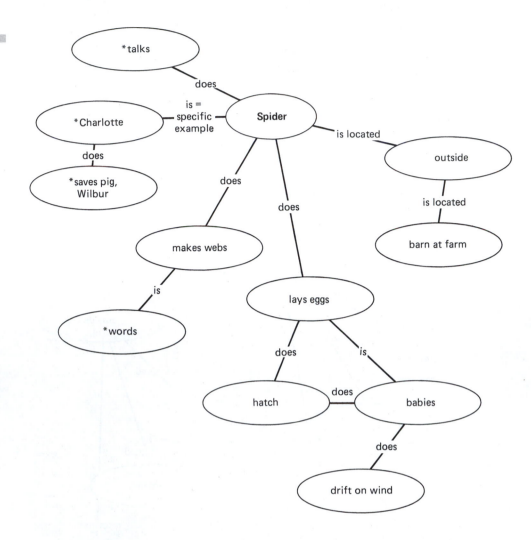

unique. For example, the spider schemas for an avid gardener, a biologist, an ento-mologist, and an expert in Anansi and other folktales are most likely to be very differ-ent from yours. As children learn, existing categories and connections are enlarged and restructured and new categories are created and modified in many particular domains. These schemas develop on the basis of individual experiences and interests.

Another schema example is shown in Figure 1.12, which illustrates a seven-year-old child's schema of "living things," a more general domain than that of Sara's spider domain. The child was given a new large tablet by his mother and was told that he could write whatever he wanted in it. One of his earliest efforts was this list of living things. Although his list is a linear display, it is easy to imagine offshoots of subdomains and perhaps even to infer connections and relationships of distinguishing properties for these more specific subdomains. Many of his entries are amusing, but they are or-ganized. His list reflects both some of the concepts he has already learned in this do-main and his ability to express these concepts in language.

Summary

This chapter started by addressing the way language develops in conversation and what conversation is. Then it moved into considering differences between oral and written

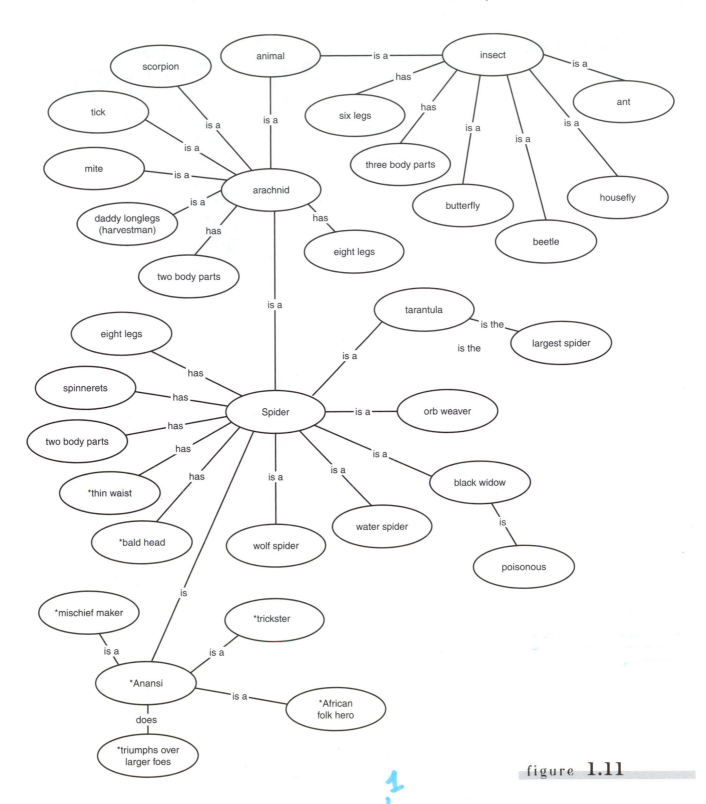

figure **1.11**

language. Following that it argued that besides the language mode, literacy needs also to address other modes of communication, particularly visual images, which are frequently incorporated with linguistic messages. Finally, it went into schemas and their development. In development, a dynamic, two-way mapping process occurs relating concepts and language and other communication modes. Children's existing conceptual schemas provide them with clues to the meanings of the wordings and visual

A two-way mapping process that relates concepts and language occurs in development.

figure 1.12

LIVING things

alagaters	ground hogs
stingray	moles
birds	ants
reatiles	bees
dad	flise
peoplle	parets
mahkeys	hous keeper
lice	termites
flees	golefer
dinodsors	tigers
mom	woodpers
kids	chiqmunks
baybeis	tertils
lions	trees
kpords	flowers
mouhtin lions	dogs
worms	cats

images (and other modes) used by others in various contexts, and the language and visual images that children experience in a range of contexts lead to modification and restructuring of their schemas.

Children do not sit on the sidelines during this process. They are active participants in the process, constantly charging into the fray. They continually learn how they can use the potential of language and other modes of the communication landscape to communicate their meanings, ideologies, and perspectives to others in their culture.

These developing language/communication abilities reflect children's evolving understandings of how communication relates to context. An integrated language perspective stands for real, authentic language use in the classroom because that is how children learn language before they enter school. It requires that the classroom provide many opportunities for children to use language for a range of purposes. The perspective also stands for including visual images and other communication modes as important, integral aspects of these genuine communication purposes. Children participate in a broad range of experiences of their choice to help them develop the sustained and deliberate attention to particular topics across the curriculum that makes systematic learning possible. In doing so, they begin to see that the various disciplines are all different ways of knowing, from history and social studies to arithmetic and other domains of mathematics. Disciplines, or content areas, represent particular cultural frames, or ways of sense-making. Members participating in these distinctive domains have constructed certain types of vocabulary, discourse, visual designs, and ideologies by which to express their meanings to others involved in the various disciplines. Making and understanding these distinctions is at the root of rich interdisciplinary and integrated teaching and learning.

Hubbard (1996); Lindfors (1999); Wells (1981, 1999)

An integrated language perspective stands for authentic language use in the classroom.

Dyson (1989); Edelsky (1986, 1991); Fried (2001); Johns (2002); Lindfors (1999)

- Disciplines are domains that are cultural frames.
- Disciplines have certain perspectives, types of discourses or genres, and particular visual designs related to them.

Making and dealing with distinctions also undergirds a multicultural perspective where children can explore and affirm the diversity of people's sense-making from various communities and worlds, as well as the various discourses/images these people use to communicate their points of view about the world. Thus, questioning and fostering a consciousness of differences makes it possible for children to see that people from various cultures can have a reciprocal impact on each other.

In this view, the various communication modes are the tools and means to support such learning, not ends in and of themselves. They are integrated in this perspective because they are integrated in real communicative use.

Cope & Kalantzis (2000); Kress (1993); Unsworth (2001)
Nieto (2000)

- An integrated language perspective affirms diversity.
- Multiple communication modes are tools for learning.

Suggested Activities

1. To enhance and help make explicit your understanding of spoken registers, collect some samples of typical conversations. With the help of other students in your class, try to tape-record people talking in different contexts of situation: buying doughnuts at a bakery, conversing over lunch, playing on the playground, and so forth. You may want to gather some samples in the classroom too. For each sample, be sure you can answer all three questions about the context of situation: What's happening? Who's participating? What role is communication playing? Transcribe as much as you can of your samples so that you can share them with others. Now analyze and compare the linguistic patterns of your and your classmates' samples. How are these patterns the same? How are they different? How is the language being used related to the factors or features of the context of situation? What other modes of communication are also present? What ideologies or values are expressed in the language/communication samples?

2. To better understand exophoric implicit wordings, go over the spoken language samples you have already collected (or obtain some new ones). Can you identify exophoric devices whose source is not the co-text but that are understood because of some factor operating in the actual situation in which the conversation took place? Typical implicit devices that can be exophoric include the following:

   a. Pronouns: *I, you, me, he, she, him, her, his, it, they, them,* and so on, including the use of *the, this, that, those, here, there,* and the like.

   b. Substitutions that refer to a class of objects (e.g., *one, ones, the same*) or to actions in a general way (e.g., *do, be, have, do it/that*).

   c. Elliptical constructions in which only part of a phrase or sentence can be completed unless some aspect in the situation is considered. (*Lots* and *more* in the conversation about the new tape recorder are elliptical because we need a feature of the tape recorder—namely, "buttons"—to complete our understanding. See Figure 1.3.)

   Did participants seem to understand these exophoric wordings in the samples? If not, what did they do to better understand each other?

See Halliday & Hasan (1976) for a more detailed discussion of implicit devices.

3. To better understand endophoric implicit wordings, review a range of different types of written text. Can you identify endophoric implicit devices or wordings whose interpretative source is part of the co-text? Refer to the list of implicit devices in Activity 2; they can be endophoric implicit wordings too. Can you find threads or chains of meanings throughout the texts? Be careful to select children's literature and other books, magazines, newspapers, and other texts found in stores and libraries. (Avoid basals or textbooks because many of these do not contain typical or good examples of written language.)

4. To better enhance and help make more explicit your understanding of different registers of written language, look at a sample of storybooks and information

books. Are there different language patterns? Are there some examples that seem to be "fuzzy"; that is, are there some information books that have some storybooklike features? Are there some storybooks that have incorporated informationlike properties? (More will be said about this in Chapter 6.) Are there certain ideologies or values being expressed in the books?

5. To better understand how language and visual modes work to express meanings in books in different genres, explore the meanings expressed in fictional and nonfictional or information books. Besides picture storybooks, look at novels as well—although not as prevalent, many novels also include illustrations or other visual designs (e.g., *Coraline* by Gaiman; *Julie of the Wolves* by George; *In the Year of the Boar and Jackie Robinson* by Lord; and *Shabanu* by Staples). How are visual images used in these books of different genre? How are they employed in nonfictional books on different topics—in history, science, and so forth?

Gaiman (2002); George (1972); Lord (1994); Staples (1989)

References

Bakhtin, M. M. (1986). *Speech genres and other late essays* (C. Emerson & M. Holquist, Eds., and V. M. McGee, Trans.). Austin: University of Texas Press.

Bates, E. (1976). *Language and context: The acquisition of pragmatics.* New York: Academic Press.

Bower, T. G. R. (1974). *Development in infancy.* San Francisco: Freeman.

Bower, T. G. K. (1978). Perceptual development: Object and space. In E. C. Carterette & M. P. Friedman (Eds.), *Handbook of perception.* (Vol. 8, pp. 83–102). New York: Academic Press.

Bromley, K., Irwin-De Vitis, L., & Modlo, M. (1995). *Graphic organizers: Visual strategies of active learning.* New York: Scholastic.

Bruner, J. (1990). *Acts of meaning.* Cambridge, MA: Harvard University Press.

Bruner, J. S. (1975a). The ontogenesis of speech acts. *Journal of Child Language, 2,* 1–19.

Bruner, J. S. (1975b). From communication to language: A psychological perspective. *Cognition, 3,* 255–287.

Bruner, J. S. (1983). *Child's talk: Learning to use language.* New York: Norton.

Bruner, J. S. (1986). *Actual minds, possible worlds.* Cambridge, MA: Harvard University Press.

Cambourne, B. (1981). Oral and written relationships: A reading perspective. In B. M. Kroll & R. J. Vann (Eds.), *Exploring speaking–writing relationships: Connections and contrasts* (pp. 82–98). Urbana, IL: National Council of Teachers of English.

Carey, S. (1985). *Conceptual change in childhood.* Cambridge, MA: MIT Press.

Carey, S. (1988). Reorganization of knowledge in the course of acquisition. In S. Strauss (Ed.), *Ontogeny, phylogeny, and historical development: Human development* (Vol. 2, pp. 1–37). Norwood, NJ: Ablex.

Carey, S. (1991). Knowledge acquisition: Enrichment or conceptual change? In S. Carey & R. Gelman (Eds.), *The epigenesis of mind: Essays on biology and cognition* (pp. 257–291). Hillsdale, NJ: Erlbaum.

Cazden, C. B. (1992). *Whole language plus: Essays on literacy in the United States and New Zealand.* New York: Teachers College Press.

Chafe, W. L. (1985). Linguistic differences produced by differences between speaking and writing. In D. K. Olson, N. Torrence, & A. Hildyard (Eds.), *Literacy, language, and learning: The nature and consequences of reading and writing* (pp. 105–123). Cambridge: Cambridge University Press.

Chafe, W. L., & Danielwicz, J. (1987). Properties of spoken and written language. In R. Horowitz & S. J. Samuels (Eds.), *Comprehending oral and written language* (pp. 83–113). San Diego: Academic Press.

Chouliaraki, L., & Fairclough, N. (1999). *Discourse in later modernity: Rethinking critical discourse analysis.* Edinburgh: University of Edinburgh.

Cope, B., & Kalantzis, M. (Eds.) (1993). *The powers of literacy: A genre approach to teaching writing.* Pittsburgh, PA: University of Pittsburgh Press.

Cope, B., & Kalantzis, M. (Eds.). (2000). *Multiliteracies: Literacy learning and the design of social futures.* London: Routledge.

Daniels, H., & Zemelman, S. (2004). *Subjects matter: Every teacher's guide to content-area reading.* Portsmouth, NH: Heinemann.

Donaldson, M. (1978). *Children's minds.* Glasgow: William Collins Sons.

Dunn, J. (1988). *The beginnings of social understandings.* Cambridge, MA: Harvard University Press.

Dyson, A. H. (Ed.). (1989). *Collaboration through writing and reading: Exploring possibilities.* Urbana, IL: National Council of Teachers of English.

Edelsky, C. (1986). *Writing in a bilingual program: Habia una vez.* Norwood, NJ: Ablex.

Edelsky, C. (1991). *With literacy and justice for all: Rethinking the social in language and education.* London: Falmer Press.

Efland, A. D. (2002). *Art and cognition: Integrating the visual arts in the curriculum.* New York: Teachers College Press.

Eggins, S. (1994). *An introduction to systemic functional linguistics.* London: Pinter.

Fairclough, N. (1989). *Language and power.* London: Longman.

Fairclough, N. (1992). *Discourse and social change.* Cambridge: Polity Press.

Foreman, G. E., & Kushner, D. S. (1983). *The construction of knowledge: Piaget for teaching children.* Washington, DC: National Association for the Education of Young Children.

Fried, R. L. (2001). *The passionate teacher.* Boston: Beacon.

Gelman, R., & Baillargeon, R. (1983). A review of some Piagetian concepts. In J. H. Flavell & E. M. Markman (Eds.), P. H. Mussen (Gen. Ed.), *Handbook of child psychology: Vol. 3. Cognitive development* (pp. 167–230). New York: Wiley.

Goldberg, M. (1997). *Arts and learning: An integrated approach to teaching and learning in multicultural and multilingual settings.* New York: Longman.

Goodman, K. S., & Goodman, Y. M. (1979). Learning to read is natural. In L. B. Resnick & P. A. Weaver (Eds.), *Theory and practice of early reading* (Vol. 1, pp. 137–154). Hillsdale, NJ: Erlbaum.

Halliday, M. A. K. (1975). *Learning how to mean: Explorations in the development of language.* London: Edward Arnold.

Halliday, M. A. K. (1977). Text as semantic choice in social contexts. In T. van Dijk & J. S. Petofi (Eds.), *Grammars and descriptions* (pp. 176–225). Berlin: de Gruyter.

Halliday, M. A. K. (1978). *Language as a social semiotic: The social interpretation of language and meaning.* London: Longman.

Halliday, M. A. K. (1982). Three aspects of children's language development: Learning language, learning through language, and learning about language. In Y. Goodman, M. Haussler, & D. Strickland (Eds.), *Oral and written language development research: Impact on the schools* (pp. 7–19). Urbana, IL: National Council of Teachers of English.

Halliday, M. A. K. (1985). *Spoken and written language.* Victoria, Australia: Deakin University Press.

Halliday, M. A. K. (1987). Spoken and written modes of meaning. In R. Horowitz & S. J. Samuels (Eds.), *Comprehending oral and written language* (pp. 55–82). San Diego: Academic Press.

Halliday, M. A. K. (1993). Towards a language-based theory of learning. *Linguistics and Education, 5,* 93–126.

Halliday, M. A. K. (1996). Literacy and linguistics: A functional perspective. In R. Hasan & G. Williams (Eds.), *Literacy in society* (pp. 339–376). London: Addison Wesley Longman.

Halliday, M. A. K., & Hasan, R. (1976). *Cohesion in English.* White Plains, NY: Longman.

Halliday, M. A. K., & Hasan, R. (1985). *Language, context, and text: Aspects of language in a social-semiotic perspective.* Victoria, Australia: Deakin University Press.

Halliday, M. A. K., & Matthiessen, C. M. I. M. (2004). *An introduction to functional grammar.* London: Arnold.

Harste, J. C., Woodward, V. A., & Burke, C. L. (1984). *Language stories and literacy lessons.* Portsmouth, NH: Heinemann.

Hasan, R. (1984a). The nursery tale as a genre. *Nottingham Linguistic Circular, 13,* 71–102.

Hasan, R. (1984b). Coherence and cohesive harmony. In J. Flood (Ed.), *Understanding reading comprehension: Cognition, language, and the structure of prose* (pp. 181–219). Newark, DE: International Reading Association.

Hasan, R. (1995). The conception of context in text. In P. H. Fries & M. Gregory (Eds.), *Discourse in society: Systemic functional perspectives* (pp. 183–283). Norwood, NJ: Ablex.

Hasan, R. (1996). *Ways of saying: Ways of meaning.* C. Cloran, D. Butt, & G. Williams (Eds.). London: Cassell.

Heath, S. B. (1983). *Ways with words: Language, life, and work in communities and classrooms.* Cambridge: Cambridge University Press.

Heath, S. B. (1996). A lot of talk about nothing. In B. M. Power & R. S. Hubbard (Eds.), *Language development: A reader for teachers* (pp. 55–60). Englewood Cliffs, NJ: Prentice-Hall.

Holdaway, D. (1979). *Foundations of literacy.* Sydney, Australia: Ashton Scholastic.

Hubbard, R. (1989). *Authors of pictures, draughtsmen of words.* Portsmouth, NH: Heinemann.

Hubbard, R. S. (1996). Invitations to reflect on our practice: A conversation with Gordon Wells. In B. S. Power & R. S. Hubbard (Eds.), *Language development: A reader for teachers* (pp. 169–180). Englewood Cliffs, NJ: Prentice-Hall.

Johns, A. M. (2002). *Genre in the classroom: Multiple perspectives.* Mahwah, NJ: Lawrence Erlbaum.

Kagan, J. (1972). Do infants think? *Scientific American, 226,* 74–82.

Karmiloff-Smith, A. (1979). *A functional approach to child language: A study of determiners and reference.* Cambridge: Cambridge University Press.

Keil, F. C. (1984). Mechanisms of cognitive development and the structure of knowledge. In R. J. Sternberg (Ed.), *Mechanisms of cognitive change* (pp. 81–99). New York: Freeman.

Keil, F. C. (1991). The emergence of theoretical beliefs as constraints on concepts. In S. Carey & R. Gelman (Eds.), *The epigenesis of mind: Essays on biology and cognition* (pp. 237–256). Hillsdale, NJ: Erlbaum.

Krashen, S. (1993). *The power of reading: Insights from the research.* Englewood, CO: Libraries Unlimited.

Kress, G. (1993). Genre as social process. In B. Cope & M. Kalantzis (Eds.), *The powers of literacy: A genre approach to teaching writing* (pp. 22–37). Pittsburgh, PA: University of Pittsburgh Press.

Kress, G. (1997). *Before writing: Rethinking the paths to literacy.* London: Routledge.

Kress, G. (2000). Design and transformation: New theories of meaning. In B. Cope & M. Kalantzis (Eds.), *Multiliteracies: Literacy learning and the design of social futures* (pp. 153–161). London: Routledge.

Kress, G. (2003). *Literacy in a new media age.* London: Routledge.

Kress, G., & van Leeuwen, T. (1996). *Reading images: The grammar of visual design.* London: Routledge.

Lee, C. D., & Smagorinsky, P. (Eds.). (2000). *Vygotskian perspectives on literacy research: Constructing meaning through collaborative inquiry.* Cambridge: Cambridge University Press.

Lemke, J. L. (1995). *Textual politics: Discourse and social dynamics.* London: Taylor & Francis.

Lindfors, J. W. (1999). *Children's inquiry: Using language to make sense of the world.* New York: Teachers College Press.

Luke, A. (1996). Genres of power? Literacy education and the production of capital. In R. Hasan & G. Williams (Eds.), *Literacy in society* (pp. 308–338). London: Addison Wesley Longman.

Mandler, J. M. (1983). Representation. In J. H. Flavell & E. M. Markman (Eds.), P. H. Mussen (Gen. Ed.), *Handbook of child psychology: Vol. 3. Cognitive development* (pp. 420–494). New York: Wiley.

Martin, J. R. (1985). *Factual writing: Exploring and challenging social reality.* Victoria, Australia: Deakin University Press.

Martin, J. R. (1992). *English text: System and structure.* Philadelphia, PA: John Benjamins.

Martin, J. R., & Peters, P. (1985). On the analysis of exposition. In R. Hasan (Ed.), *Discourse on discourse* (pp. 61–92). Wollongong, Australia: Applied Linguistics Association of Australia.

McCollum, P. (1991). Cross-cultural perspectives on classroom discourse and literacy. In E. H. Hiebert (Ed.), *Literacy for a diverse society: Perspectives, practices, and policies* (pp. 108–121). New York: Teachers College Press.

Moll, L. C. (1992). Literacy research in community and classrooms: A sociocultural approach. In R. Beach, J. L. Green, M. L. Kamil, & T. Shanahan (Eds.), *Multidisciplinary perspectives in literacy research* (pp. 211–244). Urbana, IL: National Conference on Research in English.

Nelson, K. (1986). *Event knowledge: Structure and function in development.* Hillsdale, NJ: Erlbaum.

Newkirk, T. (1989). *More than stories: The range of children's writing.* Portsmouth, NH: Heinemann.

Nieto, S. (2000). *Affirming diversity: The sociopolitical context of multicultural education.* New York: Longman.

Nystrand, M., & Wiemelt, J. (1991). When is a text explicit? Formalist and dialogical conceptions. *Text, 11,* 25–41.

Pappas, C. C. (1991a). Young children's strategies in learning the "book language" of information books. *Discourse Processes, 14,* 203–225.

Pappas, C. C. (1991b). Fostering full access to literacy by including information books. *Language Arts, 68,* 449–462.

Pappas, C. C. (1993). Is narrative primary? Some insights from kindergartners' pretend readings of stories and information books. *JRB: A Journal of Literacy, 25,* 97–129.

Piaget, J. (1926). *The language and thought of the child.* London: Routledge & Kegan Paul.

Piaget, J. (1969a). *The child's conception of the world.* Paterson, NJ: Littlefield, Adams.

Piaget, J. (1969b). *The psychology of intelligence.* Paterson, NJ: Littlefield, Adams.

Piaget, J. (1975). *The development of thought: Equilibration of cognitive structures.* New York: Viking.

Pontecorvo, C., Orsolini, M., Burge, B., & Resnick, L. B. (Eds.). (1996). *Children's early text construction.* Mahwah, NJ: Lawrence Erlbaum.

Rabinowitz, P. J. (1987). *Before reading: Narrative conventions and the politics of interpretation.* Ithaca, NY: Cornell University Press.

Rosebery, A. S., Flower, L., Warren, B., Bowen, B., Bruce, B., Kantz, M., & Penrose, A. M. (1989). The problem-solving processes of writers and readers. In A. Dyson (Ed.), *Collaboration through writing and reading: Exploring possibilities* (pp. 136–163). Urbana, IL: National Council of Teachers of English.

Rosenblatt, L. M. (1978). *The reader, the text, the poem: The transactional theory of the literary work.* Carbondale: Southern Illinois University Press.

Rumelhart, D. E. (1980). Schemata: The building blocks of cognition. In R. J. Spiro, B. C. Bruce, & W. F. Brewer (Eds.),

Theoretical issues in reading comprehension: Perspectives from cognitive psychology, linguistics, artificial intelligence, and education (pp. 33–58). Hillsdale, NJ: Erlbaum.

Schickedanz, J. A. (1986). *More than the ABCs: The early stages of reading and writing.* Washington, DC: National Association for the Education of Young Children.

Smith, F. (1982a). *Understanding reading* (3rd ed.). New York: Holt, Rinehart & Winston.

Smith, F. (1982b). *Writing and the writer.* New York: Holt, Rinehart & Winston.

Smith, F. (1997). *Reading without nonsense.* New York: Teachers College Press.

Stern, D. N. (1985). *The interpersonal world of the child.* New York: Basic Books.

Sulzby, E. (1996). Roles of oral and written language as children approach conventional literacy. In C. Pontecorvo, M. Orsolini, B. Burge, & L. B. Resnick (Eds.), *Children's early text construction* (pp. 25–46). Mahwah, NJ: Lawrence Erlbaum.

Sulzby, E., & Teale, W. (1991). Emergent literacy. In R. Barr, M. L. Kamil, P. B. Mosenthal, & P. D. Pearson (Eds.), *Handbook of reading research* (Vol. 2, pp. 727–757). White Plains, NY: Longman.

Swales, J. M. (1990). *Genre analysis: English in academic and research settings.* Cambridge: Cambridge University Press.

Tannen, D. (1985). Relative focus on involvement in oral and written discourse. In D. R. Olson, N. Torrence, & A. Hildyard (Eds.), *Literacy, language, and learning: The nature and consequences of reading and writing* (pp. 124–147). Cambridge: Cambridge University Press.

Teale, W. H., & Sulzby, E. (1986). *Emergent literacy: Writing and reading.* Norwood, NJ: Ablex.

Tierney, R. J., & Pearson, P. D. (1984). Toward a composing model of reading. In J. M. Jensen (Ed.), *Composing and comprehending* (pp. 33–45). Urbana, IL: National Conference on Research in English.

Trevarthan, C. (1979a). Descriptive analyses of infant communication behaviour. In H. R. Schaffer (Ed.), *Studies in mother–infant interaction* (pp. 227–270). London: Academic Press.

Trevarthan, C. (1979b). Instincts for human understanding and for cultural cooperation: Their development in infancy. In M. van Cranach, K. Foppa, W. Lepenies, & D. Ploog (Eds.), *Human ethology: Claims and limits of a new discipline* (pp. 530–571). Cambridge: Cambridge University Press.

Trevarthan, C. (1980). The foundations of intersubjectivity: Development of interpersonal and cooperative understanding in infants. In D. R. Olson (Ed.), *The social foundations of language and thought: Essays in honor of Jerome S. Bruner* (pp. 316–342). New York: Norton.

Trevarthan, C., & Hubley, P. (1978). Secondary intersubjectivity: Confidence, confiding and acts of meaning in the first year. In A. Lock (Ed.), *Action, gesture and symbol: The emergence of language* (pp. 183–229). London: Academic Press.

Unsworth, L. (2001). *Teaching multiliteracies across the curriculum: Changing contexts of text and image in classroom practice.* Buckingham, England: Open University Press.

Vosniadou, S., & Brewer, W. F. (1987). Theories of knowledge restructuring in development. *Review of Educational Research, 57,* 51–67.

Vygotsky, L. S. (1962). *Thought and language.* Cambridge, MA: MIT Press.

Vygotsky, L. S. (1978). *Mind in society: The development of higher psychological processes.* Cambridge, MA: Harvard University Press.

Wells, G. (1981). *Learning through interaction: The study of language development.* Cambridge: Cambridge University Press.

Wells, G. (1985). Preschool literacy-related activities and success in school. In D. R. Olson, N. Torrence, & A. Hildyard (Eds.), *Literacy, language, and learning: The nature and consequences of reading and writing* (pp. 229–255). Cambridge: Cambridge University Press.

Wells, G. (1986). *The meaning makers: Children learning language and using language to learn.* Portsmouth, NH: Heinemann.

Wells, G. (1994). The complimentary contributions of Halliday and Vygoysky to a "language-based theory of learning." *Linguistics and Education, 6,* 41–90.

Wells, G. (1999). *Dialogic inquiry: Toward a sociocultural practice and theory of education.* Cambridge: Cambridge University Press.

Wells, G., & Chang-Wells, G. L. (1992). *Constructing knowledge together: Classrooms as centers of inquiry and literacy.* Portsmouth, NH: Heinemann.

Wertsch, J. V. (1985). *Vygotsky and the social formation of mind.* Cambridge: Cambridge University Press.

Wertsch, J. V. (1989). A sociocultural approach to mind. In W. Damon (Ed.), *Child development today and tomorrow* (pp. 14–33). San Francisco: Jossey-Bass.

Wertsch, J. V. (1991). *Voices of the mind: A sociocultural approach to mediated action.* Cambridge, MA: Harvard University Press.

Wilhelm, J. D. (2004). *Reading is seeing: Learning to visualize scenes, characters, ideas, and text worlds to improve comprehension and reflective reading.* New York: Scholastic.

 ## Children's Literature

The Adventures of Spider: West African Folk Tales by J. C. Arkhurst. Illustrated by J. Pinkney. Little, Brown, 1964.

Anansi the Spider by G. McDermott. Holt, Rinehart, and Winston, 1972.

Charlotte's Web by E. B. White. Illustrated by G. Williams. Harper & Row, 1952.

Coraline by N. Gaiman. Illustrated by D. McKean. Harper-Collins, 2002.

In the Year of the Boar and Jackie Robinson by B. B. Lord. Illustrated by M. Simont. Harper & Row, 1994.

Julie of the Wolves by J. C. George. Illustrated by J. Schoenherr. Harper & Row, 1972.

The Owl and the Woodpecker by B. Wildsmith. Oxford University Press, 1971.

Shabanu: Daughter of the Wind by S. F. Staples. Knopf, 1989.

Spider and the Sky God by D. M. N. Chocolate. Illustrated by D. Albers. Troll, 1993.

Spiders by G. Gibbons. Holiday House, 1993.

Squirrels by B. Wildsmith. Oxford University Press, 1974.

Talk Talk: An Ashanti Legend by D. M. N. Chocolate. Illustrated by D. Albers. Troll, 1993.

2

Children and Teachers in an Integrated Language Classroom

In an integrated language perspective, the classroom represents an environment of authentic language/communication use; it is a culture in which language and other modes of the communication landscape are used to learn. What are the participants—children and teachers—like in such a classroom culture? In this chapter, we further refine and extend the ideas about learners, knowledge, language, and other modes of communication covered in Chapter 1 by summarizing and highlighting characteristic attributes and activities of these participants in the classroom. Chapters 3, 4, and 5 then show how to plan and implement thematic units so that the activities of classroom participants can be realized.

An integrated language perspective is child-centered in that teachers are committed to having students have a voice in their learning. As a result, teachers take on certain roles to facilitate children's ideas and to build on them. Thus, we first cover some major characteristics of both children and teachers. It will be clear that having a "child-centered" emphasis does not preclude teacher expertise and input in teaching and learning. Teachers decide on the essential questions and understandings that children are to examine and study; they provide the broad structure of routines students are to engage in; they choose the materials, books, and other resources and experiences children will use and engage in; they serve as guides or facilitators to support students' ongoing efforts in learning.

Two major features will be apparent in our discussion about children and teachers in an integrated language perspective: (1) the importance of student-directed inquiry, that is, opportunities for individual knowers to have ownership in activities and projects that enable them to construct and reconstruct knowledge based on what they already know, and (2) how this inquiry is very much a social process. We will be emphasizing *collaborative learning* and the fact that teachers have a *collaborative style of teaching*. Much of this collaborative nature of teaching and learning is revealed through classroom discourse, so later in this chapter we examine more specifically the conversational interactions between students and teachers. The root of collaboration, we will argue, involves teachers sharing authority and power with their students. Thus, collaboration has to do with notions of control, and using some examples of classroom talk we show how collaboration is realized in the culture of the integrated language classroom. In addition, as part of collaboration, we highlight an alternative discipline approach—Developmental Discipline. It fits well with the collaborative style of teaching because it stresses the ethical dimension of teachers creating caring classrooms for all children.

Characteristics of Children and Teachers

Here we discuss first the nature of children, then the role of teachers within a range of nine major interrelated characteristics.

CHILDREN *Generate and Test Hypotheses;* TEACHERS *Foster Problem Solving and Risk Taking*

CHILDREN

Children are meaning makers or semioticians, always trying to make sense of their world. Because they are active, constructive learners, they are constantly solving problems and generating and testing hypotheses. Because their hypotheses may be confirmed or disconfirmed at any time, risk taking is inherent in the process of learning. Moreover, their hypotheses are about specific content, domain of knowledge, or problem space. Hypotheses are not content free. What children already know—their schemas on a particular topic—is the basis on which their questions arise. Learning is always the result of "the having of wonderful ideas" to try out in an activity or project. Remember how Sara's earlier knowledge of spiders (in Chapter 1) became extended and differentiated as a result of the opportunity to study spiders in depth at school. The more ideas children already have on a topic—the more there is something to think about—the more ideas are generated, and the more complicated and developed their schemas become.

Meaning makers learn by generating and testing hypotheses about the world.

Smith (1997); Wells (1999, 2001)

Duckworth (1987)

TEACHERS

As has been noted, children's schemas develop through generating and testing hypotheses about language, other communication modes, and the world and by trying to figure out their own problems on a range of topics. For learning to continue in the classroom, the teacher has to provide a climate that will further foster these children's natural learning inclinations. Rather than stress that children discover the "correct" or "right" answer in the textbook or in the teacher's head, the teacher in an integrated language classroom attempts to enhance the probability of children's own discoveries. Such an atmosphere makes children comfortable enough to put their ideas on the line so that risk taking is not cut off. It is okay for them to offer their own interpretation of a story, although it may be different from those of their teacher or their peers; it is all right to use invented spelling to express their good ideas when they don't know the conventional spelling of words; it is okay to use their own everyday wordings and experiences to first tackle new science ideas and terminology. Because risk taking aims at going beyond the status quo, the modification of children's schemas and learning is more likely.

A climate conducive to taking risks is required.

Cambourne (1984); Lindfors (1999); Wells (1999); Wells & Chang-Wells (1992)

CHILDREN'S *Language/Communication and Learning Reflect Approximations;* TEACHERS *Expect and Understand Children's Approximations in Language/Communication and Learning*

CHILDREN

Children are always modifying the ideas and concepts in their schemas. Their present theories are tentative and approximate adult (or expert) views regarding a topic. Their language also includes approximations that reflect their current understanding of the conventions of language to express their ideas. Their drawing or visual designs resemble but are not quite adult depictions. Approximations are the natural consequences of learning. They are intrinsic to the ways in which children construct their knowledge. Approximations are creative constructions. They reflect the modes of expression and cultural diversity that children bring to their communication and approaches to learning. Consequently, in this book we do not refer to children's hypotheses about the world or language with negative terms such as *errors* or *mistakes.*

Approximations are inherent in the learning process.

Cambourne (1984); Fisher (1995); Holdaway (1979); Wells (1999); Wells & Chang-Wells (1992)

Lindfors (1987)

Parents accept and actually reward spoken language approximations during the preschool years. They accept their baby's protolanguage and idiosyncratic constructions (remember Mark's *jubs,* an approximation of the conventional word *birds*) and their child's designation of "doggie" for all four-legged, furry animals and their attempts to regularize all plurals and past tenses with "mouses" and "goed." They celebrate the pictures of people that their children draw, even when no bodies are present and arms

Wells (1981, 1986)

and legs may be attached to the bottom of the faces of these people. Thus, although approximations, especially in reading and writing, may not be tolerated in most traditional classrooms, they are welcomed and encouraged in an integrated language classroom because they are considered great indicators of a child's thinking and understanding at a particular time, on a particular topic, and in a particular context. Meaning makers always produce approximations.

TEACHERS

Because teachers view children as active learners who have constructed their own knowledge, they expect children's approximations in their theories about the world and about the rules of language/communication use. Approximations are the result of risk taking and children's current hypotheses and conceptions. These approximations are reflected in everything they do—how they think a machine works, why people acted the way they did years ago, what they believe an author means, what they think an illustrator is trying to "say," how to coordinate, express, and revise the information they found on a topic from the Internet and other resources in their research reports, how to spell a word, or how to figure out a word they encounter in their reading. Because approximations are based on their existing schemas and are important indicators of children's present understandings, teachers in an integrated language classroom are careful observers of how children make sense of language, other modes of communication, and the world so they know what, why, and how to teach next.

Integrated language teachers are kid-watchers and evaluate children's learning while the children are actually using language/communication in their activities and projects. Approximations are guideposts by which teachers can assess individual children's strategies and knowledge. Teachers realize that the logic by which children learn may not be the same logic as that used by adults. Consequently, they monitor children's approximations so that they know how to respond to children to further foster, sustain, and extend their present efforts. Thus, teachers are involved in an ongoing interplay between assessment and instruction. They document children's approximations made in various contexts and across time, their instructional responses to these approximations, and children's development to more mature understanding and control of conventions so that they have a valid means of accountability regarding children's learning.

CHILDREN *Use Authentic Communication for Meaningful Purposes;* TEACHERS *Demonstrate and Encourage Authentic Communication for Meaningful Purposes*

CHILDREN

From the beginning of life, children are immersed in authentic, meaningful spoken language, as well as other modes of communication. Even as babies, they are invited to be participants in communication. They do not first learn about oral language and then learn how to use it. They learn oral language and how to use it simultaneously; they learn spoken language for real, functional purposes.

Research in emergent literacy has indicated that young children who come to school already reading and writing also learned this literate behavior in this authentic, meaningful way. Parents of these children shared and discussed books with them and encouraged them to write their own messages and notes. Parents pointed out aspects of print and illustrations to their children in everyday activities and responded to their children's comments and questions that arose in purposeful, communicative events. When the conditions are right, children can learn to read and write as easily as they learn to talk and listen. Thus, in integrated language classrooms, children use authentic language and visual images for meaningful purposes: to write and illustrate a report on their study of chicks they have seen hatch, to converse with group members about

---

Margin notes:

Approximations help teachers understand children's hypotheses or schemas about the world.

Goodman (1985); Goodman & Goodman (1990); Jaggar & Smith-Burke (1985); Wilde (1997)

Falk (2000); Gredler & Johnson (2004); Powers (1996); Wells (2001)

Communication is learned through authentic use.

Edelsky (1991); Halliday (1975); Kress (1997)

Cambourne (1984); Halliday (1993); Holdaway (1979)

the words, gestures, and spatial aspects of a play they are planning to give, or to read books or Internet websites for a project they are working on.

Authentic communication is holistic. Thus, isolated drills or practice on only one part or subsystem of language (e.g., practicing phonics rules on certain letter–sound relationships, copying over and over the spelling words of the week, or underlining nouns in sentences from the language arts textbook) are not used. Instead, children learn letter–sound relationships (or graphophonemic cues) by reading real books and writing their own stories or information books; they learn how to spell through exposure to words in their reading and by trying out their invented spellings to express their own ideas in writing; they understand how nouns work by encountering those employed by authors and by using those they need in their own writing. They also realize that most texts (even on the Internet) are multimodal and that they need to pay attention to all modes of communication because all express meanings. (This learning, of course, is also supported by explicit teaching by teachers in the context of these experiences—see the prototypes in Chapter 4 and Phonics in Context*, Grammar in Context*, and Focus Lessons* in Chapter 7.)

> Newman (1991); Unsworth (2001); Wells (1999)

> Fisher (1995); Kress (2003); Routman (1996); Weaver (2002)

It is through this kind of genuine communication use that children also learn about the various modes of the communication landscape. At the same time that they are *learning* language and visual images (i.e., constructing the language and visual design systems or figuring out how symbols and images represent meanings in oral/written and visual structures) and *learning through* language/visual images (i.e., discovering how the world works in conversations and viewing with others), they are also *learning about* language and visual images themselves (i.e., becoming aware of language as an object that has elements, forms, and functions, realizing that visual design consists of various compositional features). Although they are largely tacit or subconscious, these three aspects of communicative development simultaneously interact and facilitate one another. They are social processes, learned in authentic, meaningful communication with others.

> Halliday (1982, 1993); Unsworth (2001)

TEACHERS

Authentic language/communication is a social activity; it is used for meaningful purposes. For the various communication modes to be tools for learning instead of ends in and of themselves, teachers demonstrate how something is actually done by using language and/or other communication modes in integrated language classrooms. They use real books, which include a range of visual designs, that would be found in homes, libraries, and bookstores, and they suggest ways that particular books may be useful for particular activities or projects. When they share these books with children, they read with interest, get children to predict what will happen next, wonder about an author's choice of words, consider how and why an illustrator has expressed meanings through pictures, or how photographs clarify or highlight concepts. During sustained silent reading (SSR)* time, they themselves read their own books, and then they frequently share with their students the funny or sad parts in novels and the interesting parts in nonfictional texts. They let children in on strategies that they themselves use in reading—for example, skip what they don't know, examine the pictures or other visual images to give clues to unfamiliar ideas, read more of the surrounding text to figure out or clarify an unknown word or concept, substitute words that maintain meaning for parts of a text, reread a passage, or when they can't understand a text, even drop it altogether and get another book on the same topic.

> Authentic communication is used and demonstrated by the teacher.

> Kress (2000); Kress et al. (2001); Unsworth (2001); Wells (2001)

Teachers write letters, notes, and messages to children, parents, and colleagues. They write reminders to themselves; they label articles and places in the classroom so it is easy for all to use available resources. They share their sketches of their responses to books. They are genuine responders—they acknowledge when they don't understand something children might have said, written, or depicted so that children are given opportunities to rephrase or revise to make their intentions clearer. In sum, teachers use authentic communication, and in doing so they encourage children to see

> Lindfors (1999); Mercer (1995); Wells & Chang-Wells (1992); Young (1992)

how things are done with language and other modes of communication. Authentic communication fosters children's learning about its various registers and ideologies of multimodal texts and their awareness of how such communication can be used for their own purposes to learn about the world.

CHILDREN *Integrate Modes of Communication in Their Activities/Projects;* TEACHERS *Provide Activities and Projects So That Children Can Integrate Communication*

CHILDREN

In an integrated language classroom, there are no separate speaking, listening, reading, writing, and drawing activities. The fact that children use authentic communication in the classroom means that their use of it is integrated. Their activities and projects are surrounded by conversation. These projects require reading of both linguistic and visual-image messages; writing and depicting meanings via various visual designs are needed to share the outcomes or findings of their projects. For example, a small group of children may study slugs. As they observe the slugs, they chat among themselves about what they see, what they have read about slugs, and so forth. They take notes and make drawings on their observations and about the information they have gleaned in their reading. They individually present their findings; one writing an illustrated story about slugs (titled "Sluggo"), another a more informational piece on slugs, replete with drawings that label and note the parts of slugs, and another a cartoon pictorial depiction (with captions) of the behavior of slugs expressed in a humorous way. Or they may examine "outsider viewpoints" as part of a PERSPECTIVES thematic unit (see Chapter 4). Here small groups read various novels about "outsiders" during which they critically discuss, using both written and sketched-out responses, the different perspectives and ideologies that characters might have held *and* how the authors of these texts are representing these characters' viewpoints. Subsequently, each group contributes— through both writing and drawing—the various dimensions of similarities and differences regarding viewpoints on a class Comparison Chart*. In a CYCLES unit (see Chapter 4), groups of students study plant, animal, and weather cycles. They use a range of sources in their inquiries, including Internet websites, and then share their findings via text-image PowerPoint presentations. Each group covers the major ideas for the whole class, and then a member from each group joins a new Jigsaw group to teach classmates the details. Thus, much is learned through use of integrated communication.

TEACHERS

Integrated authentic communication occurs naturally when children have many contexts in which to explore and study a range of topics and many activities and projects to engage in. For example, when a teacher provides several animals for observation and study in the classroom, children in small groups have to work together on their projects. The teacher may initially provide a range of cards listing open-ended questions for them to consider regarding these animals, or the class might have identified important questions to pursue via a K-W-L* activity. (K-W-L* is discussed in more detail in Chapter 7.) These initial observations serve as grist for the students to pose their own questions and areas of Student-Directed Inquiries*. The teacher will also place a broad spectrum of books regarding these animals near the animal centers to support the children's investigations.

Because the teacher offers activities that are centered on or guided by children, the teacher is then available to provide specific feedback to children regarding aspects of their projects. Children may follow up on a question or comment the teacher has made in their journals by subsequently reading several books or viewing relevant Internet websites and then discussing them with the teacher. The teacher is also free to facilitate in-

Communication is integrated.

Dyson (1989); Tierney & Readance (2000); Unsworth (2001); Wells (1999, 2001); Wells & Chang-Wells (1992)

Activities are provided so that the integration of communication is possible.

Alvermann et al. (2004); Moore et al. (2003); Wells (1999, 2001); Unsworth (2001)

Wells (1999, 2001); Wells & Chang-Wells (1992)

teraction between children and can guide them to consider their peers as sources of help and support in deciding if their organization of material on their topic seems to be clear and interesting to others. In such situations, therefore, children have many opportunities to take turns offering and listening to each other's ideas about what needs to be done and how to do it. When a child writes a report on a particular subtopic related to a topic another child has chosen, the children become interested conversational partners. They share their resources, pointing out parts of books or websites they have come across in their own research that may be useful for their peers on their projects. When teachers offer meaningful activities and projects, the need for integrated communication—the use of authentic language and other modes of communication—naturally arises.

CHILDREN *Have Choices and Ownership in What They Do;* TEACHERS *Foster Children's Choices and Ownership of Their Activities and Projects and Promote Children's Autonomy and Control of Their Learning*

CHILDREN

During the preschool years, children choose activities that interest them. Their purposes sustain their attention in projects and guide their motivation to understand. By owning what they do and following their own questions about topics, they are able to create new concepts and make new connections in their schemas. Children in an integrated language classroom are also provided with opportunities to initiate their own activities. They select and take on projects; they make their projects their own, thereby making their knowledge their own. It is this ownership that fosters the intellectual autonomy. "Owning" an activity, task, or project leads to knowing how, why, and what to do. As a result, children behave responsibly.

Having choices fosters ownership and autonomy.

Fried (2001); Kohn (1998); Wells (1999, 2001); Willinsky (1990)

TEACHERS

Inherent in the collaborative approach is a certain management style. Rather than control everything done in the classroom, teachers in an integrated language classroom attempt to share with their students control of what happens. They do that by providing many choices—by letting children decide what topic to pursue within a thematic unit, what questions to pose and resolve, and what ways to relate what they have learned. By accepting children's approximations, they help children represent problems to themselves, and they foster children's intellectual autonomy. Thus, the challenge of learning and education in general—children's construction of knowledge by seeking connections that will integrate different areas and by developing strategies to exploit present understandings to maximum effect—is promoted.

Providing choices is critical to fostering ownership.

Kohn (1998); Nieto (2000); Wells (1999, 2001); Willinsky (1990)

When teachers allow children to control their learning and own their activities and projects, children's feelings of self-respect are developed and they become confident in what they know. They are encouraged to be independent, self-motivated learners. The model that teachers have provided means that children learn to treat and respect their peers, who may come from a different social class or ethnolinguistic cultural group, in the same way.

CHILDREN *Collaborate with Peers and Teacher about Learning Activities/Projects;* TEACHERS *Foster Peer Collaboration and Also Collaborate with Children in Their Learning Activities/Projects*

CHILDREN

Just as children use others as resources in learning about the world during the preschool years, children in an integrated language classroom are supported through their interactions with their peers and teacher. Rather than hours of individual "seat

Children learn through collaboration with others.

Kohn (1998); Watson (2003); Wells (1986, 1999, 2001); Wells & Chang-Wells (1992)

work" where talk is forbidden, purposeful conversation among children is encouraged. For example, several children in a small group may collaborate with their group members in an activity. Perhaps they are going to do a survey regarding litter in the community. Some children will be responsible for drawing up a rough draft of the questions they will ask, others may be busy brainstorming to decide whom they should ask, and so forth. Decisions about their individual contributions to the project require negotiation. They must decide among themselves who will be doing that task. Or perhaps a problem or issue may be posed by the teacher and then examined by children in the classroom. The teacher may also ask them to consider if they think they have enough categories of people or enough questions to make the results of their survey representative. Children bring their own knowledge to bear on the problem to come up with an answer that is constructed by a group or the class as a whole.

To understand and be understood is the basis of communication and of learning in general. Individual children have had varying experiences and, therefore, may possess very different knowledge schemas on a particular topic. Thus, individual children offer different contributions to, and have different interpretations of, what is being studied. In addition, children have unique personal characteristics and come from a variety of cultural backgrounds. Such cultural and linguistic diversity means that children also bring their own complex customs or styles of interaction to their activities or projects. Children from different cultural backgrounds have different rules for communication. Because their "ways with words" may not be like those of the other children or of the teacher, collaboration is crucial. Children from different cultural communities bring different ideologies or values about life that are embedded within their ways of expressing themselves through language and other modes of communication. Negotiation is the only means by which classroom participants—children and teacher alike—can deal with their various ways of participating or interacting. This is how intersubjectivity is achieved and understanding is accomplished.

Foster (1992); Heath (1983); Lindfors (1999); McCollum (1991); Michaels (1981); Nieto (2000)

Distinctive ideologies are "inscribed" within the discourse of children's various cultural groups.

Chouliarski & Fairclough (2001); Fairclough (1989, 1992); Gee (1999)

TEACHERS

In integrated language classrooms, the teachers' goal is to create a nurturing, caring classroom community. Because they know that children learn best in social contexts with others, they foster peer collaboration in activities and projects. Students benefit when they hear different points of views, interpretations, approaches, or strategies. Also, as these collaborative groups engage in their inquiries, teachers have ample opportunities to monitor and support their efforts. They can better understand children's different cultural ways of communicating, their varying background knowledge on topics, and their diverse approaches or strategies they employ in their projects. Teachers also form a range of buddy partnerships or small groups for many purposes (see Chapter 7 regarding group formation) so that students learn how to work with *all* students in the classroom, thereby creating a community. They also interact with children in multiple ways so that they can establish trusting, personal relationships with their students.

Collaborative peer groups promote a supportive, caring classroom community.

Lee & Smagorinsky (2000); Watson (2003)

CHILDREN *Use Feedback from Peers and Teacher to Self-Regulate Their Use of Communication and Modify Their Theories;* TEACHERS *Provide Feedback That Facilitates Children's Self-Regulation of Their Schemas*

CHILDREN

When children collaborate and negotiate with other classroom participants, they are provided with countless opportunities to reconsider, reevaluate, and reformulate how and what they mean. They present their ideas (orally, in writing, or via illustrating or other means of visual depiction) on the basis of their schemas, and they take note of their peers' or teacher's responses or ideas: "That's a great idea! How about . . . ?", "I

Feedback from others develops children's schemas.

don't understand that," "What do you mean?" or "Why do you think so?", "How are you going to display that?" This feedback extends their ideas, urges them on, and requires them to clarify and justify their views. Listening to a fellow student's report or viewing his or her presentation on a particular topic, or a partner's ideas about how to explore and report on their project, sparks new questions and ideas. This self-regulation, fostered through social interaction, leads to knowledge restructuring and modification of their schemas.

Self-regulation also promotes children's *metacognitive awareness,* that is, an awareness of their own thinking. They begin to reflect on the thinking processes of communication, what they do when they talk, read, write, draw, or depict, how their interpretations may affect others, and how others' interpretations may influence their own. This is the *literate* (and *multiliterate*) thinking that empowers children because they not only learn to take advantage of the potential of various modes of the communication landscape to express their own ideas and thought processes but also because they realize how these thought processes themselves can be seen as an object that can be critically reexamined further.

TEACHERS

A collaborative style of teaching gives teachers many opportunities to provide critical feedback to children as they engage in activities and projects. Teachers go in close and listen to understand. They take children's problems seriously and attempt to address their intentions. Their questions and suggestions are related to these intentions—are contingently responsive to students' current efforts—and then children are left on their own to consider these possibilities. Teachers lead from behind; they track what children are trying to do and then provide the support that enables children to stretch and go beyond their own limits, to do on their own what they initially could not do unaided. These are called zones of proximal development (ZPD), and these interactions provide the kind of assistance children need to modify their theories and self-regulate their schemas so that they internalize their teachers' response modes and discourse practices and begin to interact with their peers in a similar manner. Children become coaches, asking for and giving useful feedback to one another.

Some of the instructional contexts that teachers provide may be teacher-directed Focus Lessons* for the whole class or a particular group (see Chapter 7). Some of these may be preplanned to launch and support a thematic unit's exploration or to set up or clarify certain routines or activities that may be unfamiliar to students. Yet, many occur as teachers provide explicit instruction in an ongoing fashion, right at the moment that students need it, based on teachers' observation of students' difficulties, misunderstandings, or approximations.

CHILDREN *Use and Learn Modes of Communication across the Curriculum;* TEACHERS *Provide Opportunities to Integrate Modes of Communication across the Curriculum*

CHILDREN

The understanding of communication is increased and intensified when children use integrated modes of communication across the curriculum. They speak, listen, read, write, and use various visual designs as they conduct a science experiment, consider problems and discover patterns in math, engage in an inquiry in social studies, or reflect on some art project. Because the content of these disciplines (or curricular domains) is different, children discover that different registers of language (both oral and written) must be employed in their projects. They also realize that particular visual designs are connected to these different language differences. Communicative competence is fostered in complex, sophisticated ways. Metalinguistic, metavisualization, and

Alvermann et al. (2004); de Boo (1999); Moore et al. (2003); Wells (1994, 1999, 2001); Wells & Chang-Wells (1992)

Useful feedback helps children develop existing schemas.

Bruner (1983, 1986); Halliday (1993); Lee & Smagorinsky (2000); Lindfors (1987); Vygotsky (1978); Wells (1999)

Teachers create ZPDs (zones of proximal development) to promote children's learning.

Routman (1996)

Language and other modes of communication are used across the curriculum.

Berkenhotter & Huckin (1995); Johns (1997, 2002); Wells (1999); Wells & Chang-Wells (1992)

Johns (2002); Pappas (1997); Pappas & Pettegrew (1998); Unsworth (2001)

metacognitive awareness—the ability to learn *about* language and visual images, the ability to consider language and images as objects of study in and of themselves, the ability to ponder about their own thinking processes, the ability to examine their own strategies in solving or approaching certain problems in science, math, or social studies—are facilitated when children recognize in a more explicit way how linguistic/visual-image choices are expressed by different genres. They are also facilitated when children realize how various disciplines, as cultural frames, reflect various ways of knowing and ideologies or values. When children can integrate information or knowledge from various curricular domains by using these disciplines' discourse genres (or practices) in undertaking their Student-Directed Inquiries*, they begin to appreciate the distinctive contributions of various disciplines in present and future inquiries. They also become more adept in deciding which genres are appropriate for sharing the findings of their inquiries. (Subsequent chapters, especially Chapters 5 and 6, cover these differences of disciplines and genres in more detail.)

TEACHERS

Various curricular areas and disciplines deal with content and domains that are expressed by different language and visual design patterns or structures. Consequently, providing opportunities to use various modes of communication across the curriculum fosters communicative competence in a natural way yet at a sophisticated level. Disciplines are cultural frames; they are best seen as certain kinds of social activities conducted by certain communities of scholars, where novelists, mathematicians, historians, geologists, chemists, and biologists participate in particular modes of engagement with life.

Integrated work provides many challenges. It is one thing to know mathematical facts, but how should these data be reported in a survey or expressed in a report on an experiment? Or if information about the Aztecs has been obtained through reading nonfictional history texts and some stories in which Aztecs are characters, how should this information about the Aztecs and their values or ideologies be presented to the class? Should it be expressed by a piece of historical fiction or by an informational report? Maybe poetry should be considered. What is best? What are the advantages and disadvantages of selecting one form over the others? What kinds of visual images or art should be included to illustrate the findings? What questions should be considered in terms of representation and accuracy in these pictures?

When children are given opportunities to use modes of communication across the curriculum, the choices abound and the decisions to be made seem endless. However, in the process, children learn about the distinctive disciplinary modes of thinking and how these areas of intellectual thought are expressed in recognized linguistic modes or genres, and that different visual images are related to these genres. Also, in drawing on knowledge from various disciplines in a particular inquiry, children are encouraged to check and compare information they have gleaned from these resources. This helps them consider the tentative nature of knowledge in various domains and discover that while genres are inherited social forms, they can change and merge. Hence, through integrated inquiries, children become aware of the generative, creative potential of language and other modes of communication.

Many ways to use modes of communication across the curriculum are provided.

Johns (1997, 2002); Unsworth (2001)

Geertz (1983); Levstik & Pappas (1992); Pappas (1997)

Halliday (1978, 1993); Kress (1997); Wells (1993, 1994, 1999)

CHILDREN *Have Sustained Time for Systematic and Reflective Inquiry on a Range of Topics;* TEACHERS *Plan and Implement Thematic Units So That Children Have Sustained Time for Systematic and Reflective Inquiry on a Range of Topics*

CHILDREN

Children's learning during the preschool years is developed in contexts in which they focus on topics and things that interest them. By engaging in activities with others who

Reflective inquiry requires sustained time.

sustain and extend these interests, children acquire amazing communicative, cognitive, and social abilities. Schooling should, therefore, plan and provide for more of these contexts of concentrated effort. However, in most traditional classrooms the entire school day is fragmented into small time slots during which teachers and children alike are on a treadmill to get it done and move along. Rather than this "cha-cha-cha curriculum," children in an integrated language classroom have ample blocks of time to explore and think and change their minds; to figure out whether their meanings are best expressed through language or visual images, or both; to consider and evaluate different points of view; to decide on their questions and how to resolve them; to read and reread; and to write and revise. Thus, they have opportunities to study a range of topics in depth and their inquiries are systematic and reflective.

TEACHERS

The use of thematic units has many advantages. It provides both depth and breadth. (Many thematic units are illustrated throughout this book, especially in Chapters 3, 4, and 5.) A thematic unit has a central theme or conceptual framework that provides overall coherence. At the same time, it provides opportunities for children to explore specific topics and domains in-depth. Because these individual and group projects are related to the theme, however, many more connections are made. Learning has a richness and a significance rarely seen when basals and textbooks determine the course of study. Thus, a thematic unit approach reflects a "less is more" philosophy by addressing the problems inherent in "teaching for coverage" that is found in traditional classrooms where students are exposed to many topics "at a clip." Through thematic units, teachers do consider various guidelines and standards at the local, state, and national levels, but they do this by posing interesting and essential questions about content and setting up a framework for inquiry in which students can examine these central concepts and questions across the curriculum.

Thematic units also allow for children's choice. Moreover, they provide the sustained time children need to pursue their topics of study. Teachers and peers can better interact and support children in their activities and projects. Having time for systematic inquiry on topics of one's choice leads to reflective thinking. There is a constant relating of what one already knows to something new. Because the children know what's familiar and what's new, new routines and connections evolve and become apparent. Children actually become more consciously aware of these new interpretations. They move into what are called *disembedded modes of thought*. That is, they are able to reflect on their modes of communication and thinking in abstraction; they can take a critical stance to their learning. This is the metalinguistic, metavisualization, and metacognitive awareness discussed in an earlier section of this chapter.

Teachers Use a Collaborative Style of Teaching

The characteristics that we have described for children can be realized in the classroom only when teachers take on a style of teaching, a particular orientation to instruction, which was hinted at in the preceding discussion. This style of teaching is often called a *dialogically organized approach*, because it allows for and privileges both the *voices* of students and the teacher in the curriculum and the classroom discourse. It enables that *dialogic inquiry* between classroom participants be enacted in thematic units.

Conversation is an important medium for instruction in the classroom. Collaborative talk especially facilitates children's learning—their construction of knowledge—for it makes possible teachers' contributions to be *contingently responsive* to learners'

Alvermann et al. (2004); Fried (2001); Moore et al. (2003); Wells (1999); Wells & Chang-Wells (1992)

Donald Graves is responsible for the apt term "cha-cha-cha curriculum" (according to Calkins, 1986).

Thematic units provide sustained time for projects and inquiries.

Alvermann et al. (2004); Fried (2001); Moore et al. (2003); Pappas (1997); Wells (1999)

Fried (2001)

Thematic units promote in-depth, not superficial "at a clip," learning.

Kohn (1998); Wells & Chang-Wells (1992)

Donaldson (1978)

A collaborative teaching style is used.

Nystrand (1997)

Pappas & Zecker (2001a, 2001b); Wells (1986, 1993, 1994, 1999); Wells & Chang-Wells (1992) present needs. Wells provides four general recommendations for teachers to guide them in engaging in the type of talk with children in which contingent responsiveness enables and empowers learning:

1. Assume that children attempt to communicate because they have something important to say; that is, take their ways of questioning, commenting, and explaining seriously. Moreover, treat these attempts as an indication of their best efforts to solve a particular problem on their own, without the aid of others.
2. Before responding, try to listen carefully to children's accounts and ask for any needed clarifications from them to understand accurately what children are trying to relate.
3. When responding, confirm or check children's meanings first—that is, attempt to achieve intersubjectivity—and then either extend or develop their accounts, or encourage children to do so themselves.
4. Try to have your contributions at or just beyond children's current understandings. That is, formulate your contributions with *both* children's present abilities and your pedagogical intentions in mind, but always be ready to modify your agenda in light of the feedback that children provide in their responses.

These recommendations reflect Vygotsky's ideas of the zones of proximal development (ZPD) that have been mentioned earlier. ZPDs are considered the best kind of social interaction and talk for learning. That is, "good learning" occurs *in* children when they are interacting *with* teachers (and in cooperation with peers).

Teachers must keep these principles from Wells in mind especially when teaching children who come from a variety of linguistic, cultural, and socioeconomic backgrounds. An appreciation of children's different "ways with words" enables teachers to capitalize on children's individual approaches to communicating (in both oral and written forms) and to learning in general. For example, children may have different ways or styles of storying. In telling of a personal experience, some may express a series of implicitly associated topics, whereas others may focus on a single, more explicit topic. Or, depending on the customs of their culture, children may have different ideas about what is meant by staying on the subject (due to different rules for relevance) or waiting their turn to talk (due to different expectations regarding the signals for when it's okay to talk), or different orientations to public performance in the classroom (due to different personal and cultural factors that influence whether children are eager or uncomfortable in performing verbally in front of a group). Teachers must accept a wide range of language behaviors as appropriate and must be open and eager to understand children's approaches to mean. They attempt to enact what is called *culturally responsive teaching*.

In the traditional classroom, the teacher-controlled initiate-respond-evaluate (IRE) pattern characterizes much of the classroom discourse interactions. When using the IRE pattern, the teacher *initiates* a sequence by calling a child to answer, then the nominated child *responds* to the initiation or questions posed by the teacher, and then the teacher *evaluates* what the child has said before calling on the next child. It is a form of discourse that interrogates students, not one in which students and teacher can have dialogues or conversations about topics. The IRE pattern is not a structure in which teachers can be sensitive to authentic communication and student-directed inquiry. It doesn't regard learners' conceptions of their tasks and the ways they plan to proceed on them so that children can be guided by the teacher to more mature understanding. Thus, the IRE interactional pattern is used sparingly in integrated language classrooms; its purpose is usually employed to promote and make possible the range of participation structures that better enables collaboration and negotiation, or to explicitly teach some strategy or skill (that the teacher has noted via his or her observations) so that they can be successful in their inquiries. (IRE and alternative non-IRE patterns will be discussed later in the chapter.)

Wells offers four guidelines for teachers to promote contingently responsive talk with children.

Vygotsky (1978)

ZPDs enable children to learn things with others that they could not learn alone.

Heath (1983); Ladson-Billings (1994); Lindfors (1999); Nieto (2000)

Cazden (2001); Lindfors (1999)

See Cazden (2001), Lindfors (1999), and Nieto (2000) for more accounts of various "ways with words."

Cazden (2001); Edwards & Mercer (1987); Mercer (1995); Young (1992)

The IRE discourse pattern has the teacher dominating all the classroom talk.

Too many whole-group, teacher-led situations tend to constrain flexibility and reduce opportunities for teachers to interact with individual children. In integrated language classrooms, children work individually, in pairs, or in small groups, and consequently the teacher can engage in more face-to-face encounters with the children. Inherent in a collaborative style of teaching is the teacher's capacity to decenter—to take the child's perspective. While children are busy in their activities or projects, the teacher is careful to ask and respond to authentic questions in order to be informed about, and helpful in, children's endeavors and to better address their concerns and difficulties. The intent of the teacher's questions is not to check if children's ideas conform with the teacher's knowledge. The more a teacher knows a domain, the greater is the risk of behaving egocentrically in relation to that knowledge. Egocentricity is more of a problem for the teacher than for children in classrooms. A collaborative style, therefore, bridges the gap between teachers' and children's schemas so that children can create their own concepts and relationships.

Teachers in an integrated language classroom see themselves as learners. As children construct their knowledge, teachers learn about their own discoveries. Children become experts on particular topics and share their knowledge with the teacher. Teachers collaborate with children who have different ways with words and learn about the ethnic and cultural complexity of our world. When teachers include books and materials to implement their thematic units, some resources may be unfamiliar to them or known only in a superficial way. Consequently, teachers learn more about content and how that content is expressed in written language and other communication modes. Teachers then see themselves as researchers of their own practice.

Teachers are learners and researchers of their own practice.

Bartolome (1994); Cazden (2001); Cochran-Smith & Lytle (1993); Pappas & Zecker (2001b)

As developers of their own programs and curricula, teachers here use their own interpretative frameworks to generate knowledge about teaching and learning. They engage in teacher research—the systematic, intentional inquiry done by them about their own classroom work. This research is *systematic* because teachers gather and record information or document certain experiences in the classroom. It is *intentional* in that the research activity is a planned endeavor, although, of course, teachers gain insights all the time about their teaching as they teach. Finally, teacher research is *inquiry* in that it stems from or generates questions to make sense of classroom life. Because of this, teachers set about their teacher research or inquiry in ways that are parallel to those they support for their students. Like their students, they engage in inquiry that is fundamentally social and constructive, for it enables teachers both to reflect on new information and to interpret the knowledge that they already have. More importantly, though teacher research is an important intellectual heuristic to individual teachers, it also plays a critical role in the formation of the growing knowledge base for teaching that can be useful to the teaching profession at large. Teacher research enables teachers to take charge of their own professional development and learning. It also equips and prepares teachers to enter the public debate at the local and national levels about the kind of education that is needed for the twenty-first century. (More will be said about teacher research in Chapters 3, 4, 9, 10, and the Guidelines for Teacher Inquiry at the end of the book.)

Teacher research is systematic, intentional inquiry.

Cochran-Smith & Lytle (1993); Hubbard & Power (2003)

Pappas & Zecker (2001a, 2001b)

Teacher inquiry is like Student-Initiated Inquiry*.

Unlike teachers in traditional classrooms who believe their job is to implement others' programs and curricula, teachers in integrated language classrooms see themselves as professionals who own and develop their programs. Children operate from their own schemas and, consequently, travel different routes in learning. Thus, a curriculum is not considered very useful when it is in some prepackaged form that has been broken down into small steps or pieces and arranged in a linear sequence to be followed by *every* child. Such a program has been made for *unidirectional transmission,* where bits or "facts" from the material are delivered *one way* straight to the presumably empty mind of the child who is considered to have no influence in learning. Instead, teachers view knowledge in integrated language classrooms as an active reconstruction that is constantly being negotiated. What happens in the classroom must, therefore, be

Nystrand (1997); Pappas & Zecker (2001a); Wells (1999); Wells & Chang-Wells (1992)

See Table 2.1.

done in a collaborative way. This collaboration-oriented approach is contrasted with the transmission-oriented approach in traditional classrooms in Table 2.1. The traditional view is sometimes called *monologically organized instruction* because the teacher's voice is so dominant and the children's voice is not heard unless it has been controlled by the teacher. The collaborative view, as already noted, allows for both the teacher and student and, therefore, is seen as *dialogically organized instruction*, which underlies a very different teacher–student relationship.

Sharing Power in Collaboration: Developing Alternative, Non-IRE Classroom Discourse Patterns

A collaborative approach to teaching involves sharing power with students.

Cummins (1994); Oyler (1996); Pappas & Zecker (2001a); Wells (1999); Wells & Chang-Wells (1992)

See Table 2.1.

Cazden (2001); Edwards & Mercer (1987); Mercer (1995); Young (1992)

In the IRE talk structure, teachers' major purpose is to "test" students' knowledge.

We have already argued that taking a collaborative style of teaching involves teachers sharing power and authority with children and that teaching and learning in traditional classrooms reflect a different stance about power and control. In traditional classrooms, the teacher is in control of what is to be learned, when, and how. Knowledge is seen to be the possession of the teacher to be transmitted to students. Thus, it is assumed in this transmission model of teaching that what is learned is a direct reproduction of what is taught because children are not viewed as having their own theories, prior knowledge, or schemas about any particular topic under consideration. Again, see Table 2.1.

Talk or classroom discourse in a traditional classroom, therefore, reflects such power and control. Teachers not only do most of the talking, but they also control how much children talk as well as the nature of their talk. The following is an example of discourse in a first-grade classroom. You will note that the structure of the talk follows the typical IRE pattern: the teacher *initiates* the talk—usually by asking questions to which he or she knows the answers—then the child *responds,* and then the teacher *evaluates* the child's response as to its correctness. Let's see how it works.

table **2.1**   Comparison of Transmission versus Collaboration Teaching and Learning

Transmission-Oriented Teaching–Learning (Monologically Organized Instruction)	Collaboration-Oriented Teaching–Learning (Dialogically Organized Instruction)
Teacher has full authority and power in implementing instruction.	Teacher shares power and authority with students in implementing instruction.
Teacher (and/or textbooks or published programs) has all the knowledge or expertise, and students are seen to have little or no knowledge or theories of their own about topics of instruction. The teacher's role is to transmit knowledge to students.	Teacher acknowledges and values students' construction of their own knowledge and cultural understandings on topics of instruction. The teacher's role involves using teacher expertise to encourage, foster, extend, and transform student meaning-making.
Teaching–learning relationship is one of transmission and reception.	Teaching–learning relationship is one of collaborative transaction.
Teacher's agendas are dominant and control what happens in the classroom.	Both teacher and student agendas are considered to be important and are negotiated in the classroom.
Teacher's voice, questions, and initiations are predominant.	Both teacher and student voices, questions, and initiations are privileged.
Traditional (default) teacher-controlled initiate-respond-evaluate (IRE) discourse patterns are predominant—that is, didactic interactions and talk are prevalent.	Dialogically organized discourse patterns (alternative to IRE patterns) are predominant—that is, collaborative interactions and talk are prevalent.
Knowledge is a given, fixed entity and instruction is, therefore, seen to "fit all."	Knowledge emerges from interaction of voices (teacher and student) and instruction is, therefore, culturally responsive.

A small group of first-grade children has been sorting some pieces of plastic food that have been placed in the middle of a small table. The task the teacher has asked the children to accomplish involves having them place each plastic food item next to one of four pictures, each of which depicts one of four food groups: fruit and vegetables, meat, dairy products, bread products. The teacher, who had been working with other small groups in the classroom, has now come to this table, chosen one of the pieces of plastic food, and handed it to Stevie.

T: What is it?

S: [Stevie shrugs his shoulders]

T: Have another look and tell me what it is.

S: It's [inaudible]. [Other children talk and teacher doesn't hear Stevie]

T: What's it look like to you?

S: Eggs.

T: Eggs?

S: Scrambled eggs.

T: It isn't eggs, scrambled eggs. I want you to take another look.

S: It's yellow.

T: Yes, it's yellow. What food is yellow?

S: Corn? [Stevie simultaneously shaking his head indicating "no."]

T: Does that look like corn?

S: No.

T: What is yellow and would be round like this if it were put on a plate ready to eat?

S: [Stevie shrugs his shoulders]

T: Well, this is pasta. You know, noodles. So where should you put this pasta? Next to what picture?

You can see how much the teacher was in control of the conversation. She asked all of the questions, even though Stevie had no idea what this plastic object was supposed to represent. She kept trying to ask questions to "help" Stevie discover the "right" answer or make better guesses, and at times the teacher even seemed to lead him to an answer—for example, corn—that he himself felt to be unlikely or "stupid." Finally, she had to tell him what it was.

There were no opportunities for *Stevie* to ask the teacher what *he* thought the plastic item might be, which probably would have been a more appropriate scenario, because the plastic pasta item did not in fact look like pasta or noodles. As the remainder of the conversation (which is not provided here) proceeded, the teacher asked even more questions to get Stevie to place the pasta next to the right food group picture (bread products). Stevie initially put it near the dairy products picture, which was the wrong answer according to the teacher. Stevie mentioned eggs and butter (which, of course, may be used in making some kinds of pasta or noodles), but that was not considered a possibility because in the teaching materials she had relied on in setting up the sorting task, pasta was listed (and shown on the picture) under the bread food group.

The point of the teacher's task and her conversation with her students was to assess what individual children had learned about the four food groups in the nutrition lessons they had covered in preceding days. (We will not consider whether the four food groups is a worthy, interesting, or challenging topic for first-grade children to learn or study.) Even though the children worked in small groups (which the teacher had been trying out in the classroom since attending some workshops on cooperative group learning), the task was just another means of transmitting the teacher's knowledge (or the textbook information) on nutrition to the children in a direct, specified way. Children's ideas or questions were not considered here; the fact that the plastic item wasn't very realistic or that noodles are sometimes made out of eggs and butter and, therefore, might be categorized under dairy products were not problems to be examined. There is no

The IRE discourse pattern is found in a transmission-oriented curriculum.

Moll (1990); Pappas & Zecker (2001a); Wells (1999); Wells & Chang-Wells (1992)

Reflective Inquiry* here—no opportunities even for the teacher to try to understand the learner's conception of the task that the teacher set up. And there was certainly no Student-Initiated Inquiry* where Stevie could have initiated his own task based on his own questions. Thus, the IRE pattern expresses certain notions about knowledge—namely, that children do not have their own theories or knowledge of their own—and as a result teachers must transmit the knowledge or information to students.

Because teachers in integrated language classrooms have a different view of knowledge—that children construct their own knowledge—teachers take on different roles in teaching so that they can better collaborate with children to assist their learning. In doing so, they develop *alternative* interactional discourse structures that are different from the traditional IRE pattern.

> Alternative non-IRE discourse structures are developed in integrated language classrooms.

The examples that follow involve discourse around classroom sessions where two teachers are reading aloud to their young primary-age children. In the left-hand excerpt, the teacher—we'll refer to her as Teacher A—has finished reading *Bear Shadow* by Frank Asch and is beginning a whole-class discussion on the book. On the right, Teacher B has begun to read aloud *Chickens Aren't the Only Ones* by Ruth Heller.

Asch (1985)

Oyler (1996); Oyler & Barry (1992)

Heller (1981)

Teacher A

T: What was the first thing the bear did to get rid of his shadow?
C1: Ran. (T does not respond)
C2: Hid behind a tree.
T: Right. He hid behind a tree. Did it work?
Cs: No.
T: Why?
C2: Because when he left the tree, the shadow was still there.
T: Uhhuh. What was the second thing he did? C3 [child's name]?
C3: Climbed the rocks.
T: Okay, rocks, but the rocks were called . . . C4 [child's name]?
C4: Cliff.
T: And did that work?
Cs: No.
T: Then what did the bear do?
C5: He went home to get his nails and hammer.
T: Okay, but what did he do with the hammer and nails, C5 [child's name]?
C5: He hammered his shadow.
T: Did it work?
Cs: No.
T: Then what did he do? . . .

Teacher B

T: The title page again. The cover, the title page, the author . . . MY SPECIAL THANKS TO, and then the name is Margaret Bradberry Ph.D.—that means she's called doctor. She's the professor of biology at a big university, San Fran—
C1: —cisco.
T: Okay, we're all set.
C2: I hope we begin.
T: CHICKENS LAY THE EGGS YOU BUY, THE EGGS YOU BOIL OR FRY OR . . .
C3: Oil
T: DYE!
C4: They die like that?
T: OR LEAVE ALONE SO YOU CAN SEE WHAT GREW INSIDE NATURALLY.
C2: Eggs.
C1: A real chick. Baby birds are called chicks.
C5: Does that really happen?
C1: Yeah, that really happens. 'Cause I had a little bird and he laid a egg and then it opened.
T: What other bird did we learn about this winter that hatches? In the Antarctic—I'll give you a big hint.
C: Penguin.
T: Penguins! Do they come from eggs?
Cs: Yes.
T: Are they a bird?
Cs: Yes.
C1: The odd bird.
T: We're going to find that out. . . .

> Teacher A uses the IRE discourse pattern of interaction.

Wells & Chang-Wells (1992)

You can see from these excerpts that Teacher A has followed a fairly strict IRE pattern in her discussion of the book she has read. She initiated all of the turns through her questions that attempted to get at information to be correctly recalled from the text. Her agenda was to "check students' comprehension" of the text, to make sure that children get the sequence of Bear's actions "right." As a result, students' responses indicate the degree to which children dutifully conform to the teacher's agenda. There is no room for considering the affective aspects of the book, for example, the humor that children apparently found in Bear's actions as they laughed and giggled during Teacher A's reading of the book, or the exploratory talk that might have emerged about the relationship of the sun and shadows and why Bear's actions were so funny. That is, there were no opportunities for children to express *their own* reactions to the book and, therefore, no opportunities for the teacher to assess what their understanding was so that she could then extend it through guided, collaborative participation.

Teacher B shows an alternative approach to reading a book with her children. The most notable difference in the discourse pattern is that students had opportunities to initiate their own responses to the book. In her response—"oil"—C3 tries to predict the upcoming text to be read; in his question, C4 queries his interpretation of the DYE of the book to mean "die." Subsequently, C1 comments on the illustration that shows a baby chick standing next to a broken eggshell. C5 wants to know if chicks really come from hatched eggs, to which C1 answers. Here, then, is another aspect of the alternative discourse approach—namely, that children feel free to talk to each other, not just to the teacher. Following this student *cross discussion*, Teacher B enters the discussion by trying to link what students had learned about a hatching bird (penguins) earlier in the year with the present opportunity to find out more about the topic. These several turns of teacher-initiated discussion are similar to the traditional IRE pattern, but note that here, in contrast to those noted in Teacher A's excerpt, the interaction follows the *children's* lead—*their* agenda. She then accepts the child's comment that the penguin is "the odd bird" and sets up a real purpose for reading the rest of the book by remarking, "We're going to find that out," namely, that other creatures—besides chickens—lay eggs.

There are many other points to make about these two excerpts. First, the fact that a teacher uses children's literature rather than a basal or textbook passage does not ensure more collaborative, non-IRE discourse interactions. Both Teachers A and B used good literature but with different results. The difference is that integrated language teachers discover and employ more viable alternatives to a transmission-oriented curriculum. Because they trust in their students' abilities and dispositions to make sense of their experiences, the teachers conceptualize the teaching–learning process in terms of collaborative transaction rather than transmission.

Second, the fact that teachers respect and encourage children's inquiry and their own responses to books does not mean that teachers have a laissez-faire attitude in teaching, that they never share their expertise and knowledge with their students, or never directly tell their students some information on a topic that students may want or need. A collaborative style of teaching takes into account both students' and teachers' agendas. There is no simple teaching formula or techniques to accomplish collaborative learning. Instead, such learning requires vigilant reflection on the part of teachers regarding their interactions with their students. Integrated language teachers are always posing important, challenging questions for themselves: How do I share my expertise or knowledge at the same time I encourage and foster my students' own construction of knowledge and expertise? How do I hear the voices of students who may come from a range of ethnolinguistic, cultural backgrounds, as well as enable them to hear my voice and, thus, mediate the mainstream culture at large? These kinds of questions are at the core of what it means for teachers to share power and authority with their students; they are basic to successful multicultural education.

In such a teaching approach, using or not using IRE or alternative non-IRE discourse patterns is not an all-or-nothing phenomenon, and although the examples we have provided here came from first-grade classrooms, each discourse type can occur in any grade. More traditional, teacher-directed IRE patterns may and do occur in integrated language classrooms. For example, they are likely to happen when certain procedures are being set up by teachers, such as when a teacher wants students to follow specific practices as they work on small-group projects during integrated work time. Or, they may be employed when teachers develop various short Focus Lessons*

Barnes & Todd (1995); Nystrand (1997); Wells (1999, 2001)

Teacher B uses an alternative, non-IRE discourse pattern of interaction.

Student initiations abound in collaborative talk.

Cross discussion is talk between students without teacher mediation.

Cazden (2001); Lemke (1990); Pappas & Zecker (2001a)

Burbules (1993); Mercer (1995); Wells (1999, 2001); Wells & Chang-Wells (1992); Willinsky (1990); Young (1992)

Collaborative transaction, not transmission

Both student and teacher agendas are considered in a collaborative style of teaching.

Bartolome (1994); Cazden (2001); Cummins (1994); Oyler (1996); Wells (1999, 2001)

See Pappas & Zecker (2001a, 2001b) for more examples of urban teachers taking on collaborative styles in teaching.

Traditional IRE patterns can occur in integrated language classrooms in certain circumstances.

to go over some aspect of students' understandings—perhaps a mathematical or scientific concept, or how to use contractions in their writing, or how to employ a particular reading strategy in doing research for a particular project, or how they may use a visual image or design to communicate meanings. These more IRE-like interactions are used when the teacher wants to set up certain rules or routines in the classroom that will enable other, more collaborative ventures with students or to instruct students more explicitly on some specific skill that has been noticed as being problematic in the teacher's ongoing observations of students' work. Thus, when and how to share their teacher expertise in student-centered and -initiated activities and inquiries always involves the "search for the best fit." There is always a *continuum* about how various discourse patterns are realized because these patterns are related to various purposes of teaching and learning. However, more often alternative, collaborative talk (an alternative non-IRE structure) occurs in integrated language classrooms because teachers are attempting to foster students' reflective inquiry and their construction of knowledge; they are promoting independent, self-motivated learners. And for peer groups as well, there will be many occasions where collaborative talk and action are accomplished. In sum, collaborative learning and a collaborative style of teaching entail constant consideration of both teacher and student agendas. Table 2.2 summarizes the major characteristics of collaborative discourse talk. (The activities at the end of the chapter can help you become more aware of how various classroom discourse patterns between teachers and students and among students in peer groups reflect issues of power, control, and knowledge.)

The Culture of the Classroom

What does it mean to say that each classroom represents a culture of its own? It means that norms are established regarding cooperation for the use of space and time, for the use of resources, and for valuing and behaving in certain ways. At the beginning of the twentieth century, Dewey wrote: "From the standpoint of the child, the great waste in school comes from his inability to utilize the experiences he gets outside of school in any complete and free way; while, on the other hand, he is unable to apply in daily life

Margin notes

Dahl et al. (2001); Reyes (1991)

Collaborative talk fosters students' construction of knowledge.

See Table 2.2.

See Activities 1 and 2.

Dewey (1956)

---

table **2.2**   **What Collaborative Discourse "Looks" Like**

- Few teacher pseudoquestions are found. Instead, genuine, authentic questions are more prevalent.
- If there is important information the teacher wants to share, he or she just tells students. The teacher avoids "fishing expeditions" to get students to "discover" the "right" answer.
- Teacher uses checking and clarifying questions to make sure to understand the intent or meaning of student remarks.
- Teacher asks open-ended, exploratory questions to foster student inquiry.
- Student initiations (their own ideas, comments, questions, etc.) are frequently found.
- Student "cross-discussion" responses (talk among students without teacher mediation) are frequently found.
- Student "intertextual" responses—ones that connect with ideas in the books used or topics of study in the classroom, as well as those that tie personal meanings constructed from experiences at their homes/communities—are frequently found.
- Teacher's "contingent" responses that sustain, extend, and transform student ideas are frequently found.
- Teacher *and* student inquiry language acts ("wondering" questions and comments) are prevalent in which knowledge is treated as tentative and open to revision and transformation.

what he is learning at school" (p. 75). Unfortunately, this description still characterizes many of our schools. In an integrated language classroom, norms are developed and realized in such a way that life in school is not so different from life out of school. Children can readily apply in school what they have learned at home, and what they have learned in school can also be used at home.

Fried (2001)

As you have seen in this chapter, the nature of learners, communication, and knowledge when viewed from this perspective means that teachers have certain roles. However, the agendas of teachers and children alike are considered and negotiated. The classroom culture is one in which teaching and learning are a collaborative enterprise. Hand-in-hand in this collaborative style of teaching is a way that teachers interact with students regarding their behavior, one that Marilyn Watson calls *Developmental Discipline*. Developmental Discipline centers on the quality of the teacher–student relationship and the ways in which it can realize the caring, nuturing quality of the total classroom environment. It integrates children's social and ethical development in daily classroom life. As such, it is a contrast to approaches (such as Assertive Discipline) that rely on rewards to encourage good behavior and punishments to discourage bad behavior. Instead, Developmental Discipline emphasizes that teachers do the following:

Development Discipline, which fosters nuturing, caring classrooms, is integral to a collaborative style of teaching–learning.

Watson (2003, page 4)

- Form warm and supportive relationships with and among their students.
- Help their students understand the reasons behind classroom rules and expectations.
- Teach any relevant skills that students might be lacking.
- Engage students in a collaborative, problem-solving process aimed at stopping misbehavior.
- Use nonpunitive ways to externally control student behavior when necessary.

This approach is one that helps *all* students—even ones who have difficulties in being productive members of the classroom culture—to feel that they belong, can make decisions, and are competent. Just as they model and demonstrate how to do academic activities or routines, teachers also model how to get along, how to interact in cooperative learning, and how to contribute as a partner or member in collaborative inquiry projects. Thus, a collaborative style of teaching and discourse, which incorporates Developmental Discipline, promotes important, critical learning—see Table 2.3.

See Table 2.3.

table 2.3 Why Collaborative Instruction/Discourse Promotes Learning

- It validates students as important sources of knowledge. They are valuable "knowers" and contributors to understandings jointly constructed in the classroom.
- It stimulates modes of cognition—*thinking* and not just remembering—that differ from the recitation found in transmission-oriented IRE instruction and discourse.
- Because it honors and privileges what students think (and not just whether students have done their homework or worksheets, etc.), teachers are able to communicate to students a higher level of expectations for learning.
- Because it allows for many opportunities for students to offer their own ideas as well as to respond to those of others (the teacher and other students), it promotes more student engagement in curricular content.
- It provides ways for a teacher to "scaffold" student learning—to really meet students' current knowledge and further extend it.
- It enables ways for teachers to encourage and respond to individual "ways with words" or communicational styles.
- It demonstrates for students strategies they can use in cooperative, collaborative work.
- Because teachers attempt to understand students' understandings, it realizes multicultural, culturally responsive pedagogy.
- It challenges—in important political ways—the commonly held deficit misconception regarding low SES students' abilities as knowers and learners.

How can such a classroom culture be realized? How are the norms or behavior patterns in such a classroom culture established? What exactly are thematic units? How can teachers develop plans around themes that provide choices for children that foster the use of integrated, authentic communication across the curriculum? How are thematic units implemented on a day-by-day basis? Chapters 3, 4, and 5 will address these kinds of basic questions so that you can better visualize how these ideas can be translated into the classroom.

 # Suggested Activities

1. To become more aware of how various discourse patterns reflect the ways power and knowledge might or might not be shared and constructed between classroom participants, collect some examples of classroom discourse. With the help of your classmates try to obtain a range of classroom contexts—ones that are whole-class or small-group teacher-led, ones that involve talk among a few students, or ones in which a teacher is talking to just one or a few students. Remember that all talk occurs in a certain context of situation, so you will need to jot down the relevant contextual information for each sample—see Activity 1 at the end of Chapter 1.

   Transcribe as much as you can of your samples so you can share them with others in your class. Now analyze and compare yours and your classmates' samples of how the discourse patterns realized the extent to which collaborative talk occurred. In all of your examples, be sure that you consider the *purposes* of the interactions that were realized by the talk and whether there were inconsistencies between the purpose and resulting discourse. Which ones followed the IRE pattern? Which ones were alternative and non-IRE in nature? In what ways was the teacher in control of the students' opportunities to talk? Did students have to follow the teacher agenda or were students able to initiate topics of their own? What was the content of these initiations? To what extent did the teacher follow up, extend, or sustain these student initiations? Was the talk different when the teacher talked to one or a few students as opposed to the whole class or a larger group? What was the peer discourse like—more collaborative or not? How were the structures of the discourse related to the *purposes* of the various interactions?

2. To better understand your own use of various discourse patterns, tape-record your own discussions with students in an elementary classroom. Pick interactions or activities or routines that will likely give you discourse examples across the continuum from teacher-directed to collaborative. For example, select interactional contexts in which you will be following *your own* agenda, offering mostly your knowledge on a topic, or where you outline certain procedures you want students to follow in doing an experiment or in discussing a particular set of books a group has read. These are likely to be more IRE-like in nature. Choose a couple of other activities or interactions in which you hope to share your power and expertise so that students can offer their own knowledge and which, therefore, will likely reflect more collaborative talk or be alternative to IRE-like discourse. These might be discussions with a group of students who may be studying particular aspects of a topic or perhaps content conferences you might have with individual students over their written drafts. Or it might even be a whole-class, teacher-led read-aloud where you are hoping to have students offer *their own* interpretations or responses on a book. Transcribe these interactions and analyze them in the ways suggested in Activity 1 above. How did they go? Did you do a good job in explaining your expertise or agenda in the teacher-directed activity or experience? Did your goals or purposes to share power and knowledge in collaboration get accomplished? Why? Why not?

References

Alvermann, D. E., Swafford, J., & Montero, M. K. (2004). *Content area literacy instruction for the elementary grades.* Boston: Pearson Education.

Barnes, D., & Todd, F. (1995). *Communication and learning revisited: Making meaning through talk.* Portsmouth, NH: Boynton/Cook.

Bartolome, L. I. (1994). Beyond the methods fetish: Toward a humanizing pedagogy. *Harvard Educational Review, 64,* 173–194.

Bayer, A. S. (1990). *Collaborative-apprenticeship learning: Language and thinking across the curriculum, K–12.* Mountain View, CA: Mayfield.

Berkenhotter, C., & Huckin, T. N. (1995). *Genre knowledge in disciplinary communication: Cognition/culture/power.* Hillsdale, NJ: Lawrence Erlbaum.

Bruner, J. S. (1983). *Child's talk: Learning to use language.* New York: Norton.

Bruner, J. S. (1986). *Actual minds, possible worlds.* Cambridge, MA: Harvard University Press.

Burbules, N. C. (1993). *Dialogue in teaching: Theory and practice.* New York: Teachers College Press.

Calkins, L. M. (1986). *The art of teaching writing.* Portsmouth, NH: Heinemann.

Cambourne, B. (1984). Language, learning and literacy. In A. Butler & J. Turbill (Eds.), *Towards a reading-writing classroom* (pp. 5–10). Portsmouth, NH: Heinemann.

Cazden, C. B. (2001). *Classroom discourse: The language of teaching and learning.* Portsmouth, NH: Heinemann.

Chouliarsaki, L., & Fairclough, N. (2001). *Discourse in late modernity: Rethinking critical discourse analysis.* Edinburgh: Edinburgh University Press.

Cochran-Smith, M., & Lytle, S. L. (1993). *Inside/Outside: Teacher research and knowledge.* New York: Teachers College Press.

Cummins, J. (1994). From coercive to collaborative relations of power in the teaching of literacy. In B. M. Ferdman, R. M. Weber, & A. G. Ramírez (Eds.), *Literacy across languages and cultures* (pp. 295–331). Albany: State University of New York Press.

Dahl, K. L., Scharer, P. L., Lawson, L. L., & Grogan, P. R. (2001). *Rethinking phonics: Making the best teaching decisions.* Portsmouth, NH: Heinemann.

de Boo, M. (1999). *Enquiring children, challenging teaching.* Buckingham, UK: Open University Press.

Dewey, J. (1956). *The child and the curriculum and the school and society* (comb. ed.). Chicago: University of Chicago Press.

Donaldson, M. (1978). *Children's minds.* Glasgow: William Collins Sons.

Duckworth, E. (1987). *The having of wonderful ideas and other essays on teaching and learning.* New York: Teachers College Press.

Dyson, A. H. (Ed.). (1989). *Collaboration through writing and reading: Exploring possibilities.* Urbana, IL: National Council of Teachers of English.

Edelsky, C. (1991). *With literacy and justice for all: Rethinking the social in language and education.* London: Falmer Press.

Edwards, D., & Mercer, N. (1987). *Common knowledge: The development of understanding in the classroom.* London: Routledge.

Falk, B. (2000). *The heart of the matter: Using standards and assessment to learn.* Portsmouth, NH: Heinemann.

Fairclough, N. (1989). *Language and power.* London: Longman.

Fairclough, N. (1992). *Discourse and social change.* Cambridge, MA: Polity Press.

Fisher, B. (1995). *Thinking and learning together: Curriculum and community in a primary classroom.* Portsmouth, NH: Heinemann.

Foster, M. (1992). Sociolinguistics and the African-American community: Implications for literacy. *Theory Into Practice, 32,* 303–311.

Fried, R. L. (2001). *The passionate teacher: A practical guide.* Boston: Beacon Press.

Gee, J. P. (1999). *An introduction to discourse analysis: Theory and method.* London: Routledge.

Geertz, C. (1983). *Local knowledge: Further essays in interpretive anthropology.* New York: Basic Books.

Goodman, Y. M. (1985). Kidwatching: Observing children in the classroom. In A. Jaggar & M. T. Smith-Burke (Eds.), *Observing the language learner* (pp. 9–18). Newark, DE: International Reading Association.

Goodman, Y., & Goodman, K. S. (1990). Vygotsky in a whole-language perspective. In L. C. Moll (Ed.), *Vygotsky and education: Instructional implications and applications of sociohistorical psychology* (pp. 223–250). Cambridge, MA: Cambridge University Press.

Gredler, M. E., & Johnson, R. L. (2004). *Assessment in the literacy classroom.* Boston: Pearson Education.

Halliday, M. A. K. (1975). *Learning how to mean: Explorations in the development of language.* London: Edward Arnold.

Halliday, M. A. K. (1982). Three aspects of children's language development: Learning language, learning through language, and learning about language. In Y. Goodman, M. Haussler, & D. Strickland (Eds.), *Oral and written language development research: Impact on the schools* (pp. 7–19). Urbana, IL: National Council of Teachers of English.

Halliday, M. A. K. (1993). Towards a language-based theory of learning. *Linguistics and Education, 5,* 93–126.

Heath, S. B. (1983). *Ways with words: Language, life, and work in communities and classrooms.* Cambridge: Cambridge University Press.

Holdaway, D. (1979). *Foundations of literacy.* Sydney, Australia: Ashton Scholastic.

Hubbard, R. S., & Power, B. M. (2003). *The art of classroom inquiry: A handbook for teacher-reseachers.* Portsmouth, NH: Heinemann.

Jaggar, A. M., & Smith-Burke, M. T. (Eds.). (1985). *Observing the language learner.* Newark, DE: International Reading Association.

Johns, A. M. (1997). *Text, role, and context: Developing academic literacies.* Cambridge: Cambridge University Press.

Johns, A. M. (Ed.). (2002). *Genre in the classroom: Multiple perspectives.* Mahwah, NJ: Lawrence Erlbaum.

Kohn, A. (1998). *What to look for in a classroom . . . and other essays.* San Francisco: Jossey-Bass.

Kress, G. (1997). *Before writing: Rethinking the paths to literacy.* London: Routledge.

Kress, G. (2000). Desgin and transformation: New theories of meaning. In B. Cope & M. Kalantzis (Eds.), *Multiliteracies: Literacy learning and the design of social futures.* (pp. 153–161). London: Routledge.

Kress, G. (2003). *Literacy in the new media age.* London: Routledge.

Kress, G., Jewitt, C., Ogborn, J., and Tsatsarelis, C. (2001). *Multimodal teaching and learning: The rhetorics of the science classroom.* London: Continuum.

Ladson-Billings, G. (1994). *The dreamkeepers: Successful teachers of African-American children.* San Francisco: Jossey-Bass.

Lee, C. D., & Smagorinsky, P. (Eds.). (2000). *Vygotskian perspectives on literacy research: Constructing meaning through collaborative inquiry.* Cambridge: Cambridge University Press.

Lemke, J. L. (1990). *Talking science: Language, learning, and values.* Norwood, NJ: Ablex.

Levstik, L. S., & Pappas, C. C. (1992). New directions for studying historical understanding. *Theory and Research in Social Education. 20,* 368–384.

Lindfors, J. W. (1987). *Children's language and learning.* Englewood Cliffs, NJ: Prentice-Hall.

Lindfors, J. W. (1999). *Children's inquiry: Using language to make sense of the world.* New York: Teachers College Press.

McCollum, P. (1991). Cross-cultural perspectives on classroom discourse and literacy. In E. H. Hiebert (Ed.), *Literacy for a diverse society: Perspectives, practices and policies* (pp. 108–121). New York: Teachers College Press.

Mercer, N. (1995). *The guided construction of knowledge: Talk amongst teachers and learning.* Clevedon: Multilingual Matters.

Michaels, S. (1981). "Sharing time": Children's narrative styles and differential access to literacy. *Language in Society, 10,* 423–442.

Moll, L. C. (1990). Introduction. In L. C. Moll (Ed.), *Vygotsky and education: Instructional implications and applications of sociohistorical psychology* (pp. 1–27). Cambridge, MA: Cambridge University Press.

Moore, D. W., Moore, S. A., Cunningham, P. M., & Cunningham, J. W. (2003). *Developing readers and writers in the content areas K–12.* Boston: Pearson Education.

Newman, J. M. (1991). Learning to teach by uncovering our assumptions. In D. Booth & C. Thornley-Hall (Eds.), *The talk curriculum.* Portsmouth, NH: Heinemann.

Nieto, S. (2000). *Affirming diversity: The sociopolitical context of multicultural education.* White Plains, NY: Longman.

Nystrand, M. (1997). *Opening dialogue: Understanding the dynamics of language and learning in the English classroom.* New York: Teachers College Press.

Oyler, C. (1996). *Making room for students in an urban first grade: Sharing authority in Room 104.* New York: Teachers College Press.

Oyler, C., & Barry, A. (1992, December). *Shared authority during teacher-led read alouds: Alternatives to the IRE pattern.* Paper presented at National Reading Conference, San Antonio, TX.

Pappas, C. C. (1997). Reading instruction in an integrated language perspective: Collaborative interaction in classroom curriculum genres. In S. A. Stahl & D. A. Hayes (Eds.), *Instructional models in reading* (pp. 283–310). Mahwah, NJ: Lawrence Erlbaum.

Pappas, C. C., & Pettegrew, B. S. (1998). The role of genre in the psycholinguistic guessing game of reading. *Language Arts, 75,* 36–44.

Pappas, C. C., & Zecker, L. B. (2001a). *Working with teacher researchers in urban classrooms: Transforming literacy curriculum genres.* Mahwah, NJ: Lawrence Erlbaum.

Pappas, C. C., & Zecker, L. B. (2001b). *Teacher inquiries in literacy teaching-learning: Learning to collaborate in urban elementary classrooms.* Mahwah, NJ: Lawrence Erlbaum.

Powers, B. M. (1996). *Taking note: Improving your observational notetaking.* York, ME: Stenhouse.

Reyes, M. de la Luz. (1991). A process approach to literacy instruction for Spanish-speaking students: In search of a best fit. In E. F. Hiebert (Ed.), *Literacy for a diverse society: Perspectives, practices, and policies* (pp. 157–171). New York: Teachers College Press.

Routman, R. (1996). *Literacy at the crossroads.* Portsmouth, NH: Heinemann.

Smith, F. (1997). *Reading without nonsense.* New York: Teachers College Press.

Tierney, R., & Readance, J. E. (2000). *Reading strategies and practices: A compendium.* Boston: Allyn & Bacon.

Unsworth, L. (2001). *Teaching multiliteracies across the curriculum: Changing contexts of text and image in classroom practice.* Buckingham, UK: Open University Press.

Vygotsky L. S. (1978). *Mind in society: The development of higher psychological processes.* Cambridge, MA: Cambridge University Press.

Watson, M. (2003). *Learning to trust: Transforming difficult elementary classrooms through Developmental Discipline.* San Francisco: Jossey-Bass.

Weaver, C. (2002). *Reading process and practice.* Portsmouth, NH: Boynton/Cook.

Wells, G. (1981). *Learning through interaction: The study of language development.* Cambridge, MA: Cambridge University Press.

Wells, G. (1986). *The meaning makers: Children learning language and using language to learn.* Portsmouth, NH: Heinemann.

Wells, G. (1993). Reevaluating the IRF sequence: A proposal for the articulation of theories of activity and discourse for the analysis of teaching and learning in the classroom. *Linguistics and Education, 5,* 1–37.

Wells, G. (1994). The complimentary contributions of Halliday and Vygotsky to a "language-based theory of learning." *Linguistics and Education, 6,* 41–90.

Wells, G. (1999). *Dialogic inquiry: Toward a sociocultural practice and theory of education.* Cambridge: Cambridge University Press.

Wells, G. (Ed.). (2001). *Action, talk, and text: Learning and teaching through inquiry.* New York: Teachers College Press.

Wells, G., & Chang-Wells, G. L. (1992). *Constructing knowledge together: Classrooms as centers of inquiry and literacy.* Portsmouth, NH: Heinemann.

Wilde, S. (1997). *What's a schwa sound anyway? A holistic guide to phonetics, phonics, and spelling.* Portsmouth, NH: Heinemann.

Willinsky, J. (1990). *The new literacy: Redefining reading and writing in the schools.* New York: Routledge.

Young, R. (1992). *Critical theory and classroom talk.* Clevedon, England: Multilingual Matters.

 ## Children's Literature

Bear Shadow by F. Asch. Prentice-Hall, 1985.
Chickens Aren't the Only Ones by R. Heller. Scholastic, 1981.

3

Planning Thematic Units

The preceding chapters have shown how children are active constructors of knowledge. In the years before entering school, children tackle tremendously complex cultural processes not only with determination but also with enthusiasm. This learning occurs in many social contexts when the child uses language for a variety of purposes to express and communicate a variety of ideas and feelings. Once children enter school, learning should build on these same foundations, regardless of their cultural background.

Thematic units reflect patterns of thinking, goals, and concepts common to bodies of knowledge. They link together content from many areas of the curriculum and depict the connections that exist across disciplines. Thematic units provide a framework for a community of learners in which all children can continue to learn language and to construct knowledge. Moreover, they provide a context for examining and reflecting on the way meaning is constructed within cultures and across cultures.

The topics chosen for thematic units are broadly based to take advantage of different ways of knowing that individual children bring to the classroom. Thematic units also provide children with many choices about how to pursue their learning. They come to feel a powerful sense of ownership as they initiate some activities and engage in others suggested by their teachers. Moreover, as children work alone or in groups, sharing, and discussing their work and the results of their inquiries, the classroom becomes a community of learners—a classroom culture—that shares ownership of a body of knowledge and understanding that has been jointly created. Teachers, too, are part of this community as they reflect on their teaching and their students' learning within this unique culture.

Such a classroom culture is created by identifying important themes or topics that are worth spending time on and that may be common to many or all subject areas. The theme of HOUSES AND HOMES developed for younger children, for example, could include information about houses in the community as well as houses around the world, imaginary houses, animal houses, or even environments for microorganisms. It could also extend to the concept of home in many cultures and an examination of the problems of homelessness in the local community. A theme of JOURNEYS might involve older children in a study of the age of exploration or the American westward movement. They could also learn about the "journeys" of molecules or nutrients at the same time that they think about journeys in their own lives or in the lives of characters in their books. They could examine the ways in which political, social, economic, and other forces can cause people to undertake journeys. In both themes, language, the arts, mathematics, science, and the social studies become vehicles for thorough exploration.

Thematic units also take advantage of the cultural diversity (the ways in which people are defined by and find identity in a certain place, region, or culture) and cultural

See Jacobs (1989); Lipson, Valencia, Wixson, & Peters (1993); Klein (2002); Morris (2003); Neilsen (1989); Short & Harste (1995); and Stevenson & Carr (1993) for additional views of integrated curriculum.

Teachers and children are part of a community of learners.

Themes provide a central focus for linking many subject areas.

universals (elements of culture common to all nations and people) inherent in U.S. society. When children enter schools, they should enter a cultural "intersection" where value is placed on what each child brings to the environment. Themes should foster a more inclusive reality by helping children become familiar with, cope with, and benefit from diversity. This means that all themes are multicultural and cross-cultural. Thus, a STRUCTURES thematic unit might consider the relationship of housing to both environmental and cultural values (such as extended families or notions of privacy) and a PATTERNS theme might include looking at patterns in art both multiculturally (diversity within a country or culture) and cross-culturally (diversity between countries or cultures). Chapter 5 includes more detailed ideas on making the curriculum more inclusive. In addition, the prototypes in Chapter 4 include specific references to multicultural and cross-cultural content.

In this book we focus on broadly based thematic units that may last for many weeks, perhaps a whole grading period. However, thematic units may include topical studies with a more concentrated focus—for example, a section on cumulative stories or on information books on a particular topic, a country, a specific kind of literature such as poetry, the works of one author or illustrator, or even a single book. Whatever the topic or length of study, the aim of any thematic unit is to choose a topic that's worth knowing about and that will provide a supportive context for meaning-making—that is, one that reflects important concepts or essential questions for students to examine in depth.

Choosing a Theme

There is no single "right" way to develop or plan a thematic unit. We present here methods for planning that can be adapted to individual teachers, classrooms, and children. These methods are guides and suggestions to be tried and modified just as a good cook learns to improve combinations of ingredients to improve the flavor of a dish.

The topic of thematic units can be chosen in a variety of ways. You will want to build units around critical questions that will engage children with important ideas and multiple points of view. You will also need to consider areas of study that link content as called for in district and state curriculum guidelines. In addition to considering critical questions and the content of the year's instruction, however, think of children as partners in the learning that is to come, and plan with their interests and enthusiasms in mind and with their active participation.

You may want to begin the year by taking full responsibility for choosing and organizing the themes and then allowing children a more active role in planning as the year progresses and you get to know the needs and interests of your particular students. However, even from the beginning, be open to the ways in which you can tie in concepts to be taught with your students' natural curiosity and excitement about the world around them. For example, a fifth-grade teacher developed a unit on CHANGES when one of his students brought in an article from the local newspaper describing a shopping center planned for nearby wetlands. The teacher channeled the children's outrage into researching questions about the local environment and about possible legal challenges. They organized a petition drive and successfully challenged the developer before the local county planning commission. Another teacher had wanted to explore water and water systems with her third and fourth graders. She wasn't sure how to organize the unit until one of her students reported that his house was being remodeled. "They're tearing out the walls, and there's all these pipes!" he exclaimed. The unit then proceeded with the children studying WATER SYSTEMS in the school and neighborhood, diagramming cross sections of water fountains and fire hydrants, studying physical properties of flush toilets and water wheels, mapping the school's water systems,

---

Thematic units allow for important exploration of points of view.

Hartoonian (1992)

Thematic units can be planned to last for several days, for many weeks, or for a whole grading period.

Jorgensen (1994)

Thematic units evolve in a variety of ways.

Topics come from important questions in the curriculum, yet consider children's interests.

Children's experiences help to shape the direction of the unit.

Levstik & Barton (2001)

figure **3.1**

Topics should allow the use of many types of resources.

Huck, Kiefer, Hepler, & Hickman (2004)

interviewing roofing (and gutter) and municipal water companies, and completing research reports on a water system. (See Figure 3.1.)

In choosing a topic for a thematic unit, pick one that is broad enough to incorporate many types of books, resources, and activities but not so broad that children lose sight of the connections that exist among areas to be explored. The topic of nutrition, for example, is likely to be required at many grade levels. However, it is too narrow for a good thematic unit. There are few, if any, works of good fiction that would fit that topic, and much as we might hope otherwise, few children would leap to study such a topic. Nutrition may, on the other hand, be explored as part of a unit of health, but health is such a broad area that it would be difficult to cover the vast amount of material in a way that builds strong schemas or domains of knowledge related to the topic. We would prefer to choose a theme like FOOD or EATING. This topic has considerable child appeal, but it does not ignore critical questions or sacrifice intellectual content.

Webbing

Choosing a topic is the first step in planning thematic units. What follows is a multi-faceted method of planning. There is no one "correct" way to proceed or one single avenue of exploration. Figure 3.2 is an overview of the major components involved in planning and developing a thematic unit. Notice that the planning is a dynamic process. As the first top "diamond" of Figure 3.2 suggests, generating key or essential questions and considering the viewpoints that you want to include will help you select materials and/or choose activities. This process often influences the nature of the theme itself. Recasting the theme may then lead to changes in materials and activities, and so forth. Once begun, the process develops as indicated by the figure, and components may be reshaped or changed as the theme is refined and executed.

Webbing is a schematic technique, the realization of a brainstorming process. A WEB is a Semantic Map*, a mental representation of concepts and relationships. Webbing allows you to extend a theme in many meaningful directions, fleshing out the topic by choosing meaningful categories and subcategories that relate to questions es-

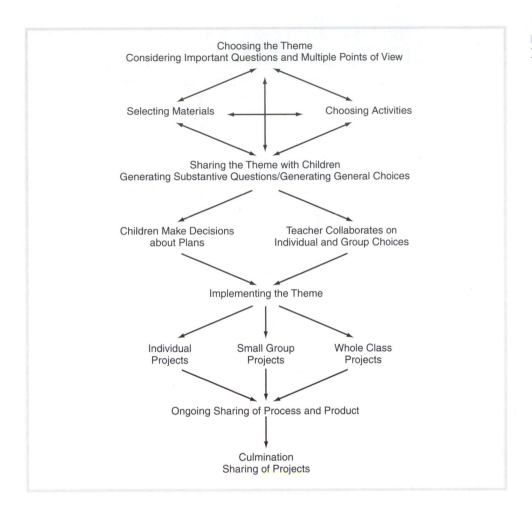

figure **3.2**
Planning for Thematic Units

sential to children's understanding of the theme. Essential questions deal with the most important issues related to a theme and help children understand the nature and purpose of their investigation. In addition, the WEB provides a picture of the possibilities of a given theme and allows you to visualize the many books, props, resources, and activities that are possible avenues of exploration for the theme.

To get the webbing process started you may want to do some free-associating and simply list everything that comes to mind in connection with a chosen theme. Doing this with a colleague or with children opens up alternative possibilities and prevents you from becoming locked into traditional ideas. As you generate lists or ideas, you will begin to see how many ideas can be grouped together in related categories that represent significant questions you want children to explore. From these, other categories or topics begin to emerge. As you brainstorm, think about ways that Reflective, Disciplined Inquiry* can help children to investigate the theme. You might want to use some of the content standards developed by organizations such as the National Council for the Social Studies, the National Council of Mathematics, and the National Council of Teachers of English to help you think about what big ideas and essential questions children might want to investigate. Also try to keep in mind titles of books and other print resources with which you are familiar, props or manipulatable materials that could give children hands-on experience with the theme, and community resources or resources in the arts that could be incorporated.

The SPACES AND PLACES web that follows began with a group of upper-elementary teachers who wanted to develop an interdisciplinary curriculum that met

Brainstorm topics with colleagues and/or children.

Consider how children can investigate concepts through Reflective Inquiry*.

state curriculum requirements. The state social studies program, for example, called for the study of local communities and the ways in which social, geographic, and economic factors affect communities. The science syllabus for this age group highlighted the study of ecosystems and the ways in which environmental conditions determine the types and sizes of populations of plants and animals within a community and affect the way the population interacts. Knowing of their students' interest in survival stories the teachers listed some of their favorite titles as a way of pursuing important questions about the interaction of people with their environment. They then listed these questions and other general concepts that children might explore as part of a unit they called "surroundings," sketching out a preliminary WEB that included activities and books that they knew they wanted to include. Figure 3.3 represents some of the preliminary planning involved in the unit. For example, one teacher had been involved in an overnight field trip to an environmental science center at his previous school and wanted children to experience some sort of outdoor activity. The school media specialist suggested including survival stories like *Shipwreck at the Bottom of the World* and *Brian's Hunt,* and she brought in several indexes of children's literature, *Adventuring with Books,* and *Kaleidoscope* to help teachers choose other fiction, poetry, and information books. The initial WEB was hung in one of the teacher's rooms as team members consulted with their students and began to flesh out the topic with other activities and books.

As the ideas "incubated" over subsequent days, a child mentioned the empty lot down the street that was full of trash. She wanted to know why the police let people dump garbage there. Another child suggested that the lot could be dangerous to the little kids walking home from the school. Their teacher suggested that this might make a good inquiry project and that they could begin by contacting someone on the city council who knew about city ordinances and planning.

In another class one girl wanted to include a favorite survival story, *From the Mixed Up Files of Mrs. Basil E. Frankweiler,* about two children surviving in the Metropolitan Museum of Art in New York City. Her teacher realized other city survival books such as *Locomotion* and *Scorpions* provided an ideal way to explore diverse points of view. Consultation with the media specialist turned up other books about city survival. Several focused on the homeless: a novel, *Monkey Island,* a picture book, *Fly Away Home,* and an information book, *No Place to Be: Voices of Homeless Children.* Other books featured urban children facing peer pressure and gang violence, *Soulfire* and *Junebug.* Thus, the question, "What factors affect human survival in an urban environment?" became an important subtheme of the unit.

Consultations with content specialists helped expand the WEB in additional directions. The district math coordinator suggested that the topic of surroundings seemed to be an ideal way to incorporate geometry or spatial concepts and that the team might want to think about city planning as a way of dividing up space using geometric shapes. The art teacher tied into these concepts with the artist's use of space, from the use of shape as an element of two- and three-dimensional space to the teaching of two-point and three-point perspective. This in turn led to questions about planning for human needs. The P.E. teacher also contributed to the idea of exploring spatial surroundings through movement activities, gymnastics, and dance. Both of the art and music teachers also suggested looking at artistic and musical interpretation's of surroundings through landscape painting and musical compositions such as "Slaughter on Tenth Avenue" or "The Grand Canyon Suite." Exploring the artist's point of view brought to mind the Harlem Renaissance and many artists and musicians affected by their cultural and physical surroundings. Here the media specialist suggested the books *Harlem* and *Appalachia: Voices of Sleeping Birds,* which talk about this topic. Thus, another essential question emerged: "How are artists and writers affected by place?"

Gradually the initial topic of surroundings grew in many directions and was reshaped into a theme that they called SPACES AND PLACES. (See Figure 3.4a.) This

---

Armstrong (2000); Paulsen (2003)

McClure & Kristo (2002); Hansen-Krening, Aoki, & Mizokawa (2003)

The first WEB is a sketch that changes as the unit progresses.

Konigsburg (1969)

Woodson (2004); Meyers (1988)

Fox (1991); Bunting (1991); Berck (1992)

Hewett (1996); Mead (1995)

A new essential question for the unit emerged.

Collaboration of teachers with different expertise can help strengthen the unit.

Myers (1996); Rylant (1991)

Once again, another essential question for the unit developed.

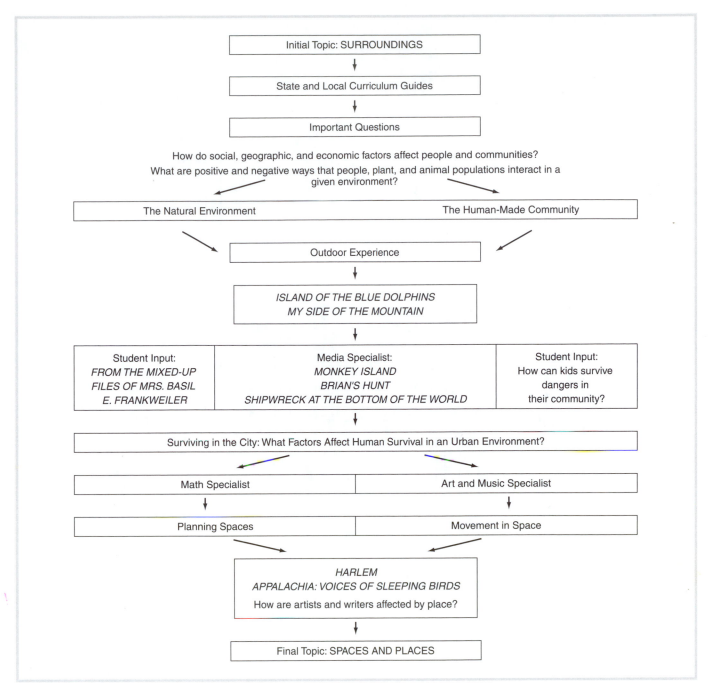

Initial Topic: SURROUNDINGS

State and Local Curriculum Guides

Important Questions

How do social, geographic, and economic factors affect people and communities?

What are positive and negative ways that people, plant, and animal populations interact in a given environment?

The Natural Environment   The Human-Made Community

Outdoor Experience

ISLAND OF THE BLUE DOLPHINS
MY SIDE OF THE MOUNTAIN

| Student Input: *FROM THE MIXED-UP FILES OF MRS. BASIL E. FRANKWEILER* | Media Specialist: *MONKEY ISLAND* *BRIAN'S HUNT* *SHIPWRECK AT THE BOTTOM OF THE WORLD* | Student Input: How can kids survive dangers in their community? |

Surviving in the City: What Factors Affect Human Survival in an Urban Environment?

Math Specialist   Art and Music Specialist

Planning Spaces   Movement in Space

HARLEM
APPALACHIA: VOICES OF SLEEPING BIRDS
How are artists and writers affected by place?

Final Topic: SPACES AND PLACES

figure **3.3**

figure, although more complex than the first sketch, only captures the possibilities of the topic at a single moment in time. The topic of SPACES AND PLACES will continue to change and to be reshaped as children and teachers encounter issues and find additional interests in the world around them. Note the essential questions under various subtopics of the theme. See Chapter 4 for more information about the role of these key questions in the prototype thematic unit WEBS.

The SPACES AND PLACES example reflects a team approach to planning thematic units, but there is no "one" way to develop themes. People tend to start in different ways. Many teachers like to involve students in the planning from the very

The unit plan will continue to evolve.

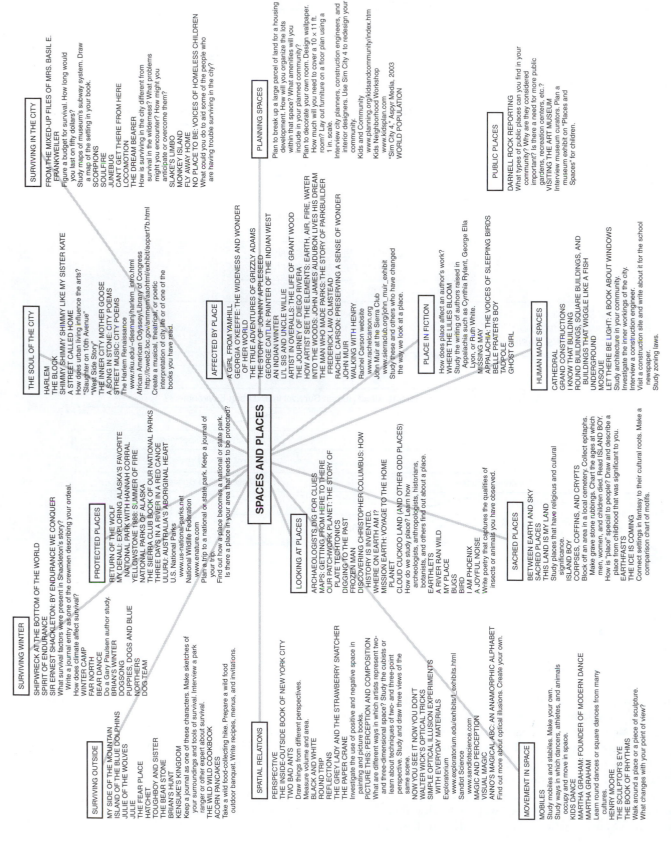

figure 3.4a

SPACES AND PLACES

SURVIVING WINTER — SCIENCE

SHIPWRECK AT THE BOTTOM OF THE WORLD
SPIRIT OF ENDURANCE
SIR ERNEST SHACKLETON: BY ENDURANCE WE CONQUER
What survival factors were present in Shackleton's story?
Write a journal entry as one of the crewmen describing your ordeal.
How does climate affect survival?
WINTER CAMP
FAR NORTH
BEAR (NORTH... study.
BRIAN'S WINTER
DOGSONG
PUPPIES, DOGS AND BLUE NORTHERS
DOG TEAM

SURVIVING OUTSIDE — SCIENCE

MY SIDE OF THE MOUNTAIN
ISLAND OF THE BLUE DOLPHINS
JULIE OF THE WOLVES
JULIE
THE FEAR PLACE
HATCHET
TOUGHBOY AND SISTER
THE BEAR STONE
BRIAN'S HUNT
KENSUKE'S KIN...
Keep a journal a... ters. Make sketches of your surroundings and tools of survival. Interview a park ranger or other expert about survival.
THE WILD WILD COOKBOOK
ACORN PANCAKES
Take a wild food-collecting hike. Prepare a wild food outdoor banquet. Write recipes, menus, and invitations.

SPATIAL RELATIONS — MATH, ART

PERSPECTIVE
THE INSIDE-OUTSIDE BOOK OF NEW YORK CITY
TWO BAD ANTS
Draw things from different perspectives.
Measure volume, area.
BLACK AND WHITE
ROUND...
REFLEC...
THE GREY LADY AND THE STRAWBERRY SNATCHER
THE PAPER CRANE
Investigate the use of positive and negative space in painting and picture books.
PICTURE THIS: PERCEPTION AND COMPOSITION
What are different ways in which artists represent two- and three-dimensional space? Study the cubists or learn about techniques of two- and three-point perspective. Study and draw three views of the same scene.
NOW YOU SEE IT NOW YOU DON'T
WALTER WICK'S OPTICAL TRICKS
SIMPLE OPTICAL ILLUSION EXPERIMENTS WITH EVERYDAY MATERIALS
Exploratorium
www.exploratorium.edu/exhibits/f_exhibits.html
Sandlot Science
www.sa...com
MAGIC A...
VISUAL M...
ANNO'S MAGICAL ABC: AN ANAMORPHIC ALPHABET
Find out more about optical illusions. Create your own.

MOVEMENT IN SPACE — SCIENCE, ART, PHYSICAL EDUCATION

MOBILES
Study mobiles
Study ways in... occupy and move in space.
KIDS DANCE
MARTHA GRAHAM: FOUNDER OF MODERN DANCE
MARTHA GRAHAM
Learn... cultu...
HENRY MOORE
THE SCULPTOR'S EYE
THE BOOK OF R...
Learn... s or square dances from many
Walk around a pla...
What changes with...

LOOKING AT PLACES — SOCIAL STUDIES, SCIENCE

ARCHAEOLOGISTS DIG FOR CLUES
MAPS: GET... THERE
OUR PATCH... E STORY OF
PLATE TE...
DIGGING T...
FROZEN MAN
DISCOVERING CHRISTOPHER COLUMBUS: HOW HISTORY IS INVENTED.
WHERE ON EARTH AM I?
MISSION EARTH: VOYAGE TO THE HOME PLANET
CLOUD CUCKOO LAND (AND OTHER ODD PLACES)
How do we... archeolog... historians, botanists, and others find out about a place.
EARTHLETS
A RIVER RAN WILD
MY PLACE
BUGS
BIRD
I AM PHOENIX
A JOYFUL NOISE
Write poetry that captures the qualities of insects or animals you have observed.

SACRED PLACES — SOCIAL STUDIES

BETWEEN EARTH AND SKY
SACRED PLACES
THIS LAND IS MY LAND
Study places that have religious and cultural significance.
ISLAND BOY
CORPSES, COFFINS, AND CRYPTS
Block off an... ery. Collect epitaphs. Make gra... at the ages at which men, wom... Read ISLAND BOY. Draw and describe a place from childhood that was significant to you.
How is 'plac...
EARTHFASTS
THE ICE IS COMING
Connect settings in fantasy to their cultural roots. Make a comparison chart of motifs.

PROTECTED PLACES — SOCIAL STUDIES

RETURN OF THE WOLF
MY DENALI: EXPLORING ALASKA'S FAVORITE NATIONAL PARK WITH HANNAH CORRAL
YELLOWST...
NATIONAL...
THE SIERR...
... OUR NATIONAL PARKS
THREE DAYS ON A RIVER IN A RED CANOE
ULURU: AUSTRALIA'S ABORIGINAL HEART
US National Parks
www.us-national-parks.net
National Wildlife Federation
www.enature.com
Plan a trip to a national or state park. Keep a journal of your trip.
Find out how a place becomes a national or state park. Is there a place in your area that needs to be protected?

THE SOUL OF THE CITY — ART, MUSIC

HARLEM
THE BLOCK
SHIMMY SHIMMY LIKE MY SISTER KATE
A STREET C...
How does urb... uence the arts?
"Slaughter on 10th Avenue"
"West Side Story"
THE INNER CITY MOTHER GOOSE
A SONG IN STONE: CITY POEMS
STREET MUSIC: CITY POEMS
The Harlem R...
www.nku.ed... intro.html
African American... Library of Congress
http://lcweb2.loc.gov/ammem/aaohtml/exhibit/aopart7b.html
Create a musical, theatrical, or poetic interpretation of city life or of one of the books you have read.

SURVIVING IN THE CITY — SOCIAL STUDIES

FROM THE MIXED-UP FILES OF MRS. BASIL E. FRANKWEILER
Figure a budget for survival. How long would you last on fifty dollars?
Study maps of museum's subway system. Draw a map of the setting in your book.
SCORPIONS
SOULF...
JUNEB...
LOCOMOTION
THE DREAM BEARER
How is surviving in the city different from survival in the wilderness? What problems might you encounter? How might you anticipate or overcome them?
SLAKE'S LIMBO
MONKEY ISLAND
FLY AWAY HOME
NO PLACE TO BE: VOICES OF HOMELESS CHILDREN
What could you do to aid some of the people who are having trouble surviving in the city?

AFFECTED BY PLACE — LITERATURE, ART, SOCIAL STUDIES

A GIRL FROM YAMHILL
GEORGIA...
OF HER...
THE TRUE...
THE STORY OF JOHNNY APPLESEED
GEORGE CATLIN: PAINTER OF THE INDIAN WEST
AN INDIAN WINTER
LI'L SIS AND UNCLE WILLIE
... LS: THE LIFE OF GRANT WOOD
THE JO... DIEGO RIVERA
HOW ARTIST SEE THE ELEMENTS: EARTH, AIR, FIRE, WATER
INTO THE WOODS: JOHN JAMES AUDUBON LIVES HIS DREAM
THE MAN WHO MADE PARKS: THE STORY OF PARKBUILDER FREDERICK LAW OLMSTEAD
RACHEL CARSON: PRESERVING A SENSE OF WONDER
JOHN MUIR
WALKING WITH HENRY
... SS AND WONDER
... ZLY ADAMS
Rachel Carson website
http://www.rachelcarson.org
John Muir at the Sierra Club
http://www...muir_exhibit
Study these

PLANNING SPACES — MATH, SOCIAL STUDIES

Plan to break up a large parcel of land for a housing development... you organize the lots within that... t amenities will you include in your... community?
Plan to decorate your own room. Design wallpaper.
How much will you need to cover a 10×11 ft. room? La... for plan using a... 1 in. scale
Interview c... ion engineers, and interior de... ers. Use only 4 to redesign your community.
Kids and Community
http://www.planning.org/kidsandcommunity/index.htm
Kids Neighborhood Workshop
http://www.kidsplan.com
"Sim City 4" Aspyr Media, 2003
WORLD POPULATION

PLACE IN FICTION — LITERATURE, ART

How does place affect an author's work?
WHERE THE LILIES BLOOM
Study the... Appala...
... ht, George Ella Lyon, o...
MISSING MAY
APPALACHIA: THE VOICES OF SLEEPING BIRDS
BELLE PRATER'S BOY
TADPOLE
GHOST GIRL.

HUMAN MADE SPACES — ART

CATHEDRAL
GRAND CONSTRUCTIONS
I KNOW THAT BUILDING
ROUND BUILDINGS, SQUARE BUILDINGS, AND BUILD... WIGGLE LIKE A FISH
MOSQU...
UNDER...
LET THERE BE LIGHT: A BOOK ABOUT WINDOWS
Study architecture in your community.
Investigate the inner workings of the city.
Interview a construction engineer.
Visit a construction site and write about it for the school newspaper.
Study zoning laws.

PUBLIC PLACES — ART

DARNELL ROCK REPORTING
What types of public places can you find in your community? Why are they considered important? Is there a need for more public gardens, recreation centers, etc.?
VISITING THE ART MUSEUM
Interview museum curators. Plan a museum ex... es and Spaces" for

---

figure 3.4b

Many teachers elicit input from students early on in developing units.

beginning. For example, you might give children copies of a thematic WEB that you have generated with only the subcategories of the topic listed. Let the children look at the WEB and circle topics they are interested in. Then give them index cards and ask them to write down things that are not on the WEB that they think of as connected to the theme and that they think would be interesting topics and questions they have about topics to pursue. Use the WEBs and cards to refine the original WEB and then work with the children to gather resources and plan activities that they think would be important to their inquiries. (See Figure 3.5.)

Themes should focus on ideas and concepts that are worth spending time on.

Some teachers like to begin to think of the theme by planning topics according to more traditional areas like math, science, art, poetry, or writing. As long as these curricula categories allow for valid exploration and inquiry of the theme by children this type of planning may be more comfortable for some, particularly beginners. However they are planned, thematic units that explore ideas worth knowing and essential questions that connect and relate ideas in important ways will likely incorporate traditional content areas in ways that mirror children's learning in the outside-the-school world. In whatever ways teachers use to develop WEBs it is important to see that a particular unit does cover traditional areas of the curriculum. The diagram in Figure 3.4b shows how understandings from traditional content areas are represented on the web of SPACES AND PLACES.

Selecting Resources

Resources should be chosen to allow children to explore many cultural perspectives.

One of the aims of a thematic unit is to provide children with wide experience with a range of resources for learning. This broad range is particularly important for exploring different cultural perspectives because not all cultural viewpoints are represented in

figure **3.5**

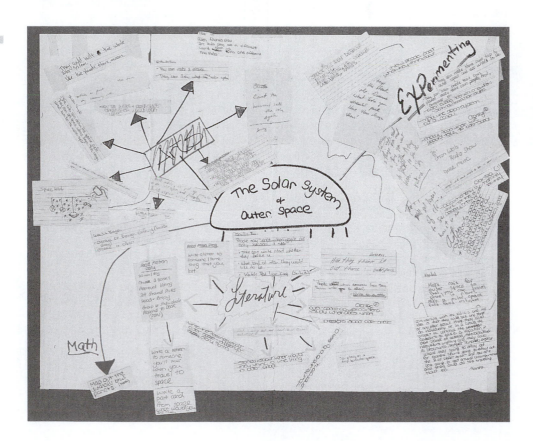

readily available books. Four major types of resources are incorporated in units. First, a thematic unit includes a variety of genres of children's literature, as well as other sources of printed information—newspapers and magazines, diaries, letters, visual artifacts, and other primary sources. Second, units make use of technological resources, a variety of media including technology systems, information, and software. These might include communication devices, websites, search engines, hypermedia such as still and moving images, and equipment such as scanners and digital cameras. Third, thematic units employ many manipulatable materials—artifacts, props, equipment, and so forth. Units also use resources from the community and the wider world: people, animals, and places that contribute to children's understanding of a theme. The arts can also contribute to the theme through the use of paintings, sculpture, crafts, music, the theater, films, and other media.

The next steps in planning a thematic unit may then be those that lead to the school or municipal library or the Internet. One of the best sources of information for gathering materials and locating electronic resources is the librarian or media specialist. These professionals are familiar with good children's books, periodicals, primary source materials, and other resources, including computer programs and simulations. They can also direct you to the many good indexes to children's materials, to archival materials, and to other technological resources. (See Table 3.1 for a list of Resources for Selecting Books and Media for Children.)

Printed Resources

Books and other printed resources that will be explored in thematic units are best chosen for their literary qualities and for their relationship to the theme. This does not preclude the use of textbooks but it does allow the teacher to make selective use of these materials and to include many of the excellent works of fiction, information books, and periodicals published for children. These resources not only allow for more critical reading on a subject but also accommodate the many reading abilities found in a heterogeneous classroom. In addition, these well-written works provide children with excellent models for their own writing.

Choose printed resources for their quality and their relevance to the theme.

Many indexes survey children's literature and other materials. (See Table 3.1.) In addition, up-to-date resources have been made available for selecting multicultural titles; the authors and editors of these titles have been careful to select titles that provide an authentic view of particular cultures, books that have been written from the point of view of an insider who knows and understands that culture well.

A broad range of resources can meet the needs of diverse cultural backgrounds.

Because we want to make more children be critical readers and to foster their learning in the various registers of written language, it is best to try to include a balance of fiction and nonfiction materials in a thematic unit. If, as you begin collecting titles, you find that there are not enough types of material to provide for a broad range of reading abilities and interests in your class, you may want to broaden the topic of your unit. For example, research on a topic of MACHINES may reveal a limited amount of suitable literature. If the topic was expanded to INVENTIONS AND INVENTORS, the scope is also expanded to include the technology of machines and other inventions, studies of the lives and struggles of inventors, research into the effects of inventions on people and communities, and the imaginary inventions of characters like Professor William Waterman Sherman in *The Twenty-One Balloons*. The change in focus assures that a wealth of materials can be found and that important relationships can be studied.

duBois (1947)

On the other hand, if you find yourself overwhelmed by titles, you may have chosen a topic that will not allow children to explore important concepts beyond a very superficial level. A theme of FEELINGS may be too general; feelings are part of our daily life experience and hard to isolate for meaningful study. In contrast, a theme of WHO AM I, CONFLICTS or CHANGES would focus on important curricular concepts and also allow children to reflect on a variety of feelings as part of the larger table **3.1**   Selecting Books and Media for Children

A to Zoo—Subject Access to Children's Picture Books (5th ed.) by C. W. Lima (Ed.). Ann Arbor, MI: Bowker, 2001.

Adventuring with Books: A Booklist for Pre-K to Grade 6 (13th ed.) by A. A. McClure & J. V. Kristo. (Eds.). Urbana, IL: National Council of Teachers of English, 2002.

Atlas of Cyberspace. www.cybergeography.org/atlas/atlas.html

American History for Children and Young Adults: An Annotated Bibliographic Index by V. VanMeter (Ed.). Littleton, CO: Libraries Unlimited, 1997.

The American Library Association Great Web Sites for Kids. www.ala.org/greatsites

Basic Collection of Children's Books in Spanish by I. Schon (Ed.). Metuchen, NJ: Scarecrow Press, 2001.

Blog-City. A free interface for publishing online diaries, scrapbooks, or photojournals. www.blog-city.com/bc

Blog*Spot. A free interface for publishing online diaries, scrapbooks, or photojournals. www.blogger.com/start

American Association for the Advancement of Science Best Science Books and AV Materials for Children and Young Adults. www.sbfonline.com/bestlists.htm

Association of Library Services to Children (American Library Association) Notable Lists (including Software and Online Subscription Services). www.ala.org/ala/alsc/awardsscholarships/childrensnotable/Default1888.htm

Book Links: Connecting Books, Libraries, and Classrooms (Bimonthly periodical. Available from the American Library Association, 50 E. Huron St., Chicago, IL 60611)

Booklist Magazine (Periodical. Available from the American Library Association, 50 E. Huron St., Chicago, IL 60611)

Choices: A Core Collection for Young Reluctant Readers (Vol. 5) by B. Fahey & M. Whalen (Eds.). Evanston, IL: John Gordon Burke, 2001.

Colonial America in Literature for Youth by J. L. Lowe and K. I. Matthew (Eds.). Metuchen, NJ: Scarecrow Press, 2003.

Educational Media Yearbook (Annual) by J. W. Brown & S. N. Brown (Eds.). Littleton, CO: Libraries Unlimited.

Elementary Science Integration Projects. www.esiponline.org

Exploring the United States Through Literature. Federal Citizen Information Center: First Gove for Kids. www.kids.gov

The Horn Book (Periodical. Available from 31 St. James Ave., Boston, MA 02108)

The Horn Book Guide (Published twice yearly. Available from 31 St. James Ave., Boston, MA 02108)

topic. If you have chosen a topic like JOURNEYS or CHANGES that could cover a very broad area, you may want to let the subcategories limit areas of inquiry, keeping in mind the students you have and making the unit more relevant to their cultural background.

As you plan a thematic unit, you may wonder how many titles are enough. We like to think that, as with chocolate, you can never have enough. Many teachers who have been teaching through thematic units for many years work with between four and five hundred books and other printed materials; their classroom libraries are supplemented by school and municipal collections. We suggest that rather than setting a specific number of titles, you plan to collect the following types of materials:

MATERIALS TO READ ALOUD

Choose the best works of literature to read aloud.

Reading aloud gives teachers the opportunity to share the best works of children's literature with their students. You may also choose materials that children might not initially read on their own. Poetry, information books, biography or autobiography, picture books, periodicals, and primary source materials should be considered for all

Informational Picture Books for Children by P. J. Cianciolo. American Library Association, 50 E. Huron St., Chicago, IL 60611, 2000.

It's the Story That Counts: More Good Books for Mathematical Learning by D. J. Whitin and S. Wilde. Portsmouth NH: Heinemann, 1995.

Kaleidoscope: A Multicultural Booklist for Grades K–8 by N. Hansen-Krening, E. M. Aoki, and D. T. Mizokawa (Eds.). Urbana, IL: National Council of Teachers of English, 2003.

The Best of Latino Heritage 1996–2002: A Guide to Juvenile Books about Latino People by I. Schon. Metuchen, NJ: Scarecrow Press, 2003.

Literature Connections to World History: K–6 Resources to Enhance and Entice by L. G. Adamson. Greenwood Village, CO: Libraries Unlimited, 1998.

National Geographic On-Line Adventures. www.nationalgeographic.com/education/online_adventures/index.htm

National Science Teachers Association Science Resources. www.nsta.org/main/sciencesites

National Wildlife Federation. www.enature.com

Our Family, Our Friends, Our World: An Annotated Guide to Significant Multicultural Books for Children and Teenagers by L. Miller-Lachman. New York: Bowker, 1992.

Portraying Persons with Disabilities: An Annotated Bibliography of Fiction for Children by D. Robertson. (Ed.). New York: Bowker, 1992.

Portraying Persons with Disabilities: An Annotated Bibliography of Non-Fiction for Children by J. Brest, Friedberg, J. B. Mullins, and A. W. Sukiennik. (Eds.). New York: Bowker, 1992.

Read Any Good Math Lately? Children's Books for Mathematical Learning by D. J. Whitin & S. Wilde. Portsmouth, NH: Heinemann, 1992.

Recreating the Past: A Guide to American and World Historical Fiction for Children and Young Adults by L. G. Adamson. Westport, CT: Greenwood Press, 1994.

Subject Guide to Children's Books in Print (Annual). Ann Arbor, MI: Bowker.

Tried and True: 500 Nonfiction Books Children Want to Read by G. Wilson & J. Moss. New York: Bowker, 1992.

Using Poetry Across the Curriculum: A Whole Language Approach by B. Chatton. Phoenix, AZ: Oryx, 1993.

Venture Into Cultures: A Resource Book of Multicultural Materials and Programs by O. L. Kuharets (Ed.). Chicago, IL: American Library Association, 2001.

World History for Children and Young Adults by V. VanMeter. Littleton, CO: Libraries Unlimited, 1991.

Your Reading: A Booklist for Junior High and Middle School by J. Brown and E. C. Stephens (Eds.). Urbana, IL: National Council of Teachers of English, 2003.

ages while chapter books and longer information books can be chosen where they are developmentally appropriate.

See Huck, Kiefer, Hepler, & Hickman (2004).

"Read-alouds" allow teachers to demonstrate the full range of responses readers might make to print. During the read-aloud time teachers can share their own and their students' emotional responses to a work, identify and respond to questions or puzzles that arise from the work, or reflect on the artistry of the writing. In addition, these read-alouds may be works that call for careful and sensitive discussion on important issues to be explored within the theme. They may also have intricacies of plot or characterization that demand careful guidance from an adult, or the shared construction of meaning that comes through group discussion or repeated readings.

For the SPACES AND PLACES theme, in addition to collecting poetry and other printed resources to read aloud, teachers chose two novels (*Julie of the Wolves, Monkey Island*) and two information books (*No Place to Be: Voices of Homeless Children* and *Corpses, Coffins, and Crypts: A History of Burial*) that they felt were good candidates for reading aloud. They also identified a list of picture books and poetry, such as *Harlem* and *Sacred Places,* that would provide good connections to important questions they

George (1972); Fox (1991)

Berck (1992); Colman (1997)

Myers (1997); Yolen (1996)

wanted to explore with the students. All these met the criteria of good literature, provided a range of cultural views of the topic, and opened up possibilities for further explorations of issues and ideas.

MATERIALS FOR GROUP ACTIVITIES

If these materials are books, you should choose them with literary qualities in mind, but they should also be good candidates for Literature Response Groups* and small group activities that don't require your direct attention. It is important that these materials be rich in possibilities for further inquiry. We want children to deal with the book as an aesthetic event and to find reasons to return to the book to explore it more deeply. We also want the book to raise critical questions about the ideologies or values that are expressed in the text, which will lead children beyond the book to make sense of alternative points of view and to make careful judgments about the wider world.

You can often find multiple copies of paperbacks that fit your theme. For the SPACES AND PLACES unit teachers and children identified seven books that they could obtain in paperback sets, *From the Mixed-Up Files of Mrs. Basil E. Frankweiler, Locomotion, Toughboy and Sister, Hatchet,* and *Island of the Blue Dolphins* (fiction) and *An Indian Winter* and *Shipwreck at the Bottom of the World* (nonfiction). In addition, teachers developed text sets, individual titles and printed materials grouped together by topics such as "place in fiction," "human-made places," and "sacred places." These materials allowed for a wide range of interests and ability levels among the children and provided broad coverage of diverse points of view and concepts important to the theme. Jackdaws*, or collections of primary source materials, which could include such printed sources as journals, letters, maps, old newspapers or advertisements, and photographs, could provide another focus for group work (see Chapter 7 for further information on Literature Response Groups* and assembling jackdaw-like packets).

Konigsburg (1969); Woodson (2004); Hill (1990); Paulsen (1987); O'Dell (1960)

Freedman (1992); Armstrong (2000)

ADDITIONAL READING MATERIALS FOR PERSONAL EXPLORATION

Reading interests of individual children in any classroom vary and should be catered to by including many other titles that may be chosen for personal enjoyment or individual research. These materials should be fun to read and may spark an interest in a special child. They can be made available for reading during sustained silent reading time and can give children the time and space to read for pleasure without having to do anything more with the book (unless, of course, they want to). Some children involved in the SPACES AND PLACES theme might choose to read about haunted places in books or periodicals or to explore mysterious places like the Bermuda Triangle. Another child might enjoy reading articles related to the theme in current newspapers and compiling a collection for other students.

Include enough resources to allow for individual interests.

PRIMARY SOURCE* MATERIALS

Primary source* materials include originals, copies, or facsimiles of such printed resources as letters, journals, maps, photographs, newspapers, magazines, advertisements, ledgers, account books, mail-order catalogs, and any other artifacts that give us firsthand information about real people who lived in other times or other places, or about the community of which we are a part today. Primary source material also includes notes of observations, transcriptions of interviews, and the like. In the SPACES AND PLACES theme, in addition to the materials mentioned earlier, teachers helped children collect maps, blueprints, city planning documents, and aerial photographs of their own community to study city planning and public spaces.

Primary Source materials can foster important inquiries.*

Technological Resources

Electronic media, including the Internet and the World Wide Web, are widely available in most schools and provide important ways to gather information and to guide and monitor ongoing inquiries. Moreover, the opportunities for collaboration among students and beyond the school community to the wider world can provide students with a critical understanding of global issues and points of view.

See Smolin & Lawless (2003) and Wolinsky (2002).

The International Society for Technology in Education has developed six basic standards of technology literacy for students in grades pre-K–12. These include the use of basic operations and concepts; the use of tools for productivity, communication, research, and problem solving; and the understanding of social issues relating to the use of technology. These standards provide a helpful framework for including the use of technological resources in thematic units. Routinely plan to use media such as overhead projectors, video cams and VCRs, and DVD players to convey information and present concepts and to provide students with organizational and presentational tools. Computers and related devices such as scanners, video cameras, and digital cameras can be used for conducting research, compiling information, and presenting information. The Internet and search engines such as Google or KidsClick! open up a wealth of sources that enhance or extend traditional printed references. Communications tools such as bulletin boards or blogs allow small groups to work together or communicate with others, and technological tools such Hyperstudio, Microsoft PowerPoint, and Inspiration can help children design and present the findings of their inquiries to audiences inside and outside the classroom. In the SPACES AND PLACES theme, teachers helped students locate many useful websites such as Habitat for Humanity and the National Wildlife Federation, and purchased Sim City 4, a city planning simulation game to work on replanning their own community. They helped children set up Blogs to work together on projects and to communicate with interested parties in their community. They made digital cameras and tape recorders available for photographing and taping the results of student inquiries and then helped the students use Hypermedia and PowerPoint to prepare their final presentations.

See http://cnets.iste.org/students/s_book.html

See www.kidsclick.org

See Blog-City www.blog-city.com/bc/; Blog*Spot www.blogger.com/start

Hands-On Resources: Artifacts, Equipment, and Props

Objects that are products of human culture—tools, machinery, and so on—or natural objects and other materials can be useful features of thematic units. These hands-on resources can provide a focus for wondering, speculating, hypothesizing, or reconstructing events concerning people's lives, both past and present. Consider how old pottery shards, Indian arrowheads, ceremonial masks, costumes, toys, and household items could serve as an entry into another time or another culture. Plan to collect headgear, footwear, and other items of clothing; shells, seeds, rocks, and other natural objects; clocks, watches, irons, toasters, pipes, hammers, beakers, test tubes, and other equipment such as tools and simple machines as a means of extending and exploring the theme. Among the equipment collected by teachers for the SPACES AND PLACES theme were wilderness survival kits, a variety of implements for measuring two- and three-dimensional space, and microscopes and magnifying glasses. Any of these could be included as props in creative dramatics, as objects for ongoing investigations, or as a springboard for focused inquiry.

Hands-on resources inspire dramatics, investigation, and inquiry.

Community Resources

Learning is not confined within the walls of the classroom but extends into the community. When children are involved in a thematic unit, they just naturally connect events and experiences in their lives outside the classroom to things that are happening in school. In addition, plan specifically to make full use of community resources—people, places, animals, and other living things—that can help strengthen children's understanding of the theme and provide access to cultural information that may not be available from printed resources. This is the time to consider the human points of view that may not be represented in printed material and to seek out people who can

Bring the community into the classroom.

Children and their families are important resources.

provide the missing voices that broaden children's understanding. The children themselves are sometimes the best source of information on a topic. Some may have had experiences that can broaden other children's awareness. Others may have unique viewpoints or understandings that shed new light on familiar ideas. Parents and other family members may also have much to contribute in the way of experience, cultural knowledge, or expertise. Plan also to include professionals, specialists, businesspeople, and others in the community who could contribute through classroom visits, interviews, or field trips. Animals and other living things are sources of information that seem to be especially appealing to children. Many thematic units can include small animals, fish, reptiles, or insects as part of the classroom environment for short periods without harm. Plants also make excellent classroom resources. Zoos, aquariums, farms, arboretums, and other such facilities, as well as the natural environments of forest, park, tidal pools, ponds, or even playgrounds, can provide the children with a wealth of learning experiences and activities. Places in the community can become classrooms as part of the thematic unit. Museums of all types and historical sites often have organized presentations and special exhibits that can be part of, or even trigger, a thematic unit. The city streets, country village, even a cemetery can provide less formal, but no less exciting, learning possibilities.

The theme of SPACES AND PLACES particularly lends itself to exploration outside classroom walls and to the use of a variety of community resources. It is ideal for urban, suburban, or rural settings and lends itself to understanding the complex factors that interact within community places. Or consider how Sara's schema of spiders and insects (discussed in Chapter 1) could have been further extended during a thematic unit on BUGS or SMALL WORLDS. Children could collect insects from home and neighborhood in "bug" jars. Various insects are sketched in different positions and, with a detailed written description, placed in a classroom display. Other children keep a daily journal of their observations of caterpillars that have spun cocoons and have been placed in a see-through box to await their metamorphosis to butterflies. You can invite several persons from the community who have an interest in insects to speak to the class. These could include one child's grandparent who collects butterflies, a local beekeeper who brings honey for the children to taste, an exterminator who arrives in a truck with a model of a huge roach perched on the top, and a local farmer who talks about the ways in which insects can help or hinder crops. The children take notes in their journals and later write up these visits in the class newspaper or use the information in research reports they are writing. Children then elect to do follow-up interviews. Some ask family members about interests or hobbies concerning insects. Others interview farmers about their favorite and least favorite insects. Still others call local pest control companies to find out the biggest pest control problem. Results of these interviews are then written up and displayed on bar graphs. The children visit a special exhibit on insects at the museum of natural history where an entomologist conducts a special hands-on tour. While in the museum, they have some time to do some "thought ramblings" in a field trip booklet (that leads to their writing a variety of poetry and short descriptive pieces), as well as interview other professional staff. Finally, as a culminating event of the unit, the children present research reports on insects to the rest of the class. Sara, of course, has chosen to do hers on arachnids.

The Arts

Another category of resources for use in thematic units involves the arts—painting, sculpture, or architecture; the decorative arts; the graphic arts; crafts; musical arts; theater, television, and film. These arts provide important visual, auditory, tactile, and kinesthetic experiences that can give rise to important understandings about a theme. The arts of other times and diverse cultures are also rich sources of information that

Include the arts as resources and as vehicles for exploring themes.

See Levstik & Barton (2001).

may be especially powerful to children of this generation. (Chapter 5 provides a wider discussion of art and music in thematic units.)

The SPACES AND PLACES theme was particularly suited to involving the arts of painting, photography, sculpture, dance, architecture, and music. The arts were rich sources of information about many American and world cultures. In addition to surveying these arts in many cultural contexts, teachers planned to make use of works by painters and photographers such as Georgia O'Keeffe, Ansel Adams (the American West) and Charles Johnson (Harlem and the rural American South of the twenties and thirties), which were inspired by their creators' intense involvement with a specific place. They looked for musical forms like jazz and rap which grew out of a cultural place. They found such musical compositions as Debussy's "La Mer" or Ferd Groffe's "Grand Canyon Suite," and paintings by Chinese artists and the American Lumninists, which were inspired by a desire to interpret space. They included works by Ben Shan, Dorothea Lange, and Diego Rivera who brought social commentary to their depictions of place. They found that the mobiles and stabiles of Alexander Calder as well as the dances of Agnes DeMille and Alvin Ailey were developed around the idea of movement in space.

Experiencing the theme of SPACES AND PLACES through these various art forms can lead children to use the arts to further explore the theme themselves or to use the arts to report back on the outcomes of their exploration of the theme. They may want to create their own mobiles or sculpture, compose a musical or theatrical presentation, choreograph a dance, or make a photo or videotaped record of their inquiries into the theme.

Planning Activities

Reflective, Disciplined Inquiry*

When you collect books and other materials for the thematic unit, consider also the many types of activities and projects from which children can choose to explore the theme. In particular, consider the kinds of activities that will raise questions that call out to be investigated, activities that will motivate children to be genuine seekers after knowledge and understanding. The discovery of a problem to solve that leads students to create and test hypotheses, explore variations on an initial problem, and think about the consequences of answers, leads to the kind of in-depth study that is the lifeblood of a thematic unit. *Reflective, Disciplined Inquiry* is the term given to this process. Reflective inquiry is more than the acquisition of knowledge and skill—they are the *tools* of inquiry. Reflective inquiry involves the following:

> Reflective, Disciplined Inquiry* gives children the tools to seek knowledge.

1. The ability to encode information—that is, to understand what information is relevant or irrelevant to solving a problem.
2. The ability to combine pieces of information, even though those pieces may at first seem unrelated.
3. The ability to compare the problem with problems previously encountered and to use those skills and concepts previously employed.

Ryan and Ellis describe the process of inquiry as recognizing a problem, selecting appropriate data sources, processing the data, and making inferences from the data. One teacher begins with a black-box problem. He asks students to watch carefully as he places a black cardboard box with tripod legs on a desk. There are several buckets immediately below the desk, and a jar of clear liquid is next to the box. The box itself has a rubber spigot spouting from the bottom front and a funnel in the center top. A student is asked to pour the liquid from the jar into the funnel, while another student

> Ryan & Ellis (1974)

monitors the spigot end. As the liquid pours into the funnel, red liquid begins to pour from the spigot—and pours, and pours—until the bucket and part of another on the floor are full.

Before discussion begins, the teacher asks students to think carefully about what they have seen, and then to draw a picture of what they think is in the black box. Over the next several days, students bring pictures to share and set up possible systems to test, which are all displayed in a center with a sign that reads "How Does It Work?" Another center has reference books about the "insides" of all sorts of machines. Some students ask to build their own black boxes and set them up for their peers to figure out. Stories of inventions are shared, new inventions are proposed, and all are used to spark student writing.

In sum, an initial problem provided the catalyst for a wide variety of learning experiences that might have been less effective if students had simply been assigned the text reading on machines. The inquiry into the problem and sufficient time to reflect on possible solutions, to discuss them, and to test hypotheses also presented a model for problem solving. So did the teacher's refusal to open the black box. Throughout the year, even after the unit was over, students continued to construct possible machines to make the box work. Their continued reflection would have been shut off if the teacher had revealed a single "right" answer. Instead, he encouraged a form of speculation similar to that used by scholars investigating all manner of "black boxes"— human cognition, prehistory, and quarks, for example.

In the foregoing example, the teacher introduced the problem and provided some of the data sources that students examined. The students then reflected on those data through discussion and the generation and testing of hypotheses. Such teacher-generated problems encourage students to engage in a wide variety of investigations that might not arise naturally in the classroom. It is important to note, however, that inquiry need not begin with a contrived problem. Students can use an inquiry approach to deal with a variety of problems. In one primary classroom, a classmate's playground accident led children to pose their own question: "How can we make a safer playground?" They decided what data they would need, organized to gather the information, and worked together to interpret the results of their study. Finally, they presented a plan to the principal and worked on an implementation committee.

In the SPACES AND PLACES unit children noticed a vacant lot near the school that was full of trash and quite an eyesore. As they became involved in a project to clean up the lot, they interviewed residents, spoke with city council members, and involved parents and other school and community members in a joint project that resulted in transforming the lot into a vegetable and flower farm. Students and residents worked jointly to clean up, cultivate, and harvest vegetables and flowers that were then distributed to elderly residents and to a soup kitchen for the homeless.

All types of disciplined reflective inquiry encourage student interaction and can generate ideas for activities. They have the additional advantage of also providing a model that can be used in seeking solutions to other problems. These activities will, in turn, suggest other books and materials; the unit may seem to be taking on a life of its own. In planning for these experiences, consider not only language but also math, social studies, the sciences, and the arts as vehicles for exploring the ideas and concepts within the scope of the thematic unit. The prototypes in Chapter 4 illustrate the kinds of projects that can be planned to include these curricular domains. In addition, Chapter 5 covers important ideas and concepts in these different curricular areas in more detail and provides further support for integrating languages across the curriculum.

Purposeful Language Activities

As you consider the many experiences that could be part of a thematic unit, you will note that language will be an important component of any activity. It is, of course, im-

Inquiries should focus on the processes of investigation.

Reflective, Disciplined Inquiry* can give children firsthand experience with problem solving.

portant to ensure that children extend their communicative competence to the fullest extent possible. During their development as competent communicators in their preschool years, children used language for many purposes in learning how to mean. They desired, demanded, socialized, personalized, wondered, imagined, and informed. If they are to continue to grow beyond the confines of their neighborhood into the context of the wider world, these activities must encompass the many situations in which oral language is used in the world and extend across cultures and into the world of print as well. A strong curriculum, therefore, must allow children to continue to express their own personal ideas. It has to provide many opportunities for children to participate in collaborative talk, in *alternative* non-IRE discourse structures (see Chapter 2).

Halliday (1975)

As you select books and other resources for the theme and the WEB begins to take shape, make sure that topics are explored through a variety of purposeful oral and written activities. A balance of these and a balance of materials are more likely to develop competent communicators and critical thinkers. These experiences help children to relate their own views and feelings through discussion, journals, editorials, reviews, and debates; to interact through letters and interviews; to inform through directions, descriptions, records, and reports; to wonder and hypothesize through experiments, observations, and theses; and to imagine through drama, poetry, and story.

Activities should provide opportunities for collaborative discussion among children and teachers.

Planning for activities such as these can occur in several ways. Activities can serve as springboards that lead children to books and other resources. At other times, a book can serve as the focus for meaningful activities, some that lead children back to the book and others that connect to other books or experiences that are part of the thematic unit. Although we illustrate this kind of planning in Chapter 4, it is helpful at this point to provide an example of how teachers might plan activities that will deepen children's response to individual books as well as to broaden their understandings of issues and concepts relating to the theme.

Plan discussion and activities that lead children back into the book.

Planning for Response to Literature

Teachers in integrated classrooms are cognizant of the importance of developing a lifelong enthusiasm for reading as well as developing the abilities necessary for strategic and fluent reading. They will, thus, include time for sustained reading in class and to give students time to reflect on their reading through response journals. Recognizing the social nature of response to literature and the need for joint meaning making, they will provide time for the informal sharing of books and peer–peer and peer–teacher discussion groups. (See Literature Response Groups* in Chapter 7.) They will want children to become aware of the linguistic aspects of all genres, and they will want to plan activities that lead children back to a fictional book, for example, to reexperience characters, settings, themes, and events they have encountered there, or to reflect on the major ways that questions, data, and arguments are explored in information books. In addition, they will want to help children reexamine books they have read to identify connections to the larger theme, to identify possibilities for further inquiry, or to consider the perspective or ideologies or values from which authors have looked at a particular topic, for example.

Take time to develop children's literary responses.

However, sometimes it is difficult to know how to help children get the most out of their literature experiences without ruining the book. Or in our efforts to integrate the curriculum sometimes we may "use" a book to *cover* curricular requirements without allowing time for aesthetic or emotional response. Moreover, there has been some debate about what characterizes authentic responses to literature. Having wrestled with these questions we would like to consider the ways in which children and adults have responded to books outside of classroom contexts. Young children take naturally to exploring their world through play and often very idiosyncratic ways. We know of a four-year-old, for example, who rarely attempted two-dimensional crayon pictures. Instead she symbolized her experiences through paper sculptures and shoe box and

Each child should be able to choose from a wide range of possible responses to a book.

matchbox pictures; her parents had to keep a steady supply of scotch tape and glue on hand for her. One of our friends remembers using the white space at the beginning of chapters to create illustrations for the novels she read as a middle-grade student; another recalls directing neighborhood productions of favorite books. These various ways of responding to books can be found among adults as well. Those of us who love to read know the pleasure of passing on the title of a favorite book to a friend or of discussing responses to books that are particularly thought provoking. In addition, some adults use other vehicles to explore their responses to oral and written literature. Documentaries, editorials, drama, and art are common forms in which adults respond to information and events in their world. Drama and dance are two forms in which story has long been transformed, while art museums of all cultures are filled with paintings and sculptures that are responses to stories. Satirists in the written and pictorial arts delight in manipulating both fiction and nonfiction. We can find humorous commentary; parodies, sequels, and prequels; updated versions; or another character's viewpoint—for example in the pages of *New Yorker* magazine or the widely popular (among adults as well as children) *The Stinky Cheese Man and other Fairly Stupid Tales*. Dressing up as characters, writing recipes, and creating maps and diagrams are also ways in which adults have chosen to respond to well-loved stories or important events. A PBS series called "Time Line" placed a T.V. news team at important historical episodes and included commercials for products invented during that time period. One only has to attend an Anime convention or read *The Dragon Lovers Guide to Pern*, a book published in response to Anne McCaffrey's "Dragon Riders of Pern" series to find similar adult reactions to fiction.

Therefore, we suggest that the keys to deepening a child's response to a book will include time to respond to it in a way each reader finds rewarding. In addition, teachers will want to help children identify connections or questions raised by books that will lead to a broader understanding of the theme. Teachers and children should agree together on the most appropriate ways to respond to a book and ways that book can contribute a topic of inquiry. These experiences should allow children to use many reading strategies (comparing and contrasting, sequencing, recalling details, and making inferences about characters), involve them in writing, drawing, speaking, and listening for many purposes, and engage them in the reflective problem solving as well.

Finally, as these activities are developed, teachers will want to consider the focus of their own classroom research and to include activities that will help them focus systematically on teaching and learning. Teachers might, for example, choose to study children's responses to cultural aspects of the theme, their responses to particular types of book, the variations in children's reading strategies, or gender differences in children's learning. In each case, teachers will want to plan specific activities that could be revealing of patterns and processes in children's learning and in their own teaching. (Examples of such activities will be highlighted in the prototypes in Chapter 4. See also "Guidelines for Teacher Inquiry.")

Organizing the Classroom for Complex Instruction

Because the thematic unit presents children with many possibilities for exploring the theme and asks that you play many roles, it is important that the physical setup of the classroom facilitates the implementation of the unit and supports inquiry and group cooperation. Whether you find yourself in a self-contained or an open classroom, whether you take responsibility for the whole day or are in a departmentalized program, your use of space can ease implementation and organization of the unit. Take time with students at the beginning of the year to discuss the setup of the classroom

Margin notes:

Scieszka (1992)

Nye (1989)

Activities should fully engage a child with a book and deepen the child's understanding of that particular book.

Activities should give teachers opportunities to learn more about their own teaching and their students' learning.

The classroom layout can facilitate learning and orchestrate group interaction.

Cohen (1994)

and how to use the space effectively and comfortably. This might, in fact, be an appropriate initiating activity for a theme of SPACES AND PLACES. Children should be made to feel ownership of the classroom and should take responsibility for its uses as well as contribute suggestions concerning its organization. However that organization finally evolves in your classroom, some features we consider important to the integrated language program in general and thematic units in particular are discussed in the following pages. Amenities such as sinks are not available in many classrooms, but the other factors such as centers can be achieved with minimum outlay as long as desks and furniture can be moved around. Moreover, involving children in the collection of supplies, materials, and in finding solutions to room layout, storage, and display problems creates an important community feeling. A group of fifth graders, for example, hung fish nets from the ceiling to display their work and invented a system of pulleys and buckets to hold art supplies, their solution to a lack of display and storage space.

Materials and Equipment

We have already mentioned the importance of an extensive classroom library supplemented by volumes from the school or municipal library as new themes are planned. In addition, the thematic unit determines the many other types of resources that are collected and displayed within the classroom at any given time. A variety of materials for writing and art activities are always desirable. These need not eat up the supply budget but can be culled from community or family sources. We have seen books created by children on the backs of wallpaper samples or used computer printouts. Beautiful collages and sculpture have been created from scrap paper, fabric scraps, feathers, sequins, beans, macaroni, paper-towel tubes, and other "found" or recycled materials. Desks, chairs, and tables should be movable so that centers can be reorganized according to the demands of a particular unit or activity. Comfortable chairs, pillows, and an old couch or area rugs can further define space and indicate quiet corners. (One lucky teacher found an old porcelain bathtub. Filled with throw pillows, it became the focal point of the reading center.) Easels, walls, and movable bulletin boards on which children's work can be displayed are essential. Rooms should be filled with children's writing, art, and other projects. Bookcases, including the type that can display books cover forward, along with storage cabinets for art supplies, science equipment, math manipulables, and other materials are also important features. Additional materials and equipment can be added according to the needs of each unit and the realities of the school budget.

Donations of furniture and materials can come from parents and other community members.

Organization of Space

Once furniture and equipment are gathered, they can be arranged into areas that suit the needs of a particular unit. Consideration should be given to the need for quiet places for individual activities such as reading, writing, teacher–child conferencing, and for centers where activities might result in more bustle. Space should be kept clear for large group gatherings and creative dramatics or movement. Some areas are permanent. The classroom library, the reading center, the listening post, the writing center where paper, writing implements, and other materials for publishing are stored, and the art center where art supplies are found and used remain unchanged across thematic units during the whole year. Other places will need to be established for ongoing inquiries; these have a temporary life. Tables are moved to certain places in the room so that children have access to the specific resources to be used and explored during a particular thematic unit. For example, places are set up where animals, insects, or plants can be observed and studied, where equipment to conduct experiments is situated, where a classroom restaurant or museum can be established, and so forth. These areas are not centers in the traditional sense and don't require a lot of teacher made materials. When

Both permanent and temporary centers are created in the classroom.

an individual thematic unit is over, much of what had been found in these temporary centers is dismantled and new centers are begun to support the activity and exploration of the next thematic unit.

Implementing the Unit

Whether planning for the unit with children from the beginning or presenting children with a WEB that is more completely planned, teachers should make children aware of their choices regarding activities and also of the contributions they might make early on. Once you begin implementing the unit, ensure that children have the opportunity to explore the theme in ways that will expand domains of knowledge. That is, a thematic unit is a tentative and flexible framework. Changes can be easily made as children's own ideas for projects and activities evolve. Part of this flexibility is accepting even a child's tangential interest. To this end, an initial agreement about what projects are to be carried out as part of the thematic unit is a useful planning and organizing tool. These agreements, which can be realized in many different ways, are means by which children and teacher are able to keep track of what children are doing and are part of the ongoing assessment and evaluation in integrated classrooms. They can provide valuable information about children's processes of learning and serve as sources for accountability. They also help make clear for children what their responsibilities are regarding completion of work and can serve as one focus for self-evaluation. (See Chapters 8 and 9.)

Initial expectations about children's work should be general in nature. Specific projects and dates are then negotiated and become more clearly defined as children have the opportunity to engage in a variety of activities that require reading and writing in a range of genres, that require using language to discuss and organize learning in various areas of the curriculum, and that require participation in various ways of knowing. It is important that children or the teacher have the opportunity to renegotiate agreements. Perhaps a child becomes excited about a particular topic and wants to do additional research. One of the other activities can be dropped to allow the time needed. Or, if a topic or an assigned book has proven too difficult, a more suitable one can be substituted. This flexibility encourages children not only to take risks but also to become aware of their capabilities, another feature of the self-evaluation process.

At the outset of each unit, you may decide on several activities that could be major avenues for introducing and exploring the theme. Each child would be expected to choose one of these projects and to choose whether to work alone or with a small group. There may need to be some negotiation here as well. If you want children to work in groups you might introduce children to projects and books and then give them time to browse through collected materials for several days. Then the children can be asked to list their top three topic and book choices. You can then form groups, attempting to give children their first or second choice. If too many children want to read the same book, you might ask for volunteers to move to other groups or promise children who ended up with their third choice a first-place slot next time. You might also consider the child's previous work and suggest options to ensure that, throughout the year, all children have the opportunity to use language for a variety of purposes while engaged with a wide range of resources. This type of planning is particularly well suited to accommodating the interests and abilities of **all** children. Grouping according to interest in a particular topic or project rather than according to so-called reading levels ensures that children will have the opportunity to work with many of their classmates during the year and that the expectations and outcomes of their learning will be a good match with their needs and enthusiasms.

Agreements can be designed to help you and students plan and to help children know what is expected of them. Due dates can be placed on the agreement to help children become self-monitoring and to aid you in pacing. There may be times when you

Agreements serve to help organize and facilitate the ongoing work of the unit.

Organizing the unit will involve negotiation as well as choice.

Thematic units can provide many ways to group children.

want children to move through activities at approximately the same pace so that all children are introduced to some aspect of the theme at the same time, or so that everyone is working on a research project at the same time. At other times this may not be crucial, and children can decide which activity to complete first.

Following are some specific agreements that you might make with children in the course of a SPACES AND PLACES theme. To introduce the theme, for example, you might want to plan activities that help children think about the scope of the unit at the same time that you help them begin thinking about important questions for their disciplined inquiries. Notice that the activities are designed to get children immediately involved in their community and to offer them opportunities to understand how a historian, poet, geographer, botanist, artist, or anthropologist might each have a unique view or method of studying a place. These understandings can be built on throughout the course of the unit.

1. Read *On This Spot: Back Through Time*. Take a walk and draw a map of the neighborhood you find yourself in. Then draw a second map or picture, imagining the neighborhood you've chosen at some point in the past, indicating what year you've chosen. Try to imagine the way the place might have looked before humans came on the scene. Include pictures of natural or human artifacts that are native or authentic to the place. — Goodman (2004)

2. Read *Island Boy*. Visit a local cemetery. Take a few minutes to sit quietly and listen to the sounds of the place. Choose one of the names on a marker and speculate about that person's life. Make a survey of people by gender and age when they died. Graph your findings. Compare an older part of the cemetery with a newer part. Make a graph comparing the average age of death from each section. Are there years in which more deaths occurred than others? Why? How has the cemetery been maintained as a special place? What other sacred places can you find out about? How do people from different cultures experience and maintain the sacred qualities of a place? — Cooney (1988)

3. Read *Earthlets: As Explained by Professor Xargle*. Observe the behavior of other "earthlings" in your environment as if you were from Professor Xargle's planet. Note the behavior in a field notebook. Include sketches. What might you conclude about the "culture" you have studied based on your observations? Publish your findings or create a museum exhibit. — Willis (1988)

4. Take a walk. Find a bird or bug to observe. Write a detailed description and note behavior in a field notebook. Share your findings. Read through Paul Fleischman's *I Am Phoenix* or *A Joyful Noise* and choose several of the poems to read chorally. Try to capture the features you observed with the sounds of language. Write your own poem for two or three voices. Share with the class. — Fleischman (1985, 1988)

5. Read *I Know That Building*. Take a walk and sketch architectural features you find in your neighborhood. Draw a composite picture that includes some of the features you found. Write an architectural guide to your neighborhood. — D'Alelio (1989)

6. Find a place outdoors and study it from three perspectives, your own, a worm's, and a bird's. Draw pictures or construct a model of your findings. Write about the scene from different points of view.

As children have time to consider the scope of the theme through introductory activities and as they choose additional activities and resources from the WEB to explore, you can guide them toward student-initiated topics and projects that will involve long-term inquiry such as the following:

1. Study the layout of your community. How has the use of land been planned wisely or unwisely? Research community and urban planning on the Internet and in your own community. Use Sim City 4 to design a new community in existing space, parceling land according to perceived needs. What aspect of your ideal community could be implemented now, and how will you achieve this? — Aspyr Media (2003)

See www.habitat.org/how/tour/1.html

2. Study organizations such as Habitat for Humanity that build low-income housing for people. Are there homes (for the elderly) or places (a children's hospital) that need sprucing up? Plan a campaign to raise funds and redecorate one of these places. Interview an interior decorator about interior design. Include plans to paint a mural and wallpaper a room so that you learn how to change scale or measure a repeated pattern.

Myers (1994)

3. Read *Darnell Rock Reporting*. Is there a place in your community that has been neglected and could be changed for the public good? Create a mural showing the changes you propose. What steps can you take to change this place? Develop a Blog to enlist community help.

4. In many of the books chosen for the theme, characters struggle to survive against a variety of odds. What are the factors that make living in different places difficult? In what ways can the climactic, geographic, economic, social, and political factors of a place influence people's lives? What is the human response to these factors? Identify someone in your community who is having difficulty surviving and the factors that make this so. What can you do to resolve some of the problems you have identified?

Finally, additional choices can be made available that meet interests and enthusiasms of individual children. The ideas presented here represent only a few of the many additional experiences that are possible as part of a theme and that individual children can select as part of their agreements:

1. Plan creative dramatics or a Reader's Theater* in response to a story or informational book. Videotape your presentation and post it on your school website.

2. Visit the art museum and make a list of its sculptures. Observe your favorite sculpture from different perspectives noting changes in light and shadow. Sketch the sculpture and write about it.

3. Interview classmates about favorite places. Write results for the class newspaper or Blog.

4. Compare settings or locations in books you are reading. Make a graffiti wall of phrases and words that authors use to describe their setting. Construct a Comparison Chart* that looks at how the authors deal with features such as physical description, or mood, and use of time in their stories and information books. How do these contribute to your enjoyment of the book? How might your understanding of the book's ideas be influenced by the author's depiction of the setting?

5. Create a PowerPoint presentation to summarize the places you have studied in this unit. Choose and record music (or compose music on the computer) that interprets these physical spaces.

6. Study small spaces through a microscope. Conduct daily observations and note changes in Sketchbook Journals*.

7. Do a study of the works of illustrators or photographers who use space in unusual ways. Find out about these people and use Hypermedia to make a display of their works, telling something about their lives and explaining their ideas.

Teachers should plan for their own inquiries as well as their students'.

In implementing the unit teachers will want to consider how they can most effectively and efficiently carry out their own research. They may want to develop an observational form or checklist for recording the responses and understandings of individual children. They may also need to plan for materials they will use that may include simple things like journals and yellow sticky pads or more complex equipment like audio or videotape recorders or audio-tape transcribing machines. Teachers may want to plan regular times for collecting data and set aside a daily period for reflecting on these data. Perhaps an informal agreement with self would be a helpful reminder to find some time each day for that kind of personal reflection. (See "Guidelines for Teacher Inquiry" at the end of the book.)

Conclusions

Through the course of a unit, children have many opportunities to share process and products concerning ongoing activities with other classmates (and with the wider community). This collaboration happens in the course of daily discussions as graphic organizers visualizing processes of investigations are developed, criteria for inquiries are discussed, and children's work is presented, published, and displayed. As knowledge is constructed and expanded, integrated language classrooms truly become communities of learning. Children not only pursue their own projects with enthusiasm, but they are also aware of and interested in the projects of their classmates. When the thematic unit culminates in the sharing of final projects, children can be encouraged to look back and reflect on their own learning and also consider the ways in which the classroom culture constructed a body of knowledge together (see the role of Learning Portfolios in this process in Chapter 9). This joining of effort and understanding is the essence of collaboration and is perhaps the most satisfying and enriching aspect of teaching and learning through thematic units. It may seem that thematic units require an inordinate amount of work. You need to remember, however, that all teaching takes time; the integrated language/thematic unit approach only means that time is used differently. Implementing any new approach takes additional time initially, but eventually teaching this way becomes second nature. In her delightful book, *A House Is a House for Me,* poet Mary Anne Hoberman begins with the simple idea of a house and then reshapes the concept of houses into new and unusual configurations. Repeated through the book is the refrain, "Once you get started in thinking this way. . ." We believe that once you start thinking in terms of thematic units, it's likely that whatever you see in the curriculum you will see in terms of meaningful connections. However you approach thematic units, the goal is to open for children the many possibilities that exist in even the simplest of ideas such as "houses" and to help move them to new and exciting insights and understandings.

Hoberman (1978)

Chapter 4 describes nine prototype thematic units to illustrate in more detail how theory from this approach gets put into action in the classroom. You will visit teachers who use this perspective at various grade levels in the elementary school and who will demonstrate how the integrated language approach can become not just another way of teaching but also an exciting and enriching way of living in the world.

References

Cohen, E. G. (1994). *Designing groupwork: Strategies for heterogeneous classrooms.* New York: Teachers College Press.

Eisenberg, M., & Berkowitz, B. (1987). *Big6* retrieved August 26, 2004 from www.big6.com

Halliday, M. A. K. (1975). *Learning how to mean: Explorations in the development of language.* London: Edward Arnold.

Hansen-Krening, N., Aoki, E. M., & Mizokawa, D. T. (Eds.). (2003). *Kaleidoscope: A multicultural booklist for grades K–8.* Urbana, IL: National Council of Teachers of English.

Hartoonian, H. M. (1992). *A guide to curriculum planning in global studies.* Wisconsin Department of Education.

Huck, C. S., Kiefer, B., Hepler, S., & Hickman, J. (2004). *Children's literature in the elementary school.* Madison, WI: Brown & Benchmark.

ISTE (International Society for Technology in Education). (2000). *National educational technology standards for students: Connecting curriculum and technology.* Retrieved August 26, 2004 from http://cnets.iste.org/students/s_book.html

Jacobs, H. (Ed.). (1989). *Interdisciplinary curriculum: Design and implementation.* Alexandria, VA: Association for Supervision and Curriculum Development.

Jorgensen, C. (1994). Creating questions that all students can answer: A key to developing inclusive curriculum. *Equity and Excellence, 2,* 1.

Klein, J. (Ed.). (2002). *Interdisciplinary education in K–12 and college.* New York: The College Board.

Kobrin, B. (1995). *Eye openers!: How to choose and use children's books about real people, places and things.* New York: Scholastic.

Levstik, L. S., & Barton, K. C. (2001). *Doing history: Investigating with children in elementary and middle schools.* Mahwah, NJ: Lawrence Erlbaum.

Lipson, M., Valencia, S., Wixson, K., & Peters, C. (1993). Integration and thematic teaching: Integration to improve teaching and learning. *Language Arts, 70,* 251–263.

McClure, A. A., & Kristo, J. V. (2002). *Adventuring with books.* Urbana, IL: National Council of Teachers of English.

Miller-Lachman, L. (1992). *Our family, our friends, our world: An annotated guide to significant multicultural literature for children.* New York: R. R. Bowker.

Morris, R. C. (2003). A guide to curricular integration. *Kappa Delta Pi Record. 39(4),* 164–167.

Nielsen, M. E. (1989). Integrative learning for young children: A thematic approach. *Educational Horizons, 68 (1),* 18–24.

Nye, J. L. (1989). *The dragonlovers guide to Pern.* New York: Ballantine Books.

Ryan, F., & Ellis, A. (1974). *Instructional implications of inquiry.* Englewood Cliffs, NJ: Prentice-Hall.

Short, K. G., & Harste, J. C. (1995). *Creating classrooms for authors and inquirers.* Portsmouth, NH: Heinemann.

"Sim City 4." (2003). Aspyr Media.

Smolin, L. I., & Lawless, K. A. (2003). Becoming literate in the technological age: New responsibilities and tools for teachers. *The Reading Teacher, 56(6),* 570–577.

Stevenson, C., & Carr, J. F. (1993). *Integrated studies in the middle grades: Dancing through walls.* New York: Teachers College Press.

Wolinsky, A. (2002). *Internet power research using the big 6 approach.* Berkeley Heights, NJ: Enslow.

Children's Literature

Acorn Pancakes, Dandelion Salad, and 38 Other Wild Recipes by J. George. Illustrated by P. Mirocha. HarperCollins, 1995.

Anno's Magical ABC: An Anamorphic Alphabet by M. Anno & M. Anno. Philomel, 1980.

Appalachia: The Voices of Sleeping Birds by C. Rylant. Illustrated by B. Moser. Harcourt, 1991.

Archeologists Dig for Clues by K. Duke. HarperCollins, 1997.

Artist in Overalls: The Life of Grant Wood by J. Duggleby. Chronicle Books, 1996.

Bear Dance by W. Hobbs. Atheneum, 1993.

The Bear Stone by W. Hobbs. Atheneum, 1989.

Belle Prater's Boy by R. White. Farrar, Straus, & Giroux, 1996.

Between Earth and Sky: Legends of Native American Sacred Places by J. Bruchac. Illustrated by T. Locker. Harcourt, 1996.

Bird by D. Burnie. Photographs by P. Chadwick. Knopf, 1988.

Black and White by D. Macaulay. Houghton Mifflin, 1990.

The Block by L. Hughes. Illustrated by R. Beardon. Viking, 1995.

The Book of Rhythms by L. Hughes. Illustrated by M. Wawiorka. Oxford, 1995.

Brian's Hunt by G. Paulsen. Random House, 2003.

Brian's Winter by G. Paulsen. Delacorte, 1996.

Bugs by N. W. Parker & J. R. Wright. Illustrated by N. W. Parker. Greenwillow, 1987.

Can't Get There From Here by T. Strasser. Simon & Schuster, 2004.

Cathedral by D. Macaulay. Houghton Mifflin, 1973.

Cloud Cuckoo Land (And Other Odd Places) by B. Lodge. Houghton, 1999.

Corpses, Coffins, and Crypts: A History of Burial by P. Colman. Holt, 1996.

Darnell Rock Reporting by W. D. Myers. Delacorte, 1994.

Digging to the Past: Excavations in Ancient Lands by W. J. Hackwell. Scribners, 1986.

Discovering Christopher Columbus: How History Is Invented by K. Pelta. Lerner, 1991.

Dog Team by G. Paulsen. Illustrated by R. W. Paulsen. Delacorte, 1993.

Dogsong by G. Paulsen. Viking, 1985.

Downsiders by N. Shusterman. Simon, 1999.

The Dream Bearer by W. D. Meyers. Amistad, 2004.

Dumpling Soup by J. K. Rattigan. Illustrated by H. Flanders. Little, Brown, 1993.

Earthfasts by W. Mayne. Dutton, 1967.

Earthlets: As Explained by Professor Xargle by J. Willis. Illustrated by T. Ross. Dutton, 1988.

Far North by W. Hobbs. Morrow, 1996.

The Fear Place by P. R. Naylor. Atheneum, 1994.

Fly Away Home by E. Bunting. Illustrated by R. Himler. Clarion, 1991.

From the Mixed-Up Files of Mrs. Basil E. Frankweiler by E. L. Konigsburg. Atheneum, 1969.

Frozen Man by Getz. David Holt, 1994.

George Catlin: Painter of the Indian West, by M. Sufrin. Atheneum, 1991.

Georgia O'Keefe: The Wideness and Wonder of Her World by B. Gherman. Simon & Schuster, 1986.

Ghost Girl by D. Ray. Clarion, 2003.

A Girl from Yamhill by B. Cleary. Morrow, 1988.

Grand Constructions by P. Ventura & G. P. Ceserani. Putnam, 1983.

The Grey Lady and the Strawberry Snatcher by M. Bang. Four Winds, 1980.

Harlem by W. D. Myers. Illustrated by C. Myers. Scholastic, 1996.

Hatchet by G. Paulsen. Bradbury, 1987.

Henry Moore: From Bones and Stones to Sketches and Sculptures by J. M. Gardner. Four Winds, 1993.

A House Is a House for Me by M. A. Hoberman. Illustrated by B. Fraser. Viking, 1982.

How Artists See the Elements: Earth, Air, Fire, Water by C. Carroll. Abbeville, 1996.

I Am Phoenix: Poems for Two Voices by P. Fleischman. Illustrated by K. Nutt. Harper, 1985.

I Know That Building! Discovering Architecture with Activities and Games by J. D'Alelio. The Preservation Press, 1989.

The Ice Is Coming by P. Wrightson. Ballantine, 1977.

An Indian Winter by R. Freedman. Illustrated by K. Bodmer. Holiday House, 1992.

The Inner City Mother Goose by E. Merriam. Simon, 1996.

The Inside-Outside Book of New York City by R. Munro. Putnam, 1985.

Into the Woods: John James Audubon Lives His Dream by R. Burleigh. Illustrated by W. Minor. Atheneum, 2003.

Island Boy by B. Cooney. Viking, 1988.

Island of the Blue Dolphins by S. O'Dell. Houghton Mifflin, 1960.

John Muir by E. Wayburn. Illustrated by T. Locker. Fulcrum, 2003.

The Journey of Diego Rivera by E. Goldstein. Lerner, 1996.

A Joyful Noise: Poems for Two Voices by P. Fleischman. Illustrated by E. Beddows. Harper, 1988.

Julie by J. George. Illustrated by W. Minor. HarperCollins, 1994.

Julie of the Wolves by J. C. George. Illustrated by J. Schoenherr. Harper, 1972.

Junebug by A. Mead. Farrar, Straus, & Giroux, 1995.

Kensuke's Kingdom by M. Morpugo. Scholastic, 2003.

Kids Dance: The Students of Ballet Tech. by J. Varriale. Dutton, 1999.

Let There Be Light: A Book about Windows by J. C. Giblin. Crowell, 1988.

Li'l Sis and Uncle Willie by G. Everett. Rizzoli, 1991.

Locomotion by J. Woodson. Puffin, 2004.

Magic and Perception: The Art and Science of Fooling the Senses by B. Friedhoffer & L. Eisenberg. Watts, 1997.

The Man Who Made Parks: The Story of Parkbuilder Frederick Law Olmstead by F. Wishinsky. Illustrated by S. N. Zhang. Tundra, 1999.

Maps: Getting from Here to There by H. Weiss. Houghton Mifflin, 1991.

Martha Graham by R. Freedman. Clarion, 1998.

Martha Graham: Founder of Modern Dance by G. Newman and E. N. Layfield. Watts, 1998.

Missing May by C. Rylant. Orchard, 1992.

Mission Earth: Voyage to the Home Planet by J. A. English & T. D. Jones. Scholastic, 1996.

Mobiles by B. Zubrowski. Illustrated by R. Doty. Morrow, 1993.

Monkey Island by P. Fox. Orchard, 1991.

Mosque by D. Macaulay. Houghton, 2003.

My Denali: Exploring Alaska's Favorite National Park with Hannah Corral by K. Corral & H. Corral. Alaska, 1996.

My Place by N. Wheatley. Kane/Miller, 1992.

My Side of the Mountain by J. George. Dutton, 1959.

National Parks of Alaska by M. Dunmire. Pegasus, 1991.

No Place to Be: Voices of Homeless Children by J. Berck. Houghton Mifflin, 1992.

Now You See It Now You Don't by S. Simon. Morrow, 1998.

On This Spot: Back Through Time by S. E. Goodman. Greenwillow, 2004.

Optical Illusion Experiments by M. DiSpezio. Sterling, 2000.

Our Patchwork Planet: The Story of Plate Tektonics by H. R. Sattler. Illustrated by G. Maestro. Lothrop, 1995.

Outside Over There by M. Sendak. Harper, 1981.

The Paper Crane by M. Bang. Greenwillow, 1985.

Perspective by J. Welton. Dorling Kindersly, 1993.

Picture This: Perception and Composition by M. Bang. Bulfinch Press, 1991.

Puppies, Dogs, and Blue Northers by G. Paulsen. Illustrated by R. W. Paulsen. Harcourt, 1996.

Rachel Carson: Preserving a Sense of Wonder by J. Bruchac. Illustrated by T. Locker. Fulcrum, 2004.

Reflections by A. Jonas. Greenwillow, 1987.

Return of the Wolf by D. H. Patent. Clarion, 1995.

A River Ran Wild by L. Cherry. Harcourt, 1992.

Round Buildings, Square Buildings, and Buildings That Wiggle Like a Fish by P. M. Isaacson. Knopf, 1988.

Round Trip by A. Jonas. Greenwillow, 1983.

Sacred Places by J. Yolen. Illustrated by D. Shannon. Harcourt, 1996.

Scorpions by W. D. Myers. Harper, 1988.

The Sculptor's Eye: Looking at Contemporary American Art by J. Greenberg & S. Jordan. Delacorte, 1993.

Shimmy Shimmy Shimmy Like My Sister Kate: Looking at the Harlem Renaissance through Poems by N. Giovanni. Holt, 1996.

Shipwreck at the Bottom of the World: The Extraordinary True Story of Shackleton and the Endurance by J. Armstrong. Crown, 2000.

Sierra Club Book of Our National Parks by D. Young. Sierra Club, 1990.

Simple Optical Illusion Experiments With Everyday Materials by M. DiSpezio. Sterling, 2000.

Sir Ernest Shackleton: By Endurance We Conquer by P. Calvert. Benchmark, 2002.

Slake's Limbo by F. Holman. Macmillan, 1974.

A Song in Stone: City Poems by L. B. Hopkins (Ed.). Photographs by A. H. Audette. Crowell, 1983.

Soulfire by L. Hewett. Dutton, 1996.

Spirit of Endurance by J. Armstrong. Illustrated by W. Maughan. Crown, 2000.

The Stinky Cheese Man and Other Fairly Stupid Tales by J. Scieszka. Illustrated by L. Smith. Viking, 1992.

Story of Johnny Appleseed by Aliki. Prentice-Hall, 1963.

A Street Called Home by A. B. L. Robinson. Harcourt, 1997.

Street Music: City Poems by A. Adoff. Illustrated by K. Barbour. HarperCollins, 1995.

Tadpole by R. White. Farrar, 2003.

This Land Is My Land by G. Littlechild. Children's Press, 1993.

Three Days on a River in a Red Canoe by V. B. Williams. Mulberry Books, 1981.

Toughboy and Sister by K. Hill. McElderry, 1990.

The Twenty-One Balloons by W. P. duBois. Viking, 1947.

Two Bad Ants by C. Van Allsburg. Houghton, 1988.

Uluru: Australia's Aboriginal Heart by K. Arnold. Clarion, 2003.

Underground by D. Macaulay. Houghton Mifflin, 1976.

Visiting the Art Museum by L. Brown & M. Brown. Dutton, 1986.

Visual Magic by D. Thomson. Dial, 1991.

Walking With Henry by T. Locker. Fulcrum, 2002.

Walter Wick's Optical Tricks by W. Wick. Scholastic, 1998.

Where On Earth Am I? by R. Gardner. Watts, 1996.

Where the Lilies Bloom by V. Cleaver & B. Cleaver. Illustrated by J. Spanfeller. Lippincott, 1969.

The Wild, Wild Cookbook by J. C. George. Crowell, 1982.

Winter Camp by K. Hill. McElderry, 1993.

World Population by N. Fyson. Watts, 1998.

Yellowstone 1988: Summer of Fire by P. Lauber. Orchard, 1991.

Prototypes for Integrated Language Classrooms

Starting a Thematic Unit

Reflective, Disciplined Inquiry*

Reflective, Disciplined Inquiry* is the underlying rationale for a thematic unit. As we mentioned in Chapter 3, the creation or discovery of a problem can lead students to generate questions, create and test hypotheses, explore variations on an initial problem, and study a theme in depth. This process is crucial to the development of a thematic unit because it helps children understand *why* they are engaged in a particular study or topic, *how* they can investigate important questions, and *how* they can "master perplexity" by making sense out of what did not initially make sense.

In an integrated language classroom, children do not pursue a topic simply because it has been assigned, but because they are perplexed; their existing schemas have been challenged or they perceive a problem to investigate. This problem or perplexity may be provoked by events in the school or community beyond the school, or it may be initiated by the teacher. In either case, a wide variety of learning experiences develops from the initiating event and provides opportunities for lively conversation and intellectual negotiation, engagement with substantive content from a variety of sources, and classroom thoughtfulness—thinking carefully and thoroughly before responding to questions or attempting to resolve problems. In sum, Reflective, Disciplined Inquiry* supports children's efforts toward informing themselves, directing their own studies, and becoming intellectually independent.

There are a number of ways to spark this kind of inquiry. Once you have organized possible activities, projects, and resources in your WEB, you have to decide where to begin. The first few moments and activities in a thematic unit set the stage for what is to come and can either generate interest, enthusiasm, and learning or create difficulties that are hard to overcome. The stage must be set with *meaning-full* work if children are to be engaged as *meaning makers*. What follows are some ideas that can be used to begin inquiry-based thematic units.

Begin with Children's Interests

As already noted in Chapter 3, children's interests can be used to inspire a thematic unit. Sometimes a vacation trip can generate interest in a study. One teacher sets up an interest center based on the seashells, sand, and seaweed brought back from a child's trip to the shore. She also arranges a selection of information books, poetry, and fiction in the center. Among these resources, she places several cards with different ques-

Reflective, Disciplined Inquiry is crucial to thematic studies.

An initiating event sets the stage for inquiry.

Atwell (1990); McGinley & Madigan (1990)

Support inquiry with a variety of genres.

tions for children to consider. The children then use the resources to choose a line of inquiry that starts them on a LIFE IN AND NEAR THE WATER thematic unit.

In another classroom, children become interested in a rhododendron branch that has been wilting in a corner. When they start asking questions about the dying plant, the teacher uses this interest as the beginning point for a WEB on the effect of water on living things. Students conduct experiments to chart changes caused by dehydration, they study the uses of dried plants, and they measure plant growth.

A butterfly cocoon brought into a second- and third-grade class has similar results, serving as the beginning point for the teacher's WEB. Throughout the thematic unit, children observe the cocoon and use reference books to help make inferences about what may emerge. The culminating activity of the unit includes the excitement of seeing the cocoon hatch and then the ceremony accompanying the butterfly's release into the wild.

In each of these instances, children's ideas and interests provide a theme for further study and elaboration. The teacher's task is to help children focus on substantive issues and the kinds of essential questions relevant to the theme. At the same time, the children's initiative generates interest and motivates in-depth inquiry around these essential questions.

Begin with an Artifact

Another way to begin a thematic unit is to present students with an artifact or use one brought in by a student or community member so that curiosity is aroused and speculation begins. One teacher introduces a unit on Japan by gathering her class about her in a semicircle and pulling a wooden mask out of a bag. As the children pass the mask around the circle and peer through its eyes, the teacher asks students to share their observations. The children then write a few lines—poetry for some, simple prose for others—about who this character might be. Several of these observations are shared, then all are mounted and displayed with the mask. Next the teacher records the students' questions about the mask on a large piece of paper and tells the children that she is going to share a book with them that comes from the same part of the world as the mask.

The teacher leads the class to discover a topic-of-interest by focusing children's attention on an unusual object and by maintaining its mystery while she draws children into another culture. Any artifact, from a fossil to a painting, can serve as the first step in implementing a thematic unit.

Begin with a Book

Literature is a rich source of ideas and starting points for thematic units. One teacher uses Eve Bunting's *Going Home* to spark interest in a thematic unit on JOURNEYS. In Bunting's book, a family returns to Mexico to visit the relatives left behind when the family emigrated to the United States. After discussing why the family in the book came to the United States and why the parents someday want to return to Mexico, students decided that they would interview immigrants in their own community. They developed a set of questions to ask: Why did you immigrate? What made you decide to come to the United States? What do you miss most about your old home? What were the most difficult parts of moving from one place to another? Did you find new opportunities here? Eventually, they organized their questions into categories and decided that one essential question they were investigating was, "How have the journeys of immigrants changed the world?" This question helped students organize the museum of immigration that concluded their study.

(1996) Bunting

Provide many opportunities for children to share in their work with peers.

Begin with Drama

Creative dramatics, role playing, and simulation can lead children to explore a theme by establishing a context for investigation and a need for research. A fifth-grade unit on AMERICANS ON THE MOVE begins when students are assigned the roles of family members on a New England farm in the 1840s who must decide whether to head for land in Kansas. To resolve the family conflict raised in the role playing, students need more information. They list some of the things they need to know: How much can they get for their present land? How much will the trip cost? How can they get to Kansas? What supplies will they need? Who else might be going? What crops can be grown there? Are there Indians already living on the land? How might these native peoples feel about the influx of new settlers?

These questions form the backdrop for organizing student inquiry and lead to the use of the computer simulation *The Oregon Trail,* to questions about the politics of pioneering across times and places, and to exploration of the body of literature about pioneers. At different points throughout the unit, dramatic techniques are used to focus on such issues as Native American rights, the power of the railroads and industry, establishment of free and slave states, Spanish and French claims in the West and North, and women's suffrage. Each of these issues raises important questions about how history is studied (Who narrates the story? Whose voice is heard or unheard?), challenges children's thinking, and furthers careful reflection on decisions made in the initial pioneer-oriented simulation.

Empowering Teachers and Children

Each of the teachers described here assumed that one of a teacher's roles is that of motivator and facilitator of learning. Teachers in the classroom know the curriculum and the children, linking both so that children are more likely to develop schemas for understanding the world, not just as it is in their immediate experience but also as it was in the past, is now elsewhere, and could be in the future. The intent is to empower children by creating a learning environment in which content, process, and intellectual excitement are connected. By encouraging reflective inquiry, teachers do not separate the processes of learning from the content learned. Instead, they link processes to specific contents or domains of knowledge. As children debate whether to move west, for instance, they use data sources specific to history—primary documents, such as diaries or letters written by actual pioneers, speeches and treaties representing native peoples, census information, period art, and music. To evaluate these sources, they learn such historical processes as cross documentation: Is this information supported by other documentation? Are there documents that give a contrary point of view? Whose perspective is gained? Whose is missing?

By role playing or participating in a simulation, they also gain skill in perspective-taking, an important element in developing historical as well as global understanding. As in the "black box" experience described in Chapter 3, children practice careful observation, inference, hypothesis making and testing, and scientific speculation. They also focus on significant themes and essential questions that do not have single or simple solutions. In short, they learn research skills by using them as they were intended to be used—to better understand the world.

Finally, the focus on identifying essential questions helps teachers and students concentrate their efforts on worthwhile content related to significant issues. Instructional time is limited; however, the possibilities for themes are limitless. There is no time for themes that cannot generate the kinds of essential questions discussed in Chapter 3. As a result, teachers need constantly to ask themselves the "so what" question. *So what* if children learn this material? What importance does this knowledge have? What essential questions does it help them answer? Does it help them more ef-

Record student questions on chart paper to encourage continued reference.

Clements, Tabachnik, & Fielder (1966)

Broderbund (2004)

Blake (1981), Feshback (1975); Shaftel & Shaftel (1982)

fectively participate in the world around them? In the prototypes that follow you will see how a variety of teachers answered these questions.

Prototypes in Action

The first steps are taken, the unit initiated, and then . . . what? Prototypes—excerpts from integrated language classrooms in action—provide an overview of what happens when teachers and children work together to explore themes and engage in the various activities that make up a school day. Nine prototypes offered in this chapter demonstrate the versatility and flexibility of this approach while spanning grade levels:

Prototype	Grade	Theme
1	K	WONDERING
2	1	SOUNDS ALL AROUND
3	2/3	JOURNEYS
4	3	CREATING COMMUNITIES
5	4	CYCLES
6	5	EXPLORING OUR ROOTS
7	6	DIGGING UP THE PAST
8	7	LANDSCAPES
9	8	PERSPECTIVES

There are samples taken from self-contained, family-grouped, and departmentalized settings, from thematic units that begin in different ways, and from teachers with very different styles of engaging children.

Each of the nine prototypes contains five parts:

- A WEB demonstrating the range of choices available to the teacher(s) and students
- A schedule demonstrating how time is used in the classroom
- An "Into the Classroom" component that follows children and teacher(s) through one entire day and portions of two other days
- A summary pointing out particular features of the prototype
- A bibliography of the books and resources referred to in the WEB

What to Look for in Prototypes: Tips on How to Read Them

The prototypes are provided in chronological order. There are some advantages in reading all the prototypes in the order presented. It enables you to compare and contrast the various features illustrating different prototypes to better observe and abstract developmental characteristics. However, the prototypes have been written so that you can skip around to read individual prototypes by focusing on a particular grade level, a certain classroom feature (e.g., family grouping or departmentalization), or a specific theme.

It is important to point out four features ahead of time so that you can read the prototypes more easily. First, the information in the component called "Into the Classroom" is presented in tables with four columns. The first column, "Time," indicates how activities are scheduled and the amount of time designated for different parts of the day. The second column, "Children," describes the activities children are engaged in, according to the time allotments depicted in the "Schedule" section of that prototype. The third column, "Teacher," highlights teacher roles, showing what the teacher does during children's activities. The fourth column, "Teacher Research," shows some of the activities related to the teacher's ongoing classroom research on teaching and learning, whereby the idea of reflective inquiry by students is extended to teachers as well. Thus, besides everyday assessment and ongoing evaluation of children's learning, each teacher is focusing on a particular inquiry during the course of the thematic unit. (See also the "Guidelines for Teacher Inquiry" at the end of the book).

Second, various classroom routines, such as Comparison Charts*, Sustained Silent Reading (SSR)*, and Big Books*, which are mentioned in these tables and elsewhere, may be unfamiliar to you. These routines, which are marked with an asterisk, are explained in more detail in Chapter 7, the "how-to" chapter.

Third, each WEB includes *essential questions*—the big questions around which an inquiry is organized. Some of these questions can be found in the headings for categories on each WEB. Others are listed on the WEB as research activities within a larger category. As you read the "Into the Classroom" sections and the WEBs, you can see how these questions are used to organize and focus student work. For instance, in the WONDERING prototype, the essential questions range from "Who am I?" to "How do I find out about my world?" The CREATING COMMUNITIES prototype involves students in exploring questions such as "What can we do to make changes in our community?" and "How do living things interact with each other in the world?"

Fourth, certain features of ongoing assessment are explicitly noted throughout the prototypes. Assessment and instruction in these classrooms are a reciprocal process—part of an ongoing interplay of teacher actions and evaluations, student learning, and teachers' everyday decisions as to what and how to teach. These kinds of interactions provide both teachers and students with information that is useful in promoting student learning. Many of these ongoing routines and assessments are described in Chapters 7 and 8. However, certain assessment strategies or terms, such as performance assessment or portfolios, are explained further in Chapter 9.

Prototype 1: Full-Day Kindergarten— WONDERING

Schedule

The WONDERING thematic unit is geared to full-day kindergarten, a time frame typical of many school districts around the country. (Table 4.1 shows a typical weekly plan for Karla's program.) The school is in an urban area that hosts a variety of cultures and socioeconomic groups. The school philosophy is community oriented and parents and families are involved in school governance and affairs on a regular basis. Karla Jones's classroom is self-contained and organized into centers. There is a large open area for creative dramatics, dance, music, and whole-class read-aloud reading. There is a library filled with books and comfortable places to read. Many of the books are on shelves, but many more are displayed cover-forward on wooden racks or tables or lined up along the floor for easy access. There is an art corner with a sink, supply cupboards, table, and several easels. A building or construction corner with large wooden blocks, a playhouse made out of plastic pipes, and sand and water tables provide many opportunities for dramatic play and scientific exploration. The classroom looks like a place where exciting things are happening. The children's artwork, writing, projects, and shared and dictated writing are displayed in every available space.

The thematic unit WONDERING began because Karla wanted to develop a unit that would allow her 5- and 6-year-olds to explore the world around them and their relationships to it, particularly in terms of the questions they had. She wanted to honor these questions and show children how wondering could lead to inquiries that might help them answer their questions.

Children learn through active exploration and participation.

table **4.1** **Weekly Schedule, Karla Jones's Full-Day Kindergarten Class**

Time	Monday	Tuesday	Wednesday	Thursday	Friday
9:00	Preparation. Children arrive and go to centers or meet informally with teacher.				
9:10	Circle time. Teacher reads book or tells story. Goes over daily schedule and individual plans.				
9:30	Integrated work time. Children work in centers. Teacher circulates or works with individuals or small groups. Choices might include experiments at the water or sand tables, art activities at the art center, play in block corner, manipulating props and materials measurement devices or sorting leaves in the science center, or dramatic play in the "playschool" and class library area.				
10:45	Snack				
11:00	Recess				
11:15	Library	Computer lab	Music	Art	Physical education
11:45	Cleanup				
12:00	Lunch and outdoor play				
12:45	Nap or rest period				
1:15	Book time: Teacher reads or works with Big Books*				
1:30	Snack time				
1:45	Integrated work time. Children work in centers. Teacher works with small groups or individuals.				
2:30	Snack time				
2:45	Whole-group time. Children engage in music, creative dramatics, movement.				
3:05	Wrap up				
3:15	Dismissal				

As Karla looked through several of the indexes to children's books, she found many titles that could be explored under the topic of WONDERING. She decided to keep the study manageable by limiting areas of study to four major areas, "Wondering About School," "Wondering About My Body," "Wondering About Numbers, Letters, and Words" and "Wondering About Time." She felt that these areas would allow her to cover major concepts called for in the kindergarten curriculum and would also provide books and activities that would satisfy kindergarteners' lively curiosity. Karla added the topic of "Wondering About Books," as she found children's particular interest in the pop-up and lift-the-flap books she had in the room. Then it seemed natural to add a study of libraries and how books are made. Finally, Karla added a topic of "Always Wondering." Here she planned to introduce new information books each week in order to determine children's inquiries for the rest of the year.

Karla had noticed last year that when she had her young kindergarteners examine and "read" the pictures and print in their books and emphasize both pictures and emergent messages in writing, they paid more attention to the print in books and were more motivated to write. She knew that some teachers and researchers felt differently about the role of pictures in early reading instruction—that is, that pictures in books were somehow barriers for young children's interest or motivation in learning the print in books. Thus, this year she planned her teacher research around this issue. As she observed children's special interest in pop-up and lift-the-flap books, she felt these books might provide further data for her teacher inquiry and added more of these types to her classroom collection. Over the course of the unit she hoped to document how her students attended to pictures and print and the connections between them as they developed as readers and writers.

See Samuels (1970) for information on the "pictures as barriers" view.

Prototype 1: Full Day Kindergarten—WONDERING

Wondering about Words

What is a word? Make a list of ideas about words.

Look at examples of environmental print. Identify as many words as you can. Start a collection of word cards or a dictionary of words that you know.

ANDY, THAT'S MY NAME

Can you find any words in your name? The names of your classmates? Make a chart listing all the words you find in your names.

WORD WIZARD
CLOWNING AROUND
OLD BLACK FLY
AUTUMN: AN ALPHABET ACROSTIC

How are words different from letters? What words do you already know? Add new words to your word collection or dictionary.

ABC I LIKE ME

Find words that begin with the same letter as your name and that also describe you. Do the same thing for someone else you know.

MERRY-GO-ROUND: A BOOK ABOUT NOUNS
KITES SAIL HIGH: A BOOK ABOUT VERBS
MANY LUSCIOUS LOLLIPOPS: A BOOK ABOUT ADJECTIVES

Create a chart of all the nouns, verbs, and adjectives you can think of.

Wondering about Alphabet Themes

B IS FOR BULLDOZER
ALPHA BUGS
THE BUTTERFLY ALPHABET
THE GUINEA PIG ABC
INTO THE A B SEA
MY BEASTIE BOOK OF ABC
FIREFIGHTERS FROM A TO Z
KINDERGARTEN ABC
EATING THE ALPHABET

Choose a new theme and compile an alphabet book of your own. Can you find or draw a picture for each letter of the alphabet that goes with your theme?

What Letter Comes Next?

ALISON'S ZINNIA

Find someone else in your class whose name comes after yours in the alphabet. Make a short buddy book on the two letters and share with the class.

Learn the ABC song.

Put objects or pictures in ABC order.

Wondering about Letters

WONDERING HOW LETTERS ARE MADE

ALPHABET UNDER CONSTRUCTION
ALBERT'S ALPHABET

Draw or make letters of the alphabet in the sand table with shaving cream, jump ropes, or your bodies.

WONDERING ABOUT ALPHABET STORIES AND PUZZLES

ALPHA BUGS
THE ALPHABET ROOM
THE HIDDEN ALPHABET
ALLIGATORS ALL AROUND. AN ALPHABET
CHICKA CHICKA BOOM BOOM
KIPPER'S A TO Z: AN ALPHABET ADVENTURE
WHAT PETE ATE FROM A–Z (REALLY!)
MISS BINDERGARTEN TAKES A FIELD TRIP WITH THE KINDERGARTEN
THE Z WAS ZAPPED
THE ALPHABET TREE

Talk about each of these books as your teacher reads them.

In small groups, make up your own alphabet story.

Q IS FOR DUCK: AN ALPHABET GUESSING GAME

Think of new phrases for each letter (e.g., Q is for Crown).

EMILY'S FIRST 100 DAYS OF SCHOOL
KINDERGARTEN COUNT TO 100
COUNTING OUR WAY TO THE 100TH DAY

Make a chart for your own school days. Count something that matches each day. Draw the things you count on your chart.

MEASURING PENNY

What are different ways to measure things in your classroom? Choose a unit of measurement and measure as many things in your classroom as you can. Make a picture chart showing the measurements from smallest to largest.

Wondering about Numbers

RAIN DANCE
TEN PUPPIES
BIG FAT HEN
1 2 3 FOLLOW ME!
CARLO LIKES COUNTING
HOW MANY BUGS IN A BOX?
CHICKA CHICKA 1, 2, 3

How high can you count?

Match pictures or number blocks with numerals.

Cool Math for Kids
www.coolmath4kids.com/little_links.html

Try out number games on the Web.

WONDERING ABOUT NUMBERS, LETTERS, AND WORDS

WONDERING

Wondering about Combining and Taking Away

FIVE CREATURES
ROCK IT, SOCK IT NUMBER LINE
UP TO TEN AND DOWN AGAIN
TURTLE SPLASH: COUNTDOWN AT THE FARM
TEN SEEDS
A CREEPY COUNTDOWN
ONE LIGHTHOUSE, ONE MOON
LOOK WHOOO'S COUNTING

Count all the objects in these books. Use unifix cubes to show how many you counted.

Make a Graph* showing how many objects you find in each of these books. Which book has the most?

WONDERING ABOUT TIME

What Makes Day and Night?

EARTH CYCLES
DAY LIGHT, NIGHT LIGHT
WHAT MAKES DAY AND NIGHT
NIGHT AND DAY
NOW SOON LATER
THE MOON SEEMS TO CHANGE

Act out the movements of the earth around the sun and the moon around the earth.

With the help of someone at home, keep a moon journal. Look for the moon every night before you go to bed. Keep a record of what you see. What shape is the moon? Where is it in the night sky in comparison to your house? Make note of the weather. Look at the sky during the day. Can you ever see the moon?

A Week

COOKIE'S WEEK
TODAY IS MONDAY
THE VERY HUNGRY CATERPILLAR
ONE MONDAY MORNING

Dictate your own story about the days of the week using one of these books as a model. Illustrate it.

A Day/A Night

TELLING TIME WITH BIG MAMA CAT

Make a clock with a paper plate and movable dial. Learn to tell time.

GIGGLE GIGGLE WAKE-UP!

Make a list of favorite rhyming word pairs from the book. Add new rhyming words to each pair. How many can you recognize when you look at the book?

MY GRANDMOTHER'S CLOCK
ONE AFTERNOON
HELLO TOES! HELLO FEET!
NEW MOON
LOOK AT THE MOON
THE PAPER BOY

Make a list of all the words for different times of day. Can you connect these to times on a clock?

Write an illustrated story about something you do every morning and every evening.

What's the Reason for Seasons?

THE REASON FOR SEASONS
SUNSHINE MAKES THE SEASONS

Make a model of the earth and the sun. Recreate the earth's journey around the sun.

The four seasons are based on the position of the earth relative to the sun, but not all people experience four distinct seasons. What seasons do you have where you live?

ERNIE DANCES TO THE DIGEREDOO

Find Arnhem Land, Australia, on a world globe. What are the six different parts of the year in Arnhem Land? What causes these six seasons? Why is it sunny and hot in December in Australia?

The Months

CHICKEN SOUP WITH RICE
A YEAR FOR KIKO
ONE MOON ONE LIGHTHOUSE
SING A SONG OF PIGLETS, A CALENDAR IN VERSE

Learn the names of the months.

Make a calendar that shows all the months at once.

Find out whose birthday is in each month. Mark it on your class calendar. Which month has the most birthdays?

TWELVE HATS FOR LENA

Make a hat for the current month.

ALWAYS WONDERING

The Year

MY LOVE FOR YOU ALL YEAR
CAPS, HATS, SOCKS AND MITTENS: A BOOK OF SEASONS
RIGHT OUTSIDE MY WINDOW
THE LITTLE ISLAND
THE SKY TREE
THE SEASONS OF ARNOLD'S APPLE TREE
THE YEAR AT MAPLE HILL FARM
APPLE VALLEY YEAR
SWING AROUND THE SUN

Make a mural or pop-up book showing what you think your school grounds will look like in fall, winter, spring, and summer.

What's the Season Now?

RED LEAF YELLOW LEAF

Make leaf rubbings.

Press leaves and make a leaf book.

WHY DO LEAVES CHANGE COLOR?
HOW DO YOU KNOW IT'S FALL?
A CHILL IN THE AIR: NATURE POEMS FOR FALL AND WINTER
AUTUMN IS FOR APPLES
IT'S FALL
FIRST FIELD GUIDE TO TREES
AUTUMNBLINGS
LEAVES! LEAVES! LEAVES!

Take a walk outdoors and collect leaves. Bring them back to the classroom and classify them by shape. How are they alike and different? How can we find out what kind of tree they came from?

Always Wondering

"I Wonder"
"Sometimes I Wonder"

Learn to say these poems in a Choral Reading*.

WHAT'S IT LIKE TO BE A FISH?
BUGS ARE INSECTS
WHAT MAKES A SHADOW?
POP: A BOOK ABOUT BUBBLES
DINOSAURS, BIG AND SMALL
IS THERE LIFE IN OUTER SPACE?

What else would you like to learn about? Make a list of things you want to find out more about. What are the ways to answer questions you have about your world? Help your teacher decide on inquiries about them for new units.

What's Your Name?

CHRYSANTHEMUM
NATHANIEL TALKING
CAN YOU GUESS MY NAME?

Find out about your name. Does it mean something? Are you named after another person? Do you have a nickname?

Make up your own name rap.

MY NAME IS YOON
MY NAME IS JORGE
SUMI'S FIRST DAY OF SCHOOL
THE NAME JAR

Has someone in your family changed his or her name? Interview family members and find out.

WHAT'S YOUR NAME: FROM ARIEL TO ZOE
MY SON JOHN
MISS BINDERGARTEN GETS READY FOR KINDERGARTEN
MY NAME IS ALICE

Make up versions of these books using the names of your classmates, family, and friends. Make a chart of classmates' names in ABC order. How many of your classmates' names can you find on the chart?

Wonder What Will School Be Like?

TIPTOE INTO KINDERGARTEN
AT SCHOOL: A LIFT-THE-FLAP LEARNING BOOK
FIRST DAY
FIRST DAY OF SCHOOL EVER
I AM NOT GOING TO SCHOOL TODAY

What do you think you will learn to do in kindergarten? Make a list to keep until the end of the year. Then check it and change it to reflect what you experienced.

WHO IS GOING TO SCHOOL TODAY?
ANNABELLE SWIFT KINDERGARTENER

How many of your classmates went to preschool? Were you ever afraid of going to school? What did you think this school would be like? Draw a picture in your Sketchbook Journal*.

MY KINDERGARTEN

How many of the activities in this book can you do? Keep track of special activities on a giant calendar.

WILL I HAVE A FRIEND?

What is a friend? How can each of us be a friend to others?

MOSES GOES TO SCHOOL

Do any of our classmates have special needs like Moses? How can you help them?

MS. MACDONALD HAD A CLASS

Sing and move to the book! Act out your own class play.

Do Animals Really Go to School?

THREE CHEERS FOR TACKY
LILY'S PURPLE PLASTIC PURSE
OFF TO SCHOOL BABY DUCK
THE AWFUL AARDVARKS GO TO SCHOOL
FROGGY GOES TO SCHOOL
MINERVA LOUISE AT SCHOOL
AMANDA PIG SCHOOLGIRL
YOKO
TIMOTHY GOES TO SCHOOL
LOOK OUT KINDERGARTEN HERE I COME
BISCUIT LOVES SCHOOL

How are these stories alike and different? Make a picture Comparison Chart*.

What Are My Rights and Responsibilities?

NO DAVID!
WHEN SOPHIE GETS ANGRY, REALY REALLY ANGRY

What rules do you have at your house? Compare your family's rules with other children's rules. Classify the types of rules. Make a Picture Graph* showing those rules that occur most often.

DAVID GOES TO SCHOOL

Do we need to have rules at school? What are some important rules you think you should have in your classroom? In the school? On the playground?

Wondering about My Teacher

MY TEACHER'S SECRET LIFE
FIRST DAY JITTERS
MISS MALARKEY DOESN'T LIVE IN ROOM 10
FIRST DAY LETTERS

Find out more about your teacher. Draw a picture with labels or captions of your teacher showing what you found out. Write a letter for your teacher to keep.

THE TEENY TINY TEACHER

After you have heard the story once, help your teacher tell it again. Make up a new teeny tiny story using Group Composed Writing*.

What Is School Like in Other Places?

THIS IS THE WAY WE GO TO SCHOOL: A BOOK ABOUT CHILDREN AROUND THE WORLD
WHERE ARE YOU GOING MANYONI?
ELIZABETI'S SCHOOL

How are these children's school experiences like yours? How are they different? Make a Venn Diagram*.

Look at pictures made by children from other countries.
www.theartgallery.com.au/kidsart.html

WONDERING ABOUT SCHOOL

What Is a Library?

THE LIBRARIAN
AUNT CHIP AND THE CRIPPLE CREEK DAM AFFAIR

What is a library? What is a librarian? Set up a library system for your class. How will you group or shelve the books? Make rules for borrowing and taking care of books. Post a sign with the rules in your class library. Take turns being the class librarian.

THE INSIDE OUTSIDE BOOK OF LIBRARIES

Take field trips to the school and public libraries. Find out how to get a library card. How do we take care of books? How do we take books out of the library?

How Is a Book Made?

WHAT DO AUTHORS DO?
WHAT DO ILLUSTRATORS DO?
HOW A BOOK IS MADE
AUTHOR: A TRUE STORY
FROM PICTURES TO WORDS: A BOOK ABOUT MAKING A BOOK

Reading Rainbow: "Simon's Book"

Where do you think the books in your classroom came from? How are books written and made?

Make a book of your own. Write and illustrate it.

WONDERING ABOUT BOOKS

Wondering about Pop-Up and Lift-The-Flap Books

BIG BUGS! GIANT CREEPY CRAWLY POP-UPS
BISCUIT LOVES SCHOOL: GIANT LIFT-THE-FLAP
COOKIE COUNT: A TASTY POP-UP
FEELY BUGS
GARAGE
HERE COME OUR FIREFIGHTERS!
OH MY A FLY!
SPOT GOES TO SCHOOL
SPOT GOES TO THE BEACH
SPOT GOES TO THE FARM
SPOT SLEEPS OVER by E. Hill
THE WIDE-MOUTHED FROG: A POP-UP BOOK
WHERE IS MAISY'S PANDA?
WHERE'S SPOT?
AT SCHOOL: A LIFT THE FLAP BOOK

What do you notice about these books? How are they different from other books?

POP-O MANIA

Choose one of the characters or a topic above and write a Group Composed Story*. Work with a partner to create one page for a class pop-up book.

WONDERING ABOUT MY BODY

What's Alive?

Make a classroom chart that has two parts. Put pictures of living things on one side. Put pictures of things that are not alive on the other side. Add to each side as you find more pictures.

Then look at the side that shows living things. Circle things that are animals in red. Circle things that are plants in green.

How Does My Body Work?

ME AND MY AMAZING BODY
HUMAN BODY
MY FIRST BODY BOOK
HEAR YOUR HEART
LOOK AT YOUR EYES

Carry out experiments described in these books. Record your findings in your Sketchbook Journal*.

How Does My Body Change?

I'M GROWING
TITCH
HUE BOY
YOU'LL SOON GROW INTO THEM, TITCH
THE BIGGEST BOY
SOMEONE BIGGER

Bring in pictures of you when you were a baby. Did your parents save any of your baby clothes or toys? How have you changed? Make a photo wall showing before and today pictures of the class.

My Insides and Outsides

THE SKELETON INSIDE YOU
YOUR SKIN AND MINE

Make a life-size model of the parts of your body. Paste pictures of different body parts in the right places on your model.

HOW MANY TEETH?
OPEN WIDE TOOTH SCHOOL INSIDE

How many teeth do you have? Make a tooth chart showing how many teeth total there are in your class. Learn how to brush your teeth the right way. Create a Group Composed* poster telling others in your school how to take care of their teeth.

MY FIVE SENSES

In small groups (with the help of an adult at home or at school) create sensory surprise boxes for taste, touch, hearing, and smell. Place five objects in each box that represent a different aspect of each sense. Make a list of words that describe the smell, taste, touch, or sound of each.

Blindfold classmates and see if they can guess what objects are in your box. Keep track of how many guesses were right. Make a Graph* to show results.

WHY I SNEEZE, SHIVER, HICCUP, AND YAWN
I WONDER WHY I BLINK? AND OTHER QUESTIONS ABOUT MY BODY
A DROP OF BLOOD

What did you learn from these books? Make a picture showing something you learned. Then make a list of other questions you have. Invite an optician, dentist, or doctor to visit.

Become an expert on one part of your body. Draw a picture diagram showing how it works. Dictate the information, with labels and captions, that you learned and put it by your diagram.

Learn the song "Head, Shoulders, Knees, and Toes." What other games and songs can you find that mention parts of the body?

My Hands

MY TWO HANDS
MY HANDS

Take fingerprints of everyone in class. How are they alike and different?

HANDS
HANDS: GROWING UP TO BE AN ARTIST

Make a "Hand" book using the outline of your hand as a model. On each page write and draw a picture of someone you know uses his or her hands. Include yourself.

THE HANDMADE ALPHABET

Learn the signs for the alphabet letters in your name.

THE MITTEN

Act out the story using props.

How can hands become helping hands? Can you think of a way to extend a helping hand to someone else today?

My Feet

MY FEET
MY TWO FEET
WHOSE SHOE?
SHOES
SHOES, SHOES, SHOES

Compare shoes of everyone in your class. Make a Real Graph* showing the breakdown of types of shoes.

NEW SHOES, RED SHOES

Tell a story about getting new shoes. Write it with illustrations in your Sketchbook Journal*.

Into the Classroom

Karla began the unit by focusing on children's names (as you have seen in the Introduction). She felt this was a good way for children to learn each other's names. She also understood that children's intense interest in names could provide the focus for their first inquiry, a study of family names. During the first days of school, Karla also concentrated on establishing expectations for behavior. She fully expected her students to become self-disciplined and provided a good-natured focus for discussion of behavior and classroom rules by reading the books *No David!, David Goes to School,* and *When Sophie Gets Angry, Really Really Angry.* Discussion in ensuing days also focused on behavioral expectations and how to help each other maintain a safe and welcoming classroom community. She also chose books about the first days of school and planned to use these to help children share their own first week's experiences.

As you read Table 4.2, you can see how the activities and books were planned so that children can become more familiar with concepts of print and the number system. They had time each day to explore books of all types and to write about their inquiries in their Sketchbook Journals*. Karla found two books that counted off the days of the school year, *Emily's First 100 Days of School* and *Counting Our Way to the 100th Day.* She shared these with the children and matched each day in each book with their own day. She invited them to add things and ways of using numbers to those that the characters in the books experience. To help them with concepts of time, such as days of the week and month, she created a huge calendar for the month of September and at the end of each day she asked different children to contribute some activities that were special to them on that day. She wrote several words to describe each child's idea on the space for that day. She also cut up a current calendar and arranged the months in linear order. She asked each child in turn to find his or her birthday (after consultation with parents) and then write it on the calendar. Karla also collected and cut up old calendars to give children a chance to sequence the months. The book *Chicken Soup with Rice* was a big hit and children quickly remembered the refrain for each of the months. Children also explored concepts about how their bodies work. They investigated the idea of living and nonliving things and brought in pictures and labels to fill in a large chart divided into three columns headed Living [Plants], [Animals], and Nonliving. They made their own stethoscopes from empty paper towel tubes and prepared for a visit from a nurse who will bring a model of a human heart and a stethoscope.

Shannon (1998, 2002); Bang (1999)

Wells (2001); Franco (2004)

Sendak (1962)

---

table **4.2**   Detailed Schedule, Karla Jones's Full-Day Kindergarten Class

DAY 10

Time	Children	Teacher	Teacher Research
Teacher Arrival 8:30		Karla arrives, takes care of paper-work and messages, and begins to set up centers. She chooses books about names and about the body to display around the room.	
Arrival 9:00	Children begin arriving at school and move to centers after they have put away their coats and lunches.	Karla greets the children and is available to talk informally. She invites them to visit the different centers she has set up so they can choose which center to work in later today. She checks off attendance and notes lunch room count as children enter the room.	

table **4.2**   Detailed Schedule, Karla Jones's Full-Day Kindergarten Class (continued)

DAY 10 (continued)

Time	Children	Teacher	Teacher Research
Circle 9:10	Children assemble on the braided rug in the open area for story time. Following the reading, children discuss plans for integrated work time.	Karla reads *A My Name is Alice*, inviting children to suggest some other objects that start with the same sound. She suggests that they might want to write a class version of the book. She then invites children to choose centers by placing each child's name in a see-through plastic shoe chart with pictures of each activity.	
Integrated Work Time 9:45	Children move to centers. Several choose to work in "playschool" area looking through pop-up books. Two pairs of children are working with Anita Sanchez, Karla's aide, on making simple pop-up books. Others are working on cutting out pictures for their own counting books. Some are in the drama corner acting out *Chrysanthemum*. One group works at matching written names with pictures of each child in the class.	Karla moves from group to group talking with children about their work and dealing with any difficulties.	Karla stops to take notes in the playschool area, observing the children's interactions with the pop-up alphabet books she has placed there.
Snack 10:45	Children clean up and put away materials. Then they move to the snack table where today's helpers have helped Karla prepare the snacks.	Karla has been talking about rules and responsibilities with the children for the past two weeks. She asks them to think about eating rules they have at home.	
Recess 11:00	The children go outside to play.	Karla and Anita Sanchez accompany the children to the playground. She finds that at this time of year, observing their play is a good way to get to know them and jots down notes about interactions and play preferences on a pad of Post-it notes.	
Group Time 11:15	The children assemble on the rug. Children enjoy telling the rest of their classmates about the history of their names and other information they have learned from their parents. Several children ask her if they can make a book of class names like *A My Name Is Alice*.	Karla chooses three children to add their own name details to the class name inquiry chart. Inviting children to watch her, she writes their information on the chart voicing each word as she goes.	
Cleanup 11:50			
Lunch 12:00			
Rest Time 12:45			
Book Time 1:15		Karla breaks children into pairs and gives a cardboard paper towel tube	

(continued)

table **4.2**   Detailed Schedule, Karla Jones's Full-Day Kindergarten Class *(continued)*

DAY 10 *(continued)*

Time	Children	Teacher	Teacher Research
Book Time *(continued)*		to one child in each pair. She asks if anyone knows where his or her heart is and what it does.	
	Children offer many ideas.		
		Karla shows them where their hearts are located and then she asks them to be very quiet. She tells each child with a tube to place it on their partner's heart and listen carefully. Karla then introduces the book *Hear Your Heart*.	
	Children are excited to actually hear their hearts beating.	She suggests that they listen to hearts of family members, friends, and pets at home. She suggests that they take their Sketchbook Journals* home and take notes on anything surprising that they find.	
Snack Time 1:30			
Integrated Work Time 1:45	Children work in centers.	Karla repeats the morning's choice-making process, suggesting that children try new centers. Once she is sure that small groups are working smoothly, she works with individual children as she has done all week, administering the Concepts of Print test.	Along with the usual scoring, Karla is looking for any evidence that children are noticing print/ picture connections.
Cleanup 2:30			
Group Time 2:45	Children gather on the rug.	Karla turns to the large calendar she has made for the month of September and asks children what day of the week it is. After they agree that it is Wednesday, she asks them to tell her some high points of their day. As she does every day, Karla writes several activities on the calendar. She then reads day 10 from the two books she has been sharing, *Emily's First 100 Days of School* and *Count Your Way to the 100th Day*.	
	The children have become intrigued by the way the two books handle number concepts differently. One points out that number labels are displayed prominently in *Emily's First 100 Days*. Another child, who is sitting close to Karla, declares that the numbers were harder to see in *Count Your Way to the 100th Day*. A third child has figured out that the number 100 is mentioned on each vignette in *Count Your Way to the 100th Day* but not in the other book.	Karla asks if they have seen any other patterns in the two books. She suggests that they think about differences and similarities as she continues to read on subsequent days.	Karla scribbles a note to herself on a Post-it note. She realizes that the children have noticed differences in graphic design in the two books. The numbers in *Emily's First 100 Days* are bold and colorful, really part of the overall visual design. In *Count Your Way to the 100th Day*, the numbers are smaller than the printed words and printed in a lighter green that is hard to see from a distance.
Dismissal 3:15			

table **4.2**   Detailed Schedule, Karla Jones's Full-Day Kindergarten Class *(continued)*

DAY 11

Time	Children	Teacher	Teacher Research
Teacher Arrival 8:30		Karla arrives, takes care of paper-work and messages, and begins to set up centers.	
Arrival 9:00	Children begin arriving at school and move to the centers after they have put away their coats and lunches. Others go to the library where they browse through books on display.	Karla greets the children and is available to talk informally. She checks off attendance and notes lunch room count as children enter the room.	
Circle 9:10	Children assemble on the braided rug in the open area for story time. They remember events and characters from some of the other school books and some of their own first-day experiences. Children are delighted with the surprise ending and tease Karla about the fact that teachers really don't get scared. The children begin asking Karla questions about her family. Children discuss plans for integrated work time.	Karla asks children to recall some other "first school days" books that they have read. She then reads *First Day Jitters,* a book with a surprise ending—it's the teacher who is scared to go to school. Throughout the story Karla asks children to make predictions about the main character. Karla relates a story about her first day ever of teaching and how scared she was. Karla volunteers some information and suggests, since they are wondering about her and Anita, that one of the small-group choices that afternoon can be to generate a list of questions they want to ask them. Karla invites children to choose centers. She has added *A My Name is Alice* along with a list of printed names to the playschool area and invites children to choose a Group-Composed Writing* task for their own class alphabet book.	
Integrated Work Time 9:30	Children move to different centers than they explored the previous day.	Anita works with a group of children on matching words to beginning sounds of their names for their alliterative alphabet book. Karla moves from group to group talking with children about their work and dealing with any difficulties. She spends most of her time with children who are in the science center listening to their heartbeats with a stethoscope as they try out different physical activities.	Karla tape-records the children's discussion as they sort out beginning letter sounds and she asks Anita to take note of any text/picture connections that they make.
Snack 10:45			
Recess 11:00		Since Anita can monitor the children on the playground, Karla can get ready for the classroom visitor	

(continued)

table **4.2**   Detailed Schedule, Karla Jones's Full-Day Kindergarten Class *(continued)*

DAY 11 *(continued)*

Time	Children	Teacher	Teacher Research
Recess *(continued)*		who has come to talk with the children. He is Greg Ryan, a nurse practitioner who has brought a scale model of a human heart and a stethoscope that he will demonstrate for the children and leave with Karla.	
Group Time 11:15	The children return from bathroom and recess break and assemble on the rug. Children talk about some of the experiments they have been doing. One child reports that he listened to the heartbeats off their mother dog and her puppies and that the puppy hearts went really fast. Others mention hearing faster heartbeats when they listened to their own hearts after jumping up and down.	Karla introduces Greg and gives the children some time to ask questions about his job. Greg then shows children the model of the heart and gives a simple explanation about how it works. He then shows them how to feel their pulse and lets each child listen to heartbeats with his stethoscope. Greg explains how different animals have different heart rates and suggests that they might want to find out what typical heart rates are for different-sized animals.	
	Children are intrigued by the idea of blood flowing through the heart. Since blood is a hot topic with young children who have seen their own blood from cuts and scrapes, the children ask Greg many questions.	He then gives them some tips on keeping their hearts healthy. Karla tells them that she has a book called *A Drop of Blood* that she will place in the class library. Greg volunteers to come back in the future and help set up a microscope where children can look at drops of blood.	
Cleanup 11:50			
Lunch 12:00			
Rest Time 12:45			
Book Time 1:15	One of the children asks if she can trace the hands of her family members at home that night.	Karla reads *Hands,* a novelty book that is cut in the shape of a hand. She then invites them to trace and cut out their own hands and draw something special that they do with their hands. Karla suggests that everyone might want to do that and promises to provide paper to take home.	
Snack Time 1:30			

table **4.2**   Detailed Schedule, Karla Jones's Full-Day Kindergarten Class *(continued)*

DAY 11 *(continued)*

Time	Children	Teacher	Teacher Research
Integrated Work Time 1:45	Children choose centers to work in that they haven't visited before.	Karla has added a center for children to trace, cut out, and color their helping hands (with Anita's help). Karla continues to meet with individual children to administer the Concepts of Print test.	
Cleanup 2:30			
Group Time 2:45	Children are focused on Greg Ryan's visit and what they learned. Children want to talk about the things that they did with numbers at home the night before.	Karla returns to the large calendar and discusses the day's events. After she writes about Greg's visit on the calendar, she reads Day 11 from three books she has been sharing.	
Wrap Up 3:05		Karla hands out several sheets of construction paper for each child to take home for hand tracings.	
Dismissal 3:15			

DAY 25

Time	Children	Teacher	Teacher Research
Circle 9:10	Children assemble for story time. Children discuss plans for integrated work time.	Karla reads *The Seasons of Arnold's Apple Tree* in preparation for a field trip the class is planning to take to an apple orchard.	
Integrated Work Time 9:30	Children move to centers. At this point in the unit they have begun a study of the seasons. Several work in a center sorting fall leaves that they have collected and trying to match pictures in a simple tree field guide. Another group is in the playschool area working in their Sketchbook Journals*. Several work outside with Anita. Others work with blocks figuring out ways to classify and group them.	Karla moves from group to group talking with children and monitoring their work. She then meets with the group in the playschool area to talk about their Sketchbook Journals*. Anita takes a small group of children out on the playground. They plan to trace their shadows at different times of the day.	Karla continues to watch for ways in which children are using verbal and visual sign systems. She asks children to look at the first page they did and compare it with the ones they are working on now. "Do you notice any differences?" she asks.
Group Time 11:15	Children are quick to compare their own experiences with their leaf collections. One of the children reports that the same author did *Hands*. The child replies that she just knows.	Karla reads *Red Leaf Yellow Leaf.* Karla asks the child why she thinks it's the same person who did *Hands*. Karla suggests that they could make a leaf-shaped book about their own leaves.	Karla makes a quick notation on a Post-it Note. She wants to talk later with the child to see what has caused her to connect two books by the same author.

Summary

Teachers are careful observers of children and facilitators of their learning.

Karla's classroom is a place where children have the opportunity to be children and explore their world in ways that make sense to them. She believes that kindergarten is a place where children learn best through play and active participation rather than through teacher-directed formal lessons. To this end, Karla is a facilitator. She observes carefully and listens closely, trying to understand how it is that her students are constructing knowledge. This is carried on throughout the day, using informal and formal observation techniques. (See Chapters 8 and 9.) In addition, she has identified the topic of emergent reading and writing as an area of interest and has carried out a systematic inquiry that documents students' use of pictorial texts and verbal text to make meaning. Through these observations and inquiries, she attempts to respond to what the children are trying to do. She demonstrates and collaborates as a fellow, and more experienced, learner.

The language that accompanies children's experiences involves and engages them in many language modes and registers. Karla believes that they are already readers and writers when they enter her classroom, so she gives them many opportunities to use language in natural, authentic ways. As they share their drawing, reading, and writing with each other and adults, they are thus able to refine and further build on the emergent literacy understandings that had been developed before they came to school.

References: WONDERING

Samuels, S. J. (1970). Effects of pictures on learning to read, comprehension, and attitudes. *Review of Educational Research, 40,* 397–408.

Children's Literature: WONDERING

ABC I Like Me by N. Carlson. Puffin, 1999.

Albert's Alphabet by A. L. Tyron. Atheneum, 1991.

Alison's Zinnia by A. Lobel. Greenwillow, 1990.

Alligators All Around: An Alphabet by M. Sendak. HarperCollins, 1962.

The Alphabet Room by S. Pinto. Bloomsbury, 2003.

The Alphabet Tree by L. Lionni. Knopf, 2004.

Alphabet Under Construction by D. Fleming. Holt, 2002.

Alpha Bugs: A Pop-Up Alphabet by D. A. Carter. Simon & Schuster, 1994.

Always Wondering by A. Fisher. HarperCollins, 1991.

A, My Name Is Alice by J. Bayer. Illustrated by S. Kellogg. Dial, 1984.

Amanda Pig Schoolgirl by J. Van Leuween. Illustrated by A. Schwenger. Dial, 1997.

Andy, That's My Name by T. de Paola. Aladdin, 1999.

Annabelle Swift Kindergartener by A. Schwartz. Turtleback, 1988.

Apple Valley Year by A. Turner. Simon & Schuster, 1993.

At School: A Lift the Flap Learning Book by P. Gervais. Chronicle, 2003.

Aunt Chip and the Cripple Creek Dam Affair by P. Polacco. Philomel, 1996.

Author: A True Story by H. Lester. Houghton, 2002.

Autumblings by D. Florian. Greenwillow, 2003.

Autumn: An Alphabet Acrostic by S. Schnur. Clarion, 1999.

Autumn Is for Apples by M. Knudsojn. Random, 2001.

The Awful Aardvarks Go to School by R. Lindbergh. Illustrated by T. C. Pearson. Viking, 1997.

Big Bugs! Giant Creepy Crawly Pop-Ups by K. Faulner. Illustrated by S. Holmes. Scholastic, 2003.

Big Fat Hen by K. Baker. Harcourt, 1994.

The Biggest Boy by K. Henkes. Illustrated by N. Tafuri. Greenwillow, 1995.

Biscuit Loves School: Giant Lift-The-Flap by A. S. Capucilli. Illustrated by P. Schories. HarperCollins, 2003.

B Is for Bulldozer by J. Sobel. Illustrated by M. Iwai. Harcourt, 2003.

Bugs Are Insects by A. Rockwell. Illustrated by S. Jenkins. HarperCollins, 2001.

The Butterfly Alphabet by K. B. Sandved. Scholastic, 1999.

Can You Guess My Name? Traditional Tales from around the World by J Sierra. Clarion, 2002.

Caps, Hats, Socks and Mittens: A Book of Seasons by L. Borden. Illustrated by L. Hoban. Scholastic, 1992

Carlo Likes Counting by J. Spaynol. Candlewick, 2002.

Chicka Chicka Boom Boom by B. Martin Jr. & M. Sampson. Illustrated by L. Ehlert. Simon & Schuster, 1989.

Chicka Chicka 1, 2, 3 by B. Martin Jr. & M. Sampson. Illustrated by L. Ehlert. Simon & Schuster, 2004.

Chicken Soup with Rice by M. Sendak. HarperCollins, 1962.

A Chill in the Air: Nature Poems for Fall and Winter by J. Frank. Simon & Schuster, 2003.

Chrysanthemum by K. Henkes. Greenwillow, 1991.

Clowning Around by C. Falwell. Houghton Mifflin, 1991.

Cookie Count: A Tasty Pop-Up by R. Sabuda. Simon & Schuster, 1997.

Cookie's Week by T. de Paola. Putnam, 1988.

Counting Our Way To The 100th Day by B. Franco. Illustrated by S. Salerno. McElderry, 2004.

A Creepy Countdown by C. Huck. Illustrated by J. A. Smith. Greenwillow, 1998.

David Goes to School by D. Shannon. Scholastic, 2002.

Day Light, Night Light by F. Branley. Illustrated by S. Schuett. HarperCollins, 1998.

Dinosaurs Big and Small by K. W. Zoehfeld. Illustrated by I. Washburn. HarperCollins, 2002.

A Drop of Blood by P. Shoers. Illustrated by E. Miller. Harper-Collins. 2004.

Earth Cycles by M. E. Ross. Millbrook, 2001.

Eating the Alphabet by L. Ehlert. Harcourt, 1989.

Elizabeti's School by E. Stuve-Bodeen. Illustrated by C. Hale. Lee & Low, 2000.

Emily's First 100 Days of School by R. Wells. Hyperion, 2001.

Ernie Dances to the Didgeridoo by A. Lester. Houghton, 2001.

Feely Bugs by D. A. Carter. Simon & Schuster, 1995.

Firefighters from A to Z by C. Demarest. McElderry, 2000.

First Day by D. D. Mackall. Harcourt, 2003.

First Day Jitters by J. Danenburg. Illustrated by J. D. Love. Charlesbridge, 2000.

First Day Letters by J. Danenburg. Illustrated by J. D. Love. Charlesbridge, 2003.

First Day of School Ever by S. Pak. Illustrated by J. U. Kim. Viking, 2003.

First Field Guide to Trees by R. Peterson. Houghton, 1998.

Five Creatures by E. Jenkins. Illustrated by T. Bogacki. Farrar, Straus, & Giroux, 2001.

Froggy Goes to School by J. London. Illustrated by Frank Remkiewicz. Viking, 1996.

From Pictures to Words: A Book about Making a Book by J. Stevens. Holiday, 1995.

Garage by S. Augarde. Charlesbridge, 2002.

Giggle Giggle Wake-Up! by N. W. Carlstrom. Illustrated by M. Sweet. Knopf, 2004.

The Guinea Pig ABC by K. Duke. Penguin, 1983.

Hands by L. Ehlert. Harcourt, 1997.

Hands: Growing Up to Be an Artist by L. Ehlert. Harcourt, 2004.

Hear Your Heart by P. Showers. Illustrated by K. Kucera. HarperCollins, 2001.

Hello Toes! Hello Feet! by A. W. Paul. Illustrated by N. B. West-cott. DK, 1998.

Here Come Our Firefighters! by C. Demarest. Simon & Schuster, 2002.

The Hidden Alphabet by L. V. Seeger. Roaring Brook Press, 2003.

How a Book Is Made by Aliki. Crowell, 1986.

How Do You Know It's Fall? by A. Fowler. Children's Press, 1992.

How Many Bugs in a Box? by D. A. Carter. Simon & Schuster, 1988.

How Many Teeth? by P. Showers. Illustrated by T. Keeley. Harper-Collins, 1991.

Hue Boy by R. P. Mitchell. Illustrated by C. Binch. Penguin, 1999.

Human Body by C. Selafosse. Scholastic, 2000.

I Am NOT Going to School Today by R. Harrison. Illustrated by J. Ormerod. McElderry, 2003.

I'm Growing by Aliki. HarperCollins, 1992.

The Inside Outside Book of Libraries by J. Cummins. Illustrated by R. Munro. Dutton, 1996.

Into the A B Sea by D. L. Rose. Illustrated by S. Jenkins. Scholastic, 2000.

Is There Life in Outer Space? by F. Branley. Illustrated by E. Miller. HarperCollins, 1999.

"I Wonder" by J. Kirby in *The Oxford Treasury of Children's Poems* by M. Harrison. Oxford, 1998.

I Wonder Why I Blink? And Other Questions about My Body by B. Avison. Kingfisher, 2003.

Kindergarten ABC by J. Rogers. Scholastic, 2002.

Kindergarten Count to 100 by J. Rogers. Scholastic, 2004.

Kipper's A to Z: An Alphabet Adventure by M. Inkpen. Harcourt, 2000.

Kites Sail High: A Book about Verbs by R. Heller. Puffin, 1998.

Leaves! Leaves! Leaves! by N. E. Wallace. Cavendish, 2003.

The Library by S. Stewart. Illustrated by D. Small. Farrar, Straus, & Giroux, 1994.

Lily's Purple Plastic Purse by K. Henkes. Greenwillow, 1996.

The Little Island by M. W. Brown. Illustrated by L. Weisgard. Doubleday, 2003.

Look at the Moon by M. Garelick. Illustrated by B. Garrison. Mondo, 1996.

Look at Your Eyes by P. Showers. Illustrated by T. Kelley. Harper-Collins, 1992.

Look Out Kindergarten Here I Come by N. W. Carlstrom. Viking, 1999.

Look Whooo's Counting by S. MacDonald. Scholastic, 2000.

Many Luscious Lollipops: A Book about Adjectives by R. Heller. Puffin, 1998.

Me and My Amazing Body by J. Sweeney. Illustrated by A. Cable. Dragonfly, 2000.

Measuring Penny by L. Leedy. Holt, 1998.

Merry-Go-Round: A Book about Nouns by R. Heller. Puffin, 1998.

Minerva Louise at School by J. M. Stoeke. Dutton, 1996.

Miss Bindergarten Celebrates the 100th Day of Kindergarten by J. Slate. Illustrated by A. Wolfe. Dutton, 1999.

Miss Bindergarten Gets Ready for Kindergarten by J. Slate. Illustrated by A. Wolfe. Dutton, 1996.

Miss Bindergarten Takes a Field Trip with Kindergarten by J. Slate. Illustrated by A. Wolfe. Dutton, 1998.

Miss Malarkey Doesn't Live in Room Ten by J. Finchler. Illustrated by K. O'Malley. Walker, 1996.

The Mitten by J. Brett. Putnam, 1998.

The Moon Seems to Change by F. Branley. Illustrated by B. Emberley & E. Emberley. HarperCollins, 1987.

Moses Goes to School by I. Millman. Farrar, Straus, & Giroux, 2000.

Ms. Macdonald Had a Class by J. Ormerod. Clarion, 2001.

My Beastie Book of ABC by D. Frampton. HarperCollins, 2002.

My Feet by Aliki. HarperCollins, 1992.

My First Body Book by C. Rice. DK, 2001.

My Five Senses by Aliki. HarperCollins, 1992.

My Grandmother's Clock by G. McGaughrean. Illustrated by S. Lambert. Clarion, 2002.

My Hands by Aliki. HarperCollins, 1992.

My Kindergarten by R. Wells. Hyperion, 2004.

My Love for You All Year Round by S. Roth. Dial, 2003.

My Name Is Jorge: On Both Sides of the River by J. Medina. Illustrated by F. V. Brock. Boyds, 1999.

My Name Is Yoon by H. Recorvits. Illustrated by G. Swiatowska. Farrar, Straus, & Giroux, 2003.

My Son John by J. Aylesworth. Holt, 1997.

My Teacher's Secret Life by S. Krensky. Illustrated by J. Adinolfi. Simon, 1996.

My Two Hands, My Two Feet by R. Walton. Illustrated by J. Gorton. Putnam, 2000.

The Name Jar by Y. Choi. Knopf, 2001.

Nathaniel Talking by E. Greenfield. Illustrated by J. G. Spivey. Sagebrush, 1993.

New Moon by P. Shea. Illustrated by C. Falwell. Mondo, 1996.

New Shoes, Red Shoes by S. Rollings. Orchard, 2000.

Night and Day by A. Grenowsky. Ilustrated by M. Lonsdale. Millbrook, 2001.

No David! by D. Shannon. Scholastic, 1998.

Now Soon Later by L. Grunwald. Illustrated by J. Johnson. HarperCollins, 1996.

Off to School, Baby Duck by A. Hest. Illustrated by J. Barton. Candlewick, 1999.

Oh My a Fly! by J. Pienkowski. Piggy Toes Press, 1989.

Old Black Fly by J. Aylesworth. Illustrated by S. Gammel. Holt, 1995.

One Afternoon by Y. Heo. Orchard, 1994.

One Lighthouse, One Moon by A. Lobel. Greenwillow, 2002.

One Monday Morning by U. Shulevitz. Sunburst, 2003.

1 2 3 Follow Me! by P. Dupasquier. Candlewick, 2002.

Open Wide, Tooth School Inside by L. Keller. Holt, 2000.

The Paper Boy by D. Pilkey. Orchard, 1999.

Pop! A Book about Bubbles by K. Bradley. Illustrated by M. Miller. HarperCollins, 2001.

Pop-O-Mania by B. Valenta. Dial, 1997.

Q Is for Duck: An Alphabet Guessing Game by M. Folsom. Illustrated by M. Elting. Clarion, 1985.

Rain Dance by K. Appelt. Illustrated by E. Chohat. HarperCollins, 2001.

The Reason for Seasons by G. Gibbons. Holiday, 1996.

Red Leaf Yellow Leaf by L. Ehlert. Harcourt, 1991.

Right Outside My Window by M. A. Hoberman. Illustrated by N. Wilton. Mondo, 2002.

Rock It, Sock It Number Line by B. Martin Jr. Illustrated by A. Cahoon. Holt, 2001.

The School Play by R. Wells. Illustrated by J. Wheeler. Scholastic, 2001.

The Seasons of Arnold's Apple Tree by G. Gibbons, Voyager, 1988.

Shoes by E. Winthrop. Illustrated by W. Joyce. HarperCollins, 1986.

Shoes, Shoes, Shoes by A. Morris. Illustrated by K. Heyman. Lothrop, 1995.

"Simon's Book," *Reading Rainbow,* episode 17 (VHS). WNED-TV & GPN Educational Media. Available at http://gpn.unl.edu/rainbow/product_index_alpha.asp.

Sing a Song of Piglets: A Calendar in Verse by E. Bunting. Illustrated by E. A. McCully. Clarion, 2002.

The Skeleton Inside You by P. Balestrino. Illustrated by T. Kelley. HarperCollins, 1989.

The Sky Tree by T. Locker. HarperCollins, 1995.

Someone Bigger by J. Emmett. Illustrated by A. Reynolds. Clarion, 2004.

"Sometimes I Wonder" in *Sometimes I Wonder if Poodles Like Noodles* by L. Numeroff. Simon & Schuster, 2002.

Spot Goes to School by E. Hill. Puffin Books, 1994.

Spot Goes to the Beach by E. Hill. Puffin Books, 1995.

Spot Goes to the Farm by E. Hill. Puffin Books, 1998.

Spot Sleeps Over by E. Hill. Puffin Books, 1996.

Sumi's First Day of School by S. Park. Illustrated by J. U. Kim. Viking, 2003.

Sunshine Makes the Seasons by F. Branley. Illustrated by G. Maestro. HarperCollins, 1985.

Swing around the Sun by B. J. Esbensen. Carolrhoda, 2003.

The Teeny Tiny Teacher by S. Calmenson. Illustrated by D. Roche. Scholastic, 2002.

Telling Time with Big Mama Cat by D. Harper. Illustrated by B. Moser. Harcourt, 1998.

Ten Puppies by L. Reiser. Greenwillow, 2003.

Ten Seeds by R. Brown. Knopf, 2001.

This Is the Way We Go to School: A Book about Children around the World by S. Bjorkman. Scholastic, 1992.

Three Cheers for Tacky by L. Munsinger. Houghton Mifflin, 1994.

Timothy Goes to School by R. Wells. Puffin, 2000.

Tiptoe into Kindergarten by J. Rogers. Cartwheel, 2003.

Titch by P. Hutchins. Aladdin, 1993.

Today Is Monday by E. Carle. Putnam, 1997.

Turtle Splash: Countdown at the Farm by C. Falwell. Greenwillow, 2001.

Twelve Hats for Lena: A Book of Months by K. Katz. McElderry, 2002.

Up to Ten and Down Again by L. C. Ernst. Morrow, 1995.

The Very Hungry Caterpillar by E. Carle. Philomel, 1983.

What Do Authors Do? by E. Christelow. Houghton Mifflin, 1997.

What Do Illustrators Do? by E. Christelow. Houghton Mifflin, 1999.

What Makes a Shadow? by C. R. Bulla. Illustrated by S. Shuett. HarperCollins, 1994.

What Makes Day and Night? by F. Branley. Illustrated by A. Dorros. HarperCollins, 1986.

What Pete Ate from A–Z (Really!) by M. Kalman. Putnam, 2001.

What's Alive? by K. Zoenfeld. Illustrated by N. B. Westcott. HarperCollins, 1995.

What's It Like to Be a Fish? by W. Pfeffer. Illustrated by H. Keller. HarperCollins, 1996.

What's Your Name?: From Ariel to Zoe by E. Sanders. Holiday, 1995.

When Sophie Gets Angry, Really Really Angry by M. Bang. Scholastic, 1999.

When Will I Read? by D. Cohen. Illustrated by L. Hoban. Greenwillow, 1997.

Where Are You Going Manyoni? by C. Stock. HarperCollins, 1993.

Where Is Maisy's Panda? by L. Cousins. Candlewick Press, 1999.

Where's Spot? by E. Hill. G. P. Putnam, 1980.

Whose Shoe? by M. Miller. Greenwillow, 1991.

Why Do Leaves Change Color? by B. Maestro. Illustrated by L. Krupinski. HarperCollins, 1994.

Why I Sneeze, Shiver, Hiccup, and Yawn by P. Berger. Illustrated by P. Meisel. Houghton, 2000.

The Wide-Mouthed Frog: A Pop-Up Book by K. Faulkner. Illustrated by J. Lambert. Dial Books, 1996.

Will I Have a Friend? by D. Cohen. Illustrated by L. Hoban. Aladdin, 1989.

Word Wizard by C. Falwell. Houghton, 1998.

The Year at Maple Hill Farm by A. Provensen & M. Provensen. Aladdin, 2001.

A Year for Kiko by F. Wolff. Illustrated by J. U. Kim. Houghton, 1997.

Yoko by R. Wells. Hyperion, 1998.

You'll Soon Grow into Them, Titch by P. Hutchins. Greenwillow, 1983.

Your Skin and Mine by P. Showers. Illustrated by K. Kuchera. HarperCollins, 1991.

The Z Was Zapped by C. Van Allsburg. Houghton, 1987.

Prototype 2: First Grade— SOUNDS ALL AROUND

Schedule

The plans for the SOUNDS ALL AROUND web are meant for a first grade in an open area school whose students represent many cultures and countries from the large urban area nearby. In the school organization, grades are grouped together in "pods"—areas that are separated from the other grades by walls but open to other classes in the grade level. The teachers work together to organize space, blocking off areas with bookcases and mobile bulletin boards. They have also found that dressmakers' cutting boards and old appliance boxes can be cut into folding display panels to help organize space and allow display of work at the perfect eye level for first graders. The teachers in the first grade pod also work well as a team, and although each takes responsibility for his or her own class, they sometimes plan themes together. They also make sure to schedule quiet times when all the teachers read aloud or all children are involved in Sustained Silent Reading (SSR)*. Table 4.3 shows the weekly schedule for Michael Silverman's first-grade classroom.

Michael planned the SOUNDS ALL AROUND unit for autumn, following the theme WHO AM I? meant to introduce children to each other, a new school year, and the school community. This first unit gave Michael an excellent opportunity to observe children as language learners, to get to know their diverse backgrounds, interests, and abilities, and to cover key social studies and science concepts related to identity and growth.

As Michael observed children in a variety of talking, reading, and writing activities during the first weeks of school, he was able to gather data about his students'

table 4.3 **Weekly Schedule, Michael Silverman's First-Grade Class**

Time	Monday	Tuesday	Wednesday	Thursday	Friday
8:00	Teacher preparation time				
8:25	Children arrive, put down chairs, get supplies, and work on assignments or read a book.				
9:00	Group time. Discuss ongoing projects, introduce new assignments, introduce new materials, or share completed work.				
9:20	Integrated work time. Children work on individual or group projects. Teacher meets with small groups or has individual conferences.				
9:45	Recess				
10:00	Book time. Read book or poem to class. Discuss or follow up with an activity.				
10:30	Integrated work time. Continue with projects begun earlier or inspired by Reading Aloud*.				
11:10	Cleanup. Put away materials, supplies, projects, and assignments in storage areas.				
11:15	Sharing. Children share work with class, or teacher shares information relevant to the unit.				
11:30	Lunch and outdoor play				
12:15	Art	Music	Library	Art	Music
1:00	SSR* (Teacher has conferences with individual children.) Twice a week children have Buddy Reading* with second graders.				
1:35	Group time. Teacher reads aloud or focuses on special activity.				
1:55	Recess				
2:10	Integrated work time				
2:45	Cleanup. Pass out papers. Evaluate the day.				
3:00	Dismissal				

Prototype 2: First Grade—SOUNDS ALL AROUND

Farmyard Sounds

THE COUNTRY NOISY BOOK

What noises would Muffin hear in your neighborhood? Make up new versions to fit the weather, a time of year, or a place.

OH, WHAT A NOISY FARM?
A FARMYARD SONG
EARLY MORNING IN THE BARN
BARNYARD BANTER
BARNYARD SONG
BARK GEORGE! MEOW!

Are the sounds these animals make the ones you expected? Make a chart of animal sounds. Draw pictures of animals that could make those sounds. Let people match the animal with the sound they think it could make.

WHO SAYS A DOG GOES BOW-WOW?

Interview people from other countries or cultures. Find out the sounds they have for these familiar animals.

COCK-A-DOODLE-MOO
"QUACK!" SAID THE BILLY-GOAT
THE COW THAT WENT OINK
THE PIG IN THE POND
OINK OINK

Act out other versions of these silly stories.

Familiar Farms

"Old Macdonald Had a Farm"
Sing this familiar song and make up new verses.

OLD MACDONALD HAD A FARM (ROUNDS)
OLD MACDONALD HAD A FARM (JONES)
OLD MACDONALD (SOUHAMI)
E-I-E-I-O
OLD MACDONALD (SCHWARTZ)
THE FARMER IN THE DELL

Read these versions. Construct a Comparison Chart*.

OLD MACDONALD HAD AN EMU

Make a list of animals you didn't know. Match them to the sounds that they make. Find out more about these Australian animals. Compose a version of the song for other countries or regions.

MS. MACDONALD HAD A CLASS
ONCE UPON MACDONALD'S FARM

Act out or retell the stories with a Puppet Show* or make up a new version.

Noisy Birds

BLACK CROW, BLACK CROW

Write your own counting book for a different bird or animal. Use a similar pattern.

COCK-A-DOODLE-DOO
COCK-A-DOODLE-DOO!
PROUD ROOSTER AND THE FOX
WHEN THE ROOSTER CROWED

Make a mural or Story Map* of the characters and events in these stories.

THE BROODY HEN
PEEP!

Plan Choral Reading* or Readers' Theater* of these stories.

Too Much Noise

How much noise is too much for you? Do some sounds make you uncomfortable? Survey classmates and create a graph showing your findings.
Can too much noise hurt you? How can you protect yourself from too much noise?
Are there places in your school or community where there is too much noise? Find out what you can do to solve the problem.

NOISY NORA
DRAT THAT FAT CAT!
TOO MUCH TALK
IT COULD ALWAYS BE WORSE
TOO MUCH NOISE
POSSUM COME A-KNOCKIN'
THE NOISEMAKERS
THE NOISY BOOK
NOISY NORA
THE NOISY BARN
BABY-O

Create dioramas and use them to retell these stories.

Buggy Sounds

What kinds of insects make noises? List all the insects you can think of. What purposes do sounds serve insects and other animals?

IN THE TALL TALL GRASS
OLD BLACK FLY
BUZZ BUZZ BUZZ
WHY MOSQUITOES BUZZ IN PEOPLE'S EARS
JOYFUL NOISE
BUZZ
CHIRPING CRICKETS
CICADA SING-SONG
THE VERY CLUMSY CLICK BEETLE

Listen to several voices read these poems. How do the sounds of the words mimic the behavior of the insects?

THE VERY QUIET CRICKET

Find out how insects and animals communicate. Is sound the only way to "talk"?

SOUNDS ALL AROUND

Noises at Night

How is noise different at night? Make a day/night comparison of noises in your house or neighborhood. Write words to describe the sounds you hear at each time.

I HEAR A NOISE
NIGHT NOISES
ONCE A LULLABY
THE SPOOKY EERIE NIGHT NOISE
WHOO-OO IS IT?

Tell a story of a noise that scared you at night.

SHADOWS OF THE NIGHT
ZIPPING, ZAPPING, ZOOMING BATS
AMAZING BATS
A FIRST LOOK AT BATS
A PROMISE TO THE SUN
I LIVED WITH BATS
BATS
BATS: STRANGE AND WONDERFUL

Bat Conservation International www.batcon.org
Study bats. How do they hear noise?

The Sound of Music

RAT-A-TAT, PITTER PAT
THUMP, THUMP, RAT-A-TAT-TAT
SCIENCE EXPERIMENTS WITH SOUND AND MUSIC
MY FAMILY PLAYS MUSIC

Listen to different types of musical instruments. Classify them as to the types of sound they make.

MUSICAL INSTRUMENTS OF THE WORLD
WHAT INSTRUMENT IS THIS?
MUSIC

Create your own classroom orchestra with simple instruments. Compose music to accompany a favorite story or poem.

Rainy Day Sounds

RAIN TALK
LISTEN TO THE RAIN

Keep a weather observation Journal* and keep track of the sounds you hear on different weather days.
Write your own weather story.

RUMBLE THUMBLE BOOM
FLASH, CRASH, RUMBLE AND ROLL

Find out what causes thunder.

Machine Sounds

"Bam, Bam, Bam"
CLICK, RUMBLE, ROAR: POEMS ABOUT MACHINES

Do Choral Readings* of some of these poems.

CRASH! BANG! BOOM!

Listen to the noises of machines in your neighborhood. Add some to the list.

Listen to the Story

Listen to storytellers, recordings of radio broadcasters, and audiotapes of poets reading their work.

How can we use our voices in interesting ways?

Tell a story and record it on audiotape. Plan a Storytelling* festival. Invite family members to come and tell stories.

Plan a Choral Reading* of some favorite poems. Use solo voices, small groups of voices, and the whole class. Change loudness and softness, and adjust pitch high and low.

Find out how sound effects are created for radio, television, or film. Create your own sound effects for a story you tell on audiotape or for a cartoon you draw.

Sounds of the Train

COUNTRY CROSSING
"Song of the Train"
"Riding on the Train"
TRAIN SONGS
TRAIN WHISTLES: A LANGUAGE IN CODE

Are there machine codes in your community? What other types of codes communicate messages?

Family Sayings

THERE'S A FROG IN MY THROAT
FIRST THINGS FIRST: AN ILLUSTRATED
   COLLECTION OF SAYINGS
SAY SOMETHING
YO! YES?
HONEY I LOVE AND OTHER POEMS
NATHANIEL TALKING
"Grandma's Bones"

Interview family members or neighbors. What are some sayings that are important to them? Make a Graffiti Wall* of sayings. Are there some from different cultures or countries that are alike?

What are conversation routines in your family? Does everyone talk at the dinner table or is everyone quiet? In your family is it all right for children to interrupt adults or should children always be quiet around adults?

Make a Comparison Chart* of talk etiquette, showing the differences and similarities that you find.

HOW YOU TALK

How are hearing and talking alike?
What were your first words?
What different languages are represented in your class? In the families of your class? Make a chart showing all the different languages spoken by the families in your class.
Find out if there are words in other languages that are similar to each other.

How We Hear

EARS ARE FOR HEARING

Study a plaster model of the ear.
Interview an audiologist and learn about audiometers.
Find out what causes ear infections.
Make a survey about how many in your class have had ear infections. How many have had tubes in their ears?
Are there things that can cause you to lose your hearing?

THE SCIENCE BOOK OF SOUND
HEARING SOUNDS
SOUNDS ALL AROUND

Conduct experiments with sound. Find out about people who work with sound.

Listen for the Sound

QUIET, PLEASE
IF YOU LISTEN
JUST LISTEN
THE LISTENING WALK
THE OTHER WAY TO LISTEN
WHEN THE WOODS HUM
GOBBLE, GROWL, GRUNT
ONCE IN THE COUNTRY

Take a walk outdoors. Listen for sounds of the natural world or the human-made world. Compile a list of all the sounds you hear that are natural or human-made. Make a picture or mural to show your findings.

Experiment with different kinds of sound. How would you categorize them?

ONE WINDY WEDNESDAY
THE QUIET NOISY BOOK
THE QUIET MOTHER AND THE NOISY
   LITTLE BOY

SPEAK UP, BLANCHE!

Think of the quietest sound you know. Make a class book of "small" sounds.

City Sounds

GARAGE SONG
CITY SOUNDS (EMBERLEY)
CITY SOUNDS (BROWN)
CITY NOISE
THE SEALS ON THE BUS

How are city sounds different from country sounds?
What are some sound problems for people who live in a city?

Instead of Sound

HANDTALK BIRTHDAY: A NUMBER AND
   STORY BOOK IN SIGN LANGUAGE
HANDTALK
THE HANDMADE ALPHABET
MOSES GOES TO SCHOOL
MOSES GOES TO A CONCERT
DAD AND ME IN THE MORNING
Where.com American Sign Language
   http://where.com/scott.net/asl

Interview someone who knows sign language. Learn to sign.
Watch Linda Bove from *Sesame Street* sign a favorite story. Learn to do it, too.

A BUTTON IN HER EAR
I HAVE A SISTER, MY SISTER IS DEAF
ANNA'S SILENT WORLD
WHAT IS THE SIGN FOR FRIEND?

How do people with hearing difficulties hear such things as alarms, doorbells, or the telephone?
Investigate inventions and other helps for the deaf. Borrow a closed-captions device from the library. Find out how it works.
Try out a TDD (Telephone Device for the Deaf). How could you help someone who cannot hear?

PUFF. . .FLASH. . .BANG!
   A BOOK ABOUT SIGNALS

Study the many ways to "talk."

Underwater and Underground

WHALE SONG
THE WHALE'S SONG
ALL ABOUT WHALES
UNDERWATER MUSICIANS
Oceanic Research Group
   www.oceanicresearch.org/
   spermwhales.htm

Jonathan Bird's Blue World
   www.ocean.com/TOC/FilmMoreINfo.
   asp?filmID=54www

Find out how whales, dolphins, and other sea creatures use sound to communicate.
Listen to whale songs and dolphin talk.

Find out about ultrasound pictures. Did you have a sound picture taken of you?
Study bat communication.
Does the earth talk? Find out how seismographs work.

Sounds in the Wild

CHICKA CHICKA BOOM BOOM
DO BUNNIES TALK?
17 KINGS AND 42 ELEPHANTS
CROCODILE BEAT
THE HAPPY HIPPOPOTAMI
IN THE TALL, TALL GRASS
IN THE SMALL, SMALL POND
DO MONKEYS TWEET?

Sounds of the World's Animals
   www.georgetown.edu/faculty/
   ballc/animals/animals.html

Create sound effects to go with one of these stories.
Find out how sound effects are created for radio and television.

HOOT, HOWL, HISS
POLAR BEAR, POLAR BEAR,
   WHAT DO YOU HEAR?
ROAR AND MORE

Make a book of wild animal noises. Write the words so they look like the sound.

understanding and awareness of reading and writing conventions—to identify their "literacy set" (see Figure 1.6 in Chapter 1). He found that many of his students readily engaged in pretend book reading and tried a variety of written forms. Still others were beginning to focus on conventional letter–sound relationships as they read and wrote. In Michael's school district, a central emphasis was placed on literacy learning in the primary grades. In addition, as a first-grade teacher he received many questions from parents who were concerned that he was not teaching phonics and spelling in familiar ways. He was knowledgeable about research in emergent reading and writing and the role of phonological awareness—the ability to segment words into sounds—as a part of this process. Michael decided to plan a unit that would give him an opportunity to demonstrate to parents his beliefs about meaningful, contextually based learning. This would also give him a way to provide his children with many opportunities to explore the sounds of spoken language at the same time that he supported their discovery of written codes.

When he found during the WHO AM I? unit that Claire, one of his students, had a sister who was deaf, he decided to plan a unit on sound that would build on the concepts from the first unit. This would give the children opportunities to explore the idea of different cultural viewpoints, in this case the culture of the deaf. A unit about sounds would also give children a natural context for developing concepts about letter–sound relationships, word knowledge, and language play. A SOUNDS ALL AROUND theme would personalize the learning at the same time that it might help children develop empathy and concern for others' ways of living, one of the key concepts in the first-grade state social studies program. Such a theme would allow excellent opportunities for teacher research and kid watching as his children engaged in a variety of emergent literacy activities. He, therefore, planned to keep notes on teacher–pupil conferences and to tape-record children's use of strategies in ongoing activities such as Big Books* sessions. As a way of helping himself identify a range of possible behaviors, he also devised an emergent reading checklist to help him keep track of children's use of specific strategies such as book awareness, cueing systems, and print and word awareness. He hoped such a checklist would be a useful tool for reporting to parents. (See Chapter 9.) The understandings gained through these processes would help him make sense of classroom life and identify and plan for individual needs.

See Goodman, Bird, & Goodman (1992, pp. 110–116) for a discussion of checklists.

As he began to develop the unit, he found that while he was able to cover some requirements of the science and math curriculum with the activities and resources he collected, the theme particularly lent itself to exploring concepts in social studies and music. While he felt comfortable developing projects and activities for the former, he was less knowledgeable about covering some of the musical concepts. He enlisted the help of Jon Petrillo, the school music specialist, who was delighted to be his coteacher. Finally, he involved Claire and her family and Ida Sylvester, a specialist in deaf education, all of whom helped him to plan activities and projects that focused on the deaf.

Integrated language teachers are good collaborators.

Into the Classroom

Michael begins the unit by bringing a large model of the human ear and a poster showing the manual alphabet that the speech pathologist Ida Sylvester has provided. He has arranged these and some other items (a conch shell, several glass bottles, a stethoscope, a drum, and a tuning fork) in a display in a corner of the room. As the children enter the room, many of them are attracted by the display. When the class gathers on the rug for morning meeting, Michael encourages them to hypothesize how they hear, asking if they can remember times when sounds seemed different. He asks the children what happens to sounds when they cover their ears. Several children talk about how sound is different when they are swimming underwater and others recall having a bad cold and getting an ear infection. One child tells how her ears got blocked up when she went for an airplane ride. Michael has planned some simple experiments with sounds for the unit, and at some point he may introduce more formal concepts of sound waves and vibrations, depending on the children's understandings. At this point, however, he asks the children to help him start a graffiti wall listing some of the kinds of sounds that they hear throughout the day. The children decide to categorize the sounds according to the places they hear them and whether the sounds are pleasant or unpleasant.

This discussion will allow Michael to introduce children to some of the topics to be explored during the course of the unit and will eventually develop into other central inquiries—the topic of noise pollution in and out of the classroom and a study of personal, family, and cultural linguistic patterns. This initial activity will also set the stage for the topic of "Instead of Sound" and provide children with the opportunities to learn about Claire's sister and other deaf people and their rich culture. Claire's mother, Mrs. Jensen, has volunteered to work with the children over several days, answering questions and teaching them the manual alphabet and simple signs. Her sister Melanie has been invited to visit later with a sign language interpreter. Michael feels that in addition to learning about alternative forms of communication, learning manual signs will provide a wonderful kinesthetic mode of representing letters for young children learning the alphabet. Mrs. Jensen has also suggested that the class explore technological and other aids, such as pets, that are available to help the hearing-impaired. Michael is hoping that as the children talk about what they have learned from their experiences, they may make suggestions for helping people in the community who have a hearing loss and also understand how they might improve the environment for the deaf and the hearing.

In addition to these important investigations, Michael has a great sense of fun and, as Table 4.4 shows, he has planned many opportunities for playing with language during the course of the unit. The topics "Familiar Farms," "Farmyard Sounds," and "Noisy Birds" incorporate favorite songs and funny characters, and he expects that many children will want to dramatize, retell, or respond to the stories with art and music of their own. Many of the books and activities offer opportunities for children to explore written codes for sounds and to see how these can be manipulated. For example, while many of the books use traditional animal sounds, such as "bow-wow" for dogs and "cock-a-doodle doo" for roosters, others such as *My Barn* by Craig Brown use "ruff-ruff-ruuuuffff" and "er-er-errrr-er-ererer-errr" instead. The patterns of these books offer the children models for making up their own versions and exploring letter–sound relationships and the concept of onomatopoeia.

Brown (1991)

Many of the books Michael has chosen use print in unusual graphic ways: The print is as much a part of the pictorial text as of the verbal text. In *Quacky Quack-Quack!* by Ian Whybrow, the animal sounds are printed in a large decorative type that flows across the page, while in Bernard Most's *The Cow That Went Oink,* the sounds are printed in speech balloons. Stories like these draw children's attention to the written language code and also offer opportunities for shared reading, Readers' Theater*, and individual or small group rereading. As Michael has planned to observe the children's emergent reading abilities during this unit, these books provide many opportunities for him to engage in kid watching and systematic data collection, using an emergent reading and writing checklist he has developed.

Whybrow (1991)

Most (1990)

table **4.4**   **Detailed Schedule, Michael Silverman's First-Grade Class**

DAY 5

Time	Children	Teacher	Teacher Research
Teacher Arrival 8:00		Michael arrives to set out special supplies. He takes time to look through children's work folders.	Michael identifies several papers that will be useful beginning writing samples. These will form a basis for comparison over time.
Children Arrival 8:25	Children arrive and begin putting away lunches. Many go to the reading corner. Several assemble	Michael greets the children, prepares the lunch count, and takes attendance.	

(continued)

table **4.4**   Detailed Schedule, Michael Silverman's First-Grade Class *(continued)*

DAY 5 *(continued)*

Time	Children	Teacher	Teacher Research
Children Arrival *(continued)*	at the display table and examine the objects that Michael set up for sound experiments.		
Group Time 9:00	Several children have brought objects that they want the others to "listen" to. These include a dried seed pod, a snake skin, and a bird's nest. They were inspired by the book *The Other Way to Listen* that Michael read several days before. They suggest that these be added to the sound center.	Michael calls on children who want to share their listening objects with the class. He suggests that they might want to write about why they chose those objects or make a label for the display. He reads a poem by Eloise Greenfield he has found called "Nathaniel Talking." He asks children if there are special sayings or "talk" in their families. He invites them to write them or dictate them for the graffiti wall during the course of the unit.	
Integrated Work Time 9:20	Children move to the work area, stopping to get supplies they need from their dishtubs (stored on shelves). Many are involved in ongoing projects begun in previous days. Four children are working on a Puppet Show* for their version of *Old Macdonald Had an Emu.* Several are working on illustrations for a Big Book* version of *In the Tall, Tall Grass.* Another group is completing a Comparison Chart* of the different illustrated versions of *Old Macdonald.* The children in Mrs. Jensen's group negotiate the new text as she demonstrates the process of composing. A group is conducting a simple experiment in which they bounce sound off different types of materials; another is making instruments out of found objects.	Michael asks for volunteers to participate in a shared writing experience with Mrs. Jensen, Claire's mother, and another group to work with him on a sound experiment. He writes the ongoing activities on the blackboard. As part of a Group-Composed Writing* exercise, Mrs. Jensen works with a group of children in writing a first draft of a new version of *A Farmyard Song.* Michael gets the sound experiment group started with an experiment in which they bounce sound off different hard and soft surfaces. He encourages them to hypothesize or predict results and gives them a simple chart to record their findings.	Later, Michael will return to observe the Group-Composed Writing* session to take notes on the children's contributions and their knowledge of written text.
Recess 9:45	The children who have been working on homemade instruments take them outside to practice.		
Book Time 10:00	Children enjoy hearing the story.	After recess Michael reads *Too Much Noise.* After the children have responded to the book, Michael asks children if they think there are places in the school or community where there is too much noise. He invites them to be on the "listen-out" and be prepared to share findings tomorrow.	
Integrated Work Time 10:30	Children continue projects begun earlier.	Michael uses the time to visit the different groups and observe children's literacy behaviors.	During his observation, Michael uses an emergent literacy observation checklist he has developed.

table **4.4**   Detailed Schedule, Michael Silverman's First-Grade Class *(continued)*

DAY 5 *(continued)*

Time	Children	Teacher	Teacher Research
Integrated Work Time *(continued)*	The children who worked with Mrs. Jensen on their version of *A Farmyard Song* begin work on illustrations for a bulletin board display.	Mrs. Jensen transfers their draft to sheets of construction paper that will accompany their drawings on the bulletin board.	
Sharing 11:15	Children share the work they've been involved in throughout the morning.	Michael asks for volunteers from several of the groups to share their morning experiences.	
Music 12:15	The children respond with a variety of words. Some describe the instruments as having happy, sad, ringy, high, and low sounds.	The children go to the music room where teacher Jon Petrillo has assembled different instruments to illustrate four major classifications of musical instruments. He breaks the children into groups, gives them time to try the instruments out, and then asks them to listen carefully and try to describe the types of sounds they hear. He makes a list of their findings and then shows them that the instruments can also be classified as wind, string, keyboard, or percussion instruments, demonstrating each one. He asks the children if they can add some of the instruments they have been making in class to these categories. He invites children to plan to incorporate simple instruments and compositions into the projects they will be doing in the coming weeks. The group brainstorms some ways that they might add more music to their activities.	
SSR 1:00	Children engage in Buddy Reading* with members of a second-grade class. Each child has brought a book to read aloud to the other child.	Michael holds individual conferences with three children. He listens to them read, takes dictation, or reads their writing with them.	Michael takes notes on the emergent literacy concepts and patterns of phonological awareness he observes during the sessions. Although he doesn't give a Modified Miscue Analysis (see Chapter 8) at this time, he jots down information about miscues and the strategies the children are using.
Group Time 1:35	The children try out some of the signs they are introduced to on the tape. Several children tell the class that they have met Claire's sister Melanie who is deaf.	Michael shows a videotape of Linda Bove from *Sesame Street* signing the story "Little Red Riding Hood." He asks how signing is another way to speak and he asks them what they know about deafness. Michael reintroduces Mrs. Jensen, Melanie and Claire's mother, who has been working with the class, and tells them she will be coming to class all week. Next week she will bring Melanie to visit the class. Mrs. Jensen does	

(continued)

table **4.4**   Detailed Schedule, Michael Silverman's First-Grade Class *(continued)*

DAY 5 *(continued)*

Time	Children	Teacher	Teacher Research
Group Time *(continued)*		several short book talks on some of the books about sign language and the deaf and hands these out to interested children.	
Integrated Work Time 2:10	Some children return to activities begun earlier. The sound experiment group and the musical instrument group change places.	Michael gets the new groups started and then meets with children who have finished activities for individual conferences.	Michael continues to collect data during these conferences. He uses the checklist he has developed, noting print and word awareness and whether he feels the child is beginning to use particular visual cues.
Cleanup/ Evaluation 2:45	Children put away supplies and join the group.	Michael asks each child what project was worked on during the day and whether it was completed. He notes which children are finished with a project and suggests some choices they might like to consider the following day. He finishes with another poem by Eloise Greenfield called "Grandma's Bones" and reminds them to ask about family sayings to add to the graffiti wall.	

DAY 6

Time	Children	Teacher	Teacher Research
Group Time 9:00	Some of the children mention that they like to read in quiet places. One of the children tells the class that his older brother likes to do homework with the radio playing and that his mother argues about this with him. Other children say that they don't mind noise when they are writing but sometimes they can't hear when Michael does experiments because of the noise from the other classes in the pod. One of the children says that sometimes the noise during lunch in the cafeteria gives her a headache.	Michael reads *The Quiet Noisy Book* and invites the children to talk about their feelings about noise and quiet. Michael suggests that they make a chart of the things they do that need quiet places and the things they do that need noisy places. He invites children to interview some of their classmates about their noise preferences.	
Integrated Work Time 9:20	Many children are involved with on-going projects. Other children elect to be involved in the activities previously done by other groups. The interview group decides they want to interview other students in the pod about whether they think they should be allowed to talk during lunch.	Michael works with one group to generate questions for their interviews. Michael suggests that they might want to interview the principal and some teachers about this issue, too.	He encourages the children to write down their questions on separate sheets of paper and takes notes on comments they make as they attempt to spell the words. He encourages them to help each other and is interested in the kind of strategies they have to share.
Book Time 10:00	The class reads through the poem together several times and then decides to make their voices loud	Michael reads the poem "Bam, Bam, Bam" by Eve Merriam. He has written it out on chart paper	

table **4.4**   Detailed Schedule, Michael Silverman's First-Grade Class *(continued)*

DAY 6 *(continued)*

Time	Children	Teacher	Teacher Research
Book Time *(continued)*	and soft and high and low in different places. One of the children suggests that they do physical movements to the poem as well as sound effects.	and suggests that the class try a Choral Reading* of the poem. He asks for their advice on changing the sound of their voices for different parts of the poem.	
Library 12:15	SSR* with library books. George reads a mystery he has been dying to finish. Several children talk about their books at the end of the time.		
Group Time 1:35	The children have many questions for both Mrs. Jensen and Claire. They want to know how Melanie became deaf and if it can happen to them. Some cover their ears with their hands to try and imagine what it is like to be deaf. Soon all the children are trying this. They have a good time learning the signs. One child says watching Linda Bove and Mrs. Jensen sign is like looking at people dancing.	Mrs. Jensen has returned to talk with the children about the hearing-impaired and how the family has learned to communicate with Melanie. She teaches them the signs for *hello*, *my*, and *name*. She asks them to think of ways that they might help people who have trouble hearing and promises to return at a later date to hear their ideas.	

DAY 10

Time	Children	Teacher	Teacher Research
Group Time 9:00	The children have found that students and teachers feel there are two important noise problems in the school. One is the noise in the open areas. A second is the noise in the cafeteria during lunchtime. In the discussion, children decide that they could put posters up in the pods to remind people to use "indoor" voices. They wonder if there is an enclosed space that classes could use for times when they might make more noise. They decide that the noisy cafeteria is a big problem and something they want to try and work on as a group.	Michael asks the group of children who have been interviewing to share the results of their study. Michael asks if there might be something they can do to solve the problem. Michael suggests that they all talk the problem over with their families and see if they can suggest some solutions. He promises more time the following day to brainstorm ideas.	
Integrated Work Time 9:20	Children continue on previous projects. One group is planning a Puppet Show* with sound effects. Another group is working with Mrs. Jensen on a sign language version of "The Three Bears."	Michael has conferences with individual children.	
Book Time 10:00	The children volunteer to use the masking device. They look for various features of print, and many can articulate the strategies	Michael reads a Big Book* version of *Thump, Thump, Rat-a-Tat-Tat.* He then uses a masking device and asks different children to use it to mask things such as a letter	Children's responses and their explanations of why and how they made choices provide useful information about strategies and

(continued)

table **4.4** Detailed Schedule, Michael Silverman's First-Grade Class *(continued)*

DAY 10 *(continued)*

Time	Children	Teacher	Teacher Research
Book Time 10:00 *(continued)*	they use in looking at the printed language. The children enjoy the idea of the marching band and decide that this is a story that they want to use their instruments with.	they know, a small word, or a word with a short *a* sound. As children carry out these tasks, he asks them to talk about why or how they made their choices. Their answers provide useful information about strategies and concepts of print.	concepts of print, as well as of their growing familiarity with phonology. Michael makes notes about individual strategies in a small notebook.

Children take action to solve real problems.

Summary

The SOUNDS ALL AROUND theme provides these first graders the means to explore the world of printed language in a variety of developmentally appropriate ways. The children's growing understanding of emergent reading and writing, concepts that Michael was able to document through his own research, was reassuring to parents and district professionals who had at first been unsure about his integrated language perspective. Just as importantly, the literature that was part of the unit was experienced and enjoyed in natural ways. Michael does not feel that he has to "use" a book or a poem to teach phonics; he knows that planned activities and the experiences the children have chosen to respond to the books naturally support the development of their literacy sets.

The unit also provides Michael's first graders with many opportunities for focused inquiry around such *essential questions* as: How does sound effect us? How can we control sounds? How can we communicate without sound? How can we use what we have learned to change our environment? As a result of their study of the effects of sound, they campaigned to have a traffic light installed in the cafeteria. When the noise level during lunchtime is acceptable, the light shows green, but when it increases, the light changes to yellow. A red light indicates that talk should stop for a minute. In realizing their ability to make changes in their school surroundings, they are learning how citizens can effect change in the larger society. Through other inquiries they have become involved in their environment in a variety of ways and gained understanding and respect for individual differences within their class and cultural differences between their classmates' families. They have discovered interesting differences in family talk at mealtimes and found several wonderful storytellers among the relatives of several children. These family members were invited to class for a storytelling festival that culminated the unit. Finally, because one of their classmates is directly affected by a sister who is deaf, they have a unique opportunity to learn firsthand about the differently abled and to participate in that special world in a personal way. The understandings the children have gained over the course of the unit not only support their growth as competent language learners but also heighten their sensitivity to the diversity in the world around them and their future role as change agents.

Children's Literature: SOUNDS ALL AROUND

All about Whales by D. H. Patent. Holiday House, 1987.

Amazing Bats by F. Greenway. Photographs by J. Young & F. Greenway. Knopf, 1991.

Anna's Silent World by B. Wolf. Lippincott, 1977.

Baby-O by N. W. Carlstorm. Illustrated by S. Stevenson. Little, Brown, 1992.

"Bam, Bam, Bam" in *Jamboree Rhymes for Everyone* by E. Merriman. Illustrated by W. Gaffney-Kessell. Dell, 1984.

Bark George! by J. Feiffer. Harper Collins, 1999.

Barnyard Banter by D. Fleming. Holt, 1994.

Barnyard Song by R. Greene. Illustrated by R. Bender. Simon, 1997.

Bats by G. Gibbons. Holiday House, 1999.

Bats: Strange and Wonderful by L. Pringle. Boyds Mills, 2000.

The Broody Hen by O. Dunrea. Doubleday, 1992.

A Button in Her Ear by A. B. Litchfield. Illustrated by E. Mill. Whitman, 1976.

Buzz by J. Wong. Harcourt, 2000.

Buzz Buzz Buzz by B. Barton. Puffin, 1979.

Chicka Chicka Boom Boom by B. Martin & J. Archambault. Illustrated by L. Ehlert. Simon & Schuster, 1989.

Chirping Crickets by M. Berger. Illustrated by M. Lloyd. HarperCollins, 1998.

Cicada Sing-Song by C. Densey. Gareth, 1998.

City Noise by K. Kuskin. Illustrated by R. Flowers. HarperCollins, 1994.

City Sounds by C. Brown. Greenwillow, 1992.

City Sounds by R. Emberley. Little, Brown, 1989.

Click Rumble Roar: Poems About Machines. Selected by L. B. Hopkins. Photographs by A. H. Audette. Crowell, 1987.

Cock-A-Doodle-Doo by F. Brandenberg. Illustrated by Aliki. Greenwillow, 1986.

Cock-A-Doodle-Doo! by J. Runcie. Illustrated by L. Lorenz. Simon & Schuster, 1991.

Cock-A-Doodle-Moo by B. Most. Harcourt, 1996.

Country Crossing by J. Aylesworth. Illustrated by T. Rand. Atheneum, 1991.

The Country Noisy Book by M. W. Brown. Illustrated by L. Weisgard. Harper, 1993.

The Cow That Went Oink by B. Most. HBJ, 1990.

Crash! Bang! Boom! by P. Spier. Doubleday, 1972.

Crocodile Beat by G. Jorgensen. Illustrated by P. Mullins. Bradbury, 1988.

Dad and Me in the Morning by P. Lakin. Illustrated by R. Steele. Whitman, 1994.

Do Bunnies Talk? by D. A. Dodds. Illustrated by A. Dubanevich. HarperCollins, 1992.

Do Monkeys Tweet? by M. Walsh. Houghton, 2000.

Drat That Fat Cat! by P. Thomson. Illustrated by A. Busby. Scholastic, 2003.

E-I-E-I-O by G. Clarke. Lothrop, 1992.

Early Morning in the Barn by N. Tafuri. Greenwillow, 1983.

Ears Are for Hearing by P. Showers. Illustrated by H. Keller. Crowell, 1990.

The Farmer in the Dell by A. Wallner. Holiday House, 1998.

A Farmyard Song by C. Manson. North-South, 1992.

A First Look at Bats by M. Selsam & J. Hunt. Walker, 1991.

First Things First: An Illustrated Collection of Sayings Useful and Familiar for Children by B. Fraser. Harper, 1990.

Flash, Crash, Rumble, and Roll by F. Branley. Illustrated by B. Emberley & E. Emberley. Crowell, 1985.

Garage Song by S. Wilson. Illustrated by B. Kaplan. Simon & Schuster, 1991.

Gobble, Growl, Grunt by P. Spier. Doubleday, 1971.

"Grandma's Bones" in *Nathaniel Talking* by E. Greenfield. Illustrated by J. S. Gilchrist. Black Butterfly Children's Books, 1988.

The Handmade Alphabet by L. Rankin. Dial, 1992.

Handtalk: An ABC of Finger Spelling and Sign Language by R. Charlip & M. B. Miller. Photographs by G. Ancona. Macmillan, 1974.

Handtalk Birthday: A Number and Story Book in Sign Language by R. Charlip & M. B. Miller. Photographs by G. Ancona. Four Winds, 1987.

The Happy Hippopotami by B. Martin Jr. Illustrated by B. Everitt. HBJ, 1991.

Hearing Sounds by S. Hewitt. Children's Press, 1998.

Honey I Love and Other Poems by E. Greenfield. Illustrated by L. Dillon & D. Dillon. HarperCollins, 1978.

Hoot, Howl, Hiss by M. Koch. Greenwillow, 1991.

How Do Our Ears Hear? by Carol Ballard. Raintree, 1998.

How You Talk by P. Showers. Illustrated by M. Lloyd. HarperCollins, 1992.

I Have a Sister, My Sister Is Deaf by J. Peterson. Illustrated by D. Ray. HarperCollins, 1984.

If You Listen by C. Zolotow. Illustrated by M. Simont. Harper, 1980.

I Lived with Bats by F. McNulty. Illustrated by L. Shiffman. Cartwheel, 1999.

In the Small, Small Pond by D. Fleming. Holt, 1993.

In the Tall, Tall Grass by D. Fleming. Holt, 1991.

It Could Always Be Worse by M. Zemach. Farrar, Straus, & Giroux, 1977.

Joyful Noise: Poems for Two Voices by P. Fleischman. HarperCollins, 1988.

Just Listen by W. Morris. Illustrated by P. Cullen-Clark. Atheneum, 1990.

Listen to the Rain by B. Martin Jr. & J. Archambault. Illustrated by J. Endicott. Henry Holt, 1988.

The Listening Walk by P. Showers. Illustrated by Aliki. HarperCollins, 1991.

Meow! by K. Arnold. Holiday, 1998.

Moses Goes to a Concert by I. Millman. Farrar, Straus, & Giroux, 1998.

Moses Goes to School by I. Millman. Farrar, Straus, & Giroux, 2000.

Ms. Macdonald Had a Class by J. Ormerod. Clarion, 1996.

Music by N. Ardley. Photographs by D. King. Knopf, 1989.

My Family Plays Music by J. Cox. Illustrated by E. Brown. Holiday House, 2003.

Nathaniel Talking by E. Greenfield. Illustrated by J. S. Gilchrist. Black Butterfly Children's Books, 1988.

Night Noises by M. Fox. Illustrated by T. Denton. Harcourt, 1989.

The Noisemakers by J. Caseley. Greenwillow, 1992.

The Noisy Barn by H. Zeifert. Illustrated by S. Taback. HarperCollins, 1991.

The Noisy Book by M. W. Brown. Illustrated by L. Weisgard. HarperCollins, 1993.

Noisy Nora by R. Wells. Dial, 1997.

Oh, What a Noisy Farm! by H. Zeifert. Illustrated by E. Bolam. Tambourine, 1995.

Oink Oink by A. Geisert. Houghton Mifflin, 1993.

Old Black Fly by J. Aylesworth. Illustrated by S. Gammell. Holt, 1992.

Old MacDonald by A. Schwartz. Scholastic, 1999.

Old Macdonald by J. Souhami. Illustrated by P. McAlindon. Orchard, 1996.

Old Macdonald Had a Farm. Illustrated by C. Jones. Houghton Mifflin, 1988.

Old Macdonald Had a Farm. Illustrated by G. Rounds. Holiday House, 1989.

Old Macdonald Had an Emu by D. Niland. Hodder and Stoughton, 1986.

Once a Lullaby by B. P. Nichol. Illustrated by A. Lobel. Greenwillow, 1986.

Once in the Country by A. Johnston. Illustrated by T. Allen. Putnam, 1996.

Once Upon Macdonald's Farm by S. Gammell. Simon & Schuster, 1981

One Windy Wednesday by P. Root. Illustrated by H. Craig. Candlewick, 1996.

The Other Way to Listen by B. Baylor. Illustrated by P. Parnall. Scribners, 1978.

Peep! by K. Luthardt. Peachtree, 2003.

The Pig in the Pond by M. Waddell & Jill Barton. Candlewick, 1992.

Polar Bear, Polar Bear, What do You Hear? by B. Martin Jr. Illustrated by E. Carle. Henry Holt, 1991.

Possum Come A-Knockin' by N. Van Laan. Illustrated by G. Booth. Knopf, 1990.

A Promise to the Sun: A Story of Africa by T. Mollel. Illustrated by B. Vidal. Little, Brown, 1992.

Proud Rooster and the Fox by C. Threadgill. Tambourine, 1991.

Puff . . . Flash . . . Bang! A Book About Signals by G. Gibbons. Morrow, 1993.

"Quack!" Said the Billy-Goat by C. Causley. Illustrated by B. Firth. Lippincott, 1986.

The Quiet Mother and the Noisy Little Boy by C. Zolotow. Illustrated by M. Simont. Harper, 1989.

The Quiet Noisy Book by M. W. Brown. Illustrated by L. Weisgard. HarperCollins, 1950.

Quiet, Please by E. Merriam. Illustrated by S. Hamanaka. Simon & Schuster, 1993.

Rain Talk by M. Serfozo. Illustrated by K. Narahshi. McElderry, 1990.

Rat-A-Tat, Pitter Pat by A. Benjamin. Illustrated by M. Miller. Crowell, 1987.

"Riding on the Train" in *Honey I Love and Other Poems* by E. Greenfield. Illustrated by L. Dillon & D. Dillon. HarperCollins, 1978.

Roar and More by K. Kushkin. Harper, 1990.

Root-A-Toot-Toot by A. Rockwell. Macmillan, 1991.

The Science Book of Sound by N. Ardley. HBJ, 1991.

Science Experiments with Sound and Music by S. Levine & L. Johnstone. Sterling, 2002.

The Seals on the Bus by L. Hort. Illustrated by B. Karas. Holt, 1998.

17 Kings and 42 Elephants by M. Mahy. Illustrated by P. MacCarthy. Dial, 1987.

Shadows of the Night: The Hidden World of the Little Brown Bat by B. Bash. Sierra, 1993.

"Song of the Train" in *One at a Time* by D. McCord. Little, Brown, 1986.

Sounds All Around by W. Pfeffer. Illustrated by H. Keller. HarperCollins, 1999.

Speak Up, Blanche! by E. A. McCully. HarperCollins, 1991.

The Spooky Eerie Night Noise by M. R. Reeves. Illustrated by P. Yalowitz. Bradbury, 1989.

There's a Frog in My Throat by L. Leedy. Holiday House, 2003.

Thump Thump Rat-A-Tat by G. Baer. Illustrated by L. Ehlert. Harper & Row, 1989.

Too Much Noise by A. McGovern. Illustrated by S. Taback. Houghton Mifflin, 1967.

Too Much Talk by A. S. Meddaris. Illustrated by S. Vitale. Candlewick, 1995.

Train Songs by D. Siebert. Paintings by M. Wimmer. Crowell, 1990.

Train Whistles: A Language in Code by H. R. Sattler. Illustrated by G. Maestro. Lothrop, 1985.

Underwater Musicians by D. M. Souza. Carolrhoda, 1998.

The Very Clumsy Click Beetle by E. Carle. Philomel, 1999.

The Very Quiet Cricket by E. Carle. Philomel, 1990.

Whale Song by T. Johnson. Illustrated by E. Young. Putnam, 1987.

The Whale's Song by D. Sheldon. Illustrated by G. Blythe. Dial, 1990.

What Instrument Is This? by R. Hausherr. Scholastic, 1992.

What Is the Sign for Friend? by J. E. Greenberg. Photographs by C. Rothschild. Franklin Watts, 1985.

When the Rooster Crowed by P. Lillie. Illustrated by N. W. Parker. Greenwillow, 1991.

When the Woods Hum by J. Ryder. Illustrated by C. Stock. Morrow, 1991.

Who Says a Dog Goes Bow-Wow? by H. De Sutter. Illustrated by S. MacDonald. Doubleday, 1992.

Whoo-oo Is It? by M. McDonald. Illustrated by S. D. Schindler. Orchard, 1992.

Why Mosquitoes Buzz in People's Ears by V. Aardema. Illustrated by L. Dillon and D. Dillon. Dial, 1975.

Yo! Yes? by C. Raschka. Orchard Books, 1993.

Zipping, Zapping, Zooming Bats by A. Earle. Illustrated by H. Cole. HarperCollins, 1995.

Websites

Bat Conservation International
www.batcon.org

Jonathon Bird's Blue World
www.ocean.com/TOC.FilmMoreINfo.asp?filmID=54

Oceanic Research Group
www.oceanicresearch.org/spermwhales.htm

Sounds of the World's Animals
www.georgetown.edu/faculty/ballc/animals/animals.html

Where.com American Sign Language
http://where.com/scott.net/asl

Prototype 3: Second/Third Grade—JOURNEYS

Schedule

Dehea Munioz's family-grouped class includes children who would be identified as second and third graders in more traditionally organized schools. Dehea's school houses a "magnet" program that emphasizes cross-cultural and multicultural studies and includes students from all over the city and from various sociocultural and economic backgrounds. The school is also managed by a site-based school council that includes parent, teacher, student, and administrative representatives. The school council decided that family grouping had many pluses, given their situation. Children of various backgrounds and abilities could more easily work together. Older children could benefit from helping younger children and acting as their tutors. The council felt that the older students' familiarity with the classroom organization could help them initiate the younger members into the routine of the thematic unit approach. This type of mentoring supports the school's goal of developing cross- and multicultural understanding by building strong personal relationships between children from disparate backgrounds. Family grouping also accommodates children with a variety of capabilities and gives them plenty of time to develop as learners. In this particular class, the teacher is responsible for teaching all subject areas except art, music, health, and physical education. (See Table 4.5.) The school staff believes in cooperative planning, however, and specialists in these subject areas enjoy extending classroom themes through their areas of expertise.

The JOURNEYS theme was the culmination of several needs and interests that Dehea saw in her school and classroom. First, the school has a long-term relationship

table **4.5** Weekly Schedule, Dehea Munioz's Second/Third-Grade Family-Grouped Class

Time	Monday	Tuesday	Wednesday	Thursday	Friday
7:30	Teacher preparation time				
8:00	Children arrive, put away coats, prepare lunch count, and take attendance.				
8:10	Group time. Initiating activity: setting the stage for individual and small-group activities for the day. Plans for the day are discussed.				
8:30	Physical education	Art	Health	Music	Library
9:30	Recess				
9:45	Integrated work time. Children work in small groups or individually. Teacher works with small groups or has individual conferences. Time is flexible.				
11:15	Math				
12:00	Lunch and outdoor play				
1:00	Book sharing. Teacher reads a book aloud. Several children talk about the books they have been reading.				
1:30	Integrated work time. Children continue work time, or teacher works with whole class.				
2:15	Group sharing. Children report on their group work. Teacher may conduct a lesson on relevant topics.				
2:45	Read Aloud* or SSR*. Teacher reads aloud or everyone engages in SSR*.				
3:00	Cleanup and dismissal				

Prototype 3: Second/Third Grade—JOURNEYS

Immigration to North America

THE LAND I LOST
ELLIS ISLAND
ELLIS ISLAND: LAND OF HOPE
HECTOR LIVES IN THE UNITED STATES NOW
THE LONG WAY TO A NEW LAND
IMMIGRANT GIRL
MY GRANDMOTHER'S JOURNEY
ALL THE LIGHTS IN THE NIGHT
WATCH THE STARS COME OUT
MAKING A NEW HOME IN AMERICA
I HATE ENGLISH
TO BE A SLAVE
HOW MANY DAYS TO AMERICA?
IMMIGRANT KIDS
WHEN AFRICA WAS HOME
HELLO, MY NAME IS SCRAMBLED EGGS
EMMA'S DRAGON HUNT
HOANG ANH: A VIETNAMESE-AMERICAN BOY
FATHER'S RUBBER SHOES
MY NAME IS MARIA ISABEL
IF YOUR NAME WAS CHANGED AT ELLIS ISLAND
THE DREAM JAR
COMING TO AMERICA
GRANDFATHER'S JOURNEY
TEA WITH MILK
HOW I BECAME AN AMERICAN
MY FREEDOM TRIP
TWO SUNS IN THE SKY
YANG THE YOUNGEST AND HIS TERRIBLE EAR
Survey: Why do people move?
Chart: Places class members have lived or visited.
Use a variety of maps to locate foreign place names
   used in the United States.
Storyteller: Stories with African roots
Interview new immigrants:
   What brought you here?
   What is most strange in new country?
   What is most missed from old country?
Comparison Chart*: Different immigrant groups and
   why they came.
Discuss difference between voluntary and involuntary
   immigration.
Have a multicultural fair: Share what has been learned
   about the people who come to America and the
   native peoples who lived here first. Make and share
   ethnic foods, art, crafts, dance, and music.

Journeys Toward Growth and Understanding

SITTI'S SECRETS
GRANDPA'S FACE
NATHANIEL TALKING
MARIA TERESA
TURTLE KNOWS YOUR NAME
HOW DOES IT FEEL TO GROW OLD?
UNDER THE SUNDAY TREE
ALL THE COLORS OF THE RACE
AT THE CROSSROADS
NOT SO FAST, SONGOLOLO
YOUNG MARTIN'S PROMISE
VIVA MEXICO
AMAZING GRACE
WORKING COTTON
MIRETTE ON THE HIGH WIRE
THE JOURNEY
TONIO'S CAT
ALICE YAZZI'S YEAR

K-W-L*: What is a journey?
Interview people of different ages:
   What is the best thing about being your age?
   What can you do now that you couldn't do before?
   What would you like to do that you can't do easily at this age?
Classroom meetings: Plan for the class's progress on theme, deal
   with interpersonal and management issues.
Current events time. Discuss current issues that concern children.
Display news items, pictures, etc. about current issues.
Write letters of concern about issues of importance.
Compare different kinds of work in community and in other parts
   of the world (i.e., Crossroads).
What kinds of work require travel? Begin bulletin board to display
   student findings.
Read biographies and compare types of personal journeys.
Make collage of things important to own journeys.
Make a life line showing important things you have learned to do
   and some challenges you have faced over time.

Getting There

FREIGHT TRAIN
ROUND TRIP
AIRPORT
BICYCLE MAN
LIFE ON A BARGE
THE ERIE CANAL
INCREDIBLE CROSS-SECTIONS
SCHOOL BUS
FLYING
JONATHAN AND HIS MOMMY
FILL IT UP
THE WAY THINGS WORK
THE SECRET LIFE OF HARDWARE
TRUCKER
TRUCK SONG
CARS AND HOW THEY GO
BIKES
CARAVAN
MAPS: GETTING FROM HERE TO THERE
WHERE ARE YOU GOING, MANYONI?
HOW MAPS ARE MADE
MAPPING OUR WORLD
MAPS IN EVERYDAY LIFE

Mechanical connections. Study how simple and
   compound machines used for household
   gadgets and tools work. Chart the national
   origins and organize by continent or region.
How would the history of the world be different
   if air travel (or cars, etc.) did not exist?
Design a new way to travel, using what you know
   about simple and compound machines. Make
   a cross-section of your invention.
Read maps to plot routes around the community.
Take a "Jonathan and Mommy" walk.
Use maps to plan a field trip.
Follow maps to explore the school or
   neighborhood.
Take a trip on a bus, train, or boat.
Design paper airplanes that can glide, do loops, etc.
Do clay boats activity: Design a boat that can
   carry the most cargo.
How much travel do you do in one day?
Categorize and chart types and purposes for travel.
Visit an airport or other transportation centers.
Make a model city. Plan for transportation, as
   well as other services. What would make your
   city a good place to visit?
Make a collage of different ways to travel.
Goods travel, too. Make a list of all places your
   clothes came from (check tags).
The world in a chocolate bar. Where do all the
   ingredients in a candy bar come from?
   Locate on map.

Migrations of First Peoples

THE PEOPLE SHALL CONTINUE
THE GIRL WHO LOVED WILD HORSES
THE MUD PONY
BABY RATTLESNAKE
KEEPERS OF THE EARTH
KEEPERS OF THE ANIMALS
SEES BEHIND TREES
WHO CAME DOWN THAT ROAD?
THE STAR PEOPLE
Map movement of native people from your area.
Video: section of Scott Momaday on Onondaga Nation.
Discuss: Why do the people of the Six Nations call themselves a
   separate nation?
Mural comparing life in three different nations.
Compare Native American journey stories with those from other cultures.

HUMAN JOURNEYS

IMAGINARY JOURNEYS

Historic Journeys in the United States

AUNT HARRIET'S UNDERGROUND RAILROAD IN THE SKY
CASSIE'S JOURNEY
DEATH OF THE IRON HORSE
THE JOSEPHINA QUILT STORY
FOLLOW THE DRINKING GOURD
DAKOTA DUGOUT
SARAH, PLAIN AND TALL
GREAT MIGRATION
SWEET CLARA AND THE FREEDOM QUILT
A TRAIN TO SOMEWHERE
ORPHAN TRAIN RIDER: ONE BOY'S STORY
COOLIES
COVERED WAGONS
HANA'S SUITCASE: A TRUE STORY
HOMESTEADING; SETTLING AMERICA'S HEARTLAND
I HAVE HEARD OF A LAND
UNDER THE QUILT OF NIGHT
NORTH BY NIGHT
ALMOST TO FREEDOM
Visit a historic site. Use trip book to collect data on life at that site,
   why people came there.
People moving in the past: Make time line of U.S. migrations.
If you were going west, what would you want to take with you?
If you were Native American, what would you want to say to these new people?
What If . . .? activity:
   What if Native Americans and European Americans had settled
   their differences peacefully?
Classroom museum: Create displays that show historic journeys.
Plan a frontier community: Give students picture map of area. What
   resources can you use? What kind of jobs will you need in your
   town? Make an ad for your town to attract new people.
Make a model of a Native American community (select group from
   your area, or near neighbor). Show how people used the natural resources.

Magical and Fantastic Journeys

THE WRETCHED STONE
THE MYSTERIES OF HARRISON BURDOCK
POSSUM MAGIC
MIRANDY AND BROTHER WIND
JUNE 29, 1999
ALADDIN AND THE ENCHANTED LAMP
THE FOOL OF THE WORLD AND THE
   FLYING SHIP
THE MAGIC HORSE
AIRMAIL TO THE MOON
ANNO'S JOURNEY
TRAVELING TO TONDO
SHEEP ON A SHIP
THE TREK
MOLASSES FLOOD
WHERE THE WILD THINGS ARE
ZORAH'S MAGIC CARPET
THE LEGEND OF THE PERSIAN CARPET
AND THE DISH RAN AWAY WITH THE SPOON
THE THREE PIGS
ME OH MAYA
THE JOURNEY OF OLIVER K. WOODMAN

Make a list of magical elements in stories.
Make a museum of literary quests.
Compare quests in book with those in popular
   children's films.
Write "What happened next . . ." after reading one of
   the magical journey stories.
Using Possum Magic as a model, write a version for
   another culture.
What foods would you eat and where would you go?
Make a collection of time travel books.
Draw a picture of a time you would like to visit. Who
   would you be? What would you like to do? Find out
   as much as you can about the time you have selected
   and share your findings with class.
"When are you?" Identify time clues in pictures.

Journeys in Traditional Literature

WHEN SCHLEMIEL WHEN TO WARSAW
EAST OF THE SUN AND WEST OF
   THE MOON
ANANSI THE SPIDER
THREE JOVIAL HUNTSMEN
THE PEOPLE COULD FLY
GREEK MYTHS
SUNDIATA
HER SEVEN BROTHERS
TAM LIN
SUN
FLIGHT
LEGENDS OF JOURNEYS
THE THREE BEARS AND 15 OTHER
   STORIES
PERSEPHONE
THE TALE OF ALADDIN AND THE
   WONDERFUL LAMP
ARTHUR, HIGH KING OF BRITAIN

Locate culture of origin for each story and
   mark on world map.
Make a story map based on one of the literary
   journeys.
Compile a list of travelers and their reasons
   for travel.
Display*: When . . .travels, it is because . . .
   Study illustrations. What do they tell about
   the time and place in the story?
Create a cartoon strip of a journey tale.
Write: If I were a story traveler. . .
Put on the Interact musical version of
   Goldilocks.

Language Travels

TALK ABOUT ENGLISH
BEN'S TRUMPET
TAKE MY WORD FOR IT
MARMS IN THE MARMALADE
WHO SAYS A DOG GOES BOW–WOW?
A WORLD OF WONDERS
PUNCTUATION TAKES A VACATION

Collect words from other languages that have
    become part of English.
On world map, place names on their country
    of origin.
Collect slang words and regional variations,
    and make a dictionary of slang or
    regionalisms. Where did these words come
    from? Why don't they stay around very long?
    Make a Graffiti Wall* to collect new words
    as they are found.
Collect language used for specific activities:
    athletics, music, etc.
Study the "language" of art and music: How
    have sounds and images journeyed around
    the world?
Collect travel words, and put on Graffiti Wall*.

Out-of-This World Journeys

THE FORGOTTEN DOOR
THE SNOW QUEEN
THE SEARCH FOR DELICIOUS
TUESDAY
HARRIETS'S HARE
SPACE RACE
THE GREEN BOOK

Create a cross-cultural space colony.
How many miles? Find out how many miles it is to
    different parts of the solar system. Place these
    "astronomical" numbers on large strips of paper
    around the room.
Make a time line of space travel.
Plan for the future. What should NASA tackle next?
Write to NASA to find out what their plans are.
Write stories about future space journeys.
Study alternative worlds in literature. What do they
    have in common?
Which might you want to visit?
Dramatize scenes from favorite fantasies.
Make a literature guide for fantasy. What are the
    characteristics of different types of fantasy? How
    are journeys used in these books?

Journeys in Art, Music, and Movement

I SPY: AN ALPHABET IN ART
I SPY A FREIGHT TRAIN: TRANSPORTATION IN ART
LINNEA IN MONET'S GARDEN
DRAWING FROM NATURE: DRAWING LIFE IN MOTION
THE TURN ABOUT, THINK ABOUT, LOOK ABOUT BOOK
WALK TOGETHER CHILDREN: BLACK AMERICAN SPIRITUALS
A VERY YOUNG DANCER

Use The Turn About . . . book, and create own turn about pictures.
Analyze art: How do artists get their work to "move"? Use art in children's books,
    as well as that of other visual artists. Look at art from all over the world.
Make art that moves. Try making mobiles, using line alone to imply motion.
Listen to journey music (e.g., "Four Seasons," "The Moldau," "Grand Canyon
    Suite," "Peter and the Wolf"). What makes the music "journey"?
Collect sounds of movement. Use tape recorders and record sounds of movement
    (footsteps, cars, wind blowing, etc.).
Make a symphony of natural movement sounds.
Make a mural of a journey using techniques studied in other artists' work.
Put "journey" poetry to music, or do Choral Readings*.
Listen to recordings of different types of vocal music. What types of journeys are
    found in songs?
Turn a journey story or poem into dance.
Learn movement that will make you healthier. Plan a fitness journey.
Make a fitness path on the school grounds or plan an obstacle course in the gym.

Numerical Journeys

ANNO'S COUNTING HOUSE
WORLD OF WONDERS: A TRIP THROUGH
    NUMBERS
MAPS AND GLOBES
SPLASH!
MOVING FROM ONE TO TEN

Work the problems in Anno's Counting House.
Create a different journey with number
    problems.
Present children with a mathematical quest.
Work on reading astronomical numbers.
Cooking math.
How numbers grow: addition and
    multiplication.
Are we there yet? Calculating mileage on maps.

Geological Migrations

ROCKS AND MINERALS
VOLCANO
HOW TO DIG A HOLE TO THE OTHER SIDE OF THE EARTH
FOLLOW THE WATER BROOK TO OCEAN
WATER'S WAY
THE MAGIC SCHOOL BUS AT THE WATERWORKS

Field trip to stream/creek. Find evidence that rocks and soil have
    moved. Take photos for exhibit.
Use sand table to observe erosion by wind and water.
Make mural of cause and effect: How volcano, earthquake, water
    change how the earth looks.
Walking trip to collect evidence that earth and rock have moved
    or been moved.
Class book: Earth Movers.
Use globe to look for evidence of continental shifts.
How does the earth's movement change people's lives? Small
    group report.
Field trip to water treatment plant.

JOURNEYS THROUGH TIME AND SPACE

NATURE'S JOURNEYS

PERSONAL JOURNEYS

Family Journeys

GOLD CADILLAC
I GO WITH MY FAMILY TO
    GRANDMA'S
RELATIVES GAME
BIGMAMA'S
TAR BEACH
ABUELA
FIRST ONE FOOT, NOW
    THE OTHER
THREE DAYS ON A RIVER
    IN A RED CANOE
STRINGBEAN'S TRIP TO
    THE SHINING SEA
NIGHT DRIVING
DIA'S STORY CLOTH
GOING HOME

Learn traveling songs.
Draw or write about a favorite
    family trip.
Make a travel brochure for a place
    you want to visit.
Make a "trip book" of journeys
    taken by class members.

Plant Migrations

PLANT
TREE
THE REASON FOR A FLOWER
PLANTS THAT NEVER EVER BLOOM
SEEDS: POP, STICK, GLIDE
HOW SEEDS TRAVEL
EAT THE FRUIT, PLANT THE SEED
DANDELION ADVENTURES

Have students plant seeds from fruit and
    vegetables they have prepared and eaten.
Collect and categorize plants by how they
    travel.
Grow plants from different beginnings: seeds,
    roots, cuttings.
Write the adventures of a seed.
Guest speaker: Plants that travel where you
    don't want them (kudzu, creeper, poison ivy).
Conduct experiments on how far a seed moves
    in a breeze.
How many plants come from a package of
    seeds? Record numbers.

Astronomical Migrations

JOURNEY TO THE PLANETS
JOURNEY INTO A BLACK HOLE
JUPITER
SATURN
SEEING EARTH FROM SPACE
LOOK TO THE NIGHT SKY
THE CONSTELLATIONS
PICTURE ATLAS OF THE UNIVERSE
COMETS

Field trip to planetarium.
Collect star charts for each month and
    trace movement.
Guest speaker: Sailing by the stars.
Make a class planetarium; read stories
    about constellations.
Act out motion of planets around the
    sun. Make a mural of solar system.
Study different planets. Write the story
    of a planet as if the planet could tell its
    own story.

Animal Migrations

BIRD
BUTTERFLY AND MOTH
MONARCH BUTTERFLIES:
    MYSTERIOUS TRAVELERS
HOME IN THE SKY
SHELL
WHERE THE WAVES BREAK
WHERE DO THEY GO? INSECTS
    IN WINTER
TOWNSEND'S WARBLER
THE MOON OF THE
    MONARCH BUTTERFLIES
MONARCH
HOW DO BIRDS FIND
    THEIR WAY?
STARTING LIFE BUTTERFLY
WHALE JOURNEY
BABY WHALE'S JOURNEY

Map bird and butterfly migrations.
Guest speaker: Why animals migrate.
Observation in school yard: Keep
    track of living things in area.
    What movement patterns can be
    observed?
Set up a living system in
    classroom and observe
    and record movement patterns.
Visit the zoo. How did animals get to
    the zoo?
Compare zoo behavior to behavior
    in the wild as seen in videos.

with a "sister school" in France. Children were already exchanging letters, pictures, and videotapes. Second, Dehea was a cross-cultural traveler herself, having lived in several countries before returning to the United States for college and work. She wanted her students to learn to see themselves as world citizens, interested in cross-cultural travel and open to people from different backgrounds. She also wanted to capitalize on the fact that many of her students had already moved a number of times as recent immigrants from Southeast Asia or having lived in several different regions of the United States or their own community. Journeys were already a part of their lives. Finally, Dehea knew from conferences with some of the parents and comments from children that many of her students had experienced hostility because of cultural differences. Dehea was aware that one of the most important opportunities for developing openness to differences is in the early elementary years. The JOURNEYS theme would allow her to begin the process of developing the cross- and multicultural perspective that was a school goal and a real issue in her students' lives.

Dehea also decided to make developing cross- and multicultural understanding the focus of her teacher inquiry during the thematic unit. Her background reading led her to look carefully at several issues. First, she was interested in the impact of "culturally conscious" books—literature that speaks from *inside* a culture, not just *about* it. Dehea found several books representing some of the cultures in her class. She decided to study the impact of these texts by analyzing the children's Literature Response Group* journals and classroom discussions. Second, Dehea decided to look at the impact of planned reflection based on multiple exposures to different cultures. Her experience led Dehea to believe that simple exposure was not enough. The children needed to reflect on what they had experienced, and they needed enough experience to begin to appreciate both cultural universals (elements of culture common to all people and nations—food, language, arts, recreation, beliefs, and the like) and cultural differences (the variety of manners, myths, and customs and institutionalized practices that develop around cultural universals). As a result, Dehea planned for regular opportunities for the children to have and reflect on cross- and multicultural experiences. She also decided to focus on five children and carefully monitor their responses in their journals and other written and oral work. The five children selected—three boys and two girls—appeared to be having difficulty with cultural differences. Two were children whose parents had expressed concern to Dehea about intolerance directed at their children in the community. Three were children who seemed to Dehea to resort to stereotyping in many of their cross- and multicultural interactions. She thought their reactions would provide her with some evidence of the impact of the thematic unit's cross- and multicultural component.

Finally, in looking over the school's curriculum guides, Dehea noted that the science curriculum required that she deal with aspects of physical and biological science, and the social studies guide called for a study of neighborhoods and communities of the past and present, with an emphasis on human interaction with the environment. As she developed her plans, she constantly looked for ways to incorporate these topics into her thematic unit, and developed a set of *essential questions* to guide her work, including the following: Why do people move? How is movement influenced by geography? How is the environment changed by people's journeys? What happens when people from different cultural backgrounds live and work in the same place? What kind of personal journeys help people grow and mature? Are there patterns to plant, animal, and geological movement? How do ideas travel?

Into the Classroom

As you enter Dehea Munioz's classroom and watch the interactions between members, you note that the use of natural resources and people in the larger community sets the stage for a wide variety of activities, including studying other cultures and customs, exploring movement in the arts, and investigating the cross-cultural and multicultural origins of English. In Dehea's school, these strands run through the entire curriculum. As children move from one level to another within the school, they encounter these concepts in increasingly diverse and complex forms. These concepts motivate enough interest and offer enough rich possibilities to support multiple encounters.

Two other features of this prototype are important to note. First is Dehea's excellent support from the specialists in art, music, and physical education, each of whom consults with Dehea and introduces a sequence of activities that encourage children to experience movement physically and aesthetically. As you will see in Day 1 of Table 4.6, these specialists also work together to help Dehea set the stage for the unit. This is an important stage if students are to generate ideas for study. By the time Dehea meets with the children to work on a class WEB, they have been immersed in some aspect of the unit all morning and are ready to think about the theme topic in more depth than if they had been asked to generate ideas "cold." Second is the way in which Dehea integrates assessment into her ongoing instruction to meet her content and process goals. As you read through the days' activities, you will note that she collects samples of children's work at different stages for their portfolios. She has specific ways in which children collect data, from Sketchbook Journals* to double-entry Journals*. She includes assessment on Day 15, when she collects both observational data and the exhibit folders.

Table 4.6 samples the first day of the JOURNEYS theme and provides an overview of how Dehea draws children into planning activities, works with the specialists, shares books with her students, and sets the stage for her own inquiry. Day 4 provides a look at the variety of science activities that have developed since Day 1. Day 15 represents a midpoint opportunity for children to communicate what they have been studying in one aspect of the unit and shows how Dehea refocuses the class to maintain momentum and keep interest in the unit high. She is particularly sensitive to the choreography of this day as she plans for quiet time to follow high-energy activities and precede guest speakers.

> Collaboration on themes includes working with art, music, and physical education teachers.

table 4.6   Detailed Schedule, Dehea Munioz's Second/Third-Grade Family-Grouped Class

DAY 1

Time	Children	Teacher	Teacher Research
Teacher Arrival 7:30		Dehea arrives to complete paperwork and get materials ready for the children. She has already arranged an interest center focusing on a terrarium containing a cocoon attached to a leafy branch. Now she sets out literature on butterflies and moths and displays activity cards with the books.	
Children Arrival 8:00	As the children come in, they place their colorful name tags in the attendance envelope. Several children are assigned to record the lunch count and attendance. Others move to the interest center to study the new addition to their classroom.	Dehea takes time to chat with individual children.	
Group Time 8:10	Children have many questions about the cocoon and have already begun looking at the books and activity cards on butterflies and moths. They volunteer many	Dehea calls children to group time, where she has a large pad of chart paper set up on an easel for Observation and Interference*. She asks the children to describe what	

(continued)

t a b l e **4.6**   Detailed Schedule, Dehea Munioz's Second/Third-Grade Family-Grouped Class *(continued)*

DAY 1 *(continued)*

Time	Children	Teacher	Teacher Research
Group Time *(continued)*	comments on what they have seen.	they have observed in the terrarium and records their comments on the chart paper under the heading "Observations." She stops several times to ask if something is really an observation (something we can test with our senses) or an inference (something we think our observations mean). She adds a new column to the chart, and heads it "Inferences."	
	Students refer to the books in the center to clarify their observations.		
	Most of the children are sure that the cocoon will produce a butterfly.		
		Dehea explains that she found the cocoon while hiking near a stream. The creature who made the cocoon, she explains, has already had a long journey and has a longer one ahead. Perhaps they will learn a bit more about the caterpillar's journey in their next class.	
Physical Education 8:30	Children line up to go to physical education.	Ruth Rabinowitz, the P.E. teacher, has been alerted to the introduction Dehea has planned for the JOURNEYS theme. She is able to combine her time this week with the music teacher, Fred Bechtel, because another class is on a field trip. She and Fred decide on a dramatic beginning for a subtheme on movement.	
	Children enter a slightly darkened gymnasium where images of butterflies flash on the walls.	Ruth and Fred use slides and two projectors to cast butterfly images on the walls. Fred's selection of music ("Rites of Spring" and "Four Seasons") fits the theme and plays softly in the background. Fred shares *The Very Hungry Caterpillar.*	
	Children listen as Fred reads.		
	Children fit their movement to the story and then to the music.	Ruth asks children to act out how they think the caterpillar felt at each stage of the story. Fred has them listen to the music and think about which music best fits each feeling. Ruth asks them to imagine themselves in a cocoon, using as little space as possible to move, struggling out of their cocoons, and then swooping and soaring with large movements, finally settling on a branch or flower.	
	They swoop and soar, wiggle, and inch their way along an imaginary branch.		
		Next, Fred teaches the class the "Inchworm" song, using an autoharp as accompaniment. He invites several of the older students who have some experience with the autoharp to accompany their classmates' singing.	
	Children sing. Several try the autoharp.		

table **4.6**   **Detailed Schedule, Dehea Munioz's Second/Third-Grade Family-Grouped Class** (*continued*)

DAY 1 (*continued*)

Time	Children	Teacher	Teacher Research
Recess 9:30	Several students decide to be cater-pillars and butterflies during recess.	Dehea meets her students to walk out to recess with them.	
Integrated Work Time 9:45	After a morning immersed in butter-flies and movement, children are ready to think about the unit as a whole. They have many questions and are excited about what they have done so far. Children have many ideas about studying co-coons and insects. Children volunteer ideas: vacation trips, moving from one home to another, and journeys into outer space. One child recalls the time another classmate was new to the school and did not speak English well. This triggers interest in jour-neys to foreign places and how in-teresting it would be to visit their sister school in France.	Dehea asks children to brainstorm the idea of JOURNEYS. She writes their ideas on a class WEB. Dehea asks questions to point them in other directions, too. She asks them about journeys they have taken—journeys that changed them just as a cocoon changes to a butterfly, journeys that were fun, or journeys that moved them from one place to another to live. She asks if they know people who go on many journeys or who might have interesting stories to tell and reminds them that they can continue to add to the WEB as new ideas come up. Dehea explains that the unit will in-volve activities connected to jour-neys and should help them to think about journeys in new ways. She summarizes some of the ac-tivities they will be involved in during the course of the unit and introduces some books with jour-neys themes.	Dehea points children toward dis-cussing cross- and multicultural journeys, her research interest during this unit.
10:15	Children volunteer for "Out-of-This-World Journeys," "Magical and Fantastic Journeys," "Getting There," and "Journeys Toward Growth and Understanding." Children look through the book se-lections, and each child chooses a story to read.	Dehea has grouped the books and asks for volunteers for each, ex-plaining the basic theme of each group of stories. Dehea has more than enough books for each group. She allows each child to choose from the ten to twelve stories available for each type of journey story. Next, she asks children to work to-gether in groups of three or four. She explains that when each child has finished his or her story, the group will take turns telling each other about the stories. As each person speaks, children are asked to think about how their stories are similar and different. Then they will decide on categories in order to construct a Comparison Chart*.	The "Journey's Toward Growth and Understanding" books form the foundation of Dehea's research on how to help children deal with cross- and multicultural issues in their own lives.
	Children read silently. As some fin-ish before other members of their group, they jot down details in their Sketchbook Journals*.	Dehea monitors SSR*, stopping to listen to several children who want to read to her. She suggests that one member in each group	Data gathering begins. As groups begin discussion, Dehea moves from group to group taking notes and observing the children at

(*continued*)

table 4.6   Detailed Schedule, Dehea Munioz's Second/Third-Grade Family-Grouped Class *(continued)*

DAY 1 *(continued)*

Time	Children	Teacher	Teacher Research
Integrated Work Time *(continued)*	Several get art paper and draw pictures from their stories. Several groups begin telling each other about their stories.	jot down details that seem to be alike in the stories.	work. She records the selections made by the five focus children.
Math 11:15	One group of children uses a yard wheel (a wheel that clicks off yards as it is rolled along a surface) to measure the distance from the office to the classroom. Several of the children are ready for a more challenging problem, and they use a map of the city to calculate distances from home to school. Some of them use a ruler to do a simple "as the crow flies" measurement. Others use their calculators to figure actual driving or walking distances. They have some difficulty with interpreting the distances on the map and ask for Dehea's help. Distances are recorded on a graph. A few children calculate their travel for the school year and decide to find out if they travel further to school than their parents travel to work.	Dehea wants children to be able to use basic measurements and to see the need for accuracy in reporting distances measured. She sets before each student the task of calculating either the distance they travel from home or bus stop to the school each day or the distance from the front office to their classroom. She also challenges some of the students to see if they can figure out their travel for the week and month. This allows her to assess understanding of days in a week, weeks in a month, and calculator functions. Dehea encourages children to use their calculators. As she moves from child to child, she monitors progress. She spends more time with the group that asks for special help, and makes notes about the specific problems they seem to be having with map reading or making calculations. She decides that she will add a selection on map reading to the WEB. As this is the first time some of the children have attempted this type of measurement, she reminds them to put their work in learning portfolios so that she and they can monitor progress on this new skill. Dehea works with the whole group on adding multiple-digit numbers. Students check their work with calculators.	
Book Sharing 1:00	Children listen to the reading, sometimes asking for clarification or to see the pictures that head each chapter. They are particularly interested in the chapter "Tank, the Water Buffalo."	Dehea begins reading *The Land I Lost*. The stories in the book are funny and touching, and Dehea hopes they will help her students understand that new immigrants to America might miss their old homes very much. In particular, Dehea wants the children to learn something about the country that was home to the parents of several of her students. Dehea suggests that someone might want to find out more about the animals in the story.	Dehea selected this book for her teacher inquiry. She thinks it will provoke considerable discussion and provide an opportunity to invite Tran's parents to class to talk about their childhoods in Vietnam. This is a culture with which the children can have multiple contacts, mediated by discussion and further study.

table **4.6**   Detailed Schedule, Dehea Munioz's Second/Third-Grade Family-Grouped Class *(continued)*

DAY 1 *(continued)*

Time	Children	Teacher	Teacher Research
Book Sharing *(continued)*	Children volunteer information about books they are reading. Some exchange books. One child shares part of a book he is writing about his dog, Edison, who got his name after chewing on a lamp cord.	Dehea asks students to share some of their own reading.	
Integrated Work Time 1:30		Dehea explains that many people have journeyed to the United States from other countries. One way of seeing the influence of these people on the United States is to notice how many words we borrow from other languages and other places.	
	One child says that his favorite foreign word is "taco." Most of the children who studied Mexico last year laugh. Others wonder what is so foreign about "taco."		
		Dehea tells them that there are many more foreign words that they use every day—they may even have lived in places named for foreign countries, cities, or people. She divides the children into groups of four or five. Each group gets a map of a different region of the United States. Their task is to see how many place-names they can find that come from other countries. They may use the globes, world maps, and atlases already in the social studies center to check their work. She reminds them that some of them are quite good at the names of different countries and cities because they have been playing *Where in the World Is Carmen Sandiego?*	
	Children work in groups to find place-names from other countries. One group wonders if such unfamiliar words as "Montauk" and "Massapequa" are foreign. The names don't appear in the class atlas, so children decide to put them in a separate category called "Strange Names." Another group finds lots of foreign names, such as Paris and Athens, but they find some that are so funny, such as Monkey's Eyebrow and Rabbit Hash, that they make a new category called "Funny Names." A third group notices two cities named Columbus and starts looking for duplications of place-names.	Dehea helps each group categorize the names they have found by regions of the world. She tells them that some of the names they have found come from native peoples who lived in the Americas long before the first settlers from other parts of the world came here. She helps one group compile a list of names used in several different places, such as Columbus, Lexington, and Middletown.	

(continued)

table **4.6**   Detailed Schedule, Dehea Munioz's Second/Third-Grade Family-Grouped Class *(continued)*

DAY 1 *(continued)*

Time	Children	Teacher	Teacher Research
Group Sharing 2:15	Children report on their group work and comment on how many names come from Europe. They locate place-name origins on the world map and wonder why they found only one name from all of Asia (China) and one from Africa (Cairo). They want to add that question to the topics on the WEB begun in the morning. Children give their pronunciations for different words. Children add "Language Travels" to the WEB and decide to collect samples of regional variations.	Dehea asks children to identify parts of the world that are often represented in U.S. place-names. Dehea adds their new question to the WEB. She also points out that pronunciations of names change as words journey from one country to another. She points out that Lima, Peru, is pronounced as if the *i* were a long *e*, while Lima, Ohio, is pronounced with a long *i*, just like lima beans. She writes several other words on the board. Dehea, whose accent differs from her students', tells them how each word is pronounced in the region where she grew up. She asks why language changes so much from location to location.	
Reading Aloud 2:45	Children listen to book. Some write in their Sketchbook Journals* or make sketches to go with the story.	Dehea reads *I Hate English,* a book about an immigrant's struggle with the English language.	Dehea is anxious to see what students have to say in their art and Journals*. These responses will give her some idea of how children are thinking about other cultures.
Dismissal 3:00	Weekly class leader reminds children that tomorrow is library day and time to return last week's books.		

DAY 4

Time	Children	Teacher	Teacher Research
Group Time 8:10	Children listen and participate in storytelling with a guest storyteller. They have found Nigeria on the world map and seen slides Jameel shared from his father's trip to West Africa. They have many questions about some of the characters in the stories. The trickster is familiar from other traditional literature they have read, and they note the similarities between the tricksters they know and those in the Nigerian tale Mr. Burton tells.	Dehea has arranged for Jameel's father, Mr. Burton, to visit class today to share stories from Nigeria. He can only stay a short while, but he has brought several small "talking drums" that he collected while traveling in West Africa. After telling one of the trickster tales from Nigeria, he plays a tape recording of African drummers and lets children try to make the drums talk.	Dehea takes careful notes on student responses, especially on the focus children in her teacher inquiry. This is the second culture to include visits from parents. Dehea notes that one focus child has just told another, "Be quiet. I need to know this stuff!"
Music 8:45	Children discover the range of sounds that can be made with different percussion instruments. They use the instruments to accompany several songs that have roots in both Africa and the United States. They especially enjoy some of the spirituals in *Walk Together Children.*	Mr. Bechtel begins class fifteen minutes late today to accommodate Mr. Burton. Mr. Bechtel has a number of percussion instruments set up for the class. He plays some modern music that uses percussion and asks children to listen for some of the similarities between	Mr. Bechtel reports to Dehea that children are interested in the music and in how the spirituals were used to send messages. Two students asked why Africans came to this country when things were so bad.

table **4.6**   Detailed Schedule, Dehea Munioz's Second/Third-Grade Family-Grouped Class *(continued)*

DAY 4 *(continued)*

Time	Children	Teacher	Teacher Research
Music 8:45 *(continued)*		modern American music and the African music Mr. Burton shared with them. Mr. Bechtel makes a note to tell Dehea of student interest in the spirituals.	
Integrated Work Time 9:45	Children begin work on trickster stories. They use the books in the reading center to remind them of the story patterns they have previously discussed. Other books help them decide on appropriate settings and figure travel routes. Several of the children place their stories in countries they have been studying.	A display of trickster stories is set up in the reading center and organized by country of origin. All the stories involve a journey of some sort. There is also a display of books with rich illustrations of different parts of the world. Dehea asks children to write their own trickster stories involving a journey of some sort. These can be illustrated and made into a book and a copy sent to thank Mr. Burton for his visit.	These stories are also a source of data for Dehea's research as they provide insight into how children understand the cultural settings for their stories.
		Dehea moves from child to child, talking with children about their stories and listening as several read what they have written.	
	A couple of children are trying to use dialogue in their stories and are uncertain in their use of punctuation.	Dehea makes a note on her own Observation Chart to pull a small group aside tomorrow to edit for punctuation in dialogue.	
		She encourages children to use their personal dictionaries and best-guess spelling so that they can get all of their ideas organized in a first draft. Tomorrow, she tells them, there will be time for peer Editing Conferences*.	
10:30 (Note: Dehea extends integrated work time today.)	Children work in small groups or individually on the following: <ul><li>A survey of trips class members have taken, with graph of results.</li><li>A world map showing routes of literary journeys in books read by classmates.</li><li>Observation of cocoon and note taking in Sketchbook Journal*.</li><li>Development of a board game based on the journey of a monarch butterfly.</li><li>Preparation for a trip to the planetarium, including collecting sky charts from local newspapers and displaying them on the bulletin board with captions based on student research.</li><li>Conducting an experiment on propulsion (balloon rockets), based on directions on the *Journey to the Planets* bulletin board.</li></ul>	At 10:30 most of the children have a rough draft of a story. Dehea tells them it is a good idea to move on to something else now and come back to the story a little later: "Give the story time to percolate in your thoughts!" Dehea directs students into individual and group activities. Dehea works with one group on how to display data they have collected. Dehea also checks the bulletin board in the science area where she has set up a display to get children ready for a simulation she is planning for the following week. Each day a new picture, question, or riddle appears on the bulletin board. Books, pamphlets, and manipulatives for experiments are displayed on the shelf below to help students follow the clues that will prepare them for their space journeys.	

(continued)

table **4.6**   Detailed Schedule, Dehea Munioz's Second/Third-Grade Family-Grouped Class *(continued)*

DAY 4 *(continued)*

Time	Children	Teacher	Teacher Research
Group Meeting 11:45	Children report on group work. The group that made the balloon rockets demonstrates, and most of the other students also want to sign up for that area.	Dehea helps make explicit the connections between student work and the JOURNEYS theme, asking students why jet propulsion would be important in space journeys. She asks if anyone could answer the riddle about an animal that propelled itself much like a rocket. She notes what still needs to be done after lunch and collects student's self-reports.	

DAY 15

Time	Children	Teacher	Teacher Research
Group Time 8:10	Children put finishing touches on the class museum of "Nature's Journeys." In addition to preparing a piece of the exhibit, each child is responsible for one part of either the museum guidebook or the tour notes used by the guides. In one corner of the room is a planetarium made from a refrigerator carton. Its insides are painted black, and students have made perforated sky charts showing constellations at different seasons of the year. A student guide reads over her notes and makes sure that visitors will be able to see the pictures and stories about the planets that are exhibited on the outside walls of the planetarium. On a table, books, children's writing and artwork, charts of butterfly metamorphosis, and the remains of the cocoon are displayed with student-created labels and photographs of the new butterfly as it stretched its wings and was released into the outdoors. Another student guide arranges the board games his peers completed and makes sure the rules are easy to see. Other displays include projects on bird migration, reports on observations of life on the school yard, movement in the class aquarium, and murals showing the impact of volcanoes and earthquakes on the	Dehea makes sure children are prepared for guests. She reminds them to use the museum guides they prepared. Dehea uses this event as a midpoint performance assessment for one of the aspects of the thematic unit. As part of the preparation for the museum opening, Dehea checks the notes and guides against the criteria she and the students developed. During the tours she will move among her students, checking their work with their guests.	

table **4.6** Detailed Schedule, Dehea Munioz's Second/Third-Grade Family-Grouped Class (*continued*)

DAY 15 (*continued*)

Time	Children	Teacher	Teacher Research
Group Time (continued)	earth's surface. Further along one wall, students have set up a hands-on science display where different types of plants and plant parts are arranged with instructions for categorizing the way plants move from one place to another. On a table near the door, student-created museum guidebooks contain a map of the exhibits, brief explanations of how the exhibits fit the JOURNEYS theme, pictures and poems, and a suggested reading list.		
Museum Opening 8:30	Children take turns as tour guides, helping younger children read stories and exhibit descriptions, and operating the planetarium. When not acting as guides, they read to one of the groups of children waiting to come to the exhibit. Stories have been selected from those written by classmates so that they fit the theme and are short enough to be completed in just a few minutes of reading.	Dehea turns on the tape recorder to play Holtz's "The Planets," as guests from other classes arrive.	
Book Sharing 9:30	Children are exhausted and pleased with their museum opening. They place their notes in folders and gather in the reading area. Children sit comfortably and listen to the story, joining in on favorite parts. They join in singing "Waltzing Matilda," one of the traveling songs Mr. Bechtel taught them. As they line up to go to the library, they are already talking about the funny words in the song.	Dehea knows the children need some time to relax and restore energy levels before moving on to other work for the day. She also wants to refocus the group so that the theme does not become stale. She selects a class favorite, *Mirandy and Brother Wind* to read. Dehea leads the class in singing "Waltzing Matilda." She tells them that after lunch they will be meeting someone who knows a great deal about the place where this song comes from and about the unusual words in it.	
Library 9:45	As they enter the library, each child tells Dehea how many steps their journey took. Children participate in the scavenger hunt, using card catalog and book-finding guides.	Dehea has the children count the number of steps it takes to complete their journey to the library. Mr. Schwartz, the librarian, greets the children and tells them that he is going to help them journey around the world. He has set up a scavenger hunt that will help them find information books about different parts of the world. Dehea returns to her class, where she collects the exhibit folders. The children still have to write self-evaluations, and then Dehea	

(continued)

table **4.6**   Detailed Schedule, Dehea Munioz's Second/Third-Grade Family-Grouped Class *(continued)*

DAY 15 *(continued)*

Time	Children	Teacher	Teacher Research
Library *(continued)*		will give each child written feedback on their performance. This information will also be sent to parents, along with samples of student work and suggestions for activities to try at home and books that might be shared.	
		Dehea pulls out a cardboard trunk decorated with pictures from all over the world. Inside are "culture clues"—a plastic beef cow, a stuffed koala, real kiwi fruit, a turtle mask, raw wool, a boomerang, and a variety of pictures representing Australia, New Zealand, and some of the surrounding South Pacific Islands.	
Group Time 10:15	Children speculate on the contents of the trunk. Several recognize the kiwi fruit, but no one knows where it is from or how it got to the United States. They ask for more clues.	Dehea asks children to observe the trunk. What do they think is in it? What clues can they use to help them guess? She reaches in one hand and pulls out a kiwi fruit. She pulls out artifacts and pictures one by one, as the children make guesses.	Dehea is especially pleased by the children's response to the pictures. They note similarities between Nigeria, Vietnam, and the places in the pictures. They are eager to provide their ideas.
	Children begin to try to figure out the problem as each new clue appears. Some of the artifacts make them think this must be a place with farms. Others notice that some of the pictures have beaches, so it must touch the ocean.	Dehea records their suggestions.	
	Someone remembers an ad for Qantas airlines and says, "They go down under!"	She pulls out a tiny stuffed koala bear.	
	Children list the possibilities as Antarctica, Australia, Tasmania, and New Zealand. They aren't sure about South Africa and think Indonesia could be "down under," too.	Dehea calls their attention to the globe, and asks what part of the world might be "down under."	
		Dehea introduces *Possum Magic* to the class and asks them to listen for some of the things they saw in the trunk. This story, she tells them, takes place down under.	
	Children listen as Dehea reads, and all call out, "Australia," when the answer becomes obvious.	Dehea tells them that their special guest this afternoon comes from Australia, and she will let him tell them more about down under. She then tells them that some of the things in the trunk were from Australia, some from New Zealand, and some from other islands in the South Pacific. Per-	While the guest is talking to the children, Dehea plans to take notes on student comments and questions. So far, her study supports her hypothesis that sustained study, multiple exposures to another culture, and time to reflect will have a positive impact on children's attitudes to their

table **4.6**   Detailed Schedule, Dehea Munioz's Second/Third-Grade Family-Grouped Class *(continued)*

DAY 15 *(continued)*

Time	Children	Teacher	Teacher Research
Math 11:15	The students work on figuring out how to divide the kiwi fruits evenly. They decide it would be easiest to divide the class into six groups, and then each group could divide one kiwi fruit into the same number of pieces as they had group members. Children work either in the math center on problems involving division or with the teacher, using manipulatives to show sets and subsets.	haps they will be able to figure out which are which. Dehea shows children six kiwi fruits: "I want you all to taste this fruit from down under, but you will need to help me make sure there is enough for everyone." She then asks the children how to divide up the fruit so that everyone gets a taste. Dehea cuts the fruit as each group tells her how many pieces it needs. She then works through the problem on the board. Some of the children are ready for division, and they are allowed to work in the math center on problems set up for them there. Most of the younger children still need practice with manipulatives, and Dehea distributes materials for them to work with.	own and others' cultures. The most effective experience seems to be the opportunity for children to meet people from other cultures. Dehea has noticed that the children treat their "international" classmates with great respect after such a visit and talk about visiting that person's home country some day.

Summary

The opportunity to work with like-minded and cooperative colleagues is certainly a plus for Dehea Munioz. She benefits from a schoolwide commitment to the goals of cross- and multicultural understanding that Dehea feels are fundamental to her teaching. It is also representative of her approach to teaching and learning that her collegial relationships benefit her students. Dehea does not pretend to know everything there is to know about each theme introduced in the course of a year. Instead, she embarks as a learner, albeit a more expert one, with her students. As a fellow learner and researcher with her students, Dehea taps resources and asks for help in constructing new knowledge as her students do. She also uses what she has learned to improve teaching and learning in her classroom. As a result, Dehea made some interesting discoveries. First, she found distinct differences in how children responded to the "culturally conscious" books she selected. The children whose cultures were represented seemed to find a voice in these books. Several children who had rarely spoken up in class began participating in Literature Response Groups*. Initially, some expressed anger about what they experienced in school and in their home neighborhoods. Their journal entries became longer and included more commentary on life in and out of school. Other students expressed surprise and sometimes distress that differences might be more than "just skin color." Dehea noted a change, however, as each international visitor came for several visits and became a classroom friend. In this role the visitor also became a "neutral" reference point for discussions of cultural differences. The children's fascination with other countries and customs also allowed them to look differently at differences closer to home. Through their joint and individual inquiries, Dehea, her students, her peer teachers, and members of the school community were better able to negotiate some of the tensions in their own cross- and multicultural community.

Exploration is a joint student and teacher venture.

Children's Literature: JOURNEYS

Abuela by A. Dorros. Illustrated by E. Kleven. Dutton, 1991.

Airmail to the Moon by T. Birdseye. Illustrated by S. Gammell. Holiday House, 1988.

Airport by B. Barton. Harper & Row, 1982.

Aladdin and the Enchanted Lamp by M. Mayer. Illustrated by G. McDermott. Macmillan, 1985.

Alice Yazzi's Year by R. Maher. Illustrated by S. Begay. Tricycle, 2003.

All the Colors of the Race by A. Adoff. Lee & Shepard, 1982.

All the Lights in the Night by A. Levine. Illustrated by J. E. Ransome. Tambourine Books, 1991.

Almost to Freedom by V. M. Nelson. Illustrated by C. Bootman. Carolrhoda, 2003.

Amazing Grace by M. Hoffman. Illustrated by C. Burch. Dial, 1991.

Anansi the Spider by G. McDermott. Holt, Rinehart, and Winston, 1972.

And the Dish Ran Away with the Spoon by J. Stevens. Illustrated by S. C. Stevens. Harcourt, 2001.

Anno's Counting House by M. Anno. Harper & Row, 1986.

Anno's Journey by M. Anno. HarperCollins, 1977.

Arthur, High King of Britain by M. Morpugo. Illustrated by M. Foreman. Harcourt, 1995.

At the Crossroads by R. Isadora. Greenwillow, 1983.

Aunt Harriet's Underground Railroad in the Sky by F. Ringgold. Crown, 1992.

Aurora Means Dawn by S. Sanders. Bradbury, 1989.

Baby Rattlesnake by T. Ata. Children's Book Press, 1989.

Baby Whale's Journey by J. London. Illustrated by J. Van Zyke. Chronicle, 1999.

Ben's Trumpet by R. Isadora. Greenwillow, 1979.

Bicycle Man by A. Say. Parnassus Press, 1982.

Bigmama's by D. Crews. Greenwillow, 1991.

Bikes by A. Rockwell. Dutton, 1987.

Bird by D. Burne. Knopf, 1988.

Butterfly and Moth by P. Whalley. Knopf, 1988.

Caravan by L. McKay Jr. Illustrated by D. Ligasan. Lee & Low, 1995.

Cars and How They Go by J. Cole. Crowell, 1983.

Cassie's Journey: Going West in the 1860s by B. Harvey. Illustrated by D. K. Ray. Holiday House, 1988.

Comets by S. Bonar. Watts, 1998.

Coming to America by B. Maestro. Illustrated by S. Ryan. Scholastic, 1996.

The Constellations by R. A. Gallant. Four Winds, 1979.

Coolies by Yin. Illustrated by C. Sooentpiet. Philomel, 2001.

Covered Wagons by V. Kay. Illustrated by A. Hudson. Millbrook, 1998.

Dakota Dugout by A. Turner. Macmillan, 1985.

Dandelion Adventures by P. Kite. Illustrated by A. Hudson. Millbrook, 1998.

Death of the Iron Horse by P. Goble. Bradbury, 1987.

Dia's Story Cloth by D. Cha. Compendium by J. Herold. Illustrated by C. Cha & N. T. Cha. Lee & Low, 1996.

Drawing from Nature: Drawing Life in Motion by J. Arnosky. Lothrop, 1987.

The Dream Jar by B. Pryor. Illustrated by M. Graham. Greenwillow, 1996.

East of the Sun and West of the Moon by D. J. MacHale. Rabbit Ears Press, 1991.

Eat the Fruit, Plant the Seed by M. Selsam. Morrow, 1980.

Ellis Island by C. Reef. Dillon, 1991.

Ellis Island: Land of Hope by J. L. Nixon. Bantam Books, 1992.

Emma's Dragon Hunt by C. Stock. Lothrop, 1984.

The Erie Canal by P. Spier. Doubleday, 1970.

Father's Rubber Shoes by Y. Heo. Orchard, 1995.

Fill It Up by G. Gibbons. Crowell, 1985.

First One Foot, Now the Other by T. dePaola. Putnam, 1981.

Flight by B. Burleigh. Putnam, 1991.

Flying by D. Crews. Greenwillow, 1986.

Follow the Drinking Gourd by J. Winter. Knopf, 1988.

Follow the Water from Brook to Ocean by A. Dorros. HarperCollins, 1991.

The Fool of the World and the Flying Ship by A. Ransome. Illustrated by U. Shulevitz. Farrar, Straus, & Giroux, 1968.

The Forgotten Door by A. Key. Scholastic, 1965.

Freight Train by D. Crews. Greenwillow, 1978.

Girls Together by S. A. Williams. Illustrated by S. St. James. Harcourt, 1999.

The Girl Who Loved Wild Horses by P. Goble. Bradbury, 1978.

Going Home by E. Bunting. Illustrated by D. Diaz. HarperCollins, 1996.

Goin' Someplace Special by P. McKissack. Illustrated by J. Pinkney. Atheneum, 2001.

Gold Cadillac by M. Taylor. Bantam, 1987.

Grandfather's Journey by A. Say. Houghton Mifflin, 1993.

Grandpa's Face by E. Greenfield. Illustrated by F. Cooper. Putnam/Philomel, 1988.

Great Migration by J. Lawrence, HarperCollins, 1993.

Greek Myths by O. Coolidge. Houghton Mifflin, 1949.

The Green Book by J. P. Walsh. Farrar, Straus, & Giroux, 1982.

Hana's Suitcase: A True Story by K. Levine. Illustrated by R. Innocenti. Whitman, 2003.

Harriet's Hare by D. King Smith. Crown, 1994.

Hector Lives in the United States Now: The Story of a Mexican-American Child by J. Hewett. Photographs by R. Hewett. Lippincott, 1990.

Hello, My Name Is Scrambled Eggs by J. Gilson. Lothrop, 1985.

Her Seven Brothers by P. Goble. Bradbury, 1988.

Hoang Anh: A Vietnamese-American Boy by D. Hoyt-Goldsmith. Holiday House, 1992.

Home in the Sky by J. Baker. Greenwillow, 1984.

Homesteading: Settling America's Heartland by D. H. Patent. Wallker, 1999.

How Do Birds Find Their Way? by R. Gans. Illustrated by P. Mirocha. HarperCollins, 1996.

How Does It Feel to Grow Old? by N. Farber. Illustrated by T. S. Hyman. Dutton, 1979.

How I Became an American by K. Gündisch. Translated by J. Skofield. Cricket, 2001.

How Many Days to America? by E. Bunting. Clarion, 1988.

How Maps Are Made by M. Branwell. Lerner, 1998.

How Seeds Travel by C. Overbeck. Lerner, 1982.

How to Dig a Hole to the Other Side of the Earth by F. McNulty. Harper, 1979.

If Your Name Was Changed at Ellis Island by E. Levine. Illustrated by W. Parmenter. Scholastic, 1993.

I Go with My Family to Grandma's by R. Levinson. Dutton, 1986.

I Hate English by E. Levine. Scholastic, 1989.

I Have Heard of a Land by J. C. Thomas. Illustrated by F. Cooper. HarperCollins, 1998.

Immigrant Girl: Becky of Eldridge Street by B. Harvey. Illustrated by D. K. Ray. Holiday House, 1987.

Immigrant Kids by R. Freedman. Dutton, 1980.

Incredible Cross-Sections by R. Platt. Knopf, 1992.

I Spy: An Alphabet in Art by L. Micklethwait. Greenwillow, 1991.

I Spy a Freight Train: Transportation in Art by L. Mickelthwait. Greenwillow, 1996.

Jonathan and His Mommy by I. Smalls-Hector. Little, Brown, 1992.

The Josephina Quilt Story by E. Coerr. Harper & Row, 1986.

The Journey by S. Stewart. Illustrated by D. Small. Farrar, Straus, & Giroux, 2001.

Journey into a Black Hole by F. M. Branley. Crowell, 1986.

The Journey of Oliver K. Woodman by D. Pattison. Illustrated by J. Cepeda. Harcourt, 2003.

Journey to the Planets by P. Lauber. Crown, 1982.

Jupiter by S. Simon. Morrow, 1985.

Keepers of the Animals by M. J. Caduto & J. Bruchac. Fulcrum, 1988.

Keepers of the Earth by M. J. Caduto & J. Bruchac. Fulcrum, 1988.

The Land I Lost by H. Q. Nhuong. HarperCollins, 1982.

The Legend of the Persian Carpet by T. dePaola. Illustrated by C. Ewart. Putnam, 1993.

Legends of Journeys by O. J. Norris. Cambridge University Press, 1988.

Life on a Barge by H. Scarry. Prentice-Hall, 1982.

Linnea in Monet's Garden by C. Bjork. R & S, 1987.

The Long Way to a New Land by J. Sandin. Harper & Row, 1989.

Look to the Night Sky by S. Simon. Puffin, 1979.

The Magic Horse by S. Scott. Greenwillow, 1985.

The Magic School Bus at the Waterworks by J. Cole. Illustrated by B. Degan. Scholastic, 1986.

Making a New Home in America by M. Rosenberg. Lothrop, 1986.

Mapping Our World by M. Branwell. Lerner, 1998.

Maps and Globes by J. Knowleton. Illustrated by H. Barton. Crowell, 1985.

Maps: Getting from Here to There by H. Weiss. Houghton Mifflin, 1991.

Maps in Everyday Life by M. Branwell. Lerner, 1998.

Maria Teresa by M. Atkinson. Illustrated by C. E. Eber. Lollipop Power, 1979.

Marms in the Marmalade by D. Morley. Carolrhoda, 1984.

Me Oh Maya by J. Scieszka. Illustrated by A. McCauley. Viking, 2003.

Mirandy and Brother Wind by P. McKissick. Illustrated by J. Pinckney. Knopf, 1988.

Mirette on the High Wire by E. A. McCully. Putnam, 1992.

Molasses Flood by B. Lent. Houghton Mifflin, 1992.

Monarch Butterflies: Mysterious Travelers by B. Lavies. Dutton, 1992.

Monarchs by C. Lasky. Photographs by C. G. Knight. Gulliver Green, 1993.

The Moon of the Monarch Butterflies by J. C. George. Illustrated by K. Mak. HarperCollins, 1993.

Moving from One to Ten by S. Halpern. Macmillan, 1993.

The Mud Pony by C. L. Cohen. Scholastic, 1988.

My Freedom Trip by F. Park and G. Park. Illustrated by D. R. Jenkins. Boyds Mills, 1998.

My Grandmother's Journey by J. Cech. Illustrated by S. McGinley-Nally. Bradbury, 1991.

My Name Is Maria Isabel by A. F. Ada. Atheneum, 1993.

The Mysteries of Harris Burdock by C. Van Allsburg. Houghton Mifflin, 1984.

Nathaniel Talking by E. Greenfield. Illustrated by J. Gilchrist. Black Butterfly, 1989.

Night Driving by J. Coy. Illustrated by P. McCarty. Holt, 1996.

North by Night: A Story of the Underground Railroad by K. Ayres. Delacorte, 1998.

Not So Fast, Songololo by N. Daly. Macmillan, 1986.

Orphan Train Rider: One Boy's Story by A. Warren. Houghton Mifflin, 1996.

The People Could Fly by V. Hamilton. Knopf, 1985.

The People Shall Continue by S. Ortiz. Children's Book Press, 1988.

Persephone by W. Hutton. McElderry, 1994.

Picture Atlas of the Universe. Rand-McNally, 1991.

Plant by D. Burne. Knopf, 1989.

Plants That Never Ever Bloom by R. Heller. Grosset & Dunlap, 1984.

Possum Magic by M. Fox. Illustrated by J. Vivas. Abingdon, 1987.

Punctuation Takes a Vacation by R. Pulver. Illustrated by L. R. Reed. Holiday House, 2003.

The Reason for a Flower by R. Heller. Grosset & Dunlap, 1983.

Relatives Came by C. Rylant. Bradbury, 1985.

Rocks and Minerals by D. J. Arneson. Kidsbooks, 1990.

Round Trip by A. Jonas. Greenwillow, 1983.

Sarah, Plain and Tall by P. McLachlan. Cranston, 1988.

Saturn by S. Simon. Morrow, 1985.

School Bus by D. Crews. Greenwillow, 1984.

The Search for Delicious by N. Babbitt. Farrar, Straus, & Giroux, 1969.

The Secret Life of Hardware by V. Cobb. Lippincott, 1982.

Seeds: Pop, Stick, Glide by P. Lauber. Crown, 1981.

Seeing Earth from Space by P. Lauber. Orchard Books, 1990.

Sees Behind Trees by M. Dorris. Hyperion, 1996.

Sheep on a Ship by N. Shaw. Houghton Mifflin, 1989.

Shell by A. Arthur. Knopf, 1989.

Sitti's Secrets by S. Nye. Illustrated by N. Carpenter. Four Winds, 1994.

The Snow Queen by H. C. Andersen. Macmillan, 1985.

Space Race by S. Waugh. Delacorte, 2000.

Splash! by A. Jonas. Greenwillow, 1995.

The Star People: A Lakota Tale by S. D. Nelson. Abrams, 2003.

Starting Life Butterfly by C. Llewellyn. Illustrated by S. Mendez. Northword, 2003.

Stringbean's Trip to the Shining Sea by V. B. Williams & J. Williams. Scholastic, 1988.

Sun by S. Simon. Morrow, 1986.

Sundiata by R. Bertol. Crowell, 1990.

Sweet Clara and the Freedom Quilt by D. Hopkinson. Illustrated by J. Ransome. Knopf, 1993.

Take My Word for It by V. Pizer. Dodd, Mead, 1981.

The Tale of Aladdin and the Wonderful Lamp by E. Kimmel. Illustrated by J. Cheng. Holiday House, 1992.

Talk about English: How Words Travel and Change by J. Klausner. Crowell, 1990.

Tam Lin by S. Cooper. Macmillan, 1991.

Tar Beach by F. Ringold. Crown, 1991.

Tea with Milk by A. Say. Houghton Mifflin, 1999.

The Three Bears and 15 Other Stories by A. Rockwell. Crowell, 1975.

Three Days on a River in a Red Canoe by V. B. Williams. Mulberry Books, 1981.

Three Jovial Huntsmen by S. Jeffers. Bradbury, 1973.

The Three Pigs by D. Weisner. Clarion, 2001.

To Be a Slave by J. Lester. Dial, 1968.

Tonio's Cat by M. Calhoun. Illustrated by E. Martinez. Morrow, 1996.

Townsend's Warbler by P. Fleischman. HarperCollins, 1992.

Train to Somewhere by E. Bunting. Illustrated by R. Himler. Clarion, 1996.

Traveling to Tondo by V. Aardema. Knopf, 1991.

Tree by D. Burne. Knopf, 1988.

The Trek by A. Jonas. Greenwillow, 1985.

Trucker by H. H. Wurmfeld. Macmillan, 1990.

Truck Song by D. Diebert. Illustrated by B. Barton. Crowell, 1984.

Tuesday by D. Wiesner. Clarion, 1991.

The Turn About, Think About, Look About Book by B. Gardner. Lothrop, 1983.

Turtle Knows Your Name by A. Bryan. Macmillan, 1989.

Two Suns in the Sky by M. Bel-Ami. Front Street, 1999.

Under the Quilt of Night by D. Hopkinson. Illustrated by J. E. Ransome. Simon & Schuster, 2001.

Under the Sunday Tree by E. Greenfield. Harper & Row, 1988.

A Very Young Dancer by J. Krementz. Dell, 1986.

Viva Mexico by A. Palacios. Steck-Vaughn, 1992.

Volcano: The Eruption and Healing of Mount St. Helens by P. Lauber. Bradbury, 1986.

Wagon Wheels by B. Brenner. Illustrated by D. Bolognese. Harper & Row, 1978.

Whale Journey by V. French. Illustrated by I. Flather. Zero, 1998.

Walk Together Children: Black American Spirituals by A. Bryan. Aladdin, 1981.

Watch the Stars Come Out by R. Levinson. Illustrated by D. Goode. Dutton, 1985.

Water's Way by L. W. Peters. Illustrated by T. Rand. Little, Brown, 1991.

The Way Things Work by D. Macaulay. Houghton Mifflin, 1988.

When Africa Was Home by K. L. Williams. Orchard Books, 1991.

When Schlemiel Went to Warsaw by I. B. Singer. Farrar, Straus, & Giroux, 1986.

Where Are You Going, Manyoni? by C. Stock. Morrow, 1993.

Where Do They Go? Insects in Winter by M. Selsam. Four Winds, 1982.

Where the Waves Break: Life at the Edge of the Sea by A. Malnig. Nature Watch Books, 1985.

Where the Wild Things Are by M. Sendak. Harper & Row, 1963.

Who Came Down That Road? by G. E. Lyon. Illustrated by P. Catalanotto. Orchard, 1992.

Who Says a Dog Goes Bow-Wow? by H. De Zutter. Illustrated by S. MacDonald. Bantam, 1993.

Working Cotton by S. A. Williams. Harcourt Brace Jovanovich, 1992.

A World of Wonders by J. P. Lewis. Illustrated by A. Jay. Dial, 2002.

World of Wonders: A Trip Through Numbers by S. Ockenga & E. Doolittle. Houghton Mifflin, 1988.

The Wretched Stone by C. Van Allsburg. Houghton Mifflin, 1991.

Yang the Youngest and His Terrible Ear by L. Namioka. Little, Brown, 1992.

Young Martin's Promise by W. D. Myers. Steck-Vaughn, 1992.

Zorah's Magic Carpet Ride by S. Czernecki. Hyperion, 1996.

Prototype 4: Third Grade— CREATING COMMUNITIES

Schedule

CREATING COMMUNITIES takes place in a rural area that is experiencing rapid change.

Connie Bedar's third grade is located in a historic building in the county seat of a midwestern state. Many of the children are from farming families that have lived and worked there for several generations. However, the recent opening of a Japanese auto plant nearby and the infusion of a large refugee population have added a diverse mix of cultures to the community.

Because there are no art or music specialists, Connie and the other third-grade teacher, Jennifer Reilly, arrange their schedules so that Connie teaches art and her colleague teaches music. They schedule planning time during the children's P.E. and library periods. (See Table 4.7)

Connie feels strongly that her students need to understand their community and how it is connected to the world. As a result, she tries to bring the community into the school and students into the community as often as possible. At the beginning of the year, children told Connie that history was their least favorite subject, declaring it boring and not useful. Because Connie is determined to help children see the relevance of history and other social studies to their lives, she has focused her teacher inquiry on building student interest in this area. Connie has a collection of picture books about different communities that she plans to use as models for creating their own commutable **4.7** Weekly Schedule, Connie Bedar's Third-Grade Class

Time	Monday	Tuesday	Wednesday	Thursday	Friday
7:30	Teacher arrival and setup				
8:00	Children arrival and "jobs" time				
8:10	Whole-class activity	Whole-class activity	Physical education/ library	Art/music	Whole-class activity
9:15	Integrated work time				
10:00	Recess				
10:15	Integrated work time				
11:30	Literature				
12:00	Lunch				
12:45	Math	Math	Math	Math	Math
1:30	Art/music	Individual or group time	Individual or group time	Individual or group time	Physical education/ library
2:00	Cleanup				
2:05	Whole-group time				
2:30	Dismissal				

nity book. She is also particularly interested in the success that some teachers have had with "Foxfire" types of oral history projects, especially in small communities such as hers. As a result, a major part of her teacher inquiry is the effect of writing and publishing an illustrated community history.

Into the Classroom

The idea for the theme CREATING COMMUNITIES began with a look at the third-grade curriculum standards. The social studies standards focused on local history and culture, whereas the science curriculum called for a study of animal behavior and habitats. At first, Connie thought that communities might be too broad a topic to deal with in a single thematic unit. As she planned, however, Connie decided to emphasize aspects of community most directly related to the third-grade science and social studies curriculum and to the local community. As you read through Table 4.8, you will notice that on Day 1, Connie uses a whole-class activity that generates a lot of discussion about what makes a community. Later she will look at various aspects of urban and rural communities with a view toward helping children analyze their own community. Connie also moves the concept of community into the area of science immediately after children have considered it in terms of human communities. On Day 1, students are also engaged in a study of an ant farm that Connie has placed in the science center. Connie emphasizes the move to science by changing the room into "Bedar Laboratories." The children love the role playing and easily adapt to the rules for laboratory behavior, including inventing some rules of their own. Also notice that Connie helps make the study of community history relevant to the present day by placing students in Literature Response Groups to study communities with which they are very familiar, "Neighborhoods" and "The School Community." These topics will provide plenty of practice in reading easy-to-read and short chapter books by popular authors. Connie feels that wide reading of these books will give her third-graders additional opportunities to become fluent readers.

Connie also schedules a separate time each day to work on literature and mathematics. These are flexible time periods, and on Day 15 she substitutes a special program for the math time period. Generally, however, Connie tries to provide intensive work in both areas every day.

Prototype 4: Third Grade—COMMUNITIES

HABITATS AS COMMUNITIES

POND
BUTTERNUT HOLLOW POND
COLORFUL CAPTIVATING CORAL REEFS
A FOREST COMMUNITY
ONE SMALL SQUARE: BACKYARD
ONE SMALL SQUARE: WOODS
LIFE IN A POND
SAGUARO MOON: A DESERT JOURNAL
A FOREST COMMUNITY
CITY PARK
Exploring Pond Habitats
  www.naturegrid.org.uk/pondexplorer/pond-cross.html
Virtual Tide Pool
  www.pbs.org/wnet/nature/edgeofsea/tidepool.html
U.S. Environmental Protection Agency: Habitat
  Protection
  www.epa.gov/owow/oceans/coral/about.html
Find out about the interactions between plants and animals
  in a habitat in your community (e.g., a pond, wetlands, a
  tidal pool). How many species of animal do you observe
  there? How do plants and animals interact and support
  each other? Draw a flow chart or Semantic Map*
  showing connections among each of the species.
Create an I-movie or video presentation about the habitat
  modeled on *National Geographic* or *Nature*
  presentations.

GETTING AROUND THE COMMUNITY

MY MAP BOOK
MAPS AND GLOBES
AS THE CROW FLIES: A FIRST BOOK OF MAPS
Draw a bird's-eye-view map of your neighborhood. Include places that are important to you and include
  them on a map key. Write a description of one of the places on your map.
MAPPING PENNY'S WORLD
THERE'S A MAP ON MY LAP
ME ON THE MAP
MAPS AND MAPPING MAPS AND GLOBES
SMALL WORLDS: AN INTRODUCTION TO MAPS
Find out how cartographers work. What are the different types of maps you could use to represent your
  community?
Measure the perimeter of your school yard and the school building. Draw a map of your school grounds to
  scale. Include other key features and represent them accurately. How is this map different from the one
  you drew of your neighborhood?
Look at a map of your community. Find your own street on the map grid. Place markers for everyone in
  the community.
Browse through the Yellow Pages and make a list of places. Note their addresses and then find them on the
  street grid. Find different routes to get to the places from your school. Write directions. Ask a parent to
  drive you to one of the places following your directions.

MapQuest
www.mapquest.com
Use MapQuest to find driving directions from your address to the places you selected. Compare your
  directions to those from MapQuest.

MY PLACE
Find maps of your community that go back in time.
Create your own version of MY PLACE using the maps and findings from your community study as
  resources.
Study public transportation in your community. Plan a trip from your home to a museum, historical site,
  stadium, zoo, or park by public transportation, using schedules and maps. On a street map of your
  community, compare the time and distance for your trip if taking public transportation, private car, riding
  your bike, or walking. Can you find a safe route to ride or walk from place to place?

Studying Other Animal Communities

Carry out an in-depth study of one of the animal groups
  below. Create a picture glossary, chart, or diagram to
  show what you learn about each animal. Be sure that
  you include what these animals are like, what they eat
  (and who eats them), their habitats, and so forth.
What characteristics about each species indicate that
  these animals are part of a community?
Design a poster presentation to show how your animal
  is part of a community.

ANIMAL COMMUNITIES

THE LIFE AND TIMES OF THE HONEYBEE
HONEYBEES (Heiligman, Milton)
BRILLIANT BEES
World Almanac for Kids
  www.worldalmanacforkids.com/explore/animals/
  bee.html
Beekeeping Homepage
  http://ourworld.compuserve.com/homepages/
  Beekeeping

GORILLAS
Gorillas Online
  http://staff.washington.edu/timk/gorillas
CHIMPANZEES
THE CHIMPANZEES I LOVE: SAVING THEIR
  WORLD AND OURS
AMONG THE WILD CHIMPANZEES (VHS)
Jane Goodall Institute
  www.discoverchimpanzees.org

WOLVES
GROWING UP WILD: WOLVES
WOLF
International Wolf Center
  www.wolf.org/wolves/index.asp
Nova: Wild Wolves
  www.pbs.org/wgbh/nova/wolves

WHALES! STRANGE AND WONDERFUL
British Columbia Killer Whale Program
  www.killerwhale.org
  www.killerwhale.org/fieldnotes/clans.html
DOLPHIN
WILD ABOUT DOLPHINS
DOLPHINS
Dolphin Research Center
  www.dolphins.org

ANT CITY
THE LIFE AND TIME OF THE ANT
IT'S AN ANT'S LIFE
ANTS
A COLONY OF ANTS
ANTS (Fleischer, Greenaway)
LEAF-CUTTING ANTS
ARE YOU AN ANT?
As a whole class create a K-W-L chart about ants and
  ant communities.
Then use the ant books and other resources to find
  information about ant communities. Make an
  illustrated semantic map of what you have learned.
Kits at The Nature Store
  www.thenaturestore.com/livekits.htm
Find or purchase an ant colony and learn how to care
  for it. Observe the ants in your colony, keeping
  track of daily observations in a science journal. Did
  you learn anything from your observations that you
  didn't learn from the books you read? Write up your
  findings in an illustrated information book for other
  third graders.

Our Community

THE BEST TOWN IN THE WORLD

Draw a picture of your favorite thing about your community and write a description.

Compare your picture to others in the class. What are the types of places you enjoy? Brainstorm a list of "best" things about your own community. Devise a list of things you'd like to find out more about.

MY NEW YORK

CITY OF ANGELS: IN AND AROUND LOS ANGELES

ON THIS SPOT: BACK THROUGH TIME

THE CITY BY THE BAY: A MAGICAL JOURNEY AROUND SAN FRANCISCO

I LIVE IN TOKYO

I LIVE IN BROOKLYN

Read one these books in your Literature Response Groups*. Share your responses in your Sketchbook-Journal*. What different aspects of community does your book describe? Make a list of categories and then share them with the whole class. Choose topics from the categories that you want to use to study your own community.

Break into small groups to study each of the topics you decide on. What resources will you use to find out more about your category? Invite community members to provide information for your inquiries.

Assemble your findings in a large illustrated book adapting the formats of the books you read.

COMMUNITY CLOSE UP

Choose one of the following two topics and read as many of the books as you can. Then work in small groups to complete suggested activities.

Neighborhoods

WHEN MULES FLEW ON MAGNOLIA STREET

AMELIA LENDS A HAND

OH NO, NOAH

THE FOUR UGLY CATS IN APARTMENT 3D

MYSTERIOUS MISS SLADE by D. King-Smith Crown, 2000.

ARK IN THE PARK

ANDY RUSSELL, NOT WANTED BY THE POLICE

THE KEY COLLECTION

TIPPY LEMMEY

Read books that are set in neighborhoods.

Draw Character Portraits* or Character Sociograms* of the characters.

Plan a TV talk show interview with the main characters from these books.

How is the neighborhood described in these books alike and different from your own?

Make a chart listing the types of problems students face in the different books. Are they the same or different from the problems that exist in your neighborhood? How is a neighborhood a community and how can you help make it a better place for everyone?

WHAT IS A COMMUNITY?

CREATING COMMUNITIES

I GOT COMMUNITY

WHAT IS A COMMUNITY FROM A TO Z

What is a community? What do peer groups, playground groups, sports teams, families, and communities have in common? How are they different? Create a chart showing what you think. Add features and make changes to the chart as you study communities.

The School Community

ROBERT AND THE BACK-TO-SCHOOL SPECIAL

STARTING WITH ALICE

THE GOLD THREADED DRESS

A CRAZY MIXED-UP SPANGLISH DAY

JUDY MOODY GETS FAMOUS

MATH RASHES: AND OTHER CLASSROOM TALES

THE YEAR OF MISS AGNES

SURVIVING BRICK JOHNSON

DOGGONE . . . THIRD GRADE

7 × 9 = TROUBLE

ROBERT AND THE WEIRD AND WACKY FACTS

DEAR WHISKERS

MEAN MEAN MAUREEN GREEN

HORRIBLE HARRY AND THE MUD GREMLINS

Read books that have school settings.

Draw Character Portraits* or Character Sociograms* of the characters.

Plan a creative drama presentation in which each main character arrives at your school as a new student.

Make a chart listing the types of problems students face in the different books. Are they the same or different from the problems in your school? How is the school a community and how can you help make it a better place for everyone?

Cultures in the Community

BLOCK PARTY

MY CHINA TOWN

TAR BEACH

ABUELA

HARLEM

THE BLOCK

UPTOWN

A STREET CALLED HOME

SMOKY NIGHT

MADELENKA

ON THE TOWN A COMMUNITY ADVENTURE

Each of these books depicts a different culture that is part of a larger community.

Study the many cultures that have contributed to your community, past and present.

Create a quilt that represents these contributions.

U.S. Census Bureau
www.census.gov/acs/www

See if you can find the census report for your community or one close to where you live. Learn how to read the tables and charts. Adapt the categories of the U.S. Census to your own school community and take a school census (with the permission of your principal).

CHARTS AND GRAPHS

Display your findings in a table or graph.

Community Needs

JACKSON JONES AND THE PUDDLE OF THORNS

HOWIE BOWLES AND UNCLE SAM

THE THUMB IN THE BOX

SEEDFOLKS

Visit your city hall or town council and attend a council meeting.

Find out how city government works.

In addition to the city council, what departments help run the city? Choose a job that you might like to do someday and find out what that person does.

Interview city council members and others about problems in your community. Plan and role play a city council meeting that will deal with problems you found out about in your research. As a class choose one problem and develop an action plan for change. Carry it out.

Music in the Community

THIS LAND IS MY LAND

FROM SEA TO SHINING SEA by A. Cohn. Scholastic, 1993.

Music has been important to many generations of Americans. What music is important to your community and why? Interview family members and older members of the community about types of music and particular songs that were important to your community's past. Catalog types of music, cultural preferences, and songs by decade. Compile an auditory record of music to accompany your community book.

table **4.8**   Detailed Schedule, Connie Bedar's Third-Grade Class

DAY 1

Time	Children	Teacher	Teacher Research
Teacher Arrival 7:30		Connie checks her mail and organizes materials for the day.	
Children Arrival 8:00	Children enter room and greet teacher and peers. They go immediately to jobs; check on the class animals, take attendance, and water plants. Several cluster around an ant farm that Connie has installed in the science center, along with a collection of books about ants.	Connie greets the children, talks individually with several, and collects permission slips for a walking trip.	
Whole-Class Activity 8:10	Students volunteer ideas such as their town, their church, their neighborhood, and so on.	Connie reads *I Got Community* and *What Is a Community from A to Z*. She asks children to help her to brainstorm their thoughts about what a community is and lists their ideas on the board. She then asks them to meet in small groups to create Comparison Charts* of the types of communities the children brainstormed. She asks each group to choose categories for comparing characteristics that make each group a community.	
Integrated Work Time 9:15	Most of the children have worked on Comparison Charts* before and know the routine.	Connie monitors student work, asking questions when a group seems stuck.	
Recess 10:00			
Integrated Work Time 10:15	Children finish work on their Comparison Charts* and each group shares their findings.	Connie takes note of understandings (and misunderstandings) about communities.	
Literature 11:30	Children contribute ideas.	Connie introduces a K-W-L* technique to find out what children know about ants.	
	Children take notes in their Sketchbook Journals*. Following the reading, they help Connie fill in the chart with new things they learned. Several of those who have been looking at the ant farm add a few additional facts.	Connie then reads *Ant City*. She then asks children to help her fill in the chart.	
Lunch 12:00			
Math 12:45	Children create designs using fractional parts of geometric shapes. For homework, they are to see how many geometric shapes and fractions of shapes are in one room.	Connie introduces geometric shapes and how changing them can create interesting designs. She collects children's work and displays it.	
Individual or Group Time 1:30	Children look through the books and return to their desks to read the	Connie introduces children to the chapter books about neighborhoods and schools. She gives Book Talks* on several of the titles and gives them the	

table **4.8**   Detailed Schedule, Connie Bedar's Third-Grade Class *(continued)*

DAY 1 *(continued)*

Time	Children	Teacher	Teacher Research
Individual or Group Time *(continued)*	book of their choice. Connie plans to discuss books they have been reading.	rest of the time to browse through the titles and choose one that they want to read. She tells them that rather than reading just one book to share in Literature Response Groups* during this study, they will be reading, discussing, and comparing as many books as they can.	
	One child suggests that that means they will be a reading community.		
Cleanup 2:00	Children put all work away and gather at the front of the room.		
Group Time 2:05		Connie leads a discussion of the day's work and how it relates to the CREATING COMMUNITIES theme. She reminds them of their class walking trip the next day and hands out the directions for making an ant farm.	
Dismissal 2:30			

DAY 2

Time	Children	Teacher	Teacher Research
Teacher Arrival 7:30		Connie makes sure that everything is in order for their class walking tour.	
Children Arrival 8:00	Several children have gathered at the ant farm and make notes in their Sketchbook Journals*. Two children say they found signs of ants on their way to school.	Connie greets the children and parent helpers and talks individually with several of them.	
Whole-Class Activity 8:10	Children gather supplies for walking trip, meet their assigned team of reporters, and confirm jobs. Some students have already made a map to guide the walking tour of the town where the school is located. Children sketch pictures of building decoration and architecture that they see. They make note of the types of businesses that occupy the different buildings and which buildings are unoccupied. They note a cornerstone on the county courthouse that reads 1887. They also point out modern devices like streetlights and traffic lights that may not have been there originally. They note the presence of window air conditioners, of fresh paint on one storefront, and a "For Lease" sign on another.	Connie has divided the children into groups based on some of the community categories they discussed the day before. She reminds children of their jobs and makes sure that the parent volunteers all have the right group of five children and the right maps and assignments.	Connie keeps a small notebook for recording her observations of students as they work in the community. Connie moves from group to group, noting questions and discoveries in her notebook. The walking trip provides her with plenty of data about student enthusiasm for their own community.
	One group gathers natural material and found objects to be used for an art project. Another group takes texture rubbings from manhole covers, the		

(continued)

table **4.8**   Detailed Schedule, Connie Bedar's Third-Grade Class *(continued)*

DAY 2 *(continued)*

Time	Children	Teacher	Teacher Research
Whole-Class Activity *(continued)*	cornerstone on the courthouse, even an out-of-state license plate. The mechanic at the gas station stops to chat and ends up giving an interview. Their excitement is contagious and they stay on task and are not ready to return to class when the trip is over.		
Literature 11:30	Children listen to the book. They discuss how the town in the story compares with their community.	Connie reads *The Best Town in the World*. She asks the children to help her make a list of the types of things author Byrd Baylor mentioned in the book. She tells them they will work on organizing their findings from their walk after lunch.	
Lunch 12:00			
Math 12:45	Children work in pairs to complete graphing exercises using some of the data they collected on their walk.	Using a multimedia projector, Connie teaches a lesson with a computer program on Graphing*.	
Individual or Group Time 1:30	Children work in groups on projects begun during the morning walk. Some of their ideas include the following: • Make a chart showing the businesses in the town center. • Make a map of the downtown area. • Create a mural of the town. • Make a "dictionary" of interesting architectural features they found.		
Cleanup 2:00			
Whole-Group Time 2:05	Children enjoy the idea of fold-out pages and one suggests that they could have pages like that in their book. Several of the children have parents who work in the nearby auto plant and recognize that the book *I Live in Tokyo* is about a city in Japan, not the United States.	Connie reads *My New York* and Book Talks* other books she has collected that give first-person accounts of different big cities. She tells them that these books could serve as models for their own community book.	
Dismissal 2:30			

DAY 7

Time	Children	Teacher	Teacher Research
Children Arrival 8:00	Many children are looking through the collection of city books Connie has assembled.		

table **4.8**   Detailed Schedule, Connie Bedar's Third-Grade Class *(continued)*

DAY 7 *(continued)*

Time	Children	Teacher	Teacher Research
Whole-Class Activity 8:10	Because the book takes great leaps backward in time on the island of Manhattan, children see new possibilities for looking back in time in their own community.	Connie reads *On This Spot; Back Through Time*. Connie helps them think about how they might research their community's past. Connie asks children to begin thinking about what categories or major questions they want to address in their community book.	
Integrated Work Time 9:15	Groups and individuals work on finishing the projects that grew out of their community walk.	Connie moves from group to group monitoring progress.	
Recess 10:00			
Integrated Work Time 10:15	Children finish their projects and get ready to present them to the rest of the class in the afternoon.	Connie conferences with five individual children. She listens to them read and then they talk about the book together. Connie makes notes about strategies and comprehension in her journal.	
Literature 11:30		Connie reads *My Tokyo*. She tells the children that she feels they are ready to make decisions about what topics they want to include in their community book.	
	After much discussion, the children decide on People in the Community, Places in the Community, History of the Community, and Jobs in the Community.	Connie suggests that they might also include a topic of The Future of the Community, looking at needs and possible changes that may occur by the time they are adults.	Connie scribbles notes on children's attitudes during the discussion. She will add to her journal during lunch.

Summary

Like many of the other teachers described in these prototypes, Connie provides a variety of opportunities for students to work together in small groups and to share their work with the wider community. The Community Book project provided an opportunity for student inquiry and received a great deal of attention in the community. Community members enjoyed being interviewed for stories so much that they dug old items out of attics and called students to come see unusual crafts and artifacts or hear stories. Connie found several local businesses that were willing to provide seed money to create color copies of the book and to give every child in the school a copy. Additional copies were sold on a cost-only basis. Adults stopped children on the street to comment on their writing and artwork or simply to tell the students that their work was enjoyed. The children developed an enormous sense of pride as they saw their work getting this kind of attention, and older community members were pleased to have their past respected and made part of the children's present. This was particularly useful for children from the more rural parts of the community and for those from immigrant cultures. Although some were shy about the more traditional ways of some of their family members, the oral history and newspaper projects made their relatives celebrities.

Obviously not every school is set in a town where the modern and traditional meet in such distinctive ways. Nonetheless, schools in other locales have equally interesting communities around them that can provide similar laboratory experiences.

Connie's teacher research not only supported her notion that local problems will engage children's interest and lead them to better understand larger social issues but also demonstrated the power of real audiences for student work.

Children's Literature: CREATING COMMUNITIES

Abuela by A. Dorros. Penguin, 1991.

Amelia Lends a Hand by M. Moss. American Girl, 2002.

"Among the Wild Chimpanzees" (VHS). National Geographic, 1997.

Andy Russell, Not Wanted by the Police by D. Adler. Harcourt, 2001.

Ant City by A. Dorros. HarperCollins, 1987.

Ants by P. Fleischer. Benchmark, 2002.

Ants by T. Greenaway. Raintree, 2001.

Are You an Ant? by J. Allen. Illustrated by T. Humphries. Kingfisher, 2004.

Ark in the Park by W. Orr. Holt, 2000.

As the Crow Flies: a First Book of Maps by G. Hartman. Aladdin, 1993.

The Best Town in the World by B. Baylor. Turtleback, 1986.

The Block by L. Hughes. Illustrated by R. Beardon. Viking, 1995.

Block Party by M. Singer. Illustrated by S. Roth. Knopf, 2004.

Brilliant Bees by L. Glaser. Illustrated by G. W. Holland. Millbrook, 2003.

Butternut Hollow Pond by B. J. Heinz. Millbrook, 2000.

Charts and Graphs by W. Clemson & D. Clemson. Two-Can Publishing, 2002.

Chimpanzees by R. Stetoff. Benchmark, 2003.

The Chimpanzees I Love: Saving Their World and Ours by J. Goodall. Scholastic, 2001.

The City by the Bay: A Magical Journey around San Francisco by T. Brown. Chronicle, 1998.

City of Angels: In and around Los Angeles by J. Jaskol. Dutton, 1999.

City Park by W. Davis. Illustrated by J. L'Hommedieu. Children's Press, 1997.

A Colony of Ants by R. Spilsbury and L. Spilsbury. Heinemann, 2003.

Colorful Captivating Coral Reefs by D. Patent. Walker, 2003.

A Crazy Mixed-Up Spanglish Day by M. Montes. Scholastic, 2003.

Dear Whiskers by A. Nagda. Holiday, 2001.

Doggone . . . Third Grade by C. McKenna. Holiday, 2002.

Dolphin by N. Davies. Raintree, 2001.

Dolphins by D. Greenberg. Benchmark, 2003.

A Forest Community by E. Massie. Raintree Steck-Vaughn Publications, 2000.

The Four Ugly Cats in Apartment 3D by M. Sachs. Atheneum, 2002.

The Gold Threaded Dress by C. Marsden. Candlewick, 2002.

Gorillas by S. Simon. HarperCollins, 2000.

Growing Up Wild: Wolves by S. Markle. Atheneum, 2001.

Harlem by W. D. Myers. Illustrated by C. Myers. Scholastic, 1997.

Honeybees by D. Heiligman. National Geographic, 2002.

Honeybees by J. Milton. Grosset, 2003.

Horrible Harry and the Mud Gremlins by S. Kline. Viking, 2003.

Howie Bowles and Uncle Sam by K. Banks. Farrar, Straus, & Giroux, 2000.

I Got Community by M. Cooper. Illustrated by D. Gottlieb. Holt, 1995.

I Live in Brooklyn by M. Takabayashi. Houghton, 2004.

I Live in Tokyo by M. Takabayashi. Houghton, 2001.

It's an Ant's Life by S. Parker. Reader's, 1999.

Jackson Jones and the Puddle of Thorns by M. Quattlebaum. Sagebrush, 1995.

Judy Moody Gets Famous by M. A. MacDonald. Candlewick, 2001.

The Key Collection by A. Cheng. Holt, 2003.

Leaf-Cutting Ants by H. Frost. Pebble, 2002.

The Life and Times of the Ant by C. Micucci. Houghton, 2003.

The Life and Times of the Honeybee by C. Micucci. Houghton Mifflin, 1997.

Life in a Pond by A. Fowler. Children's Press, 1996.

Madelenka by P. Sis. Farrar, 2000.

Mapping Penny's World by L. Leedy. Holt, 2000.

Maps and Globes by J. Knowlton. HarperCollins, 1986.

Maps and Mapping by D. Chancellor. Kingfisher, 2004.

Math Rashes: And Other Classroom Tales by D. Evans. Front Street, 2000.

Me on the Map by J. Seeney. Dragonfly, 1998.

Mean, Mean Maureen Green by J. Cox. Holiday, 1999.

My China Town by C. Mak. HarperCollins, 2003.

My Map Book by S. Fanelli. HarperCollins, 1995.

My New York by K. Jakobsen. Little, Brown, 1994.

My Place by N. Wheatley. Kane Miller, 1994.

Mysterious Miss Slade by D. King-Smith. Crown, 2000.

Oh No, Noah! by J. Hurwitz, North South, 2002.

One Small Square: Backyard by D. M. Silver. Illustrated by P. J. Wynne. Learning Triangle Press, 1993.

One Small Square: Woods by D. M. Silver. Illustrated by P. J. Wynne. Learning Triangle Press, 1995.

On this Spot: Back through Time by S. E. Goodman. Greenwillow, 2004.

On the Town: A Community Adventure by J. Caseley. Greenwillow, 2002.

Pond by G. Morrison. Houghton, 2002.

Robert and the Back-to-School Special by B. Seuling. Cricket, 2002.

Robert and the Weird and Wacky Facts by B. Seuling. Cricket, 2002.

Saguaro Moon: A Desert Journal by K. J. Pratt-Serafini. Dawn Publications, 2002.

Seedfolks by P. Fleischman. HarperCollins, 1997.

7 × 9 = Trouble by C. Mills. Farrar, Straus, & Giroux, 2002.

Small Worlds: An Introduction to Maps by K. R. Young. Scholastic, 2002.

Smoky Night by E. Bunting. Illustrated by D. Diaz. Harcourt, 1994.
Starting with Alice by P. R. Naylor. Atheneum, 2002.
A Street Called Home by A. Robinson. Harcourt, 1997.
Surviving Brick Johnson by L. Myers. Clarion, 2000.
Tar Beach by F. Ringgold. Random House, 1991.
There's a Map on My Lap by T. Rabe. Random House, 2002.
This Land Is My Land by W. Guthrie. Illustrated by K. Jakobsen. Little, Brown, 1998.
The Thumb in the Box by K. Roberts. Groundwood, 2001.

Tippy Lemmey by P. McKissack. Simon & Schuster, 2003.
Uptown by B. Collier. Holt, 2000.
Whales! Strange and Wonderful by L. Pringle. Boyds Mills, 2003.
What Is a Community from A to Z by B. Kalman. Crabtree, 2000.
When Mules Flew on Magnolia Street by A. Johnson. Knopf, 2000.
Wild about Dolphins by N. Davies. Candlewick, 2001.
Wolf by M. Leach. Raintree, 2002.
Wolves by C. Economos. Chelsea, 2003.
The Year of Miss Agnes by K. Hill. Simon & Schuster, 2000.

Websites

Kits at the Nature Store
www.thenaturestore.com/livekits.htm

US Census Bureau
www.census.gov/acs/www

Prototype 5: Fourth Grade—CYCLES

Schedule

Steve Williams teaches in a self-contained classroom in the suburbs of a large urban area. (Table 4.9.) The school district has had a history of innovative educational programs although recent federal regulations have put pressure on administrators and teachers to conform to standards and teach to state performance tests. Steve has always been particularly interested in science and wanted to plan at least one thematic study that would immerse his fourth graders in science inquiries. He also wanted to prepare his students for the language arts proficiency test that would be given in early spring. He planned the CYCLES theme for the beginning of the second semester of the year to give his students extensive exposure to narrative and information texts. He felt that thoughtful engagement with good children's literature would provide the types of

table 4.9 **Weekly Schedule, Steve Williams's Fourth-Grade Class**

Time	Monday	Tuesday	Wednesday	Thursday	Friday
	Teacher preparation time				
9:00	Children arrive and go to centers or meet informally with teacher.				
9:10	Group meeting				
9:30	Integrated work time				
10:55	Cleanup				
11:00	Recess				
11:15	Library	Music	Art	Computer lab	Physical education
11:45	Literature				
12:15	Lunch				
12:45	SSR* Teacher Conferences with individual children				
1:05	Book Talks: Several children share books they have been reading.				
1:15	Math				
2:00	Integrated work time. Children continue working on projects.				
2:45	Cleanup				
2:50	Reading Aloud*				
3:15	Dismissal				

Prototype 5: Fourth Grade—CYCLES

CIRCUITS, DIALS, GEARS, AND WHEELS

What do you know about circuits, dials, gears, and wheels? Brainstorm things you know and questions you have.

Discovery Box

Take apart old clocks or machines that use gears. Draw the pieces and write about how you think they might work.

THE NEW WAY THINGS WORK

SWITCH ON SWITCH OFF

ELECTRONICS LAB

ELECTRICITY AND MAGNETISM

HOW DO YOU LIFT A LION?

THE MAGIC SCHOOL BUS AND THE ELECTRIC FIELD TRIP

POWER UP: EXPERIMENTS, PUZZLES, AND GAMES EXPLORING ELECTRICITY

ZAP IT! EXCITING ELECTRICITY ACTIVITIES

GEAR UP: MARVELOUS MACHINE PROJECTS

WHEELS AT WORK: BUILDING AND EXPERIMENTING WITH MACHINES

LEVERS, WHEELS, AND PULLEYS

MACHINES

WHEELS AND CRANKS

ROBOTS RISING

Machines: Mind-boggling experiments you can turn into science fair projects.

Playground Physics
http://lyra.colorado.edu/sbo/mary/play

Conduct experiments with circuits, gears, or wheels. Create a poster to go with your project explaining the steps you took and the results. Build a robot or other invention using what you've learned.

LIFE CYCLES IN THE WORLD AROUND YOU

Break into groups to study animal, plant, or weather cycles. Carry out research and hands-on explorations and experiments. Present your findings to the whole class in a PowerPoint presentation. After each group identifies key concepts in its study, conduct a Jigsaw to teach the concepts to other class members.

Life Cycles of Plants

THE SKY TREE

FROM FLOWER TO FRUIT

FROM SEED TO PLANT

THE LIFE AND TIMES OF THE APPLE

THE LIFE AND TIMES OF THE PEANUT

How do plants and animals grow and adapt?

What changes represent a natural part of the life cycle?

Observe, draw, and describe bean plant growth from seed to mature plant.

Life Cycle of Animals

INCREDIBLE LIFE CYCLES

CHICKS AND CHICKENS

EGG TO BIRD (CYCLES OF LIFE)

A SALAMANDER'S LIFE

FROG

"Eyewitness Video: Amphibian"

THE BUTTERFLY

Which of these animals relies on plant life to survive? Make a chart showing connections between animal and plant life cycles.

Observe changes in the chicken, butterfly, or frog cycle directly. Keep a daily Sketchbook Journal* of observations noting changes over time.

Create a butterfly garden, incubate eggs, or stock a polliwog aquarium. Observe, draw, and record daily changes in a Sketchbook Journal*.

Children's Butterfly Site
www.mesc.usgs.gov/resources/education/butterfly/bfly_intro.asp

Educational Science Co.
http://educationalscience.com

Kits at The Nature Store

The Water Cycle

WATER (TRUE BOOKS: NATURAL RESOURCES)

FROM STREAM TO OCEAN

DOWN COMES THE RAIN

WATER DANCE

THIS IS THE RAIN

A DROP OF WATER: A BOOK OF SCIENCE AND WONDER

Carry out experiments that show how the water cycle works.

NASA Observatorium
http://observe.arc.nasa.gov/nasa/earth/hydrocycle/hydro3.html

Water Science for Schools
http://ga.water.usgs.gov/edu/watercycle.html

Describe the steps in your experiments and what you found in your Sketchbook Journal*.

Weather Cycles

WEATHER WATCH! HOW WEATHER WORKS

WEATHER

STORMS

TORNADOES

THE MAGIC SCHOOL BUS INSIDE A HURRICANE

HURRICANE WATCH

"Eyewitness Video: Weather"

Hurricane Hunters
www.hurricanehunters.com

Weather Wiz Kids
www.weatherwizkids.com

Compare the steps in the water cycle to storm cycles. Present your findings in a PowerPoint presentation.

NATURAL CYCLES

Destruction and Renewal

VOLCANO: THE ERUPTION AND HEALING OF MT. ST. HELENS

YELLOWSTONE FIRES: FLAMES AND REBIRTH

SUMMER OF FIRE: YELLOWSTONE 1988

Wildland Fires in Yellowstone
www.nps.gov/yell/technical/fire

Diagram the cycle of rebirth after these two disasters—volcano eruption and wildfires—showing the emergence of new life forms.

National Forest Service
www.smokeybear.com/only_you.asp

What are good and bad forest fires? Develop a TV talk show about the pros and cons of wildfires and controlled fires.

What destructive natural forces threaten your community? What steps can your class take to ensure that your own community is safe from wildfires or other natural disasters?

Go and Come Back

INTERRUPTED JOURNEY: SAVING ENDANGERED SEA TURTLES

INTO THE SEA

LIFE CYCLE OF A SEA TURTLE

THE SALMON

LIFE CYCLE OF A SALMON

COME BACK SALMON

Journey North Website
www.learner.org/jnorth/Migrations

How do sea turtle and salmon life cycles form a home/away/home pattern? Make a picture glossary of one of the animals and a map showing its life cycle journeys. Find out what problems the animal encounters in the modern world. Make a list of threats to the animal's future.

MUSICAL CYCLES

Watch the video version ON THE DAY YOU WERE BORN. Create your own musical composition to reflect your studies of the human life cycle.

What type of music is circular in nature?

Compile a CD of musical cycles.

Learn circle dances. Mark a map with places in the world where people enjoy circle dances.

Dance Companies on the Web
www.dancer.com/dance-links/other.htm#World

STORY CYCLES

THE FOUR CORNERS OF THE SKY: CREATION STORIES AND COSMOLOGIES FROM AROUND THE WORLD

How do people around the world understand the structure of the universe? Make a Comparison Chart* of motifs from these stories.

WHERE THE WILD THINGS ARE

PETER RABBIT

Make a Story Map showing the plot progression of these two picture books. Make a display of other picture books that follow a home/away/home pattern.

CIRCLE OF MAGIC Series

THE DREAM STEALER

THE SHERWOOD RING

ROWAN AND THE TRAVELERS

THE HOBBIT: OR THERE AND BACK AGAIN

THE THIEF LORD

How do cycles and circles figure in these books? Create a mural (with captions) showing the patterns you have found.

CYCLES

Create a cycle graffiti wall. Write and draw words, phrases, and images that you connect to the concept of cycles.

What would you do if you had a chance to live forever? Take the role of a young girl or boy, a mother or father, or a business man or woman and write an argument for or against the possibility. Role play your decisions.

TUCK EVERLASTING

Keep reactions to the book in a Sketchbook Journal*. Write down things you notice about Babbitt's use of language. Make predictions about the story.

Draw a pastel picture in response to the book's prologue.

Write a missing-child description of Winnie.

Draw a portrait of the man in the yellow suit.

After her conversations with Tuck and Jessie, write Winnie a letter advising her what to do.

Hold a mock trial for Tuck. Present evidence for and against his innocence.

Compare the book to the movie. Make a Venn Diagram* showing how they are alike and different. Write a critique of the strengths and weaknesses of both.

Election Cycles

The League of Women Voters
www.lwv.org

Congress for Kids
www.congressforkids.net

Find out about voting in your community and state. How often are elections held?

How many people in your community voted in the last election? Brainstorm ways to get more people to vote.

VOTE!

CANDIDATES, CAMPAIGNS, AND ELECTIONS

AMERICA VOTES

FRIENDLY FOES; A LOOK AT POLITICAL PARTIES

RUNNING FOR OFFICE: A LOOK AT POLITICAL CAMPAIGNS

Break into small groups to do the election related activities.

Birth

THE TROUBLE WITH BABIES

GROVER G. GRAHAM AND ME

ANASTASIA KRUPNIK

ALL ABOUT SAM

How do older siblings react to younger brothers or sisters in these books? Form new groups with classmates who have read each of the other books. Make Comparison Charts*.

What is your place in your own family hierarchy? Write a story about your family from a sibling's point of view. (Team up with a classmate if you are an only child.)

Death and Dying

LIFE TIMES

THE MOUNTAINS OF TIBET

BLACKBERRIES IN THE DARK

CASSIE BINEGAR

MISSING MAY

THE FRIENDS

SUN AND SPOON

What was the relationship of each of these characters to the person that died? What were the stages of grief they went through? Who or what helped them eventually accept the death of a loved one?

Read the obituary and memorial page in your local newspaper. Write an obituary for each of the characters who died.

CIVIC CYCLES

Recycling

WHERE DOES THE GARBAGE GO?

RECYCLE!

RE-CYCLES

TAKING CARE OF THE EARTH: KIDS IN ACTION

Interview students to see who recycles and what they recycle. Display findings on a graph.

Survey your community to see what type of recycling occurs. Is there something more you could be doing? Come up with an advertising campaign to convince community members of the importance of recycling.

DUCK FOR PRESIDENT

THE GRIZZLY GAZETTE

DORK ON THE RUN

GIRL REPORTER ROCKS POLLS

CROWN ME!

THE KID WHO BECAME PRESIDENT

How are elections portrayed in these books? Compare these fictional versions to how elections are held in your community.

HUMAN LIFE CYCLES

ON THE DAY YOU WERE BORN

How is the birth of a new baby celebrated in your family?

Find out about birth and birthday customs around the world at Teaching.com www.iecc.org

Birthday Traditions from Around the World www.kidsparties.com/traditions.htm

ISLAND BOY by B. Cooney

What are the life stages covered in the book? Choose one of the three topics, BIRTH, GROWING OLDER, DEATH and DYING, that follow to study and at least one of the books listed in each to read and discuss in a Literature Response Group*.

After you have studied these topics and books, find out about how births and deaths are celebrated in your community. Then conduct research on what people in other countries and cultures do. Make Semantic Maps* or Graphs* showing the results of your findings and describing what you find in words and pictures.

Growing Older

What do you know about the aging process? Write a description of what you think you'll be like when you are 70. Draw a picture of yourself at 70.

Make a list of words describing senior citizens. After you read the books below, see if you want to add anything to your list.

GRANNY THE PAG

THE HOUSE OF WINGS

THE EXILES

OLIVE'S OCEAN

GRANNY TORTELLI MAKES SOUP

A YEAR DOWN YONDER

CHILD OF THE OWL

THIEF OF HEARTS

THE COOK'S FAMILY

What special relationships do young characters have to older people in these books? Note the characteristics of the older people on a Comparison Chart*. Include things like physical descriptions, hobbies, occupations, and emotional support.

Is there an older person in your life? Write a description of that person and what your relationship means to you.

Are there older people in your community who could use your help or who could help you? Invite members of the older generation to become part of your classroom community. Adopt a retirement home and make regular visits. What can you learn from these older people?

Saying Goodbye

SAYING GOODBYE: A SPECIAL FAREWELL TO MAMA NKWELLE

CORPSES COFFINS AND CRYPTS: A HISTORY OF BURIAL

FUNERALS: RITES OF PASSAGE

LET'S TALK ABOUT GOING TO A FUNERAL

LIFE'S END

Visit a funeral home and find out how burials or cremations are arranged and carried out. Is your family willing to talk about plans for the end of life? If so, what plans are in place? If someone you know dies, what suggestions can you make for a ceremony or ritual that would be meaningful to you?

Visit a local cemetery and study the gravestones and memorials. Make a list of epitaphs. Calculate how many years each person lived and calculate average life span. Make a chart showing the number of children, women, and men who died in a given year and at what age they died. What conclusions could you draw about deaths in different eras?

strategies they would need to do well on the tests. He consulted the state science standards and found a number of standards that he could cover under the CYCLES umbrella, particularly in the life sciences and the physical sciences. He also felt the need to speak to 9- and 10-year-olds' burgeoning interests in the world around them and to the questions they have about themselves, their extended families, and their futures. CYCLES allowed him to give his students opportunities to explore the many books about the human life cycle and involve them in inquiries about a range of science topics. Because children had also been interested in the election process that had taken place the previous November, Steve decided to include the topic of voting cycles. When he told children that they would be studying CYCLES as a theme, his students immediately thought of "recycling" as a possible inquiry so he added that topic to his plan. Finally, Steve enlisted the physical education teacher to help plan a study of circle dances from around the world, and the children came up with the idea of collecting and learning rounds for a performance and concert to showcase their CYCLES studies. Jan Nord, the music teacher, gave Steve *The Round Book* to use as a resource, and a group of children volunteered to select rounds that they wanted to learn.

MacDonald & Jaeger (1999)

Because so much of the unit would involve children in science inquiries, Steve was determined to involve children in developing their research skills. He had been working with the children all year on gathering and processing data from secondary sources. Now he wanted to include firsthand observations and the Internet as sources of information. He decided to focus his teacher inquiry on the children's strategies for gaining information from websites and how this process was different from getting information from books or observations. He wanted to know what kind of criteria the children established and used and how they integrated this information with information from other sources. After the children had broken into groups and chosen a "Life Cycles in the Natural World" topic to study, Steve told the children that he hoped they would make extensive use of the Internet along with other sources. Steve then provided each group with a tape recorder and asked them to tape their small-group meetings as their studies progressed. He added these data to direct observations noted in his journal.

Into the Classroom

In preparation for the study Steve contacted parents with information about the scope of the theme. He wanted to make sure that families were comfortable with the topics of aging, death, and dying as well as with birth and wanted parents to be alerted to children's questions and interests. He was gratified at the support he received, including an offer from one of the children's uncles to bring the class to his funeral home. Steve then began the CYCLES theme by asking the children to brainstorm the topic of wheels on a large sheet of chart paper. After they had generated a variety of words and phrases, he took out Natalie Babbitt's *Tuck Everlasting* and read the prologue, asking children to listen for words, phrases, and images that they might want to add to the chart. He then turned the focus to the three characters that were introduced in the prologue—Ma Tuck, Winnie, and a stranger—and asked them to tell what they thought each character might be like. He then broke the children into three groups with each group taking the role of one of those characters. Steve then asked the children to write what they would do if they discovered a pool of water that would allow them to live forever. Steve then had volunteers from each group come up and role play a discussion about the pros and cons of living forever. The children were well able to consider the consequences of such an event and, thus, were introduced to the sensitive topics of birth, death, and dying that they would explore in subsequent weeks. As Steve read *Tuck Everlasting* aloud, they chose one "Human Life Cycle" topic to study in depth.

Babbit (1975)

Steve began his science inquiries with an exploration of mechanical cycles. He collected everyday machines, wires, gears, wheels, and other objects in a discovery box and gave children time and tools to take them apart. He asked them to speculate on how the idea of cycles carried over into the area of technology in their Sketchbook Journals*. This activity then led to numerous experiments with electricity, magnetism, and machines. As children gained insights into these concepts, they wanted to build an invention of their own. Steve suggested that they break into small groups to design and build a working robot or vehicle.

We enter the classroom on Day 16 of the CYCLES study. Children have finished with presentations of their hand-made machines and are preparing to begin their study of natural life cycles. They are also continuing their studies of "Human Life Cycle" topics and are looking forward (with a few misgivings) to a visit to a local funeral home. (See Table 4.10.)

table 4.10   Detailed Schedule, Steve Williams's Fourth-Grade Class

DAY 16

Time	Children	Teacher	Teacher Research
Teacher Arrival 8:00		Steve arrives and sets aside Plant, Animals, Water, and Weather cycle books that he will introduce to children later in the morning.	
Children Arrival 9:00	Children arrive and begin putting away lunches.	Steve greets the children.	
Group Meeting 9:10	Several children think of the water cycle they had studied the previous year.	He asks them to take out their Sketchbook Journals* and take some time to write and draw about what cycles they think of in the natural world around them.	
	One child draws a diagram to represent electricity. Their study of *Tuck Everlasting* probably influences several to mention the solar system and the cycle of seasons.	Steve discusses their ideas with them. Steve introduces children to the four natural life cycles topics they will study by showing children some of the books he has collected.	
	Most children know that they can find information on the World Wide Web.	Then he asks them if there are any other places they might find information about the topics.	Steve has his notebook open to jot down children's understandings about research resources.
Integrated Work Time 9:30	Two groups of children work on Comparison Charts* tied to their human life cycles books.	Steve circulates among the groups. Steve asks the children to spend some of their work time looking through the books he has selected for their inquires. He wants them to decide on the topics they want to work on by the following day.	
	A third group is making Comparison Charts* of funeral and burial customs in places around the world.		
Cleanup 10:55			
Recess 11:00			
Specials 11:15	Children go to the library.	The media specialist introduces the children to the use of the Kids Click search engine at www.kidsclick.org.	Steve takes notes throughout the lesson.
	Many already know about search engines such as Google.	Steve suggests that they take turns using library computers to see	

(continued)

table **4.10**   Detailed Schedule, Steve Williams's Fourth-Grade Class *(continued)*

DAY 16 *(continued)*

Time	Children	Teacher	Teacher Research
Specials *(continued)*		what resources might be available for each of the topics in their inquiries.	He will be observing children who are working at computers.
Literature 11:45	The children are enjoying the book and several relate the character of the grandmother to an older person they know.	Steve continues reading *The Exiles,* a book about a summer four English girls must spend with their eccentric grandmother.	
Lunch 12:15			
SSR* 12:45	Children read materials of their choice. Several are reading one of the natural life cycles books.	Steve conferences with individual children.	
Math 1:15	Pairs of children take turns trying the simulation while others work on worksheets Steve has printed off the Internet.	Steve introduces children to the idea of organizing information through a simulation called Dream Car Math. He hopes the concepts learned here will carry over into their inquiries.	
Integrated Work Time 2:00	Children continue work from that morning.	Steve conferences with individual children.	
Cleanup 2:45			
Reading Aloud* 2:50	Children listen quietly or sketch or write in their Sketchbook Journals*.	Steve reads from *Rowan and the Travelers,* a book he has chosen as part of a study on literary cycles.	
Dismissal 3:15			

DAY 20

Time	Children	Teacher	Teacher Research
Group Meeting 9:10		Steve gathers the children together and hands out Post-it notes. He asks children to write down their first and second choices for their inquiry topics.	
Integrated Work Time 9:30	Children work on finishing Comparison Charts*.	Steve works on sorting the children into inquiry groups.	
Cleanup 10:55			
Recess 11:00			
Specials 11:15	The children are fascinated by the idea of setting a picture book to music, especially noting the unusual instruments like seashells.	The music teacher shows children a video called *On the Day You Were Born,* the story of the Minneapolis Symphony's collaboration with author Debra Fraser.	
Literature 11:45	The "Growing Older" group presents their Comparison Chart* to the rest of the class.	Steve leads the group in comments and discussion.	

table **4.10**   Detailed Schedule, Steve Williams's Fourth-Grade Class *(continued)*

DAY 20 *(continued)*

Time	Children	Teacher	Teacher Research
Lunch 12:15			
SSR* 12:45			
Math 1:15	Children continue working on date organization.	Steve moves around the room to monitor individual understanding.	
Integrated Work Time 2:00	Children seem to understand that if they are doing research and writing about real things, they have to make sure their facts are right.	Steve announces the members of each inquiry group. He asks them to think of how the reports of their inquiries will be different from other types of presentations. He then asks children to get into their groups with the books he has collected. He asks them to spend the rest of the time browsing through the books and then to develop a list of criteria for books they use for research.	He makes notes about their understanding of fiction and nonfiction genres.
Cleanup 2:45			
Reading Aloud* 2:50		Steve reads from *Rowan and the Travelers*.	
Dismissal 3:15			

DAY 23

Time	Children	Teacher	Teacher Research
Group Meeting 9:10	Each group chooses a leader to report on their inquiries.	Steve asks for progress reports and fills in a large Status of the Class* chart.	
Integrated Work Time 9:30	Children break into their groups and then into pairs to work on individual contributions to their inquiry reports. Some are creating flow charts or diagrams to illustrate the cycle that they are studying. Others are writing descriptive labels for the charts. One group is working on a three-dimensional model of a hurricane.	Steve moves around the class monitoring progress. He then calls individual children up for a reading conference.	
Specials 11:15	Children use their computer lab time to continue the research for their inquiries.		Steve moves from station to station talking with children and taking notes.
Literature 11:45		Steve reads from *Come Back Salmon*, the story of how a class of fifth graders launched a river cleanup and how salmon subsequently returned to spawn.	
	Children are intrigued by the outcome achieved by these students. They suggest that there might be something in their own area that they could get involved with.	Steve suggests that this would be a great way to end their CYCLES study.	

Summary

The careful planning that went into the CYCLES unit gave children new opportunities for inquiry and a deepening understanding of the use of multiple data sources. The topic also helped to deepen their understanding of important ideas as they focused on such *essential questions* as: How do cycles and circular patterns affect us as human beings and how we live our lives? How do cycles occur in our social and political lives? What life cycles exist in the world of nature and how do these cycles affect the way we live? What do cycles mean in the world of machines and technology? What questions do all these areas raise for our future?

Steve was pleased at the progress children made in developing criteria for looking at different sources of information. He was also pleased at the maturity with which the children dealt with the sensitive topics of aging and dying. His teacher research project, Steve felt, provided insights into the learning processes of fourth graders. His documentation allowed him to pinpoint areas that required further instruction and to present these positive outcomes to parents and other professionals. Steve was also confident that the sustained reading practice that the children experienced with a variety of text structures as well as the critical thinking they engaged in would, with some direct coaching on test-taking techniques, help them to do well on the upcoming proficiency tests.

Children's Literature: CYCLES

All about Sam by L. Lowry. Houghton Mifflin, 1988.

America Votes by L. Granfield. Illustrated by S. Bjorkman. Kids Can, 2003.

Anastasia Krupnik by L. Lowry. Houghton Mifflin, 1979.

Blackberries in the Dark by M. Jukes. Knopf, 1985.

The Butterfly Life Cycles series by S. Crewe. Steck-Vaughn, 1998.

Candidates, Campaigns, and Elections by L. Scher & M. O. Johnson. Scholastic, 2004.

Cassie Binegar by P. MacLachlan. HarperCollins, 1982.

Chicks and Chickens by G. Gibbons. Holiday, 2003.

Child of the Owl by L. Yep. HarperCollins, 1977.

Circle of Magic series by T. Pierce. Scholastic (multiple titles).

Come Back Salmon by M. Cone. Sierra Club, 1992.

The Cook's Family by L. Yep. Putnam, 1998.

Corpses, Coffins, and Crypts: A History of Burial by P. Colman. Holt, 1997.

Crown Me! by K. Lay. Holiday House, 2004.

Dork on the Run by C. Corman. HarperCollins, 2003.

Down Comes the Rain by F. M. Branley. Illustrated by J. G. Hale. HarperCollins, 1997.

The Dream Stealer by G. Maguire. Clarion, 2002.

A Drop of Water: A Book of Science and Wonder by W. Wick. Scholastic, 1997.

Duck for President by D. Cronin. Illustrated by B. Lewin. Simon & Schuster, 2004.

Egg to Bird (*Cycles of Life* series) by C. Scrace. Watts, 2002.

Electricity and Magnetism by P. Adamczyk. Usborne, 1994.

Electronics Lab by B. Bach. Silver Dolphin, 2001.

The Exiles by H. McKay. Simon & Schuster, 1992.

"Eyewitness Video: Amphibian" (VHS). DK, 1995.

"Eyewitness Video: Weather" (VHS). DK, 1996.

Follow the Water from Brook to Ocean by A. Dorros. HarperCollins, 1991.

The Four Corners of The Sky: Creation Stories and Cosmologies from around the World by S. Zeitlin. Illustrated by C. Raschka. Holt, 2000.

Friendly Foes; A Look at Political Parties by K. M. Kowalski. Lerner, 2004.

The Friends by K. Yumoto. Dell, 1998.

Frog by B. Watts. Creative, 2003.

From Flower to Fruit by A. O. T. Dowden. HarperCollins, 1984.

From Seed to Plant by G. Gibbons. Holiday, 1991.

Funerals: Rites of Passage by M. Ross. Heinemann, 2003.

Gear Up: Marvelous Machine Projects by K. Good. Lerner, 2003.

Girl Reporter Rocks Polls by L. Ellerbee. Avon, 2001.

Granny the Pag by N. Bawden. Clarion, 1996.

Granny Tortelli Makes Soup by S. Creech. HarperCollins, 2003.

The Grizzly Gazette by S. Murphy. HarperCollins, 2003.

Grover G., Graham, and Me by M. Quattlebaum. Delacorte, 2001.

Henry's First Moon Birthday by L. Look. Atheneum, 2001.

The Hobbit: Or There and Back Again by J. R. R. Tolkien. Houghton Mifflin, 1966.

The House of Wings by B. Byars. Viking, 1972.

How Do You Lift a Lion? by R. E. Wells. Albert Whitman, 1996.

Hurricane Watch by F. Branley. HarperCollins, 1985.

Incredible Life Cycles by T. Knight. Heinemann, 2003.

Interrupted Journey: Saving Endangered Sea Turtles by K. Lasky. Photographs by C. Knight. Candlewick, 2001.

Into the Sea by B. Guiberson. Holt, 1996.

Island Boy by B. Cooney. Turtleback, 1991.

The Kid Who Became President by D. Gutman. Scholastic, 1999.

Let's Talk about Going to a Funeral by M. Johnson. Powerkids Press, 2003.

Levers, Wheels and Pulleys by J. Farndon. Benchmark, 2002.

The Life and Times of the Apple by C. Micucci. Orchard, 1992.

The Life and Times of the Peanut by C. Micucci. Houghton Mifflin, 2000.

Life Cycle of a Salmon by A. Royston. Heinemann, 2000.

Life Cycle of a Sea Turtle by B. Kalman. Turtleback, 2002.

Life's End by D. Chapman. Raintree/Steck-Vaughn, 2001.

Life Times by B. Mellonie & R. Ingpen. Bantam, 1983.

Machines by C. Gifford. Kingfisher, 2000.

Machines: Mind-Boggling Experiments You Can Turn into Science Fair Projects by J. VanCleave. John Wiley, 1993.

The Magic School Bus and the Electric Field Trip by J. Cole. Illustrated by B. Degen. Scholastic, 1997.

The Magic School Bus Inside a Hurricane by J. Cole. Illustrated by B. Degen. Scholastic, 1996.

Missing May by C. Rylant. Orchard, 1992.

The Mountains of Tibet by M. Gerstein. HarperCollins, 1997.

The New Way Things Work by D. Macaulay. Houghton Mifflin, 1998.

Olive's Ocean by K. Henkes. Greenwillow, 2003.

On the Day You Were Born by D. Fraser. Harcourt, 1991.

Power Up: Experiments, Puzzles, and Games Exploring Electricity by S. Markle. Atheneum, 1989.

Recycle! A Handbook for Kids by G. Gibbons. Little Brown, 1992.

Re-Cycles by M. E. Ross. Millbrook, 2002.

Robots Rising by C. Sonenklar. Holt, 1999.

The Round Book by M. MacDonald & W. Jaeger. Linnet, 1999.

Rowan and the Travelers by E. Rodda. Greenwillow, 2001.

Running for Office: A Look at Political Campaigns by E. Landaus. Lerner, 2004.

A Salamander's Life by J. Himmelman. Scholastic, 1998.

The Salmon by S. Crewe. Sagebrush, 1979.

Saying Goodbye: A Special Farewell to Mama Nkwelle by I. Onyefulu. Millbrook, 2001.

The Sherwood Ring by E. M. Pope. Houghton Mifflin, 2001.

Sky Tree by T. Locker. HarperCollins, 1995.

Storms by M. Maslin. Raintree, 2000.

Summer of Fire: Yellowstone 1988 by P. Lauber. Orchard, 1991.

Sun and Spoon by K. Henkes. Greenwillow, 1997.

Switch On Switch Off by M. Berger. HarperCollins, 2001.

Taking Care of the Earth: Kids in Action by L. Pringle. Boyds, 1996.

The Thief Lord by C. Funke. Scholastic, 2002.

Thief of Hearts by L. Yep. HarperCollins, 1995.

This Is the Rain by l. M. Schaffer. Illustrated by J. Wattenberg. Greenwillow, 2001.

Tornadoes by S. Simon. HarperCollins, 2002.

The Trouble with Babies by M. Freeman. Holiday, 2002.

Tuck Everlasting by N. Babbitt. Farrar, Straus, & Giroux, 1975.

Volcano: The Eruption and Healing of Mt. St. Helens by P. Lauber. Simon & Schuster, 1996.

Vote! by E. Christelow. Clarion, 2004.

Water (True Books: Natural Resources) by C. Ditchfield. Children's Press, 2003.

Water Dance by T. Locker. Harcourt Brace, 1997.

Weather by S. Simon. HarperCollins, 1993.

Weather Watch! How Weather Works by R. Rupp. Story Kids, 2004.

Wheels and Cranks by D. Glover. Rigby Interactive Library, 1997.

Wheels at Work: Building and Experimenting with Machines by B. Zubrowski. Morrow, 1986.

Where Does the Garbage Go? by P. Showers. HarperCollins, 1993.

A Year Down Yonder by R. Peck. Dial, 2000.

Yellowstone Fires: Flames and Rebirth by D. H. Patent. Photographs by W. Munoz. Holiday House, 1990.

Zap It! Exciting Electricity Activities by K. Bood. Lerner, 2003.

Prototype 6: Fifth Grade— EXPLORING OUR ROOTS

Schedule

Karen Beeman teaches fifth grade in a bilingual program in a predominantly Mexican/Mexican American urban midwestern school. All the students speak Spanish at home, but their level of English proficiency varies. Identity is one of the most important issues Karen's students must deal with in her classroom and in the larger community. Being a Latino in an urban area is very complex, with success or failure dependent on such variables as socioeconomic status, the family's motivation for migrating, place of origin, length of time in the United States, and treatment by mainstream Americans. Some of Karen's students identify themselves as "American" because they have witnessed the discrimination, embarrassments, and difficulties their parents have endured for being "Mexican." They try not to identify with many aspects of Mexican culture. Often they lose touch with their home language and culture and as adolescents have

"Identity" can be complex for ESL students.

difficulties dealing with identity issues. Karen wanted to incorporate a positive stance toward Latin America in the classroom, identifying and studying what is not often publicly spoken about (language differences, culture shock, identity crisis, and discrimination) so that students would be more energized to learn and would grow both personally and academically. She had also noted that her students learned a great deal more when content was linked to their personal issues and concerns.

Karen weighed many variables in designing her thematic unit, most important of which were the students' cultural identity and language. The theme EXPLORING OUR ROOTS was first conceived as a way of incorporating all these issues into the classroom and linking students' personal experiences to academic subject areas. The unit covers some of the fifth-grade curriculum objectives in Karen's district but goes further by merging aspects of Mexican and American cultures. Karen feels particularly strongly about this issue. She was born to American parents in Mexico and attended bilingual schools through high school, so she had struggled with some of the same issues her students faced. Because of her concerns about identity issues, Karen's teacher research focused on students' reactions to studying identity issues. She plans to observe any changes in students' attitudes, particularly on the student-created segregation between "brazers" (a word coined in the community, based on the Spanish *braceros* and connoting something akin to "wetback"), more Americanized Mexican Americans, and the "mainstream" English-speaking fifth graders who also attend the school. To see if the quantity and quality of reading and writing increased as a result of studying identity issues, Karen plans to keep a journal of observations to focus on activities where students naturally tend to group themselves heterogeneously, mixing recent immigrants with those who had been in the United States longer. She also plans to document the relationship between classroom activities and discussion and students' efforts to work on community issues. Finally, Karen hopes to share her observations with parents and colleagues in hopes that her work would be the beginning of a school-wide plan. (See Table 4.11.)

Into the Classroom

Because the theme EXPLORING OUR ROOTS deals with issues of conquest, encounter, and the blending of cultures, Karen has begun it right after Columbus Day.

table **4.11**   Weekly Schedule, Karen Beeman's Fifth-Grade Bilingual Class

Time	Monday	Tuesday	Wednesday	Thursday	Friday
9:00	Student/teacher duties (attendance, lunch tickets)				
9:10	Integrated work time. Reading, writing, and social studies.				
10:35	Art	Music	Gym	Integrated work time	Library
11:30	Crafts/Art reflective of EXPLORING OUR ROOTS				
12:00	Reading Aloud*				
12:20	Lunch				
12:50	SSR*				
1:25	Integrated work time. Math, science, and art.				
2:30	Dismissal				

The unit begins with a glimpse into the roots of Mexican culture. Though there are many areas of Mexican culture that could begin the theme, Karen concentrates on the Aztecs, who survived by creating a novel irrigation and anti-erosion form of agriculture by making islands (or *chinampas*) in the Lag Texcoco with mud from the lake bottom. This symbol of creating roots in the chinampas appealed to Karen and so the theme begins with a simulation of the chinampas. Students then delve into various aspects of culture, family, art, history, and agriculture. The primary focus is on family roots and elements that form culture throughout time. Social studies and reading/writing are integrated easily in the activities about family, cuisine, and identity. Math and science are also integrated through activities that enable students to analyze the Mayan place-value system and then study their own community to highlight its strengths and improve its weaknesses. Parents and the community are essential participants in this thematic unit. Students rely on them for data and help in planning for the future. Many activities bring in parents and community members to share their expertise and visions.

The unit is planned for three months of study. Throughout the unit, most morning integrated work time begins with a structured activity or discussion planned by Karen. Frequently, the activity is a Focus Lesson*. The Focus Lessons* include such things as examining writing or comparing trade book and textbook versions of the same events. Other times Karen uses class meetings to review information or highlight exciting things that happen in the classroom. Class meetings also provide a forum for student-led demonstrations of work in progress or for hearing a guest speaker. A variety of group work takes place. Some projects are student initiated and lead to small group work; other projects involve small groups in contributing a part of a larger project (i.e., writing the bilingual cookbook). Throughout the day, students work in integrated activities. Mornings, however, usually focus on reading, writing, and social studies and afternoons on science and math. Students also analyze their surroundings and plan activities that move them into the community as active participants in its betterment. Finally, the unit culminates in a celebration of both American and Mexican cultures. Food from the cookbook is shared, a play presented, and other projects exhibited.

Karen must carefully choreograph the use of language in this unit. The bilingual program in which she works is a transitional, late-exit program. Students are heterogeneously mixed according to their English proficiency. Some are about to be moved into programs in which all instruction is in English. Others have just arrived from Mexico with no English. They receive instruction in Spanish in major content areas; their more English-fluent peers also benefit from ongoing instruction in Spanish. As a result, major explanations and discussions are conducted by Karen in Spanish, especially at the beginning of the year. Reading in both languages is done daily, both aloud by the teacher and individually or in small groups. Because Karen feels that it is unreasonable to expect students to speak one language specified by the teacher when all people in the classroom are bilingual, an explanation may be given in Spanish but students may respond in either language. Many group activities are also carried out utilizing both languages. However, Karen must also monitor students' English language proficiency, so she carefully orchestrates some activities so that they are carried out in each language. For example, when working on writing with the students, Karen finds that two variables influence the choice of language for writing: (1) the language of the materials used as references and (2) the language preference of the audience. If writing on family issues, such as the interviews in this unit, the writing tends to be in Spanish; when the audience is the English-speaking classroom to whom students present their projects, students write in English regardless of their English proficiency. (See Table 4.12.)

Class meetings can be important forums for sharing.

Prototype 6: Fifth Grade—EXPLORING OUR ROOTS

Identity Roots

CHILDREN AND THE YUCATAN
MY MEXICO/MÉXICO MÍO
PASSPORT TO MEXICO
THE STORIES JULIAN TELLS
BLESS ME, ÚLTIMA
TALES OF FAR NORTH
THE HOUSE ON MANGO STREET
. . . AND NOW MIGUEL
HELLO, AMIGOS!
MEXICAN PROFILES: BILINGUAL BIOGRAPHIES FOR TODAY
CESAR CHÁVEZ
BARRIO GHOSTS
HARVESTING HOPE. THE STORY OF CEASAR CHAVEZ
IN THE DAYS OF THE VAQUEROS; AMERICAS FIRST COWBOYS
THE POT THAT JUAN BUILT
VOICES FROM THE FIELD: CHILDREN OF MIGRANT WORKERS
    TELL THEIR STORIES
MY NAME IS JORGE: ON BOTH SIDES OF THE RIVER

Write your autobiography.
Interview a person you respect and write a short biography.
Write about your experiences. How are they alike or different from
    those of children in Mexico or other parts of the United States?
Invite a person you admire from the community to speak to the class.
Write about what you would like to be doing in 10 years.

Me and My Family

THE HUNDRED PENNY BOX
GATHERING THE SUN
IN MY FAMILY/EN MI FAMILIA
MAMA'S BIRTHDAY SURPRISE
LOCAL NEWS
THE WALLS OF PEDRO GARCIA
BLUE WILLOW
IMMIGRANT KIDS
EL LIRÓN SIN NOMBRE
FAMILY PICTURES
LA HISTORIA DE ERNESTO
AL OTRO LADO DE LA PUERTA
RAMONA AND HER FATHER
ANNIE AND THE OLD ONE
LOVE TO MAMÁ: A TRIBUTE TO
    MOTHERS
IF THE SHOE FITS
I SPEAK ENGLISH FOR MY MOM
THE COMPOSITION
FIRST DAY IN GRAPES

Trace your family's migration to the United
    States and/or around the United States on a
    map. Chart their migration on a time line.
Interview relations about life in Mexico
    compared with that in the United States.
Write about your home town using maps and
    historical references.

Celebration Roots

ARROZ CON LECHE
FIESTA! CINCO DE MAYO
TOO MANY TAMALES
THE SPIRIT OF TIO FERNANDO
PIÑATA MAKER
FIESTA USA
LA BODA
PABLO REMEMBERS
CALAVERA ABECEDERIO
CLATTER BASH: A DAY OF THE
    DEAD CELEBRATION
FELIPA AND THE DAY OF THE
    DEAD
FIESTA FIREWORKS
BIG BUSHY MOUSTACHE

Research Mexican *posadas*
    (celebrations); write an explanation
    and present one to the school.
Make a year-long calendar, marking
    celebrations in both Mexico and
    the United States. How does each
    reflect the culture of its country of
    origin?
Prepare a show reflecting games and
    oral traditions of both cultures.

EXPLORING OUR ROOTS

Literary Roots

CANTO FAMILIAR
NEIGHBORHOOD ODES
VERSITLAN
THE DAY IT SNOWED TORTILLAS
ANTONIO MACHADO Y LOS NIÑOS
JUAN RAMÓN JIMÉNEZ Y LOS NIÑOS
CUENTOS JUVENILES DE AMÉRICA
CINDERELLA
RED RIDING HOOD
THREE LITTLE PIGS
LA VOZ DE COATL
LA MONTAÑA DEL ALIMENTO
FOLK TALES: FOUR PLAYS FOR THE CLASSROOM
TORTILLAS PARA MAMÁ AND OTHER NURSERY RHYMES
I AM PHOENIX: POEMS FOR TWO VOICES
EL LIBRO DE LAS ADIVINANZAS
THE WOMAN WHO OUTSHONE THE SUN/LA MUJER
    QUE BRILLABA AUN MÁS QUE EL SOL
THE WITCH'S FACE
THIS TREE IS OLDER THAN YOU ARE
SOL A SOL: BILINGUAL POEMS
ANGELS RIDE BIKES AND OTHER FALL POEMS/
    LOS ANGELES ANDAN EN BIBCICLETA Y OTROS POEMAS
    DE OTONO
CALLING THE DOVES/EL CANTO LOS PALOMAS
IGUANAS IN THE SNOW/IGUANAS EN LA NIEVE
A MOVIE IN MY PILLOW/UNA PELÍCULA EN MI ALMOHADA
THE UPSIDE DOWN BOY/EL NINO DE CABEZA
THIS TREE IS OLDER THAN YOU ARE

WÁCHAELE!
HORSES HOOVES AND CHICKEN FEET: MEXICAN FOLK TALES
THE LITTLE GOLD STAR: A SPANISH AMERICAN CINDERELLA
JABUTI: A TRICKSTER TALE FROM MEXICO
JUAN BOBO GOES TO WORK
THE STORY OF COLORS/LA HISTORIA DE LOS COLORES
LAUGHING OUT LOUD, I FLY/A CARCAJADAS YO VUELO

Make a play of a favorite tale and present it.
Compare and contrast origins of folktales—use maps and
    historical references.
Write a poem or tale reflective of your culture.
Identify the main components or a folktale and write a
    retelling or present an oral Storytelling* version.

Establishing Roots for the Future

THIS HOME WE HAVE MADE/ESTA CASA QUE HEMOS HECHO

Create a plan to actively work on issues in the community that are
    important to you. Negotiate how to implement your plan. Enlist
    school, community, and parental support.
Suggestions:
    Conduct a survey of fourth–sixth graders about their community
        concerns. Write up results for the class paper.
    Conduct a survey of classroom parents and see what their major
        concerns are. Are they similar to yours? How can you work together?
    Invite area leaders to speak about your concerns. Try to enlist their help.
    Begin a letter-writing campaign to city officials to urge them to act on
        your concerns.

Culinary Roots

TORTILLA FOR EMILIA
NEW JUNIOR COOKBOOK
210 RECETAS DE COCINA INTERNACIONAL
VOY A COCINAR
COCINA NAVIDEÑA MEXICANA
COOKING THE MEXICAN WAY
THE TORTILLA BOOK
EVERYBODY COOKS RICE
ESPECIALIDADES DE LA COCINA MEXICANA
THE TORTILLA FACTORY

Write a (bilingual) class cookbook to sell.
Mark a day to celebrate cooking traditions. Invite
　　special people.
Analyze why and how the cuisines of the United
　　States and Mexico are different.

Indigenous Roots

CORN IS MAIZE
THE FLAME OF PEACE: A TALE OF THE AZTECS
AZTEC INDIANS
LA MÚSICA DE LA CHIRÍMIA
BUFFALO DANCE: A BLACKFOOT LEGEND
POPOL VUH
DE TIGRES Y TLACUACHES: LEYENDAS ANIMALES
LA CIVILIZACIÓN MAYA
EL MAÍZ TIENE COLOR DE ORO
THE MONKEY'S HAIRCUT, AND OTHER STORIES TOLD BY THE MAYA
MITOS Y LEYENDAS
MONTEZUMA AND THE AZTECS
LEYENDAS MEXICANAS
MAYA
THE ANCIENT MAYA
THE WITCH'S FACE
PEOPLE OF CORN
RABBIT IN THE MOON　www.halfmoon.org
DAILY LIFE IN ANCIENT AND MODERN MEXICO CITY

Build a model of an indigenous living area.
Study the calendars of the Mayans and Aztecs and analyze them
　　mathematically.
Make a time line of events affecting indigenous people. Begin with pre-
　　Columbian time. Chart changes on tables and graphs.
Write and illustrate your own version of the Aztec tale of settlement in the
　　valley of Mexico.
Compare Mexican indigenous myths and legends and Native American
　　myths and legends. Use a Graphic Organizer*.
Invite a Native American and/or indigenous Mexican to class to discuss his
　　or her heritage.

My Family Roots

GOING HOME
ME AND MY FAMILY TREE
THE GREAT ANCESTOR HUNT
WHERE DID YOU GET THOSE EYES? A GUIDE TO
　　DISCOVERING YOUR FAMILY HISTORY
GROWING OLDER
EL ABUELO TOMÁS
AMÉRICA IS HER NAME
BEFORE WE WERE FREE
COLIBRI
THE CIRCUIT
THE COLOR OF MY WORDS
CUBA 15
DAUGHTER OF THE MADRUGADA
ESPERANZA RISING
FLIGHT TO FREEDOM
HOW TÍA LOLA CAME TO VISIT/STAY
XOCHITL AND THE FLOWERS/ XOCHTL, LA NIÑA DEL LAS FLORES

Make a Comparison Chart* of these books. What types of circumstances led to the
　　characters' journeys? Note countries of origin on a map. Document the oral
　　history of someone in your family or community who took a similar journey
　　to America.

Make a family tree and photo gallery across as many
　　generations as possible, either for yourself or for
　　someone in your community.
Document the oral history of an older person in your
　　family or community.

Life Support Roots

PRIETTA AND THE GHOST WOMAN
JOURNEY OF THE NIGHTLY JAGUAR
QUETZAL: SACRED BIRD OF THE CLOUD FOREST
POPPY SEEDS
BEING A PLANT
PLANT EXPERIMENTS
WATER PLANTS
PLANTS
A FIRST LOOK AT THE WORLD OF PLANTS
COLOR DE TIERRA
COME SPRING
EXPERIMENTOS ATMOSFÉRICOS
AIR
NATURE'S WEATHER FORECASTERS
OBSERVANDO EL CLIMA
STORMS
WATER (WEBB)
WATER (BUNSTON)
WATER FOR THE WORLD
WHAT MAKES IT RAIN?
WEATHER EXPERIMENTS
FLASH, CRASH, RUMBLE AND ROLL
IT'S RAINING CATS AND DOGS: ALL KINDS OF WEATHER
　　AND WHY WE HAVE IT
LAS CHINAMPAS: UNA TÉCNICA AGRICOLA MUY
　　PRODUCTIVA
GATHERING THE SUN: AN ALPHABET IN SPANISH AND ENGLISH

Write a booklet describing the chinampas for class visitors.
Investigate why certain herbs and plants are grown in Mexico
　　and not the United States.
Classify plants. Develop a plant key for identification purposes.
Conduct experiments on different rooting systems of plants.

Artistic Roots

DIEGO
FRIDA KAHLO
JOSEPHINA
FOLK TOYS AROUND THE WORLD AND HOW TO MAKE THEM
WHEN CLAY SINGS
THE FLAME OF PEACE: A TALE OF THE AZTECS
FRIDA

Make a craft reflecting either U.S. or Mexican culture.
Compile a collection of favorite Mexican and U.S. crafts. Write a manual
　　explaining how to make them and how they reflect their culture.
Study traditional and modern artists in the United States and Mexico.
　　Experiment with their styles in your own art.

Neighborhood Roots

ANY SMALL GOODNESS; A NOVEL OF THE BARRIO
BARRIO: JOSÉ'S NEIGHBORHOOD
PETTY CRIMES

Make a map of your own neighborhood. On a legend, list places that are
　　unique to the neighborhood. Using one of these books as a model make
　　a picture book about your neighborhood.

table **4.12**   **Detailed Schedule, Karen Beeman's Fifth-Grade Bilingual Class**

DAY 1

Time	Children	Teacher	Teacher Research
Student/ Teacher Duties 9:00	Children take care of assigned duties. Attendance, lunch count taken, library books returned, and homework collected.	Prior to students' arrival, Karen posted an "EXPLORING OUR ROOTS" web on the wall. The WEB presented a compilation of suggestions children had made, along with some of Karen's ideas.	
	Children add activities to the WEB and negotiate ideas with peers. Ricky adds "Research recycling centers and set one up in the classroom," and Catherine suggests writing and illustrating an Aztec legend.	As children enter the room, Karen supervises assignments and responds to students who have written to her on the Message Board*.	
Integrated Work Time 9:10		Karen gathers the children around her. She places a large plastic sweater box, potting soil, rock, and stones the students have brought in, pitted chiles and epazote (an herb from Mexico), and beans.	
	Children share what they learned in interviewing their parents about the chinampas in Mexico City. They jot down notes of the creation of the chinampas.	She begins by asking the children what they learned in interviewing their parents. Karen records questions for small-group discussion and investigation.	Karen makes mental notes of students' comments and plans to use some of what they say in the sections of the theme on family and cultural knowledge.
	The volunteers work with Karen to create several model chinampas, using class discussion to guide their work.	The sharing and discussion are led in Spanish by Karen, though some students interject English, too. Karen and student volunteers begin to create a model of the chinampas.	
	Students move into small groups, select roles, decide on resources and begin working on the following: • Why the chinampas were important to the Aztecs. • Where the idea for the chinampas came from. • The destruction of the chinampas. • Why it might be important to study ancient people such as the Aztecs. • What the Spaniards thought of the chinampas and the Aztecs. Any group that finishes early goes to their EXPLORING OUR ROOTS Sketchbook Journals* and writes reactions to the morning activities. Each group reports to the whole class on their investigation and discussion.	Karen organizes cooperative learning groups, models with a group the roles students will use, and introduces the questions students will investigate. Questions are introduced in Spanish, but students may speak in the language most comfortable to them as long as everyone understands, including those with the least English.	Karen keeps notes on which students have decided to work together, and moves between groups, listening to discussions and focusing on students' perceptions of and possible identification with the Aztecs.

table **4.12**   Detailed Schedule, Karen Beeman's Fifth-Grade Bilingual Class *(continued)*

DAY 1 *(continued)*

Time	Children	Teacher	Teacher Research
Music 10:35	Students watch a video (in Spanish) on the Aztecs that explains Aztec culture: family, agriculture, religion, food, art, music, and dance.	Karen and the music teacher have planned this time to connect the music with the EXPLORING OUR ROOTS unit.	
	Students discuss the video:	Karen leads a brief discussion in Spanish after the video. She focuses on the relevance of the Aztecs to the lives of the students and tries to bring out their background knowledge on indigenous peoples of Mexico and Latin America.	Later, Karen reflects on the following questions:
	Ernesto: "Teacher, the movie says the Indians were smart, but I thought they were dumb. Why do people think they're dumb?"		• How much cultural knowledge do students have?
	Maribel: "Mi mamá me contó que los indios vivian muy saludable-mente y sabian curar todo. No tenian tanta violencia y enfermedad como nosotros." (My mother told me the Indians lived very healthy lives and knew how to heal many things. They didn't have as much illness and violence.)	Karen suggests that they add a time line of events affecting indigenous people to their WEB.	• How important is that knowledge to them?
		The music teacher says that the Aztecs also had a rich artistic tradition, including music and dance, then she introduces students to instruments that may have been used by Aztecs and versions that are still used today.	• How do students' different perceptions about their cultural identity come out in the discussions?
Crafts/Art 11:30	Students move to groups, following Karen's instructions. They discuss the possible uses of different artifacts and the meaning of the symbols. Some recognize forms from the video on the Aztecs.	As children return to class, Karen places a set of pictures and artifacts on the center of each group of tables. She asks students to study the material in each group and then decide what each item might be used for and figure out what the decorations on each item represent.	
Reading Aloud* 12:00	Students offer predictions, comments, and reactions to the book.	Karen reads *La Música de la Chirimia* to the class.	
SSR* 12:50	Students take ten minutes to look at the new books in the room and select one to read during SSR*. They then read and write to the teacher about their reading in their Sketchbook Journals*.	Karen explains that she would like the students to be reading about topics related to the EXPLORING OUR ROOTS theme during SSR* and has brought a number of books they might want to try.	Karen logs books being read by students and later reviews and responds to Sketchbook Journals*, keeping track of student comments related to her teacher research interests.
Integrated Work Time 1:25	Students join groups. In front of each group is a large piece of chart paper and pens. They participate in the discussion led by Karen and then work in smaller groups to discuss the following:	Karen asks students to group themselves. She then facilitates whole-group discussion on the neighboring community. She asks what they think the strengths and weaknesses of the community are.	
	• Five major strengths of the community.		
	• Five major weaknesses of the community.		
	• What the community should be like.		
	• Five ways we could improve the community.		

(continued)

table 4.12   Detailed Schedule, Karen Beeman's Fifth-Grade Bilingual Class *(continued)*

DAY 1 *(continued)*

Time	Children	Teacher	Teacher Research
Integrated Work Time *(continued)*	The resulting discussion is lively and generates many possibilities for community projects, including working with the priests to sit down with the gang members and stop the shooting, and cleaning up the garbage by the aqueduct.	Karen records suggestions, noting that no decision will be made today. This is a brainstorming session. Later, they can pick a project they really want to work on.	
Dismissal 2:30			

DAY 5

Time	Children	Teacher	Teacher Research
Student/ Teacher Duties 9:00	Children carry out morning duties.	Karen had previously noted that her students were not accustomed to reading and writing recipes. Though their parents had a wealth of culinary expertise, most did not use recipes. Karen decided to tap into the parents' knowledge and introduce the students to a new written genre. She has asked students to write a recipe that reflects a special meal from their family.	
Integrated Work Time 9:10	Children bring their recipes to the whole-group portion of integrated work time. As they gather around Karen, they find sets of measuring cups, measuring spoons, utensils, and mixing bowls. Students help Karen remember directions for the recipes. One of the students tells Karen that her mother learned to cook from her father's mother. The only time she uses a recipe is if the food is not Mexican and is all new to her.	Karen demonstrates a cooking recipe, highlighting the directions and quantities of measurement. She explains orally what she is doing, with no written recipe. She then asks students to talk her through the same recipe.	
	Students select one of the recipes from each group and use water to practice measuring out quantities. They try to write clear instructions for others to follow. They also estimate equivalencies and measure to confirm their estimates.	Karen reviews measurements with students, including some equivalencies (e.g., 2 cups = 1 pint). Karen asks students if they would like to make a bilingual cookbook and asks them to think about what might be involved in doing so (i.e., editing, illustrating, publishing, and distributing).	
	Each group rewrites their recipes in English and Spanish.		
	Small group reports on community issues are presented today on the results of the following: • Survey of other students in the school on community concerns	Karen monitors group reports, making sure that everyone who wants to gets a chance to participate.	Karen is very excited about this part of the theme. Parents have been interested, as have community leaders. A local priest has told students he will ask for support from

table **4.12**   Detailed Schedule, Karen Beeman's Fifth-Grade Bilingual Class *(continued)*

DAY 5 *(continued)*

Time	Children	Teacher	Teacher Research
Integrated Work Time *(continued)*	• Parent survey • Interview with two area leaders • Interview with leader of community center in area Students decide that they want to combine two projects, both their celebration of EXPLORING OUR ROOTS planned for the end of the unit and a thank-you for those who have helped in their community project.	Karen leads a discussion of the results of the group studies, asking where the students want to go from here. Karen agrees to student suggestion, and planning begins for this new venture.	the parish if students decide to pursue their plan for a community cleanup. The city council member for the area has volunteered equipment to help, too. Part of Karen's research interest was in whether this study would connect outside the school setting and this is exciting evidence that it has.

Summary

While Karen Beeman's classroom is officially bilingual, the issues she faces are not unfamiliar to many teachers in areas where more and more students acquire English as a second language. As with Dehea Munioz (Prototype 3), she is concerned about the cultural identities of her students and with the impact that entering a different culture has on their success in and out of school. Like Dehea, Karen also has cross-cultural experience and recognizes the points of dissonance for students. As the unit progressed, Karen found that focusing her *essential questions* on issues such as identity, migration, bilingualism, conquest, and subjugation—What are our major concerns about our community? How can we work together to make our community better?—seemed to make school relevant and appealing to her students. Children went out into the neighborhood; the neighborhood was invited into the school. Multiple audiences for children's written, oral, and artistic productions helped to break down some of the barriers between groups of children. Karen's documentation of her and the students' experience allowed her to argue for more schoolwide attention to issues of cultural identity. The students' public performances provided concrete evidence to parents and school personnel that students were both interested in and capable of handling these issues. Finally, Karen noted that her students became more adept at register switching (using the language appropriate to the situation), more comfortable in using both Spanish and English in their studies, and more likely to see bilingualism as a positive attribute.

Children's Literature: *EXPLORING OUR ROOTS*

Air by A. Webb. Franklin Watts, 1986.

Al Otro Lado De La Puerta by M. Medero. Editorial Novaro, 1982.

América Is Her Name by L. J. Rodriguez. Illustrated by C. Vasquez. Curbstone Press, 1998.

The Ancient Maya by I. F. Glum. Benchmark, 1996.

. . . and Now Miguel by J. Krumgold. Harper & Row, 1953.

Angels Ride Bikes and Other Fall Poems/Los ángeles andan en bicicleta y otros poemas de otoño by F. X. Alarcon. Illustrated by E. Salvidor. Atheneum, 2002.

Annie and the Old One by M. Miles. Illustrated by P. Parnell. Little, Brown, 1971.

Antonio Machado Y Los Niños by J. M. Garrido Lopera. Everest, 1983.

Any Small Goodness: A Novel of the Barrio by T. Johnston. Illustrated by R. Colon. Blue Sky, 2001.

Arroz Con Leche: Popular Songs and Rhymes From Latin America by L. Delacre. Scholastic, 1989.

Aztec Indians by P. McKissack. Children's Press, 1985.

Barrio Ghosts by E. Cervantes & A. Cervantes. New Readers Press, 1988.

Barrio: José's Neighborhood by G. Ancona. Harcourt, 1998.

Before We Were Free by J. Alvarez. Knopf, 2002.

Being a Plant by L. Pringle. Crowell, 1983.

Big Bushy Moustache by G. Soto. Illustrated by J. Cepeda. Knopf, 1998.

Bless Me, Ultima by R. A. Anaya. Tonatiuh International, 1972.

Blue Willow by D. Gates. Viking, 1948.

La Boda: A Mexican Wedding Celebration by N. Van Lann. Illustrated by A. Arroyo. Little, Brown, 1996.

Buffalo Dance: A Blackfoot Legend by N. Van Loan. Little, Brown, 1993.

Calavera Abecederio: A Day of the Dead Alphabet Book by J. Winter. Harcourt, 2004.

Calling the Doves/El Canto Los Palomas by J. F. Herrara. Illustrated by E. Simmons. Children's Book Press, 2001.

Canto Familiar by G. Soto. Illustrated by A. Nelson. Harcourt, 1995.

Cesar Chavez by R. Franchere. Illustrated by E. Thollander. Crowell, 1970.

Children of the Yucatán by F. Staub. Carolrhoda, 1996.

Las Chinampas: Una Técnica Agrícola Muy Productiva by J. Aguilar. Arbol Editorial, S. A. de C. V., 1982.

Cinderella, Or the Little Glass Slipper by C. Perrault. Illustrated by E. LeCain. Bradbury, 1973.

The Circuit: Stories from the Life of a Migrant Child by F. Jiménez. University of New Mexico Press, 1997.

La Civilizacion Maya by S. Gerson & S. Goldsmith. Trillas, 1988.

Clatter Bash: A Day of the Dead Celebration by R. Keep. Peachtree, 2004.

Cocina Navideña Mexicana by E. O. de Sanz. Editorial Continental, 1987.

Colibri by A. Cameron. Farrar, Straus, & Giroux, 2003.

Color De Tierra by I. Suarez de la Prida. Editorial Amaquemecan, S. A. de C. V., 1987.

The Color of My Words by L. Joseph. HarperCollins, 2000.

The Composition by A. Skarmeta. Illustrated by R. Alfonso. Groundwood, 2000.

Cooking the Mexican Way by R. Coronado. Lerner, 1982.

Corn Is Maize: The Gift of the Indians by Aliki. Crowell, 1976.

Cuba 15 by N. Osa. Delacorte, 2003.

Cuentos Juveniles De América by M. Vich Adell (Ed.). Gente Nueva, 1974.

Daily Life in Ancient and Modern Mexico City by S. Cory. Illustrated by R. Webb. Runestone, 1999.

Daughter of the Madrugada by F. Wood. Delacorte, 2002.

The Day It Snowed Tortillas by J. Hayes. Mariposa, 1986.

De Tigres Y Tlacuaches: Leyendas Animales by M. Kurtycz. Editorial Novaro, 1981.

Diego by J. Winter. Translated by A. Price. Illustrated by J. Winter. Knopf, 1994.

210 Recetas De Cocina Internacional by V. Ramos Espinoza. Editorial Diana, 1979.

El Abuelo Tomás by S. Zavrel. Ediciones S. M., 1987.

El Libro de las Adivinanzas by C. Bravo-Villasante. Editorial Minon, 1984.

El Lirón Sin Nombre by J. Moran. Illustrated by C. Buskuets. Susaeta Ediciones, S. A., 1983.

El Maíz Tiene Color de Oro by S. Martinez-Ostos. Editorial Novaro, 1981.

Especialidades de la Cocina Mexicana by A. de la Rosa. Editores Mexicanos Unidos, 1981.

Esperanza Rising by P. M. Ryan. Scholastic, 2003.

Everybody Cooks Rice by N. Dooley. Illustrated by P. I. Thornton. Carolrhoda, 1991.

Experimentos Atmosféricos by V. Webster. Children's Press, 1986.

Family Pictures/Cuadros de Familia by C. L. Garza. Children's Book Press, 1990.

Felipa and the Day of the Dead by B. Müller. North South, 2004.

¡Fiesta! Cinco de Mayo by J. Behrens. Children's Press, 1986.

Fiesta Fireworks by G. Ancona. Lothrop, 1998.

Fiesta U.S.A. by G. Ancona. Lodestar, 1995.

First Day in Grapes by L. K. Perez. Illustrated by R. Casilla. Lee & Low, 2002.

A First Look at the World of Plants by M. E. Selsam. Walker, 1978.

The Flame of Peace: A Tale of the Aztecs by D. Lattimore. Harper and Row, 1987.

Flash, Crash, Rumble and Roll by R. M. Branley. Crowell, 1964.

Flight to Freedom by A. Veciana-Suarez, Scholastic, 2002.

Folk Tales: Four Plays for the Classroom by L. Swinburne & S. Bank. Walker, 1989.

Folk Toys Around the World and How to Make Them by V. Fowler. Prentice-Hall, 1984.

Frida by J. Winter. Scholastic, 2002.

Frida Kahlo by R. M. Turner. Little, Brown, 1993.

Gathering the Sun: An Alphabet in Spanish and English by A. F. Ada. Illustrated by S. Silva. Lothrop, 1997.

Going Home by E. Bunting. Illustrated by D. Diaz. HarperCollins, 1996.

The Great Ancestor Hunt: The Fun of Finding Out Who You Are by L. Perl. Clarion, 1989.

Growing Older by G. Ancona. Dutton, 1978.

Harvesting Hope. The Story of Ceasar Chavez, by K. Krull. Illustrated by J. Mair. Clarion, 2003.

Hello, Amigos! by T. Brown. Henry Holt, 1986.

La Historia de Ernesto by M. Company. Ediciones S. M., 1986.

Horses Hooves and Chicken Feet Mexican Folk Tales by N. Philip. Illustrated by J. Mair. Clarion, 2003.

The House on Mango Street by S. Cisneros. Vintage Contemporaries, 1989.

How Tía Lola Came to Visit/Stay by J. Alvarez. Knopf, 2001.

The Hundred Penny Box by S. B. Mathis. Puffin, 1986.

I Am Phoenix: Poems for Two Voices by P. Fleischman. Harper & Row, 1985.

If the Shoe Fits by G. Soto. Illustrated by T. Widener. Putnam, 2002.

Iguanas in the Snow/Iguanas en La Nieve by F. X. Alarcon. Illustrated by M. C. Gonzalez. Children's Book Press, 2001.

Immigrant Kids by R. Freedman. Dutton, 1980.

In My Family/En Mi Familia by C. L. Garza. Children's Press, 1996.

In the Days of the Vaqueros: America's First Cowboys by R. Freedman. Clarion, 2001.

I Speak English for My Mom by M. Stanek. Illustrated by J. Freidman. Whitman, 1989.

It's Raining Cats and Dogs: All Kinds of Weather and Why We Have It by F. M. Bradley. Houghton Mifflin, 1987.

Jabuti: A Trickster Tale from Mexico by G. Dermott. Harcourt, 1999.

Josephina by J. Winter. Harcourt Brace, 1996.

Journey of the Nightly Jaguar: Inspired by an Ancient Mayan Myth by B. Albert. Illustrated by R. Roth. Atheneum, 1996.

Juan Bobo Goes to Work by M. Montes. Illustrated by J. Cepeda. HarperCollins, 2000.

Juan Ramón Jimenez y los Niños by J. R. Ramirez. Everest, 1980.

Laughing Out Loud, I Fly/A carcajadas you vuelo by J. F. Herrera. Illustrated by K. Barbour. HarperCollins, 1998.

Leyendas Mexicanas by R. Morales. Aguila, S. A. de Ediciones, 1968.

The Little Gold Star: A Spanish American Cinderella by R. D. San Souci. Illustrated by S. Martinez. HarperCollins, 2000.

Local News by G. Soto. Harcourt Brace, 1993.

Love to Mamá: A Tribute to Mothers by P. Mora. Illustrated by P. Barragán. Lee & Low, 2001.

Mama's Birthday Surprise by E. Spurr. Illustrated by F. Davalos. Hyperion, 1996.

Maya by P. McKissack. Children's Press, 1985.

Me and My Family Tree by P. Showers. Crowell, 1978.

Mexican Profiles: Bilingual Biographies for Today by J. Nava & M. Hall. Aardvard Media, 1974.

Mitos y Leyendas translated and adapted by J. Oleza. Ediciones Gaisa, 1968.

The Monkey's Haircut, and Other Stories Told by the Maya by J. Bierhorst. Morrow, 1986.

La Montaña del Alimento adapted by H. Rohmer. Illustrated by G. Carrillo. Children's Book Press, 1988.

Montezuma and the Aztecs by N. Harris. Bookwright, 1986.

A Movie in My Pillow/Una Película en mi almohada by J. Argueta. Children's Book Press, 2003.

La Música de la Chirimia by J. A. Volkmer. Carolrhoda, 1991.

My Mexico/México Mío by T. Johnston. Illustrated by F. J. Sierra. Putnam, 1996.

My Name is Jorge: On Both Sides of the River by J. Medina. Boyds Mills, 1999.

Nature's Weather Forecasters by H. R. Sattler. Nelson, 1978.

Neighborhood Odes by G. Soto. Illustrated by D. Diaz. Harcourt Brace, 1992.

New Junior Cookbook by *Better Homes and Gardens*. Meredith, 1989.

Observando El Clima by A. Ford. Everest, 1982.

Pablo Remembers: The Fiesta of the Day of the Dead by G. Ancona. Lothrop, 1993.

Passport to Mexico by C. Irizarry. Franklin Watts, 1987.

People of Corn: A Mayan Story by M. Gerson. Illustrated by C. Golembe. Little, Brown, 1995.

Petty Crimes by G. Soto. Harcourt, 1998.

The Piñata Maker by G. Ancona. Harcourt Brace, 1994.

Plant Experiments by V. Webster. Children's Press, 1982.

Plants by L. Bender. Gloucester Press, 1988.

Popol Vuh translated by A. Recinos. Fondo de Cultura Económica, 1982.

Poppy Seeds by C. R. Bulla. Crowell, 1955.

The Pot That Juan Built by N. Andrews-Goeble. Illustrated by D. Diaz. Lee & Low, 2003.

Prietita and the Ghost Woman/Prietita y la Llorona by G. Anzaldúa. Illustrated by C. Gonzalez. Children's Press, 1996.

Quetzal: Sacred Bird of the Cloud Forest by D. H. Patent. Illustrated by N. Waldman. Morrow, 1996.

Ramona and Her Father by B. Cleary. Illustrated by A. Tiegreen. Morrow, 1977.

Red Riding Hood by J. Marshall. Dial, 1987.

Sol a Sol: Bilingual Poems by L. M. Carlson. Illustrated by E. Lisker. Holt, 1998.

The Spirit of Tio Fernando/El Espiritin de Tio Ferando: A Day of the Dead Story/Una Historia del Dia de los Muertos by J. Levy. Translated by T. Mlawer. Illustrated by M. Fuenmayor. Whitman, 1995.

The Stories Julian Tells by A. Cameron. Pantheon Books, 1981.

The Story of Colors/La historia de los colores by S. Marcos. Illustrated by D. Dominquez. Cinco, 1999.

Storms by R. Broekel. Children's Press, 1982.

This Home We Have Made/Esta Casa Que Hemos Hecho by A. Hammond & J. Matunis. Crown, 1993.

This Tree Is Older Than You Are: A Bilingual Gathering of Poems and Stories with Paintings by Mexican Artists by N. S. Nye. Simon & Schuster, 1995.

Three Little Pigs by P. Galdone. Seabury, 1970.

Too Many Tamales by G. Soto. Illustrated by E. Martinez. Putnam, 1993.

The Tortilla Book by D. Kennedy. Harper & Row, 1975.

The Tortilla Factory by G. Paulsen. Illustrated by R. W. Paulsen. Harcourt Brace, 1995.

Tortilla for Emilia by M. Angeles. Sundance, 1992.

Tortillas para Mamá and Other Nursery Rhymes by D. Griego. Holt, Rinehart & Winston, 1981.

The Upside Down Boy/El nino de cabeza by J. F. Herrera. Illustrated by E. Gomez. Children's Book Press, 2000.

Versitlan by R. López Moreno. Presencia Latinoamericana, S. A., 1983.

Voices from the Fields: Children of Migrant Workers Tell Their Stories by S. B. Atkin. Little, Brown, 2000.

Voy a Cocinar by M. Lasa. Sitesa, 1988.

La Voz de Coatl by L. Ramos. Editorial Novaro, 1983.

Wáchaele! Poetry and Prose on Growing Up Latino in America by I. Stavans. Cricket, 2001.

The Walls of Pedro Garcia by K. McColley. Delacorte, 1993.

Water by B. Bunston. Silver Burdett, 1982.

Water by A. Webb. Franklin Watts, 1986.

Water for the World by F. M. Branley. Crowell, 1982.

Water Plants by L. Pringle. Crowell, 1975.

Weather Experiments by V. Webster. Children's Press, 1982.

What Makes It Rain? The Story of a Raindrop by K. Brandt. Troll, 1982.

When Clay Sings by B. Baylor. Macmillan, 1972.

Where Did You Get Those Eyes? A Guide to Discovering Your Family History by K. Cooper. Walker, 1988.

The Witch's Face: A Mexican Tale by E. A. Kimmel. Illustrated by F. V. Broeck. Holiday House, 1993.

The Woman Who Outshone the Sun/La Mujer Que Brillaba Aun Mas Que el Sol by R. Zubizarreta, H. Rohmer, & D. Scheter. Illustrated by F. Olivera. Children's Book Press, 1991.

Xochitl and the Flowers/Xochtl la niña del las flores by J. Argueta. Illustrated by C. Angel. Children's Book Press, 2003.

Prototype 7: Sixth Grade—
DIGGING UP THE PAST

Schedule

Interact (1974); ESS (1974)

DIGGING UP THE PAST begins with a simulated experience—two archaeological digs—and uses the "unearthing" of artifacts to draw children into an exploration of the processes used to define and resolve problems in various domains. The unit is designed to incorporate the world studies curriculum typical of many sixth-grade programs into a larger unit on the interpretation of human, plant, and animal remains. The major *essential question* in this theme is "How do we know what happened in the past?" It builds on the foundation of independent reading and research begun in earlier years, with the intent of helping children further develop their understanding that knowledge is a human construction subject to change and interpretation, and that students and teachers alike participate in making and interpreting knowledge.

The unit also makes use of a commercial simulation, *Dig* (a unit developed by Interact), and *Bones*, an Elementary Science Study (ESS) science program. Although commercial materials are not necessary to the theme, they do provide resources that are otherwise unavailable or difficult to obtain. Two "digs" initiate the unit. The first is a wastebasket excavation that introduces children to the process of excavation and interpretation of data. The second is the simulation *Dig* that involves students in the replication of an archaeological excavation. These activities take approximately one week, with about forty-five minutes to an hour per day devoted to the digs.

Although it has become common to departmentalize at sixth grade, the teacher in this class, Caitlin Cooper, works in a self-contained sixth grade in a school noted for its integrated language curriculum. Her schedule is given in Table 4.13.

Caitlin has been developing this unit over the past several years. Over time and as a direct result of her teacher inquiries, her plans have changed. Caitlin now puts more emphasis on methodology as a category that cuts across both science and social stud-

table **4.13**   Weekly Schedule, Caitlin Cooper's Self-Contained Sixth-Grade Class

Time	Monday	Tuesday	Wednesday	Thursday	Friday
8:00	Opening exercises				
8:10	Forum. Children gather to share work, group plan, and learn about activity choices for the day.				
8:30	Integrated work time. Children sign up to work in various areas, participate in special projects (i.e., digs). Opportunity for problem solving, creative thinking, self-expression, communication, and content engagement.				
9:50	Special classes: art, music, physical education, library				
10:30	Recess				
10:45	Integrated work time				
12:00	Lunch				
12:45	SSR*				
1:00	Forum. Whole-group experiences that include introducing new material, guest speakers, writing/editing workshops, math reviews, and the like.				
2:00	Integrated work time				
2:30	Cleanup, announcements, and dismissal				

ies. She finds that this better supports a Reflective, Disciplined Inquiry* approach and makes more explicit the kind of attention she wants to pay to how knowledge is acquired in specific domains. She now helps students report on how they acquired information, not just on the product of their research. She also makes more explicit the connections between the work her students do this year and their prior studies of American history in fifth grade. She found that her students were not making these connections on their own and were confused as to when events in American history happened in relation to world history. Finally, she has added a section called "Burying the Present" not only to capitalize on student interest in burial practices in ancient civilizations but also to move her students beyond a fascination with the techniques of mummification or buried treasures to current practices and issues, including waste management and land use. This year Caitlin intends to continue her research into how students become more reflective inquirers. To better understand how children are approaching problems in the different disciplines, Caitlin requires that her students keep a specific type of Journal* in which they record problems they are investigating, the approaches and sources that are working best, and the problems they are encountering in their work.

Into the Classroom

Students move among work centers distributed throughout the room and a central grouping of tables and chairs arranged for projects using reading and writing. We begin on Day 6, after children have worked with the excavations. (See Table 4.14.) Caitlin uses most of the morning on this day to establish the idea of interpretation of artifacts and to set the stage for the later introduction of the *Bones* unit and a study of fossils and geological interpretation. She has done some background reading on the use of fossilized bones in studying early humans and on the controversies surrounding the interpretation of human remains. Caitlin's plans also call for inviting an anthropologist to class. The traditional task of the guest expert is to deliver a speech (with short discussion afterward) and then leave. In this case, however, Caitlin has asked the guest to talk about the concept of culture and serve as consultant to the children as they develop their own island cultures. Caitlin may be the only teacher assigned to this classroom, but she regularly invites guests to provide other points of view, different types of expertise, and a range of audiences for children's work. During this unit guests include, in addition to the anthropologist, an architect, a storyteller, several parents who have traveled to the areas being studied, a dancer, and international students from a nearby university.

Invite guests to serve as consultants for student work.

   Another project that involves students in interpreting data and communicating their results is the development of a museum of prehistory and the creation of artifacts and documents related to a student-developed culture. (Compare this to the "Nature's Journeys" museum in Prototype 3.) In each case, children simulate the activity of experts in a domain. They have recourse to some of the same data that an expert might have, and they can consult experts as they develop their ideas. They make approximations in their interpretations in the same ways that they use approximations in other forms of communication. Caitlin is anxious to see if this activity will show up in the student inquiry reports. She also encourages this type of intellectual risk taking by sharing literature such as Ray Bradbury's short story "History Lesson," in which the tentative nature of historical interpretation and the possibility of error are humorously pointed out.

Bradbury (1974)

   Between Days 6 and 10, students use a teacher-developed simulation to construct an island culture and begin reconstructing plant and animal histories. Portions of the schedule of Day 20 highlight the continued development of the theme as children prepare to share their findings.

Building a Prehistory Museum

HOMINIDS: A LOOK BACK AT OUR ANCESTORS
WHERE THE FOREST MEETS THE SEA
TYRANNOSAURUS REX AND ITS KIN
FROM MAP TO MUSEUM
TRACES OF LIFE
THE KINGFISHER BOOK OF THE ANCIENT WORLD

Include Displays* of the development of plants and animals.
Make a geological clock.
Display size comparisons of plants and animals over time.

Animals

THE BONE WARS
THE PUZZLE OF THE DINOSAUR-BIRD
DINOSAURS AND THEIR YOUNG
DIGGING UP DINOSAURS
TYRANNOSAURUS WAS A BEAST
DINOSAURS DOWN UNDER AND
    OTHER FOSSILS FROM AUSTRALIA
TRAPPED IN TAR
DINOSAUR PARENTS, DINOSAUR
    YOUNG. UNCOVERING THE MYSTERY
    OF DINOSAUR FAMILIES
GREAT DINOSAUR EXPEDITIONS AND
    DISCOVERIES: ADVENTURES WITH
    THE FOSSIL HUNTERS
"Dinosaur Hunters" (VHS)

Do *Bones* unit in ESS.
Make a time line of an animal species.

Plants

MOONSEED TO MISTLETOE

Make plaster fossils.
Collect plant fossils and label them for
    a Display*.
Make a plant history of the world.
    What are the oldest plants on earth?
    The newest?

Music and Dance

Learn music and dance
    from other cultures.
Invite guests to help
    identify patterns in
    music by region.
Investigate how music
    and dance are used
    in the cultures studied.

FOSSIL REMAINS

Arts and Crafts

PAINTERS OF THE CAVES

Try crafts from cultures
    studied.
Make a Display* of crafts
    indigenous to the cultures
    you study.
List all the ways you can find
    that art is used in your own
    culture.
Use found objects and recycle
    them into art.
Set up a class museum of world
    art.

SCIENCE

THE ARTS

DIGGING UP THE PAST

METHODOLOGY

Architecture as a Time Line

UNBUILDING
CATHEDRAL
CITY
MILL
PYRAMID
PROVINCETOWN
GREAT MOMENTS IN ARCHITECTURE
LEBEK: A HANSEATIC CITY OF
    NORTHERN EUROPE THROUGH
    THE AGES

See if you can unravel the mysteries behind the
    building of the pyramids, Stonehenge, or the
    ancient Mayan buildings. Think of an interesting
    way to share your discoveries.
Make a Display* of distinctive architectural
    features from different times and cultures.
    Look for evidence of these features in
    American culture.

THE CHANGING CITY
THE CHANGING COUNTRYSIDE

Use either of Muller's books, and trace the history of
    one feature of the changing landscape.
Write a story about a person living in any of the places
    you've read about in these books. Do as a
    performance assessment.
Theory building: How is architecture related to:
• the natural environment
• people's religious beliefs and other values
• technological development

In the Social Sciences

"History Lesson"
MOTEL OF THE MYSTERIES
DIGGING TO THE PAST
THE BOYS' WAR
LETTERS OF A WOMAN HOMESTEADER
THE BONE DETECTIVES
FROZEN MAN
FINDING THE LOST CITIES
SHIP
BURIED IN ICE
ARCHEOLOGISTS: EXPLORERS OF
    THE HUMAN PAST
ARCHEOLOGY FOR KIDS:
    UNCOVERING THE MYSTERIES OF
    OUR PAST
"Mysteries of Mankind" (VHS)

Do a wastebasket excavation.
Do simulation DIG.
Collect articles on "garbageology"—the study
    of landfills.
Interview different social scientists about their
    work (anthropologist, archaeologist,
    sociologist, etc.).
Conduct an observation of human interaction.
Study the different types of information that
    can be gathered from Primary Sources*.
Create a Jackdaw*.

In the Sciences

WHITE BEAR, ICE BEAR
TRACKING WILD CHIMPANZEES
BEAVER AT LONG POND
THE COMPLETE FROG
PLACES OF REFUGE
WATCH OUT FOR SHARKS!
BORN FREE
MUMMIES, DINOSAURS, AND
    MOON ROCKS
INTO THE SEA
PROBING VOLCANOES
FOSSIL FISH FOUND ALIVE:
    DISCOVERING THE COELACANTH
ON SHIFTING GROUND: THE
    STORY OF THE CONTINENTAL
    DRIFT

View films/videos of scientific studies
    (Goodall in Africa, Cousteau on the
    Calypso, and other field researchers).
How do scientists study plants and
    animals?
Interview scientists about their work.
Plan and conduct a study of a
    classroom pet or pets. Keep field notes,
    and make a final report. Take photos
    for support data.

Information Books

MUMMIES MADE IN EGYPT
EARLY HUMANS
LIFE THROUGH THE AGES
THE BLACK DEATH
CALLIOPE: WORLD HISTORY
  FOR YOUNG PEOPLE

Write a history of your island culture.
Compare burial and other practices
  and beliefs between cultures.
Make a "life through the ages" book
  for your culture. Illustrate.
Study influence of ancient Africa and
  Asia on western cultures.
Look for common patterns in ancient
  and modern cultures.

Traditional Literature

IN THE BEGINNING
WORDS FROM THE MYTHS
SHAMROCKS, HARPS, AND SHILLELAGHS
SWEET AND SOUR: TALKS FROM CHINA
ORACLE BONES, STARS, AND WHEELBARROWS:
  ANCIENT CHINESE SCIENCE AND TECHNOLOGY
DAUGHTER OF EARTH

Compare folktales, myths, and legends from other cultures.
Hypothesize a type of folktale for a culture (e.g., an island
  culture might have water sprites).
Write a catalog of common themes, characters, and so on
  in traditional literature.
Write a tale that would fit your island culture.
Collect folklore from your own area/region; compare with
  those from other places.
Analyze: What do these tales tell us about values of different
  cultures?

Historical Fiction

I, TUT
HIS MAJESTY, QUEEN HATSEPSHUT
THE EYE IN THE FOREST
SETH OF THE LION PEOPLE
DAWN WIND
THE STRONGHOLD
THE SAMURAI'S TALE
THE AMETHYST RING
MALU'S WOLF
A WAY OF HIS OWN
BOY OF THE PAINTED CAVE
RETURN TO THE PAINTED CAVE
ANOOKA'S ANSWER
WARRIOR SCARLET

How have different authors visualized the
  past? What evidence do they use? What
  is their point of view? Are there instances
  of presentism or anachronisms?
Write a piece of historical fiction that could
  come from your island culture.
Discuss: Slides of "developed" and
  "developing" cultures. Is "development"
  always "progress?"

LITERATURE

MATH

Field Math

Find out how math is used in archaeological
  and anthropological work.
Set up problems from your island culture and
  share them via computer with your
  classmates.
Invent a base system for your culture.
Make size comparisons of plants and animals.

Problem Solving

INCREDIBLE CROSS-SECTIONS

Express size comparisons as fractions,
  decimals, and ratios.
Calculate proportions for museum
  Displays*.
Figure the cost benefit of recycling
  in the school.
Weigh recycled goods; calculate resale.

Interpreting Cultures

SHAKA, KING OF THE ZULUS
DAWN WIND
THE STRONGHOLD
LOST AND FOUND
THE LAND I LOST
FAMILIES
MUMMIES, TOMBS, AND TREASURE
STEPPING ON THE CRACKS
THE MYSTERY OF THE MAYA:
  UNCOVERING THE LOST CITY OF
  PALENQUE
STONEHENGE: DIGGING
  FOR THE PAST
WHO CAME FIRST? NEW CLUES TO
  PREHISTORIC AMERICANS

"Lost Kingdoms of the Maya" (VHS)
"Mysteries of Egypt" (VHS)
The Rabbit in the Moon (Mayan culture)
  www.halfmoon.org
 Mummy, *National Geographic*
  www.nationalgeoraphic.com/features/96/
  mummy
Mr. Dowling's, Electronic Passport
  (Ancient Africa)
  www.mrdowling.com/609ancafr.html
Ancient Africa
  www.plaza.k12.nd.us/webguests/Africa
Make a catalog of ways in which cultures take
  care of necessities.
What values do these choices represent?
Write a set of "Laws for Cross-Cultural
  Travelers."
Create a traveler's guide to a culture or country.
  Be sure to let the traveler know about customs
  that could cause misunderstandings.
Make a comparative time line for cultures and
  countries from different regions of the world.
Do parallel culture studies: Begin with island
  culture and real-world parallels.
Trace evidence of cultural diffusion in your own
  community.
Study families in a cross-cultural perspective.
Conduct an in-depth study of several cultures
  over time.

SOCIAL STUDIES

Inventing Culture

BAAA
BARMI: A MEDITERRANEAN CITY
  THROUGH THE AGES
CRANBERRIES
THE IGLOO
THE PUEBLO

Construct an island culture. How will
  you meet your basic needs? Use the
  resources in the environment?
Prepare geographic and historic reports,
  decide on government, and so on.
Write documents, laws, create art,
  literature, music.
Communicate and trade with others.
Provide evidence that your creations
  are possible by finding parallels in
  past or present.

Burying the Present

CARTONS, CANS, AND ORANGE PEELS:
  WHERE DOES OUR GARBAGE GO?
RECYCLOPEDIA

Investigate ways your community deals with waste.
Investigate cross-cultural issues of
  pollution/waste disposal.
Create a school plan for recycling.
Debate: Should a local industry be able to dump
  waste into a lake that is a major tourist attraction?
Visit a recycling center and/or a water treatment plant.

table **4.14**   Detailed Schedule, Caitlin Cooper's Self-Contained Sixth-Grade Class

DAY 6

Time	Children	Teacher	Teacher Research
Forum 8:10	Children make a chart of what can be known or inferred from artifacts, using digs and slides of Viking dig as data.	Caitlin shares parts of *Digging to the Past* and asks students what other digs they know of. She shows slides of the Viking excavation, Yorvik, at York, England.	Caitlin's teacher inquiry begins here, as she presents the idea of archaeology as a form of data collection and points out the methods explained in *Digging to the Past.*
Integrated Work Time 8:30	Children select a settlement location on Mystery Island and list factors influencing their decisions. Breaking into groups based on location, they discuss what it would take to survive in their group's area. Each group takes a clan name and begins to plan for the kind of civilization that they will be able to develop in that area.	Caitlin distributes a map of an uninhabited island and asks children to select a location where they could survive. Each group is then given a list of supplies they will have to work with. After students have worked in groups, Caitlin leads a discussion of problems encountered and ideas tried. She calls on a student to record some of the considerations each clan must deal with. This is posted in the room for student reference throughout this activity.	
Literature 9:50	Children listen to a story and discuss connections to interpreting artifacts.	Caitlin shares the "History Lesson" and participates in discussion.	
Integrated Work Time 10:15	Children try to identify artifacts from their state's prehistory and infer their use.	A specialist from the local museum brings artifacts to class and leads a discussion of how the museum staff reconstructs the past and builds displays based on fragments from the past.	
Whole Group Activity 11:00	Children observe slides and discuss the observations that led to the archaeologist's misinterpretations of the artifacts in the slides.	Caitlin follows up the guest talk with a slide show based on *Motel of the Mysteries,* a spoof on artifact interpretation.	
Integrated Work Time 11:20	Children return to their clans and work on developing their culture, using some of the ideas gathered during the earlier part of the morning.	Caitlin moves among groups, asking questions and listening to students' discussions.	
Forum 1:00	Children work in pairs to identify groups of bones. They measure bones and calculate the possible size of the creature.	During this period, Caitlin introduces a new type of artifact—bones—using the ESS unit *Bones.*	
Integrated Work Time 2:00	Children work in pairs or individually on the following: • Comparing traditional literature from ancient cultures • Investigating arts and crafts common to ancient cultures • Using *Tyrannosaurus Was a Beast* as a model for writing poems about the creatures reconstructed during forum • Making size Comparison Charts* of features of Mystery Island	Caitlin works with small groups for part of this period and conducts several Reading Conferences* for the rest of the time.	Caitlin's emphasis here is on how to use different sources. She asks students to keep track of the sources they use and to remember to record both their sources and why they chose particular sources in their Journals*.

table **4.14** Detailed Schedule, Caitlin Cooper's Self-Contained Sixth-Grade Class *(continued)*

DAY 10

Time	Children	Teacher	Teacher Research
Forum 8:10	Children listen to a story.	Caitlin reads portion of *The Bone Wars*.	
Integrated Work Time 8:30	Children are conducting inquiries into a variety of topics. They have engaged in source sharing discussions, developed specific questions, and used a variety of data sources.		As students have engaged in inquiries throughout the unit, Caitlin has systematically introduced them to different research techniques. Now Caitlin wants them to focus more carefully on the process of researching as well as the final product. She reminds them that good researchers want to know about the process because it helps them evaluate the product. She reminds them to use their double-entry Journals* to take notes.
	Children listen and talk with the guest. They take notes as she talks, leaving enough room for their own questions and comments. They then move into centers, including:	Guest anthropologist speaks about what a "culture" is and responds to student questions.	
	• *Mystery Island.* Present part of their culture to the anthropologist and use expert help in solving problems.	The anthropologist works with small groups as they rotate into the Mystery Island center.	
	• *Plants.* Organize a plant history that connects plants and agriculture with human culture.	Caitlin works with the plant history group as they organize data.	Caitlin is particularly interested in observing how students handle this stage of their inquiry.
	• *Literature.* Create a Comparison Chart* of "origin" stories from different cultures. Note how plants and animals are explained in these stories.	Caitlin brings a pomegranate and a copy of *Daughter of Earth* to share with this group. After everyone tastes the seeds and discusses whether they were worth the months in Hades, Caitlin calls students' attention to several other "origin" myths and to Hamilton's *In the Beginning*, a collection of creation stories from around the world.	
	• *Animal observations.* View video on Jane Goodall's work and begin to read *Born Free*.	Caitlin enters this area as the video ends and talks with the students about careful observation of live animals, then introduces *Born Free*.	Later, Caitlin will collect samples of student observation reports as part of her inquiry.
Art 9:50	Children construct mosaics similar to those in illustrations of ancient Greece and Rome, except that they use symbols representing different aspects of their island cultures.	An art specialist works with the class and plans some of her activities to coincide with units Caitlin has developed.	
Integrated Work Time 10:45	Children rotate between groups.	Caitlin continues as during the first integrated work time.	
Forum 1:00	Students working with a base 5 number system present their work to the class, giving some base 5 problems. Three students share their most recent writing.	Caitlin helps as students do base 5 problems, congratulating those who figure it out: "Looks as if you're ready to try another base system!" She also joins in the	

(continued)

DAY 10 *(continued)*

Time	Children	Teacher	Teacher Research
Forum *(continued)*		discussion of the writing presented, using an overhead to answer questions about quotations and paragraphing in dialogue.	
Integrated Work Time 2:00	Students work in centers.	Caitlin works with small groups and then holds a Reading Conference* on *The Stronghold* and *Dawn Wind*.	

DAY 20

Time	Children	Teacher	Teacher Research
Forum 8:10	A small group reports on their ten-day study of Ethel, the classroom guinea pig. They have made charts of growth and a video of Ethel's behavior. The class discusses the study and compares it to the video on Goodall and to *Born Free*. They decide that several comparison studies would be useful and begin to plan how to conduct them.	Caitlin encourages other animal studies. When two children suggest a study of sixth graders, she tells them to think about what their questions might be to guide the study, how they would collect data, and how they would protect their "subjects' " privacy. She suggests they submit a plan to the class for discussion and approval.	Caitlin takes notes on student work. She is especially interested in how the children deal with ethical issues at this point. She makes a note to remind herself to show them guidelines for human subjects research.
Integrated Work Time 8:30	Several new groups have grown from previous work, including: • *Museum group.* Construction is under way on a diorama-type museum of the prehistoric world. Students have designed exhibits to compare interpretations of what the prehistoric world was like. They have found conflicting accounts in reports about the work of pale-oarchaeologists Don Johannsen and Richard Leakey. • *Architecture.* After working with the art teacher, students are preparing a report "The Bones of Buildings," using *Unbuilding* and *Incredible Cross-Sections* as models for planning their report. • *Human culture.* Three groups have each looked at a different culture and are now collaborating on a way to share the results of their studies. • *Leaders.* After questions of leadership arose in the Mystery Island activity, a group of students decided to study the influence of different types of leaders in history and is		Many of these activities serve as both performance assessment and data in Caitlin's study. As she has gathered data throughout the unit, several issues seem particularly salient. First, she wants to see how (or if) children represent or account for differing interpretations in their final reports. Second, she wants to see how children handle the different genres they will use in reporting their studies. Third, she wants to see whether they report both process and results. Performance assessment also provides Caitlin with rich data for her own inquiry.

For the Human culture row, the Teacher column reads:

Caitlin works carefully with this group in planning how to share their findings. This will be used as a performance assessment. Children have conducted several studies throughout the unit, and received regular feedback from peers and from Caitlin. Caitlin uses these group tasks to assess children's progress toward two of the major goals for the unit—

table **4.14**   Detailed Schedule, Caitlin Cooper's Self-Contained Sixth-Grade Class (continued)

DAY 20 (continued)

Time	Children	Teacher	Teacher Research
Integrated Work Time (continued)	preparing a news conference with Shaka Khan, Mao Ze-dong, Saladin, Henry VIII, and Franklin D. Roosevelt.	learning to use and understand the processes for solving problems in various domains and using content appropriately and accurately.	
Forum 1:00	Author's Chair*. Students share some of their writing with peers.	Caitlin participates in listening to and discussing each author's work.	Caitlin takes notes on peer evaluations related to appropriateness of genre.

Summary

Departmentalized teaching requires careful team planning and coordination of efforts by an entire team of teachers, but a teacher in a self-contained classroom such as Caitlin must also use her planning periods wisely. She must be constantly alert to student interests and possible extensions. She makes extensive use of the services of the school librarian and the surrounding community for human and material resources, and works with the art, music, and P.E. teachers to enrich her themes. Caitlin also spends time carefully organizing her room and thinking about her students' needs. She uses a variety of methods and media, especially videotapes. Sometimes children watch prepackaged programs and often they make their own. In this way, Caitlin capitalizes on early adolescents' fascination with the video medium to promote careful observation and support their inferences, as well as to help them recognize and appreciate the perspective of the filmmaker.

The advantage of this type of self-contained, integrated approach to study is the ease with which Caitlin and her students can cross and relate disciplinary categories. Time is as flexible as the class's inclinations and the requirements of their studies. In addition, Caitlin can pursue long-term research goals in which she revises her teaching strategies, documents student response, and adjusts thematic units accordingly. As a result of her teacher research during this thematic unit, Caitlin finds that the students' "I-Search" reports are especially useful for student self-evaluation. For instance, she discovers that, while students can *report* other interpretations, they become confused in *evaluating* the merits of different interpretations. She notes that students seem to confuse interpretation and opinion and are reluctant to evaluate something that "is his opinion, but I don't agree with it."

Children's Literature: DIGGING UP THE PAST

Africa (Cultural Atlas for Young People Series) by J. Murray. Checkmark, 1990.

The Amethyst Ring by S. O'Dell. Houghton Mifflin, 1983.

Anooka's Answer by M. Cowley. Clarion, 1999.

Archeologists: Explorers of the Human Past by B. Fagan. Oxford, 2003.

Archeology for Kids: Uncovering the Mysteries of Our Past by R. Panchyk. Chicago Review Press, 2001.

Baaa by D. Macaulay. Houghton Mifflin, 1989.

Barmi: A Mediterranean City through the Ages by X. Hernandez & P. Comes. Houghton Mifflin, 1992.

Beaver at Long Pond by W. T. George and L. B. George. Illustrated by L. B. George. Greenwillow, 1988.

The Black Death by J. Day. Franklin Watts, 1989.

The Bone Detectives: How Forensic Anthropologists Solve Crimes and Uncover Mysteries by D. Jackson & C. Felllenbaum. Little, Brown, 1996.

The Bone Wars by K. Lasky. Morrow, 1988.

Born Free by J. Adamson. Random House, 1974.

Boy of the Painted Cave by J. Denzel. Philomel, 1988.

The Boys' War: Confederate and Union Soldiers Talk about the Civil War by J. Murphy. Houghton Mifflin, 1990.

Buried in Ice by O. Beattie & J. Geiger. Illustrated by J. Wilson. Scholastic, 1992.

Calliope: World History for Young People by R. Baker & C. Baker, III (Eds.). Cobblestone. (Periodical)

Cartons, Cans, and Orange Peels: Where Does Our Garbage Go? by J. Foster. Houghton Mifflin, 1991.

Cathedral by D. Macaulay. Houghton Mifflin, 1977.

The Changing City by J. Muller. Atheneum, 1977.

The Changing Countryside by J. Muller. Atheneum, 1977.

City by D. Macaulay. Houghton Mifflin, 1974.

The Complete Frog: A Guide for the Very Young Naturalist by E. A. Lacey. Illustrated by C. Santoro. Lothrop, 1988.

Cranberries by W. Jaspersohn. Houghton Mifflin, 1991.

Daughter of Earth by G. McDermott. Delacorte, 1984.

Dawn Wind by R. Sutcliffe. Walck, 1962.

Digging to the Past: Excavations in Ancient Lands by W. J. Hackwell. Scribner's, 1986.

Digging Up Dinosaurs by Aliki. Crowell, 1981.

"Dinosaur Hunters" (VHS). National Geographic, 2004.

Dinosaur Parents, Dinosaur Young. Uncovering the Mystery of Dinosaur Families by K. Zoehfled. Illustrated by P. Carrick and B. Shillinglaw. Clarion, 2003.

Dinosaurs and Their Young by R. Freedman. Illustrated by L. Morill. Holiday House, 1983.

Dinosaurs Down Under and Other Fossils from Australia by C. Arnold, Photographs by R. Hewett. Clarion, 1990.

Early Humans by N. Merriman. Knopf, 1989.

The Eye in the Forest by W. Steele & M. Steele. Dutton, 1975.

Families: A Celebration of Diversity, Commitment and Love by A. Jenness. Houghton Mifflin, 1990.

Finding the Lost Cities by R. Stefoff. Oxford, 1997.

Fossil Fish Found Alive: Discovering the Coelacanth by S. M. Walker. Carol Rhoda, 2003.

From Map to Museum: Uncovering Mysteries of the Past by J. Anderson. Photographs by G. Ancona. Morrow, 1988.

Frozen Man by D. Getz. Illustrated by P. H. McCarty. Holt, 1994.

Great Dinosaur Expeditions and Discoveries: Adventures with the Fossil Hunters Dinosaur Library, 1993.

Great Moments in Architecture by D. Macaulay. Houghton Mifflin, 1978.

His Majesty, Queen Hatsepshut by D. S. Carter. Lippincott, 1987.

"History Lesson" by R. Bradbury. In *Transformations 2: Understanding American History through Science Fiction.* Fawcett Crest, 1974.

Hominids: A Look Back at Our Ancestors by R. Sattler. Illustrated by C. Santoro. Lothrop, 1988.

The Igloo by C. Yue and D. Yue. Illustrated by D. Yue. Houghton Mifflin, 1993.

Incredible Cross-Sections by S. Biesty. Knopf, 1992.

In the Beginning by V. Hamilton. Illustrated by B. Moser. Harcourt Brace Jovanovich, 1988.

Into the Sea by B. Z. Guiberson. Illustrated by A. Berenzy. Holt, 1996.

I, Tut: The Boy Who Became Pharaoh by M. Schlein. Four Winds, 1979.

The Kingfisher Book of the Ancient World by H. M. Martell. Kingfisher, 2001.

The Land I Lost by H. Q. Nhuong. HarperCollins, 1982.

Lebek: A Hanseatic City of Northern Europe through the Ages by X. Hernandez & J. Ballonga. Illustrated by R. Corni. Houghton Mifflin, 1991.

Letters of a Woman Homesteader by E. P. Stewart. Houghton Mifflin, 1982.

Life through the Ages by G. Caselli. Putnam, 1987.

Lost and Found by J. P. Walsh. Andre Deutsch, 1985.

"Lost Kingdoms of the Maya" (VHS). National Geographic, 1997.

Malu's Wolf by R. Craig. Orchard, 1995.

Mill by D. Macaulay. Houghton Mifflin, 1983.

Moonseed to Mistletoe: A Book of Poisonous Wild Plants by C. Lemer. Morrow, 1988.

Motel of the Mysteries by D. Macaulay. Houghton Mifflin, 1980.

Mummies, Dinosaurs, and Moon Rocks: How We Know How Old Things Are by J. Jesperson & J. Fitz-Randolph. Illustrated by B. Hiscock. Atheneum, 1996.

Mummies Made in Egypt by Aliki. Crowell, 1979.

Mummies, Tombs, and Treasure by L. Perl. Houghton Mifflin, 1990.

"Mysteries of Egypt" (VHS). National Geographic, 2001.

"Mysteries of Mankind" (VHS). National Geographic, 1997.

On Shifting Ground: The Story of the Continental Drift by J. S. Kidd and R. A. Kidd. Facts on File, 1997.

The Mystery of Maya: Uncovering Lost City of Palenque by P. Lourie. Boyds Mills, 2001.

Oracle Bones, Stars, and Wheelbarrows: Ancient Chinese Science and Technology by F. Ross, Jr. Illustrated by M. Goodman. Houghton Mifflin, 1982.

Painters of the Caves by P. Lauber. National Geographic, 1998.

Places of Refuge by D. Patent. Clarion, 1992.

Probing Volcanoes by L. Lindop. Millbrook, 2003.

Provincetown by M. Oliver. Edited by J. Wheatcroft. Press Alley, 1987.

The Pueblo by C. Yue & D. Yue. Illustrated by D. Yue. Houghton Mifflin, 1990.

Pyramid by D. Macaulay. Houghton Mifflin, 1975.

The Puzzle of the Dinosaur-Bird by M. Schlein. Illustrated by M. Hallett. Dial, 1996.

Recylopedia by R. Simons. Houghton Mifflin, 1993.

Return to the Painted Cave by J. Denzel. Philomel, 1997.

The Samurai's Tale by E. C. Haugaard. Houghton Mifflin, 1990.

Seth of the Lion People by B. Pryor. Morrow, 1988.

Shaka, King of the Zulus by D. Stanley & P. Vennema. Illustrated by D. Stanley. Morrow, 1988.

Shamrocks, Harps, and Shillelaghs by E. Barth. Illustrated by U. Arndt. Houghton Mifflin, 1982.

Ship by D. Macaulay. Houghton Mifflin, 1993.

Stepping on the Cracks by M. Hahn. Houghton Mifflin, 1992.

Stonehenge: Dipping for the Past by C. Malone. Oxford, 2002.

The Stronghold by M. Hunter. Harper & Row, 1974.

Sweet and Sour: Tales from China by C. Kendall & Y. Li. Illustrated by S. Felts. Clarion, 1979.

Traces of Life by K. Lasky. Illustrated by W. Powell. Morrow, 1989.

Tracking Wild Chimpanzees by J. Powzyk. Lothrop, 1988.

Trapped in Tar: Fossils from the Ice Age by C. Arnold. Photographs by R. Hewett. Clarion, 1987.

Tyrannosaurus Rex and Its Kin by H. K. Sattler. Illustrated by J. Powzyk. Lothrop, 1988.

Tyrannosaurus Was a Beast by J. Prelutsky. Illustrated by A. Lobel. Greenwillow, 1988.

Unbuilding by D. Macaulay. Houghton Mifflin, 1983.

Warrior Scarlet by R. Sutcliff. Walck, 1958.

Watch Out for Sharks! by C. Arnold. Photographs by R. Hewett. Clarion, 1991.

A Way of His Own by T. A. Dyer. Houghton Mifflin, 1985.

Where the Forest Meets the Sea by J. Baker. Greenwillow, 1988.

White Bear, Ice Bear by J. Ryder. Illustrated by M. Rothman. Morrow, 1988.

Who Came First? New Clues to Prehistoric Americans by P. Lauber. National Geographic, 2003.

Words from the Myths by I. Asimov. Dutton, 1969.

Other Resources

Elementary Science Study (ESS). (1974). *Bones.* New York: McGraw-Hill.

Interact. (1998). *Dig.* Lakeside, CA: Learning Through Involvement.

Prototype 8: Seventh Grade—LANDSCAPES

Schedule

Grace Choi is a teacher in a suburban middle school with dual certification in English and social studies. Her school district has established a humanities block for seventh graders that provides an extended ninety-minute period with one teacher to cover English language arts and social studies. Although these students are from middle-class and upper-middle-class families, they also represent a diverse population of longtime residents and newer immigrant cultures that have settled around and work in the adjacent large city. The past year Grace and several other content area teachers had written and received a grant from their district for a weeklong planning session in cross-disciplinary collaboration. They used the time and the money budgeted for materials to plan a theme of LANDSCAPES that would include standards-based content in English, social studies, science, and mathematics.

Grace began the year with a theme of EXPLORATIONS. In that unit she had built on and reviewed sixth-grade studies of the prehistorical and ancient world that would lead students into studies of ancient and medieval civilizations required by the seventh-grade social studies standards. In the earlier unit on EXPLORATIONS she included a review of archeology and archeological methods and an exploration of emerging civilizations worldwide during the period between 1000 B.C. and 500 C.E. She felt that this exploration helped students understand that civilizations were flourishing all over the world during that time, although we don't have full archeological and historical records for all these civilizations. She wanted students to understand that previous beliefs about these cultures were due in part to beliefs by some Western scientists that rich civilizations could not have developed in places like South Africa. Also, such beliefs resulted from the destruction of artifacts and records due to climate changes, warfare, and colonization.

Grace planned the LANDSCAPES unit to center around an in-depth study of Greek and Roman civilizations that was, thus, grounded in the broader understandings of worldwide history. She wanted students to understand how issues they face in their own lives were also present in earlier civilizations. She also hoped that her students could begin to appreciate how past civilizations and cultures still influenced the world in which they lived.

In a weeklong workshop the previous June, Grace and other humanities teachers worked with seventh-grade science and mathematics teachers to coordinate the theme of LANDSCAPES so that outside the humanities block, students would also explore mathematical landscapes and geographical landscapes. As you visit Grace's classroom, keep in mind that students are also conducting inquiries in earth science and geometry. (See Tables 4.15 and 4.16.)

Grace has decided to focus her inquiry on students' understandings of genres. She has found copies of two books, *The Greek News* and *The Roman News,* that present

Powell & Steele (1999); Langley & DeSouza (1996)

Prototype 8: Seventh Grade—LANDSCAPES

Greek and Roman Landscapes

In small groups, use print-based resources and websites to conduct in-depth studies of civilizations of Greece and Rome. Focus on information about government, the arts, daily life, warfare, science, and mathematics. Present your findings in class versions of ROMAN NEWS and GREEK NEWS.

British Museum websites
www.thebritishmuseum.ac.uk/pee/peehome.html
www.thebritishmuseum.ac.uk/world/world.html

Greece

YOUR TRAVEL GUIDE TO ANCIENT ROME
ANCIENT GREECE (Morris, Solway)
A DICTIONARY OF THE ANCIENT GREEK
EYEWITNESS: ANCIENT GREECE
ANCIENT GREEK HOMES/JOBS/WAR AND WEAPONS
OLYMPIA: WARRIOR ATHLETES OF ANCIENT GREECE
"Great Cities of the Ancient World: Athens and Ancient Greece" (VHS)
The Ancient Greek World, University of Pennsylvania
www.museum.upenn.edu/Greek_World
The Ancient Greeks
www.arwhead.com/Greeks
National Geographic Reading Expeditions: Civilizations Past to Present, Greece
www.nationalgeographic.com/education/readingexpedsWE41204.html
Hellenic Ministry of Culture
www.culture.gr/2/21/toc/index.html
See Discovery Channel School lessons plans for additional websites
http://discovery.com/lessonplans/ancienthis.html#6-8

Rome

YOUR TRAVEL GUIDE TO ANCIENT ROME
EVERYDAY LIFE IN ANCIENT ROME
ANCIENT ROME
EYEWITNESS: ANCIENT ROME
ANCIENT ROMAN HOMES/WAR AND WEAPONS/WOMEN
WOMEN IN ANCIENT ROME (MacDonald, Nardo)
NATIONAL GEOGRAPHIC READING EXPEDITIONS: ROME
THE ROMAN ARMY: THE LEGENDARY SOLDIERS WHO CREATED AN EMPIRE
THE ROMAN ARMY
ROME IN SPECTACULAR CROSS SECTION
"Great Cities of the World: Rome and Pompeii" (VHS)

HISTORICAL LANDSCAPES

LANDSCAPES

Myths and Epics

ROMAN MYTHS
A GIFT FROM ZEUS
PEGASUS
PEGASUS THE FLYING HORSE
HEROES AND MONSTERS OF GREEK MYTH
KING MIDAS: THE GOLDEN TOUCH
ARACHNE SPEAKS
I AM ARACHNE: FIFTEEN GREEK AND ROMAN MYTHS
GREEK MYTHS
TALES OF THE GREEK HEROES
THE MACMILLAN BOOK OF GREEK GODS AND HEROES
D'AULAIRES' BOOK OF GREEK MYTHS
ATALANTA'S RACE
JASON AND THE GOLDEN FLEECE
ARIADNE AWAKE
CUPID AND PSYCHE
DAUGHTER OF EARTH
OLYMPIANS
WINGS
GREEK MYTHS FOR YOUNG CHILDREN
FABULOUS MONSTERS
"Greek Gods" (VHS)

Create a pantheon of Greek gods and goddesses and their Roman counterparts. Draw illustrations and write brief descriptions for each pair on a mural.

Look for examples of Greek and Roman myths in modern life. What references do you find in other fiction? In advertising? In products?

LITERARY LANDSCAPES

A New Look at Old Stories

LOST IN THE LABYRINTH
QUIVER
APHRODITE'S BLESSING
INSIDE THE WALLS OF TROY
SIRENA
WAITING FOR ODYSSEUS

How have authors of these books incorporated myths into their novels? How have they developed characterization, plot, setting, and theme from the original? Choose a myth you have read and expand it into a longer story. How will you include these elements of fiction in your writing?

Journeys through the Landscape

THE ODYSSEY OF HOMER
TALES FROM THE ODYSSEY
THE CHILDREN'S HOMER
BLACK SHIPS BEFORE TROY
THE ILIAD AND THE ODYSSEY
HOMECOMING

How has the motif of the journey influenced modern fiction? Compare elements in the ODYSSEY to Voigt's HOMECOMING. How many connections can you find? Draw a story map for each book including relevant symbols in the mode of ancient maps. See examples at the British Library site:
www.bl.uk/collections/map_manuscripts.html

Look for similar home/away/home patterns in modern fiction. Create a website showing connections. Make a list of titles to post on the Internet.

Historical Settings

SECRETS OF VESUVIUS
THIEVES OF OSTIA
DETECTIVES IN TOGAS
MYSTERY OF THE ROMAN RANSOM
THE EMPEROR'S WINDING SHEET
EAGLE OF THE NINTH

How is historical fiction different from nonfiction you have been reading?

What do authors of historical fiction owe their readers? Develop a list of criteria for evaluating historical fiction; then apply them to these titles.

Write a work of historical fiction set in ancient Greece or Rome. Use primary and secondary sources to construct your setting. Include source notes and an author's note. Use images, illustrations, pop-ups, or other visual modes to complement your writing.

EXPLORING ARTISTIC/ ARCHITECTURAL LANDSCAPES

CITY: A STORY OF ROMAN PLANNING AND CONSTRUCTION
THE STORY OF ARCHITECTURE
EYEWITNESS: BUILDING
AN ANCIENT GREEK TEMPLE
AMAZING BUILDINGS
ROMAN AMPHITHEATERS
THE PARTHENON
THE COLISEUM AND THE ROMAN FORUM
ROME IN SPECTACULAR CROSS SECTION
THE STORY OF ARCHITECTURE

Benaki Museum, Athens
www.benaki.gr/index-en.htm

The Metropolitan Museum of Art Greek and Roman Collections
www.metmuseum.org/collections/department.asp?dep=13

NOVA Roman Baths
www.pbs.org/wgbh/nova/lostempires/roman

What were the contributions of Greece and Rome to architecture and art?

Use books and websites to compile a visual record of architectural features developed in Greece and Rome. Find and photograph examples in your community.

Study art forms such as mosaics, ceramics, and painting. Create your own work of art based on a Greek or Roman myth you have read.

Mapping the Landscape

MAPS AND MAPPING
MAPS AND GLOBES
A+ PROJECTS IN EARTH SCIENCE
BE YOUR OWN ROCK AND MINERAL EXPERT

How do we describe the features of landscapes? In small groups carry out mapping inquiries suggested in these books and create different types (relief, topographical, etc.) of maps of your school neighborhood.

Altapedia.com
www.atlapedia.com

Geo-Globe: Interactive Geography www.thinkquest.org/library/site_sum.html?tname=10157&url=10157

International travel maps and books www.itmb.com

CIA World Factbook www.cia.gov/cia/publications/factbook/index.html

National Geographic www.nationalgeographic.com/index.html
http://plasma.nationalgeographic.com/mapmachine

How is the land affected by changing weather patterns? How does this affect human civilizations? Connect historical changes in climate to the rise and fall of ancient civilizations on a timeline.

What are ways in which land features and climate have influenced history?

Climate Change from BBC Weather Center www.bbc.co.uk/climate

NATURAL LANDSCAPES

Arty Facts: Planet Earth and Art Activities

Conduct experiments about rocks and minerals:

To demonstrate how seismic waves work in causing earthquakes and other underground explosions

To illustrate how volcanic plugs work in volcano eruptions

To show how sedimentary layers develop

To depict how tectonic plates collide

To demonstrate how crystals grow

To illustrate how gold nuggets may grow in sediments

To depict how an animal body becomes a fossil

Create displays to show the steps in your experiment and your findings.

Conduct an inquiry on one of the earth science topics (Caves and Caverns, Rocks and Minerals, or the Changing Earth). Report your findings in a poster session. Include drawings, diagrams, samples, pop-ups, and models to clarify your findings.

THE LANDSCAPE BENEATH YOU

Caves and Caverns

CAVE (Silver, Siebert)
CAVES
CAVES AND CAVERNS
LIMESTONE CAVES (Davis, Gallant)
PAINTERS OF THE CAVES
HIDDEN WORLDS: CAVES
CAVES: UNDERGROUND WORLDS
THE WORLD OF CAVES, MINES, AND TUNNELS

National Caves Associations
http://Cavern.com

MATHEMATICAL LANDSCAPES

Geometry in the Landscape

Study the contributions of Greece to the field of geometry.

Learn congruence, properties of two- and three-dimensional figures, and the properties of triangles, including the use of the Pythagorean Theorem.

THE ELEMENTS OF POP-UP: A POP-UP BOOK FOR ASPIRING PAPER ENGINEERS

Use mathematical processes and ideas from THE ELEMENTS OF POP-UP to create drawings and three-dimensional models of Greek and Roman architecture and architectural features.

The Changing Earth

ON SHIFTING GROUND: THE STORY OF THE CONTINENTAL DRIFT
OUR PATCHWORK PLANET: THE STORY OF PLATE TECTONICS
SHAPING THE EARTH
VOLCANO: THE ERUPTION AND HEALING OF MT. ST. HELENS
VOLCANOES (Branley, Morris, Simon, Sipiera)
GEYSERS: WHEN THE EARTH ROARS
HOW MOUNTAINS ARE MADE
THE DANCE OF THE CONTINENTS
EARTH: THE MAKING OF A PLANET
EARTHQUAKES (Branley, George, Pope, Simon)
"Mysteries Underground" (VHS)
"Volcano" (VHS)

Earthquake Hazards Program
http://earthquake.usgs.gov/4kids/learning/adv.html

The Savage Earth
www.pbs.org/wnet/savageearth

Volcano World
http://volcano.und.nodak.edu

Rocks and Minerals

ROCKS AND MINERALS (Oldershaw, Parker, Riciutti, Symes)
SHAPING THE EARTH
STORIES IN STONE: THE WORLD OF ANIMAL FOSSILS
UNDER THE GROUND
MUD MATTERS
IF YOU FIND A ROCK
A LOOK AT MINERALS: FROM GALENA TO GOLD
A LOOK AT ROCKS: FROM COAL TO KIMBERLITE
HIDDEN UNDER THE GROUND: THE WORLD BENEATH YOUR FEET
"Splendid Stones" (VHS)
"Eyewitness—Rock and Mineral" (VHS)

The Mineral Gallery
http://mineral.galleries.com/default.htm

MINING PERSONAL LANDSCAPES

A MANGO-SHAPED SPACE
MIND GAMES
GOSSIP TIMES THREE
LOSING IS NOT AN OPTION
WHIRLIGIG
RUBY ELECTRIC
KEEPERS OF THE NIGHT

How do the characters in these books explore their inner landscapes? What is the event that causes introspection and how does each character achieve self-insight? Write about an event when you were forced to look inward.

table **4.15**   Weekly Schedule, Grace Choi's Middle School Schedule

Time	Monday	Tuesday	Wednesday	Thursday	Friday
8:15	Humanities				
9:05					
9:55	Enriched English				
10:45	Planning				
11:35	Lunch				
12:25	Enriched English				
1:15	Humanities				
2:05					
2:50	Dismissal				

table **4.16**   Weekly Schedule for One of Grace Choi's Classes of Seventh-Grade Students

Time	Monday	Tuesday	Wednesday	Thursday	Friday
8:15	Humanities				
9:05					
9:55	Math				
10:45	Art	Music	Art	Music	PE
11:35	Language				
12:25	Lunch				
1:15	Science				
2:05	Health				
2:50	Dismissal				

information about ancient Greece and Rome in a magazine or newspaper format. After students have chosen the topics for their inquiries, Grace shares the two books with them and asks them to present the results of their inquiries in the same format. She suggests that students study the books carefully (along with modern-day newspapers) and make note of all the different genres they find. She tells them that she will expect a similar range in their own reports. She will observe their group work, conference with individuals, and then study their final projects to see what they understand about different verbal and visual genres.

Into the Classroom

On the first day of the unit Grace made the transition from the EXPLORATIONS theme to the LANDSCAPES theme by showing students the A&E video "The Greek Gods." (See Table 4.17.) Following the video, Grace asks the students to compile a list of gods and their main identities that they remembered from the video. She then introduced them to a collection of Greek and Roman myths and asked them to read as many as they can for the next several days. She suggested that, as students read, they brainstorm any modern-day products or associations that they can think of that are associated with Greek and Roman mythology. She then introduced them to an overhead of the LANDSCAPES web and suggested that they begin thinking about the topics (government, trade and industry, the military, architecture, women's and children's roles, etc.) that they want to pursue for their individual inquiries.

Day 5 sees the students immersed in reading Greek and Roman myths and choosing the topics that they will study in their inquiries.

table **4.17**   **Detailed Schedule, Grace Choi's Seventh-Grade Humanities Block**

DAY 10

Time	Children	Teacher	Teacher Research
Homeroom 8:00 to 8:15	These students are in Grace's first humanities block.	Grace takes attendance as the school announcements are broadcast.	
Group Meeting 8:15–8:30		Grace introduces students to novels that are retellings or versions of Greek myths and epics. She provides Book Talks* on several novels and invites students to browse through them during the week. They will be choosing one book to read with a Literature Response Group* that Friday.	
Integrated Work Time 8:30–9:20	Students take out the materials they have been collecting from newspapers, magazines, and other sources that carry the names of Greek and Roman gods and goddesses. They have categorized the materials into types such as outer space, consumer products, businesses, and popular culture.		
	Several groups are working on organizing the materials into Comparison Charts* with labels, photographs, and hand-drawn pictures.	Grace moves from group to group discussing their progress and making suggestions about format.	
	Two other groups are working on two murals, Character Portraits*—one of Greek gods and goddesses and the other of the Roman pantheon. Both groups have coordinated the order in which each figure will be depicted so that they can match Greek and Roman characters that bear the same characteristics.		
Group Time 9:20–9:50	Students are delighted with the idea of translating characters from myths into a news format and are intrigued by the visual graphics that go with it. "That's a lot like Manga," one exclaims (a Japanese form of graphic novel).	Grace calls the students together for a group meeting and takes out *The Greek News, The Roman News, USA Today,* and the local daily paper. She reads sections of *The Greek News* that relate to the gods they have been studying and then shows them other sections of the book.	
	Students immediately think of comics, sports articles, and news stories.	She asks students to help her make a list of the different types of things they would find in a newspaper.	Grace is jotting down notes as the students discuss the parts of a newspaper. She will use these notes and the class list as part of her data.
		Grace asks them to spend the rest of the period looking at the materials she has brought in small groups and come up and add to the list as they identify other features.	

(continued)

table **4.17**   Detailed Schedule, Grace Choi's Seventh-Grade Humanities Block *(continued)*

DAY 10 *(continued)*

Time	Children	Teacher	Teacher Research
Group Time *(continued)*	Students take to the project enthusiastically. One boy says, "Wow, I never thought I'd find history fun!"	She explains that they will be doing inquiries on Greek and Roman civilizations and she wants them to present their findings in a format like *The Greek News*.	

DAY 15

Time	Children	Teacher	Teacher Research
Group Time 8:15–8:45	Each group reports on the subtopics they have decided on. Their plan is to break into smaller groups to cover each of the topics in depth.	Grace has divided the class into two major groups, one to study Greek civilization and the other to study Roman. Grace reminds students of the work they had started the previous week and asks for progress reports. She calls attention to the list of newspaper genres they have generated. She urges them to narrow down the types of features they want to use in their final reports and to have duties assigned to each person by the end of the week. (Who will do the artwork? Who will do the writing? What other jobs may be necessary?)	Grace takes notes as the students report.
Integrated Work Time 8:45–9:50	Students break into small groups to work on assignments.		Grace moves from group to group making notes on any discussion related to genre.

DAY 25

Time	Children	Teacher	Teacher Research
8:15–9:50	Students are finishing up their research for their inquiries. Each large group is meeting together for a progress report. *The Greek News* group has decided to cover Famous Greek People, Women and Children in Ancient Greece, War and Warriors, and Architecture and the Arts. *The Roman News* group has decided on Everyday Lives, Architecture, The Military, and Sports. They now finalize plans for the format of each subtopic.	Grace moves among groups to listen to discussions, answer questions, and make suggestions. Grace has put together bins of art materials for the students to use: construction paper, tempera paint, glue, scissors, and drawing materials.	Grace has provided both groups with tape recorders to record their discussions. She will add these data to her other research data.

Summary

Seventh graders can be consumed with their own personal worlds in ways that can shut down enthusiasms for the study of history. By helping students to find links between modern-day products and their roots in ancient mythology Grace created a real enthusiasm in her "consumer culture" adolescents. She felt that similar links between past and present were made throughout the course of the study—between modern-day issues and issues in the past, between modern-day characters and characters in the past, between literary structures and those of the past, and between modern language and languages of the past. Furthermore, Grace felt that the LANDSCAPES theme also provided her students with an important framework for upcoming studies of the Middle Ages in cultures in Asia, the Americas, Africa, the Middle East, India, and Europe, thus returning to and continuing the broad cross-cultural timeline begun in the EXPLORATIONS unit.

Finally, an evaluation meeting among teachers at the end of the unit showed overwhelming enthusiasm for this approach to curriculum development. The group decided to continue their end-of-the-year planning meetings and to include all grade-level teachers and the school media specialist in order to build on the integrated curriculum they had begun in LANDSCAPES that year.

Children's Literature: LANDSCAPES

Amazing Buildings by P. Wilkinson. Illustrated by P. Donati. DK, 1993.

Ancient Greece by N. Morris. Peter Bedrick, 2000.

Ancient Greece by A. Solway. Oxford, 2001.

Ancient Greek Children (*People in the Past* series) by H. Middleton. Heinemann, 2003.

Ancient Greek Homes (*People in the Past* series) by H. Middleton. Heinemann, 2003.

Ancient Greek Jobs (*People in the Past* series) by H. Middleton. Heinemann, 2003.

An Ancient Greek Temple by J. Malam. Peter Bedrick, 2001.

Ancient Greek War and Weapons (*People in the Past* series) by H. Middleton. Heinemann, 2003.

Ancient Greek Women (*People in the Past* series) by H. Middleton. Heinemann, 2003.

Ancient Roman Homes (*People in the Past* series) by R. Williams. Heinemann, 2002.

Ancient Roman War and Weapons (*People in the Past* series) by R. Williams. Heinemann, 2003.

Ancient Roman Women (*People in the Past* series) by R. Williams. Heinemann, 2003.

Ancient Rome by A. Solway Illustrated by P. Connolly. Oxford, 2001.

Aphrodite's Blessing: Love Stories from Greek Myths by C. McLaren. Atheneum, 2002.

A+ Projects in Earth Science by J. VanCleave. Wiley, 1999.

Arachne Speaks by K. Hovey. Illustrated by Blair Drawson. McElderry, 2001.

Ariadne Awake by D. Orgel. Viking, 1994.

Arty Facts: Planet Earth and Art Activities by J. Cooper. Crabtree Publishing, 2002.

Atalanta's Race by S. Climo. Clarion, 1995.

Be Your Own Rock and Mineral Expert by M. Pinet and A. Korkos. Sterling, 1997.

Black Ships before Troy by Rosemary Sutcliff. Delacorte, 1993.

Cave by D. M. Silver. Illustrated by P. J. Wynne. McGraw-Hill, 1997.

Caves by D. Siebert. HarperCollins, 2000.

Caves and Caverns by G. Gibbons. Harcourt, 1993.

Caves: Underground Worlds by Jeanne Bendick. Holt, 1995.

The Children's Homer by P. Colum. Simon, 1982.

City: A Story of Roman Planning and Construction by D. Macaulay. Houghton Mifflin, 1983.

The Coliseum and Roman Forum by M. Whittock. Heinemann, 2002.

Cupid and Psyche by M. C. Craft. Morrow, 1996.

The Dance of the Continents by R. Gallant. Benchmark, 1999.

Daughter of Earth by G. McDermott. Delacorte, 1984.

D'Aulaires' Book of Greek Myths by I. d'Aulaire & E. P. d'Aulaire. Doubleday, 1962.

Detectives in Togas by H. Winterfeld. Harcourt, 2002.

A Dictionary of the Ancient Greek World by D. Sacks. Oxford, 1997.

Eagle of the Ninth by R. Sutcliff. Walck, 1954.

Earth: The Making of a Planet by R. Gallant. Illustrated by C. Schuberth. Cavendish, 1998.

Earthquakes by F. Branley. Illustrated by R. Rosenblum. HarperCollins, 1994.

Earthquakes by M. George. Creative Education, 1997.

Earthquakes by J. Pope. Illustrated by I. Moores. Copper Beech Books, 1998.

Earthquakes by S. Simon. Morrow, 1991.

The Elements of Pop-Up: A Pop-Up Book for Aspiring Paper Engineers by D. A. Carter. Simon & Schuster, 1999.

The Emperor's Winding Sheet by J. P. Walsh. McMillan, 1974.

Eyewitness: Ancient Greece by A. Person. DK, 2000.

Eyewitness: Ancient Rome by S. James. DK, 2000.

Eyewitness: Building by P. Wilkinson. DK, 2000.

"Eyewitness—Rock and Mineral" (VHS). DK, 1992.

Fabulous Monsters by M. Williams. Candlewick, 1999.

Geysers: When the Earth Roars by R. Gallant. Watts, 1997.

A Gift from Zeus by J. Steig. HarperCollins, 2001.

Gossip Times Three by A. Koss. Dial, 2003.

"Great Cities of the Ancient World: Athens and Ancient Greece." (VHS). Questar, 1994.

"Great Cities of the World Rome and Pompeii" (VHS). Questar, 1993.

"Greek Gods" (VHS). A & E, 2000.

Greek Myths by O. E. Coolidge. Houghton Mifflin, 2001.

Greek Myths for Young Children by M. Williams. Candlewick, 1995.

The Greek News by A. Powell & P. Steele. Candlewick, 1999.

Heroes and Monsters of Greek Myth by R. Evslin. Laurel Leaf, 1994.

Hidden Under the Ground: The World Beneath Your Feet by P. Kent. Dutton, 1998.

Hidden Worlds: Caves Under the Ground by P. de Bourgoing. Illustrated by D. Bour. Scholastic, 2000.

Homecoming by C. Voigt. HarperCollins, 1974.

How Mountains Are Made by K. W. Zoehfeld. Illustrated by J. Hale. HarperCollins, 1995.

I Am Arachne: Fifteen Greek and Roman Myths by E. Spires. Illustrated by M. Gerstein. Farrar, Straus, & Giroux, 2001.

If You Find A Rock by P. Christian. Illustrated by B. H. Lember. Harcourt Brace, 2000.

The Iliad and the Odyssey by M. Williams. Candlewick, 1998.

Inside the Walls of Troy by C. McLaren. Simon & Schuster, 2004.

Jason and the Golden Fleece by L. E. Fisher. Holiday House, 1990.

Keepers of the Night by K. W. Holt. Holt, 2003.

King Midas: The Golden Touch by Demi. McElderry, 2002.

The Kingfisher Book of the Ancient World by H. M. Martell. Kingfisher, 2001.

Limestone Caves by W. Davis. Children's Press, 1997.

Limestone Caves by R. Gallant. Watts, 1998.

Look At Minerals: From Galena to Gold by J. S. Kittinger. Watts, 1998.

Look At Rocks: From Coal to Kimberlite by J. S. Kittinger. Watts, 1998.

Losing Is Not an Option by R. Wallace. Knopf, 2003.

Lost in the Labyrinth by P. Kindl. Houghton Mifflin, 2002.

The Macmillan Book of Greek Gods and Heroes by A. Low. Aladdin, 1994.

A Mango-Shaped Space by W. Mass. Little, Brown, 2003.

Maps and Globes by J. Knowlton. Illustrated by H. Barton. HarperCollins, 1986.

Maps and Mapping by D. Chancellor. Kingfisher, 2004.

Mind Games by J. M. Crumwell. Houghton Mifflin, 2003.

Mud Matters by J. Dewey. Photographs by S. Trimble. Cavendish, 1998.

"Mysteries Underground" (VHS). National Geographic, 1997.

The Mystery of the Roman Ransom by H. Winterfeld. Harcourt, 2002.

The Odyssey of Homer by B. Picard. Oxford, 2001.

Olympia: Warrior Athletes of Ancient Greece by D. Blacklock. Illustrated by D. Kennett. Walker, 2001.

Olympians: Great Gods and Goddesses of Ancient Greece by L. E. Fisher. Holiday House, 1984.

On Shifting Ground: The Story of the Continental Drift by J. S. Kidd, J. S. Kidd, & R. A. Kidd. Facts on File, 1997.

Our Patchwork Planet: The Story of Plate Tectonics by H. R. Sattler. Illustrated by G. Maestro. Lothrop, 1995.

Painters of the Caves by P. Lauber. National Geographic, 1998.

The Parthenon by L. du Temple. Lerner, 2003.

Pegasus by M. Mayer. Illustrated by K. Craft. HarperCollins, 1998.

Pegasus: The Flying Horse by Jane Yolen. Illustrated by M. Li. Dutton, 1998.

Quiver by S. Spinner. Knopf, 2002.

Rocks and Minerals by C. Oldershaw. Dorling Kindersley, 1999.

Rocks and Minerals by S. Parker. Dorling Kindersley, 1997.

Rocks and Minerals by E. Riciutti. Scholastic, 1998.

Rocks and Minerals by R. F. Symes. Photographs by C. Ketes. Knopf, 1988.

Roman Amphitheaters by D. Nardo, Watts, 2002.

The Roman Army by D. Blacklock. Illustrated by D. Kennett. Walker, 2004.

The Roman Army: The Legendary Soldiers Who Created an Empire by D. Blacklock. Walker, 2004.

Roman Myths by G. McCaughrean. McElderry, 2001.

The Roman News by A Langley & P. DeSouza. Candlewick, 1996.

Rome in Spectacular Cross Section by S. Solway. Illustrated by S. Beisty. Scholastic, 2003.

Ruby Electric by T. Nelson. Atheneum, 2003.

Secrets of Vesuvius by C. Lawrence. Roaring Brook, 2002.

Shaping the Earth by D. Patent. Photographs by W. Muñoz. Clarion, 2000.

Sirena by D. J. Napoli. Scholastic, 1998.

"Splendid Stones" (VHS). National Geographic, 1997.

Stories in Stone: The World of Animal Fossils by J. S. Kittinger. Watts, 1998.

The Story of Architecture by F. Milo. Illustrated by S. Baril. Peter Bedrick, 2001.

Tales from the Odyssey: Books One to Six by M. P. Osborne. Hyperion, 2004.

Tales of the Greek Heroes by R. L. Green. Turtleback, 1995.

Thieves of Ostia by C. Lawrence. Roaring Brook, 2001.

Under the Ground by C. Delafosse. Illustrated by P. De Hugo. Scholastic, 1999.

"Volcano" (VHS). National Geographic, 2003.

Volcano: The Eruption and Healing of Mt. St. Helens by P. Lauber. Bradbury Press, 1986.

Volcanoes by F. Branley. Illustrated by M. Simont. HarperCollins, 1985.

Volcanoes by N. Morris. Crabtree, 1995.

Volcanoes by P. P. Sipiera & D. M. Sipiera. Children's Press, 1998.

Volcanoes by S. Simon. Morrow, 1995.

Waiting for Odysseus by C. McLaren. Simon & Schuster, 2000.

Whirligig by P. Fleischman. Holt, 1998.

Wings by J. Yolen. Illustrated by D. Nolan. Turtleback, 1997.

Women in Ancient Rome by F. MacDonald. Peter Bedrick, 2000.

Women in Ancient Rome by D. Nardo. Lucent, 2000.

The World of Caves, Mines, and Tunnels by S. Hoare. Illustrated by B. Hogarth. Peter Bedrick, 1999.

Prototype 9: Eighth Grade—PERSPECTIVES

Schedule

Ed Tyson teaches in an urban area with a large multicultural and diverse socioeconomic population. He covers two sections of communication arts and social studies with eighth graders each day (as well as two sections of a special writing lab to seventh graders). This double block of time allows Ed ninety uninterrupted minutes with each group of eighth graders. As you saw in the Introduction, Ed's school is a departmentalized middle school that has grade-level pods in which particular groups of students in a grade have the same teachers. (See Tables 4.18 and 4.19.) Ed chose the theme of PERSPECTIVES to zero in on major understandings in the language arts and social studies that will also allow him to speak to state standards in the English language arts and social studies. State social studies standards call for coverage of American history and Ed has decided to look at the early history of the United States and the development of the Constitution by engaging students in some of the very diverse and sometimes divisive perspectives that led to the Revolutionary War and later to the Civil War. He also wants to provide students with a deeper understanding of how the Constitution grew out of different perspectives into the profoundly important document that it is today. The PERSPECTIVES theme also allows Ed's students to explore critical ideas about point of view in their own lives and in fiction and nonfiction. As they

table **4.18** Weekly Schedule, Ed Tyson's Middle School Schedule

Time	Monday	Tuesday	Wednesday	Thursday	Friday
9:00	Communication arts				
9:50	Social studies				
10:40	Writing lab				
11:30	Lunch				
12:20	Communication arts				
1:10	Social studies				
2:00	Planning period				
2:50	Writing lab				
3:35	Dismissal				

table **4.19** Weekly Schedule for One of Ed Tyson's Classes of Eighth-Grade Students

Time	Monday	Tuesday	Wednesday	Thursday	Friday
9:00	Communication arts				
9:50	Social studies				
10:40	Math				
11:30	Lunch				
12:20	Art				
1:10	Computer lab				
2:00	Science				
2:50	Physical education				
3:35	Dismissal				

Prototype 9: Eight Grade—PERSPECTIVES

Looking to Outer Space

ADVENTURE IN SPACE: THE FLIGHT TO FIX THE HUBBLE

ASTEROIDS, COMETS, AND METEORS

COSMIC PHENOMENA

COMETS, METEORS, AND ASTEROIDS

DEEP SPACE OBSERVATION SATELLITES

DESTINATION: JUPITER

DESTINATION: MARS

DESTINATION: SPACE

EARTH AND SPACE

ESCAPE FROM EARTH: VOYAGES THROUGH TIME

EXPLORING OUR SOLAR SYSTEM

GUIDE TO SPACE

HOME ON THE MOON: LIVING ON A SPACE FRONTIER

THE HUBBLE SPACE TELESCOPE

HUBBLE SPACE TELESCOPE: EXPLORING THE UNIVERSE

MARS

MERCURY AND VENUS

THE MOON

NASA

SCIENCE PROJECT IDEAS ABOUT THE MOON

SCIENCE PROJECT IDEAS ABOUT THE SUN

THE SOLAR SYSTEM: SATURN

URANUS, NEPTUNE, AND PLUTO

ZERO G: LIFE AND SURVIVAL IN SPACE

Hubble Telescope
http://hubblesite.org/

NASA
www.nasa.gov/audience/forstudents/
5-8/features/index.html

In small groups, choose topics about outer space to study in depth. Keep track of your inquiries and get feedback from the class via a class Internet blog.

THE ELEMENTS OF POP-UP

Using pop-up book ideas and other resources, create models or other displays for a class science museum. Write illustrated brochures and other ways to share your findings. Make posters, letters of invitation to local TV stations, and other ways to advertise the museum.

LOOKING BEYOND THE EARTH

Looking Back at Earth: Global Warming

GLOBAL WARMING

GLOBAL WARMING: THE THREAT OF EARTH'S CHANGING CLIMATE

ACID RAIN

AIR POLLUTION

ATMOSPHERE: SEA OF AIR

KEEPING THE AIR CLEAN

THE OZONE LAYER

HOW WE USE AND ABUSE OUR PLANET: AIR AND ENERGY

World Meteorological Organization
www.wmo.ch

NASA
www.kids.earth.nasa.gov/air.htm

Choose topics related to global warming (e.g., ozone layer, the greenhouse effect, acid rain) to study. Report your findings via models, written texts, and visual designs for the classroom science museum.

I WANT TO BE AN ENVIRONMENTALIST

Friends of the Earth
www.foe.org

How can you help Earth? Contact the Friends of the Earth (FOE) for information on protecting life on Earth. Share your ideas and create plans of action.

ARTISTIC PERSPECTIVES

Impossible Perspectives

NOW YOU SEE IT NOW YOU DON'T

SIMPLE OPTICAL ILLUSION EXPERIMENTS WITH EVERYDAY MATERIALS

What is the science behind optical illusions? Prepare a video explaining how optical illusions work. Create your own two- and three-dimensional illusions to fool viewers.

The Mathematical Art of M. C. Escher
www.mathacademy.com/pr/minitext/escher/
index.asp#intro

Study the art of Escher. How did he use mathematics to create his work? Create your own Escher-like images using polyhedra, tessellations, and a Moebius strip.

ANNO'S ALPHABET

WALTER WICK'S OPTICAL TRICKS

How did Anno and Wick make use of the principles explored by Escher? Use their techniques to create models for your video on optical illusions.

Nonrealistic Perspectives

ABORIGINAL ART OF AUSTRALIA: EXPLORING CULTURAL TRADITIONS

DREAMINGS: THE ART OF ABORIGINAL AUSTRALIA

AFRICAN ARTS AND CULTURE

PAINTER'S EYE: LEARNING TO LOOK AT CONTEMPORARY AMERICAN ART

CHUCK CLOSE UP CLOSE

ART ATTACK: A SHORT HISTORY OF THE AVANT GARDE

Look at art that doesn't try to depict the world realistically. What are the beliefs and traditions that have influenced these art forms? Create a PowerPoint presentation that compares similar subject matter across the realm of realism and abstract art. Provide descriptive labels and your personal responses.

HEART TO HEART: NEW POEMS INSPIRED BY TWENTIETH CENTURY ART

Read and discuss these poems. Write your own poems to one of the works of art studied above.

Through a Child's Eyes

How are forms that children draw echoed in the art of past and present? Collect drawings from preschoolers. Study and classify the ways they use lines and shapes. Find evidence of these in art of the past and present. Display your findings in a visual chart.

GRAPHIC PERSPECTIVES

MAUS: A SURVIVOR'S TALE

LITTLE LIT: FOLK AND FAIRY TALE FUNNIES

SAND LAND

UG, BOY GENIUS OF THE STONE AGE AND HIS SEARCH FOR SOFT TROUSERS

PERSPOLIS: THE STORY OF A CHILDHOOD

THE SANDMAN; ENDLESS NIGHTS

How do each of these graphic novels deal with point of view and characterization? How is the experience of reading them different from a novel in words alone? Develop a set of criteria for evaluating graphic novels. Create your own graphic novel based on one of the books you have read.

Spatial Perspectives

EYEWITNESS PERSPECTIVE

Study the Renaissance artists who discovered and used mathematical perspective. Print out reproductions of some of their works. Find the lines of perspective that they must have used. Draw over the reproduction to show their technique.

Leo Battista Alberti
http://easyweb.easynet.co.uk/giorgio/vasari/
albert/alberti.htm

Fillippo Brunelleschi
www.greatbuildings.com/architects/
Filippo_Brunelleschi.html

Masaccio
www.kfki.hu/~arthp/bio/m/masaccio/
biograph.html
www.artchive.com/artchive/M/masaccio.html

Learn to use the techniques of perspective developed by these and other Renaissance artists to draw a scene from three different perspectives.

POLITICAL PERSPECTIVES

THE UNITED STATES CONSTITUTION AND THE BILL OF RIGHTS

The U.S. Constitution online
www.usconstitution.net/index.html

The Work of the Continental Congress and the Constitutional Convention
http://lcweb2.loc.gov/ammem/bdsds/bdexhome.html

Our Documents Initiative
www.ourdocuments.gov/index.php?flash=true&

Study the deliberations surrounding the writing of the Constitution. What were the two main opposing parties at the dawn of the U.S. government? How did they reach a compromise when writing the Constitution? How have political parties evolved in the course of U.S. history? What are the major political perspectives in the United States today? Compare these to earlier political parties. What are party platforms and how are they enacted in government?

THE GREAT LITTLE MADISON

ABIGAIL ADAMS: WITNESS TO A REVOLUTION

IN PURSUIT OF LIBERTY: THE STORY OF AMERICA'S BILL OF RIGHTS

THE BILL OF RIGHTS: THE FIRST TEN AMENDMENTS OF THE CONSTITUTION

What were Madison's views on the Constitution? Research the views of other members of the Constitutional Convention.

Who were prominent women at the time of the Constitutional Convention? Assume that women were given the right to vote and were delegates to the convention. Take the role of one prominent person, male or female. Research the views held by that person and participate in your own class Constitutional Convention in that role.

NOTHING BUT THE TRUTH

What are your constitutional rights as a student? Study cases in which the courts have debated the rights of students in issues such as censorship.

VOTE FOR LARRY

HOPE WAS HERE

JUDE

How are these characters involved in political issues? Compare ways in which the authors have woven political viewpoints into their plots. Make a Comparison Chart*.

PERSPECTIVES

PERSONAL PERSPECTIVES

Study different types of opinion pieces in the media, including editorials and book, film, music, and TV reviews.

Analyze the different styles of editorial writing in several different newspapers: The New York *Times*, *USA Today*, and your own local newspaper. www.nytimes.com/pages/opinion/index.html
www.usatoday.com/news/opinion/front.htm

How is editorial writing different from reporting? Choose a major event/problem from one of the books you are reading. Write a front-page news report about the event. Then write an editorial that deals with the same event.

Take one of the issues you have studied in this unit. Write an editorial or op/ed piece for the local newspaper.

Compile a collection of printed and TV movie or book reviews. Look at nationally known TV review personalities such as Roger Ebert. www.suntimes.com/index/ebert.html

Develop a video book review of one of the books you read above.

Study techniques of persuasion used in advertising.
www.entrenet.com/~groedmed/namedu/adtech.htm
www.idahoptv.org/ntti/nttilessons/lessons2001/wells.html
www.propagandacritic.com

Locate examples of each of the different types of propaganda techniques in TV or magazine ads. Create a poster informing others in your school of these techniques. Then devise your own ads for one of the books (or objects) in this unit using the same techniques.

OUTSIDE LOOKING IN

THE OUTSIDERS
FREAK THE MIGHTY
THE SKIN I'M IN
PROBABLY STILL NICK SWENSON
I CAN HEAR THE MOURNING DOVE
HOW I WONDER WHERE YOU ARE
THE MISFITS
BIG MOUTH AND UGLY
SPEAK
SHADOW PEOPLE
RATS SAW GOD
TRIBES

Choose one of these titles to read in a small-group literature circle or book club. Keep track of your written and pictorial reactions in your Sketchbook Journal*. Create Character Sociograms* to represent relationships. Write a description of the main character from another character's viewpoint. What are the qualities and circumstances that seem to set these character's outside the "in group"? What are their reactions? Are you an outsider or insider?

Create a class Comparison Chart* to compare/contrast ideas from all books along these questions and others.

The Columbine school massacre was carried out by teens who felt marked as outsiders. Many schools now have zero- tolerance policies for behavior that they consider deviant. See discussion surrounding such policies at Law for Kids.

Law for Kids
www.lawforkids.org/QA/School/ School47.cfm?MaxRows=12

Take the role of one of the outsiders in the books above and write an editorial for or against such policies. Use the Bill of Rights to support your position.

Law for Kids: The Bill of Rights
www.lawforkids.org/LawDocs/BillofRights.cfm

Present a TV Talk Show* interviewing various characters about the ethical issues they face and how they might resolve them.

EXPLORING DIFFERENT PERSPECTIVES

Choose one of the Cultural, Gender, First Person, or Alternate perspectives sets of books to study. Read as many titles from your set as you can. Keep track of your reactions in your Sketchbook Journal*.

Discuss your books in a small-group, Literature Response Group*, or book club and then work together to develop activities as suggested. Finish your small-group studies with a whole-class look at MULTIPLE PERSPECTIVES.

Alternate Perspectives

THE TRUE STORY OF THE THREE LITTLE PIGS AS TOLD BY A. WOLF
BEAST
THE MAGIC CIRCLE
DATING HAMLET: OPHELIA'S STORY
ROMEO AND JULIET: TOGETHER (AND ALIVE) AT LAST
APHRODITE'S BLESSING: LOVE STORIES FROM GREEK MYTHS
WAITING FOR ODYSSEUS

How did the authors of these books create believable stories from other characters' points of view? Create Character Portraits* of the protagonists and antagonists. Choose a famous folktale, myth, or play and develop a short story from the antagonist's point of view.

Perspectives From Different Genders

I FEEL A LITTLE JUMPY AROUND YOU
THE PIGMAN
WHEN MY NAME WAS KEOKO
THE KINGS ARE ALREADY HERE
WHEN THE BOUGH BREAKS
SOLDIER BOYS
FLIPPED
TOGETHER, APART
DELIVER US FROM EVIE
AM I BLUE? COMING OUT FROM THE SILENCE

What are the parameters of views in these books? How are differing perspectives relating to gender conveyed by authors of fiction?

What constitutional issues are involved in gender perspectives? Based on the books you have read, create a questionnaire that surveys differing perspectives in your school and community and problems that may surround them. Report the results through graphs and a descriptive report and suggest a plan for conflict resolution if needed.

First-Person Perspectives

STONECUTTER
ALICE, I THINK
ANGUS, THONGS AND FULL FRONTAL SNOGGING
WHO THE MAN
IN SPITE OF KILLER BEES
THE GOSPEL ACCORDING TO LARRY
GIRL COMING IN FOR A LANDING: A NOVEL IN POEMS

Study the use of first-person voice in fiction. What are the strengths and weaknesses involved in writing in the first person? Study the use of dialogue in these books. Provide examples of dialogue that seem especially believable. Now find examples of poorly written dialogue in these or other first-person novels.

Think of an issue or problem common to students in your school. Write a short story (with illustrations) about this issue from the first- and third-person perspectives. What are the demands of the different types of writing?

REAL OR IMAGINARY PERSPECTIVES IN WAR

Fact or Fiction?

DEAR AMERICA SERIES: THE WINTER OF RED SNOW
MY NAME IS AMERICA SERIES: THE JOURNAL OF EDMUND PEASE

Read titles from these series that are set in the Revolutionary or Civil War. Are these authentic first-person narratives? What has the publisher done to suggest that these books are factual?

When authors of historical fiction write in the first person, what do they owe their audiences?

Put yourself in the place of an editor developing a historical fiction series. Develop criteria for this type of fiction. How can you help the audience for the series become critical readers? How does the issue of using primary versus secondary sources fit in this development?

Compare the DEAR AMERICA and MY NAME IS AMERICA books to THE AMERICAN REVOLUTIONARIES: A HISTORY IN THEIR OWN WORDS; FREDERICK DOUGLAS: IN HIS OWN WORDS; YANKEE DOODLE BOY, WE WERE THERE TOO!; and YOUNG PEOPLE IN U.S. HISTORY or to authentic journals you can find in historical archives.

American Memory Archives
http://memory.loc.gov/ammem/collections/ finder.html

Search manuscripts using the search term "diary."

The Modern World

WAITING FOR THE RAIN
THE MIDDLE OF SOMEWHERE: A STORY OF SOUTH AFRICA
CHAIN OF FIRE
JOURNEY TO JO'BURG
THE OTHER SIDE OF TRUTH
HABIBI
A STONE IN MY HAND

What are points of contention in societies around the world today? Locate areas of conflict on a world map. What are the major issues that grow out of conflicting perspectives? Choose four to five areas of conflict and break into small groups to study issues. Present your findings to the rest of the class using a format found on serious TV talk shows that present two sides of an issue.

TALKING PEACE: A VISION FOR THE NEXT GENERATION

What organizations are working to solve conflicts? How are they doing it?
http://gbgm-umc.org/nwo/99ja/teens.html

The Ulster Project www.ulsterproject.org

Seeds of Peace http://seedsofpeace.org

Develop your own action plan for solving problems in the areas you studied. Present them on a class website.

Cultural Perspectives

Looking from Within a Culture

BEHIND THE MOUNTAINS
A SUITCASE OF SEAWEED
BORN CONFUSED
CUBA 15
FINDING OUR WAY
A GROUP OF ONE

What are the themes that connect these works of fiction? How are young adults in cultures outside the United States different from you? How are they the same? Make a Venn Diagram* of likenesses and differences.

Looking at Culture from the Outside

SHABANNU
GO AND COME BACK
A GIRL NAMED DISASTER
GRAB HANDS AND RUN
THE OTHER SIDE OF TRUTH

What can authors writing from within a culture contribute that outsiders cannot? Is it possible for outsiders to portray different cultures authentically? How can writers and readers from outside a culture know if stereotypes are perpetuated? Develop a list of criteria for writers and readers of multicultural fiction. Post it on your class website.

Collect music to serve as the score for a Readers' Theater* from two of the books, one from each set of books/perspectives.

Multiple Perspectives

JINX
BULL RUN
BRONX MASQUERADE
BAT 6
SEEDFOLKS
BIG TALK POEMS FOR FOUR VOICES
BREAKOUT
"Twilight Los Angeles" (VHS)
"Bridge and Tunnel" Sarah Jones's website www.sarahjonesonline.com

These books and the performance pieces by Anna Deavere Smith and Sarah Jones present multiple perspectives on one or more themes. How have the authors crafted believable voices? Plan Readers' Theater* readings of these books. Then return to your small groups and write and perform a dramatic presentation that summarizes some aspect of the four different perspectives you studied. Convey important concepts as well as themes in your presentation.

The American Past

The Revolutionary War

MY BROTHER SAM IS DEAD
THE FIGHTING GROUND
JUMP SHIP TO FREEDOM
RABBLE IN ARMS
JOHNNY TREMAIN
THE FIFTH OF MARCH: THE STORY OF THE BOSTON MASSACRE
CAST TWO SHADOWS: THE REVOLUTIONARY WAR IN THE AMERICAN SOUTH
JUST JANE
TIME ENOUGH FOR DRUMS

The Civil War

WITH EVERY DROP OF BLOOD
THE RIVER BETWEEN US
THE SLOPES OF WAR
BEFORE THE CREEKS RAN RED
HEAR THE WIND BLOW. A NOVEL OF THE CIVIL WAR
THE LAST SILK DRESS
AMELIA'S WAR
SOUND THE JUBILEE

Explore perspectives in books about the Revolutionary War and the Civil War. How were perspectives of the loyalists different from the revolutionaries? Yankees from Southerners? Whites from African Americans? Men from women? How do authors portray these issues relating to the different sides in each of the wars? How does first-person or third-person perspective affect your response to the books? Create a mural (with captions) that displays the various perspectives and what you have learned about them.

How do the times in which authors are writing shape their personal perspectives on the stories they are telling? Note particularly MY BROTHER SAM IS DEAD and JOHNNY TREMAIN. What were the original publication dates and what events surrounded the authors as they wrote?

BULL RUN

Read aloud the multiple perspectives on the first battle of the Civil War as Fleischman provides it in this book. Choose one of the books above and take the characters and one event from the book. Write a Readers' Theater* script. Use primary and secondary sources in addition to the book to create authenticity in the setting and events.

explore perspectives from many cultures, genders, genres, and literary voices, Ed's students are asked to develop and apply criteria to their own reading and to employ those criteria to writing many genres on their own. In addition, Ed hopes to link topics covered in the literature the students read to the issues in social studies, particularly to constitutional issues of today.

Ed sees many possibilities in extending the theme of PERSPECTIVES to other content areas. Because his eighth graders have a whole semester of art (then a second semester of music), he has teamed up with art teacher Reenie Cooper to explore the concepts of perspectives in art. He has also alerted members of the math and science faculty to his plans. Several teachers have agreed to link concepts in their own fields to the timing of the PERSPECTIVES theme. Maria Ruiz, who teaches science to his students, saw exciting links to eighth-grade standards in space sciences and planned studies for students. Maria has set up an Internet Blog for all to interact around inquiries on outer space, whose findings will consist of a science museum for others in the school. Ernie Kaminsky, the math teacher in the pod, is developing a unit on ratios and beginning algebra to support the math that students will need to create models in the science class. He also saw connections to the visual perspectives topic and made several suggestions by having students study the invention of mathematical perspectives and optical illusions.

Ed's own teacher inquiry focused on the personal perspectives of his diverse group of adolescents. He has long been aware of the cliquish, sometimes intolerant, tendencies in the population he teaches. He was interested to see what a concrete focus on differing points of view would have on his students' own abilities at conflict resolution and on their ability to appreciate the diverse viewpoints held by students and their families and cultural communities. His initial questions included, "What cultural understandings do students bring to class?" "What happens as students attempt to take on points of view that are different from their own?" "How do these perspectives change over the course of the year?" Beginning with the outsiders study, Ed kept a notebook of observations of students' reactions, comments, and small-group interactions. He also asked students in groups to keep a written record of the major points in their group discussions and to tape-record some of their sessions. Ed used the recordings and photocopies or digital photos of their work to add richness to his inquiry.

Ed began the unit with the topic of "Outsiders." This had always been a favorite study with his students in years past and he felt that the whole idea of who is "outside" and who is "inside" would be a good way to get students interested in perspective and point of view. The books he chose also contained important themes of interest to adolescents and he felt he could link ethical issues raised in the books to the larger society that surrounded both the fictional characters and his own students.

Into the Classroom

We begin with the fourth week of the unit after students have completed the role playing and editorial writing activity that ended the "Outsiders" study. (See Table 4.20.) As Ed had expected, the students were particularly passionate about the rights of the characters they had read about, and there was much discussion about the pressure each of them felt from parents, their ethnic cultures, and the wider society to conform to societal norms. Ed hoped to link their interest to the study of American history as required by state social studies standards. As we enter the classroom the students have begun to study "Real and Imaginary Perspectives in War" and the differing points of view that led to the two greatest conflicts in American history. Ed wants the students to begin to think critically about an author's point of view, the reliability of point of view in fiction and nonfiction, and the use of primary sources such as letters and diaries in the study of history. He also wants students to apply the idea of voice and point of view in their own writing. He feels that a study of the conflicting points of view that led to the American Revolution and Civil War would be easier to relate to now that they had studied the topic of outsiders.

At the same time students continue to work with Reenie Cooper in art, Maria Ruiz in science, and Ed Kazminsky in math on their PERSPECTIVES-related projects.

table **4.20**   **Detailed Schedule, Ed Tyson's Eighth-Grade Communication Arts Block**

DAY 13

Time	Children	Teacher	Teacher Research
Small-Group Work Time 9:00–10:00	There is at least one person in each group who insists that real children wrote the diaries in other times. This makes for lively discussion as students find evidence to support their opinions.	Ed has broken the students into smaller groups to read and discuss multiple copies of titles from two popular series of diaries from American history. Although these were fiction, they looked very much like authentic writing of real people and he was curious to see what students' reactions were. He asks each group of students to make a Two-Column Chart* and make a list of factual and fictional events.	Ed monitors groups and takes notes on conflict resolution.
Group Time 10:35	Some students argue that the journal writer's name on the cover, the epilogue, and illustrations at the end means it was true. One student points out that the title page inside the book lists the name of a favorite author.	Ed asks for reports from each of the groups. A discussion about how to sort out fact from fiction ensues. Ed helps students develop a list of criteria for determining fact from fiction. He suggests they consult the media specialist and the Internet later. Ed has brought in some collections of primary source diaries and documents that have been collected together in book form. He lends out some of the materials to students and assigns others to use the media center, library, or home computer to search for first-person documents from the Revolutionary War and the Civil War. He wants them to compare the diaries they've been reading to primary source materials from the same eras. He will then help them to develop a list of criteria for other students to use when evaluating the authenticity of works of fiction and nonfiction. This activity is designed to lead into the study of conflict in the American past and in the global society of today and the reading of fiction and nonfiction about these topics.	

(continued)

table **4.20**   Detailed Schedule, Ed Tyson's Eighth-Grade Communication Arts Block (*continued*)

DAY 30

Time	Children	Teacher	Teacher Research
Group Meeting 9:00–9:20	Most students have finished reading and discussing their books and are now deciding on follow-up activities. The group reading about modern-day conflicts has decided to do further research into the conflicts surrounding the fiction books they've read. They want to write the script for a movie video highlighting different world conflicts and suggesting solutions. One of the Revolutionary War groups has decided to create a mural with captions to represent important factors in the development of the war. One of the Civil War groups wants to develop a story about the Battle of Gettysburg and to work it in to a Readers' Theater* script using *Bull Run* as a model. Another group wants to develop a pictorial newspaper detailing causes of the war.	Ed holds a short group meeting to check on progress of the different Literature Response Groups* that are studying "Real and Imaginary Perspectives in War."	Ed takes note of the student's enthusiasm for presenting information from so many different points of view and in so many different genres.
Integrated Work Time 10:35	One group is finishing up their discussion of *My Brother Sam Is Dead* and *Johnny Tremain*. Other students go to work on group projects.		

DAY 40

Time	Children	Teacher	Teacher Research
Group Meeting 9:00– 10:35	The final presentation is given by the group that read *The Slopes of War* and studied the Battle of Gettysburg. They present their Reader's Theater* script of the battle. Since students have been so heavily engaged with the topic, they had many ideas to contribute.	Ed invites discussion, questioning students about the process that they went through to develop their script. He then asks them to recall their "Outsiders" work and the research they did on student rights. He asks them to summarize some of the things they learned about their rights as students and their rights as citizens of the United States. Were these the same thing? Ed then introduces four works of fiction about adolescents involved in constitutional or electoral processes: *Jude, Vote for Larry,*	

table **4.20**   Detailed Schedule, Ed Tyson's Eighth-Grade Communication Arts Block *(continued)*

DAY 40 *(continued)*

Time	Children	Teacher	Teacher Research
Group Meeting *(continued)*		*Nothing but the Truth,* and *Hope Was Here.* He informs students that as they will be reading these books, along with biographies, information books, and other resources about the U.S. Constitution and the Bill of Rights, he wants them to understand how the documents were created, how they were affected by the Revolutionary War and the Civil War, and how these documents affected their own lives.	

Summary

The departmentalized schedule that we have come to expect in most middle and high schools allows teachers with special expertise to cover the advanced concepts that are necessary for disciplines such as science, math, and social studies. On the other hand, such departmentalization and short class periods can fragment learning and fail to find bridges across traditional disciplines. Ed's school has found what it feels is a good solution. By organizing students in pods, teachers can ensure more cohesion across the curriculum and students feel nurtured by a small community of professionals. Moreover, because he is responsible for both language arts and social studies, Ed has the advantage of longer blocks of time for students to engage with important ideas.

Ed feels satisfied that the PERSPECTIVES theme accomplished many of his personal goals, and he felt the state standards in social studies were met and exceeded over the course of the study. He also felt that students gained a better understanding of literary techniques as they examined first-person and third-person points of view in their reading and used such techniques in their writing. Results of his teacher inquiry led Ed to believe that students' sensitivity to different points of view extended beyond their own adolescent culture to a deeper understanding of conflict and conflict resolution, human rights, fact and opinion, and fiction and nonfiction. He will continue his research for the rest of the year to see if he can determine how the study of PERSPECTIVES transformed student attitudes and activism.

Children's Literature: PERSPECTIVES

Abigail Adams: Witness to a Revolution by N. Bober. Atheneum, 1995.

Aboriginal Art of Australia: Exploring Cultural Traditions by C. Finley. Lerner, 1999.

Acid Rain by L. Petheram. Bridgestone Books, 2003.

Adventure in Space: The Flight to Fix the Hubble by E. Scott. Photographs by M. Miller. Hyperion Books, 1995.

African Arts and Culture by J. Bingham. Raintree/Steck-Vaughn, 2004.

Air Pollution by R. L. Donald. Children's Press, 2001.

Alice, I Think by S. Juby. HarperCollins, 2003.

Am I Blue? Coming Out from the Silence by M. Bauer. HarperCollins, 1995.

Amelia's War by A. Rinaldi. Scholastic, 2002.

The American Revolutionaries: A History in their Own Words by M. Meltzer. Crowell, 1987.

Angus, Thongs, and Full Frontal Snogging by L. Rennison. HarperCollins, 2001.

Anno's Alphabet by M. Anno. Crowell, 1975.

Aphrodite's Blessing: Love Stories from Greek Myths by C. McLaren. Atheneum, 2002.

Art Attack: A Short History of the Avant Garde by M. Aronson. Clarion, 1998.

Asteroids, Comets, and Meteors by R. Kerrod. Lerner Publications, 2000.

Atmosphere: Sea of Air by R. A. Gallant. Benchmark Books, 2003.

Bat 6 by V. E. Wolff. Scholastic, 1998.

Beast by D. J. Napoli. Atheneum, 2000.

Before the Creeks Ran Red by C. Reeder. HarperCollins, 2003.

Behind the Mountains by E. Danticat. Scholastic, 2002.

Big Mouth and Ugly by J. C. Oates. HarperCollins, 2002.

Big Talk Poems for Four Voices by P. Fleischman. Candlewick, 2000.

The Bill of Rights: The First Ten Amendments of the Constitution by D. L. Hudson, Jr. Exodus, 2002.

Born Confused by T. D. Hidier. Scholastic, 2003.

Breakout by P. Fleischman. Cricket, 2003.

Bronx Masquerade by N. Grimes. Dial, 2002.

Bull Run by P. Fleischman. HarperCollins, 1995.

Cast Two Shadows: The Revolutionary War in the American South by A. Rinaldi. Harcourt, 2002.

Chain of Fire by B. Naidoo. Illustrated by Eric Velasquez. HarperCollins, 1990.

Chuck Close Up Close by J. Greenberg & S. Jordan. Abrams, 1998.

City of Light, City of Dark by Avi. Illustrated by B. Flocca. Orchard, 1995.

Comets, Meteors, and Asteroids by S. Simon. Morrow, 1994.

Cosmic Phenomena by G. Vanin. Firefly Books, 1999.

Creating the Constitution: The People and Events That Formed the Nation by D. Weidener. Enslow, 2002.

Cuba 15 by N. Osa. Delacorte, 2003.

Dating Hamlet: Ophelia's Story by L. Fiedler. Holt, 2002.

Deep Space Observation Satellites by J. Sherman. Rosen Publishing, 2003.

Deliver Us from Evie by M. E. Kerr. HarperCollins, 1995.

Destination: Jupiter by S. Simon. HarperCollins, 1998.

Destination: Mars by S. Simon. HarperCollins, 2000.

Destination: Space by S. Simon. HarperCollins, 2002.

Dreamings: The Art of Aboriginal Australia by P. Sutton. George Braziller, 1997.

Earth and Space by L. Howell, K. Rogers, & C. Henderson. Usborne Publishing, 2001.

The Elements of Pop-Up: A Pop-Up Book for Aspiring Paper Engineers by D. Carter & J. Diaz. Simon & Schuster, 1999.

Escape from Earth: Voyages through Time by P. Ackroyd. Dorling Kindersley, 2003.

Exploring Our Solar System by S. Ride & T. O'Shaughnessy. Crown, 2004.

Eyewitness Perspective by A. Cole. DK, 1994.

The Fifth of March: The Story of the Boston Massacre by A. Rinaldi. Gulliver, 2004.

The Fighting Ground by Avi. HarperCollins, 1984.

Finding Our Way by R. Saldana, Jr. Random, 2003.

Flipped by W. Van Draanen, Knopf, 2001.

Freak the Mighty by R. Philbrick. Scholastic, 2001.

Frederick Douglas: In His Own Words by M. Meltzer. Harcourt, 1995.

Galaxies by S. Simon. Morrow, 1988.

Girl Coming in for a Landing: A Novel in Poems by A. H. Wayland. Knopf, 2002.

A Girl Named Disaster by N. Farmer. Orchard, 1996.

Global Warming by C. Oxlade. Bridgestone Books, 2003.

Global Warming: The Threat Of Earth's Changing Climate by L. Pringle. Sea Star, 2001.

Go and Come Back by J. Abelove. DK, 1998.

The Gospel According to Larry by J. Tashjian. Holt, 2001.

Grab Hands and Run by F. Temple. Scholastic, 1993.

The Great Little Madison by J. Fritz. Putnam, 1989.

A Group of One by R. Gilmore. Holt, 2001.

Guide to Space by P. Bond. DK, 1999.

Habibi by N. S. Nye. Simon & Schuster, 1997.

Hear the Wind Blow. A Novel of the Civil War by M. D. Hahn. Clarion, 2003.

Heart to Heart: New Poems Inspired by Twentieth Century Art by Jan Greenberg. Abrams, 2001.

Home On the Moon: Living On a Space Frontier by M. J. Dyson. National Geographic, 2003.

Hope Was Here by J. Bauer. Putnam, 2000.

How I Wonder Where You Are by C. Lynch. Knopf, 2001.

How We Use and Abuse Our Planet: Air and Energy by A. Haswell. Thameside Press, 2000.

The Hubble Space Telescope by M. W. Carruthers. Franklin Watts, 2003.

Hubble Space Telescope: Exploring the Universe by M. D. Cole. Enslow, 1999.

I Can Hear the Mourning Dove by J. Bennett. Scholastic, 1997.

I Feel a Little Jumpy around You: A Book of Her and His Poems Collected in Pairs by N. S. Nye & P. Janeszcko. Simon & Schuster, 1999.

I Want to Be an Environmentalist by C. O. Grace. Harcourt, 2000.

In Pursuit of Liberty: The Story of America's Bill of Rights by R. Freedman. Holiday, 2003.

In Spite of Killer Bees by J. Johnston. Tundra, 2001.

Jinx by M. Wild. Walker, 2002.

Johnny Tremain by E. Forbes. Houghton Mifflin, 1943.

The Journal of James Edmund Pease by J. Murphy. Scholastic, 1998.

Journey to Jo'burg by B. Naidoo. HarperCollins, 1986.

Jude by K. Morgenroth. Simon & Schuster, 2004.

Jump Ship to Freedom by J. Collier & C. Collier. Delacorte, 1981.

Just Jane by W. Lavendar. Harcourt, 2002.

Keeping the Air Clean by J. Baines. Steck-Vaughn, 1998.

The Kings Are Already Here by G. Freyman-Weyr. Houghton, 2003.

The Last Silk Dress by A. Rinaldi. Laurel Leaf, 1999.

Little Lit: Folk and Fairy Tale Funnies by A. Spiegelman & F. Mouly. HarperCollins, 2000.

The Magic Circle by D. J. Napoli. Dutton, 1993.

Mars by R. Korrod. Lerner Publications, 2000.

Maus: A Survivor's Tale by A. Spiegelman. Pantheon, 1986.

Mercury and Venus by R. Kerrod. Lerner, 2000.

The Middle of Somewhere: A Story of South Africa by S. Gordon. Orchard, 1990.

The Misfits by J. Howe. Atheneum, 2001.

The Moon by M. W. Carruthers. Franklin Watts, 2003.

My Brother Sam Is Dead by J. Collier & C. Collier. Delacorte, 1981.

NASA by S. Tocci. Franklin Wattts, 2003.

Nothing But the Truth by Avi. HarperCollins, 1993.

Now You See It Now You Don't by S. Simon. Morrow, 1998.

The Other Side of Truth by B. Naidoo. HarperCollins, 2002.

The Outsiders by S. E. Hinton. Viking, 1967.

The Ozone Layer by R. L. Donald. Children's Press, 2001.

Painter's Eye: Learning to Look at Contemporary American Art by J. Greenberg & S. Jordan. Delacorte, 1994.

Perspolis: The Story of a Childhood by M. Satrapi. Pantheon, 2004.

The Pigman by P. Zindel. HarperCollins, 1968.

Probably Still Nick Swenson by V. E. Wolff. Simon & Schuster, 2002.

Rabble in Arms by K. Roberts. Doubleday, 1947.

Rats Saw God by R. Thomas. Simon & Schuster, 1996.

The River Between Us by R. Peck. Dial, 2003.

Romeo and Juliet Together (and Alive!) at Last by Avi. Harper-Collins, 1988.

Sand Land by A. Toriyama. Viz Communications, 2003

The Sandman: Endless Nights by N. Gaiman. DC Comics, 2003.

Science Project Ideas about the Moon by R. Gardner. Enslow, 1997.

Science Project Ideas about the Sun by R. Gardner. Enslow, 1997.

Seedfolks by P. Fleischman. HarperCollins, 1999.

Shabannu Daughter of the Wind by S. Staples. Knopf, 1989.

Shadow People by J. MacDonald. Delacorte, 2000.

Simple Optical Illusion Experiments with Everyday Materials by M. DiSpezio. Sterling, 2000.

The Skin I'm In by S. Flake. Hyperion, 2000.

The Slopes of War by N. Perez. Houghton, 1990.

The Solar System: Saturn by R. Birch. Chelsea Clubhouse, 2004.

Soldier Boys by D. Hughes. Atheneum, 2001.

Sound the Jubilee by S. Forrester. Puffin, 1997.

Speak by L. H. Anderson. Puffin, 2001.

A Stone in My Hand by C. Clinton. Candlewick, 2002.

Stonecutter by L. Watts. Houghton Mifflin, 2002.

A Suitcase of Seaweed by J. Wong. McElderry, 1996.

Talking Peace: A Vision for the Next Generation by J. Carter. Turtleback, 1995.

Time Enough for Drums by A. Rinaldi. Laurel Leaf, 2000.

Together, Apart by D. Gray. Houghton, 2002.

Tribes by A. Slade. Knopf, 2002.

The True Story of the Three Little Pigs as Told by A. Wolf by J. Scieszka. Viking, 1990.

"Twilight Los Angeles" (VHS) by A. D. Smith. Twilight Distributed by PBS, 2000.

Ug, Boy Genius of the Stone Age and His Search for Soft Trousers by R. Briggs. Knopf, 2002.

Uranus, Neptune, and Pluto by R. Kerrod. Lerner Publications, 2000.

Vote for Larry by J. Tashjian. Holt, 2004.

Waiting for Odysseus by C. McLaren. Atheneum, 2000.

Waiting for the Rain by S. Gordon. Orchard, 1987.

Walter Wick's Optical Tricks by W. Wick. Scholastic, 1998.

We Were There Too! Young People in U. S. History by P. Hoose. Farrar, Straus, & Giroux, 2001.

When My Name Was Keoko by L. Park. Clarion, 2002.

When the Bough Breaks by A. Myers. Walker, 2000.

Who the Man by C. Lynch. HarperCollins, 2003.

With Every Drop of Blood by J. Collier & C. Collier. Delacorte, 1981.

The Winter of Red Snow: The Revolutionary War Diary of Abigail Jane Snow by K. Gregory. Scholastic, 1996.

Yankee Doodle Boy: A Young Soldier's Adventures in the Revolutionary War as Told by Himself by J. P. Martin. Holiday House, 1995.

Zero G: Life and Survival in Space by P. Bond. Cassell, 1999.

Conclusions

Each of the teachers visited in the prototypes in this chapter is a unique individual in strength, interests, and enthusiasm. Some are more likely to think initially in disciplinary or curricular categories when planning; others prefer to follow a theme across categories first and attend to disciplinary or curricular requirements later. Some work well in teams or in open classrooms; others enjoy the flexibility of self-contained or family-grouped settings. Despite these and other differences, there are also commonalities among them that identify their classrooms as integrated language environments. First, these classes are distinguished by the joint participation of adults and children in meaning making. Dehea Munioz, for instance, regularly involves children in planning at the outset of a thematic unit so that they see themselves as active participants not just in learning about something or someone but in selecting what to learn about. As a result, her plans evolve over the course of the unit as student investigations trigger new questions for inquiry. Dehea is also a researcher in her own right. As the thematic unit progresses, she introduces specific experiences or information, collects data on student responses, analyzes those responses, and develops theories supported by her research, thereby better learning how to support student learning.

Distinguishing features of integrated language classrooms.

A related feature of these integrated language classrooms is a different view of error. Children hypothesize, make approximations, develop theories, and test them against new data. Their hypotheses and theories may not be supported by these new data, and their approximations may be refined as they learn more, but that is the nature of learning. Hypothesis-making requires risk, and these classes provide a context within which intellectual risk taking is encouraged, supported, and expected. Caitlin Cooper depicts this perspective as her students first develop the tools of archaeological observation and inference and then use those tools to construct their own civilization. Other teachers in the prototype also encourage hypothesizing that points children toward assuming responsibilities in the larger community.

> Teachers and children in these classes develop a different view of "error" and intellectual risk taking.

Teachers in integrated language classrooms see themselves as child developmentalists rather than teacher technicians. They are professionals responsible for developing a child-centered curriculum that has solid intellectual content. Child developmentalists know that content and context are inseparable. They strive to arrange the kind of context that fosters student engagement in their process of building theories about the world. These classrooms are full of participants, not recipients. Children are the active makers of meaning.

> Teachers become child developmentalists rather than technicians.

These classroom contexts are filled with a range of materials, but they are not expensive resources. Rather, they are gathered from many sources, including materials donated by or borrowed from families, friends, acquaintances, and other members of the community. Books and print resources are easily obtained from libraries. As pointed out in Chapter 3, experienced integrated language teachers frequently use approximately 400 to 500 books during a thematic unit. Space does not allow us to list that many books on the WEBs. Consequently, the WEBs in this chapter include only a portion of the books available on these themes.

> Integrated language classrooms are content rich and community oriented.

Related to this feature of resources is the way the community serves as a resource. An important characteristic of the integrated language classrooms you have seen here is how frequently the boundaries between the community and the classroom are crossed. Time after time, the community is brought into the classroom to provide expertise or help. Parents and friends and children from other classes join class participants to celebrate and support children's efforts. Children go on field trips into the community to gain important information and data for their projects. In turn, the larger community provides a real audience for student work. Through this two-way process, the classroom culture is enlarged and expanded, and bridges are constructed to span the gulf between the school and the world at large.

Finally, the various classroom and teaching arrangements depicted here are not specific to a particular grade or age. A teacher working on a seventh- or eighth-grade team in a middle school setting, for instance, would be more likely to use patterns such as those that could be found in a fourth- and fifth-grade departmentalized setting than those in the sixth-grade self-contained model. Obviously, ideas from one prototype can be used in others, and activities set up for younger children can often be adapted for use with older students, and vice versa. Classrooms, as with any human community, change over time. What is crucial is that each of these teachers constantly seeks to enrich children's lives by making them more interested and able learners.

References

Atwell, N. (Ed.). (1990). *Coming to know: Writing to learn in the intermediate grades.* Portsmouth, N. H.: Heinemann.

Barr, R., Barth, J., & Shermis, S. S. (1977). *Defining the social studies (Bulletin No. 51).* Washington, DC: National Council for the Social Studies.

Bergen, D. (Ed.). (1987). *Play as a medium for learning and development: A handbook of theory and practice.* Portsmouth, NH: Heinemann.

Blake, D. W. (1981). Observing children learning history. *The History Teacher, 14,* 533–549.

Clements, M., Tabachnik, R., & Fielder, W. (1966). *Social study.* New York: Bobbs-Merrill.

Feshback, N. D. (1975). Empathy in children: Some theoretical and empirical considerations. *Counseling Psychologist, 4,* 25–30.

Goodman, K., Bird, L., & Goodman, Y. (1992). *The whole language catalog: Supplement on authentic assessment.* Santa Rosa, CA: American School Publishers.

Hartoonian, M. (1992). *A guide to curriculum planning on global studies.* Milwaukee: Wisconsin Department of Public Instruction.

McGinley, W., & Madigan, D. (1990). The research "story": A forum for integrating reading, writing, and learning. *Language Arts, 67,* 474–483.

Perry, T., & Fraser, J. (1993). *Freedom's plow.* London: Routledge.

Ryan, F., & Ellis, A. (1974). *Instructional implications of inquiry.* Englewood Cliffs, NJ: Prentice-Hall.

Shaftel, F. R., & Shaftel, G. (1982). *Role playing in the curriculum* (2nd ed.). Englewood Cliffs, NJ: Prentice-Hall.

Sims, R. (1982). *Shadow and substance: Afro-American experience in contemporary children's fiction.* Urbana, IL: National Council of Teachers of English.

Spears-Bunton, L. A. (1990). Welcome to my house: African-American and European-American students' responses to Virginia Hamilton's "House of Dies Drear." *Journal of Negro Education, 59,* 566–576.

Stone, L. C. (1986). International and multicultural education. In V. Atwood (Ed.), *Elementary social studies: Research as a guide to practice (Bulletin No. 79,* pp. 34–54). Washington, DC: National Council for the Social Studies.

5

More Ideas to Integrate the Curriculum

Two major characteristics of the integrated language perspective are the use of oral and written language across the curriculum and the integration of the various curricular areas. Chapters 3 and 4 explained how this integration is accomplished through thematic units. This chapter provides more specific details and ideas to help teachers integrate language and content in five curricular areas: social studies, science, mathematics, art, and music. In each curricular area, there are two emphases: (1) a brief overview of current views, principles, and concepts, and (2) more ideas for ways to integrate language within and across the curriculum.

Social Studies

What Is Social Studies?

See the National Council for the Social Studies' website, www.ncss.org, for more resources on the teaching and learning of social studies.

We see social studies as the integration of the processes of learning about people as they arrange to live together in groups, and the content of history and the social sciences as they relate to these human activities. How children learn and what they learn are both fundamental parts of social studies. In the social studies, children learn to recognize and evaluate social data, build causal theories, draw conclusions, and make and challenge generalizations about human behavior. These are important behaviors in a culturally diverse society in an interdependent world. Students need to make *informed* and *reasoned* decisions, not just to enhance their individual lives—although this is certainly important—but also to enable them to better work for the public good. Thus, the basic subject matter and constant focus of the social studies are people *in community*. Social studies connects children to the world, whether engaging them in studying family history, looking at the influences of the Nile River on Egyptian society and how Egyptians have attempted to control those influences, or in examining the economic, social, and political impact of urbanization in a developing nation. In our perspective, social studies is often the core of the integrated curriculum, for it provides powerful themes for study and opportunities for children to engage in important conversations about race, class, gender, ideology, and the distribution of power in human societies. Because these issues divide societies, they are among the most controversial—and potentially interesting—parts of the curriculum. As a result, social studies is one of the most powerful contexts within which children use all the forms of language discussed in previous chapters. Sometimes however, this feature of social studies makes teachers, as well as some students and parents, uncomfortable. This explains, at least in part, why social studies is too often reduced to its least interesting and least contro-

Gamberg, Kwak, Hutchings, & Altheim (1988); McGinnis (n.d.); NCSS (1994)

Social studies connects children to the world.

Levstik & Barton (2001)

versial aspects. In too many classrooms, social studies is little more than perfunctory studies of topics such as community helpers or transportation, without any real attention to the human consequences of social studies content. But if we are to prepare students to live in community with others, to make informed and reasoned decisions, and to participate fully in a democratic society, we cannot ignore controversies. Instead, we can use the social studies to help children develop the knowledge, skills, and attitudes necessary to understand and cope with controversy. In the context of an integrated curriculum, then, social studies gains an importance that it often lacks in the traditional classroom.

Like science, social studies is not a single discipline but an integration of content, concepts, and generalizations from a number of disciplines. Social studies generally draws on history, geography, anthropology, sociology, political science, economics, psychology, and the arts. Combining these disciplines encourages children to see the way in which these forces together influence human activity. Figure 5.1 shows the way content from several disciplines can pose different questions to be used in exploring a single theme. The integrated nature of social studies, however, makes it more complicated to define than science, due in part to the multiple perspectives or purposes that can be attributed to this curricular area. As a result, teachers need to think carefully about building a classroom context that supports social studies.

Building the Social Studies Context

LINKING PROCESS AND CONTENT

As we have already mentioned, social studies involves integrating the processes of learning about history, the social sciences, and the arts with content drawn from each domain. This is a crucial idea in understanding the place of social studies in an integrated curriculum. Good teaching focuses on helping students learn important organizing ideas. Because each of the component fields within social studies focuses on different, though related, organizing ideas, students need plenty of opportunity to study the content of each field; they also need to learn *how* each field acquires and organizes knowledge. The

> Social studies is an integration of content, concepts, and generalizations from several disciplines.
>
> Barr, Barth, & Shermis (1977); Maxim (1987); Stodolsky (1988)

> See also Barr, Barth, & Shermis (1977) and Barth (1996) for a discussion of the implications of differing definitions of social studies.

> Cope & Kalantzis (2000); Downey & Levstik (1988); Levstik & Pappas (1987, 1992); Wilson & Wineberg (1988)

> "Knowing" in a domain is more than remembering discrete "facts."

figure **5.1**

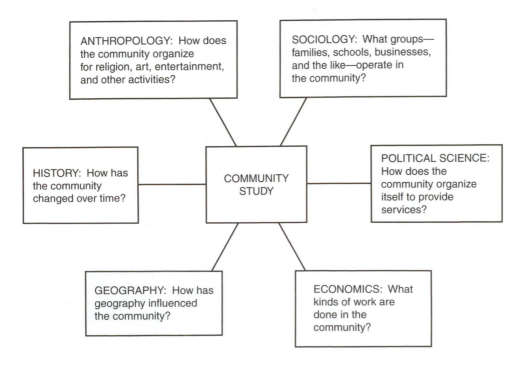

ANTHROPOLOGY: How does the community organize for religion, art, entertainment, and other activities?

SOCIOLOGY: What groups— families, schools, businesses, and the like—operate in the community?

HISTORY: How has the community changed over time?

COMMUNITY STUDY

POLITICAL SCIENCE: How does the community organize itself to provide services?

GEOGRAPHY: How has geography influenced the community?

ECONOMICS: What kinds of work are done in the community?

way knowledge is constructed in history, for instance, is quite different from the way in which scientists understand chemistry. A scientist can observe the way in which hydrogen combines with oxygen to produce water and can generate laws based on this observation. A historian can never observe the phenomena under investigation. Instead, history is constructed from the partial residue of the past. The historian constructs a plausible explanation of how that residue fits into the past but cannot construct laws to explain this phenomenon. History is particularistic and resists our attempts to construct a full account of the past. Yet, making sense of history is critically important for the goal of history education is to enable students to participate in democratic life.

These are very different ways of thinking about evidence, hypotheses, and proofs. For children to develop understanding in social studies, they need to understand these differences. They need experience in using and interpreting various kinds of social data from history, the social sciences, and the arts. Yet process alone is not social studies. No matter what processes are used, there is always a subject of study—the question or content under investigation. In addition, not all subjects are equally worthy of study. Given the limited amount of time and the almost infinite variety of topics that can be studied in any school year, part of the teacher's obligation is making sure that the topics studied are worthwhile. Thus, the teacher might ask, with regard to content, if selected topics help children:

View a period or culture from the perspective of those who live or lived in that time and place.

Recognize the impact of interactions between humans and the environment.

Develop deeper understanding of themselves and others as individuals and members of groups.

Act as knowledgeable, critically minded citizens.

Resist prejudice and avoid stereotyping.

Critically evaluate social data and interpretations of social data.

From this perspective, time spent investigating apples or bears may not seem worthwhile, despite some possibilities for helping children learn to use the processes of gathering and analyzing data or communicating findings. On the other hand, consider the possibilities from both process and content perspectives when third-grade children study a problem in their community.

No More Litter

Children in a mountainous rural district were engaged in a thematic unit centered on their community and containing the areas outlined in Figure 5.1. After touring the community, they discussed a real problem in their area: the illegal dumping of trash and garbage. They thought that something ought to be done about the garbage that littered their hillsides, but they were not sure what that could be or if children could make any difference. Their teacher suggested that they investigate and collect data to help them decide. She then arranged a series of field trips to garbage collection sites: illegal dumps, the county landfill, and a recycling center. The children planned and collectively wrote interview questions, recorded their observations and interviews, and then set about analyzing their data. Their teacher encouraged them to express their findings in a variety of ways. Soon the classroom was full of captioned artwork detailing what had been found. Some children made a mural showing how the plants and animals might feel about all the garbage. The trees, birds, and even the sun commented on how awful the litter was. Only germs, maggots, and rats had good things to say. The children had been researching in information books, and they shared their findings about the relationship of germs, maggots, and rats to garbage.

VanSledright (2002)

History is interpretation based on the residue of the past.

Barton & Levstik (2004); VanSledright (2002)

Gamberg, Kwak, Hutchings, & Altheim (1988)

NCSS (1994); NCSS Focus Group (1992)

Harlan (KY) Elementary School (1986)

See Berson (2004) for a fourth-grade inquiry on "The Trashing of Our Community" in which digital photography was employed.

Children study an authentic problem and record their observations.

Next, the class began a recycling campaign. Their trip to the recycling center had convinced them that this would have several benefits. Not only would it clean up the environment, but they could also earn money to pay for the videotapes they were using. The second grade sponsored a can-collecting contest in the school, and they soon were recycling huge numbers of aluminum cans. They also began writing a play about a community where it was illegal not to litter. They made up songs and dialogue and constructed props as a way to convince the rest of their school to participate in an antilitter campaign.

Children participate in alleviating a problem.

The next step was to visit their local government representatives to find out what was being done about the litter problems. They discovered that their county had begun an adopt-a-spot campaign to encourage a sense of responsibility and ownership about the environment. The class adopted their school yard to educate others in the community about their responsibility. Before long, the children had edited their tapes, selected artwork and writing as well as musical background, and produced a videotape called *No More Litter*. The tape was used at parent–teacher meetings to encourage adults to join the adopt-a-spot program.

Consider what these children accomplished in terms of the goals of social studies:

Accomplishing the goals of social studies

1. The topic had power and reality for them. It helped them understand the diverse factors that shape societies (geography, history, sociology, and economics).
2. The unit allowed the children to critically examine a public issue in their community and act as knowledgeable, critically minded citizens by helping to alleviate that problem (citizenship and political science).
3. They learned something about the community services available to help people take care of such basic problems as garbage disposal and recycling (economics, political science, and sociology).
4. They discovered that elected officials shared their concerns and were willing to work with the community to solve problems (political science).
5. They learned what resources could be used to investigate a problem, how to critically evaluate those resources, and how to effectively communicate their findings to other people (reflective inquiry).
6. They learned to see the problem from the perspective of different community members and interest groups (history, economics, sociology, and psychology).

At the end of this unit, the children had a sense of efficacy rather than defeat. They had discovered a powerful motivation for using their writing and reading skills, and as a result, they improved the very skills that had caused them problems in their previous schooling. Finally, this thematic unit broke down the walls between school and the surrounding world.

Levstik & Barton (2001); VanSledright (2002).

Little would have happened if the children had not had time to study in-depth and reflect on what they had learned, ask new questions, and select ways to respond to their findings.

DEPTH

For children (and adults) to understand a particular cognitive domain, they need enough time to study in such depth that they begin to build theories about how knowledge in that domain is used. They need to see how particular information fits in the larger context of a domain. In geography, for instance, how does one piece of information (the location of a mountain range) relate to another (a low density of population)? What can one find out about people by knowing and developing understanding? Providing context means providing an opportunity to study something in-depth as the second-grade children studied the problem of litter in their community. To have depth, a topic must have *extensiveness;* that is, it must be rich enough to generate subtopics, activities, and interest. Study is equally important in that it encourages the kind of thinking that relates to theory building in a domain. As a result, social studies is not

Carey (1985a, 1985b); Daniels & Zemelman (2004); Keil (1984); Newmann et al. (1995); Whitin & Whitin (1997); Wells (1999)

Context can facilitate depth.

Hyde & Bizar (1989); Levstik & Barton (2001)

Gerwin & Zevin (2003)

Social studies is a way of asking and answering questions.

Using incongruity

Freedman (1980)

Levinson (1997)

Looking at history as interpretation

Meltzer (1964)
Hurmence (1982)

Teachers gather resources.

Riis (1971)

Children share findings and chart results.

Children create their own texts.

just the accumulation of information but also a "mystery" in that a spirit of openness and investigation exists. It involves a way of asking questions about a subject and a way of answering and understanding the answers. Some incongruity or anomaly must, therefore, strike children as they encounter the social studies. Read the following account of a classroom and think about how the teacher uses incongruity to involve children in thinking about interpretation in the social studies.

Immigrant Children

As part of a thematic unit titled MIGRATIONS, a teacher brought a selection of books on U.S. immigration into his fifth-grade classroom. He hoped to generate interest in a recurrent theme in American history and a current topic of debate in the surrounding community. He brought one of his favorite books, *Immigrant Kids* by Russell Freedman, to share orally. As he read to the class, he pointed out the photographs that illustrated the text. One picture of a child bathing in a metal sink generated a good deal of discussion; children noted how difficult it would be to keep clean and how little privacy families would have had in the tenement pictured. Some days later, as the teacher shared *Watch the Stars Come Out* by Rikki Levinson, one of the children called attention to Diane Goode's illustration of a child bathing in a metal sink in a New York tenement—clearly based on the photograph they had seen earlier. The children were amazed at the difference between Goode's soft pastel treatment of the same scene that the photographer had captured in all its squalor. At this point, the teacher saw an opportunity to help children look at the interpretive nature of historical reporting. He gathered other examples of authors and illustrators who treated issues of voluntary and involuntary immigration. He brought to the classroom Meltzer's *In Their Own Words,* a compilation of the memories of enslaved African Americans, and Hurmence's *A Girl Called Boy,* a historical fiction based on slave narratives. He also located copies of the slave narratives preserved at the State Historical Society so that a group of students could study these books' source material. He found collections of pictures of the ethnic and tenement neighborhoods of Manhattan that were taken by Jacob Riis at the turn of the century and published in *How the Other Half Lives,* a photo essay on illegal immigration by Ashabranner, and photographs from the collection.

Students also located reference material in the school and public library and in their textbooks and set to work analyzing the varying interpretations in the sources. One group developed charts to show the following:

The sources for information used by authors and illustrators

The ways in which illustrations were used to help interpret information

The types of interpretations authors used

Specific information selected for inclusion or omission

Evidence of point of view (ideological perspective, bias, distortion)

Soon these fifth graders were developing criteria for evaluating information books and historical fiction. (See Figure 5.2.) The children went on to create their own information books and historical fiction based on their studies and the criteria they had developed. One of their texts was titled *How to Read History.* As a result of their study, these children had learned a great deal about the interpretive nature of history:

1. They were engaged in comparing and contrasting interpretations that would not only help them understand the history of immigration but also serve them well when they studied other history and read historical literature.
2. They learned to look for certain types of errors, bias, and misinterpretation—an important part of understanding history and the social studies.
3. They learned some of the ways in which historical information can be "mythologized" and misunderstood.

figure **5.2**

Criteria	Biography	History	Historical Fiction
Conversation	Not invented.	Must have evidence.	Invent only for fictional characters.
Order of events	Can't change if it's true.	Definitely can't change.	Only for made-up events.
Invented actions	Not for real people.	Never. Infer with support.	Yes, as long as it doesn't change history.
Invented people	No. Maybe disguise the identity of real people.	No. Must be based on evidence.	Yes. Put invented people in real situations.

Visualizing the Social World

Part of the impact of the MIGRATIONS theme came through visual images—photographs, paintings, and drawings—that gave immigration not only a human face but also a material world. The visual arts provide information about clothing, work and leisure activities, gender roles, religious practices, household goods, and children's play. A student can study the faces of immigrant children as they pick over rags, work in sweatshops, or walk among the vendors on Hester Street in New York. In the same way, pictures of the bleak, windswept Gila River Relocation Center in Arizona make vivid the indignities of Japanese internment. One photograph of a long line of people waiting in the blowing dust to use the latrines in the camp speaks volumes to students. Similarly, Wendall Minor's paintings in *Mojave* and *Heartland* provide students with powerful images of American landscapes.

Visual images provide different vantage points, or perspectives, from which to view the world and make explicit some of the powerful emotions that often defy words to fully express. They are also accessible to even very young children. This does not mean that visual images are always simple to comprehend. Think about how challenging it can be to "read" the imagery in, say, a painting by Chagall or Magritte. Even relatively "realistic" paintings can be interpreted at many different levels and in many different ways. Beyond their aesthetic purposes the arts are also social and ideological data. Gheeraert's painting of Queen Elizabeth I standing astride a map of the world is not just a picture of a historical figure, anymore than Steen's *The World Upside Down* is only a picture of a social gathering. Each provides social and political commentary—a perspective on the social world—that is neither wholly aesthetic nor the whole picture of a particular time, place, or person. One teacher finds *The Kids' Art Pack* a helpful resource here. He began with a picture—Ford Madox Brown's *The Last of England*—and set of questions from the book. In the picture, a somber couple sits in the foreground, clasping hands and gazing back toward England from the deck of a ship. The questions require students to look closely, speculating on how the two main figures might be feeling, what the woman is holding in her left hand (a baby's hand), the significance of the name of the ship (*El Dorado*), the weather, and other details in the painting. Students then construct an interpretation of the "story" told in the painting. Finally, their teacher shares the event that inspired the painting—emigration to Australia in 1855—and engages the class in a discussion of how the artist captured that event and some of its accompanying emotions.

The visual arts also shape popular opinion and behaviors by boosting consumerism, discouraging particular personal or social habits, memorializing people and events, and encouraging participation in various activities. Depictions of individuals, groups, or events have enormous influence on the ways in which students think about

Albert & Groth (1997); Barton & Levstik (1996)

Seibert (1988); Seibert (1990)

Barton (2001); Mitchell (1994)

Visual images can be interpreted in many ways.

Van der Meer & Whitford (1997)

The visual arts shape popular opinion and behaviors.

Barton (2001); Barton & Levstik (1996); Foster, Hoge, & Rosch (1999); Kammen (1996)

Images should show the complexity and diversity of human life.

See Barton (2001) for ways to analyze historical photographs.

The arts are a form of problem solving.

The arts transform information into visual representation.

the social world. Think about the impact of pictures of waif-like models on young girls' body image, the stereotyping of Arabs as bomb-throwing terrorists in different media, or of World War II propaganda posters presenting the Japanese as a "yellow peril." Perhaps most powerfully, consider the ways in which images from television and film influence students. After looking at pictures representing five hundred years of American history, children from kindergarten through sixth grade identified a picture of a 1950s' drive-in restaurant as the "Happy Days" picture. They also recognized other aspects of material culture from television shows or in popular movies that depicted historical events. Sometimes this helps children in sequencing events in time; sometimes visual images perpetuate stereotypes, myths, and oversimplifications of the social world.

Because social studies in the integrated curriculum should make people next door as well as those in other times, places, and circumstances real to children, it is important to find visual images that present people as complex beings who share the students' humanity. When carefully selected, such images provide important social data to children. They help children answer such questions as: What is it like to live in this time or place? What is it like to be this person? To feel this way? And, perhaps most significantly, images help children visualize what it means to be fully human in a diverse and interdependent world.

Besides their use as social data, however, the arts are also an important form of problem solving. In one class, students studying American history were asked to see if they could come up with a multicultural time line of ten events they considered to be significant in American history. After considerable debate about what constituted a "multicultural" time line as well as what constituted "significance," students set about building their time lines. Their teacher asked that they use illustrations and captions rather than long explanations for each point on the time line. First, the students collected a set of events that they all thought was significant. Next, they began sorting these events into time periods. They debated about whether an event or individual was significant multiculturally or only for one group. Once they had settled on ten events or individuals, they set about deciding how to illustrate the significance of each. This turned out to be an important discussion; in order to depict the *significance* of an event, they had to understand it well enough to *symbolize* it. One group, for instance, drew a slave breaking out of manacles to represent the Emancipation Proclamation. Another group drew the face of a Native American and placed arrows next to the face. At the top of the downward-pointing arrow, the students printed the population of Native Peoples in the Americas at the time of Columbus's arrival; at the bottom of that arrow, they listed the population one hundred years later. The other arrow, pointing up, began with the population of Europeans after Columbus's arrival and then one hundred years later. Once the time lines were complete, the class discussed each group's choices. By this time they could provide solid support for their choices, explain their significance, and discuss the challenges inherent in telling a multicultural story while accurately depicting the impact of each individual and event. The time lines provided a lively forum through which students expressed their moral judgments as well as their historical analyses.

In another classroom, students working on a DIGGING UP THE PAST theme also sought to transform linguistic information into visual representation. After collecting evidence of cultural diffusion in their small, largely rural community, they decided to develop a map that traced certain practices from other countries and other parts of the United States to their community. First, they used digital cameras to take photographs of cultural artifacts and practices in their community. Their pictures included a restaurant and two grocery store signs, photographs of international cookbooks in the local library, names from storefronts, pictures of themselves, of their homes, and public art. They grouped these images into categories—What We Eat, How We Dress, Celebrations, Language, and Built Environment—and used the computer to create collages for each category. They designed their explanatory text as a series of letters and postcards that could be attached to the large map. They also designed symbols to indicate how each practice or artifact made its way to their community. A couple of students experimented with digitally enhancing their photographs to dress local people in clothing representing some of their countries of origin. In the end, they created a visually exciting map that kept their peers and families interested for some time. The students came away from the experience with a better understanding of the sources of their own cultural practices and a growing awareness of how cultural diffusion operates, even in relatively homogeneous communities.

Technology helps students manipulate visual images.

See Berson (2004) for the use of digital photography in inquiry.

Avoiding Social Studies Mythologies and Stereotypes

Helping children see the ways in which history and the social sciences use social data and the kinds of problems that can arise in these domains is an important way to help children recognize mythologized information. Unfortunately, the tendency to simplify complex subject matter for children has often resulted in a social studies curriculum that is little more than an accumulation of myths and misunderstandings. Children learn about such a complex figure as Abraham Lincoln only that he freed the slaves, split rails as a boy, and grew to be a very tall man in a stovepipe hat. Lincoln as a person is lost. As we mentioned earlier, one of the purposes of social studies in an integrated curriculum is recapturing the humanity of such people not by presenting children with historical "dirty linen" but by connecting them with real people so that they can better understand the nature of their nation's and the world's past, present, and possible future. Few people are entirely heroic or completely unassailed by doubts, whether they are children or famous adults. Social studies can provide a context in which to look at the decisions both good and bad that people have made and to see how they responded to the challenges life offered them.

Freeman & Levstik (1988)

Oversimplification leads to misunderstanding.

Egan (1979); Zarnowski (1997)

Connect children with real people and provide a context for studying human decision making.

One of the most popular units in one teacher's third-grade class is MEETING CHALLENGES. She and her third graders interview people in the community selected by the students as people who meet challenges in a variety of ways, not only firefighters and police officers but also news reporters, who talk about the challenges of accurately reporting the news, and people who have met physical challenges. In addition, the teacher sets up a "history roundtable" in which children learn about figures from the past, with an emphasis on the challenges they met (e.g., Should Rosa Parks have moved to the back of the bus? Should Washington have been king? Why did Lindbergh think he should/could fly across the Atlantic?). Children come to the roundtable in character, prepared to talk to each other and to classmates about how they might respond to these historical challenges. They use a variety of literature as background material and often end by asking very interesting questions. One boy, for instance, found George Washington most admirable. But, he wondered, why had Washington continued to own slaves? The class discussed the possibility of a person's being heroic in some ways but not in others. Could such a person still be a hero? they debated, concluding that most people probably were not heroic all the time.

Encourage children to see history as the story of people meeting challenges.

These children chose their heroes and heroines not because they were presented with myths but because they were beginning to understand the strengths and weaknesses of the people they admired. Aside from this being a more accurate view of history as well as of human nature, children can also better imagine themselves meeting challenges and overcoming weaknesses.

Encourage children to see themselves as able to meet challenges.

Today's world is diverse and interconnected. Unless students are able to understand diverse cultures, both locally and globally, they cannot appreciate the issues that affect their lives. They will not be able to make informed decisions about economic, political, and environmental issues. Too frequently, only very superficial treatment of complex cultures is found in the social studies curriculum. Such a narrow approach leads to focusing on the strangest or most bizarre customs of a culture or on the most "primitive" people of the region. When cultures are seen only as "weird" or exotic,

Merryfield (2004)

Substantive culture learning promotes students' understanding of diverse cultures locally and globally.

barriers to substantive culture learning occurs. Substantive culture learning consists of teaching both cultural similarities and differences. This perspective is characterized by the following ways: (1) it develops skills in perspective consciousness by helping students recognize and understand underlying assumptions and values in their own and others' perspectives and how they change over time; (2) it fosters ways to recognize stereotypes by assisting students to identify and directly address stereotypes; (3) it uses primary sources from cultures/regions under study by enabling students to utilize a range of literature, documents, artifacts, newspapers, websites, and so on, and to interact with people from the culture; (4) it fosters the understanding of the intersections of prejudice and power by encouraging students to study prejudice and discrimination within and across diverse world regions, as well as how people resist such discrimination; and (5) it promotes the understanding of dynamic change and increasing global interconnectedness by helping students make sense of how cultural norms change over time, including how connections exist between economic, political, cultural, and environmental factors and themselves and people in other cultures. With such culturally responsive teaching, students can explore cultures critically—they are armed with strategies for pursuing important issues of social justice in their own communities and country, as well as globally.

Attending to the Language and Images of Social Studies

Cope & Kalantzis (2000); Hyde & Bizar (1989)

All the foregoing examples describe language use in the content areas that constitute the social studies. A teacher in an integrated language classroom seeks ways to use language across the curriculum, but that means attending to the uses of language peculiar to many knowledge domains. What is the language of geography, for instance? How are symbol systems used on maps and globes to transmit geographic information and a sense of place? What do place-names tell us about human geography?

Sobel (1998)

See Chancellor (2004) and Hammond's (2001) *Discovery Maps* for more information about maps and mapping.

A short activity using one symbol system—maps—may point out the way language shows the interconnectedness of our world. You need only a map of your state. Lay the map out and begin to look for names borrowed from other places. In one small section of central Kentucky, for example, you can locate Paris and Versailles. Ohio has Lima, Cadiz, and Schoenbrun. Where in the world did the place-names in your state come from? What parts of the world predominate? Are there also names borrowed from Native Americans? You may want to try this with a map of Australia. What could account for this geographic phenomenon?

Part of the teacher's job is to help children learn to use the vocabulary of history and the social sciences intelligently. There should be opportunities for children to express what they are learning in charts, graphs, and maps and in informational genres. They should have experience taking surveys and talking about the limitations of survey methods. (Did the survey really ask the right questions? Who answered the survey? Are they representative?) When children use the data sources common to each of these fields, they can use these sources as models for communicating the results of their studies. Children studying immigration produce maps of migration patterns and bar graphs comparing immigration from and to different parts of the world. They may collect historic photographs from their own community along with oral history interviews and create a history of local immigration that includes a table of contents and bibliography. In other words, they use the language of historians and social scientists to talk about these domains of knowledge.

In addition, students may decide to represent what they have learned in genres less commonly associated with a particular domain. These could include such things as letter writing between real or imagined historical personages (e.g., an East German and a West German discussing the problems of reunification) or to individuals outside the classroom (e.g., pen pals or relatives) describing what students are learning. They could include scripts for radio and TV plays to be tape-recorded or videotaped; speeches, plays, and skits to be performed; or filmstrips to be produced. Or they could include annotated catalogs of artifacts (e.g., the dress of men and women of pioneer America or eating utensils from different cultures) or calendars, each page containing a drawing and text related to a topic (e.g., a calendar of archeology or technological change). And finally, as we mentioned earlier, not all representations need be written. Paintings, murals, mobiles, dioramas, maps, musical compositions, and drama can be powerful forms through which children share learning. Images depict meanings in different ways from those expressed in written language. Students need scaffolding in analyzing photographs, for example, to appreciate what they see in them (observation) and what they conclude about this study of photographs (interpretation). Ideologies require critical examination: Whose faces are present? Whose are absent? In what circumstances and roles are different persons depicted?

Beaty (1997); Barton (2001); Berson (2004); Sobel (1998)

See Library of Congress's website, http://memory.loc.gov/ammem/ndlpedu/educators/workshop/discovery/guid4.html, for a guide for photo analysis.

Perspectival Social Studies

Any time students represent what they have learned—and any time they pick up a source to help them learn—they must deal with *perspective*. At the beginning of this book, we outlined our perspective—our point of view and basic assumptions—about language and learning. However, whether authors explicitly explain their perspective or not, *all texts represent some worldview.* There is no such thing as *just the facts*. Someone sorts through the available data, perceives some facts as more relevant than others, organizes those facts, and presents his or her interpretation in a written narrative, a museum exhibit, a piece of art, or in the classroom. A series of nineteenth-century photographs of sod houses and homesteaders on the Kansas "frontier," for instance, represents a very different perspective or interpretive stance than would an exhibit that focused on the life of Kickapoo Indians in Kansas during the same period, or one that interspersed images of homesteaders with images of the Kickapoo people.

All texts represent some worldview.

Appleby, Hunt, & Jacob (1994); Kammen (1996); Levstik (1986, 1987)

As perspectives change, so too do interpretations. Consider, for instance, the lack of attention given in the past to women in history and much of the social sciences. While many of the facts about women's lives were there all along, it was not until people began asking different questions about the social world that they began assigning new significance to those facts. Gradually, scholarship not only included but sometimes focused on women's activities. As a result, the old assumptions, as well as the interpretations that accompanied them, altered. You can see similar patterns in the treatment of other previously underrepresented groups. If we did not regularly revise the questions we ask and the data we use in making sense out of the world, we would be trapped in old ideologies, less able to think about changes in the present or future because we have incomplete or erroneous information. Social studies *must* be subject to revision—to hearing new voices, rethinking old assumptions, and searching for more complete evidence. There can be no "last word"—instead, revision and reinterpretation are basic to social studies.

Social studies must be subject to revision.

In order to help children recognize how perspective shapes interpretation teachers have to carefully consider how to select the books and other resources used in instruction. One primary teacher carefully orchestrates a FAMILY theme so that children can see that a variety of family structures and relationships are normal. She and her students discuss different types of family members—uncles, aunts, cousins, stepparents, mothers, fathers, and siblings—as well as different types of family arrangements and family activities. In order to help students understand some of these differences, she uses a variety of literature. She introduces the topic of family travel with two books, *Night Driving,* a gentle story about a father and son as they take a nighttime road trip, and *Nine for California,* a humorous nineteenth-century stagecoach journey in which a resourceful mother averts a series of potential disasters. Later, when discussing how families care for each other, she shares *When We Married Gary,* a warm story about two little girls and their new stepfather, *Mountain Wedding,* about another blended family

Coy (1997)

Levitan (1997)

Hines (1997)

Gibbons (1997)

Cameron (1997)

McLerran (1997)

Participatory research links children, parents, teachers, and the community.

whose transition to unity is a little rockier and quite humorous, and *More Stories Huey Tells*, a little boy's stories about his engaging family. Through these and other stories, the teacher tries to establish a sense of positive family relationships and mutual responsibilities. Students then create lists of things families can do to work well together and suggestions for strategies to use when things are not going well. The class talks about how different family members might view the same events differently and how that can sometimes cause problems. They listen to *The Year of the Ranch* about a family's move to Arizona and the different ideas members of the family have about their year on the ranch. Finally, the teacher invites parents or other interested adults to participate in a special project with students in the class. This is a *participatory research* project in which children and adults work together on a project of their choice. In this case, some of the participants wrote books about a time when the child and adult had worked together on something important. Others wrote and illustrated posters of favorite memories from childhood. One parent and child wrote a poem together about a trip they had made to the mother's childhood home in Venezuela, and then each made an illustration of the poem. Their pictures provoked considerable conversation in the class about how differently each had remembered some parts of the trip. This project was very popular with the children, whether they worked with their own parents or some other adult, but it was also an eye-opener for the teacher. As a result of this classroom interaction, she found adults in the community much more supportive of her work, more willing to talk to her about children's work, and more willing to volunteer in the school. As each year passes, more and more adults show up. Interestingly, some parents continue with the program even after their own children have moved on in school. These volunteers ensure that every child in the class has an adult with whom to work. As a result, social studies instruction includes the perspectives of many community members as well as the teacher and children in the class.

Teacher as Learner

With seven areas—history, geography, anthropology, sociology, political science, economics, and psychology—and multiple perspectives on each one to consider, the elementary teacher may not have a great deal of background in any single field related to social studies. Although this is often seen as a disincentive for teaching social studies, it is also an opportunity to try a role other than that of dispenser of information. Traditionally, many elementary teachers rely on the textbook to delineate the curriculum and to form the boundaries of knowledge. The teacher's role in that case is to help children acquire the information that is within those boundaries. The teacher and the children share the same source of information, and the teacher has the "answers" at least insofar as the text and teacher's guide provide them. However, an integrated approach to the curriculum proposes a different way of looking at the teacher's role. There is no way a teacher can know everything there is to know about the topics that can come up in the course of a thematic unit. As a result, the teacher studies the topics with the children as a fellow learner. The teacher is a more sophisticated learner and probably has more background knowledge to bring to bear in trying to understand a new area, but the task is a joint endeavor by students and teacher. This dramatically alters the teacher's stance. Think about a teacher as one who engages in the following four activities.

Teachers are both decision makers and fellow learners.

ARRANGING OPPORTUNITIES FOR CHILDREN TO THINK CRITICALLY ABOUT THE CONTENT OF SOCIAL STUDIES
Observe how this fourth-grade teacher leads children to clarify their understanding of the geographic concept of desert through a Sketch to Stretch* exercise.

The children begin by drawing what they imagine a desert to look like. Most of the children include sand (yellow), snakes, lizards, and cacti. One child draws a tent strung between two saguaro cactus plants and surrounded by people in turbans and long robes. After the class discusses what features they think most deserts have in common and lists some of the areas of uncertainty, the teacher records the results on chart paper as a Semantic Map*. (See Figure 5.3.) She also asks that they save their pictures until the end of the investigation.

During the next class session, a guest from Yemen shares slides of the desert and other features of Yemen. The children are surprised by pictures of corrugated tin houses surrounded by a brown, stony, and arid landscape. They have many questions to ask, and later they add to and amend their semantic map considerably. (See Figure 5.4.)

The teacher shows a short filmstrip of the high tableland in the desert sections of Arizona and Nevada. The children express surprise at the difference between the black hills of Nevada and the red landscape of parts of Arizona. As they add more information

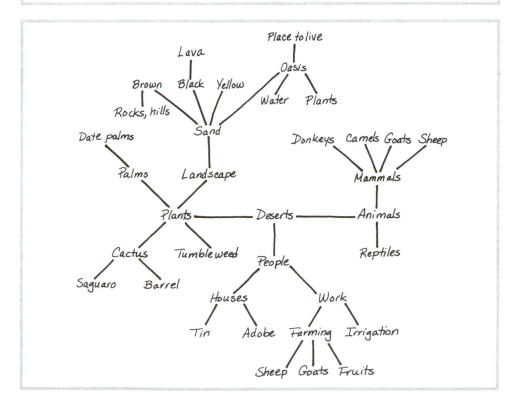

figure **5.3**

figure **5.4**

Teachers learn to elicit student questions.

Barton (2001)

Teachers learn to arrange for incongruities.

Merryfield (2003)

Children learn to distinguish between observation and inference and between supported and unsupported claims.

to their semantic map, they become involved in a debate about whether saguaro cactus grows in all deserts. The teacher asks them to work in groups to construct questions that still need to be asked about deserts. She suggests that they think about the pictures they drew on the first day of their discussion. What questions would help them to make their pictures more accurate?

After the small groups have developed their questions, the teacher leads a debriefing session, during which the children share their work and begin to organize their questions and to consider the sources they can use to find answers.

Another way to launch inquiry is to use sets of photographs from a particular time period that are organized around different topics—businesses, schools or education, leisure activities, transportation, technology, and so forth. Small groups first write down their expectations or what they are likely to find in the photographs and whether these ideas would be the same as today or whether they are apt to be different from now. Then they carefully examine the photographs and note down what they actually see (again categorizing their ideas as to whether items listed are like today or not) and compare their findings with their anticipated ones. Further analysis consists of indicating when students think the photographs in a set were taken along with their reasons for their determinations. Such analysis leads to generating questions for inquiry that can be explored by other resources. That is, their initial photograph investigation provokes a mystery to be solved.

PROVIDING CHALLENGES TO ASSUMPTIONS

Most of us prefer to let our assumptions go unchallenged, and we work hard to fit new information into old schemas. For children to enrich their schemas relative to social studies, some entrenched ideas must be challenged and other possibilities presented. The teacher must find out what children know about a topic and what assumptions, or schema, they already have in place. The teacher in the foregoing example did this by asking children to draw their ideas of a desert. The teacher's next task is to deal with the anomalies or incongruities—the discrepant events—that do not fit with the children's existing schema.

A fifth-grade teacher found that his students were sure that the work of men on the frontier was much more strenuous and difficult than that done by women. The teacher did not tell students that their information was inadequate. Instead, he brought in diary excerpts describing a day's work done by a young mother on the Oregon frontier. He also brought in several artifacts: kitchen implements necessary for meal preparation and reproductions of period clothing borrowed from a costume shop. These artifacts caused children to question their assumptions because it became clear that household work on the frontier was considerably more taxing than they had assumed.

At the beginning of a unit on the Middle East, a teacher asked seventh-grade students to write and draw words and images that they associate with women of the Middle East. Most students depicted Middle Eastern women as Arab, veiled, uneducated, and hidden away. Using maps, statistics of religious diversity across the region, and online newspapers and magazines, students created a collage of information about girls' and women's lives in this part of the world that directly addressed and disrupted their initial stereotypes and misinformation.

HELPING CHILDREN FORMULATE QUESTIONS AND GENERATE OPINIONS

As children confront discrepant events and begin to think about problems and issues to explore, the teacher helps them formulate their questions so that when it is time to communicate findings and draw meaning from their study, children will be able to make supported claims and understand the claims made by others. One simple activity that helps older children distinguish between observing data and drawing inferences based on those data involves the concepts of developed and less-developed countries. The teacher introduces the terms and asks for student response in listing the characteristics or properties of each classification (thus establishing the existing schema). Next, a series of eight to ten slides showing scenes in countries generally considered developed (e.g., United States, England, Germany, and Russia) and developing (e.g., Rwanda, Indonesia, Philippines, and Yemen) are shown, but the slides contradict the stereotypes. A U.S. slide shows a poor rural area without electricity or indoor plumbing, and an Indonesian slide pictures a large, modern city. Children are asked to quickly classify the scene in each picture as either developed or developing. After they have done so, the slides are shown again and discussed so that the problems with these common terms are demonstrated and students are forced to think differently about how parts of the world are categorized.

ORGANIZING RESOURCES FOR STUDENT INQUIRY

As topics are chosen for investigation, the teacher must also be prepared to search out multiple sources at a variety of levels for student use. This is not as daunting a task as it may at first seem. A number of organizations are anxious to help teachers provide good materials for social studies. The National Geographic Society has launched an extensive program to improve the instruction of geography, including their National Geographic Kids Network Project from Technical Education Research Centers, Inc., while State Councils on Economic Education and the American Bar Association provide materials, activities, and support for teachers who want to include more economic and law content. Historical agencies provide suggested activities and materials for use in classrooms. Some colleges and universities have programs that link international students with area classrooms so that students can meet and talk with people from other cultures. In addition, private and public funds support centers for the dissemination of information in many areas of the social studies, from history and civics to global studies. The resources are there; teachers are the vital link between resources and students.

> All of these organizations have websites.

> Links with colleges and universities can match classrooms with international students studying in the United States.
>
> Kraus International (1992)

Obviously, no single book can suggest everything there is to do in a field as diverse as social studies. The activities suggested here will get you started in thinking about how to use social studies as the context for integrating the curriculum.

References: Social Studies

Albert, M., & Groth, J. (1997). Arts alive in the development of historical thinking. *Social Education, 61*, 42–44.

Appleby, J., Hunt, L., & Jacob, M. (1994). *Telling the truth about history*. New York: Norton.

Barr, R., Barth, J., & Shermis, S. S. (1977). *Defining the social studies*. (Bulletin No. 51). Washington, DC: National Council for the Social Studies.

Barth, J. (1996). NCSS and the nature of social studies. In O. L. Davis (Ed.), *NCSS in retrospect* (pp. 9–19). Washington, DC: National Council for the Social Studies.

Barton, K. C. (2001). A picture's worth: Analyzing historical pictures in the elementary grades. *Social Education, 65*, 278–283.

Barton, K. C., & Levstik, L. S. (1996). "Back when God was around and everything": The development of elementary children's understanding of historical time. *American Educational Research Journal, 33*, 419–454.

Barton, K. C., & Levstik, L. S. (2004). *Teaching history for the common good*. Mahwah, NJ: Lawrence Erlbaum.

Beaty, J. J. (1997). *Building bridges with multicultural picture books*. Portsmouth, NH: Heinemann.

Berson, M. J. (2004). Digital images: Capturing America's past with the technology of today. *Social Education, 68*, 214–219.

Carey, S. (1985a). *Conceptual change in childhood*. Cambridge: MIT Press.

Carey, S. (1985b). Are children fundamentally different kinds of thinkers and learners than adults? In S. B. Chipman, J. W. Segal, & R. Glaser (Eds.), *Thinking and learning skills: Research and open questions* (Vol. 2, pp. 485–517). Hillsdale, NJ: Erlbaum.

Cope, B., & Kalantzis, M. (Eds.). (2000). *Multiliteracies: Literacy learning and the design of social futures*. London: Routledge.

Daniels, H., & Zemelman, S. (2004). *Subjects matter: Every teacher's guide to content-area reading*. Portsmouth, NH: Heinemann.

Downey, M., & Levstik, L. S. (1988). Teaching and learning history: The research base. *Social Education, 52*, 336–342.

Egan, K. (1979). What children know best. *Social Education, 43*, 130–139.

Foster, S. J., Hoge, J. D., & Rosch, R. H. (1999). Thinking aloud about history: Children's and adolescents' responses to historical photographs. *Theory and Research in Social Education, 27*, 179–214.

Freeman, E., & Levstik, L. (1988). Recreating the past: Historical fiction in the social studies curriculum. *Elementary School Journal, 88*, 329–337.

Gamberg, R., Kwak, W., Hutchings, M., & Altheim, J. (1988). *Learning and loving it: Theme studies in the classroom.* Portsmouth, NH: Heinemann.

Gerwin, D., & Zevin, J. (2003). *Teaching U.S. history as mystery.* Portsmouth, NH: Heinemann.

Harlan (KY) Elementary School (1986). *No more litter* [Videotape made by third grade class]. Harlan, KY: Author.

Hyde, A. A., & Bizar, M. (1989). *Thinking in context: Teaching cognitive processes across the elementary school curriculum.* White Plains, NY: Longman.

Kammen, M. (1996). Some patterns and meanings of memory distortion in American history. In D. L. Schacter (Ed.), *Memory distortion: How minds, brains, and societies reconstruct the past* (pp. 331–345). Cambridge: Harvard University Press.

Keil, F. C. (1984). Mechanisms of cognitive development and the structure of knowledge. In R. J. Stemberg (Ed.), *Mechanisms of cognitive development.* New York: Freeman.

Kraus International. (1992). *Social studies: Curriculum resource handbook.* Millwood, NY: Author.

Levstik, L. S. (1986). The relationship between historical response and narrative in a sixth-grade classroom. *Theory and Research in Social Education, 14,* 1–15.

Levstik, L. S. (1989). Historical narrative and the young reader. *Theory Into Practice, 28,* 114–119.

Levstik, L. S., & Barton, K. C. (2001). *Doing history: Investigating with children in elementary and middle schools.* Mahwah, NJ: Lawrence Erlbaum.

Levstik, L. S., & Pappas, C. C. (1987). Exploring the development of historical understanding. *Journal of Research and Development in Education, 21,* 1–15.

Levstik, L. S., & Pappas, C. C. (1992). New directions for studying historical understanding. *Theory and Research in Social Education, 21,* 369–385.

Maxim, G. W. (1987). *Social studies and the elementary school child* (3rd ed.). Columbus, OH: Merrill.

McGinnis, K. (n.d.). *Educating for a just society.* St. Louis, MO: The Institute for Peace and Justice.

Merryfield, M. M. (2003). A global education framwork for teaching about the world's women. *Social Education, 67,* 10–16.

Merryfield, M. M. (2004). Elementary students in substantive culture learning. *Social Education, 68,* 270–273.

Mitchell, W. J. T. (1994). *Picture theory.* Chicago: University of Chicago Press.

National Council for the Social Studies (NCSS). (1994) *NCSS National Standards.* Washington, DC: National Council for the Social Studies.

National Council for the Social Studies (NCSS) Focus Group. (1992). *Initial response to national history standards.* Unpublished document, Washington, DC: National Council for the Social Studies.

Newmann, R., Secada, W., & Whlage, G. (1995). *A guide to authentic instruction and assessment: Vision, standards and scoring.* Madison, WI: Wisconsin Center for Educational Research.

Riis, J. (1971). *How the other half lives.* New York: Dover.

Sobel, D. (1998). *Mapmaking with children: Sense of place education for the elementary years.* Portsmouth, NH: Heinemann.

Stodolsky, S. S. (1988). *The subject matters.* Chicago: University of Chicago Press.

VanSledright, B. (2002). *In search of America's past: Learning to read history in elementary shools.* New York: Teachers College Press.

Wells, G. (1999). *Dialogic inquiry: Towards a sociocultural practice and theory of education.* Cambridge: Cambridge University Press.

Whitlin, P., & Whitlin, D. (1997). *Inquiry at the window: Pursing the wonders of learners.* Portsmouth, NH: Heinemann.

Wilson, S. M., & Wineberg, S. S. (1988). Peering at history through different lenses: The role of disciplinary perspectives in teaching history. *Teachers College Record, 89,* 525–539.

Zarnowski, M. (1997). It's more than dates and places: How nonfiction contributes to understanding social studies. In R. A. Bamford & J. V. Kristo (Eds.), *Making facts come alive: Choosing quality nonfiction literature K–8.* Norwood, MA: Christopher-Gordon.

Children's Literature: Social Studies

A Girl Called BOY by B. Hurmence. Clarion, 1982.

Discovering Maps: A Children's World Atlas and Guide to Map Reading. HammondWorld Atlas, 2001.

Immigrant Kids by R. Freedman. Dutton, 1980.

In Their Own Words by M. Meltzer. Crowell, 1964.

The Kids' Art Pack by R. Van der Meer & R. Whitford. DK Publishing, Inc., 1997.

Maps and Mapping by D. Chancellor. Kingfisher, 2004.

Mojave by D. Seibert. Illustrated by W. Minor. Crowell, 1988.

More Stories Huey Tells by A. Cameron. Farrar, 1997.

Mountain Wedding by F. Gibbons. Morrow, 1997.

Night Driving by J. Coy. Holt, 1997.

Nine for California by S. Levitan. Orchard, 1997.

Sierra by D. Seibert. Illustrated by W. Minor. Crowell, 1990.

Watch the Stars Come Out by R. Levinson. Illustrated by D. Goode. Dutton, 1987.

When We Married Gary by A. G. Hines. Greenwillow, 1997.

The Year of the Ranch by A. McLerran. Viking, 1997.

Science

What Is Science?

Sagan (1978)

Science encompasses many domains.

Carl Sagan once suggested that human beings are predisposed by intellect, emotional makeup, and evolution to be interested in those things we label science. Science is a categorical label used to encompass such domains as biology, chemistry, physics, and geology. Most significantly, science is a way of knowing. In fact, some people prefer to talk about "sciencing" rather than "science." Advocates of sciencing emphasize that science is more than a collection of facts and formulas; science is a way of dealing with and ordering experience, usually by rigorous investigation of physical and biological phenomena. Because experience rarely arranges itself tidily into discrete disciplines, much of modern science crosses disciplinary boundaries. You are probably familiar with biochemistry as a cross-disciplinary category, but you may be less used to thinking about the science of social science—the search for the patterns and processes that influence the way in which people think and behave. Much of our discussion of how children think and learn is drawn from scientific studies of such cross-disciplinary phenomena, as recognized by some of the science programs designed for elementary schools. One of these, the Biological Sciences Curriculum Study (BSCS), explains its stance this way:

> Children should learn about science, technology, and health as they need to understand and use them in their daily life and as future citizens. Education in the elementary years should sustain the natural curiosity of children, allow exploration of their environments, improve explanations of phenomena in their world, develop understanding and use of technology, and contribute to informed choices in their personal and social lives.

"Sciencing" implies active participation in investigations.

Carin & Sund (1985); Kyle, Bonnstetter, Gadsden, & Shymansky (1988); Saul et al. (2002)

Bybee, Ellis, Muscsella, & Robertson (1988)

Learning science includes making informed choices about health and technology.

Blocks to Learning Science

If science is intrinsically interesting as a forum for children's exploration of the natural world, why do many students leave school thinking of science as dull and hard? Several factors account for the problems some students have with science. First, there is growing evidence of differential treatment and opportunities in science teaching. Teachers often have different levels of expectation for boys and girls and for children from some racial, ethnic, or socioeconomic groups. Sometimes this shows up in the roles assigned to students during science instruction. Boys tend to be assigned—or take—more active roles, girls more passive ones. In addition, parents, peers, the media, and some curriculum materials may reinforce these roles for females and minority students. Another problem is that science is too often taught as vocabulary, not problem solving. It is taught in the abstract, with an emphasis on "getting it right" rather than on posing questions, taking intellectual risks, or learning from mistakes. As a result, too many children come to fear science and avoid it whenever possible.

An integrated language perspective approaches science quite differently. Science is seen as more than information accumulation. In this perspective, doing science has values in common with doing social studies, encouraging wonderment, curiosity, openness to new ideas, and skepticism. As with social studies, the prime motive behind doing science is to provide children with a variety of ways of finding out about the world and themselves.

Mullis et al. (1988)

Guzzetti (2003); Krueger & Sutton (2001); Martin et al. (2005)

Teachers often have different levels of expectation for boys and girls as well as children of color.

Saul et al. (2002); Whitin & Whitin (1997)

Science is more than information accumulation; learning science involves maintaining a sense of wonder.

Science as a Way of Knowing

Perhaps it will help to think about teaching and learning science as having six major elements.

Components of sciencing

SCIENCE IS A WAY OF THINKING

Science offers a unique way of looking at the world and of asking questions, gathering, representing, and interpreting data, and explaining findings. Scientific thinking involves particular attitudes that include making judgments based on adequate data, striving to be rational and analytical, and maintaining a sense of wonder at the complexity and beauty of the universe. You have probably learned to call this process the scientific method. What you may not have considered is that science is also a process of false starts and fortunate accidents. Sometimes presentations of the "scientific

Chaillé & Britain (2003); Saul et al. (2002); Scott (1992); Whitin & Whitin (1997)

method" make it seem that inquiry in science is a neat, linear pathway to knowledge, rather than the exhilarating though riskier and more halting exploration of pathways that sometimes turn into blind alleys and accidents that sometimes turn into insights.

SCIENCE IS A WAY OF PROBLEM SOLVING

Doris (1991); Fritzer & Bristor (2004); Saul et al. (2002)

Science draws on and constructs the body of facts, principles, laws, and theories that attempts to explain physical, biological, and behavioral phenomena. This body of knowledge is both the framework for scientific understanding and thinking and the "product" of the sciencing process. It is the outcome of inquiry—a way of solving problems related to the natural world. When science is presented as a finished product, or as a set of simple steps, we misrepresent the power of this discipline. Authentic learning in science involves children in confronting anomalies, formulating questions, dealing with unanticipated results, and offering possible explanations. Thus, science is not a static knowledge or enterprise—the joy of science is the wonderful rush of new and continuous information.

SCIENCE IS A LIVING TENSION BETWEEN THEORY AND OBSERVATION

Varelas (1996); Whitin & Whitin (1997)

As scientists work, they create theories based on observation and alter those theories as new observations—data—reveal new information. There is always a productive tension between theory and data. This tension encourages a willingness to revise and abandon theories in the face of new information and is an important component of sciencing in the classroom. Science involves a dynamic, ongoing, reciprocal theory–data "dance."

SCIENCE USES A RANGE OF WAYS TO REPRESENT AND VISUALIZE DATA

Bromley et al. (1995); Helm & Katz (2001); Kress et al. (2001); Lemke (1998, 2003)

See Lehrer & Schauble (2002) for examples of investigating with real data in the classroom.

Science is very multimodal. Science is a way of thinking; it is a way of saying and seeing. Besides the written message, science texts are filled with a range of visual designs—figures, graphs, charts, diagrams, and so forth. Thus, a major aspect of being a scientist is using representational forms, both in the process of investigations and in the dissemination of findings.

SCIENCE INCLUDES A TECHNOLOGICAL COMPONENT

Fritzer & Bristor (2004)

Technology uses knowledge from science to accomplish tasks and solve problems. Sometimes, too, technology creates new problems, and people are faced with moral and ethical dilemmas. Children as well as adults must learn to examine the benefits and risks of this aspect of sciencing and to understand the relationship between science, technology, health, and society. In addition, technology is a problem-solving tool in science. Children engage tools for measuring or drawing, for looking closely, and for imagining alternatives. These tools help children look more closely at their world but also require attention to their appropriate uses and possible limitations.

SCIENCE INVOLVES A SOCIAL COMPONENT

Carter (1991); Martin et al. (2005); Merryfield (1991)

Science is a human activity that is influenced by social interests and ideology.

Science is a human activity that is influenced by social interests and ideology. Science and technology have complex global social ramifications. Current social, political, technological, and ecological choices affect the possible futures available to the world's people. The nuclear accident at Chernobyl, for instance, affected food crops and animals from Norway to Italy. Increased population in California affects water resources as far away as Colorado. Science education helps children envision the social impact of scientific and technological knowledge. A unit on CHANGES, for instance, would include not only how something changed but also the social impact of that change: not simply *can* we build a dam to stop flooding but *should* we do so? Not can we use fiber optics to increase telecommunications but what will be the social impact of this technological change?

You may have noticed some similarities between this definition of science and the previous definition of social studies. Both fields stress the integration of process and content, of a way of thinking about the world and of observing and building theories about what we observe. Both emphasize the recognition of problems and the central role of perspective in social and scientific inquiry. Thus, there is "science" in the social sciences, and there are social issues in the sciences. There are also differences that make it useful to consider separately these two ways of knowing.

Science is essentially a search for explanatory laws and principles—a search rarely possible in history and not always possible in the other social sciences. Gravity operates according to laws that do not respond to changing social conditions, political upheavals, or economic trends. Little in social studies can be said to be subject to physical laws. Science attempts to control social factors so that results can be generalized beyond a specific event; history and the social sciences often seek to understand and explain specific events. There are places where these two parts of the curriculum intersect—in ecology, for instance—but each also offers a particular way of knowing that can challenge children to think in increasingly mature ways. Think about the difference in approach taken in the No More Litter example, which used a social studies theme, and the following example that approaches an environmental issue from a more science-like perspective.

Fritzer & Bristor (2004); Hyde & Bizar (1989)

Science looks for generalizations; history studies the particular.

Water Cleanup

A sixth-grade class in Iowa became concerned about pollution in their community's water supply. Their reading had led them to conclude that suds and phosphates were a contributing factor. In class discussions, the children hypothesized that laundry detergents must be putting the suds into the streams and rivers. Several had seen evidence of suds at the water treatment plant, and others had observed overflowing washers and rinse water full of suds going into drains. They wanted to find out if there were some detergents that did not make as many suds.

McShane (1988)

Building hypotheses

The enterprising teacher arranged for the donation of a washing machine, and a parent set up a suds collector. The class then made arrangements with the school janitor to use white cotton cleaning cloths of equal size. Students decided that they would need to test the cleaning power of detergents as well as the suds production, especially if they were to convince others to use lower sudsing detergents. With this in mind, they decided to test a variety of stains: catsup, mustard, motor oil, salad dressing, lipstick, marker and ballpoint pen inks, tea, coffee, chocolate, soil, and blood.

Testing hypotheses

The next steps involved setting up procedures for testing and recording results. The students were most concerned about the importance of using scientific methods and procedures. They tried to keep their work accurate by maintaining the same brands for making stains and ensuring that the same amount of the staining substance was used in each trial. They set up a data sheet for recording each trial that included information about the water temperature, brand of detergent, type of stain, amount of suds in the wash and rinse cycles, and results of a litmus test.

Controlling variables

Interviews with a representative from the local sewage treatment plant helped students understand some of the social and environmental problems that resulted from excessive sudsing and phosphates. Interviews with parents helped them understand the consumer's dilemma when there is a choice between better cleaning power in a detergent and fewer pollutants in the public's water. Finally, the children shared their results with the community, letting others know how each detergent in their study had fared and how clean the low-sudsing detergents got laundry.

Studying community impact

Consider what these children accomplished in terms of the goals of sciencing:

Meeting the goals of sciencing

1. Like the litter study for the younger children, this topic dealt with how people managed their environment, especially in making decisions about the uses of technology versus protecting the environment (technology, ecology, and society).
2. The methods used in designing the study—establishing hypotheses, gathering and analyzing data, and reporting results—engaged children in learning and using the scientific method essential to sciencing.

3. As part of their study, children drew on content from various sciences. They investigated the impact of suds and phosphates on water environments and on the humans who used the water (biology). The children studied the action of detergents as they interacted with water, stains, and cloth (chemistry). They also learned something about the machinery used to conduct the experiments (physics).

4. They learned that problems in science do not always have simple, clear-cut solutions. This is a point of intersection with social studies, where human interests conflict and problems are not easily resolved.

5. They learned that the process of solving one problem in science frequently raises other questions, so that sciencing is a continuous feature of living.

USING THE LANGUAGE OF SCIENCE

One of the hallmarks of the language of science is the ability to communicate ideas and share information with accuracy and clarity. Throughout this study, students had opportunities to do just that. They wrote letters, set up their experiments, wrote descriptions of observations, represented them, and wrote reports of their data. They referred to other sources: library references, technical material from manufacturers, and expert testimony. They cooperated with people in the community: the companies that donated goods and services, the parent who helped set up the suds-gauging machine, and their peers. For eight weeks, these children conducted a rigorous, controlled study into a real problem in their community. Because it was a real problem, and because the results would be shared publicly and could have significant social impact, accuracy and clarity were crucial. In addition, they had to read other scientific writing as well as other forms of public writing: government reports and newspaper articles. Thus, there were many models for student reporting.

This scientific investigation could also have been integrated into a larger study of the community or of ecology, or it could have spurred a series of investigations into water purity historically, culturally, and scientifically. Certainly, the students had to be aware of the social and economic issues related to their study, especially as they engaged in debate and discussion about cleanliness versus decreased pollutants.

DEPTH

As you have probably gathered by now, understanding in a cognitive domain requires depth. Their teacher knew that an eight-week study would require enough time to really think about the investigation, plan carefully, and conduct accurate tests. At the end of eight weeks, the children knew a great deal more than which low-sudsing detergent was the most effective cleaning agent. It might have been possible to give them that information based on EPA tests. What they had learned, however, was how to "know" in science. They were building the scaffolding that would support future learning in science and help them to evaluate other scientific claims. Imagine, for instance, that these children were watching a commercial for a detergent that got clothes "whiter than white." What problems might they have with such claims? What questions might they have about supporting evidence? How might they understand such issues of water quality as the salt content in rivers and streams? They are likely now to think very differently about these issues because they have had an opportunity to think in depth about related issues and to build a framework for understanding new information. Depth also allows children to understand the connections between "pure" science and the applications of science that we call technology.

Science and Technology

We all take much of science for granted, especially as it relates to technology. One primary teacher, inspired by Macaulay's *The Way Things Work*, decided to try a thematic unit built around MACHINES. She remembered wondering as a child how a pencil

---

Seeing science as an aspect of living

Communicate ideas and share information with accuracy and clarity.

Gee (2004); Rutherford & Ahlgren (1990); Scott (1992); Saul et al. (2002)

See Saul (2004) for the many ways that science involves language and literacy.

Making cross-curricular connections

Doris (1991); Hyde & Bizar (1989); Reardon (2002a)

Claims and evidence are critical features of science inquiry.

Connecting "pure" science to its applications

Macaulay (1988)

sharpener worked and what made the toaster pop. She was sure from watching her young students that they shared her interest in the way things work. To begin the unit, the teacher gathered a number of machines that were easily dismantled and safe for small children to experiment with. She arranged a machine center in the room and laid out a manual meat grinder, pencil sharpener, coffee grinder, eggbeater, flour sifter, and pepper mill. She then gathered the children around her in a circle on the floor and introduced the concept of the wheel. While children experimented with moving objects of various shapes across the floor, the teacher asked: "Why is it easier to move the toilet paper roll and the ball than the cracker box and the block? How could you use the roll or ball to move the box?" As children made suggestions, the teacher put several wheeled vehicles in the circle. "Are there any shapes like the paper roll on these vehicles?" Children quickly identified the wheels and proceeded to load the wagons and trucks with boxes and blocks.

Establish an interest center, encourage initial exploration and experimentation, and use questions to move explorations in new directions.

At this point, the teacher shared the section of Macaulay's book about wheels. Over the next several days, children kept track of all the ways in which they observed wheels being used. They also used construction toys (e.g., Erector sets and LEGO blocks) to build wheeled vehicles. They drew pictures of new uses for wheels and collected pictures from magazines to make wheel collages.

Use information books as a resource.

Their teacher pointed out that many of the things they had worked with were machines. She asked the children to separate some of the things that used wheels into two categories: one to include wheels used as machines and the other to include wheels that were not machines (e.g., a single disc attached to nothing). There was much discussion as children tried to decide what constituted a machine. With help from the teacher and *The Way Things Work*, they wrote this definition: "A machine does work. Some parts of machines move."

- Provide practice with examples and nonexamples.
- Help children construct definitions.

With this definition written on chart paper, the students set to work listing all the machines they could find in their classroom. For homework, they listed all the machines they could find in one room at home. Before long, children began bringing in samples of machines to add to the collection in the machine center. As this unit progressed, students tried using a variety of machines. They took machines apart and tried to figure out how they worked. They used information books to help them understand machines, built machines to do various simple tasks, and drew machines for doing work in the future. They wrote about, talked about, and experimented with machines. Their teacher left messages for them in the center, asking them to think about such questions as: How is an eggbeater like a meat grinder? or Can you find a machine that uses a ratchet?

Maintain excitement and enthusiasm.

See also Lind & Milburn (1987) for another good example of a primary unit on MACHINES, Chaillé & Britain (2003) for a unit on HOW DOES IT MOVE, and Shaw & Dybdahl (1996) for a unit on WHEELS.

Teachers' Roles in Sciencing

If children are engaged in the kind of sciencing described, it soon becomes clear that they are, as Carl Sagan suggests, disposed to be curious about the area we label science. It is also clear that we are talking about a particular kind of activity that requires teachers to present activities across the sciences (physics and chemistry as well as biology and geology), structured to engage all children in identifying, posing, and attempting to solve problems. The teacher described earlier did this by arranging the machine center and making sure that everyone participated. Another teacher began a unit on MOVEMENT by hanging a large animal mobile labeled "How Do I Move?" In each case, materials are organized so that children not only are bound to ask questions but also know how to set about answering those questions. There are materials, time, and a place to work, and the teacher interjects carefully considered questions. When one group of children struggles to decide how to organize their observations of animal movement, the teacher provides three possible models: Hoban's *A Children's Zoo*, a book that matches a picture of an animal with descriptive words, Greenway's *Animals Q & A: How Do I Move?*, a book with a question-and-answer format,

Doris (1991); Martin et al. (2005); Rutherford & Ahlgren (1990)

Science should engage all children.

Chaillé & Britian (2003)

Children need materials, time, and a place to work.

Hoban (1985)
Greenway (1992)

Ehlert (1993)
Watts & Parsons (1993)

Consciously give girls active roles in sciencing.

Guzzetti (2003); Martin et al. (2005); Mullis et al. (1988)

Chaillé & Britain (2003); Saul et al. (2002)

Providing organizational help

Pearce (2002)

Reardon (2002b); Saul et al. (2002); Shaw & Dybdahl (1996); Whitin & Whitin (1997)

Doris (1991); Scott (1992); Whitin & Whitin (1997)

and Ehlert's *Nuts to You!*, a combination of collage and poetry depicting the behavior of a squirrel. In another group, the teacher helps children make model sycamore (or maple) seeds that spin like helicopters. When it appears that two boys are taking over the task, she intervenes, asking the girls to demonstrate the task for new group members. She then sets up an activity that involves finding plants whose seeds "work like a parachute" or "stick to fur or cloth" and carefully balances the working groups to make it less likely that one group or one person will dominate. She also uses literature, films, and guest speakers to introduce her students to a variety of male and female scientists from various racial and ethnic backgrounds. Perhaps most importantly, the teacher listens to her students' questions, monitoring herself to make sure that she does not allow one child or group of children to dominate the discourse in her classroom.

Children's scientific investigations do not develop in a vacuum. Instead, they are nurtured through carefully planned experiences, including some teacher presentation to individuals, small- and whole-class groups modeling from literature as well as from peer observation, judiciously chosen teacher questions, and regular opportunities for individual and group reflection. Students, thus, acquire scientific knowledge and thinking processes as they repeatedly engage in science in many different contexts. In addition, teachers provide organizational help—the kind of scaffolding that allows students to be both independent and accountable for their work.

QUESTION BOARD

A fifth-grade teacher finds that a "question board" is a useful tool. He found that many questions came up in class that would be worth later investigation but were too often lost in the press of ongoing work. Now he uses a large piece of laminated oak tag. Two types of questions are raised: *research questions* that can be answered by researching what someone has already done and would be answered by reading books or checking various websites, and *testable questions* that students themselves tackle by answering via observation or experimental inquiry. Students can select individual or small-group investigations, if they choose, or the whole class may decide to pursue one or more of these questions as part of a new theme. Replications of the second type, testable questions, are also encouraged and shared.

CLASS JOURNALS

One teacher uses a "Wonder Journal*." This is a class journal that functions much as the question board does. As children pursue an investigation, they share their "wonders"—unanswered questions about observations they have made. These wonderings often inspire other children to respond, adding their own observations and inferences to the journal. Other teachers may use a "Scientist's Notebook" or "Science Journal*." These have blank pages (or pages that have a blank section and a section of lines) so that students' writing and drawings can be included. The notebooks/journals can be used all year for the inquiries in each unit or for each particular inquiry.

SCIENTISTS' MEETINGS

One of the ways that new information is refined and disseminated is through meetings. Recall how Maria Ruiz in the PERSPECTIVES unit—see Introduction—had weekly meetings around the outer space inquiries. Teachers find scientists' meetings a useful way to share and refine children's investigations. They can be whole-class debriefings or to check the status of student inquiries; they can serve as a forum for one or two students' presentations of their work. As students listen, ask questions, and talk about what they hear, they may jot down questions or responses in their own notebooks/journals. In these meetings, students indicate what their next plans are and the names of people with whom they might collaborate. Sometimes students decide to replicate an investigation done by another child; sometimes they decide to try another tack related to a problem raised during the meeting.

READING, WRITING, AND DRAWING ABOUT SCIENCE

Like adult scientists, children read, write, and draw about science. Reading or hearing read different genres of science writing helps students imagine different ways of writing (and drawing) about their own work. A group of third-grade students used typical and fuzzy informational books—two versions of *From Caterpillar to Butterfly, Monarch Butterfly of Aster Way,* and *Becoming Butterflies*—to create displays (illustrated depictions and captions) to show the changes that occur in becoming butterflies. Another group of sixth graders read a set of typical and fuzzy nonfiction books, as well as stories and poems, on mice and rodents and used ideas from Jennifer Dewey's *Rattlesnake Dance* to create their own book combining mythology, stories, and science about the mice they were observing in their own classroom. Students were careful in how to use the appropriate illustrations to complement the various genres in their book. In addition to books about science, children need to read and hear about books written by or about scientists. For example, a group of students studying the environment near their own school particularly enjoyed Swinburne's *Once a Wolf: How Wildlife Biologists Fought to Bring Back the Gray Wolf.*

Helm & Kartz (2001); Kress et al. (2001); Saul (2003)

See Lake (2000) and Neutze (2002) for books and websites for science inquiries.

Legg (1998); Heiligman (1996); Ring (1999); Rockwell (2002)

Dewey (1997)

Swinbourne (1999)

Science as a Way of Doing

As you can see from the preceding discussion, science is learned in the doing. As children act on objects, they begin to build theories based on their actions and observations. We are not describing a simple "hands-on" approach to science. Manipulating objects is necessary but not sufficient in and of itself. Certainly children learn most readily about things that are directly accessible to their senses, but there is evidence that simply performing tasks using concrete objects does not necessarily mean that children understand the scientific content or the relationship of that content to any other situation or context. Children's experiences need to be linked to particular contexts—the themes and questions we have already discussed—but they also need opportunities to express their experiences in a variety of ways, to apply what they have learned to novel situations, to receive appropriate feedback from teachers and peers, to reflect on that feedback, and then to make adjustments and try again. In sum, children need time to build theories, test them, revise them, and represent them. Reading and referring to a range of informational texts in books and websites and writing up scientific explanations and depicting data via visual images related to hands-on explorations also support their building these theories.

Science is learned in the doing.

- Link experiences to context.
- Provide opportunities to apply learning in novel situations and time to build, test, revise, and represent theories.

Goldman & Bisanz (2002); Pappas et al. (2003)

Reading and writing informational texts in books and websites inform and extend hands-on exploration and support theory building.

In shifting from a science curriculum that emphasizes information accumulation to one that concentrates on the quality of children's understanding, starting simply is a key idea. Begin with questions and topics that are interesting and familiar to children. In the WONDERING prototype, children address the question, "How does my body work?" Several books are read aloud and children try out the explorations that are suggested in the books. They also consider the insides and outsides of bodies, along with books and hands-on explorations, then move to examining how bodies change or grow. Throughout these sets of science inquiries are many occasions to use math in meaningful ways—measuring, graphing, and so forth.

Start simply.

Many science inquiries often lead to more social studies concerns. For example, in PERSPECTIVES, Ed Tyson's science colleague began addressing only outer space topics, but students began to be concerned with global warming, which is a worldwide concern for all inhabitants of the planet (see the Introduction chapter). Questions from one activity often generate questions that cut across the curriculum. The teacher anticipates many of these possibilities in developing a planning WEB, yet is prepared to move in unanticipated directions, led by careful observation of students and the recognition that children's own questions may generate powerful activities and good science. This kind of activity is motivating and challenging, and it provides an excellent context for integrating science across the curriculum. It is also an approach that appears more likely to improve the participation of females and others underrepresented in science.

- Connect explorations to themes and other parts of the curriculum.
- Anticipate the unexpected.

See the National Science Teachers Association's website, www.nsta.org, for more resources on the teaching and learning of science.

References: Science

Bromley, K., Vitis, L. I., & Modlo, C. (1995). *Graphic organizers.* New York: Scholastic

Bybee, R., Ellis, J. D., Muscella, D., & Robertson, W. C. (1988). *New designs for elementary school science: A study conducted by the Biological Sciences Curriculum Study (BSCS).* Colorado Springs: Colorado College.

Carin, A. A., & Sund, R. B. (1985). *Teaching modern science.* Columbus, OH: Merrill.

Carter, C. (1991). Science-technology-society and access to scientific knowledge. *Theory Into Practice, 30,* 273–279.

Chaillé, C., & Britain, L. (2003). *The young child as scientist: A constructivist approach to early childhood science education.* Boston: Pearson Education.

Doris, E. (1991). *Doing what scientists do: Children learn to investigate their world.* Portsmouth, NH: Heinemann.

Fritzer, P., & Bristor, V. J. (2004). *Science content for elementary and middle school teachers.* Boston: Pearson Education.

Gee, J. P. (2004). Language in the science classroom: Academic social languages as the heart of school-based literacy. In W. Saul (Ed.), *Crossing borders in literacy and science instruction: Perspectives on theory and practice* (pp. 13–32). Newark, NJ: International Reading Association.

Goldman, S. R., & Bisanz, G. L. (2002). Toward a functional analysis of scientific genres: Implications for understanding and learning processes. In J. Otero, J. A. Leon, & A. C. Graesser (Eds.), *The psychology of science text comprehension* (pp. 19–50). Mahwah, NJ: Lawrence Erlbaum.

Guzzetti, B. J. (2003). Girls in science; Creating symmetrical opportunities for acquiring scientific literacy. In W. Saul (Ed.), *Crossing borders in literacy and science instruction: Perspectives on theory and practice* (pp. 111–122). Newark, NJ: International Reading Association.

Helm, J. H., & Katz, L. (2001). *Young investigators: The project approach in the early years.* New York: Teachers College Press.

Hyde, A. A., & Bizar, M. (1989). *Thinking in context: Teaching cognitive processes across the elementary school curriculum.* White Plains, NY: Longman.

Kress, G., Jewitt, C., Ogborn, J., & Tsatsarelis, C. (2001). *Multimodal teaching and learning: The rhetorics of the science classroom.* London: Continuum.

Krueger, A., & Sutton, J. (Eds.). (2001). *EDThoughts: What we know about science teaching and learning.* Aurora, CO: Mid-continent Research for Education and Learning.

Kyle, W. C., Bonnstetter, R. J., Gadsden, T., & Shymansky, J. (1988). What research says about hands-on science. *Science and Children, 25(7),* 39–40, 52.

Lake, J. (2000). *Literature and science breakthroughs: Connecting language and science skills in the elementary classroom.* Markham, Canada: Penbroke Publishers.

Lehrer, R., & Schauble, L. (2002). (Eds.). *Investigating real data in the classroom: Expanding children's understanding of math and science.* New York: Teachers College Press.

Lemke, J. L. (1998). Multiplying meaning: Visual and verbal semiotics in scientific text. In J. R. Martin & R. Veel (Eds.), *Reading science: Critical and functional perspectives on discourses of science* (pp. 87–113). London: Rutledge.

Lemke, J. L. (2003). The literacies of science. In W. Saul (Ed.), *Crossing borders in literacy and science instruction: Perspectives on theory and practice* (pp. 33–47). Newark, NJ: International Reading Association.

Lind, K. K., & Milburn, M. J. (1987). Mechanized childhood. *Science and Children, 25(5),* 322–333.

Martin, R., Sexton, C., Franklin, T., with Gerlovich, J. (2005). *Teaching science for all children: An inquiry approach.* Boston: Pearson Education.

Merryfield, M. M. (1991). Science-technology-society and global perspectives. *Theory Into Practice, 30,* 288–293.

Mullis, I., Jenkins, B., Berry, R., Champagne, A., Penick, J., Raizen, S., Weiss, I., & Welch, W. (1988). *The science report card: Elements of risk and recovery.* Princeton, NJ: Educational Testing Service.

Neutze, D. (2002). Resources for resourceful teachers. In Saul et al. (Eds.), *Science workshop: Reading, writing, and thinking like a scientist* (pp. 115–136). Portsmouth, NH: Heinemann.

Pappas, C. C., Varelas, M., Barry, A., & Rife, A. (2003). Dialogic inquiry around information texts: The role of intertextuality in constructing scientific understandings in urban primary classrooms. *Linguistics and Education, 13(4),* 435–482.

Pearce, C. (2002). Inquiry: A classroom model. In Saul et al. (Eds.), *Science workshop: Reading, writing, and thinking like a scientist* (pp. 39–73). Portsmouth, NH: Heinemann.

Reardon, J. (2002a). Science workshop: Capturing the essense of scientific inquiry. In Saul et al. (Eds.), *Science workshop: Reading, writing, and thinking like a scientist* (pp. 17–38). Portsmouth, NH: Heinemann.

Reardon, J. (2002b). Writing: A way into thinking science. In Saul et al. (Eds.), *Science workshop: Reading, writing, and thinking like a scientist* (pp. 86–100). Portsmouth, NH: Heinemann.

Rutherford, F. J., & Ahlgren, A. (1990). *Science for all Americans.* New York: Oxford University Press.

Sagan, C. (1978). *Address given at the 26th annual national convention of the National Science Teachers Association,* Washington, DC.

Saul, W. (Ed.) (2004). *Crossing borders in literacy and science instruction: Perspectives on theory and practice.* Newark, NJ: International Reading Association.

Saul, W., Reardon, J., Pearce, C., Dieckman, C., & Neutze, C. (2002). *Science workshop: Reading, writing, and thinking like a scientist.* Portsmouth, NH: Heinemann.

Scott, J. (1992). *Science & language links: Classroom implications.* Portsmouth, NH: Heinemann.

Shaw, D. G., & Dybdahl, C. S. (1996). *Integrating science and language arts: A sourcebook for K–6 teachers.* Needham Heights, MA: Allyn & Bacon.

Varelas, M. (1996). Between theory and data in a 7th grade science class. *Journal of Research in Science Teaching, 33(3),* 229–263.

Whitin, P., & Whitin, D. (1997). *Inquiry at the window: Pursuing the wonders of learners.* Portsmouth, NH: Heinemann.

Children's Literature: Science

A Children's Zoo by T. Hoban. Mulberry Books, 1985.

Animals Q & A: How Do I Move? by S. Greenway. Ideals Children's Books, 1992.

Becoming Butterflies by A. Rockwell. Walker & Co., 2002.

From Caterpillar to Butterfly by D. Heiligman. HarperCollins, 1996.

From Caterpillar to Butterfly by G. Legg. Franklin Watts, 1998.

Get It in Gear: The Science of Movement by B. Taylor. Random House, 1991.

Monarch Butterfly of Aster Way by E. Ring. Trudy, 1999.

Nuts to You! by L. Ehlert. Harcourt Brace Jovanovich, 1993.

Once a Wolf: How Wildlife Biologists Fought to Bring Back the Gray Wolf by S. R. Swinburne. Boston: Houghton Mifflin, 1999.

Plants: A Creative Hands-on Approach to Science by C. Watts & A. Parsons. Macmillan, 1993.

Rattlesnake Dance: True Tales, Mysteries, and Rattlesnake Ceremonies by J. O. Dewey. Boyds, 1997.

The Way Things Work by D. Macaulay. Houghton Mifflin, 1988.

World Water Watch by M. Koch. Greenwillow, 1993.

Mathematics

Recent research in mathematics gives validity to the integrated language perspective in helping children learn math. Having opportunities to use math as a tool, an aid to tackle a problem, or the means to accomplish a project within a thematic unit of study, is consistent with what we know about how children learn mathematical understandings during the preschool years and form mathematical knowledge in out-of-school activities in general.

Besides being emergent readers and writers, it is clear now that young children during the preschool years are also emergent mathematicians. Preschoolers engage in a variety of everyday activities that involve numbers: playing store-bought games or those invented by parents and children (e.g., counting stairs), watching educational TV shows (e.g., *Sesame Street*), helping parents on shopping trips, discussing how long it is till supper or till they get to Grandma's house, and noting how many floors yet to go in an elevator to the doctor's office. Moreover, numbers depicting the cost of products, mileage and speed limits, and the like are frequently incorporated into the public print of the signs and labels of our culture. As a result of this exposure, even two- and three-year-olds have considerable competence in counting objects. By the age of four, most children extend their early counting knowledge to comparing and reproducing number sets and to addressing simple arithmetic problems with small sets. When kindergartners begin school, they have already constructed important mathematical understandings; they have considerable arithmetic prowess on which to build and extend.

> Emergent mathematicians
>
> Gelman & Gallistel (1978); Hughes (1986); Saxe (1988a, 1988b); Saxe, Guberman, & Gearhart (1987)

In this new view of the emergent mathematician, language plays an important role. In fact, the origin of numbers can be traced to one of the earliest uses of language by the child. There is ample evidence to show that babies' early utterances of "up," "more," "all gone," and so on represent functional expressions that also serve as precursors of numbers in children's subsequent language. Relying on the number words (and numerals) found everywhere in their world and used repeatedly in interactions with themselves and others, children try to make sense of what they see and hear by employing their versions of "counting" to answer their own questions of how many or how much. That is, the development of mathematical understandings is also learning through language. Thus, the view that children learn mathematics principally through math lessons in school—and then only when they enter what Piaget has described as the concrete operational stage of development—has been questioned by cognitive developmentalists, mathematicians, and mathematics educators alike.

> Language is integrally related to early understanding of math.
>
> Nesher (1988)

> Piaget (1952, 1953)

A critical aspect of the recent views on the development of mathematical understandings is the importance of sociocultural influences on the process. That parents and others engage young children in everyday activities and games involving mathematical concepts and that these interactions support the children's efforts in learning

> Donaldson (1978); Gelman & Gallistel (1978); Lave, Murtaugh, & de la Rocha (1984)

> Social–cultural factors affect mathematical development.

There is a shift from performance techniques to reasoning and thinking about math.

Burns (1992); Hyde & Hyde (1991); Mokros, Russell, & Economopoulos (1995); Rutherford & Ahlgren (1990); Van de Walle (2004)

Borasi & Siegel (2000); Cobb, Yackel, & Wood (1991); Hiebert et al. (1997)

National Council of Teachers of Mathematics (NCTM) (1989)

See NCTM's website, www.nctm.org, for further information and resources on teaching and learning mathematics.

math suggest that similar collaborative experiences are needed in the classroom to strengthen and extend these understandings. Another important related issue is the movement from the performance of techniques to a more reflective way of knowing. Rather than emphasize a curriculum in which children practice or perform techniques to get "right" answers, the current view envisions a curriculum in which children develop an understanding and critical awareness of how and when to use mathematical techniques as well as why they work and how they are developed. Such a curriculum requires personal interpretation and invention, with opportunities to read, talk, and write about others' views and opinions on mathematical problems and issues. Thus, controversy, ambiguity, doubt, and risk taking all play important roles in the development of children's understandings and their attitudes toward mathematics. Moreover, these experiences contribute to their appreciation of the value of mathematics as a discipline and a certain way of knowing.

This new view can be seen in the key goals that the National Council of Teachers of Mathematics (NCTM) has set for students of mathematics in the 1990s:

1. To learn to value mathematics
2. To become confident in their ability to do mathematics
3. To become mathematical problem solvers
4. To learn to communicate mathematically
5. To learn to reason mathematically

These goals are radically different from those found in traditional classrooms but consistent with those fostered in integrated language classrooms. The following section underscores the importance of a problem-solving atmosphere in mathematics teaching and learning. The last two sections cover more ideas for integrating mathematics in thematic units and other ways in which mathematics can be incorporated in language and literacy activities.

Promoting a Problem-Solving Atmosphere in Mathematics

Math is a system of relationships.

Rutherford & Ahlgren (1990); Van de Walle (2004)

Ma (1999)

Mathematics is essentially the science of patterns and relationships. This *relational understanding* is the major objective in the teaching and learning of mathematics. It consists of helping children develop (1) mathematical ideas or concepts—*conceptual knowledge;* (2) a facility with the symbolism, rules, and methods of performing mathematics processes—*procedural knowledge;* and (3) connections between the methods/symbols and the corresponding concepts—*connections between conceptual and procedural knowledge.* Thus, fostering relational understanding in children requires that they know both the what and the why of mathematics. Traditionally school mathematics instruction has implied that there is a right way to do mathematics, and too frequently the symbolic method to produce mathematical results has been separated from the meaning. Facility with computation does not ensure that children have the ability to know when to use those skills when they encounter a particular problem. When children are seduced solely into the symbolism of math, they cannot create and recreate math relationships in their minds. Knowing mathematics means being able to use it in purposeful ways.

Thus, in integrated language classrooms, problem solving—the spirit of inquiry—is promoted. The challenge is to provide motivating problems that spark children's natural curiosity in a safe and supportive environment so that they can develop and use the mathematical skills and strategies they will need to solve real-life problems.

A problem-solving atmosphere in math requires a different role for the teacher.

The teacher dominated initiate–respond–evaluate (IRE) discourse has to be replaced with more collaborative talk. (See Chapter 2.)

Such a problem-solving curriculum has a different role for the teacher. The teacher cannot control instruction by being the key person to provide information, explain concepts or skills, or give examples. The teacher cannot direct all classroom interactions in an IRE-like discourse fashion—asking all of the questions, leading all of the discussions, and prompting student responses to the "right" answers. Instead, the teacher shares power with children by providing inquiry-based opportunities for them to grapple with problems on their own, search for strategies and solutions that make sense to them, and learn how to evaluate their results. Thus, choosing and using "good problems" is a critical feature of the integrated approach. Good problems are ones that have multiple routes to resolution, thereby encouraging children to express their thinking and approximations about the mathematical concepts underlying computational procedures while leading them to encounter new and unfamiliar mathematical territory that is an important curricular agenda or goal of the teacher. That is, solving good problems leads children to relational understanding because it is accomplished through collaborative talk where teachers are able to assess children's sense of these problems and then provide contingent, responsive feedback.

Learning is never an all-or-nothing enterprise. In a good problem-solving activity, children develop a tentative understanding of the concept(s) involved. As they engage in additional activities, more sophisticated and elaborate thinking evolves as they see and appreciate more connections. They also begin to view mathematical knowledge not as a stable body of facts but as a dynamic process of inquiry constructed by human, social activity—where uncertainty and conflict lead to a search for a more refined understanding of the world.

Children learn math best when the math they encounter is embedded in meaningful activities, where their problems involve real purposes for using and exploring math. In thematic units, children can analyze complex problems, arrive at reasonable solutions, and justify and evaluate the effectiveness of their solutions. In these contexts children care about the results and outcomes of their math activity.

Using Mathematics in Projects in Thematic Units

Like any symbolic system, mathematics involves both pure and applied aspects. The pure aspects are the abstractions of the symbolic language of mathematics (its concepts, principles, and theories); the applied aspects are the variety of ways mathematics explains the physical world and helps us in various everyday social interactions. These aspects are not separate. In fact, in the history of mathematics, new abstract formulations of mathematics have almost always been developed because specific situations or problems had to be addressed. These new notions have subsequently found applications to many other situations or problems. Before coming to school, children's knowledge of pure mathematics has been acquired in a dynamic, interactive way and anchored in applied circumstances. Unlike traditional classrooms, where frequently only pure or abstract math is emphasized, integrated language classrooms incorporate both aspects of math. In various thematic units, children continue to learn the abstract aspects of math *within* meaningful problem-solving contexts that facilitate their understanding of, and thinking about, mathematical concepts.

Math consists of many concepts and topics: number sense, numeration, and number systems; fractions and decimals; measurement, geometry, and spatial sense; estimation; statistics and probability; and algebra. Though only a hint of the possibilities can be provided here, mathematizing—using mathematics as reasoning and as active problem solving—is an integral feature of all the suggestions presented.

GRAPHING*

Graphing* can be used in practically any and every thematic unit and by children at any level in the elementary and middle school. In developing graphs, children compare, count, add, and subtract. Other mathematical operations such as multiplying and dividing are also possible in organizing data in a systematic way to discover patterns. Graphs can be the result of surveys children have conducted on a range of topics or issues. Graphs may come about when children have opportunities to observe

---

Problems need to be selected so that children's current math understandings can be assessed and extended.

Borasi & Siegel (2000); Hyde & Hyde (1991); Lampert (1991); Ma (1999); Van de Walle (2004)

Problem solving and math inquiry encourage children to view mathematics as a humanistic discipline shaped by cultural and personal values.

Borasi & Siegel (2000); Ridener & Fritzer (2004)

Borasi & Siegel (2000); Ma (1999); Van de Walle (2004)

Ridener & Fritzer (2004)

See Zaslavsky (1998, 2003) for useful ideas for incorporating math ideas along various across-the-curriculum multicultural thematic units.

See also Cordeiro (1988) for an example of a sixth-grade unit on infinity.

Clemson & Clemson (2002); King (1998);
Nagda & Bickel (2002)

See Moline (1996) for lots of ideas for
incorporating graphs.

data accumulation in the course of a thematic unit, for example, in gathering specific information in particular scientific experiments or conducting interviews or surveys related to a social studies issue. Several books written for children (e.g., *Getting the Facts, Charts and Graphs,* and *Tiger Math*) are useful tools in constucting graphs.

Graphing* activities can easily be incorporated in any of the prototypes in Chapter 4. In the CREATING COMMUNITIES unit, graphs can show how children get from one space to another—how many children in the class go to school by walking, by car, or by bus. This unit could collect this information for the whole school and expand the number of space categories beyond school into community spaces such as stores or entertainment places. Moreover, in the "Animal Communities" section of this unit, ideas from *Tiger Math* can be used to incorporate aspects about ants, honeybees, wolves, whales, and so forth. In JOURNEYS, children plant various kinds of seeds, roots, and cuttings and chart daily growth. Graphs showing and comparing growth patterns of propagation could be constructed. Information on types of and purposes for travel could also be organized and displayed through a graph in the JOURNEYS unit.

Older children can develop more complex graphs that incorporate percentages, averages, and other complex mathematical operations rather than those that may rely mostly on adding and subtracting. For example, in a fourth-grade version of the LET'S EAT! thematic unit, children could keep journals of their food consumption for a week and plot their average number of calories for each day of the week and contrast the average number of calories consumed through nutritious food versus junk food. They might also explore various types of graphs to display their data in bar graphs, line graphs, circle graphs, and especially computer-generated graphs. In the eighth-grade PERSPECTIVES, children could collect slang and other expressions about "outsiders" for a dictionary as part of their study of the "Outsiders" subtheme. Besides this dictionary, they could document the percentage of use of certain expressions to exclude others by students at different grades, as well as the ways in which these wordings make students feel.

In sum, graphs can be incorporated in many ways in any thematic unit. Teachers can consider Graphing* activities as part of planning a WEB. Although you could review the prototype WEBs in Chapter 4 and brainstorm a range of other possibilities, some of the most valuable graphs are those that evolve spontaneously. Recognizing the natural opportunities in the classroom allows for an integration of math with every curricular area. A growth graph can be developed when children notice some pollywogs with developed feet and others with less-developed feet. Contrasting the books that have been read on various topics within a unit, charting miles traveled by various explorers, and depicting types of foods eaten by people in various regions or countries all incorporate various Graphing* activities that require meaningful mathematical experiences for children across the curriculum. As children learn to use graphs to answer purposeful questions about their world and to make sense of the data they collect, they extend their knowledge of the communication potential of graphs—they learn graphs, learn about graphs, and learn through graphs.

Graphing opportunities should be planned for, but many can also emerge spontaneously.

See Chapter 7 for more information on graphing.

Whitlin, Mills, & O'Keefe (1990); Mills, O'Keefe, & Whitlin (1996)

MEASUREMENT

Only a few ideas of the limitless possibilities for measurement can be presented here. Various cooking activities, which can be incorporated in most units, readily incorporate measurement of ingredients: liquids such as milk, water, and oil; solids such as butter or shortening; particles of "matter" such as flour and sugar. As children follow various recipes, they begin to understand fractions and comparable amounts. The doubling or tripling of recipes requires estimating and confirming equivalencies of particular ingredients.

Food measurement

In the CYCLES prototype (in the "Water Cycle" subtheme) many water experiments and other activities are incorporated that could have children measuring water and other liquids. Various containers that have both cup and milliliter markings could be available for measuring water. Comparing English and metric liquid and dry measurements could be included in a primary-grade LET'S EAT! unit. Children could bring in weight information for various packaged and canned goods from the grocery store and then try to represent these weights (in terms of pounds and grams) by using scales and a range of objects in the classroom.

As you may have already noted, measurement is usually an initial step of Graphing*, especially when linear measurement is involved. Measuring the growth of plants from seeds, for example, is a prerequisite to graphing plant differences in the JOURNEYS and CYCLES units. It is important that children have opportunities to use both the English and metric systems in linear measurements. In a SPACES unit, for example, children could measure their favorite spaces at home (the length and width of their room, their bed, etc.) in inches, feet, and yards *and* in centimeters and meters. Older children could consider the notion of perimeter by figuring out the perimeters of objects in the various spaces in the classroom. Lots of measuring is required in the various displays constructed in the science museum in the "Outer Space" subtheme in PERSPECTIVES (see also the eighth-grade vignette in the Introduction chapter).

"Body Spaces" could also be explored in both the WONDERING and SPACES thematic units (as well as other units such as TAKING CARE, where taking care of the environment, others, and your body, etc., were explored). Children's heights, as well as lengths and widths of various body parts, could be measured. For older children, the concept of circumference could be explored by measuring the circumferences of children's waists, heads, wrists, or thighs. Having children estimate the sizes of their body parts and then compute how far off their "real" measurements are adds even more to these problem-solving activities. The LANDSCAPES unit provides many opportunities for measurement to create various maps.

Measurement of time can frequently be incorporated in a range of thematic units. In a FLIGHT unit, children using a stopwatch can chart the time it takes their miniature parachutes, which are attached to objects of various weights, to land from the top of the playground equipment. A study of some of the timed events from the *Guinness Book of World Records* can lead children to track their everyday events to identify their own records. In a thematic unit on IT'S ABOUT TIME, encouraging children to determine the time elapsed by noting both the hands on an analog clock and the digits on a digital clock helps them to begin a study of the ways people have described time.

Many scientific experiments involve the measurement of time. In a unit on DISAPPEARING ACTS, older elementary students studied a range of topics: various magic tricks and magicians such as the famous Houdini, certain aspects of pollution (many materials are not easily biodegradable and are, therefore, not good disappearing acts), and famous missing persons such as Amelia Earhart. They also timed the evaporation rates of various liquids (water, oil, alcohol, and soapy water). Another possible scientific activity is an exploration of the disappearing acts (the "demise" of soapy bubbles) and an examination of why certain bubbles last longer than others. Measuring various transformations is frequently an integral aspect of the careful observation required also in the process of sciencing. In sum, measurement can be easily incorporated in various ways in thematic units. Just as in Graphing*, possible measurement ideas should be considered ahead of time in planning WEBs, but more natural opportunities emerge frequently if the teacher is alert enough to spot and support them.

FOSTERING GEOMETRIC AND SPATIAL SENSE

In traditional elementary classrooms, geometry is usually limited to children learning the labels of various geometric shapes, and in the older grades, sometimes memorizing formulas to compute the area of various shapes. However, when engaged in activities and experiences in various thematic units, children can be encouraged to think about and analyze the shapes in more meaningful ways. The formula for calculating the area of a rectangle is much more understandable when children are asked to determine the

Contrasting English and metric systems

Add estimation to measurement activities.

Time measurement

Burns (1992); Mokros, Russell, & Economopoulos (1995); Pappas & Bush (1989); Van de Walle (2004)

dePaola (1975, 1979, 1982)

area of a construction paper "rug" to cover the bottom of a diorama constructed as an extension of a book they have read. Other such constructions—making Strega Nona's house (found in dePaola's *Strega Nona, Big Anthony and the Magic Ring,* and *Strega Nona's Magic Lessons*) or the houses of the *Three Little Pigs*—require that children visualize the three-dimensional nature of geometric figures. As part of a fourth-, fifth-, or sixth-grade SPACES unit, children's attempts to construct accurate scaled-down versions of their favorite spaces at home can foster a concentrated effort to understand geometric and spatial sense. This project also means that children employ a range of measurements, deal with ratios, and apply certain algebraic expressions. This is required also in the PERSPECTIVES unit as students create three-dimensional pop-up space dislays (see Chapter 1). Children gain similar understandings when, after having architects and city planning personnel come to visit the classroom in a HOUSES thematic unit, they decide to design and construct a model of a town depicted in a story or in a nonfictional text in social studies.

See Borasi & Siegel (2000) for an example of an integrated inquiry-based geometry unit for middle school students.

In a thematic unit such as DESIGNS AND PATTERNS, children are able to explore geometric figures in depth. Besides studying the symmetrical patterns of plant and animal organisms and various crystal formations, children examine all kinds of patterns and geometric designs. Children construct many patterns and designs by using a range of material (pennies, buttons, seeds, small sticks, attribute blocks, LEGO blocks, etc.) and then describe them through writing or illustrations so that others can try to replicate them. Musical patterns are examined, patterns of three in stories are compared, and quilts are designed using various geometric shapes. Children use rubber bands to construct shapes on student-made or commercially made geoboards and compasses to make circles. They construct various triangular designs as well as pentomino or hexomino puzzles. They use dot or centimeter paper to make hexagons or equilateral triangles to create tessellating patterns. Geometry circuit boards are set up to show various geometric shapes, arranged so that when a match is made, a bell rings.

Geometric understandings can be fostered not only in thematic units in which geometric sense is a major focus. The development of a range of geometric concepts (e.g., shape, size, symmetry, congruence, and similarity in two- and three-dimensional space) along with the appropriate geometry vocabulary can also be fostered in many other units when teachers are aware of the possibilities. These understandings and experiences in geometric thinking provide an important foundation for learning the more formal generalizations in geometric relationships in the upper grades.

Burns (1992); Van de Walle (2004)

OTHER MISCELLANEOUS IDEAS FOR INTEGRATING MATH

There are many everyday routines in which children can use math in the classroom. Giving children responsibility for various routine tasks such as taking roll, keeping track of lunch or milk money or book orders, or distributing materials fosters mathematical understandings. Understanding of decimals is developed when real money is computed and handled for real purposes. There are many opportunities for dealing with money in thematic units as well. Money can be exchanged in grocery stores or restaurants set up in the classroom in units such as LET'S EAT! Children can trade and sell stocks in hypothetical accounts as part of a DISAPPEARING ACTS unit. Store-bought and student-made games also provide many opportunities for developing the concept of number and other mathematical principles. (Games are discussed in the next section as well.)

Give children responsibilities for everyday "housekeeping" activities that involve math.

Having many manipulatives available for children to use encourages many kinds of mathematical understandings. We know of a kindergarten teacher who fosters the idea of number sets by having children tell how many sets (of ten, three, four, etc.) of blocks are counted out when they work in the construction area. The teacher observes the strategies the children employ and intervenes to support their efforts or to point out how peers' sets are different or equivalent. By the end of the year, most of these children know that two sets of ten blocks are equivalent to four sets of five blocks.

See Kamii (1985) for examples of using games in a first-grade classroom and Zaslavsky (1998, 2003) for a variety of multicultural games for children at many grades.

What is important in these mathematical activities and experiences is that children recognize the socially constructed nature of mathematical knowledge—that alternative interpretations and debate are integral elements of the discipline. Moreover, underlying these authentic problem-solving approaches is the expectation that *all* children—boys *and girls* from diverse ethnolinguistic backgrounds—will not only be attracted to such mathematical sense making but will also be confident in developing mathematical understandings.

Many ways to use math are possible in the classroom no matter what the thematic unit is. Ideas that more directly integrate language and literacy are suggested in the following pages.

Language, Literacy, Visual Images, and Mathematics

FOSTERING TALK ABOUT MATH

Speaking and listening are naturally integrated in children's discussions of mathematical concepts. Comparing information obtained or accumulated as part of projects fosters mathematics as a way of knowing. In small groups or as whole class, they debate how, when, and why certain mathematical operations are appropriate for the issues being investigated. Addition, subtraction, multiplication, division, fractions, and decimals are not pursued as separate subjects of math. In real-life situations, problems frequently require solutions that integrate several techniques. Consequently, children have to talk about and consider others' views when they decide which mathematical operations are necessary.

Talk about the illustrations in books that center around math topics often helps students bring up good questions about math and helps students better understand math concepts. To further math talk, many teachers regularly gather a range of text sets of children's literature having math concepts in them and have children read and discuss them in Literature Response Groups*. In these small-group discussions, students talk about what they don't understand or what seems puzzling to them, explain math ideas in their own words, use open questions ("What did you notice?" "What did the story remind you of?"), and ask their own questions that they then attempt to answer. In these experiences, students understand that math is an integrated part of living; they make personal connections with math. They realize that math can be an intrinsically rewarding topic that they can learn and think about. (Ideas for using literature books for teaching math follow.)

INTEGRATING READING, WRITING, AND DRAWING ABOUT AND AROUND MATH

Many opportunities for reading and writing about math are also possible in an integrated language classroom. Reading, writing, and drawing occur when children jot down survey data or organize their various calculations in Sketchbook Journals* and then share these illustrated notes with others. The construction of graphs (a type of visual image) also incorporates reading and writing. Reading and writing reports of scientific experiments or other investigations include opportunities to express and comprehend mathematical data. Constructing and playing games as extensions of books read and studied in class can also provide meaningful occasions to apply and use math. Board games (which frequently include visual images) may depict important significant events of a story or a biography or stages of transformation in an experiment on animal and plant growth. As children decide on and write their directions so that others can play, particular mathematical operations are considered and clarified. Players then develop these mathematical understandings as they try to comprehend and follow the directions.

Many teachers include specific math Journals* in which children are encouraged to write about the difficulties they might have with math problems, to record new

Margin notes

Borasi & Siegel (2000); Hiebert et al. (1997); Hyde & Hyde (1991); Ma (1999); Van de Walle (2004)

Math anxiety and avoidance are greatly reduced for all children when there are many meaningful math experiences.

See Lehrer & Schable (2002) for ways of incorporating real math data into classroom investigations.

Discussion of math problems fosters math understandings.

Borasi & Siegel (2000); Corwin et al. (1996); Ma (1999)

See Thiessen & Matthias (1992) and Whitlin & Wilde (1992, 1995) for lists of mathematical books to use in these small-group discussions. Ridener & Fritzer (2004) also provide both children's books and websites.

Whitlin & Wilde (1995)

Borasi & Siegel (2000); Burns (1995); Daniels & Zemelman (2004); Fulwiler (1980, 1982); Moline (1996)

Countryman (1992)

learnings, and to compare and contrast various procedures or strategies to solve problems. These journals serve as personal records of the experience of doing mathematics. Beginning a school year by having children write their own mathematics autobiography provides teachers, as well as the students themselves, many insights into children's views and attitudes toward math. Asking students to tell about their accomplishments or disasters, and what they like or do not like about math, reveals ideas about their thinking on the nature of mathematics, as well as their abilities to learn and understand it. It also uncovers their perceptions of how they have been taught math in school and how math has functioned in their out-of-school, everyday life. Using these ideas, teachers have a better sense about individual students' beliefs, needs, interests, and feelings regarding math and are, therefore, able to develop appropriate instruction.

Another possible way for children to do both reading and writing of math is through Student-Directed Inquiries* on math topics of choice. "Math search" papers can cover a range of topics, such as African mathematics, ancient math, paper folding, paradoxes, tessellations, gambling, numerology, and the work of M. C. Escher, that both teachers and students can develop together. Besides generating initial questions to guide and frame their inquiries and papers, children can also address other questions on the process of their inquiry: what they knew and didn't know before the inquiry, what they did to find out about their topic of inquiry, and what they learned and did not learn from their study. (See Organizing/Monitoring Student-Initiated Inquiry* in Chapter 7 for more ideas on implementing math inquiry projects.) The purposeful reading, writing, and drawing involved in studying these math topics encourage in-depth relational thinking.

USING "MATHEMATICAL" LITERATURE BOOKS

As already noted, many wonderful books that have mathematical concepts in them can be included in thematic units. Later we suggest only some of the possibilities.

Two books to use for primary grades cover math for 100 days of school. *Emily's First 100 Days of School* by Rosemary Wells tells what happens at school for the first 100 days from the perspective of Emily, a young rabbit. Each day—day 1, day 2, and so on—the children make a new number and when they arrive at 100, they have a party! *Counting Our Way to the 100th Day* by Betsy Fanco is a book of 100 poems and each poem covers 100 of something—various 100 things that can be counted (e.g, leaves, picnic pests, names, and so forth). After being read aloud a number day or a poem, children could engage in their various open-ended extensions of the number ideas in each book.

Murphy has written several books about everyday events for primary-grade children that help demystify math. *A Pair of Socks* is a concept book that has a striped sock looking for its missing mate. *Give Me Half! Understanding Halves* explains fractions by having a brother and sister figure out how to divide a pizza or cookies into halves so they can share equally. *Get Up and Go!* concretely introduces time lines by depicting the minutes a young girl uses to get ready for school. Other books in this Mathstart series cover a range of math concepts and topics—for example, *The Penny Pot* (about the counting of coins); *Super Sand Castle Saturday* (about aspects of measurement); *Coyotes All Around* (about how you can add up numbers in your head by simple rounding).

There are many other math literature series: the Pigs and Math books (e.g., *Pigs Will Be Pigs, Pigs on a Blanket,* and *Pigs Go to the Market*), the Marilyn Burns Brain Day Books (e.g., *The Greedy Triangle* and *A Cloak for the Dreamer*); and the Sir Cumference books (e.g., *Sir Cumference and the Dragon of Pi* and *Sir Cumference and the Great Knight of Angleland*).

Older elementary children enjoy *Math Curse*, which presents a girl who begins to see how almost everything in her life can be seen as math inquiry, even choosing what she will wear that day. Also, *Counting on Frank* could be used for many ages. It is a humorous book in which a boy is always measuring, figuring out, and musing about mathematics and things around the house. He calculates how many Franks (his dog)

Margin notes

Math autobiographies

See Burns (1995) and Borasi & Siegel (2000) for other authoring ideas in math.

Student-Directed Inquiry* can occur around math topics, too.

Borasi & Siegel (2000); Countryman (1992); Macrorie (1988)

Freedman & Person (1998)

Wells (2000)

Franco (2004)

Murphy (1996a, 1996b; 1996c)

Murphy (1998, 1999, 2003)

Axelrod (1997, 1998, 1999)

Burns (1994); Friedman (1994)

Neuschwander (1999a, 1999b)

Scieszka (1995)

Clement (1991)

could fit in his room or how long of a line an average ballpoint pen can make before running out of ink. He estimates that if he "accidentally" knocked down fifteen peas off his plate for the last eight years, the peas would now be at the level of the tabletop. Because all of these books have to do with familiar, everyday events, children can extend the books by writing and illustrating their own stories that involve a mathematical point of view.

Math literature books show children how math is embedded in real life.

Another book, *The King's Chessboard* by David Birch, is a story that takes place in ancient India. The King of Deccan is so pleased with his wise man's services that he wishes to give him a reward. The wise man does not think he needs a reward, but the king is insistent. The wise man reflects, and then noting the king's chessboard, asks the king for the number of grains of rice that would be required if one grain were placed on the first square, two on the second square, four on the third square, and so on for all 64 squares on the chessboard. Because the king isn't sure how much rice would be necessary, and because he is too proud to let on to anyone that he doesn't know, he grants the wise man's request as his reward. With only half the squares accounted for, however, the royal granaries are nearly bare from meeting the requirements of the reward. In *One Grain of Rice* by Demi, a similar plot and setting are found, but this time it is a village girl name Rani who teaches a raja what it really means to be wise and fair.

Birch (1988)

Demi (1997)

As children discover how the king finds a way to save face and get over being outwitted by the wise man and how the raja is fooled by a young girl to address her people's hunger, they begin to reflect on the mathematical power of a simple request. Extensions of this book could involve children in posing other "simple" requests that require different kinds of mathematical patterns—adding 10 or some other number for each chessboard square, for example. These could be incorporated in stories or expressed by short descriptions of various patterns (e.g., on day 1 there are ten pennies; on day 2, twenty; day 3, fifteen; day 4, twenty-five; then thirty-five, thirty, and so on) for other classmates to figure out. Possible mathematical abstractions can be considered by children because the abstractions are begun in a meaningful way and are initiated and controlled by the children.

Mitsumasa Anno has several books incorporating various mathematical concepts. In *Anno's Hat Tricks*, Anno and Nozaki introduce children to the deductive reasoning that is the basis of binary logic. As the hatter encourages Shadowchild (the reader) to play tricks about red and white hats, the power of "if" is explained as it is used by computer programmers, mathematicians, and other scientists. Children enjoy making their own hats to dramatize the book or writing plays to illustrate other examples of the process of elimination and binary logic.

Nozaki & Anno (1985)

In Anno's *Mysterious Multiplying Jar*, Anno and his son, Masaichiro, illustrate the concept of factorials in a manner that children with a basic understanding of multiplication can grasp. Like a cumulative folktale, the authors present an island in a sea; and on that island, two countries; and in each country, three mountains; and so on up to ten jars. How many jars altogether? Well, there were 10! jars. As children discover a new function of the exclamation point, they begin to realize how it signals a special kind of numerical relationship. The !, called a *factorial,* means that the number it follows stands for the product of that number multiplied by the next smaller number, multiplied by the next smaller number, and so forth all the way down to 1. Extensions can involve children in trying to figure out other real-life scenarios that depict factorials (e.g., the possible arrangements of the desks of four students). In addition, because the Anno book is like a cumulative tale, a study of some of these folktales leads children to discover how the part–whole relationship in these tales compares with the relationships of the mathematical factorial idea. Sometimes this investigation can result in children's writing a new genre—"cumulative factorial" tales.

Anno & Anno (1983)

Several books for older elementary and middle-grade children make math fun and help break down the mystique around math. In *Fractals, Googols, and Other Mathematical Tales* and *The Adventures of Penrose the Mathematical Cat,* Theoni Pappas has

Pappas (1993, 1997)

Tahan (1993); Enzenberger (2000)

Schwartz (1998)

Williams (1982, 1983, 1984)

Conford (1988, 1989, 1991)

Viorst (1978)

Chardiet & Maccarone (1991)

Goldberg (1992)

Maestro (1993)

Wyatt & Hinden (1991)

Barkin & James (1990); Wilkinson (1989); Bernstein (1992)

Burns (1975)

See *Math for Smarty Pants* by Burns (1982) and Zaslavsky (1998, 2003) for even more games and activities in various mathematical areas.

Mathematical literature books come in all genres.

Gray (1988)

Tang (2001)

Penrose the cat involved in real-life tales about the use of mathematics. Two longer novels—*The Man Who Counted* and *The Number Devil*—focus on math puzzles in life. In the first book, a scribe documents in "memoir" fashion the mathematical adventures of a fellow traveler—the Man Who Counted—as he resolves various disputes of problems on their journey to Baghdad. The second book tells about how Robert, a boy who hates math, encounters a clever number devil in his dreams that makes Robert learn about the wonder of number. *G Is for Googol* is a math alphabet book that covers a range of math concepts in interesting ways. Besides enjoying these books, they also could serve as prototypes for students to write their own tales or math alphabet book. Although not picture books, all include illustrations, so thinking about how students might include illustrations in these student-constructed books provides opportunities for them to make text–visual image connections.

The topic of money is a good one to incorporate in many thematic units, and many books, both fiction and nonfiction, are available to support children's inquiries in this domain. Because children become aware of money at an early age, and because the economy is so much in the news, books can help them begin to learn about fiscal responsibility. Vera Williams has three books—*A Chair for My Mother, Something Special for Me,* and *Music, Music for Everyone*—in which Rosa, her mother, and her grandmother save in a jar her mother's tips from her job as a waitress at the Blue Tile Diner, and other extra family money, to buy various items. Ellen Conford also has several chapter books about Jenny Archer, who tries to raise money in some interesting but not always popular ways: *A Job for Jenny Archer; What's Cooking, Jenny Archer?;* and *Can Do, Jenny Archer.* Other books of fiction cover money topics that children can relate to. In Viorst's *Alexander, Who Used to Be Rich Last Sunday,* Alexander squanders his money in foolish ways; in *Martin and the Tooth Fairy* by Chardiet and Maccarone, buying children's teeth to make a profit from the tooth fairy is foiled; and in *Alice* by Whoopi Goldberg, Alice's dream-come-true sweepstakes ends up a scam.

A range of nonfictional titles about money also appeals to children. Maestro's *The Story of Money* traces the history of money and shows how the medium of money has changed from salt to electronic cards. *The Money Book* by Wyatt and Hinden is a paperback that covers a range of topics—even some unusual ones, such as collectibles, betting, and charity. Several books—*Jobs for Kids; Making Cents: Every Kid's Guide to Money;* and *Better Than a Lemonade Stand*—cover innumerable ways children can earn money or begin a business for profit.

Another informative book that children love is *The I Hate Mathematics! Book* by Marilyn Burns. A range of activities convinces children that math can be fun and that there is more to math than arithmetic. Topology (the study of surfaces) is examined in "A Topological Garden," exponential growth is introduced in "Doing Dishes," and a palindrome is discovered in "The Perfect Palindrome." Children can reenact in the classroom many of the tricks and games described in the book. Trying them out on the unsuspecting in other classes or at home can lead to shared writings about reactions. Because the activities are frequently illustrated by cartoons, children are sometimes spurred to use this medium to express other math tricks they have discovered.

As already noted, mathematical literature books are written in a range of genres. There are poetry books, such as *One, Two, Three, and Four—No More?.* Here Catherine Gray's verses and Marissa Moss's illustrations depict various animals in combinations of the first four numbers, thereby providing a delightful introduction of simple numeration, addition, and subtraction for young mathematicians. *The Grapes of Math* includes mind-stretching math riddles that require children to make sense of both the pictures and text. Besides reading these verses over and over, children can extend the book in many ways. They can make stick or other animal puppets and dramatize these arithmetical operations. They can also write their own verses, using other animals and mathematical operations that involve numbers over four. Older elementary children can try writing similar verses or riddles (or ones that use other kinds of poetic structures or that focus on objects or people rather than animals, or make use of picures that depict the gist of the the riddles), using other operations, such as multiplication and division. Writing verses that incorporate mathematical notions can be part of children's Sketchbook Journals* as they engage in various projects in thematic units throughout the year.

There are "fuzzy" books as well, where the language of various genres is incorporated or intermingled (see more about "fuzzy" books in Chapter 6). In *Emeka's Gift: An African Counting Story,* Ifeoma Onyefulu has Emeka setting off to visit his grandmother in the next village. The book is storylike in that he is engaged in various events and has conversation with people on his journey. He meets, for example, three women on their way to the market who stop to say hello. Then as he passes through the market and sees many things that Granny would like, he worries whether she will understand that he has no money to buy anything for her. Stunning photographs of Emeka's village in southern Nigeria are included (rather than illustrations) and various topics about the village related to the storyline, such as markets, are further explained in informational "boxes" (e.g., "Markets are important meeting places . . .").

Onyefulu (1995)

WRITING AND ILLUSTRATING STORY PROBLEMS

One of the best ways children can make mathematics meaningful is to write (and illustrate) their own story problems. These can be constructed and collected in every thematic unit throughout the year, perhaps in a special journal designated for this purpose. Ideas are generated as the children read a range of genres and investigate problems across the curriculum. For example, they can incorporate their mathematical data by spinning a yarn using the characters and episodes in a story they are enjoying. Problems can be expressed by describing the behaviors of animals or by relating historic events. As writers, children begin with a solution and then work backward to construct an interesting problem. As readers of their peers' problems, they do the opposite: They begin with trying to figure out the problem and work toward the solution. These reading, writing, and illustrating experiences, and the spirited discussions surrounding them, are invaluable mathematical problem-solving activities.

Burns (1995); Countryman (1992); Daniels & Zemelman (2004); Mills, O'Keefe, & Whitlin (1996); Moline (1996); Whitlin & Wilde (1995)

Writing (and illustrating) their own mathematics book for children in other classes or for children next year provides opportunities to display and reflect on what they know about math. Math becomes meaningful, even for kindergartners, as they try to explain and illustrate the mathematical concepts and procedures they know so that other children can understand them. By sketching classroom and real-world scenarios, children come up with interesting and novel ways to express these mathematical understandings.

See Van den Brink (1987) for a good classroom example of the writing and illustrating by first graders of their own arithmetic books.

Summary

In an integrated classroom, problem solving is emphasized across the curriculum. Both pure and applied aspects of mathematics are integrated so that relational understanding is developed. Math is concrete and meaningful because it has to do with real-world problems and scenarios. Because math activities and experiences make sense to children, the mathematical concepts they acquire by being engaged in these activities serve as launch pads for expanding these concepts to greater levels of abstraction in meaningful ways. As children discuss the process of mathematical operations or techniques, they examine their appropriateness; risk taking is fostered when they consider and evaluate alternative methods. They also learn the diverse ways that mathematical meanings are expressed through the "language" and "visual images" of mathematics and its genre-specific forms and structures: graphs, proofs, definitions, algorithms, and equations.

Teachers need to demonstrate mathematical operations, strategies, models, or approaches to problems in Focus Lessons* (see Chapter 7) and/or have regular sessions in which math is the focus. Rather than spend a lot of rote exercises on many problems,

Andersen (1993); Daniels & Zeleman (2004); Hyde & Hyde (1991); Moline (1996); Zaslavsky (1996)

Learning math involves learning various math genres.

Moline (1996); Mousley and Marks (1991)

> The coherence of problems in meaningful contexts is emphasized.

children tackle and have practice with a smaller number of problems in-depth. In so doing, they develop an appreciation of the coherence of a problem and the process involved in attempting to solve it. Children see math as a powerful way of knowing and themselves as confident mathematicians.

References: Mathematics

Borasi, R., & Siegel, M. (2000). *Reading counts: Expanding the role of reading in mathematics classrooms.* New York: Teachers College Press.

Burns, M. (1992). *About teaching mathematics: A K–8 resource.* White Plains, NY: Cuisenaire Co. of America.

Cobb, P., Yackel, E., & Wood, T. (1991). Curriculum and teacher development: Psychological and anthropological perspectives. In E. Fennema, T. P. Carpenter, & S. J. Lamon (Eds.), *Integrating research on teaching and learning mathematics* (pp. 83–119). Albany: State University of New York Press.

Cordeiro, P. (1988). Playing with infinity in the sixth grade. *Language Arts, 65,* 557–566.

Corwin, R. B., Storeygard, D., & Price, S. L. (Eds.). (1996). *Talking mathematics: Supporting children's voices.* Portsmouth, NH: Heinemann.

Countryman, J. (1992). *Writing to learn mathematics: Strategies that work, K–12.* Portsmouth, NH: Heinemann.

Daniels, H., & Zemelman, S. (2004). *Subjects matter: Every teacher's guide to content-area reading.* Portsmouth, NH: Heinemann.

Donaldson, M. (1978). *Children's minds.* Glasgow: William Collins Sons.

Freedman, E. B., & Person, D. G. (1998). *Connecting informational children's books with content area learning.* Boston: Allyn & Bacon.

Fulwiler, T. (1980). Journals across the disciplines. *English Journal, 69,* 14–22.

Fulwiler, T. (1982). Writing: An act of cognition. In C. W. Griffin (Ed.), *New directions for teaching and learning: No. 12. Teaching writing in all disciplines* (pp. 15–26). San Francisco: Jossey-Bass.

Gelman, R., & Gallistel, C. R. (1978). *The child's understanding of number.* Cambridge, MA: Harvard University Press.

Hiebert, J. (1984). Children's mathematics learning: The struggle to link form and understanding. *Elementary School Journal, 84,* 497–513.

Hiebert, J., et al. (1997). *Making sense: Teaching and learning mathematics with understanding.* Portsmouth, NH: Heinemann.

Hughes, M. (1986). *Children and numbers: Difficulties in learning mathematics.* New York: Basil Blackwell.

Hyde, A. A., & Bizar, M. (1989). *Thinking in context: Teaching cognitive processes across the elementary curriculum.* Oxford: Longman.

Hyde, A. A., & Hyde, P. R. (1991). *Mathwise: Teaching mathematical thinking and problem solving.* Portsmouth, NH: Heinemann.

Kamii, C. K. (1985). *Young children reinvent arithmetic: Implications of Piaget's theory.* New York: Teachers College Press.

Lampert, M. (1991). Connecting mathematical teaching and learning. In E. Fennema, T. P. Carpenter, & S. J. Lamon (Eds.), *Integrating research on teaching and learning mathematics* (pp. 121–152). Albany: State University of New York Press.

Larke, P. J. (1988). Geometric extravaganza: Spicing up geometry. *Arithmetic Teacher, 36,* 12–16.

Lave, J., Murtaugh, M., & de la Rocha, O. (1984). The dialectic of arithmetic in grocery shopping. In B. Rogoff & J. Lave (Eds.), *Everyday cognition: Its development in social context* (pp. 67–94). Cambridge, MA: Harvard University Press.

Lehrer, R., & Schauble, L. (Eds.). (2002). *Investigating real data in the classroom: Expanding children's understanding of math and science.* New York: Teachers College Press.

Ma, L. (1999). *Knowing and teaching elementary mathematics.* Mahwah, NJ: Lawrence Erlbaum.

Macrorie, K. (1988). *The I-search paper.* Portsmouth, NH: Boynton/Cook.

McCallum, R., & Whitlow, R. (1994). *Linking mathematics and language: Practical classroom activities.* Markham, Ontario, Canada: Pippin.

Mills, H., O'Keefe, T., & Whitlin, D. (1996). *Mathematics in the making: Authoring ideas in primary classrooms.* Portsmouth, NH: Heinmann.

Mokros, J., Russell, S. J., & Economopoulos, E. (1995). *Beyond arithmetic: Changing mathematics in the elementary classroom.* Palo Alto, CA: Dale Seymour Pulications.

Moline, S. (1996). *I see what you mean: Children at work with visual information.* York, ME: Stenhouse.

Mousley, J., & Marks, G. (1991). *Discourse in mathematics.* Victoria, Australia: Deakin University Press.

National Council of Teachers of Mathematics (1989). *Curriculum and evaluation standards for school mathematics.* Reston, VA: Author.

Nesher, P. (1988). Precursors of number in children: A linguistic perspective. In S. Strauss (Ed.), *Ontogeny, phylogeny, and historical development: Human development* (vol. 2, pp. 106–124). Norwood, NJ: Ablex.

Pappas, C. C., & Bush, S. (1989). Facilitating understandings of geometry. *Arithmetic Teacher, 36,* 17–20.

Piaget, J. (1952). *The child's conception of number.* London: Routledge & Kegan Paul.

Piaget, J. (1953). How children form mathematics concepts. *Scientific American, 189,* 74–79.

Ridener, B., & Fritzer, P. (2004). *Mathematics content for elementary and middle school teachers.* Boston: Pearson.

Rutherford, F. J., & Ahlgren, A. (1990). *Science for all Americans.* New York: Oxford University Press.

Saxe, G. B. (1988a). Candy selling and math learning. *Educational Researcher, 17,* 14–21.

Saxe, G. B. (Ed.). (1988b). *New directions for child development: No. 41. Children's mathematics* (pp. 55–70). San Francisco: Jossey-Bass.

Saxe, G. B., Guberman, S. R., & Gearhart, M. (1987). *Social processes in early number development* (Monograph No. 52, Serial No. 216). Society for Research in Child Development.

Thiessen, D., & Matthias, M. (1992). *The wonderful world of mathematics: A critically annotated list of children's books in mathematics.* Reston, VA: National Council of Teachers of Mathematics.

Van den Brink, J. (1987). Children as arithmetic book authors. *For the Learning of Mathematics, 7,* 44–47.

Van de Walle, J. A. (2004). *Elementary and middle school mathematics: Teaching developmentally.* Boston: Pearson.

Whitlin, D. J., Mills, H., & O'Keefe, T. (1990). *Living and learning mathematics: Stories and strategies for supporting mathematical literacy.* Portsmouth, NH: Heinemann.

Whitlin, D. J., & Wilde, S. (1992). *Read any good math lately? Children's books for mathematical learning, K–6.* Portsmouth, NH: Heinemann.

Whitlin, D. J., & Wilde, S. (1995). *It's the story that counts: More children's books for mathematical learners, K–6.* Portsmouth, NH: Heinemann.

Zaslavsky, C. (1998). *Math games and activities from around the world.* Chicago: Chicago Review Press.

Zaslavsky, C. (2003). *More math games and activities from around the world.* Chicago: Chicago Review Press.

Children's Literature: Mathematics

The Adventures of Penrose the Mathematical Cat by T. Pappas. Wide World Publishing, 1997.

Alexander, Who Used to Be Rich Last Sunday by J. Viorst. Illustrated by R. Cruz. Atheneum, 1978.

Alice by W. Goldberg, Illustrated by J. Rocco. Bantam, 1992.

Anno's Hat Tricks by A. Nozaki & M. Anno. Philomel, 1985.

Anno's Mysterious Multiplying Jar by M. Anno & M. Anno. Illustrated by M. Anno. Philomel, 1983.

Better Than a Lemonade Stand by D. Bernstein. Illustrated by R. Husberg. Beyond Words, 1992.

Big Anthony and the Magic Ring by T. dePaola. Harcourt Brace Jovanovich, 1979.

Can Do, Jenny Archer by E. Conford. Illustrated by D. Palmisciano. Little Brown, 1991.

A Chair for My Mother by V. Williams. Greenwillow, 1982.

Charts and Graphs by W. Clemson & D. Clemson. Two-Can Publishing, 2002.

A Cloak for the Dreamer by A. Friedman. Illustrated by K. Howard. Scholastic, 1994.

Counting on Frank by R. Clement. Gareth Stevens, 1991.

Counting Our Way to the 100th Day by B. Franco. Illustrated by S. Salerno. Margaret K McElderry Books, 2004.

Coyotes All Around by S. J. Murphy. Illustrated by S. Bjorkman. HarperCollins, 2003.

Emeka's Gift: An African Counting Story by I. Onyefulu. Dutton, 1995.

Emily's First 100 Days of School by R. Wells. Hyperion Books, 2000.

Fractals, Googols and Other Mathematical Tales by T. Pappas. Wide World Publishing, 1993.

G Is for Googol: A Math Alphabet Book by D. M. Schwartz. Illustrated by M. Moss. Tricycle Press, 1998.

Get Up and Go! by S. J. Murphy. Illustrated by D. Greenseid. HarperCollins, 1996.

Getting the Facts by A. King. Copper Beech Books, 1998.

Give Me Half! Understanding Halves by S. J. Murphy. Illustrated by B. Karras. HarperCollins, 1996.

A Grain of Rice by H. C. Pittman. Hastings House, 1986.

The Grapes of Math by G. Tang. Illustrated by H. Briggs. Scholastic, 2001.

The Greedy Triangle by M. Burns. Illustrated by G. Silveria. Scholastic, 1994.

The I Hate Mathematics! Book by M. Burns. Illustrated by M. Hairston. Little, Brown, 1975.

A Job for Jenny Archer by E. Conford. Illustrated by D. Palmisciano. Little, Brown, 1988.

Jobs for Kids by C. Barkin & E. James. Illustrated by R. Doty. Lothrop, 1990.

The King's Chessboard by D. Birch. Illustrated by D. Grebu. Dial, 1988.

Making Cents: Every Kid's Guide to Money by E. Wilkinson. Illustrated by M. Weston. Little, Brown, 1989.

The Man Who Counted: A Collection of Mathematical Adventures by M. Tahan. Illustrated by P. R. Baquero. Translated by L. Clark and A. Reid. W. W. Norton Co., 1993.

Martin and the Tooth Fairy by B. Chardiet & G. Maccarone. Illustrated by G. B. Karas. Scholastic, 1991.

Math Curse by J. Scieszka. Illustrated by L. Smith. Viking, 1995.

Math for Smarty Pants by M. Burns. Illustrated by M. Weston. Little, Brown, 1982.

The Money Book by E. Wyatt & S. Hinden. Illustrated by A. Levin. Tambourine, 1991.

Music, Music for Everyone by V. Williams. Greenwillow, 1984.

The Number Devil: A Mathematical Adventure by H. M. Enzensberger. Illustrated by R. S. Berner. Translated by M. H. Helm. Henry Holt, 2000.

One Grain of Rice: A Mathematical Folktale by Demi. Scholastic, 1997.

One, Two, Three, and Four—No More? by C. Gray. Illustrated by M. Moss. Houghton Mifflin, 1988.

A Pair of Socks by S. J. Murphy. Illustrated by L. Ehlert. HarperCollins, 1996.

The Penny Pot by S. J. Murphy. Illustrated by L. Cravath. HarperCollins, 1998.

Pigs Go to the Market: Fun with Math and Shopping by A. Axelrod. Illustrated by S. McGinley-Nally. Aladdin Paperbooks, 1999.

Pigs on a Blanket: Fun with Math and Time by A. Axelrod. Illustrated by S. McGinley-Nally. Aladdin Paperbooks, 1998.

Pigs Will Be Pigs: Fun with Math and Money by A. Axelrod. Illustrated by S. McGinley-Nally. Aladdin Paperbacks, 1997.

Sir Cumference and the Dragon of Pi: A Math Adventure by C. Neuschwander. Illustrated by W. Geehan. Charlesbridge, 1999.

Sir Cumference and the Great Knight of Angleland: A Math Adventure by C. Neuschwander. Illustrated by W. Geehan. Charlesbridge, 1999.

Something Special for Me by V. Williams. Greenwillow, 1983.

The Story of Money by B. Maestro. Illustrated by G. Maestro. Clarion, 1993.

Strega Nona by T. dePaola. Prentice-Hall, 1975.

Strega Nona's Magic Lessons by T. dePaola. Harcourt Brace Jovanovich, 1982.

Super Sand Castle Saturday by S. J. Murphy. Illustrated by J. Gorton. HarperCollins, 1999.

Tiger Math: Learning to Graph from a Baby Tiger by A. W. Nagda & C. Bickel. Henry Holt, 2000.

What's Cooking, Jenny Archer? by E. Conford. Illustrated by D. Palmisciano. Little, Brown, 1989.

Art and Music

Langer (1978)

Gardner (1982)

Language and the arts are our humanistic vehicles for constructing and conveying meaning. Langer has argued that, whereas language is linear and the arts nonlinear, both are branches of the same root. Language is a way of naming and the arts a way of knowing. Gardner suggests that through language and the arts the human mind creates, revises, transforms, and "recreates wholly fresh products, systems and even worlds of meaning."

Arnheim (1974)

In Western mainstream cultures, the attention of educators has been on the acquisition of verbal language and the teaching of "literacy." We cannot afford, however, to ignore the potential of the arts for constructing and representing ourselves and our particular culture. Arnheim has called this potential the neglected "gift of comprehending through our senses" (p. 1). The arts seem to be integrally intertwined with children's need to make sense of themselves and their world through symbols. Very young children quickly pick up the intonation or musical patterns of various registers of language. They sing little rhymes to themselves, savoring the sounds and patterns of words. They create metaphors and tell stories as they explore their world. They exhibit an astonishing creative artistry in the manipulation of the elements and principles of the visual arts. We also know that artistic expression seems to enable children in the creation of oral and written texts.

Caldwell & Moore (1991)

Davenport (1999); Dyson (1986); Olshansky (1994); Short, Kaufman, & Kalm (2000)

Gee (2000)

Gardner (1982)

Thus, there is good reason to include the arts as natural vehicles for exploring the topics in thematic units. We need, argues Gardner, "to acknowledge forms and intensities of thought other than" those traditionally valued by our school systems (p. 214). Yet too often arts education has been considered a frill. If not the first to be eliminated in the face of budget cuts, it is limited to the production of art and music (i.e., students engaged in making art or music) only once a week for twenty minutes to an hour in a room apart from the day-to-day business of the classroom.

Donmoyer (1995)

Arts curricula have been reexamined.

In recent years, however, a broadening and redefining of arts education curricula have occurred. Arts educators have increasingly made efforts to put the arts at the center of the school restructuralization movement. This revitalization of the arts has taken several directions. In the visual arts, an approach called discipline-based art education (DBAE) has grown out of a collaboration between Elliott Eisner and the Getty Center for Education in the Arts. DBAE programs call for experiences in four major areas: art making, art history, art criticism, and aesthetics. According to Eisner, there are four things people do with art: "They make it, they understand it, they make judgments about it and they appreciate it" (p. 7). He suggests that when children make pots out of clay coils, for example, they should have the opportunity to think about proportion and technique, to consider the feelings conveyed when pots are delicate or heavy, and to make connections to the uses and forms of pots in other times and cultures.

Aesthetics raises the question: What is art and what is my response to it?

Brandt (1988a)

Another approach to arts education has developed out of the work of Howard Gardner and his colleagues at Harvard Project Zero, a group that has had major influence on arts research and education. In contrast to DBAE, these educators suggest that art training should be based in "spontaneous emotional activities, attunements, discernments, appraisals, and imaginary experiments of the child" (p. 20). Gardner argues that such an approach focuses on the arts as alternative ways of knowing, and it emphasizes artistic production as a central focus of the curriculum interwoven with strands of perception (discrimination) and reflection (introspection and critical analysis about productive and perceptual endeavors). The heart of arts education, he argues, should be "the capacity to handle, to use, to transform different artistic symbol systems—to think with and in the materials" (p. 163).

Gardner's work has been especially helpful in clarifying how teachers can respond to the child's artistic development in ways that are similar to their response to the child's development of language systems. He suggests, for example, that across cultures the years from two to about seven are spent "coming to grips with the world of 'symbols.'" During this time "the child's capacity to use, manipulate, transform and comprehend various symbol systems matures at a ferocious pace" (pp. 211–212). These young children should be given every opportunity to explore media and forms of expression in a way that allows natural processes to unfold. Older children, however, become increasingly aware of the culture in which they live and become occupied with the rules and standards of those around them. Thus, the type of experimentation with art forms and the lack of conformity children exhibit before formal schooling begin give way to a period of wanting to know how to make a drawing look "real" or a song sound "right." At this point, a teacher can step in with experiences that help children gain mastery of various techniques and media at the same time they introduce them to questions and concepts regarding standards and criticism. In addition, by introducing children to many different cultural traditions teachers can broaden the range of possibilities children see for their own art making.

Giving the preteenager a knowledge of techniques and a familiarity with various media should make it less likely that during the critical years of adolescence, when teens begin to recognize the range of the finest art and performance that exists, they give up because they cannot measure up. If instead they see their work within the context of broad cultural and historical traditions, it is more likely that they will remain willing participants in the arts throughout their lives.

Certainly, there seems to be room for ideas from both DBAE and Project Zero as teachers plan to integrate the arts across the curriculum. We have already explored the arts as resources in thematic units in Chapter 3, specifically in SPACES AND PLACES, which included the study of many aspects of two- and three-dimensional space in art and explored movement in space as it relates to art, music, and dance. Such themes also allow children to study paintings, sculptures, and musical compositions and to consider how artists, choreographers, and composers have explored and represented space in their creations throughout history and across cultures. Furthermore, because the arts exist in historical, cultural, and political contexts they become important sources for Reflective, Disciplined Inquiry*. In Chapter 4, many of the prototypes represent collaboration between art, music, and physical education specialists and the classroom teacher.

Because of the limitations of space in this book, we cannot deal with the wide range of genres that exist within the scope of the disciplines called the arts. In Chapter 7, we look at the language-related arts of drama and literature. In the remainder of this section we look more closely at two of the arts—visual art and music—as vehicles for exploring and responding to the content in thematic units and as domains of knowledge in their own right. However, we encourage teachers to explore other art forms such as movement and dance through websites and other resources.

Because the arts often require special skills or talents as well as specialized knowledge, you may feel a bit intimidated by developing experiences that involve children with techniques used in art and music production or in discussing their critical, historical, or aesthetic dimensions. There are many excellent resources that will boost your confidence and suggest practical methods for developing art and music activities. Some of these resources are included in the bibliography of Books for Exploring the Arts that follows, along with books that engage children in various ways of thinking and experiencing these art forms.

Gardner (1988)
Gardner (1980, 1982)

Gardner (1982)

See proceedings of a joint DBAE, Project Zero conference in Winner & Hetland (2000).

The arts are resources and vehicles for learning.

See Levstik & Barton (2000).

Gee (2000)

See Bang (1991); Barrett, McCoy, & Veblen (1997); McFee and Degge (1980); and Upitis (1990) for help in understanding and applying concepts about art and music.

Resources for Exploring the Arts (Including Dance and Movement)

THE VISUAL ARTS

Agee, J. (1988). *The Incredible Painting of Felix Clousseau*. New York: Farrar, Straus, & Giroux.

Aronson, M. (1998). *Art Attack: A Short Cultural History of the Avant-Garde*. New York: Clarion

Belton, S. (2003). *Pictures for Miss Josie*. Illustrated by G. Christie. New York: Greenwillow.

Berry J. (1996). *Rough Sketch: Beginning*. Illustrated by R. Florczak. San Diego: Harcourt Brace.

Bonafoux, P. (1992). *A Weekend with Rembrandt*. New York: Rizzoli International.

Capek, M. (1996). *Murals, Cave, Cathedral to Street*. Art beyond Borders series. Minneapolis: Lerner.

Carle, E. (1992). *Draw Me a Star*. New York: Philomel.

Christelow, E. (1999). *What Do Illustrators Do?* New York: Clarion.

Cocca-Leffler, M. (2001). *Edgar Degas: Paintings That Dance*. New York: Putnam/Grosset.

Corain, L. (1995). *Giotto and His World*. New York: Peter Bedrick.

Crispino, E. (1996). *Van Gogh*. New York: Peter Bedrick.

Cummings, P., (Ed.). (1999). *Talking with Artists: Volume Three*. Boston: Houghton Mifflin.

de Trevino, E. B. (1965). *I, Juan de Pareja*. New York: Farrar, Straus, & Giroux.

dePaola, T. (1991). *Bonjour, Mr. Satie*. New York: Putnam.

Dewey, J. O. (1996). *Stories on Stone: Rock Art: Images from the Ancient Ones*. Boston: Little, Brown.

Dionetti, M. (1996). *Painting the Wind*. Illustrated by K. Hawkes. Boston: Little, Brown.

Duggleby, J. (1998). *Story Painter: The Life of Jacob Lawrence*. Chronicle.

Everett, G. (1992). *Li'l Sis and Uncle Willie: A Story Based on the Life and Paintings of William H. Johnson*. Illustrated by W. H. Johnson. New York: Rizzoli International.

Fritz, J. (2001). *Leonardo's Horse*. Illustrated by by H. Talbot. New York: Putnam.

Geisert, A. (1997). *The Etcher's Studio*. Boston: Houghton Mifflin.

Greenberg, J. (2001). *Heart to Heart: New Poems Inspired by Twentieth Century American Art*. New York: Abrams.

Greenburg, J., & Jordan, S. (1995). *The American Eye: Eleven Artists of the Twentieth Century*. New York: Delacorte.

Greenburg, J., & Jordan, S. (1998). *Chuck Close, Up Close*. New York: Delacorte.

Greenburg, J., & Jordan, S. (2000). *Frank O. Gehry: Outside In*. New York: DK.

Greenburg, J., & Jordan, S. (2001). *Vincent Van Gogh: Portrait of an Artist*. New York: Delacorte.

Janson, H. W., & Janson, A. F. (1997). *History of Art for Young People*. New York: Abrams.

Konigsburg, E. L. (1967). *From the Mixed-up Files of Mrs. Basil E. Frankweiler*. New York: Atheneum.

Konigsburg, E. L. (1967). *The Second Mrs. Giaconda*. New York: Atheneum.

Krull, K. (1995). *Lives of the Artists: Masterpieces, Messes (and What the Neighbors Thought)*. Illustrated by K. Hewitt. San Diego: Harcourt Brace.

Lattimore, P. N. (1991). *The Sailor Who Captured the Sea: The Story of the Book of Kells*. New York: HarperCollins.

Lionni, L. (1991). *Matthew's Dream*. New York: Knopf.

Llorente, P. M. (1993). *The Apprentice*. Illustrated by J. R. Alonso. New York: Farrar, Straus, & Giroux.

Lyons, M. E. (1996). *Painting Dreams: Minnie Evans Visionary Artist*. Boston: Houghton Mifflin.

Lyons, M. E. (2000). *Catching the Fire: Philip Simmons, Blacksmith*. Boston: Houghton Mifflin.

Macaulay, D. (2000). *Building Big*. Boston: Houghton Mifflin.

McClintock, B. (1996). *The Fantastic Drawings of Danielle*. Boston: Houghton Mifflin.

Micklethwait, L. (1991). *I Spy: An Alphabet Book in Art*. New York: Greenwillow.

Micklethwait, L. (1999). *A Child's Book of Art: Discover Great Paintings*. New York: DK.

Nye, N. S. (1995). *This Tree Is Older Than You Are: A Bilingual Gathering of Poems and Stories from Mexico with Paintings by Mexican Artists*. New York: Simon & Schuster.

Nye, N. S. (1998). *The Space Between Our Footsteps: Poems and Paintings from the Middle East*. New York: Simon & Schuster.

Paterson, K. (1979). *Bridge to Terabithia*. New York: HarperCollins.

Presilla, M. E. (1996). *Mola: Cuna Life Stories and Art*. New York: Holt.

Ray D. K. (2001). *Hokusai: The Man Who Painted a Mountain*. New York: Farrar, Straus, & Giroux.

Richardson, J. (1997). *Looking at Pictures: An Introduction to Art for Young People*. New York: Abrams.

Ringgold, F. (1993). *Dinner at Aunt Connie's House*. New York: Hyperion.

Rochem, D. (1998). *Art Around the World: Loo-Loo, Boo and More Art You Can Do*. Boston: Houghton Mifflin.

Romei, F. (1996). *Leonardo Da Vinci*. New York: Peter Bedrick.

Rubin, S. G. (2003). *Degas and the Dance: The Painter and the Petits Rats, Performing Their Art*. New York: Abrams.

Say, A. (1996). *Emma's Rug*. Boston: Houghton Mifflin.

Severance, J. B. (2000). *Skyscrapers. How America Grew Up*. New York: Holiday.

Shaw, M., & Gal, L. (1996). *Tiktala*. New York: Holiday House.

Sills, L. (1993). *Visions: Stories about Women Artists*. Niles, IL: Whitman.

Sills, L. (2000). *In Real Life Six Women Photographers*. New York: Holiday House.

Stanley, D. (1996). *Leonardo Da Vinci*. New York: Morrow.

Stanley, D. (2000). *Michelangelo*. New York: HarperCollins.

Streissguth, T. (1999). *Mary Cassatt: Portrait of an American Impressionist*. Minneapolis MN: Carolrhooda.

Sullivan, C. (1992). *Children of Promise: African American Literature and Art for Young People*. New York: Abrams.

Sullivan, C. (1994). *Here Is My Kingdom: Hispanic-American Literature and Art for Young People*. New York: Abrams.

Tames, R. (2001). *Auguste Rodin*. Life and Work of series. Portsmouth NH: Heinemann.

Temko, F. (2001). *Traditional Crafts from Japan*. Minneapolis: Lerner.

Venezia, M. (1998). *Alexander Calder*. Getting to Know the World's Greatest Artists series. New York: Children's Press.

Wilson, E. (1994). *Bibles and Bestiaries: A Guide to Illuminated Manuscripts*. New York: Farrar, Straus, & Giroux.

Wright-Frierson, V. (1996). *A Desert Scrapbook: Dawn to Dusk in the Sonoran Desert*. New York: Simon & Schuster.

MUSIC

Adoff, A. (1995). *Street Music: City Poems*. Illustrated by K. Barbour. New York: HarperCollins.

Anderson, M. T. (2001). *Handel: He Knew What He Liked*. Illustrated by K. Hawkes. Boston: Candlewick.

Ardley, N. (1995). *A Young Person's Guide to Music*. New York: DK.

Brett, J. (1991). *Berlioz the Bear*. New York: Putnam.

Fenner, C. (1995). *Yolanda's Genius*. New York: McElderry.

George-Warren, H. (2001). *Shake Rattle & Roll: The Founders of Rock & Roll*. Illustrated by L. Levine. Boston: Houghton Mifflin.

Haskins, J. (1996). *The Harlem Renaissance*. Brookfield, CT: Millbrook.

Haskins, J. (2001). *One Nation under a Groove: Rap Music and Its Roots*. New York: Hyperion.

Hopkins, L. (1997). *Song and Dance*. Illustrated by C. M. Taylor. New York: Simon & Schuster.

Krull, K. (1993). *Lives of the Musicians: Good Times, Bad Times (and What the Neighbors Thought)*. Illustrated by K. Hewitt. San Diego: Harcourt Brace.

Lester, J. (2001). *The Blues Singers: Ten Who Rocked the World*. Illustrated by L. Cohen. New York: Hyperion.

MacLachlan, P. (1988). *The Facts and Fictions of Minna Pratt*. New York: HarperCollins.

Martin, B. Jr. (1994). *The Maestro Plays*. Illustrated by V. Radunsky. New York: Holt.

Monceaux, M. (1994). *Jazz, My Music, My People*. New York: Knopf.

Moss, L. (1995). *Zin! Zin! Zin! A Violin*. Illustrated by M. Priceman. New York: Simon & Schuster.

Myers, W. D. (2003). *Blues Journey*. Illustrated by C. Myers. New York: Holiday.

Namioka, L. (1992). *Yang the Youngest and His Terrible Ear*. Illustrated by K. de Kiefte. Boston: Little, Brown.

Paterson, K. (1985). *Come Sing, Jimmy Jo*. New York: Dutton.

Philip, N. (1995). *Singing America: Poems That Define a Nation*. Illustrated by M. McCurdy. New York: Viking.

Pinkney, A. D. (2001). *Duke Ellington*. Illustrated by B. Pinkney. New York: Hyperion.

Pinkney, A. D. (2003). *Ella Fitzgerald: The Tale of a Vocal Virtuoso*. Illustrated by B. Pinkney. New York: Hyperion.

Pinkney, B. (1994). *Max Found Two Sticks*. New York: Simon & Schuster.

Raschka, C. (1992). *Charlie Parker Plays Be Bop*. New York: Orchard.

Raschka, C. (1997). *Mysterious Thelonious*. New York: Orchard.

Ryan, P. M. (2003). *When Marian Sang, The True Recital of Marian Anderson, The Voice of a Century*. Illustrated by B. Selznick. New York: Scholastic.

Schroeder, A. (1996). *Satchmo's Blues*. Illustrated by F. Cooper. New York: Doubleday.

Silverman, J. (1996). *Just Listen to This Song I'm Singing: African American History through Song*. Brookfield, CT: Millbrook.

Steig, W. (1994). *Zeke Pippin*. New York: HarperCollins.

Strickland, M. (1993). *Poems That Sing to You*. Illustrated by A. Leiner. Honesdale, PA: Wordsong.

Voigt, C. (1983). *Dicey's Song*. New York: Atheneum.

Williams, V. B. (1984). *Music, Music for Everyone*. New York: Greenwillow.

Wilson, C. (1996). *The Kingfisher Young People's Book of Music*. New York: Kingfisher.

Wolfe, V. E. (1991). *The Mozart Season*. New York: Henry Holt.

DANCE AND MOVEMENT

Ancona, G. (1998). *Let's Dance*. New York: Morrow.

Augustyn, F., & Tanaka, S. (2001). *Footnotes; Dancing the World's Best-Loved Ballets*. Brookfield, CT: Millbrook.

Carlstrom, N. W. (1993). *How Does the Wind Walk?* Illustrated by D. K. Ray. New York: Macmillan.

Cauley, L. B. (1992). *Clap Your Hands*. New York: Putnam.

Esbensen, B. (1995). *Dance with Me*. Illustrated by M. Lloyd. New York: HarperCollins.

Gauch, P. L. (1994). *Tanya and Emily in a Dance for Two*. Illustrated by S. Ichikawa. New York: Philomel.

Giovanni, N. (1996). *The Genie in the Jar*. Illustrated by C. Raschka. New York: Holt.

Gray, L. M. (1995). *My Mama Had a Dancing Heart*. Illustrated by R. Colon. New York: Orchard.

Haskins, J. (1992). *Black Dance in America*. New York: HarperCollins.

Hughes, L. (1995/1954). *The Book of Rhythms*. Illustrated by M. Wawiorka. New York: Oxford.

Isadora, R. (1993). *Lili at Ballet*. New York: Putnam.

Jessel, C. (2000). *Ballet School*. New York: Viking.

Jones, B. T., & Kuklin, S. (1998). *Dance*. New York: Hyperion.

King, S. (1993). *Shannon: An Ojibway Dancer*. Illustrated by C. Whipple. Minneapolis: Lerner.

Kuklin, S. (1989). *Going to My Ballet Class*. New York: Bradbury.

Lowery, L. (1995). *Twist with a Burger Jitter with a Bug*. Illustrated by P. Dypold. Boston: Houghton Mifflin.

Martin, B., & Archambault, J. (1986). *Barn Dance*. Illustrated by T. Rand. New York: Holt.

Noll, S. (1987). *Jiggle Wiggle Prance*. New York: Greenwillow.

Pinkney, A. D. (1993). *Alvin Ailey*. Illustrated by B. Pinkney. New York: Hyperion.

Rodanas, K. (1994). *Dance of the Sacred Circle: A Native American Tale*. Boston: Little, Brown.

Ryder, J. (1996). *Earthdance*. Illustrated by N. Gorbaty. New York: Holt.

Schaefer, C. L. (1996). *The Squiggle*. Illustrated by P. Morgan. New York: Crown.

Schick, E. (1992). *I Have Another Language, the Language Is Dance*. New York: Macmillan.

Tadjo, V. (1988). *Lord of the Dance: An African Retelling*. New York: Lippincott.

Tamar, E. (1996). *Alphabet City Ballet*. New York: HarperCollins.

Van Laan, N. (1993). *Buffalo Dance: A Blackfoot Legend*. Illustrated by B. Vidal. Boston: Little, Brown.

Varriale, J. (1999). *Kids Dance: The Students of Ballet Tech*. New York: Dutton.

Walsh, E. S. (1993). *Hop Jump*. San Diego: Harcourt Brace.

WEBSITES

American Treasures   http://lcweb.loc.gov/exhibits/treasures

Andrew Mellon Foundation and The Art Museum Consortium
    www.artstor.org

Art Museum Network   www.amn.org

The Classical Music Archives
    www.classicalarchives.com/index.html

Eiteljorg Museum of American Indians and Western Art
    www.eiteljorg.org

Getty Museum   www.getty.edu/museum

Harvard's Fogg Museum
    http://artmuseums.harvard.edu/fogg/index.html

The Hermitage   www.hermitagemuseum.org

The Met for Kids   www.metmuseum.org/explore/index.asp

Metropolitan Museum Collections
    www.metmuseum.org/collections/index.asp

Mr. Dowling's Electronic Passport (Ancient Africa)
    www.mrdowling.com/609ancafr.html

National Women's History Museum   www.nmwh.org

San Francisco Museum of Modern Art   www.sfmoma.org

San Francisco Symphony for Kids   www.sfskids.org

Smithsonian   www.si.edu

Smithsonian American Art [see also African Art, Museum of the American Indian, Natural History Museum, National Gallery, Freer C=Gallery and Sackler Gallery]
    http://nmaa-ryder.si.edu/collections/index.html

Smithsonian Encyclopedia
    www.si.edu/resource/faq/start.htm

Smithsonian Music Encyclopedia
    www.si.edu/resource/faq/nmah/music.htm

Tate Museum   www.tate.org.uk

Tretyakov Museum   www.tretyakov.ru

University of California Museum of Paleontology
    www.ucmp.berkeley.edu/collections/other.html

Victoria and Albert Museum   www.vam.ac.uk/nal/index.html

Virtual Renaissance
    http://library.thinkquest.org/3588/Renaissance

Walker Museum of Art   www.walkerart.org

Whitney Museum of Art   www.whitney.org

World Wide Art Gallery www.theartgallery/cp,.au/kidsart.html

Specialists are resources and team members.

Consider also the artists within your own community as resources. With support from corporate sponsors, many museums and arts groups are developing outreach programs for local schools. School districts often have artist-in-residence programs that can provide children with a valuable firsthand look at the creative process inherent in the production of a work of art. In the light of our new understanding about children's conceptions of the arts and the call for developing their critical and aesthetic awareness, it seems especially important that children see these artworks evolve over time rather than simply examine or listen to the finished product.

Don't hesitate to enlist the support of your school or district's art and music specialists. They have expertise in developing critical, aesthetic, and historical perspectives for children in their respective fields, and you should enlist them as team members and resource persons for all thematic units. They can suggest composers, musicians, and musical compositions or art and artists from many historical periods that can be incorporated into the units. They may also have libraries of recordings or art reproductions, or know of other sources that they would be willing to share with the children. They themselves may be practicing artists or know of artists who can share their work and processes with the children. At other times, a theme may suggest some important critical or aesthetic factors to the specialists on which they can expand during their time with the children. Such would be the case in a unit when an art teacher introduces children to op art, or when a music teacher concentrates on critical factors such as dynamics and crescendo.

In a PATTERNS unit an art teacher introduced children to American quilt-making traditions that began in Africa and are realized today in the work of artists like Faith Ringgold. Themes can also provide specialists with the opportunity for developing experiences with special techniques. A theme of SPACES for older children can provide the opportunity for teaching different techniques in two- or three-point perspective so that they could represent views of a scene or an object from below or above.

Art or music can often serve as the focus in a thematic unit (a subtopic on the books of a particular illustrator or on exploring art or music through books) or as a springboard to a unit. For example, an art teacher might work with a classroom teacher to coordinate a study of "changing languages" with an exhibit of alphabet books from many countries that is on view at the art museum. A middle school music teacher helped classroom teachers develop a unit for studying American history through American music.

Thus, keep in mind the important role played by artists in the community and by the art and music specialists in your school. The following classroom activities can serve as foundations, easily laid by teachers, that will allow the specialists to build further expertise and understanding in the realms of art and music.

Art and Music Makers

Art and music are not simply tools for teaching concepts in other content areas but ways of knowing these concepts. They allow children to explore a theme, act on it, and transform it. The integrated language classroom thus provides many opportunities to create art and music and many materials and avenues of expression. Try to make available as full a range of materials and instruments as the school budget will allow and encourage children to consider their use as they choose ways to explore a given theme. These would include simple musical instruments and basic art supplies as well as donated items and found objects. For your wish list consider the use of computers or synthesizers that would allow children to compose, play, read, and listen to music as well as to learn notation and orchestration, and to experiment with the sounds of various instruments. Or consider how the Internet and CD-ROM would allow children to have immediate access to the art of the world's great museums.

> Children learn through the languages of art and music.
>
> See Barrett, McCoy, & Veblen (1997); Upitis (1990); and Walther (1981) for other ideas.

Made readily available, the simplest materials and instruments can give children the means for creating a variety of art and music in response to themes being studied. As part of the subtheme "Exploring Nature" in an EXPLORATIONS unit, for example, first graders may want to translate sounds and rhythms they noted on a nature walk into a symphony of sounds using child-made instruments or some of the simple percussion instruments. Some children may choose to make block prints, gluing natural objects such as leaves and grasses to cardboard, inking them with a brayer (a roller used in printing), and then pressing a sheet of construction paper onto the inked surface. Others may want to create a natural hanging by suspending found objects from a stick with yarn and weaving twigs, grasses, and other elements into this warp.

As part of a TIME theme, children may take a simple and familiar tune such as "Twinkle, Twinkle, Little Star," and play it on recorders, then change it into a morning or afternoon song, or a summer or winter song, varying tempo, pitch, and dynamics. They can then listen to Ferde Grofe's "Grand Canyon Suite," which depicts different times of day, or listen to the variations that Mozart wrote for "Twinkle, Twinkle, Little Star."

Brandt (1988b)

Children involved in a theme of CHANGES, having decided to do a painting of a local scene, could discuss what colors or media to choose to express changes at different times of the day, or seasonal or weather changes. By thinking about the ways that colors can affect feelings or the way that qualities of media such as acrylic or watercolor paints can convey meaning, children can also be led to appreciate the choices made by artists such as Claude Monet or Winslow Homer, who spent much of their careers depicting the changing light in landscapes and cityscapes.

Books often weave into a story a musical or artistic theme that suggests a musical or artistic response. Reading about "Sea Journeys" (as a subtheme of JOURNEYS) may lead children to listen to the many musical interpretations of the sea, then create their own sea symphony with voice and instrument. As part of a study of "Personal Journeys," children can read Gary Paulsen's *Dogsong,* in which a young Inuit boy, Russel, braves the arctic wilderness in search of himself and his cultural heritage. They may then seek to interpret the story through a melody and instrument that represent Russel's song or through a monochromatic painting, using shades and tints of blue not only to represent the frigid arctic landscape but also to convey the mood of the character's isolation.

Paulsen (1985)

Students involved in the theme DIGGING UP THE PAST may want to make sketches of animal symbols found on fragments of Native American pottery, noting the abstraction of form and pattern. They may then choose to create their own artifacts by building clay coil pots and decorating them with their own personal symbols. A group of children could create a ceramic tile mural or a mosaic of key events and understandings gleaned from their study. Others may read John Bierhorst's *A Cry from the Earth: Music of North American Indians,* a book that suggests and presents Native American instruments, songs, dances, and masks that were part of music making. It could serve as a springboard for some remarkable art and music activities. These last suggestions, many of which incorporate music making, dance, and art, could serve to summarize a unit such as DIGGING UP THE PAST in ways that are every bit as effective as writing a research report. However art and music making are incorporated into the integrated classroom, they provide children with a richness of expression and an added depth of understanding. Although there is not space enough here to include detailed instructions for art and music projects, we have summarized some of the activities that would be possible as part of a thematic unit.

Bierhorst (1979)

The arts can be used to summarize a unit.

Music and Art as Ways of Knowing

Music

Listen to or sing theme-related music.

Do finger plays and movement exploration.

Compose music to interpret stories or poems.

Choose theme music for a story or novel.

Orchestrate poems for Choral Reading*.

Make instruments.

Listen to sounds in nature or sounds in the city; represent pitches and rhythms on a musical scale.

Collect old song lyrics. What do these say about the time in which they were written?

Compare musical forms in your own culture.

Compare musical taste and music makers in other cultures.

Art

Weave natural objects into wall hangings.

Create a class theme quilt out of embroidered panels.

Draw a map for a work of fiction.

Make a sculpture out of cardboard and plastic pipe.

Create character portraits out of clay.

Make a diorama or shoe box scene in miniature.

Create a collage to represent a book or concept.

Paint a mural of a theme's important ideas.

Sculpt papier-mâché masks.

Illustrate with watercolor or other media.

Sketch with charcoal or pastel chalk.

Make linoleum or meat-tray prints.

Make batik or crayon-resistant wall hangings.

Compare art forms in your own culture.

Compare art tastes and artists in other cultures.

Compare illustrators' media and styles.

Talking about Art and Music

When children are involved in the production of various forms of art and music, they gain control over such media as clay, watercolor, and pastels or such simple instruments as the human voice, recorder, percussion, and string instruments. In addition, they may begin to think about the expressive properties inherent in these art forms. Having time to explore a given instrument or medium in-depth gives children opportunities to think about themselves as choice makers as they seek to express meaning through an art form.

They may come to understand that they may choose an element of art or music for its literal property (a piece of music has tempo, while a painting has shapes), but that element also has expressive or metaphorical properties (a fast tempo can convey tension or the hectic pace of life, while a rectangular shape can convey weight or repose).

Encourage children to reflect on and talk about their experiences with the arts. It is through talk that questions essential to aesthetic understandings can be raised: Does art have to be beautiful? Do we have to know what a piece of music is "about" to enjoy it? Can truth be found in fiction? Talk also provides children with the experience necessary for developing critical awareness: What makes this picture more effective than that? What criteria do I apply when I listen to a new piece of music?

Talk provides a focus for developing aesthetic and critical awareness or for reflecting on art forms.

Being able to talk with children about the arts does not require expert knowledge in any of these disciplines. Teachers can ask some simple but powerful questions that will help children to think about the emotive power of art and music, which is another key to developing aesthetic awareness: Why did you choose watercolor instead of tempera paint for your painting? Did you choose these colors for a particular reason? What were you thinking about as you looked at (listened to) that picture (song)? How did that painting (composition) make you feel? Why would you say that? Young children will probably respond with idiosyncratic reasons: I chose red because I like red. However, older children begin to understand the stylistic choices available to them and other artists: I chose red because I was feeling angry. In addition, teachers may want to use some of the critical vocabulary associated with the forms of each particular discipline in the same way they use words such as word, sentence, character, setting, story, or report in discussing the elements and forms of language. Such words or terminology help children begin to think about how artists or musicians convey meaning through a given art form, which in turn can provide fertile ground for developing aesthetic and critical awareness.

Gardner & Winner (1982)

To illustrate how this might be done, let us take an art form that is already a familiar part of integrated language classrooms and show how talking about picture books can develop an aesthetic awareness in children. It may seem surprising to think that such a familiar object as a picture book could be considered an art form, but today's picture books are part of an artistic tradition dating at least as far back as 1300 B.C. to the Egyptian Book of the Dead. During the Middle Ages, the book illustrator or painter was held in equal esteem with the painter and sculptor, and well into the nineteenth century religious or cultural stories were often the subject matter of paintings and sculpture. With today's sophisticated printing techniques, book illustration is attracting many talented artists who are working in a variety of original media (e.g., watercolor, pen and ink, stitchery, or collage) that is then reproduced by means of printing techniques.

As an art form the picture book is a combination of image and idea in a sequence of turned pages. When words are present, they support the pictures just as the pictures extend and enhance the meaning of the words. When we have closed the best picture books, we experience something that is much more than the sum of the parts.

Marantz (1983)

Studying the art of the picture book has advantages over studying reproductions of paintings or listening to recordings of a symphony. A reproduction of a painting may not be faithful to the color of the original, and the texture of the painting's surface cannot be accurately reproduced. More important, the size of the original may have a great impact on the viewer's response, yet reproductions are seldom faithful to a painting's original size. The picture book, on the other hand, keeps its integrity as an art object. It does not matter if we cannot see the original artwork, because these originals were created so that they could be photographically reproduced and bound together within the covers of the book.

When you are talking with children about the art of the picture book, it may be helpful to connect children's experiences in making choices in their own art to the choices made by the artist seeking to convey some visual meaning. Just as writers use words and sentences to create character, setting, theme, and mood in a story, illustrators use line,

Kiefer (1995); Sipes (1998)

shape, color, value, and texture to convey these same properties. As previously mentioned, the elements of art have their objective, or exemplified, qualities (lines can be jagged or curving, while shapes can be sharp-edged or biomorphic) and their expressive qualities (jagged lines convey a feeling of excitement or danger, while curved lines seem restful or rhythmic). These elements are chosen and composed according to the principles of design: balance, rhythm, repetition, variety, unity, and eye movement. In a painting, of course, these elements and principles are present only on a single pictorial plane. In a picture book the artist can use elements and principles to unify the entire book and bring added power to the final art object.

An illustrator is also concerned with the technical aspects of book production. The artist's choice of original media, typeface, endpapers, pictorial content, or viewpoint can add meaning and depth to the book. Likewise, illustrators may also rely on historical or cultural conventions—aspects of art that have come to be identified with a particular period or culture. When adapted by an illustrator, these conventions can add to our understanding of a tale set in the past or a distant place. Paul Zelinsky in his illustrations for Susan Isaacs' American tall tale, *Swamp Angel,* used aspects of early American portraiture and landscape painting borrowed from itinerant painters called limners. He chose very different conventions for *Rapunzel.* This tale, with its roots in Northern Europe, is visualized by Zelinsky through the forms, textures, and lighting of Renaissance painting. Ed Young uses devices and perspectives reminiscent of Chinese silk screen paintings in books like *Lon Po Po.* Not only do these adaptations of historical and cultural conventions help make children more sensitive to the many choices available to an artist, but they also provide possibilities for connecting art in the classroom to art in the museum.

Understandings of style in picture books will help teachers bring the best picture books into their classrooms and add depth to discussions about them. These ideas are also applicable to music and the other arts. Notice, for example, how concepts of form and composition such as movement, balance, mood, harmony, repetition, pattern, and motif are present when we talk about either music, literature, or art. In all these areas the composer, the writer, and the artist must make choices in order to convey meaning, just as children make choices in constructing their world.

It is not always necessary or profitable to teach these elements to children or to expect them to apply abstract stylistic labels. Instead, aesthetic understandings grow in the broader context of the integrated language classroom. In the act of creating art, music, or writing, children may come to see how various elements convey and enhance meaning. In discussing these art forms, they acquire the words for talking about their elements and mechanics. In observing and talking with artists, musicians, and other professionals, they become more insightful about their own processes of creation. We hope that they will use these understandings to broaden the scope of the art forms that provide enjoyment, and we also hope that they will become increasingly sophisticated in their search for quality.

Art and Music in the Wider World

The suggestions for using art and music in the integrated classroom are highly compatible with recent trends in arts education. The knowledge represented by art and music extends beyond the range of a single genre such as painting or choral performance to encompass broader domains. Take the case of children engaged in making clay pots. In addition to producing, perceiving, and reflecting on the art of ceramics and considering the aesthetic, historical, and critical ramifications of pottery, children can come to understand how the decoration on a piece of pottery represents accurate Primary Source* material and gives us access to the culture and social structure of other times, sometimes in the absence of any written history: What legend is retold on the surface of the Greek vase? What symbols were important to Native Americans of the Southwest? Moreover, as they create their own pottery, children must think about the

---

*Sidebar notes (left margin):*

See Kiefer (1995) for a more detailed discussion of elements of art in picture books.

Isaacs (1994)

Zelinsky (1997)

Young (1989)

Children discover style by being choice makers.

See Grallert (1991).

Children develop understandings beyond the range of a single work or single art discipline.

object's use as a container: Will it hold liquids or solids? Will it be used for cooking or storage? They will gain experience with concepts of volume, mass, and density. They will have a chance to consider the object's weight in relation to its structure and form: Will it stand up if the bottom is narrow and the top wide? They will be able to consider the physical makeup of soils, to note changes in matter, and to think about chemical changes that may occur during the firing process: Is a pot more likely to hold liquids after it is fired? Why might it explode in the kiln? What happens to the colors in glazes during the firing? They must consider an object's placement in space and contrast two- and three-dimensional space: When does an object have not only a bottom and a top but also a front and a back? Such powerful understandings are possible through other arts experiences as well and form the basis for the suggestions we have made in this chapter. These understandings show how children learn art and music as domains of knowledge. Their experience with certain media, such as clay or watercolor, or percussion instruments or voice, helps them to explore more specific domains in different ways. Figure 5.5 is a visual summary of the ways in which art and music encompass and connect to many domains of knowledge.

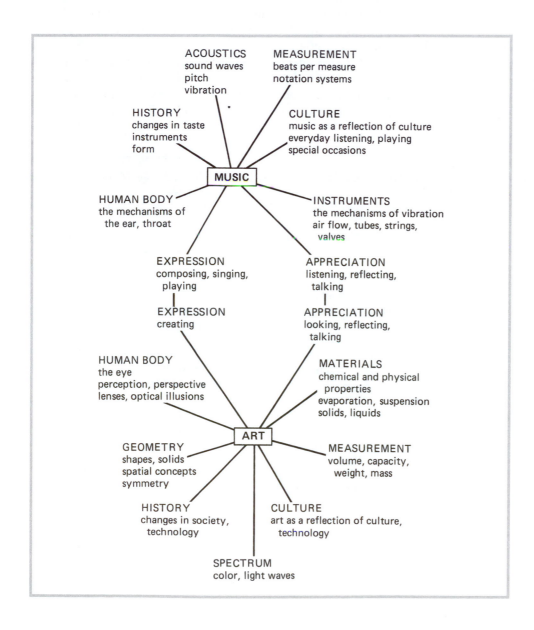

figure **5.5**

Interrelations between Domains of Knowledge in Music and Art

Part of helping children to develop an aesthetic awareness involves helping them to become sensitive to the sights and sounds in the world around them and to look and listen with a practiced eye and ear. In an integrated language classroom, children's experiences with art and music can develop their sensitivities in a variety of subtle ways. Sketching objects or scenes as a prelude to writing, for example, may make children more aware of small nuances of detail, pattern, or texture that they can describe with words. Discovering the details or visual subplots that many illustrators include in pictures, children may look more carefully at the world around them, noting, for example, the subtle changes taking place in the tadpole aquarium or in the textures and colors of an early spring day.

As children gain experience as makers of music, they may become more sensitive to the qualities of the human voice that they can use in Reading Aloud* or creative dramatics. As they listen to music, they may become aware of the subtle effects of such qualities as pitch and volume on their understandings and feelings when they listen to a sales pitch or the evening news. This attention to detail and the aesthetic qualities of the world can lead to a heightened concern with the environment (both in and out of the classroom) and with their own work. A sensitivity to musical sound, for example, can lead to greater understanding of noise in the outside world and its positive and negative effects on the emotions. Involvement with the visual arts can help sensitize children to pollution and urban clutter.

However you and your students get involved and whatever the outcomes, art and music need to happen frequently for children of all ages. Limiting children's involvement with the arts deprives them of a powerful means of expression and understanding and the fullest opportunity for knowing themselves and their world.

The arts make children more sensitive to sensory aspects of the world around them.

References: Art and Music

Arnheim, R. (1974). *Art and visual perception: A psychology of the creative eye.* Berkeley: University of California Press.

Bang, M. (1991). *Picture this: Perception and composition.* Boston: Bullfinch Press/Little, Brown.

Barrett, J. R., McCoy, C., & Veblen, K. K. (1997). *Sound ways of knowing.* New York: Schirmer Books.

Brandt, R. (1988a). On discipline-based art education: A conversation with Elliott Eisner. *Educational Leadership, 45(4),* 6–9.

Brandt, R. (1988b). On assessment in the arts: A conversation with Howard Gardner. *Educational Leadership, 45(4),* 30–34.

Caldwell, H., & Moore, B. H. (1991). The art of writing: Drawing as preparation for narrative writing in the primary grades. *Studies in Art Education, 32,* 207–219.

Davenport, J. D. (1999). The arts: A means for developing literacy. *The Delta Kappa Gamma Bulletin, 66(1),* 11–15.

Donmoyer, R. (1995). The arts as modes and methods of teaching: A (borrowed and adapted) case for integrating the arts across the curriculum. *Arts Education Policy Review, 96(5),* 14–20.

Dyson, A. H. (1986). Transitions and tensions: Interrelationships between the drawing, talking, and dictating of young children. *Research in the Teaching of English, 20,* 379–409.

Ewens, T. (1988). Flawed understandings: On Getty, Eisner and DBAE. In J. Burton, A. Lederman, & P. London (Eds.), *Beyond DBAE: The case for multiple visions of art education* (pp. 6–22). North Dartmouth, MA: University Council on Art Education.

Gardner, H. (1980). *Artful scribbles: The significance of children's drawings.* New York: Basic Books.

Gardner, H. (1982). *Art, mind, and brain: A cognitive approach to creativity.* New York: Basic Books.

Gardner, H. (1988). Towards more effective arts education. *Journal of Aesthetic Education, 22,* 157–167.

Gardner, H., & Winner, E. (1982). Children's conceptions (and misconceptions) of the arts. In H. Gardner (Ed.), *Art, mind, and brain: A cognitive approach to creativity* (pp. 103–209). New York: Basic Books.

Gee, K. (2000). *Visual arts as a way of knowing.* York, ME: Stenhouse.

Grallert, M. W. (1991). Working from the inside out: A practical approach to expression. In M. R. Goldberg & A. Phillips (Eds.), *Arts as education* (pp. 79–90). Cambridge, MA: Harvard Educational Review.

Kiefer, B. (1995). *The potential of picturebooks: From visual literacy to aesthetic understanding.* Columbus, OH: Merrill/Prentice Hall.

Langer, S. (1978). *Philosophy in a new key.* Cambridge, MA: Harvard University Press. (Originally published in 1942)

Levstik, L. S., & Barton, K. C. (2000). *Doing history: Investigating with children in elementary and middle schools.* Mahwah, NJ: Lawrence Erlbaum.

McFee, J. K., & Degge, R. M. (1980). *Art, culture and environment: A catalyst for teaching.* Dubuque, IA: Kendall Hunt.

Olshansky, B. (1994). Making writing a work of art: Image making within the writing process. *Language Arts, 71(5),* 350–357.

Short, K., Kaufman, G., & Kahn, L. H. (2000). "I just need to draw.": Responding to literature across multiple sign systems. *The Reading Teacher, 54(2),* 160–171.

Sipes, L. R. (1998). Learning the language of picturebooks. *Journal of Children's Literature, 24(2),* 66–75.

Upitis, R. (1990). *This too is music.* Portsmouth, NH: Heinemann.

Winner, E., & Hetland, L. (2000). *Beyond the soundbite; Arts education and academic outcomes.* Los Angeles: The Getty Center.

Children's Literature: Art and Music

A Cry from the Earth: Music of North American Indians by J. Bierhorst. Four Winds, 1979.

Dogsong by G. Paulsen. Bradbury, 1985.

Make Mine Music by T. Walther. Little, Brown, 1981.

Swamp Angel by S. Isaacs. Illustrated by P. Zelinsky. Dutton, 1995.

Lon Po Po by E. Young. Philomel, 1989.

Rapunzel by P. Zelinsky. Dutton, 1997.

6

Learning about Written Language

Chapter 1 provided a preliminary review of the theoretical foundation of the integrated language perspective. The following four major interrelated principles were emphasized:

Children (all humans) are active, constructive learners.

Knowledge is organized and constructed by individual learners through social interaction.

Language is organized in different ways and in different patterns or registers because it is used for different purposes in different social contexts.

Language is but one mode of the communication landscape—others, especially visual meanings, are involved in much of the multimodal communication in our society.

This chapter builds on and extends the third and fourth principles—the variation of communication—by focusing more on the nature of written texts (including images) and processes of using them. Although this chapter concentrates on the last two principles, the other two are involved in our discussion as well, because all four are interrelated and cannot be separated.

Registers of Written Language

What Is a Genre?

In the previous chapters we have argued that it is important for children to have many opportunities to use a range of written genres in the classroom. We have argued that a major advantage of the use of a thematic unit is that such an approach provides a means to accomplish this. However, what is really meant by the term *genre*? You probably have met this term in English literature courses during which you have read and studied various written genres such as short stories, odes, sonnets, novels, novellas, and plays. We will use *genre* much more broadly, not only to include these literary genres but also to incorporate the potentially limitless number of written texts available in our culture.

Although we focus mostly on written texts in this chapter, our meaning of genre also includes a similar limitless range of spoken texts. Our culture consists of a variety of structured activities occurring in a range of contexts of situation. When the particulars in these situations are similar, the spoken texts constructed by participants end up

The range of written genres is limitless.

There are many spoken genres, too.

being similar and having a similar form or organization. When the factors in these situations are different, the spoken texts related to these contexts result in different forms and organizations. Think of the kinds of texts and the types of discourse patterns that are used when people participate in service encounters, such as shopping in stores or markets, buying stamps or sending packages at post offices, or buying tickets at travel agencies. Contrast these texts with the kind of spoken language employed when people visit a doctor, consult with a lawyer, or perhaps seek advice from a university academic advisor. Now consider the language patterns that are likely to occur in very different activities: when people attend a party, have lunch with friends at a restaurant, participate in a religious service, or conduct a public meeting.

Can you "visualize" the variations of spoken language—the different registers of language—in these examples? Can you "sense" similarities or commonalities and differences in these examples? Certain texts appear to be similar or go together into certain sets or categories because they seem to be part of certain socially ordered activities serving similar purposes. For example, the texts in the service encounters might resemble each other even though different "goods"—groceries, stamps, or plane tickets—might be bought and sold. Moreover, this set of texts would be somewhat different from the discourse patterns in which we seek a service from a professional such as a physician or lawyer. And both of these sets would be very different from the text registers of a party or lunch at a restaurant with friends. We can call these various categories of texts—these similar sets, ways, or registers of using language—*genres*.

Just as there are numerous kinds of spoken genres, there are numerous types of written genres. Besides the literary ones already mentioned, there are mysteries, westerns, fantasies, science fiction, historical fiction, romances, biographies, poems, how-to manuals, editorials, advertisements, information books, commentaries, business letters, newsletters, recipes, and reviews of books, films, and movies, and so forth.

Thus, prior knowledge, in terms of both our direct experiences and activities of life and our verbal (oral and written) experiences and encounters, contributes to the development of genres. Thus, the recurring situations in which people interact and enact social activities give rise to regularities in texts. Schemas of content and form converge because genres have to do with *what* is "sayable" along with *when* and *how* it is said or written. That is, genres are types or classes of communicative events or texts.

Genres—spoken or written—have two characteristics that at first glance appear to be contradictory. First, genres are *stable*. They have fixed elements or patterns: A story is organized in a different way from an essay, which in turn is different from a recipe. Genres are stable because they do certain jobs in our culture, allowing us to choose from a range of genres to communicate various intentions.

Although they are stable, genres always involve *change* because we put together various available options from different genres in a different way or borrow elements or features from different genres in new, novel ways; we create new subgenres. Because we frequently have new language goals or purposes to be accomplished in everyday life, aspects of the patterns of genres are altered. Genres are *evolved* and *evolving systems*.

The generic characteristics of stability and change lead to predictable and creative texts. A particular text is always a new, creative instance of some genre, but at the same time it is always predictable, being in some sense "old hat" for its users. Thus, genres are inherited social forms, but they are also historical entities that change and merge.

The Organization of Written Genres

The predictability and creativity, or novelty, of written texts in particular genres are owed to their linguistic organization. Authors do not simply sequence words, sentences, and paragraphs in a random, helter-skelter fashion. Instead, they structure their

---

Bakhtin (1986); Cope & Kalantzis (1993, 2000); Halliday & Matthiessen (2004); Halliday & Hasan (1985); Hasan (1995); Johns (1997, 2002); Swales (1990)

A genre is a conventional way of using language.

Both nonverbal and verbal experiences contribute to the development of genres.

Hasan (1995); Halliday & Matthiessen (2004); Kress (1993); Swales (1990)

Genres are stable patterns of language use.

Genres reflect change in patterns of language use.

Bakhtin (1986); Martin (2001); Kress (1993); Pappas & Pettegrew (1998); Chouliaraki & Fairclough (1999)

Stability in generic patterns leads to predictability in texts; change in generic patterns leads to creativity in texts.

Genres consist of organized linguistic schemes.

The organization of genres is related to how language is used for social activities.

Wildsmith (1971, 1974)

Hasan (1985a)

Texture involves meaning relations.

texts in particular ways that are influenced by the purposes they want the language to accomplish. In doing so, they draw on their language of the linguistic conventions of various genres.

The Textural Patterns of Written Texts

Let's consider again the storybook *The Owl and the Woodpecker* and the information book *Squirrels* that were discussed in Chapter 1. Each of these texts represents a typical example of its respective genre; that is, everyone would agree that *The Owl and the Woodpecker* is a storybook and that *Squirrels* is an information book. We have already observed (in Chapter 1) that each possesses different linguistic patterns or *textural* differences. That is, the storybook has linguistic patterns (identity chains) to refer to the *same* characters or objects (woodpecker, owl, or woodpecker's tree, for example) in the text, whereas the information book includes patterns (coclassification chains) in which the same classes of objects or animals (in our case, squirrels) are referred to in the text. Other aspects of texture were mentioned—the use of the past tense in the story versus the present tense in *Squirrels,* and the fact that this information book contains many more descriptive constructions than does the story.

If we looked at these two texts from these two genres, and at other texts that are typical examples of the genres, we would probably notice even more linguistic differences. You were surely aware of these linguistic differences in storybooks and information books even before you read this textbook, but you probably have never examined them in any explicit way. This chapter points out other linguistic patterns of a range of written genres—patterns that you already know about in a tacit or subconscious way—to render them more explicit and make you more aware of the nature of written genres. This awareness enables teachers to know how to select books of various genres for children to read in the classroom and to know how to respond to children as they attempt to read and write in various genres.

The Global Structure of Written Texts

Genres are also organized in global ways.
Pappas (1991)

Hasan (1984, 1985b, 1996)
Storybook genre

Hasan (1984, 1996)

Besides textural differences, texts of written genres are structured in a more global way; they are organized into big "chunks," which vary for different genres. Each genre has a shape, or global structure, of its own. For example, stories are typically formed into elements according to what many researchers call a *story grammar.* Although researchers have described and labeled the components of these global frameworks in different ways, the schemes are very similar. We use the framework (and terminology) developed by the linguist Ruqaiya Hasan, who has studied the language of bedtime stories in depth.

According to Hasan's scheme, there are chunks or elements that every story must have to be considered a story, and there are optional elements that a particular story may or may not include. The elements she calls the Initiating Event, Sequent Event, and Final Event are the necessary (or obligatory) elements in this framework, and the Placement, Finale, and Moral are optional. Remember, these elements are not just one sentence or event but also big chunks of text that may include many events or sentences. The elements that are found in the storybook *The Owl and the Woodpecker* are described and illustrated in Table 6.1. There is another optional element that could be included in a storybook but not realized in this storybook. It is:

The optional Moral element, not found in *The Owl and the Woodpecker,* could also be included in storybooks.

- *Moral*—provides a moral statement or claim.

Thus, when you review storybooks, you would want to see if you can recognize the ways in which these elements—the Placement, the Initiating Event, the Sequent Event, the Final Event, the Finale, *and* the Moral—are realized in them.

Storybooks have to do with interpersonal understandings, how characters' goals interrelate and how their plans to achieve these goals mesh or clash. This genre shapes its table **6.1**   Global Elements in *The Owl and the Woodpecker*

Description of the Global Elements	Examples from *The Owl and the Woodpecker*
Placement—an author may introduce or "place" characters on "stage" in the story, provide time or locale information, relate what characters habitually do, talk about certain attributes of characters, and so on (optional).	"Once upon a time" information, as well as something about the locale ("in a forest, far away") and about the habitual behavior of the woodpecker character ("lived in a tree in which he slept all night and worked all day"), is included.
Initiating Event—the conflict or problem of the story emerges.	The owl, who has sleeping and working habits that are the opposite of those of the woodpecker, moves into a nearby tree. The woodpecker's daily tapping keeps the owl awake and he becomes so bad tempered that something has to be done.
Sequent Event—a recount of characters' attempts to resolve the problem or conflict.	Other animals in the forest have a meeting and decide that the owl has to leave, because the woodpecker was there first. One night, they try to push down his tree while the owl is out hunting, with no success.
Final Event—resolution of the problem or conflict.	
Finale—a restoration of the habitual or normal state of affairs (optional).	The tree is blown down by a terrible storm. Fortunately, however, the owl, who had been sound asleep and was not aware that he was in danger, is saved by the woodpecker's tapping, and the owl and the woodpecker remain "good friends all the rest of their lives."

message so that inferences about human beliefs, purposes, or motives can be expressed. In contrast, the information book genre does not involve specific characters and their goals, personal motives for action, and the like. As a result, just as a different texture exists, the information book genre has a different global structure or a different "grammar." We use Pappas's scheme to describe this genre which, like Hasan's story framework, has both necessary global chunks, or elements, that every information book has to include and optional elements that particular information books may or may not express. Table 6.2 shows the global elements that were found *Squirrels*. There are other elements—all optional ones—that could be realized in information books. They are:

Information book genre

Pappas (2002, in preparation)

Other optional elements, not found in *Squirrels*, could be included in information books.

- *Prelude*—offers an introductory preface (often reflecting quasi-story language) that precedes the obligatory Topic Presentation element. (See *The Honey Makers* by Gibbons where both honeybees and the human honey makers are put on stage sort of like a story before the Topic Presentation begins.)

  Gibbons (1997)

- *Category Comparison*—compares or discusses different members of the class or topic that a book is about. (See *The Squirrel* by Lane where red and gray squirrels are compared.)

  Lane (1981)

- *Historical Vignette*—provides some historical information regarding the topic. (See *A Seed Is a Promise* by Merrill where a short historical episode tells of how a Canadian miner dug in the frozen earth and found very old tiny seeds that then grew.)

  Merrill (1973)

- *Experimental Idea*—explains a possible experiment that could be done that is related to the topic. (See *Feel the Wind* by Dorros where an experiment is described to study the strength of the wind in two conditions—riding on a bicycle into the wind and riding with the wind.)

  Dorros (1989)

- *Addendum*—includes, after the obligatory Final Summary element, extra topic-related information that is realized in very different genres, for example, maps, table **6.2**   Global Elements in *Squirrels*

Description of the Global Elements	Examples from *Squirrels*
Topic Presentation—the topic of the text is presented or introduced.	The topic of squirrels is presented.
Description of Attributes—a description of the attributes of the class or topic the book is about.	That squirrels are furry, have long bushy tails, strong back legs, two big front teeth, and so on are described.
Characteristic Events—characteristic or habitual or typical process/events are expressed.	How squirrels live and build homes, use their tails, have babies, what they eat, and so on are explained.
Final Summary—summary statements are made about the information covered in a book.	Summarizes that if you walk in the woods, you might see squirrels jumping and frolicking on trees or hiding a store of nuts.

Gibbons (1991)

Fowler (1992)

Aronsky (2002)

an experiment, directions to make something, a list of questions/answers, and so on. (See *From Seed to Plant* by Gibbons where directions to raise bean plants are provided.)

- *Recapitulation*—recaps information in the book (frequently, important vocabulary used in the book). (See *It Could Still Be Water* by Fowler where vocabulary terms such as *liquid, solid,* and *vapor* are listed, each near a small picture.)
- *Illustration Extension*—provides explanations about illustrative objects or displays in books via wordings, for example, labels, captions, keys. (See *All About Frogs* by Aronsky where a series of captions are used to note the illustrated stages of the metamorphosis of tadpoles to frogs.)

Because more optional elements can be found in information books, this genre is more complex than storybooks. Not all of the optional elements are found in each book, but there are lots of ways to make such books have variation and still be part of the genre. It is important to make note of the last optional element—the Illustration Extension. These extra wordings near images (labels, captions, keys, etc.) are called the minor text. This minor text and the array of visual images found in these books make the information book genre distinctly different from the storybook. The storybook has pictures, but not the same kind as the information book does.

In summary, these two generic schemes, for both storybooks and information books, are provided to illustrate how two genres are organized and how they differ with respect to their global patterns. These schemes also have other organizational features. For example, each generic text structure has rules for how the global elements are ordered, specifically whether elements have a fixed or flexible order. For example, the Moral story element, if included, must always follow the Final Event of the story. However, if the story also includes the Finale global element, the Moral element can come either before or after the Finale. The Placement (if included), the Initiating Event, the Sequent Event, and the Final Event have a fixed order, following one another as listed in Table 6.1.

The generic scheme for information books also has fixed and variable aspects of order. The Topic Presentation is usually the first element—unless the Prelude is included—but the order of the next two elements shown in Table 6.2—Description of Attributes, Characteristic Events (and Category Comparison, if it is included)—can vary. The Final Summary always follows all of these, and the Addendum, Afterword, and Recapitulation (if one or two are included) always end the book.

Another characteristic of generic schemes is whether certain elements can be discrete, separate chunks or interspersed in other elements. Both of the generic schemes discussed have such features. The story scheme allows for the possibility that in certain stories Placement information can be interspersed in the Initiating Event. The infor-

Part of a genre's organization is the order of its elements.

The order of elements can be fixed or variable.

Certain elements of a generic scheme can be discrete or interspersed.

mation book generic scheme permits even more interspersion. The Topic Presentation can be interspersed in any one of the three elements—Description of Attributes, Characteristic Events, or Category Comparison—and any of these three can be interspersed in each other. The Illustration Extension, which is a very commonly found optional element, can be interspersed throughout all of the elements.

You already know about this structure of storybooks and information books, although the organization of these two written genres and many others may seem complicated when it is described in this explicit way. Nevertheless, these generic text structures provide a sense of stability. Knowledge of these schemes makes texts more predictable and comprehensible to readers. Reading a range of written genres to children and providing many opportunities for children themselves to read texts of various genres help them internalize knowledge of the shape, rhythm, and flow of the various registers, or genres, of written language. Moreover, experiences with various genres provide children with a wide range of models to draw on in their own writing. Thus, children are now able to extend their communicative competence and expertise as semioticians to include meaning making in written language.

Although generic schemes have structure, order, and specificity, they also allow for the creation of new texts that show variation and novelty. We have noted how creativity in particular texts can occur through the inclusion of certain optional elements, changes in their order, or interspersion of some elements in others. The potential for creativity in written texts is even greater, however. Creativity in written texts can be best understood and appreciated by examining texts from other written genres and by developing a general model of genres.

Learning about various generic schemes helps readers and writers.

Allen (2000); Calkins (1994, 2001); Moore et al. (2003); Smith (1988, 1997)

Newkirk (1989); Pappas (1993a, 1993b)

A General Model of Written Genres

We have already mentioned that the storybook *The Owl and the Woodpecker* and the information book *Squirrels* are typical texts from their respective genres. In reading or reviewing them, no one would disagree that the former is a storybook and the latter an information book. However, many texts are not so clear-cut or typical. There are many "fuzzy," or atypical, texts. Let's consider two texts—*Mouse* by Sara Bonnett Stein and *Panda* by Susan Bonners—to illustrate the notion of "fuzziness." Figure 6.1 shows the first part of each text.

The Owl and the Woodpecker and Squirrels are typical examples of their genres.

Some texts are "fuzzy" examples of genres.

Stein (1985); Bonners (1978)

As you review the texts in Figure 6.1, consider whether these texts are information books or storybooks. To the left of the two excerpts are the abbreviations of possible global elements from the two genres. (See the key at the bottom of Figure 6.1.) The dotted lines indicate pages in the books. First, approach each as an example of the storybook genre. The first four pages of *Mouse* seem like a Placement. A mouse is introduced, and the actions of the mouse—where she lives and how she makes her nest—could be considered habitual behavior. The last page of the excerpt could be seen as the beginning of the Initiating Event in which a baby is born. A similar case can be made for *Panda*. A sort of Placement can be established for the first three pages of the excerpt, in which a panda is introduced and habitual information is included. The Initiating Event also begins with the birth of an offspring. Moreover, in each text, identity chains for the mouse and panda can be established, which is a textural feature of the storybook genre.

Now consider each text as an example of the information book genre. The first page of each book seems to be a Topic Presentation, each presenting the topic, mouse and panda, respectively. The second page begins the second global element. In *Mouse* this is the Characteristic Event, whereas in *Panda* it could be either Description of Attributes with information from the Characteristic Event in it or the other way around. Although it seems that identity chains are involved in each, neither book has the theme

Mouse

P? TP?   A mouse lives in a dark closet where the family never sees her.

CE?   She makes her nest of soft things she finds in the closet—white stuffing, blue wool, red cloth.

The outside of the nest is round, with a hole just big enough for a mouse to get through.

The inside of the nest is hollow, just the right size for the mouse and her babies.

When the nest is finished, the mouse is ready to have her babies. Her belly tightens.

IE?   She pushes out a wet, pink baby in a thin wrapper.

Panda

P?TP?   In a mountain forest of southwestern China, a giant panda sits in a birch tree.

DA/CE?   Snowflakes fall on her black and white fur, but she does not look for shelter.

She has lived in snow most of her life.

IE?   Early one autumn, she found a den in a rocky mountainside. There she made a nest out of broken bamboo stalks. While frosty winds blew through the forest, she gave birth to her cub.

KEY
From the Storybook Genre:
Global Elements   P—Placement
                    IE—Initiating Event
From the Information Book Genre:
Global Elements   TP—Topic Presentation
                    DA—Description of Attributes
                    CE—Characteristic Events

figure **6.1**

Source: Stein, 1985; Bonners, 1978

Mouse and *Panda* include features from the storybook and information book genres.

An atypical text can be coherent, comprehensible, and of high quality.

Typical texts are found in the "peaks" of genre mountains.

Atypical texts are found in the "slopes" or "valleys" of genre mountains.

Siebert (1988)

of "human" conflict that characterizes stories. However, *Mouse* is in the present tense, a textural feature of the information book genre, and *Panda* begins with the present tense but switches to the past tense.

Thus, these are "fuzzy" or atypical texts because they do not fit clearly in either genre. They seem to have some features of each genre; thus, they lie where the boundaries of these genres overlap. To help you visualize this overlap, Figure 6.2 uses genre "curves" or "mountains" to both depict the typical texts of each genre (*The Owl and the Woodpecker* and *Squirrels*) and the more atypical or fuzzy texts (*Mouse* and *Panda*).

The fact that a text is atypical does not mean that it is necessarily less coherent or comprehensible or of low quality. It is because authors have knowledge of the structure and features of various genres that they are able to select and write a text that is creative, novel, and interesting. Thus, we need a model of genres that can deal with such creativity.

Genres do not have absolute boundaries, as Figure 6.2 shows. Real texts are not the result of all-or-nothing formulas. Instead, some texts are typical of particular genres; they lie in the shaded part of the genre mountains—at the "peaks"—and are very distinctively different from typical texts of other genres. Other texts reflect degrees of atypicality and are less distinctive; they lie on the nonshaded "slopes" or "valleys" of the genre mountains or where the genre mountains overlap and intersect.

Consequently, our model of genres has to depict these characteristics of texts that are a matter of degree. We cannot go into every type of text in this chapter, but let's try to extend Figure 6.2 to consider other genres. First, how should we treat the genres of poetry and how-to manuals? We add these genres to the storybook and information book genres by placing them in multidimensional space. Figure 6.3 depicts this by adding two new genre mountains.

Now, let's consider two atypical texts that show overlap between genres. The first is the book *Mojave* by Diane Siebert (1988). The first two pages of this book about the Mojave Desert—an area that covers thousands of square miles of southern California, southern Nevada, and small portions of Utah and Arizona—are reprinted here.

figure **6.2**

figure **6.3**

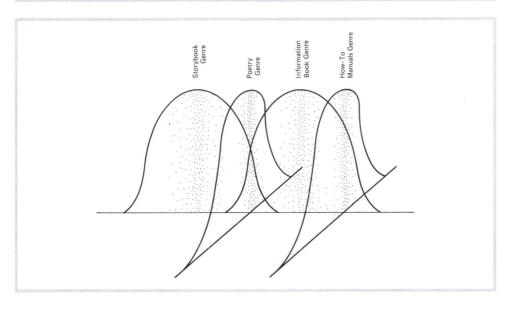

Mojave

> *I am the desert.*
> *I am free.*
> *Come walk the sweeping face of me.*
>
> *Through canyon eyes of sandstone red*
> *I see the hawk, his wings outspread;*
> *He sunward soars to block the light*
> *And casts the shadow of his flight*
> *Upon my vast and ancient face.*
> *Whose deep arroyos boldly trace*
> *The paths where sudden waters run—*
> *Long streams of tears dried by the sun.*
>
> *I feel the windstorm's violent thrust;*
> *I feel the sting of sand and dust*
> *As bit by bit, and year by year,*
> *New features on my face appear.*

The book goes on by talking about mountain ranges (that "crease my face"), lakes, the animal jacks, dust "devils" (winds or storms), and so forth. Can you see how this text is atypical? In what ways is it fuzzy? Is it like an information book because it

Mojave includes features from the information book, poetry, and personal narrative genres.

provides information about the Mojave Desert, the creatures that live there, the vegetation, the sand and sun, and how the desert changes with the seasons? However, this information is expressed by lyrical prose and a poetic register. Thus, there is an overlap of information book and poetry features. We could even make the case that *Mojave* also has some features of yet another genre, that of the personal narrative (a genre not included in Figure 6.3). That is, the message seems also to be communicated through the experiences of an "I"—in this case, the "I" being the desert.

Another book, *The See-Through Zoo: How Glass Animals Are Made* by Suzanne Haldane, also shows fuzziness. Unlike excerpts from the other books, the excerpts that follow start with page 8, then skip to other parts of the book.

The See-Through Zoo: How Glass Animals Are Made

Glass is made from materials that could be found in any backyard: sand, soda, ash, and lime. Yet from these familiar ingredients, objects both ordinary and unique have been fashioned for many thousands of years. (p. 8)

In a large open area, several paces from where the craftsmen work, the furnace is fired up to the melting temperature of 2600°F—more than ten times the heat needed to boil water.

At night, while the glassmakers are home sleeping, the batch is cooked. During the ten to twelve hours it takes to fuse—melt and blend—the ingredients, the intense heat must be kept constant, or the furnace will be damaged and the glass ruined. . . .

Too hot ever to touch, the molten glass, now referred to as "metal," is ready to be worked.

Two people are needed to turn metal into animals. One is the teacher, the other the pupil.

The master craftsman is called the gaffer, from an old English word meaning grandfather.

He has had years of experience and familiarity with glass. Guided only by his imagination, he pulls and pushes the glass into the shapes of more than fifty different animals, using a variety of tools.

His helper, called a gatherer because he collects or gathers the glass, assists and learns from the master. (p. 15)

The two artisans must work fast. They are always racing against time, because glass cools rapidly, and below a certain temperature it can no longer be shaped.

Tiny animals may be pulled and pinched into shape in a matter of seconds. But larger animals, especially those composed of several pieces of metal, must be reheated before the addition of each piece, because hot glass will only stick to hot glass. . . . (p. 18)

An animal starts as a ball of molten glass. The gaffer begins most animals at either the head or tail. Cats, horses, and unicorns begin at the head; dolphins, sharks, and seals at the tail.

When making an elephant, however, the gaffer begins with the body. . . . (p. 19)

These excerpts illustrate that the book is like an information book in that it provides an account of what glass is made of, how it is made, and so forth. It also includes features of a how-to manual in that it describes the step-by-step work of a master glassmaker (the gaffer) and his assistant (the gatherer) in fashioning glass animals in general and a glass elephant specifically. Thus, this text seems also to overlap genres.

Authors create typical texts of particular genres as well as atypical texts that reflect overlapping genres. Our model must, therefore, have a multidimensional perspective to explain both the typicality *and* the overlap, or atypicality, of texts in a range of genres.

Discussions of genres are frequently simplified by depicting them as two large all-or-nothing categories, such as fiction and nonfiction or narrative and expository. Unfortunately, many texts do not fit easily into these categories. Although most fiction is narrative, a personal narrative is not fiction. What about biography? Or letters? Or

Haldane (1984)

The *See-Through Zoo* includes features from the information book and how-to manual genres.

Classifying all texts into two large genres is too simplistic.

figure **6.4**

newspaper stories? They are narrative, but they are nonfiction. Two major categories or general types of genres cannot account for the complexity and the range of the genres present in our culture.

When we consider the subgenres, it is clear that no two-category model will work. Are mysteries, fantasies, westerns, science fiction, or historical fiction part of the storybook genre or genres on their own? What is the distinction between biographies and historical fiction? How do they overlap? How do recipes and reports of science experiments overlap with information books and how-to manuals? How do epics, sonnets, and odes relate? Where should letters—personal and business letters, thank-you notes, and invitations—fit? Figure 6.4 tries to depict such a model of genres. (Activity 1 at the end of the chapter can help you explore more about the multidimensional, overlapping aspects of written genres.)

See Activity 1.

The Ideology of Texts/Genres: Examining the "Element" of Description in Different Genres

In Chapter 1, we talked about how ideologies—our values, biases, and perspectives—are embedded in the texts that we read and write. Sometimes ideology is very apparent and easy to spot; sometimes it is very subtle and hard to detect. And it isn't necessary to consider ideology in an explicit way in every text that students read or write. Nevertheless, we want to give you some more examples of how ideology is expressed so that you can be alert to consider it when it might be relevant to do so.

We extend this discussion by examining how the "element" of description is realized in different kinds of genres. This exploration also gives us another way to show both the conventionality and the complexity of linguistic patterns in written language. (This section also provides background to Teaching Grammar in Context* in Chapter 7.)

All texts express ideology—values, biases, points of view, and power in relation to others.

Coe, Lingard, & Teslenko (2002); Chouliaraki & Fairclough (1999); Fairclough (1989, 1992); Lemke (1995); Luke (1988); Nodelman (1996); Stephens (1992)

Halliday & Matthiessen (2004)

Lexicogrammar is a term that incorporates the content or vocabulary expressed by linguistic patterns of texts/genres.

Relational processes or verbs are attributive processes, identifying processes, and possessive processes.

Eggins (1994); Halliday & Matthiessen (2004); Pappas & Pettegrew (1998)

First Discovery Books (1991)

Many descriptive constructions depict what things are like.

Many descriptive constructions depict how things are done.

Claybourne (1994)

Gibbons (1984)

Halliday & Martin (1993)

Description in advertisements is frequently expressed through short sentences that "assume" relational processes.

We also introduce a new term—*lexicogrammar*—which emphasizes several ideas. First, when we talk about *grammar,* we are talking about patterns or constructions at the text (and genre) level. Too frequently, *formal grammar* has meant solely focusing on parts of speech or types of sentences, isolated from the context of reading and writing texts. Second, grammatical constructions are not concerned with form alone; they consist of certain vocabulary, or *lexis.* Certain kinds of vocabulary or content words are related to different kinds of texts or genres. Thus, the use of *lexicogrammar* better explains how texts do what they do in the world. Finally, it is our attention on these lexicogrammatical patterns expressed in texts and genres that enables us to understand how ideology or perspective might manifest itself.

Description is found in many genres. It is especially found in factual genres, which we will examine first, because the major purpose of this broad class is to explore the world around us, focusing on what things are like or how things are done. Then we will see how it occurs in fiction.

Description in Factual Genres

Certain types of lexicogrammatical patterns are prevalent in factual texts. For example, refer again to Figure 1.5 in Chapter 1 that shows the beginning of the typical information book *Squirrels.* You will note that there is a density of constructions that includes relational processes, or verbs. These are attributive processes ("he *looks* happy and mischievous") and possessive processes ("he *seems to have* little socks on his feet"). We have mentioned other kinds of lexicogrammatical patterns in *Squirrels:* the fact that these processes are expressed as "timeless" verbs in simple present tense; and the idea that a class of an animal, namely, squirrels, is included (as opposed to a particular woodpecker or owl, which we saw in *The Owl and the Woodpecker*). Other typical information books include similar features. For example, some of the early sentences of *The Ladybug* are "The ladybug *is* an insect./Ladybugs *are* often red with black spots./Like all insects, the ladybug *has* six legs." And the first sentence of *Tunnels* is: "Most tunnels *are* long holes dug underground." Thus, these three features of lexicogrammatical structure (constructions that include relational processes, present-tense verbs, and class or generic nouns) are characteristic in the description in the information book genre.

So far we have illustrated descriptive constructions that include relational processes and depicted *what things are like.* However, description can also be expressed by action verbs or processes. For example, in the book *Squirrels,* the last sentence in Figure 1.5 (in Chapter 1)—"Squirrels live in trees."—begins the beginning of the global element Characteristic Events (see Table 6.2). Other characteristic actions or behavior—they *build* homes, *scamper* up and down trees, *leap* through the air, *gather* nuts and acorns, and so forth—all describe *how things are done.* In *How Do Bees Make Honey?* similar constructions are found: "Honeybees *live* together in big groups called colonies," "[Some honeybees] *build* honeycomb nests out of wax." When the things being described are nonliving things, such as in *Tunnels,* the processes or verbs in the lexicogrammatical constructions function as actions of use (e.g., "People *dig* tunnels . . .").

Thus, these are some of the major lexicogrammatical structures that are description in the information book genre. They are also predominant in description found in many adult factual reports and scientific genres.

The factual genre of advertisements also realizes description to a great extent. In an advertisement of a necklace, for example, a company first names the product—THE CLASSIC HEART—and then provides many lexiogrammatical constructions of description: "Timeless symbol of love," "Tender and eternal," "Original yet enduring," "Definitely romantic." Note that many of these sentences "break" the common "rule" where a sentence *must* have a subject and verb. Yet all of them work as description. Most of the sentences in the advertisement represent relational processes, despite the fact that these key verbs are absent and they and other language must be understood.

For example, in the first sentence above, an identifying process is involved ([the classic heart *is* the] "timeless symbol of love") and the next one "has" an attributive process ([the classic heart *is*] "tender and eternal").

Thus, the lexicogrammatical structures here are both similar to and different from the ones in the information book texts. We have already discussed in Chapter 1 the possible ideological implications of some of the wordings in *Squirrels,* namely, the use of "happy and mischievous" and having "little socks on his feet," as well as the predominance of singular masculine pronouns to refer to squirrel (instead of *it* or *its*). Ideological issues are much more blatant in the advertisement. The elliptical structures serve to emphasize the emotionally laden vocabulary, thereby enticing readers of the ad to become customers of the product.

What if someone had bought such a heart and then had it stolen? How different the descriptive words would be if a description of it was needed for an insurance or police report (two other factual genres). Here the owner would have used relational constructions, but he or she would have used alternative wordings to describe the physical features of the heart—shape, size, color, and so forth. Thus, the owner would not have used "tender and eternal," "original yet enduring," and "definitely romantic"!

Thus, when descriptions are realized in various factual genres, they are similar but different. See also how the description was accomplished in the fuzzy or atypical texts in this chapter (e.g., how the Mojave Desert or the construction of glass animals was described). Moreover, note how very different ideology or values may be present in the language used in these texts and other examples provided in this section.

Description in Fictional Genres

Description occurs in fictional texts as well, but because the major aim of these genres is to entertain or amuse readers, the lexicogrammatical patterns are realized differently. Characters and their motivations and feelings or reactions influence action and drive the plot. In fiction, description depicts the places that characters go, the objects they come across, or the other characters they meet. These descriptions are woven into the text along with lexicogrammatical constructions that include a different type of verb called *mental* processes. There are three classes of mental-process verbs: *cognition* (verbs of thinking, knowing, understanding), *affection* (verbs of liking, fearing, hating), and *perception* (verbs of seeing, hearing). For example, there is a mental process in sentence 3 in Figure 1.4 in Chapter 1—"Owl . . . *liked* to work all night and sleep all day." That is, the description of how things were done (note the past tense) is connected to the character's verb of affection toward this characteristic behavior.

In the beginning of the storybook *Amelia's Road,* it is stated that Amelia hated roads. They are described via an attributive relational process, then Amelia's mental reactions to them are included: "*Los caminos,* the roads, were long and cheerless. They never went where you *wanted* them to go."

In the fictional novel *Child of the Owl,* the character Casey is sent to Chinatown to live with her grandmother, Paw-Paw. Although her parents had been raised in Chinatown, this was Casey's first time. Note again how Casey's mental responses are interwoven with the description of Chinatown.

> I didn't know what to make of the buildings. . . . They were mostly three- or four-story stone buildings but some had fancy balconies, and others had decorations on them like curved tile roofs . . .—one building had bright yellow balconies decorated with shiny, glazed purple dolphins—and there was a jumble of neon signs, dark now in the daytime, jammed together. Most of the buildings, though, had some color to them— bright reds and rich golds with some green thrown in.
>
> But it was the people there that got me. I don't think I'd ever seen so many Chinese in my life before this.

Mental processes are verbs of cognition, affection, and perception.

Eggins (1994); Halliday & Matthiesen (2004); Pappas & Pettegrew (1998)

Altman (1993)

Yep (1977)

The first sentence includes two mental processes of cognition ("didn't know" and "make of" [think]). Then the description is realized by past-tense constructions having several relational processes (e.g., "they *were* . . . three- or four-story stone buildings"; "one building *had* bright yellow balconies"). In the last two sentences of the excerpt, Casey's reaction to the Chinese people in Chinatown is expressed through all three types of mental processes—affection ("*got* me"), cognition ("don't *think*"), and perception ("I'd *seen*").

Thus, the lexicogrammatical patterns in each of the fictional examples of fictional description are unlike those found in factual genres. Description in fictional genres generally uses the past tense (except in dialogue); it deals with particular people, places, and objects. Description is steeped in human mental reactions. As a result, the human values are also more apparent. For example, we know how Amelia and Casey feel about the places they find themselves.

Description in fictional texts/genres is frequently interwoven with human mental reactions and responses.

Summary

Written genres are *products* of our culture, but these products are the result of various social *processes* that have certain purposes or goals. Genres are organized to provide both *stability* (they have certain fairly predictable elements and an accepted sequence, and so forth) and *change* (although they are somewhat "fixed," they reflect new versions of structure and sequence elements in novel and creative ways). *Typical texts* of a particular genre reflect that genre as a whole; they are exemplars for which consensus can be found. However, many *atypical* texts exist as well; they are borderline cases or instances of subgenres that contain features of one or more other genres.

Genres are products of social processes.

Because of the complexity of written genres, their lexicogrammatical structures cannot be taught in direct, formal ways; otherwise, children will be misled and given only part of the story. They will miss out and never understand the creativity, limitless options, or potential of language. However, if teachers have an awareness of the various conventions of a range of written genres, they can support and foster children's processes of reading and writing them. They can provide many examples of both typical and atypical texts, point out and compare their elements and features, and facilitate children's comprehension and composition of texts of a variety of genres. They can help children learn to look at how values are being expressed in books they read and write. (See Teaching Grammar in Context* in Chapter 7 for some of the possibilities; see also Activity 2 for ways to examine ideology of texts.)

See Activity 2.

The Reading and Writing Processes

In Chapter 1 we discussed the involvement of the reader and writer in processing or using written texts. It was emphasized that both reading and writing are meaning-making process—that is, both readers and writers bring meaning (based on their schemas) to texts. In this chapter, we extend and expand on these important ideas by looking further into each of these two processes. Then, because so many texts are multimodal, we explore the characteristics and features of visual images. Finally, we put written and visual messages together by reconsidering the reader/viewer–writer/illustrator that we examined in Chapter 1.

The Reading Process

Booth (2001); Goodman (1967, 1997); Smith (1988, 1997); Moore et al. (2003)

Reading is a constructive, problem-solving process. Readers pose problems or ask questions about the text. Inherent in this process is *prediction,* a set of reader expectations. Readers predict what print means—reading consists of informed guesses. They confirm their predictions or they resolve or answer the problems they pose, or they disconfirm their initial predictions and have to set new hypotheses or consider new questions or problems about the meaning of the text. In this process, readers understand or partially comprehend the text.

Using a variety of strategies, readers use the linguistic clues or "cues" provided by the author. The type of genre the author has chosen is a particular source of these clues. Readers employ these clues to build or construct their own useful, personal world of the text. They structure their own knowledge or schema regarding that text. Thus, from the reader's point of view meaning is not in the text itself but arises during the interaction—or what many researchers call the *transaction*—between the written words of the text and the reader. Let's try to get an idea of this transaction by considering the following passage about Rocky and then examining some important issues regarding it.

Rocky slowly got up from the mat, planning his escape. He hesitated a moment and thought. Things were not going well. What bothered him most was being held, especially since the charge against him had been weak. He considered his present situation. The lock that held him was strong but he thought he could break it. He knew, however, that his timing would have to be perfect. Rocky was aware that it was because of his early roughness that he had been penalized so severely—much too severely from his point of view. The situation was becoming frustrating; the pressure had been grinding on him for too long. He was being ridden unmercifully. Rocky was getting angry now. He felt he was ready to make his move. He knew that his success or failure would depend on what he did in the next few seconds.

Well, who is Rocky? Most readers answer "a wrestler" or "a prisoner" (or "a convict"). How did you respond? This passage has been used in research studies in which some subjects were asked, before reading, to take the perspective that Rocky is a wrestler, and some, that Rocky is a prisoner. After the reading, they were asked to answer questions about the passage. The subjects answered the same questions differently, depending on the perspective. In another study, in which the subjects were not asked to take a particular perspective, the researchers got similar findings. Subjects again responded differently to the same questions. In this study the subjects were college students majoring in either physical education or sociology. What is interesting about these findings is that the subjects' answers corresponded to their major. Without being asked to do so, most of the physical education majors took the perspective that Rocky was a wrestler, whereas the sociology students most frequently viewed Rocky as a prisoner.

How can we account for these different reader responses? These readers read the same text—the same words—so the meaning cannot be said to reside totally in the text. Instead, individual readers had different transactions with the text. Some readers with whom we have shared this passage have also reported that Rocky was a horse or a dog. We have even gotten the answer "a kindergartner" from a teacher in a recent workshop with early elementary teachers. In this setting, we were discussing and evaluating how much the bits of language—letters, sounds, words, and so on—were emphasized in the reading lessons in the basal readers used in their schools. Take a kindergartner's point of view and read the passage again.

This Rocky passage was constructed by researchers for a particular experiment. If it were found in any other context, we would probably not consider it complete. It seems to be the beginning of a story in which an author may possibly include many flashbacks to fill in important circumstances or pertinent events in Rocky's life. If it is a story, the subgenre is unclear from the passage as it stands; maybe it's a mystery.

Nevertheless, by using this passage, several important points can be made about the reading process. First, readers use prior knowledge or experience about the world and language to construct meaning. In other words, they construct meaning by bringing meaning *to* the text. Notice that individual words from the passage—*mat, escape,*

Beers (2003); Goodman & Burke (1985)

Cazden (1992); Nystrand (1986, 1987); Pappas & Pettegrew (1998)

Transaction
Lytle & Botel (1988); Rosenblatt (1978, 1989); Hunsberger & Labercane (2002); Karolides (1992, 1997); Pappas & Barry (1997); Weaver (2002)

Anderson, Reynolds, Shallert, & Goetz (1977)

Carey, Harste, & Smith (1981)

Different readers have different interpretations of "Rocky."

Readers use prior knowledge to understand texts.

charge, lock, and so forth—have different meanings depending on whether the perspective of a wrestler or prisoner (or horse, dog, or kindergartner) is taken. The same is the case for the individual sentences. That is, different readers were concerned with different predictions and different questions and answers before, during, and after reading the Rocky passage. This means that, although people might *think* that reading proceeds in a bottom-up or part-to-whole (from letters to words to sentences, etc.) process, the opposite is the case. Because reading is more of a top-down, whole-to-part process, comprehension is a relative—not an absolute, all-or-nothing—phenomenon. In other words, more than one interpretation is possible in transactions with texts.

Second, although varied responses are possible for a particular text, it is not the case that everything goes. No one reading the Rocky passage would say that Rocky is a beautician or a florist. The language and organization of the text are more like a "blueprint." The text offers openness, but it also provides control or constraints. We know, for example, that the Rocky passage is not the beginning of a text that belongs to the poetry, information book, or how-to manual genres.

Third, readers' transactions and interpretations are influenced by factors of social context, including both the background of the reader—cultural, economic, gender, personal, and so on—and the actual situation in which the reading occurs. Remember that the researchers asked the subjects in the study to take on different roles for Rocky. Remember that the sociology and the physical education majors responded to the task without having been asked to take a specific perspective. What personal and situational factors were affecting the teacher's response to the Rocky passage?

The term *transaction*, thus, emphasizes the active meaning-making flavor of the reading process, or how readers experience or "evoke" the text. When children learn to read or use written texts across the curriculum, they acquire the conventions or genres of particular disciplines, the different "ways of knowing," and the various domain-specific rules of evidence for history, science, math, art, and so forth. At the same time, they develop some general approaches to reading across the curriculum. This range of transactions with text is outlined in Table 6.3.

These transactions reflect the ways in which children engage with and respond to texts before, during, and after reading. One type of transaction is the *emotional, experiential,* and *autobiographical* responses of readers—what stands out (or is salient) for them when they read particular texts. *Connective* transactions have to do with readers' linking prior knowledge of experiences and texts with ideas in texts and fitting these new ideas within their present schemas of various topics or experiences. *Descriptive* and *analytic* transactions are those in which features of texts are noted and authors' actual structures or wordings—their specific linguistic choices—are examined. *Interpretive* and *elaborative* transactions deal with the sense-making, problem-solving strategies readers employ to predict, consider, infer, explain, ponder, and question ideas to decide what texts mean for them. *Evaluative* transactions are considerations of appropriateness regarding texts, whereby readers assess authors' ideas and arguments and their effectiveness in relating or expressing their messages to decide whether particular texts are "good" or not or whether certain ideologies or values are presented. Finally, *self-reflective* transactions involve readers' noting and monitoring their own processes of reading.

Thus, in reviewing Table 6.3, you will note that these types of transactions involve a range of reader experiences and questions. These questions, which can be at an awareness level that is tacit or subconscious or more explicit, depend on readers' purposes for reading—whether they are reading for pleasure during Sustained Silent Reading* (see Chapter 7), skimming quickly to decide if a particular book will provide useful information for a project they are doing, or reading to get answers to specific questions for a report or to participate in a discussion with peers. Thus, there is no hierarchy or order in these transactions. Many occur simultaneously, overlapping and affecting each other. Some predominate in reading particular genres—in reading a storybook versus a biography versus a how-to manual. Some happen because of specific contextual factors.

Smith (1997); Weaver (2002)

The comprehension of texts is a relative phenomenon.

Rosenblatt (1978, 1989)

- The characteristics of a text affect readers' interpretations of that text.
- Personal and immediate situational factors affect readers' interpretations of texts.

Reading involves social reader–text transactions.

Geertz (1983); Cope & Kalantzis (2000); Martin (1990); Moore et al. (2003)

- A range of transactions is possible in reading.
- These transaction categories have been taken from Lytle and Botel (1988).

Emotional, experiential, and autobiographical transactions
Connective transactions

Descriptive and analytic transactions

Interpretive and elaborative transactions

Evaluative transactions

Self-reflective transactions

Reader questions about a text can be tacit or explicit.

- Many transactions can occur at the same time.
- Transactions are influenced by the genre involved.

table **6.3**   **Types of Transactions with Text**

Types	Definitions	Sample Questions
Emotional, experiential, and autobiographical	Initial response, showing involvement with the text; identifying and/or empathizing. Experiencing the text by using mental/sensory imagery.	What stands out for me? How do I feel about this?
Connective	Linking text with prior experiences, with attitudes and ideas and similar texts, and other ideas within the text; making analogies.	What does this text make me think of? Remind me of? How does this text fit with what I already know about this subject?
Descriptive and analytic	Noticing features of the text, e.g., choice or function of particular words, syntax, or length of sentences; functions of sentences or paragraphs in the text; characters and events; tone; type of discourse; style; use of metaphor or other figures of speech; author's arguments.	How does this text work? What's going on here? What does it say?
Interpretive and elaborative	Using reasoning or problem-solving strategies to construct meaning, resolve doubts, and make sense of text; hypothesizing; making predictions, asking questions; using evidence to confirm or disconfirm a hypothesis or prediction or to answer own questions. Explaining, exploring, making inferences; questioning and defining intentions, problems, themes, and symbols. Creating, revising, and adding to text. Pondering implications of ideas, including incongruities, discrepancies, ambiguities, and omissions.	What does this text mean? What might be added here? Omitted? Changed? Where can I apply these ideas? How valid/reliable is this argument?
Evaluative	Evaluating the text according to criteria related to appropriateness, effectiveness, difficulty, relevance, importance of content, or form.	Does this make sense? How [good] is this? What do I agree/disagree with?
Self-reflective	Noticing one's own processes of reading; monitoring or keeping track of current understandings of words, sentences, or discourse level meanings; noticing conflicts between text and own knowledge and beliefs.	What am I doing as I read? What questions do I have? What do I understand? Not understand?

Source: Lytle & Botel, 1988.

Summary

Reading is an active, constructive, social meaning-making process that consists of a range of transactions with texts during which readers ask questions, monitor understanding or partial understanding of particular texts, and take control of their reading processes. Transactions such as these foster abilities to question the authority of texts and to read critically and creatively. Moreover, when children are monitoring and evaluating their reading, they reflect about their thinking. Metacognitive awareness is enhanced.

The Writing Process

The writing process is also an active, constructive, social, meaning-making enterprise. Drawing on their own schemas (which include their knowledge of the language system and the conventions of a range of written genres), writers create texts for readers to use. Because they have to decide what to include in their texts and how to express their messages, the writing process itself engenders in writers new ideas and insights, new meanings, and a deeper thinking.

Cazden (1992); Lytle & Botel (1988)

There are just as many misconceptions about the writing or composing process as there are about the reading process. As a result, instruction in writing has persisted in emphasizing the mechanics of the *product* and the language *parts*—the formation of letters, spelling of words, grammatical relationships between words, and so on—rather than the *whole* of the writing *process* (that is, writers' efforts at meaning making in the creation of texts). To become writers, children need many opportunities from the beginning to write a range of meaningful, authentic texts, rather than to be kept busy with the isolated assigned exercises to "practice writing" that are found in many traditional classrooms.

Current research in writing has changed to emphasize the process of writing and to describe how real writers go about constructing texts. This does not mean that the product and parts of language are ignored. Instead the product, including the ideologies and values expressed in it, is considered *within* the process.

The writing process has been described (but sometimes in different terms) as consisting of prewriting, drafting, revising, editing, and publishing. These five activities are not to be seen as linear, discrete steps or stages of a single composing process. Instead, just as reading involves interacting, simultaneously occurring transactions or experiences, the activities or experiences of writing are also dynamic, and frequently they simultaneously affect and interact with one another. Thus, to counteract the idea that composing is a single, neat, lock-step sequence, act, or process, we consider these five activities different dimensions, aspects, or *experiences of writing* for constructing or creating texts.

Experiences of Writing

PREWRITING EXPERIENCES

The prewriting experience, sometimes called the rehearsal experience, is more than just what precedes or motivates writing. Instead, prewriting includes almost anything and everything. In some sense, writers' schemas—all their experiences—can be seen as prewriting. Prewriting is generating and exploring, recalling and rehearsing, and relating and probing ideas, as well as planning, thinking, and deciding. Prewriting experiences occur when we talk and listen during discussions, presentations, written passages read aloud, brainstorming sessions, and so on. They happen while we read, skim, research, observe experiments or demonstrations, and see films and videotapes. Drawing and sketching constitute prewriting experiences. Moreover, prewriting experiences consist of writing itself: jotting down notes or questions, sketching out patterns or connections between ideas, constructing Semantic Maps* on a topic, charting or outlining commonalities and differences in observations, and transcribing others' talk. Thus, prewriting is an ongoing experience, not some distinct period of writing. It can occur and interact simultaneously with the other writing experiences yet to be described.

DRAFTING EXPERIENCES

Drafting involves attempts to create or construct a whole text. Unlike the language fragments jotted down during brainstorming, discussion, or observation, drafting consists of spontaneous experiences in producing connected discourse. *Drafting* is a better term than *writing* because it reflects the tentative nature of the text so constructed. It is a matter of trying to get the ideas down, frequently quickly because the mind is always faster than the pen (or the keys of the typewriter or computer). Leaving blanks when the "right" word doesn't pop immediately to mind or periodically suspending concerns about audience sometimes enables a writer to deal with this time factor. Also, during drafting, the writer tries not to worry too much about spelling and punctuation, knowing that the text produced will be reconsidered, crossed out, changed, arranged, and elaborated on. Drafting can be interrupted by prewriting experiences; it can also occur concurrently with revising experiences.

REVISING EXPERIENCES

Revising experiences have to do with attempts of "re-visioning." They are occasions to re-think, re-view, re-see, re-make, re-construct, and re-create the text. Revising is also

---

Atwell (1998); Booth (2001); Calkins (1994); Fletcher & Portalupi (2001); Lensmire (2000); Moore et al. (2003); Smith (1997)

Current views of writing emphasize the process of writing.

Writing activities or experiences are dynamic and interactive.

Prewriting experiences (sometimes called rehearsal experiences)

Drafting experiences

The word *drafting* implies tentativeness.

Revising experiences

Revising consists of the "re-visioning" of a writer's meanings.

an ongoing activity that can happen during prewriting (as ideas are being simultaneously generated and revised or reexamined) and during drafting (as ideas are being reconsidered so that certain wordings are chosen or selected over others).

Revising experiences also frequently occur subsequently to or interspersed with drafting experiences; that is, revising exists after or in between the production of sections of text. Revision is an effort to stand back to interact with the text. The writer becomes a reader when the text is reread and its meaning reconsidered to decide whether the writer's intentions or message has been expressed clearly. This is also when other readers (the teacher and peers) may interact—or transact—with the text and provide specific information and feedback about its effect on them. Readers' expectations and questions about the text may lead to more drafting as well as more prewriting experiences.

> Chapters 7 and 8 cover conferences in more detail.

EDITING EXPERIENCES

> Editing experiences

Editing experiences are those that are intended to "clean up" the draft of a text so that its message is stated in the most comprehensible way, using the most appropriate language possible. Editing involves shaping the message, perhaps changing sentences, or condensing, deleting, or combining them. It can involve replacing one word with another to make it "fit" better or be more vivid. In addition, the tone or style of the text as well as spelling, punctuation, and grammar is checked during editing. Teachers and children may set up different rules or systems for editing experiences. Peer groups and self-editing procedures are frequently established. The important point about editing is that it is done in the context of children's own writing, not as a separate, isolated exercise.

> Chapters 7 and 8 cover editing in more detail.
>
> Editing concerns are addressed *within* the context of the child's writing.

PUBLISHING EXPERIENCES

> Publishing experiences

Publishing consists of sharing. The publishing of final drafts takes various forms in the classroom and differs from classroom to classroom. It is different in the nature of the final product and how it is shared. With respect to the product itself, some publishing experiences require only that the children rewrite their texts in their best handwriting. Other publishing entails the teacher, a parent volunteer, or the student typing the final draft. The final draft may have a special cover, or it may be placed in a special format for display. Sometimes the publishing of final drafts ends up in classroom, school, community, or even national newspapers and magazines.

Because publishing has to do with sharing in general, publishing experiences are not limited to the publishing of final drafts. Thus, any of the children's writing experiences can be "published." Prewriting experiences—plans for projects, questions to be investigated, Semantic Maps* on a topic from small-group brainstorming sessions—can be shared; drafts and edited copies can be responded to by peers, the teacher, or the whole class. Moreover, as for final drafts, publishing experiences can occur with a range of audiences within the classroom or beyond—with other classes of the school or others in the community.

> Publishing is sharing.

Summary

Like reading, writing is an active, constructive, social meaning-making process. It consists of a range of writing experiences in the construction of texts from a variety of genres. Writing entails ownership. Writers are given opportunities to take control of the composing process; they decide on their own topics and determine for what purposes their writings are to accomplish, through which genres their texts are to be formed, and for which audiences their messages are to be expressed. In the writing experiences described, the text as a product is a concern but the process of the construction of that text as well as thinking about that process is also emphasized.

> Ownership is an important feature of the writing process.

The Nature of Visual Images

Kress (2003); Kress et al. (2001); Kress & van Leeuwen (1996); Unsworth (2001)

Now that we have looked at the reading and writing processes in which readers and writers are engaged to create written language, it is important to explore the elements and characteristics of visual images that are so frequently incorporated with written messages in multimodal texts. Providing pictures or images to illustrate the features we describe later would be most helpful for you to understand the nature of visual images. However, because of space constraints in the book, and because permissions for reproducing images are so expensive, we can only include a few here. And, what we do present, we have *sketched out* ourselves. We are not used to examining the various features or characteristics of images, so a lot of what is talked about in this section is likely to be quite new for you, as well as the terminology employed to describe the meanings depicted in images. The rationale we presented about seeing the linguistic features we covered in Chapter 1 and earlier in this chapter as being tacit, but something you already know, applies to considering visual images. It is probable that many of the ideas discussed here may also be already "known" in some sense. However, if you are going to help students be capable of viewing images and creating them on their own, it is important that you try to make these tacit understandings about images more explicit for yourself.

In Chapter 1, we provided the following reconfiguration of the concept of context of situation for verbal–visual, multimodal texts:

Reconfiguration of the context of situation from a multimodal perspective

What is happening?

Ideational/representational patterns verbally and visually construct the ideas or content of the communication message—the nature of events, the objects and participants, and the circumstances in which they happen.

Who is taking part?

Interpersonal/interactive speakers/listeners, readers/writers, and viewers and what is viewed and has been constructed by illustrators.

What role is communication playing?

Textual/compositional meanings are concerned with how meanings are expressed by text and image—the relative emphasis or distribution of the information being expressed among elements of the text and image.

We use the concepts from each question that relate to visual images to organize this section—representational meanings, interactive meanings, and compositional meanings.

Representational Meanings

Representational meanings have to do with content of images.

Representational meanings have to do with depicting the content of the world. This content is depicted in different ways, ones around actions or events, ones that display classification, ones that show part–whole relationships, and ones that show participants as objects changing over time.

Event images

IMAGES THAT SHOW EVENTS

Pictures, illustrations, and photographs often show participants involved in various "events" or actions. Participants can be people or animals (or mythical creatures), as well as inanimate objects, such as furniture, buildings, cars, and natural phenomena like trees, water, or plants. In addition, in diagrams, participants can be boxes or circles. Actions in images are indicated by "action lines" or vectors. Images can be Transactional so that these vectors from an Actor participant can be directed toward another participant called a Goal. Figure 6.5A shows such an image. Here, the person is the Actor and the Goal is the wagon, with the action vector being one of pulling. Lots of such images are found

Transactional images

in illustrations or photographs in a range of genres. In stories a child might be depicted building a sand castle, stacking blocks, or moving puzzle pieces. In each case, the child would be the Actor, with the action vectors ("building," "stacking," and "moving") directed toward the Goals of sand castle, blocks, and puzzle pieces. Informational texts might show someone planting seeds, a squirrel eating acorns, or children rolling marbles down ramps. Similar Actor-action vector-Goal pattern structures would be found in such images. However, not all images involving actions depict a Goal—that is, in these images, there is an Actor, but there is no apparent participant to whom the action is directed. Such an image is called Nontransactional. Figure 6.5B shows a Nontransactional structure—a frog that is jumping or leaping with no Goal depicted. Again, we could envision many pictures that would show only Actors—a child, bird, squirrel, worm—involved in actions (vectors)—running, flying, scurrying, burrowing.

Nontransactional images

IMAGES THAT CLASSIFY

Classification images

Some images classify by organizing participants into certain categories. These images represent participants in terms of "kinds of" relations or taxonomies. One type of this kind of image is called a Covert Taxonomy where a set of participants (Subordinates) is depicted, but the Superordinate, the actual category, is not included—it is implied. Figure 6.6A shows several feathers but the Superordinate class or category—bird feathers—is not included. Overt Taxonomies are images when the Superordinate is present. These are often found as tree diagrams or certain flowcharts. Figure 6.6B shows a tree diagram of states of matter, which is the Superordinate participant, with solids, liquids, and gases as Subordinate participants.

IMAGES THAT SHOW PART–WHOLE RELATIONSHIPS

Part–whole images

There are lots of images (especially in informational texts) that show part–whole relationships. These are usually an object with its labeled parts. The object, person, or animal is the Carrier, and the parts are Possessive Attributes. Such an image—called a Structured Analytical image—is shown in Figure 6.7A. The flower is the Carrier with the various labeled parts as the Possessive Attributes. An image can be a Structured

figures **6.5A** and **6.5B**
Images That Show Events

Transactional Image   Nontransactional Image

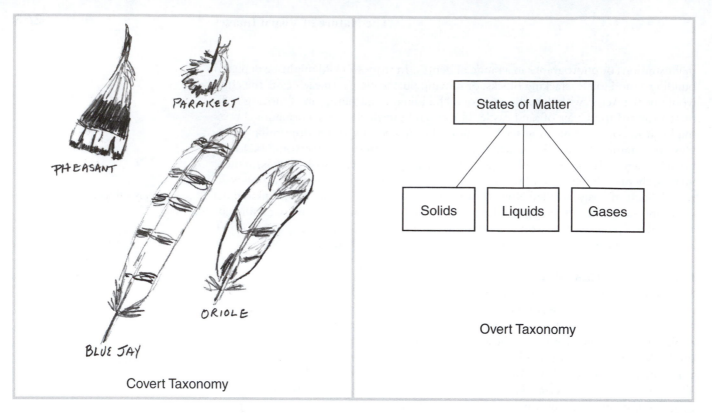

figure 6.6A and 6.6B
Images That Classify

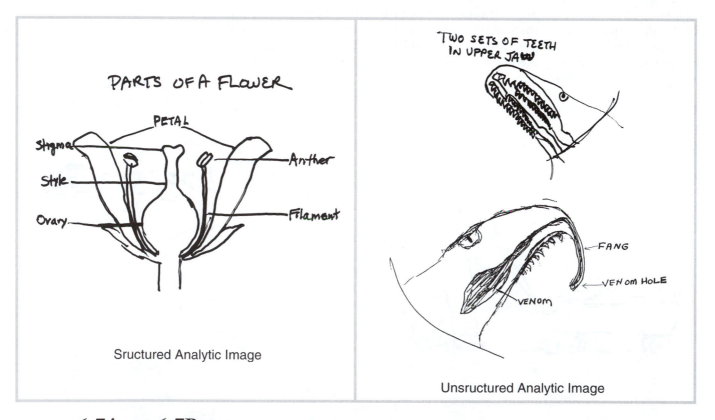

figure 6.7A and 6.7B
Images That Show Part–Whole Relationships

Analytical one even if no labels are present. For example, photographs in fashion magazines or catalogs may show a model wearing various kinds of clothing and/or accessories. The model would be the Carrier and the various pieces of clothing/accessories would be the Possessive Attributes. (The picture of a squirrel from *Squirrels* discussed in Chapter 1 is another example.) An Unstructured Analytic image shows Possessive Attributes (the parts) but not the whole Carrier itself. This kind of image often occurs when there is a zooming in or magnifying of some part of the whole (a feature of CD-ROMs that enables a viewer to zoom in to see particular parts more clearly). Figure 6.7B shows a zoom-in of the two sets of teeth in the upper jaw of a snake and the venom/fang of a rattlesnake.

Wildsmith (1974)

TIME LINES

Time-line images

Time Lines depict stages of a sequence of things. Figure 6.8 provides a series of pictures that show how a fully grown caterpillar changes over time by first sitting on a leaf stem, then hanging by a silk thread, then changing into a pupa, and then finally growing into a butterfly inside the pupa. Story maps that depict through pictures the major actions of a story and time lines created in social studies to show major events in a particular historical period are examples of Time Lines. Stages of a process over time are sometimes depicted (e.g., the building a tunnel in *Tunnels* or packaging of milk in *The Milk Makers*).

Gibbons (1984, 1985)

Interactive Meanings

Interactive meanings or relations have to do with the interactions between the producers (which we have called illustrators in Chapter 1) and viewers of images. Several dimensions are involved in such interactions and are briefly described next:

Interactive meanings depict illustrator–viewer relations.

- **Visual Demands and Offers:** Images that contain humans, humanlike creatures, or animal participants whose gaze seems to be directed straight to the viewer are called Demands. That is, it is as if the participant is demanding attention from a viewer. In Demands, the viewer enters into some kind of imaginary interpersonal relationship with the represented "gazing" participant. In contrast, when images of participants do not gaze directly at the viewer, and no imaginary relationship exists, such images are considered as Offers. Here what is depicted is offered as if the viewer is an impersonal onlooker.
- **Social Distance:** The distances that people have with others depend on the nature of their social relationships. To understand the social distance aspects between the viewer and participants depicted in images, consider and visualize various real life, social interactions with others. For example, in intimate relationships we are likely to be physically close and would have the faces of these

figure **6.8**

Time Line

others in our vision. With others with whom we have personal relations but are not intimate, our field of vision would consist of these others' bodies waist up. Then, with strangers, we keep at a distance and our field of vision would likely consist of these others' full bodies. These social distances between the viewer and the represented participants in images are realized via close-up, medium, and long shots (or some intermediate position). That is, participants can be portrayed close up (as if they are personally close to a viewer), or depicted as a long shot (as if a far social relationship to a viewer), and so forth. Moreover, nonhuman participants (buildings, landscapes) can also be seen in a "social distance" way.

- *Attitude:* Represented participants can be depicted so that images either reflect involvement with the viewer—a frontal angle—or indicate detachment with the viewer—an oblique angle.

- *Power:* If represented participants are seen from a high angle with the viewer looking down on them, then these participants are seen as if the viewer has power over them. In contrast, when they are represented from a low angle, the participants are depicted as if they have power over the viewer. Eye-level angle depicts an equality between represented participants and the viewer.

- *Realism:* Viewer judgment about whether an image is real, "naturalistic," or credible—its modality—is influenced by various factors. For example, color (high color saturation versus black and white) of an image would be considered more naturalistic. Contextualization of an image also affects naturalistic modality—that is, an image of an animal in a tree or other aspects of its habitat would be considered to have higher modality and, therefore, be more naturalistic than the same animal without a background and surrounded only with white space. The level of detailed features also affects modality and judgments of realism.

- *Objective Images:* Cutaways are considered objective from the point of the perspective of the viewer because these images show more than what is observable on the surface from any usual viewer position. The surface of a represented participant is somehow peeled off or removed to reveal what is hidden. Cross sections, which also show what cannot usually be observed, are also objective images.

Compositional Meanings

Compositional meanings deal with layout.

Compositional meanings involve the layout of images in texts. Three elements or concepts are discussed—information value, framing, and salience.

INFORMATION VALUE

Left and Right. In the layout of texts—on a page, within a page, or over a double-page spread—what is placed on the left is usually considered as being more familiar. This familiar information is referred to as the "given information." In contrast, what is placed on the right-hand side is considered less familiar and, therefore, the "new information." Within images, a similar pattern usually exists—that is, the information on the left is familiar and given and that on the right is new.

Top and Bottom. Information value also exists in images in terms of whether elements are placed on the top or bottom of a page. Usually those elements that depict more generalized, abstract, conceptual information are found on the top, and the more familiar and concrete information is on the bottom.

Center-Margin. A center element offers central information, and margins are considered subordinate or peripheral elements to the center image. A triptych, another type of center-margin layout, consists of three distinct images in a row. Again, the center is the nucleus of information and the margins express contextualizing information.

FRAMING

The concept of framing refers to the ways in which elements or groups of elements within a layout may be disconnected or marked off from each other or may be connected or joined together. When elements are marked off and disconnected, they are seen to be strongly framed; whereas when elements are more integrated, they are considered to be weakly framed. Framing can be accomplished by the use of frames or borders around elements, as well as by discontinuities of color or shape or by white space. Connectedness can be depicted by the use of vectors from within images and through the overlapping and superimposition of images.

SALIENCE

Certain elements in images have salience due to a range of factors (e.g., the elements' relative size, their color, their sharpness of contrast, location in the foreground, distinctive framing, and so forth). Humans, humanlike creatures, and animals tend to be viewed as salient.

See also Nodelman (1988) and Winters & Schmidt (2001) for more ideas on how different colors, lines, shapes, and so on in images depict various meanings.

Summary

We have not presented an exhaustive account of the nature of images. However, the preceding description provides a sense of how meaning-making systems are employed in images. Different types of images are found in different written genres. Moreover, as written messages reflect ideologies or values, so do visual images. That is, in written texts, the reader and writer ask questions such as: Whose voices do I hear? Whose voices do I represent? How are, or should, voices be expressed? Whose voices are absent? In visual images, the viewer and illustrator ask: Whose "faces" do I see? Whose faces do I represent? How are, or should, faces be expressed? Whose faces are absent? See Activity 3 to explore ways to apply these ideas to multimodal texts of different genres.

See Kress & van Leeuwen (1996) and Unsworth (2001) for more details about images.

Ideologies are reflected in images, too.

See Activity 3.

The Reader/Viewer–Writer/Illustrator Contract Reconsidered

Now that we have looked at reading and writing separately, and the nature of images, it is important to reconsider again the relationships or connections between the reading/viewing and writing/illustrating processes that we discussed in Chapter 1. Table 6.3 covered transactions with text as a reader. Such transactions involve visual images as well. Thus, the same types of transactions—emotional, experimental, and autobiographical; connective; descriptive and analytic; interpretive and elaborative; evaluative; and self-reflective—with their respective sample questions, also apply to a viewer who engages in the images in a multimodal text. Moreover, similar processes occur for a writer and an illustrator, the creator of visual images. Using their own experiences and knowledge of a topic, writers compose verbal messages for readers. Depending on the purpose of the meanings they want to communicate, texts are organized according to some genre and reflect ideologies or values for their reader audiences. Illustrators are also concerned with communicating their experiences and knowledge for viewers. That is, in representing Actors, Goals, Carriers, Possessive Attributes, and so forth, and in depicting participants so as to have an interacting affect on viewers, illustrators also compose.

Unsworth (2001)

Thus, there are similarities in the ways by which both readers/viewers and writers/illustrators activate the semantic potential of a multimodal text. This bridge between the reader/viewer and writer/illustrator and the connections between the reading/viewing and writing/illustrating processes are shown in Figure 6.9 by the arrows

figure **6.9**

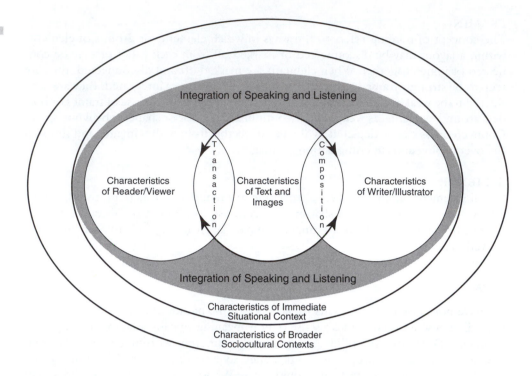

around the top and bottom of the multimodal text circle. These processes are constructive, meaning making, and social. As Figure 6.9 shows, three characteristics or influences involved in the use of multimodal texts are: (1) the characteristics of the reader/viewer and writer/illustrator (knowledge, attitudes, skills, values, etc.), (2) characteristics of the text and image (the genre of text/type of image, text/image structure, the content or topic expressed/represented, etc.), and (3) the characteristics of the social context (the immediate situational context—perhaps a certain context in a certain classroom—*and* the broader sociocultural contexts such as school, home, neighborhood, town/city, state, region, nation, and culture). Surrounding this contract is the integration of speaking and listening (depicted in Figure 6.9 by a shaded area). Thus, this figure represents the essence of what is meant by an *integrated* language perspective. You may want to review how that integration was realized in the classroom prototypes in Chapter 4. (Activity 4 at the end of this chapter can help you become more aware of this integration in the prototypes.)

See Activity 4.

Summary

This chapter began by examining the nature of written genres. All genres—spoken and written—emerge in a culture as conventional responses to particular and recurrent situations because texts accomplish social action. We have emphasized written genres in this chapter, and we have discovered that genres are organized in various ways because they serve different jobs in our culture. To understand both the stability and the change inherent in genres, a general model of genres that included both typical and atypical texts was presented. Then, by examining how the element of description is realized in various factual and fictional genres, the complexity of lexicogrammatical patterns of different texts was considered, along with how these structures express various ideological stances or perspectives.

The processes of using written texts were examined next. First reading, and then writing, was addressed. Subsequently, the nature of visual images was discussed. Conventions about images also exist and are employed by viewers and illustrators. These images are also constructive and social. In considering the nature of images, along with written messages, and their function in multimodal texts, a reconsideration of the reader/viewer–writer/illustrator contact was summarized. Table 6.4 further summarizes some of the major factors that readers/viewers and writers/illustrators engage in during these integrated processes. (See Table 8.8 in Chapter 8 for how to think of these factors in terms of analyzing written multimodal texts.)

table **6.4**   Reader/Viewer and Writer/Illustrator Factors

Factors Regarding the Written-Language Message	Factors Regarding the Visual-Image Message
Content or Ideational Factors	
• Registers or genres follow different sets of conventions.	• Different types of images follow different sets of conventions by depicting participants in events, classifying ideas, representing part–whole relationships, or reflecting time sequences.
• Texts reflect different purpose, audience, and ideology realized by different registers.	• Images reflect different purpose, audience, and ideology realized by different conventional features.
• Different genres use different types of images.	• Different types of images are used in different genres.
• Texts are organized so that the sequence of ideas makes sense.	• Elements of images are spatially orchestrated to make sense.
• Sufficient information is included for understanding ideas or topic.	• Sufficient information is included for understanding ideas or topic.
• Major and minor texts (labels, captions, keys) next to images express content or ideas.	• Images often include minor texts to provide or explain details about them.
• Information in the written message is related to that depicted in images in various ways (e.g., to reinforce ideas, to offer different ideas, to further elaborate on ideas).	• Information in the visual-image message is related to that depicted in written language in various ways (e.g., to reinforce ideas, to offer different ideas, to further elaborate on ideas).
Physical Presentation or Layout	
• Placement and organization of "chunks" of print on pages, depending on genre (e.g., novels, advertisements, poems, recipes, electronic hypertexts, catalogs, how-to manuals, science procedures, etc.).	• Placement and organization of images or elements within images that indicate different information relationships (e.g., familiarity versus newness; concrete versus abstractness; centrality versus marginality; etc.).
• Symbols and other aspects of print reflect importance or impact (e.g., bullets, underlining, boldness, size and type of font, etc.).	• Elements in images depict salience (e.g., color, size, location, sharpness of contrast, etc.).
• Framing of blocks of print to indicate relative connectedness with other blocks of print or with images.	• Framing of images to indicate relative connectedness with other images or with blocks of print.
• Use and placement of headings and minor text (e.g., labels, captions, keys, diagrams, etc.).	• Use of borders around headings or lines, arrows, or other nonlanguage symbols near minor text (e.g., labels, captions, keys, diagrams) related to images.
• Use of medium aspects of language (e.g., directional principles of print; punctuation, spelling, and other print conventions—spacing, hyphens, asterisks, abbreviations, paragraphs, etc.).	• Positioning of participants in images to interact with viewers (e.g., the nature of gaze, close-up versus long shot, angle, modality, etc.) to reflect visual attention, social distance, attitude, power, realism, and objectiveness.

Suggested Activities

1. To help you explore more fully the multidimensional, overlapping nature of written genres, collect a range of written genres with the help of classmates. Choose texts from many sources—books, magazines, and newspapers, for example—and put them in two piles, one having typical texts, the other having atypical or fuzzy texts. (This activity is similar to Activity 4 in Chapter 1, where you collected storybooks and information books. However, here you are not limiting your examination of texts to two genres.) See if you can identify typical texts that everyone would agree belong to a particular genre. Discuss why you think they are typical. Try to look at the language patterns—both the global chunks and the textural organizations—that seem to be involved. Now consider your atypical or fuzzy texts. How are they atypical? What is the nature of the overlap? That is, what genres seem to be involved in the language patterns?

2. To get experience in spotting possible ideologies or values in texts, examine the texts you have collected with this in mind. How are people, places, objects, or events represented? In which texts or genres is ideology easy to recognize? In which texts or genres is it difficult to find? Why? Do you and your classmates have different interpretations regarding the ideology so identified (or not)?

3. To help you understand the various characteristics of images and how images depict representational, interactive, and compositional meanings, examine a range of images in multimodal texts of different genres. In partners or small groups, try to identify these features of images. Then examine how verbal and visual meanings in these texts are related. Is one mode more prominent in different genres? How are ideologies reflected in visual images?

4. To help you make more explicit the integration of speaking, listening, reading, viewing, writing, and illustrating processes in classroom contexts, review the prototypes in Chapter 4. Try to identify instances in which integration occurred. See if you can classify these experiences.

References

Allen, J. (2000). *Yellow brick roads: Shared and guided paths to independent reading 4–12.* Portland, ME: Stenhouse.

Anderson, R. C., Reynolds, R. E., Schallert, D. L., & Goetz, T. E. (1977). Frameworks for comprehending discourse. *American Educational Research Journal, 14,* 367–381.

Atwell, N. (1998). *In the middle: New understandings about writing, reading, and learning—A guide for teachers 6–12.* Portsmouth, NH: Boynton/Cook.

Bakhtin, M. M. (1986). *Speech genres and other late essays* (V. W. McGee, Trans.). Austin: University of Texas Press.

Beers, K. (2003). *When kids can't read: What teachers can do.* Portsmouth, NH: Heinemann.

Booth, D. (2001). *Reading and writing in the middle years.* Portland, ME: Stenhouse.

Calkins, L. M. (1994). *The art of teaching writing.* Portsmouth, NH: Heinemann.

Carey, R., Harste, J., & Smith, S. (1981). Contextual constraints and discourse processes: A replication study. *Reading Research Quarterly, 16,* 201–212.

Cazden, C. B. (1992). *Whole language plus: Essays on literacy in the United States and New Zealand.* New York: Teachers College Press.

Chouliaraki, L., & Fairclough, N. (1999). *Discourse in later modernity: Rethinking critical discourse analysis.* Edinburgh: University of Edinburgh.

Coe, R., Lingard, L., & Teslenko, T. (Eds.). (2002). *The rhetoric and ideology of genre: Strategies for stability and change.* Cresskill, NJ: Hampton Press.

Cope, B., & Kalantzis, M. (Eds.). (1993). *The powers of literacy: A genre approach to teaching writing.* Pittsburgh, PA: University of Pittsburgh Press.

Cope, B., & Kalantzis, M. (Eds.). (2000). *Multiliteracies: Literacy learning and the design of social futures.* London: Routledge.

Eggins, S. (1994). *An introduction to systemic functional linguistics.* London: Pinter.

Fairclough, N. (1989). *Language and power.* London: Longman.

Fairclough, N. (1992). *Discourse and social change.* Cambridge: Polity Press.

Fletcher, R., & Portalupi, J. (2001). *Writing workshop: The essential guide*. Portsmouth, NH: Heinemann.

Geertz, C. (1983). *Local knowledge: Further essays in interpretive anthropology*. New York: Basic Books.

Goodman, K. S. (1967). Reading: A psycholinguistic guessing game. *Journal of the Reading Specialist, 6*, 126–135.

Goodman, K. S. (1997). Putting theory and research in the context of history. *Language Arts, 74*, 595–599.

Goodman, Y. M., and Burke, C. (1985). *Reading strategies: Focus on comprehension*. New York: Richard C. Owen.

Halliday, M. A. K., & Hasan, R. (1985). *Language, context, and text: Aspects of language in a social-semiotic perspective*. Victoria, Australia: Deakin University Press.

Halliday, M. A. K., & Martin, J. R. (1993). *Writing science: Literacy and discursive power*. Pittsburgh, PA: University of Pittsburgh Press.

Halliday, M. A. K., & Matthiessen, C. M. I. M. (2004). *An introduction to functional grammar*. London: Arnold.

Hasan, R. (1984). The nursery tale as a genre. *Linguistic Circular, 13*, 71–102.

Hasan, R. (1985a). The texture of a text. In M. A. K. Halliday and R. Hasan, *Language, context, and text: Aspects of language in a social-semiotic perspective* (pp. 70–96). Victoria, Australia: Deakin University Press.

Hasan, R. (1985b). The structure of a text. In M. A. K. Halliday & R. Hasan, *Language, context, and text: Aspects of language in a social-semiotic perspective* (pp. 52–69). Victoria, Australia: Deakin University Press.

Hasan, R. (1995). The conception of context in text. In P. H. Fries & M. Gregory (Eds.), *Discourse in society: Functional perspectives* (pp. 183–283). Norwood, NJ: Ablex.

Hasan, R. (1996). *Ways of saying: Ways of meaning*. In C. Cloran, D. Butt, & G. Williams (Eds.). London: Cassell.

Hunsberger, M., & Labercane, G. (2003). *Making meaning in the response-based classroom*. Boston: Allyn & Bacon.

Johns, A. M. (1997). *Text, role, and context: Developing academic literacies*. Cambridge: Cambridge University Press.

Johns, A. M. (2002). *Genre in the classroom: Multiple perspectives*. Mahwah, NJ: Lawrence Erlbaum.

Karolides, N. (Ed.). (1992). *Reader response in the classroom: Evoking and interpreting meaning in literature*. White Plains, NY: Longman.

Karolides, N. (Ed.). (1997). *Reader response in elementary classrooms: Quest and discovery*. Mahwah, NJ: Lawrence Erlbaum.

Kress, G. (1993). Genre as social process. In B. Cope & M. Kalantzis (Eds.), *The powers of literacy: A genre approach to teaching writing* (pp. 22–37). Pittsburgh, PA: University of Pittsburgh Press.

Kress, G. (2003). *Literacy in a new media age*. London: Routledge.

Kress, G., Jewitt, C., Ogborn, J., & Tsatsarelis, C. (2001). *Multimodal teaching and learning: The rhetorics of the science classroom*. London: Continuum.

Kress, G., & van Leeuwen, T. (1996). *Reading images: The grammar of visual design*. London: Routledge.

Lemke, J. L. (1995). *Textual politics: Discourse and social dynamics*. London: Taylor & Francis.

Lensmire, T. J. (2000). *Powerful writing: Responsible teaching*. New York: Teachers College Press.

Luke, A. (1988). *Literacy, textbooks, and ideology*. London: Falmer Press.

Lytle, S. L., & Botel, M. (1988). *PCRP II: Reading, writing and talking across the curriculum*. Harrisburg: Pennsylvania Department of Education.

Martin, J. R. (1990). Literacy in science: Learning to handle text as technology. In F. Christie (Ed.), *Literacy for a changing world* (pp. 79–117). Victoria: Australian Council for Educational Research.

Martin, J. R. (2001). A context for genre: Modelling social processes in functional linguistics. In J. de Villiers & R. J. Stainton (Eds.), *Communication in linguistics, Volume one, Papers in honour of Michael Gregory* (pp. 287–327). Toronto: Editions du Gref.

Moore, D. W., Moore, S. A., Cunningham, P. M., & Cunningham, J. W. (2003). *Developing readers and writers in the content areas K–12*. Boston: Pearson Education.

Newkirk, T. (1989). *More than stories: The range of children's writings*. Portsmouth, NH: Heinemann.

Nodelman, P. (1988). *Words about pictures: The narrative art of children's picture books*. Athens: University of Georgia Press.

Nodelman, P. (1996). *The pleasures of children's literature*. White Plains, NY: Longman.

Nystrand, M. (Ed.). (1986). *The structure of written communication: Studies in reciprocity between writers and readers*. Orlando, FL: Academic Press.

Nystrand, M. (1987). The role of context in written communication. In R. Horowitz & S. J. Samuels (Eds.), *Comprehending oral and written language* (pp. 197–214). San Diego: Academic Press.

Pappas, C. C. (1991). Fostering full access to literacy including information books. *Language Arts, 68*, 449–462.

Pappas, C. C. (1993a). Is narrative "primary"? Some insights from kindergarteners' pretend readings of stories and information books. *Journal of Reading Behavior, 25*, 97–129.

Pappas, C. C. (1993b). Questioning our ideologies about narrative and learning: Response to Egan. *Linguistics and Education, 5*, 157–164.

Pappas, C. C. (2002, December). *Identifying and describing the information book genre: The analysis of discursive features of both typical and atypical texts*. Paper presented at the National Reading Conference, Miami, FL.

Pappas, C. C. (in preparation). *Learning written genres: A social-semiotic perspective*. Cresskill, NJ: Hampton Press.

Pappas, C. C., & Barry, A. (1997). Scaffolding urban students' initiations: Transactions in reading information books in the Read-Aloud curriculum genre. In N. Karolides (Ed.), *Reader response in elementary classrooms: Quest and discovery* (pp. 215–236). Mahwah, NJ: Lawrence Erlbaum.

Pappas, C. C., & Pettegrew, B. S. (1998). The role of genre in the psycholinguistic guessing game of reading. *Language Arts, 75*, 36–44.

Rosenblatt, L. M. (1978). *The reader, the text, the poem*. Carbondale: Southern Illinois University Press.

Rosenblatt, L. M. (1989). Writing and reading: The transactional theory. In J. Mason (Ed.), *Reading and writing connections* (pp. 153–176). Boston: Allyn & Bacon.

Smith, F. (1988). *Understanding reading* (4th ed.). Hillsdale, NJ: Lawrence Erlbaum.

Smith, F. (1997). *Reading without nonsense.* New York: Teachers College Press.

Stephens, J. (1992). *Language and ideology in children's fiction.* London: Longman.

Swales, J. M. (1990). *Genre analysis: English in academic and research settings.* Cambridge: Cambridge University Press.

Unsworth, L. (2001). *Teaching multiliteracies across the curriculum: Changing contexts of text and image in classroom practice.* Buckingham, England: Open University Press.

Weaver, C. (2002). *Reading process and practice.* Portsmouth, NH: Heinemann.

Winters, C. J., & Schmidt, G. D. (2001). *Edging the boundaries of children's literature.* Boston: Allyn & Bacon.

Children's Literature

All About Frogs by J. Aronsky. Scholastic Press, 2002.

Amelia's Road by L. J. Altman. Illustrated by E. O. Sanchez. Lee & Low Books, 1993.

Child of the Owl by L. Yep. HarperTrophy, 1977.

Feel the Wind by A. Dorros. HarperCollins 1989.

From Seed to Plant by G. Gibbons. Holiday House, 1991.

The Honey Makers by G. Gibbons. William Morrow, 1997.

It Could Still Be Water by A. Fowler. Children's Press, 1992.

How Do Bees Make Honey? by A. Claybourne. Illustrated by S. Allington & A. Spenceley. Usbourne Publishing, 1994.

The Ladybug and Other Insects by First Discovery Books. Translated from French by C. Cramer. (American edition by L. Goldsen). Scholastic, 1991.

The Milk Makers by G. Gibbons. Macmillan, 1985.

Mojave by D. Siebert. Illustrated by W. Minor. Crowell, 1988.

Mouse by S. B. Stein. Illustrated by M. Garcia. Harcourt Brace Jovanovich, 1985.

The Owl and the Woodpecker by B. Wildsmith. Oxford University Press, 1971.

Panda by S. Bonners. Delacorte, 1978.

The See-Through Zoo: How Glass Animals Are Made by S. Haldane. Pantheon Books, 1984.

A Seed Is a Promise by C. Merrill. Illustrated by S. Swan. Scholastic, 1973.

The Squirrel by M. Lane. Illustrated by K. Lily. Dial Press, 1981.

Squirrels by B. Wildsmith. Oxford University Press, 1974.

Tunnels by G. Gibbons. Holiday House, 1984.

More How-To: Action Approaches in Integrated Language Classrooms

This chapter provides more how-to details of some of the routines, activities, and experiences through which inquiry in integrated language classrooms is realized. Traditional schooling often separates the process of learning from the content to be learned, having generally depended on a model of information accumulation. Children are expected to learn and remember information about particular subjects without necessarily understanding the nature of the information learned, how it came to be accepted as a part of a particular domain, or how to evaluate it relative to other information. You probably remember classes like these. In science, perhaps, you memorized definitions for terms or formulas intended to explain work and force. Too frequently, though, you did not conduct experiments with machines that could do work or with levers and pulleys that could lessen the force exerted to do a particular type of work. You may have been able to pass the exam, but you didn't really understand the underlying concepts related to the terminology. Much of what you learned probably became dated before you ever had a chance to fit it into some schema to help you explain the forces that operate in the natural world. Not so very long ago, children dutifully memorized that "an atom is the smallest indivisible piece of matter"—not very useful in light of fission and fusion and atomic weapons of frightening power.

Recent research on human cognition suggests that this old model of acquiring information is an inadequate way to teach and learn. Instead, there is mounting evidence that process and content are inextricably bound. The schemas that provide intellectual "scaffolding" for new learning are *situated*—built through experience with a particular body of knowledge in a particular context. Further experience—education—builds our repertoire of knowledge and contexts and allows us to think more abstractly and maturely.

As a result, it is not enough to go through the motions of problem solving in a sort of cookbook approach. Instead, teachers must make time for discussion and reflection. Rather than assign children a problem for homework, collect the results the next day, and move on, teachers need to guide children's research and help select appropriate resources for study. Children need to work collaboratively and to have opportunities to think out loud with a responsive teacher and peer audience; they need to revise, rethink, and test ideas to learn from and with their peers. They need to communicate with one another to consider what things mean. What difference does it make, for instance, if children clean up their school playground as part of an antilitter campaign? What difference does it make if children learn to recognize bias in a newspaper report? What use are these skills in their lives?

This is not just a "good citizen" view of education and learning. Reflection puts research and learning into the larger context of the world beyond the schoolroom walls. It is also both a communal and a personal endeavor. Children build their own

Many traditional school practices separate process from content.

The traditional information accumulation model is outmoded.

Kirshner & Whitson (1997); Lave & Wenger (1991); Lee & Smagorinsky (2000); Rogoff (1990); Vygotsky (1978); Wells (1999, 2001a)

Children need collaborative reflection.

Fried (2001); Wells (1999, 2001b); Wood (1998)

Children are adaptive experts.

Cope & Kalantzis (2000); de Boo (1999); Levstik & Barton (2001); Saul et. al (2002); Wells (1999, 2001a)

Activities herein are selective.

Activities herein are suggestions.

Activities herein are interrelated and integrated.

Figure 7.1 depicts the organization of the activities in the chapter.

Good & Brophy (1999); Levstik & Barton (2001); Newmann et al. (1995); Wertsch (1998)

Fried (2001); Young (1994)

meanings, try them on teacher and peers, and in the process, revise these meanings or find ways to defend them. They are adaptive experts: They learn what it takes to argue for a position and what constitutes adequate evidence. They participate in the give and take and excitement of a community of learners where thinking is respected and good ideas are shared. The activities described in this chapter, many of which have already been mentioned, suggest ways to foster the development of a community of learners. Many of the techniques employed in these activities use kid-watching procedures, which are discussed in even more detail in Chapter 8. The learning portfolios and other methods of evaluation and accountability are discussed in Chapter 9.

Three caveats, however, need to be pointed out. First, the activities or experiences presented do not constitute an exhaustive list. We have been selective, trying to include critical activities that show the range of implementation across the curriculum. Integrated language teachers (and children) are constantly discovering new ways and new activities to implement their own teaching and learning goals. Consequently, what is provided here should be considered only as examples of the possibilities. Second, the activities are only suggestions of how to manage a classroom. It is assumed that these ideas will be modified and reshaped by particular teachers and children to meet particular purposes and circumstances. Finally, we are forced to describe these activities separately and linearly, but it is important not to conceive of them as such. In reality, most of the time these activities are incorporated into other activities, which is one of the reasons that the perspective is called "integrated." In sum, the spirit of this chapter is to describe activities so you have enough information to put into action in the classroom some of the principles of the integrated language perspective.

Some of the activities are grouped together under a broad category. For example, Graphic Organizers* is a general category consisting of four types of activities: Semantic Maps*, K-W-L*, Comparison Charts*, and Venn Diagrams and Two/Three-Column Charts*. Two large categories include reading and writing activities and experiences, respectively. Certain experiences (e.g., Reflective, Disciplined Inquiry*, Student-Directed Inquiry*, Collaborative/Cooperative Groups*, Primary Sources*, Observation and Inference*, and Graphic Organizers*) are explained first because they represent more basic or universal processes and strategies that underlie or incorporate many of the other activities. Status of the Class*, Message Board*, and Focus Lessons* are covered last because their use is more widespread in the classroom. Figure 7.1 depicts this organization and will help you locate a particular activity or experience within the chapter.

Reflective, Disciplined Inquiry*

As we discussed in Chapter 3, Reflective, Disciplined Inquiry* is the lifeblood of a thematic unit. It links process and content in the kind of in-depth study characteristic of thematic learning. Note that this approach has three major parts. First, an *inquiry* sets up an investigation into a question or set of questions that has power for a particular group of children. You can see some of the ways in which this is done by reading the prototypes in Chapter 4. We call these "essential" questions because they are crucial to the success of an inquiry. They do not have single or simple solutions, and many lead children into a variety of other explorations along the way to resolving the original concern. Equally importantly, they are linked to the kinds of questions characteristic of the disciplines or domains within which children are inquiring.

Once a problem or question is raised, children gather relevant data and use such processes as observation, inference, classification, measurement, ordering, and hypothesizing to analyze the data and propose possible solutions or answers. The processes are similar to those generally referred to as the scientific method.

figure 7.1

Organizational Chart for
Chapter 7 Activities and
Experiences

FOSTERING INQUIRY

Reflective, Disciplined Inquiry*
Organizing/Monitoring Student-Directed Inquiry* Projects
Collaborative/Cooperative Groups*
Primary Sources*
Jackdaws*
Observation and Inference*
Graphic Organizers*
      Semantic Maps*
      K-W-L*
      Comparison Charts*
      Venn Diagrams and Two/Three Column Charts*

LITERACY ACTIVITIES AND EXPERIENCES

Reading Activities and Experiences	Writing Activities and Experiences
Reading Aloud*	Journals*
Retellings*	Dialogue Journals*
Sustained Silent Reading (SSR)*	Sketchbook Journals*
Buddy Reading*	Group-Composed Writing*
Book Talks*	Teacher-Led Group-Composed Writing*
Literature Response Groups*	Peer-Led Group-Composed Writing*
Reading Conferences*	Author's Folders*
Big Books*	Writing Conferences*
CLOZE*	Content Conferences*
Say Something*	Editing Conferences*
Coding Text*	Publishing Experiences*
	Dummy Books and Text-Image Templates*
	Displays*
	Bookmaking*
	Author's Chair*

DEVELOPING A REPERTOIRE OF LITERACY STRATEGIES

Teaching Phonics/Spelling in Context*
Teaching Grammar in Context*

EXTENDING LITERACY STRATEGIES

Sketch to Stretch*
Graphing*

Book Extensions*	Drama Experiences*
Plot Profiles*	Improvisation*
Character Sociograms*	Television News Broadcasts and
Character Portraits*	Talk Shows*
	Puppet Shows*
	Choral Reading*
	Reader's Theater*
	Story Theater*

Status of the Class*
Message Board*
Focus Lessons*

Ellis provides this description of an inquiry conducted by a second-grade class: Ellis (1986)

    One morning, members of a second-grade class were excitedly telling their teacher and each other about a near accident that had occurred at a pedestrian crossing next to the school. A primary-age child was nearly struck by a car as she was crossing the street. The students exclaimed that the intersection was dangerous, especially during the winter months when ice and snow were present. The teacher asked the students if they would like to conduct an investigation of the intersection to see how dangerous it really was and to see if they could suggest ways to make it safer. The class agreed that this would be a worthwhile project. The class wrote a *statement of the problem* as follows: How can our school crossing be made safer? With the teacher's help, the class decided to use the following data sources in their research: a model of the intersection; the intersection itself; other students in the school; school staff members, including teachers, custodians, the principal, and the secretary; local residents; photographs of the intersection; and drivers who use the intersection. Working all together as well as in teams over the course of several weeks, the class *gathered data* through interviews, observation of traffic flow, timing the speed of cars near the intersection, and taking pictures of pedestrian, bicycle, and automobile traffic at peak crossing times before and after school. The students *processed their data* with a photo essay of the intersection, summaries of interviews, drawings of the intersection depicting the various problems they had discovered, and charts showing the volume of foot, bicycle, and auto traffic at peak hours. They *made the following inferences*:

1. The crossing is dangerous, especially for younger children, and a safety awareness campaign is needed.
2. Four safety patrol students should be placed on duty rather than two, the present number.
3. Larger, more visible warning signs should be posted along the streets leading to the intersection.
4. The crosswalk lines should be repainted.

Their report was given to the school principal and to the police department. The students were pleased to see that all four of their recommendations were enacted. (pp. 197–199)

As children engage in this study, they create a number of documents, including surveys, graphs, and charts. Some children may have more trouble than others with these forms. Although the teacher may not notice some of these problems by simple observation, the children discuss their projects in their Journals* (or Sketchbook Journals*) and the teacher can respond with suggestions and specific help—perhaps a Focus Lesson*—if a problem is shared by several students. In addition, children may include some of the work from this project in a learning portfolio that is shared with the teacher as part of an evaluation of their work conducted during the study.

Cope & Kalantzis (2000); Levstik & Barton (2001); Newmann et al. (1995)

A second important feature of inquiry in an integrated setting is that it is *disciplined*. In other words, children learn to recognize how different intellectual communities decide what counts as knowledge, how knowledge is acquired, and what purposes it serves within scholarly communities and in the larger world. Knowledge about freshwater ecosystems, for instance, may be gained and used rather differently by a child setting up an aquarium, a city planning commission debating development along a stream, or a research scientist studying mayflies. In order to better help children build their intellectual schema, it is not enough to acquire information; rather, children need to understand the goals, standards, and procedures of study characteristic of the field or fields within which they are investigating. As they do so, they ask better questions, make better sense out of the information they do acquire, and better understand the uses to which information is put in the larger community. They also learn to use multiple sources in inquiries and be critical in evaluating information in terms of the values of authors or informants and the strength of evidence, especially if conflicting information emerges.

Hyde & Bizar (1989); Saul et al. (2002)

A final and crucial part of this approach is *reflection*. Some people call this time to think and discuss *debriefing*. We use both terms. In the intersection example, for instance, the teacher may debrief for ten minutes after the investigation is concluded by asking children to consider the processes used, their applicability to other problems, and the uses to which they can put their conclusions. In addition to this final debriefing, reflection occurs throughout a study. Some teachers take five or ten minutes at the end of a work period to reflect with students about problems and successes encountered during that time. Sometimes a spokesperson for each group working on a project will briefly report to the rest of the class; sometimes groups or individuals are encouraged to share information they have found that would be relevant to another person or group. Teachers facilitate this sharing by knowing what the children are working on and by encouraging them to consult other students and resources in the room. (Debriefing can also occur through Internet blogs—see the Introduction.)

In one sixth-grade class the teacher encourages the development of peer "experts." As the children read a variety of historical literature in preparation for selecting History Day projects, the teacher keeps track of areas where one child's study will help someone else. A child reading about medicine, for instance, came across information on Elizabeth Blackwell, a pioneer in women's entry into medicine, which was useful to another student reading about women in nontraditional occupations. The teacher organized a Literature Response Group* to include both these students so that they had an opportunity to share their information and expertise. At other times, when children asked the teacher questions, she referred them to a student "expert" who had been reading in that area and could be a knowledgeable resource. The teacher also encouraged children to develop particular expertise by asking them to read up on a subject that no one else seemed to know much about: "I'd like you to read this book on David Ben-Gurion. No one else seems to have discovered him, and we will need that background if we are going to discuss what's happening in the Middle East. Could you be our Ben-Gurion expert?" Soon children looked for peer expertise without teacher suggestion and sought opportunities to develop expertise themselves. In a first-grade class the teacher documents the two books that children take home each day. Then, in read-alouds or during discussions around science and social studies activities, she looks for ways to connect the individual experts' knowledge of particular authors and content ideas to the current ones being examined.

Reflection can also be encouraged by involving children in tackling ambiguous problems that may not be a part of a larger thematic unit, such as inventing a new language and a form for writing it, proving that the earth is moving, designing a better human being, and drawing a picture of democracy. These types of activities are exercises in divergent thinking. Children are challenged to think about multiple ways of solving problems rather than converge on a single solution. Each problem is grist for the mill of reflection and an opportunity to use a variety of symbol systems to communicate complex ideas.

Levstik (1986)

Ellis (1986)

Organizing/Monitoring Student-Directed Inquiry* Projects

We have argued that an essential feature of the integrated language perspective is how much Reflective, Disciplined Inquiry* is fostered and promoted throughout the curriculum. However, organizing and keeping track of various Student-Directed Inquiry* projects, where students pose and pursue their own questions or subtopics in which they do in-depth studies within a particular thematic unit, are necessary for successful collaborative teaching and learning to occur. Figure 7.2 depicts the major components of a model of an inquiry-centered curriculum. There are five major phases of the inquiry process, with various experiences or activities aligned to each of them. Note that throughout peer and teacher collaboration occurs, creating a community of inquiry. The various activities listed for each phase are not to be seen as exhaustive or exclusive but instead are noted to illustrate the characteristic flavor of the specific inquiry phases.

Daniels & Zemelman (2004); de Boo (1999); Fried (2001); Wells (1999, 2001)

UNIT THEME				
Identifying Topics and Generating Questions	**Engaging in Research Activities**	**Synthesizing and Interpreting Information**	**Presenting/ Publishing Inquiry Findings**	**Reviewing and Critiquing for Evaluation and Future Speculation**
• Whole-class K-W-L* or other brainstorming activity to identify subtopics and questions. • Overviewing by browsing print-based and other materials in the room (e.g., photographs, maps, artifacts, science apparatus) that will be important for upcoming investigations. • Forming inquiry partners—buddy pairs or small groups.	• Finding relevant multiple sources (primary and secondary). • Reading, notetaking, and creating images to express and depict meanings constructed in using resources. • Conducting hands-on explorations, observing, surveying, interviewing, etc. • Creating initial Graphic Organizers* to display initial ideas or answers to posed questions. • Deciding on responsibilities among inquiry partners in investigations.	• Reorganizing information and data via new Graphic Organizers*. • Drafting of text and images—deciding on genres and types of visual designs to be used. • Deciding on major and minor text (labels, captions, keys, etc.). • Using Dummy Books or Text-Image Templates* to determine how information is to be expressed and depicted. • Deciding on responsibilities among inquiry partners in drafting.	• Editing drafts of text and images. • Deciding on final layouts of inquiry products. • Determining the format of sharing of inquiry projects. • Inviting school and outside guests for sharing or setting up arrangements to present findings elsewhere in the community. • Deciding on responsibilities among inquiry partners in sharing.	• Reviewing what has been learned via the "L" of K-W-L* or other debriefing activity. • Further critiquing of presentations or publications. • Final assessment of both process and product of inquiry project. • Identifying further questions or speculations that may have emerged.
LAUNCHING	CONDUCTING	ORGANIZING FOR COHERENCE	SHARING	REFLECTING
Peer and Teacher Collaboration				

figure **7.2**

Phases of Inquiry

Launching Phase

Generate questions for subtopics for inquiry.

Essential questions deal with the most important ideas and issues related to a theme.

Launching Phase: Identifying Topics and Generating Questions

The first step in Student-Directed Inquiry*, of course, is to somehow launch the inquiries. This involves students identifying and choosing the topics they want to study. In developing the thematic unit, the teacher has already offered many invitations. However, more brainstorming sessions with students are usually done to consider additional possibilities. K-W-L* techniques are useful here to identify what children already know and what they want to find out about. Providing a period of overviewing (i.e., giving students a few days to browse through books and other sources and review a copy of a particular WEB) also helps in the process of selecting topics that students will find challenging and engaging and in beginning the process of question generation. Another idea is for students to sketch out ideas based on scanning through books, plus various objects or artifacts that might be gathered for use as primary materials (e.g., photographs or maps) or props or apparatus to be used in experiments. This initial identification of topics/questions is usually classwide, from which inquiry partners choose subtopics/questions to study.

Not until this initial list of possible topics/questions has been generated are children ready to identify essential questions and select subsets of those topics/questions for small-group, partner, or individual inquiry. (Even if students have individual inquiries, teachers often still create small inquiry groups so children will be supported during the process.) At this point, teachers frequently ask students to prioritize several questions they would want to investigate on an index card or sign-up sheet that shows the various possibilities the class has come up with. The teacher then goes over student lists and assigns the topics, trying to accommodate children's top choices. Obviously, some negotiation will be necessary because the teacher will want students to investigate as many of the subthemes of the unit as possible and to incorporate different perspectives on the topic. This last point is very important. If children do not select topics representative of different perspectives, their work may reinforce myths and stereotypes. Moreover, if there isn't enough interest expressed by individual students regarding the subtopics, it will be hard to sustain authentic research. Also, the availability of books and resources is a consideration. If many children choose the same topic, there will not be enough materials to go around to support their inquiries.

Levstik & Barton (2001); Wells (1999; 2001b)

It is important to note that without sufficient time for question generation, students may generate questions that are not worth investigating. Once some initial topics are identified and inquiry partners formed, new tentative questions might be generated by partners. They might create their own K-W (of K-W-L*) charts that now are more focused on the subtopics. Or Two-Column Charts* (sometimes called T-Charts) where students list "what I know" and "what I wonder" might be employed. Getting feedback from peers and the teacher, then, helps in facilitating worthwhile and interesting questions to sustain inquiry. Sometimes using another T-Chart in which children pose "big questions" and "small questions" aids their ability to find the "meaty" questions to pursue.

Question generation takes time.

Harvey (1998); Harvey & Goudvis (2000)

Many teachers have students choose at least two inquiry projects during a particular thematic unit, one individual and one small group. This is another opportunity to incorporate different perspectives. (See "Collaborative/Cooperative Groups*" in this chapter for further information on managing small groups.) Again, children need help in selecting inquiry projects that are manageable in the time set aside for research.

Conducting the Inquiry Projects: Engaging in Research Activities

Once questions have been chosen and assigned, many teachers then ask students to develop a proposal regarding their inquiry projects. Figure 9.3 in Chapter 9 shows the kind of information that is usually asked of students. Teachers have found that having students complete such a proposal helps both students and teachers in many ways. First of all, by having students put down questions they have or things they want to find out about, they tend to take their inquiry projects seriously. It assists students in deciding if the topic they have chosen is going to be as interesting and challenging for them as they had initially thought. In completing the form, students sometimes realize that something else might be better for them to study. Consequently, there is plenty of time for them to revise their project topic before putting too much effort into it. As teachers look at the books and other resources listed on the proposals, they can also determine whether other books are needed, whether students are likely to encounter multiple, supportable interpretations, or whether some system might have to be devised to share other types of books. Moreover, the proposals give teachers important information in the beginning about problems students might have so that they can resolve problems before getting bogged down in difficult dilemmas that are hard to overcome. Also, by having students consider the nature of sharing their findings, teachers can see how well students are thinking ahead about their projects. Sometimes there may be a requirement set forth about this aspect of a project, for example, that some of the findings have to be in writing and with visual images, or that the findings need to be written in a certain genre that a teacher may want to focus on during the thematic unit (biographies or informative reports, etc.). Thus, the proposal enables teachers to remind students early

Conducting Phase

on about such requirements as well as help them find the best, most interesting, or novel ways to "publish" the findings of their inquiry. It is also important at this point to consider what sorts of genres children may be thinking about using. Sometimes children find it difficult to switch from the informational genres used to collect data to the genres they decide they want to use in sharing their findings. Turning data into an interesting presentation in the sharing phase may require Focus Lessons* to help children think about the requirements of different genres. Making this information explicit helps children be strategic in selecting genres that are more likely to maintain rather than subvert their focus on the essential questions.

If inquiry projects are to be conducted by small groups rather than by individuals, then the teacher can easily modify the proposal form to ask what individual group members have decided to take responsibility for. Consensus on this issue and on the other areas included on the form helps clear up many initial difficulties members might have so that groups indeed become cooperative and collaborative.

As students work on their inquiry projects—as they research and inquire, compose and construct, and then begin to see outcomes—ongoing documentation and self-evaluation are asked of them. Teachers have several ways to do this. At the beginning of each day or before an integrated work time set aside for inquiry projects, the teacher may use Status of the Class* checks or review individual or group status reports, including Journals* that are created especially for the particular inquiry. At the end of the day or work time, students record actual accomplishments and future plans. Some teachers have students complete a special inquiry evaluation form each day (see Figure 7.3). This is kept in a special folder with the rest of the work being done on the inquiry project. Whatever system is set up, periodic evaluation of where students are in

Inquiry requires ongoing documentation and self-evaluation.

Atwell (1998)

figure 7.3

INQUIRY LOG	
Activity:	Names:
What question(s) did you try to answer today?	
Explain what you did to answer your question(s).	What sources did you use today?
What did you discover today?	What new questions are you curious about?
Are you pleased with your results today?	How would your group rate your work together? Great 10 9 8 7 6 5 4 3 2 1 0 terrible

their projects—what problems they might have and need help on, what they have accomplished already, or what they might need to do next—helps teachers collaborate and provide important responsive feedback. It also enables teachers to know when they might need to have conferences with students or conduct Focus Lessons*.

Various activities occur in the conducting phase of inquiry. Students will be involved in reading, notetaking, and/or creating visual images to express and depict the information gathered. Moreover, hands-on explorations or observations (during field trips or visits to people/places in their community) may be done. In addition, students may decide to survey or interview. Analysis of visual images (e.g., historical photographs) is also possible in this phase. Initial Graphic Organizers* (e.g., Semantic Maps*, Comparison Charts*, various flowcharts, or time lines) to express and depict ideas found in various sources are constructed. New T-Charts might be utilized to indicate "questions" and "answers" or "what's interesting" and "what's important."

Harvey (1998); Harvey & Goudvis (2000); Wilhelm (2004)

Organizing for Coherence: Synthesizing and Interpreting Information

Some synthesizing and interpreting information is accomplished in the preceding phase, but here these practices are really emphasized. In this phase students attempt to organize their information and data to create coherence. They put aside irrelevant information to hone in on the more significant data. Again, Graphic Organizers* may be utilized—redoing Semantic Maps*, or making new Two-Column T-Charts* to merge their earlier "answers" (from the "questions/answers" chart) with their "what's interesting" and "what's important" chart information, as well as synthesizing data from the multiple sources they used during the previous phase. The use of the many possible Graphic Organizers* helps students to focus on finding answers to their questions and expressing them in their own voice, rather than students writing down verbatim or plagiarizing from textual sources.

Organizing for Coherence Phase

Inquiry requires synthesis and interpretation.

This is the phase of drafting—trying to write up their information and data and sketching out possible visual images to include. Consideration of the appropriate genre structures is made. Many peer and teacher–student Content Conferences* occur as students struggle to express and depict their meanings. Focus Lessons* are used by teachers to scaffold the difficulties students seem to face in these drafting practices. Moreover, teachers in the older grades will also be interested in how students refer to and cite information from various authors or sources, so putting together this documentation is also a factor of drafting. As students begin to complete drafts of text and images, they also think about how they should be positioned in the products of their inquiries—books, collages, displays, posters, or PowerPoint or slideshow presentations. Creating Dummy Books or other Text–Image Templates* offers ways for them to best decide the layout of their inquiry findings. Determining the major and minor text (labels, captions, keys, etc., next to images) is an important aspect of the drafting and layout processes.

Johnson (1997); Kiefer (1995); Moline (1996); Shulivitz (1985)

In the cases of group inquiries, decisions as to who is to write up and draw what parts of the group's work are made. Sometimes students will have been able to parcel such responsibilities in the preceding stage. But sometimes individual students in a group may need to gather the data from other members' information to accomplish their own contribution of the findings.

Sharing Phase: Presenting and Publishing Inquiry Findings

Editing of student drafts and images are done in this phase as a necessary precurser to sharing. Either Peer or Teacher–Student Editing Conferences* occur to go over students' grammar, punctuation, spelling, and so forth. Consideration of compositional

Sharing Phase

factors in images (see Chapter 6) are also made. Focus Lessons* may also be incorporated by teachers to address particular challenges students face in editing.

Now that the products of inquiry are in good shape, students are ready to share their findings. Presentations can take many formats. Students may create a museum display in the classroom (or another place in the school); they could read excerpts from their writing; they may show PowerPoint or slideshow presentations; they may provide short overviews of collages they have created; they may do demonstrations of various experiments they have conducted. Thus, sometimes students share the actual products (or excerpts of them) or sometimes they fashion a different format to showcase their findings to make their reports, texts, or images more engaging for audiences. All of these decisions and work are done in this phase and then implemented in the actual sharing events.

Students may invite guests—other students or parents—for presentations. They may invite community members to join them, or they may present out in the community—at another school, at a school board meeting, at a local community group that is interested in the topic they have investigated. Finding and presenting for natural audiences what they have discovered make their inquiries authentic and important.

Reflecting Phase: Reviewing and Critiquing for Evaluation and Future Speculation

A final evaluation of the inquiry project is an integral feature of Student-Directed Inquiry* projects and an important opportunity for children to reflect on their work. Frequently, this evaluation includes ways for both teachers and students to assess a student's work. Criteria categories—usually created collaboratively—are developed to assess the knowledge, understandings, or content of what students have learned, various skills or strategies students might have acquired in the process of conducting their inquiry projects, and students' attitudes toward their learning and work on the inquiry topic or other aspects of the project. Assessment can be given in the more traditional way by giving an A, B, C, and so on for each criterion and then a final grade. Or other rating systems are more frequently used—Excellent, Satisfactory, and Needs Work; or Outstanding, Satisfactory, and Improving (or Working On)—capture positively children's beginning understandings, skills, or strategies. Rubrics that outline various processes and skills ahead of time are now used to help review and critique the many facets of inquiry. Beside each rating, students are asked to provide a "comment." This important self-evaluation feature helps both teachers and students better understand a student's own rationale and perspective on his or her learning and areas to work on in upcoming inquiries.

Many teachers have conferences with students over these final evaluations, especially if the students' and the teachers' assessments are very different, although teachers usually report that most students are quite honest about their assessment, so discrepant ratings are rarely seen. For small-group inquiry projects, student evaluations of their own and their group members' contributions regarding the content of their inquiry as well as how each evaluated the group social processes in doing the project would also be included. (See "Collaborative/Cooperative Groups*" for more details.)

Students may also engage in whole-class review or debriefing activities—completing the class or student "L"—what they have learned—of the K-W-L* chart. Teachers may also have students complete Semantic Maps* that incorporate what they have learned not only in their own inquiries but also from those of classmates. Sometimes teachers new to inquiry projects worry about all students learning a particular area of content when individual students or groups delve into (in depth) only one set of subtopics/questions. Such maps or other reviewing or debriefing practices reassure teachers that students learn from everyone in the class in such inquiry projects.

Fried (2001)

Reflecting Phase

Inquiry projects need to be evaluated for content, process, and student attitude.

See Harvey (1998) for a listing of possible areas to include in rubrics.

Another feature of this phase of reflection is to identify new questions or speculate on new questions that may have emerged or new topics of inquiry to pursue. Such reflection makes clear to students the ongoing nature of inquiry.

Collaborative/Cooperative Groups*

One of the characteristics of an integrated perspective, and of a more inclusive curriculum, is collaborative/cooperative learning. This is so for several important reasons. One of the goals of an integrated perspective is the development of individuals who can live together in a democratic, multicultural, and nonracist manner. Cooperative learning *can* teach children important skills for living and working in such a manner. When organized in specific ways, cooperative learning increases student interest and engagement; students may also have greater opportunities for understanding than in more traditional, whole-class organizations. In addition, Reflective, Disciplined Inquiry* relies on group investigation to (1) maximize student participation in identifying and investigating the kinds of questions discussed in earlier chapters, (2) provide opportunities for extensive interaction and collaboration among group members, (3) provide opportunities for the use of multiple abilities, and (4) assign competence to all. Finally, cooperative learning is an authentic and important way of developing understanding in settings outside of schools. Cooperation is often necessary in order to bring different skills and abilities to bear in solving problems. Yet all of us have observed groups in which participation in and influence on tasks were unequal. Rather than reduce status hierarchies, these groups reinforce them. In order to transform *group work* into *cooperative learning* teachers must be more explicitly aware of what is involved in creating a collaborative community. At the end of Chapter 2, we spoke of Developmental Discipline as a major approach to realize such classroom community. Many ideas in this view are also incorporated here.

Cohen (1994, 1998); Sharan & Sharan (1992)

Cohen (1994, 1998); Cohen et al. (1994); Schaps & Solomon (1991); Sharan & Sharan (1992)

Watson (2003)

Address Status Inequities

Race, class, gender, and ethnicity are often related to status hierarchies—social rankings within a group. In addition, status may be related to perceived abilities—in reading, athletics, or music, for instance. These perceptions of unequal status affect cooperative work, just as they affect many other areas of children's lives because they influence teachers' and other students' expectations of competence. Altering status inequities is not easy but it *is* essential if all students are to benefit from cooperative learning. Reorienting children begins with attention to creating multiple ability tasks for heterogeneous groups and assigning competence to all (particularly low-status) students.

Status perceptions affect cooperative work.

Begin by thinking about which of the essential questions in a theme best lend themselves to group rather than individual investigation. Consider whether a task:

Multiple abilities task
Cohen (1994, p. 68)

- Has more than one answer or more than one way to solve a problem
- Is intrinsically interesting and rewarding
- Allows different students to make different contributions
- Uses multimedia
- Involves sight, sound, and touch
- Requires a variety of skills and behaviors
- Requires reading and writing
- Is challenging

Organize cooperative groups for maximum interaction. In a group of four or five it is most likely that all students will have an opportunity to interact; larger groups tend to discourage full participation while groups of three tend to pair off and leave one isolated. While there may be occasions when students select their own groups,

Radenich & McKay (1995); Sharan & Sharan (1992)

overall this tends to reinforce rather than reduce status hierarchies. Instead, compose groups so that they are mixed in terms of status hierarchies (i.e., academic achievement, gender, race). Sometimes teachers organize these groups; other times students list several options and the teacher composes the groups to reflect these interests. (See below for other tips on forming groups.)

Cohen (1994, 1998)

Delegate authority. Cooperative learning necessitates the redistribution of power and authority in a learning community. The teacher cannot be the sole arbiter and authority in the classroom when children are working at multiple tasks. Instead, children develop a set of *cooperative norms* with *procedural roles* for their group work. Basic cooperative norms include: "You have the right to ask anyone else in your group for assistance," and "You have the duty to assist anyone in your group who asks for help." Some teachers develop charts that present these norms with descriptions of "What it looks like" in practice, so that children have reminders in view during work times. These teachers also use some of the kid-watching procedures described earlier to monitor group behavior. In this way they can provide specific feedback, either to individuals or groups about the way they are working.

> Establish cooperative norms and procedural roles for group investigations.

Procedural roles—facilitator, recorder/reporter, materials manager—transfer authority to students. Instead of waiting for rescue by their teacher, students must manage their own work. The teacher intervenes when either the system has broken down or students have exhausted other options. Specific procedural roles depend on the age and experience of the children involved, as well as on the nature of the task. Generally, however, groups need a facilitator whose task is to see that all group members get the help they need. It is important to note here that procedural roles do not mean that a task is divided among group members; rather, individuals must discuss their work with the group. Thus, the facilitator might ask the group to provide specific help to a member or remind the group that certain tasks remain to be completed. The materials manager is not responsible for all the materials; rather, he or she is responsible for helping the group deal with materials responsibly. It is equally important to rotate procedural roles. As children practice different roles, they grow in competence and confidence and are perceived differently by their peers.

> Procedural roles depend on age, experience, and the nature of the task.

Task descriptions are also an important feature of delegating authority. Traveling from group to group explaining tasks is not an efficient or effective use of teacher time. Instead, teachers in integrated language classrooms rely on written (sometimes with diagrams or visuals) or taped instructions and individual and group reports. Chapters 4, 5, 7, and 9 include examples of different types of reports. Often these tasks are developed in cooperation with students. At least initially, teachers usually need to help students design tasks that require multiple abilities.

Cohen (1994, 1998)

Make a low-status student the group expert. As we mentioned earlier, one way to change status hierarchies is to assign competence to low-status students. Generally this means careful observation so that the teacher can take advantage of a student's display of competence and make it public. This can happen within the context of group work—the teacher notes that a student has a good idea but is not getting a hearing. The teacher steps into the group, calls attention to the idea, and then departs. Or it can happen as part of the debriefing when the teacher calls attention to the contributions of specific individuals in the class. It is important that these contributions be real rather than contrived (i.e., "Jean does such *neat* work") and that they are relevant to the work of the group. Sometimes it is difficult to capture such moments spontaneously. As a result, some teachers purposively arrange for a low-status student to develop expertise that will be needed by a group. One sixth-grade teacher, for instance, regularly asks students to become "class experts." Because she plans individual as well as group work times, children have time to develop their expertise. While all students are expected to become expert at something related to an ongoing theme, she is especially careful to give low-status students tasks where their expertise will be necessary to future group work. She asked one student, for instance, to become an expert on Golda Meir because the class was about to start a project on the Middle East. She asked

Brandt (1991); Pierce & Gilles (1993)

another student if he would become "expert" on Middle Eastern architecture and a third to work on music. In each case she provided appropriate materials and directions so that the children would be successful. Later, as cooperative groups developed, these students could make major contributions. In fact, their expertise was often solicited by other groups as well. To facilitate this type of interaction, the teacher kept a chart of "class experts." Some students who had some facility with relevant languages (German, Arabic, Hebrew) were listed, along with children who had topical expertise (on different forms of Islam and Judaism, for instance), or specific technical skills (making maps to scale, using Photoshop on the computer, editing for punctuation). Group facilitators were reminded to use the expert list when their group needed help. Remember that this technique only works if the students truly develop competence. Simply suggesting that a child become expert is not enough, especially when that child may not feel confident of his or her abilities, or when other children perceive him or her as incompetent. Instead, the teacher must support the development of expertise through the wise allocation of time, resources, and attention. It is the teacher's obligation to provide opportunities to develop expertise and then to call that expertise to the attention of the class in ways that support its use in group interactions.

Teachers provide opportunities for children to develop expertise.

Establishing or Forming Collaborative/Cooperative Groups*

Two essential features mark cooperative activity: It has goal similarity and it reflects positive interdependence in that a particular cooperative group is successful because its members work together.

There are two major types of Collaborative/Cooperative Groups*. The first type is short term and more informal in nature, and the second type is characteristically more formal and long term. Informal, short-term groups are used when small groups of students may do short activities involving brainstorming ideas, such as K-W-L* or Semantic Map* activities, or work on approaches to solving, say, certain math problems. The group efforts are then shared with the whole class. Short-term collaborative groups also occur frequently during shared or Buddy Reading*, Say Something* activities, or peer conferencing around student writing. In other words, this first type of Collaborative/Cooperative Groups* may be seen to be ongoing in the classroom where membership of the group is frequently changing and of short duration. Thus, membership in this type of cooperative group is usually created spontaneously by students or simply determined by who may be sitting next to each other when a particular activity is initiated.

Dalton (1985); Hill & Hill (1990)

The second type of Collaborative/Cooperative Group* is more formally constituted and long term—if not for the whole duration of a thematic unit, then for a large portion of it—because these groups engage students in major projects or work. The following remarks concern mostly this second type of Collaborative/Cooperative Group*, although the ideas presented are good to keep in mind when thinking about the informal, short-term groups, too.

The most successful groups are usually those that are formed around a common interest: the desire to read and talk about the same book in Literature Response Groups* or to pursue the same questions or topics in a Student-Directed Inquiry* project. Topics are identified and selected and students are assigned to groups as for Student-Directed Inquiry* projects (described earlier). Although the groups are determined mostly through common interests, an important factor that influences the teacher's grouping decision is diversity in membership. Diversity is considered enriching in integrated language classrooms, so teachers try to make sure that students in particular groups are different—in gender; in ethnic, racial, and cultural background; and in academic *and* social abilities.

Diversity is an important factor in forming groups.

Delpit (1995)

Many children want to work with their friends and may be initially disappointed by not being placed with them. Several strategies are useful. First, talk about the classroom as a community all the time (and especially on the first day of school), stressing how important it is for everyone to get to know each other, so that students will expect to be working with lots of different groups during the school year. Second, point out that there will be many opportunities to work not only with old friends in the first type of collaborative group mentioned earlier—that is, in a peer Writing Conference* or in shared or Buddy Reading*—but also with new friends in other groups. Finally, many teachers also consider this friend issue more directly by asking students to indicate three or four people they would like to work with. This is usually done at the same time that students list their preferred topics for their inquiry projects so that teachers can consider this information when they look at students' interests—as well as at the diversity concerns. In this way, teachers can have each student in a group with at least one person that the student wanted to work with and avoid the problem of having any student being isolated or not chosen.

Having students work on topics that they have chosen usually overcomes a lot of other problems that might occur due to the membership of the groups. That is why grouping around common interests is so successful. However, groups can be formed in other ways. In the beginning of the year, when students do not know each other very well, teachers might establish groups by going around the room or down the class list and counting one, two, three, four, and so forth or by having students pick out a piece of colored paper from a hat, each color indicating a particular group. Or, especially later in the school year, teachers might actually use the criterion of working with someone new as a major means of establishing group membership. In these latter cases, common interests would nevertheless still be a focus.

In sum, in any system of forming Collaborative/Cooperative Groups*, interest and diversity are the important issues to keep in mind. Negotiation with students is very likely, so keeping track of various group membership over the course of a thematic unit and school year is extremely crucial to this end.

Group Process

Group process should be an integral part of real, worthwhile content and authentic purpose. That is, children should *never* be involved in contrived activities set up solely for the sake of "doing cooperative groups." However, if students are not used to working in Collaborative/Cooperative Groups*, there may be a need to scaffold students as they learn how to talk and act in groups. Of course, teacher demonstration and modeling will be an important way to get this done. Through various teacher–student conferences or through periodic teacher interactions in small inquiry groups, teachers are able to ask questions or respond to students in the ways they want students to behave and interact. Another way to help students learn how to work responsibly is for the teacher to work with a small group on group procedures in what one teacher called a "fishbowl technique." Here the teacher and the small group sit in the middle of the room with the rest of the class circled all around them so that all students can see and hear. Then the small group models and demonstrates the way the group process should be enacted. Discussion following the demonstration clears up further questions or concerns students might have.

Explicit directions or instruction via Focus Lessons* is yet still another way students can learn the process and procedures of groups. After the teacher's lesson, groups would try out these routines, followed by debriefing and evaluation. Some teachers find that videotaping group work helps during the debriefing. One teacher, for instance, noticed that boys often dominated small-group decision making. When she mentioned this observation in a debriefing session the boys were sure that girls had talked as much as they. The class agreed that they needed to videotape their group work so they could have more data about how boys and girls tended to work in groups. Over the next several days a student teacher in the classroom videotaped several types of interactions: small groups of mixed gender, as well as single-gender groups, and whole-class discussions. The children reviewed the tapes and concluded that there were indeed some problems. Not only did some boys dominate in small groups, but also they found that their teacher tended to call most often on these same boys during whole-class discussion. They also noticed several other things that seemed to be problems in group work. Finally, the class worked to establish new routines to ensure more equitable participation during group work and class discussions. In addition to assigning various roles to group members, they made "turn tickets" to help their teacher call on boys and girls more evenly.

Asking children to notice such specific behaviors in the group and to take turns in having various roles and processes is frequently helpful, especially for students who may be unfamiliar with groups. Consider asking children to serve in one of the following roles:

> See Hill & Hill (1990) for other ideas for roles group members can take.

Summarizer: Retells or recounts main ideas members made.

Recorder: Writes down the group ideas, frequently asking, "Is this what you said?" or "How should I write that idea down?"

Encourager: Encourages by pointing out good points, making sure that everyone has a turn.

Organizer: Tries to keep group members on task, reminds members about problems to be solved or specific ideas to be considered, and indicates when members agree on points or when there are different views that the group has to resolve.

Children can also indicate specifically when they know someone has finished talking, encouraged someone, given specific information to back up points, or used quiet voices or constructive feedback. Making these positive social skills explicit for them in the beginning helps students begin to learn how to work effectively by letting them know what is expected of them and what their responsibilities are as members in a group. Teachers need to develop relationships with all children for this to occur. Intervening in nonpunitive ways (not putting names on the board for misbehavior) may be required for some children who have difficulties in being productive in group work.

> Watson (2003)

Teachers need to realize that students will internalize these social skills gradually. Students may have to be periodically reminded until these skills become internalized, but if teachers refer to these roles or the specific behaviors, children slowly and surely learn to act responsibly in groups.

Evaluating Group Work and Process

Some of the foregoing ideas involve students in evaluating group process. Many teachers, as part of their general assessment and evaluation program, have students evaluate the work and participation in long-term Collaborative/Cooperative Groups*. (See "Organizing/Monitoring Student-Initiated Inquiry* Projects" in this chapter.) At the end of the day or group work, teachers set aside five to ten minutes for students to complete an evaluation sheet that covers both the content of the participants' work and the social skills or group process strategies they displayed. The following kinds of information are elicited:

The group's accomplishment, listing some of the important ideas and contributions that were made by individual members.

Problems that came up and how the group handled or resolved them.

New plans that the group has made, with individual responsibilities, if appropriate.

The ways in which each member helped the others in the group.

The group skills that the members have to work on next time.

Thus, these explicit ongoing group evaluations also foster students' development of the kinds of social skills necessary for meaningful Collaborative/Cooperative Groups*.

See Watson (2003) for more details on building classroom communities via Developmental Discipline.

Summary

Collaborative/Cooperative Groups* are not a panacea. Problems and mishaps will still occur, but it is through working through these misunderstandings that the classroom becomes a community. Students learn how to deal with the problems, and in doing so, they learn much more. Collaborative groups promote problem-solving and social skills as well as foster the kind of learning that cannot be done alone but that can be accomplished with support. Moreover, well-functioning collaborative groups help students learn about and understand others' perspectives, which undergirds important goals of multicultural education. The success of these groups builds the classroom community.

Primary Sources*

Barton & Levstik (2004); Gerwin & Zevin (2003); Levstik & Barton (2001)

History is constructed from the residue of the past. Historians interpret and reinterpret history on the basis of the primary sources that are available to them and on the historiographic or interpretive framework in which the historian operates. The historian uses primary sources—public documents, private papers, newspapers, and artifacts produced during the period under study—and constructs a story to explain the causes and effects of past events. The historian's story, or interpretation of the past, is a secondary source.

Forbes (1943); Collier & Collier (1974)

We see the past filtered through the perspective of the historian, and so our history changes as we change. Even the way history is presented to children changes. Thus, a historical novel such as *Johnny Tremain,* written before the Vietnam War, provides a very different perspective on the American Revolution from that of *My Brother Sam Is Dead,* a novel about the same era but written as America was just coming out of a war in Southeast Asia and reinterpreting its past in light of that traumatic event. Such interpretations are important because they are one way in which we explain ourselves as a culture and as human beings. They provide us with a historical memory and a record of how we have developed over time.

Unfortunately, however, this may be the only history many of us ever encounter. We too easily assume that a secondary historical account is "the way it really was." We forget that history is interpretative and that interpretation is tentative, pending new information. Because of this, it is important for children to understand the sources used by historians in constructing history.

See two interactive websites—dohistory.org, for an online diary, and americanhistory2.si.edu/ourstory/tryonline/indix.cfm, to support students using primary sources as historians.

A variety of Primary Sources* are available and appropriate for use with children, especially in grades 4 and up. Local historical societies, archives, and many libraries preserve primary sources in the form of old newspapers, letters, diaries, military papers, census records, period magazines, catalogs, and so forth. Photocopying such documents is relatively inexpensive and can provide children with the raw material for doing their own historical interpretation. It is also possible to buy packaged primary source material at historical sites and museums and from commercial producers.

One of the skills children learn in working with Primary Sources* is careful consideration of the strengths and weaknesses of various sources, possible biases, and inaccuracies. Children should be encouraged to confirm information gathered in one source by reference to other primary and secondary sources and to recognize the difference between a primary source that comes from the time studied and a secondary source that is an interpretation of the past based on an analysis of primary sources.

One way to help older children recognize the differences between primary and secondary sources is to begin with a Primary Source* such as Figure 7.4, a "slave narrative" or transcript of an interview with a person formally enslaved. (Such interviews were conducted during the 1930s as part of President Roosevelt's Works Progress Administration and are a major source of firsthand accounts of slavery.) Put the slave nar-

figure 7.4

Source: Courtesy of the Ohio Historical Society, Columbus, Ohio

Reporter—Betty Lugabill   Allen County
Editor—Harold Pugh   District 10
Supervisor—R. S. Drum   Ex-slaves

Kisey McKimm Ex-Slave 83 Years

I was born in Bourbon County, sometime in 1853, in the state of Kaintucky where they raise fine horses and beautiful women. Me'n my Mammy, Liza'n Joe, all belonged to Marse Jacob Sandusky the richest man in the county. Pappy, he belonged to the Henry Youngs who owned the plantation next to us.

Marse Jacob was good to his slaves, but his son, Clay was mean. I remember once when he took my Mammy out and whipped her 'cuz she forgot to put cake in his basket, when he went huntin'. But that was the last time, 'cuz the master heerd of it and cussed him like God had come down from heaven.

Besides doin' all the cookin' she was the best in the county, my Mammy had to help do the chores and milk fifteen cows. The shacks of all the slaves was set at the edge of a wood, an' Lawse, honey, us chillun used to have to go out 'n gatha all the twigs 'n brush 'n sweep it jes' like a floor.

Then the Massa used to go to the court house in Paris 'n buy sheep an' hogs. Then we used to help drive them home. In the evenings our Mammy took the old clothes of Mistress Mary 'n made clothes for us to wear. Pappy, he come ovah to see us every Sunday, through the summer, but in the winter, we would only see him maybe once a month.

The great day on the plantation was Christmas when we all got a little present from the Master. The men slaves would cut a whole pile of wood for the fire place 'n pile in on the porch. As long as the whole pile of wood lasted we didn't have to work but when it was gone, our Christmas was over. Sometimes on Sunday afternoons, we would go to the Master's honey room 'n he would give us sticks of candied honey, an' Lawd chile was them good. I ate so much once, I got sick 'nough to die.

Our Master was what white folks call a miser. I remember one time, he hid $3,000, between the floor an' the ceilin', but when he went for it, the rats done chewed it all up into bits. He used to go to the stock auction every Monday, 'n he didn't wear no stockings. He had a high silk hat, but it was tore so bad, that he held the top 'n bottom together with a silk neckerchief. One time when I went with him to drive the sheep home, I heard some of the men with kid gloves call him a "hill-billy" 'n make fun of his clothes. But he said, "don't look at the clothes, but look at the man."

One time, they sent me down the road to fetch somethin' 'n I heard a bunch of horses comin'. I jumped over the fence 'n hid behind the elderberry bushes, until they passed, then I ran home 'n told them what I done seen. Pretty soon they come to the house, 125 Union solders an' asked for something to eat. We all jumped round and fixed them dinner, when they finished, they looked for Master, but he was hid. They was gentlemen 'n didn't bother or take nothin'. When the war was over the Master gave Mammy a house an' 160 acre farm, but when he died, his son Clay told us to get out of the place or he'd burn the house an' us up in it, so we left an' moved to Paris. After I was married 'n had two children, me an' my man moved north an' I've been here ever since.

rative on an overhead transparency and read it with the class, then analyze it in terms of reliability. Can this source be trusted? What things about this source might concern you if you were a historian writing about slavery? Some of the things children may notice include the age of the person interviewed (slavery ended after the Civil War; interviews were conducted in the 1930s; many of the ex-slaves were in their eighties and nineties and would have been quite young during slavery); concern with whether this person's experience was typical; and who conducted the interview (if the interviewer was white—a likely possibility—would an African American person who had lived through slavery be likely to trust the interviewer?).

Next, provide students with secondary historical reports of slavery. Milton Meltzer's *In Their Own Words* is a compilation of slave narratives edited and interpreted

Meltzer (1964)

Lester (1968)

Hurmence (1982)
McKissack & McKissack (1994)

See Barton (2001) for ways to analyze historical photographs.

by the author. How has he used the primary sources? Which parts of Meltzer's work are primary and which interpretative? Then give the children a nonfiction narrative based on slave narratives—perhaps Julius Lester's *To Be a Slave*. How have the primary sources been interpreted here? What purpose may the author have had in writing this narrative?

Finally, have students read Belinda Hurmence's *A Girl Called BOY*, a novel that also uses slave narratives as background for a story of slavery, or the McKissacks' *Christmas in the Big House, Christmas in the Quarters*, an informational storybook based on primary sources about antebellum plantation life. The children discuss the ways in which the authors seem to have used the primary sources and their purposes in doing so. Can they recognize the primary parts of the novel? How, for instance, has Hurmence woven historical information into the fictional tale of a girl who is taken back in time and mistaken for an escaped slave? How do the McKissacks use historical information to highlight the contrast between life for European Americans and life for enslaved African Americans?

A similar procedure can be used for other types of primary sources such as photographs. After viewing the picture of a sorghum mill (see Figure 7.5), children are asked to list five observations (observations can be tested by the senses). Be clear that these are observations and *not* inferences—conclusions based on observation—at this point. Working in small groups, the students try to construct three inferences that can be supported by their observations. After a debriefing in which these inferences are shared with the class, each group resumes work and makes a list of additional information needed to confirm or disconfirm their hypotheses (inferences). At this point, the teacher can introduce further evidence or allow the children to search for it or explain that the picture shows part of a sorghum-making operation. Not every activity needs to extend for long periods. In this case, the purpose may be to provide practice in analyzing primary source material, not in initiating a study of farm technology. Children

figure 7.5

A 1930s' Sorghum Mill Worked by Mule

Source: Photograph courtesy of the Kentucky Department for Libraries and Archives, Frankfort, Kentucky can also use Primary Sources* to compare with descriptions in their textbooks. A text passage on the "surprise" attack on Pearl Harbor, for instance, can be compared to earlier news reports that the Japanese were preparing for just such an attack. Various map projections of the world can be used to initiate a discussion of what maps tell us about how people viewed the world at different times. A single coin can be analyzed as a primary source as well. If you were a person who knew nothing of American society, what could you learn by carefully analyzing a penny, a copy of *My Weekly Reader*, or a Barbie doll, for that matter? Jackdaws* provide one way to organize these and other activities using Primary Sources*.

See the "Social Studies" section in Chapter 5 for more information on primary sources.

Jackdaws*

Jackdaws* are collections of primary and secondary source material, background information, and teaching suggestions for historical and contemporary topics. Commercial Jackdaws* are of this type and are generally geared for high school students. Commercial Jackdaws* can be easily adapted for use in the intermediate and middle school grades and are relatively inexpensive. However, a teacher or the children can also construct Jackdawlike packets.

Jackdaw(™) is the commercial name for a series of Primary Source* and activity packets covering a wide range of topics in world and U.S. history.

Teacher-Made Jackdaws

A teacher can create a Primary Source* packet modeled on the Jackdaws* and geared to specific classroom needs. Because Jackdaws* concentrate on one topic or perspective in a fair degree of detail, they are important ways to provide students with multiple perspectives on larger topics.

PRIMARY GRADES SOURCE PACKET

A Jackdaw* for younger children might begin with a book such as Peter Spier's *Tin Lizzie* and contain advertisements for cars from Model T's to present models, along with road maps from different eras, pictures of gas stations and roadside merchandising such as drive-throughs, and "before and after" pictures of small towns bypassed by freeways, or connected to other places by roads and cars. Some secondary sources on the history of automobiles (e.g., "coffee table" books with well-done illustrations and clear captions) and suggested activities for children can help students study the history of automotive transportation and talk about the impact of the car on people's lives.

Spier (1978)

INTERMEDIATE AND MIDDLE SCHOOL GRADES SOURCE PACKET

Unlike the primary source packet that includes several perspectives in one Jackdaw*, this intermediate/middle school packet concentrates on a single historical perspective. Many manuscript collections contain the papers of private individuals of historic interest. In an EXPLORATIONS thematic unit the teacher might gather the letters and journal of a young woman embarking on a trip west into a packet that includes other primary sources related to American expansion in the nineteenth century: descriptions of the area the young woman was leaving, copies of newspaper descriptions of western lands and eastern problems, and prints from *Harper's* and *Leslie's* magazines of covered wagons and Native American communities in the west. The teacher would also include such sources as information about political conditions, lists of supplies recommended for travelers, a price list for some of these goods, and illustrations of fashions for men, women, and children. A few guide questions can be attached to each source so that children have some help in reading a document or picture. These sources are then used by the students as the raw material for constructing a biographical novel of the young woman's journey and settlement in the west. In doing so, children also have

Harper's and *Leslie's* were popular illustrated magazines of the Civil War era.

See Barton (2001) for schemes for analyzing historical photographs.

Stratton (1981); Schlissel (1982)

access to historical novels about the period and to fine secondary sources such as *Pioneer Women: Voices from the Kansas Frontier* and *Women's Diaries of the Westward Journey,* among others.

Student-Made Jackdaws*

See also Weber (1989) for many other Jackdaw* ideas.

The second type of Jackdaw* is constructed by students as a way of representing what they have learned in studying a particular topic or in response to a piece of literature. After children have studied the history of automobiles, they may want to put together Jackdaw* histories of their own—of cooking stoves, for instance, to go with the DIGGING UP THE PAST theme. Generally, students need some guidance in this activity. One teacher explains that children can pack a "trunk" (a cardboard box) with items to represent a particular story they have read. In a sense, these children reconstruct Primary Sources*.

Fritz (1958)

A child who read *The Cabin Faced West* by Jean Fritz makes a box that looks like an old traveling trunk and fills it with homemade dolls based on those in the story, along with a diary that might have been written by the main character and parts of a letter from "back home." Another turns a shoe box into a replica of an old lunch box similar to those carried by the women in *Rosie the Riveter* by Penny Colman. She

Colman (1995)

fills the lunch box with "artifacts" of women's work during World War II: postcards showing old recruitment posters for war work, a kerchief similar to that worn by Rosie, miniature tools and airplanes, and copies of old articles about war work, along with classified ads.

Myers (1997)

Two older children fascinated by Walter Dean Myers's *Harlem* borrow a worn instrument case from the band director and fill it with Langston Hughes's poetry, a tape of blues singers, "then and now" pictures of Harlem, and a taped interview with a local jazz musician.

Such student-created Jackdaws* allow children to represent in interesting and informative ways what they have learned while accommodating children of varying strengths and interests. The Jackdaws* also give the teacher feedback on the kinds of observations children are making and the accuracy of their inferences. One young boy's reconstruction of an 1867 journal, for instance, included reference to stopping off at a saloon to watch the football game on television. His teacher saw this as evidence of a lack of information on technology and made a note to introduce a unit on TECHNOLOGY that would include time lines of inventions.

Observation and Inference*

Although most process skills seem fairly self-evident, children as well as adults have some difficulty distinguishing between observation and inference. Observation has to do with using our senses to obtain information—or data—about objects and events, whereas inference is what we do when we interpret these data to make predictions or hypotheses or draw conclusions about them. Distinguishing between the two is usually not a problem. We don't really need to distinguish between the observations and inferences that lead us to leap out of the way of a car barreling down the road in our direction. At other

Abruscato (2004)

times, however, the distinction between what we actually *observe*—what we can discover with our senses—and what we *infer*—the meaning we give to what we observe—is crucial, particularly in social studies and science.

Observation and Inference* in Social Studies

We may observe a person of another race or ethnic group as we go about our daily business. Our observation may include seeing skin color, facial features, or clothing. We may notice the aroma of perfume or aftershave or hear the sound of a different language or dialect. But we often infer a number of things that have little to do with our actual observation. Instead, our prejudices and stereotypes interfere with observation, and we may make negative inferences that are unsupported by careful observation.

    Young children are as prone to leap to inferences without careful observation as any of us. As teachers, however, we have an opportunity to help hone their observation skills and insist on supported inferences. You will have noted that there are a number of activities in the prototypes in Chapter 4 that provide children with opportunities to observe and build supported inferences, and you have seen from the discussion of Reflective, Disciplined Inquiry* how crucial this distinction can be.

    We have evidence that as early as fourth grade children have developed specific attitudes and ideas about other races, genders, and ethnic groups. These attitudes are often the result of limited observation and experience. In the early years, however, teachers have a wonderful opportunity to build a body of observation and experience that can lead to more open-mindedness as children come in contact with a wider variety of people. Some teachers try to introduce young children to representatives from other cultures, or they do some lessons on African Americans in February (Black History Month) and women in March (Women's History Month). These short-term experiences are interesting but probably do little to change stereotypes. Instead, what seems to work best is consistent, long-term experience. For instance, instead of inviting guests from six different countries for six different visits, try arranging for a person from one culture to come to class for several visits. Talk with the children about their observations after each visit. You will probably notice a change over the course of their acquaintance with their guest. In initial visits, children tend to concentrate on the most unusual features of the visitor. However, over time, they have opportunities to observe other things—that the person enjoys soccer, has a pesky younger sibling, or loves chocolate—that are the common denominators of human contact.

    In the same way, do not limit content about people of color, ethnic groups, or experiences with gender roles to a specific month or week. Instead, provide many opportunities for children to see all sorts of people in a variety of roles and situations. The point is to help children search for commonalities, as well as for the deeper differences that not only add interest and variety to human experience but also can cause misunderstandings between people. With young children you might start with Peter Spier's *People,* focusing on the myriad ways in which people develop such cultural universals as clothing, shelter, recreation, and food. Ask children to think about things they do that might seem strange to someone from another country, from another part of their own country, or from their own class. When older children study a topic such as the settlement of California, ask them to imagine how Native Americans might write the history of this era. Or look at the American Revolution through the eyes of an African American—either free or enslaved—in the colonies. How might a European American or African American woman explain the women's rights movement of the nineteenth century? How might a Haitian describe current U.S. immigration policy?

    Of equal importance, help children to see beyond color, ethnicity, and gender to the unique individual. It is easy enough for children to recognize that all members of the same class do not have the same taste in music or clothes, do not share the same religion or belief system, or exhibit the same interests or abilities. They are less likely, however, to recognize individual differences in other groups. This is part of the reason it is so important, not only to invite people from a variety of different groups into the classroom, but also to maintain a rich collection of literature, visual images, and artifacts that represents variety *within* as well as *between* groups.

    An idea from anthropology is useful here. Anthropologists working in foreign cultures attempt to make the strange familiar. We ask you to help children make the familiar strange: to look with new eyes at phenomena they encounter every day so that they can observe more carefully, infer more justifiably, and learn more richly.

*Margin references:*

Byrnes (1988); Sonnenschein (1988); Stone (1986); Wilson (1987)

Takaki (1993)

Spier (1980)

Delpit (1995); Hollins (1996); Ladson-Billings (1994)

See Barton (2001) for ways to observe and interpret historical photographs.

Abruscato (2004); de Boo (1999); Saul et al. (2002); Whitin & Whitin (1997)

Alberti, Davitt, Ferguson, & Repass (1974)

Obviously, Observation and Inference* are not limited to multicultural, cross-cultural, or gender-related interactions. Careful observation is crucial to any social study. Think, for instance, about the careful observation conducted by the children studying the dangerous intersection or by those studying the problem of litter in their community. In each case, children's careful, accurate observations led to better-supported inferences and, thereafter, to better-conceived responses to the problems under investigation. As you read the next section on Observation and Inference* in science, you will find other examples of these processes in practice.

Observation and Inference* in Science

Careful observation is, of course, essential to good science. It was careful observation that led Newton to infer the laws of gravity, Archimedes to deduce the laws of displacement of liquids, and Galileo to conclude that the earth circles the sun. Before Galileo humans had believed—inferred—that the earth was the center of a solar orbit. Such inferences are common to children, too. Perhaps you remember thinking that the moon followed you as you drove along the highway on a clear night or recall wondering why people on the "bottom" of the world did not fall off.

When Elementary Science Study (ESS) developers tested some of their procedures while they were preparing their classroom materials and teachers' guides, they discovered that "seeing" isn't always "observing." In one third-grade class, students tried to chill water with crushed ice. Their observations were intended to lead them to conclude that "there is a minimum temperature below which an ice-water mixture will not go, regardless of the quantity of ice and snow added to it" (p. 27). Despite several opportunities to observe that this was the case, the children persisted in thinking that the temperature would drop as more snow or ice was added. It took multiple experiences before children began to accept the evidence gathered from their experiments and to interpret that evidence so as to change their original inferences.

The open-mindedness crucial to science obviously takes practice. In another ESS activity, children observed what happened when they put various objects on ice. Ice cubes and small objects such as pennies, chalk, paper clips, washers, and wooden cubes were distributed, and children were asked to observe what happened when these objects were placed on an ice cube. The teacher helped the children organize their observations as follows:

Didn't Sink In	Sank in a Little	Sank in a Lot
pieces of candle	wood	money
eraser (rubber)	stone	paper clips
pieces of chalk		thumbtacks
		washers

In their Journals*, the children speculated about the reasons for these differences—they made inferences—and then planned further experiments to see if their inferences were supported.

Other simple Observation and Inference* activities in science include having the teacher or a student perform an activity while the other students observe carefully. For instance, the demonstrator holds up two white envelopes of equal size. The first envelope is placed against the cabinet and falls to the floor. The second envelope is placed against the cabinet and stays put. Once the observation period ends, children write down and discuss three or four observations. Part of the discussion is separating statements of inference such as "There is glue on one envelope" from statements of observation such as "One envelope is still on the cabinet." Once the class establishes a set of observations, they begin to construct hypotheses or inferences that could explain the observations. Depending on the time available, the teacher can either ask children to create envelopes that will behave as the ones in the demonstration or allow them to suggest further tests of inferences. They may want to see if the "sticking" envelope will also adhere to a wooden cabinet, or they may want to compare the weights of each envelope. None of the student tests should permit opening or destroying the envelopes.

Summary

Any number of similar activities can be constructed to help children develop their ability to make the kind of careful observations and supported inferences basic to understanding phenomena. Sometimes teachers introduce these activities in Focus Lessons* in preparation for a task students want to accomplish or to initiate a new theme. Sharing the short amusing book *Dr. Xargle's Book of Earthlets* can introduce (or review) the distinction. This book has a creature, Dr. Xargle, teaching a class (presumably of other creatures) all about the nature of Earthlets. As the teacher reads the book, students use a Two-Column Chart* (or T-Chart) having a left-hand "Observations" column and a right-hand "Inferences" column to jot down their ideas expressed in the book—for example, that "Earthelets are patted and squeezed" (observation) and "Earthlets are patted and squeezed so they won't explode" (inference). Discussion around the students' responses fosters the understandings.

    Another example comes from a fourth-grade classroom where the teacher hung several birdfeeders outside the classroom window. She also made a journal labeled "Bird Observation Journal," and hung it by the window. As children wrote in the journal and talked in class meetings, they learned different ways of "looking closely," and observation/inference activities became an important part of the ongoing theme. For instance, children decided that their observations might be more accurate if two people watched the same event or if the observer talked into a tape recorder or used a video camera. In addition, they created a site map to help locate observations and created a set of abbreviations to use when recording observations. In these ways, observation and inference become techniques that allow children to accomplish their own inquiry goals, although in these two examples, asking children to draw their observations would also be a good idea. Encouraging children to "look closely" and transfer their observations by drawing the details also facilitates observation skills, which then aids them in making sense of inferences.

Willis (2002)

Harvey (1998); Reddy et al. (1998)

Sedgwick (2002)

Graphic Organizers*

Graphic Organizers* are visual displays that enable children to organize and represent meanings, ideas, and concepts on a topic, especially while they are engaged in Reflective, Disciplined Inquiry*. They can be used for many purposes: to activate prior knowledge on a topic to be studied or read about and then to show new concepts, connections, or vocabulary that developed as a result of an investigation on that topic; to depict (as a prewriting experience) the meanings or ideas to be included in a piece of writing; to share ideas on a topic or domain in small-group or whole-class discussions to gain feedback; or to present (or "publish") the findings of a systematic study or analysis done in an inquiry. Just as they reflect different purposes, Graphic Organizers* can also take on different forms. We cover four types: Semantic Maps*, K-W-L*, Comparison Charts*, and Venn Diagrams* and Two/Three-Column Charts*.

    Although Graphic Organizers* can be realized by various forms and may fulfill various purposes, all activities involving Graphic Organizers* have similar features: They all elicit children's own ideas, wordings, and meanings so that children are put into the center of their own learning. They frequently also provide a means for children to share and build on each other's ideas. Hearing others' ideas fosters divergent thinking, and children's own schemas on a topic are likely to be modified or altered. Thus, Graphic

See Tierney & Readence (2000) for another discussion of Graphic Organizers*.

Organizers* demonstrate ways to depict knowledge already acquired and to show directions to new learning.

Semantic Maps*

Semantic Maps* encourage children to think about what they already know and then try to build on and extend that knowledge. Semantic Maps* also are organized in ways that call attention to the relationship between ideas of particular topics by categorizing and connecting wordings, pictures, or concepts. As indicated, Semantic Maps* can also include pictures for they depict meanings. (More about pictures at the end of this section.)

Semantic Maps* were used in Chapter 1 to illustrate schemas—our mental models of our knowledge—and to depict how Sara developed a schema of the domain of spiders. The WEBs depicted in Chapter 4 are also types of Semantic Maps*. To illustrate how Semantic Maps* can be demonstrated in the classroom, let's recall Sara's increasingly complex understanding of the domain for "spider" (in Chapter 1) and the way her teacher built on that understanding by planning a thematic unit on BUGS (in Chapter 3). During the unit, Sara's teacher asked the children to brainstorm about what they know about spiders. As they jotted down ideas, the teacher encouraged them to try to list those words that seemed to go together. (Or before their brainstorming, the teacher could have suggested some general categories—what spiders look like, what they do, and where they are found.) Then, on the board or a large sheet of chart paper, the teacher began listing the children's ideas about spiders.

Discussion about words and their categories is one of the most valuable aspects of developing a Semantic Map* while children verbalize, and perhaps argue about, their understanding of already existing schemas. Once the children's categories have been listed on the Semantic Map*, the teacher can help them find labels for the categories. Figure 7.6 illustrates the type of Semantic Map* that can result. Notice that many of the terms may have been contributed by children who had been doing a lot of reading and writing about spiders.

Semantic Maps* are also called Concept Maps.

Bromley et al. (1995); Harvey (1998); Harvey & Goudvis (2000); Moline (1996); Wilhelm (2004)

Semantic Maps* focus on relationships between ideas and concepts.

See also Revel-Wood (1988) for a good classroom example of Semantic Maps* and Kress et al. (2001) for ones in science classrooms.

figure **7.6**
A Semantic Map* on Spiders

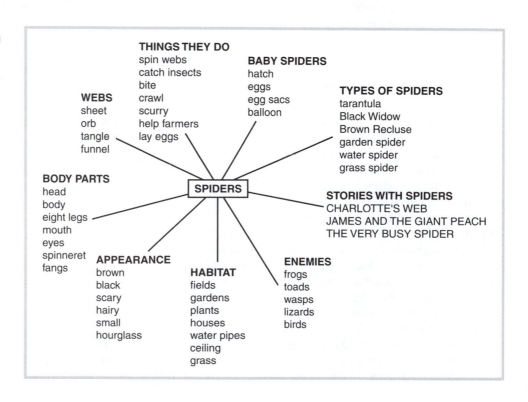

Semantic Maps* can be developed before children start a study, perhaps when they begin some initial observations of some spiders that have been brought into the classroom or seen at a local zoo. Following the discussion of the first map, children engage in some individual research and reading with the goal of enlarging and extending the original map. They then construct a second map and compare the new information they have been able to add. Or instead of writing ideas directly on the board or paper, the children can place them on brainstorming cards or strips and then organize them on a bulletin board with thumbtacks or on a portion of the board with masking tape "loops." As children study the topic, they write down another idea and decide where it should be placed on the map. The advantage of the strips is that children can physically place an idea in one category and then move it if they decide that it is best listed under a different, or new, category. Through the process, the teacher helps children find or change labels for existing categories and to distinguish subtle differences in categories and classes. Thus, the use of strips enables children to construct an ongoing Semantic Map* in a dynamic way. (They also serve as a spelling resource for students' writing during the unit.)

The finished map represents a summary of prior and new information.

Semantic Maps* can be constructed in terms of questions or key themes to be considered in an inquiry. In the CREATING COMMUNITIES thematic unit, small groups are studying different animal communities (e.g., ants, bees, gorillas, chimpanzees, wolves, whales, and dolphins). In a whole-class brainstorming session, children have identified six major questions about the animals to guide their inquiries: What do they look like? How they behave or act? Where/how do they live? What do they eat? Who eats them? Interesting facts? Figure 7.7 shows the type of Semantic Map* the teacher developed for the groups.

Ongoing, dynamic Semantic Maps* support the knowledge building during inquiry projects in a unit.

Children are asked to tell, or write individually, what they think they already know regarding each question. New information will be added as children read independently a range of books and view websites on the topic (see materials listed on the WEB in Chapter 4) to see what else they can find out about these animal communities. The teacher also urges them to be on the lookout for new questions to consider, suggesting that they can staple on a new page for such questions and new information. Children know that following their reading they will come back to the Semantic Map* to confirm or refine their original ideas and to add new information that they have found. During their reading, they may also jot down key facts or ideas, and maybe also pictures, in their Sketchbook Journals*.

figure 7.7
Animal Community Semantic Map

When the group comes together following their reading, they reexamine each question. First, they discuss their original ideas and determine if these were confirmed or contradicted by their reading. If confirmed, a star or asterisk is placed by that line. Using a marker of a different color helps children recognize the difference between prior knowledge and new information. If an original idea was a misconception, it is crossed out. Then new information gained from the reading is added under each question. Other questions (e.g., What are similarities among the animals?) are also considered as the small groups share with each other. The discussion surrounding the Semantic Map* activity is important. Children may have to go back to the books or websites they have used to support their points of view. They must verbalize and clarify important understandings in the process of negotiating and constructing the map.

Semantic Maps* can be used for a range of purposes. For example, they can be used to document and organize children's observations of snails or to note the transformations involved in a scientific experiment. They can depict various time lines—the major events in the life of a historical figure or in a particular historical period. They can be used as a prewriting experience or as a publication of a small group's (or an individual's) study of a topic. For example, Figure 7.8 shows Latisha's map on creatures that are partners or that help each other (see Latisha's illustrated draft in Chapter 8). A Semantic Map* can be constructed for one book or for a general topic on which information is acquired through reading many books or through other sources such as careful observation and interviews with experts. Semantic Maps* can also be completed for fictional stories or books in which characters, motives, actions, and outcomes are depicted.

As noted earlier, Semantic Maps* can also consist either entirely of pictures or a combination of words and pictures. For young children, struggling readers and writers, and second-language learners, pictures in Semantic Maps* offer anchors of meanings to talk about and to further develop. For example, the major events of a story (or chapter) can be depicted by a series of pictures with lines or arrows to show their sequence. Students can also add labels or captions to these pictures. Thus, the pictures

Bromley et al. (1995); Daniels & Zemelman (2004); Lehrer & Schauble (2002); Moline (1996)

Goldberg (1997); Hendrick (1997); Johnson (1997); Sedgwick (2002)

figure **7.8**

Latisha's Semantic Web

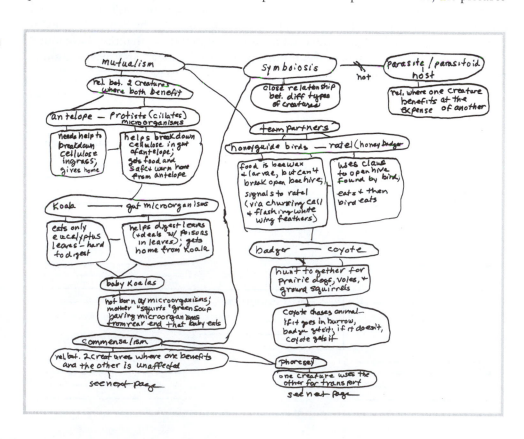

help children visualize a story read or a story to be written. Both comprehension and composing processes can be fostered. Semantic Maps* with pictures can be used across the curriculum: Students can illustrate math story problems or depict mathematical relations; they can show time lines of the growth of a plant or the changes from caterpillar to butterfly (see the example in Chapter 6); they can show the parts of spiders, flowers, scientific apparatus (with labels) to depict part–whole relationships (see again Chapter 6); and so forth.

K-W-L*

Developed by Ogle to help teachers focus on the experiences readers bring to text, K-W-L* began as a framework for actively engaging readers with informational texts. Prior to reading about a particular topic, the blackboard or a sheet of paper is divided into three columns headed "What We Know," "What We Want to Find Out," and "What We Learned and Still Need to Learn." As children brainstorm all the things they already know about the topic, teachers might ask, "Where did you learn that?" or "How could you prove that?" In general, though, all contributions offered by children are accepted for they will have opportunities to verify any initial misconceptions or misunderstandings.

Once children have listed what they know about a topic, they will want to consider what type of information they think they will find as they read. As they list their ideas, the teacher can help them categorize the information in broad subtopics similar to the approach described for Semantic Maps*.

Because this first part of K-W-L* should result in rich discussion and argument, it is likely that individual interests and questions about the topic will arise for each child. Thus, the second step, "What We Want to Find Out," should help each child identify those questions and interests that will be brought to their individual reading and record their questions on individual K-W-L* sheets. The questions help guide each child's reading and then provide a focus for filling in the third column, "What We Learned and Still Need to Know."

Often teachers use the K-W-L* strategy to launch inquiry projects—see Figure 7.2 and the earlier discussion of the Launching Phase of the inquiry process. Thus, here students are not restricted to one book but would consider multiple sources in inquiries. Specifying those resources has led to some additions to the K-W-L* scheme. Sometimes it gets modified to K-W-W-L, where the extra "W" represents "Where can I learn this?", or an extra "H" (K-W-H-L) to signify the "How am I going to learn?" or "How can I learn?". When the K-W-L* is used in inquiry projects, students' questions are grouped and individual students are asked their preference for investigation. The teacher then tries to match student interest with questions to be explored. (See this process under Launching Phase.)

K-W-L* is also equally effective when they are considering other nonprint sources—hands-on explorations, observations, surveys and interviews, historical photographs, websites, and so forth. The technique is, thus, well suited for use by small groups or an entire class and allows children to explore a variety of reading materials on a particular topic. In some classes, too, teachers use K-W-L* charts a bit differently. For a science workshop, for instance, one class substitutes *Wonder* for *Want to Know,* because *wonder* better conveys the attitude toward scientific inquiry the teacher encourages. In this class, too, children keep individual K-W-L* charts. When they work on individual or small-group projects, they first list five things they already know about a topic and five things they wonder about the topic. After reading, listening to a presentation, or conducting an experiment, they fill in the Learn column. The completion of the "L" can also be done at the end of in-depth inquiry projects—during the Reflecting Phase (see Figure 7.2). Also, another extra "Q" may be included (K-W-L-Q) to consider "What new questions do I know?".

Ogle (1986); Harvey (1998); Tierney & Readance (2000)

K-W-Ls* can help launch inquiry projects.

Bromley et al. (1995); Bryan (1998); Wood & Dickinson (2000)

Allen (2000)

Comparison Charts*

Comparison Charts* allow children to compare and contrast ideas and information.

Comparison Charts* also involve examinations of likenesses and differences among ideas, events, characteristics, and so forth. Comparison Charts* may take a number of forms. Sometimes they may be used to focus characters, events, motifs, and themes within a single story or novel or the characteristics, features, and attributes in informational materials. At other times, they can be useful in comparing books, events, or properties within a given theme. Comparison Charts* give children opportunities to work individually with texts and then to pool and share details of their reading with their peers in a small group or with the whole class. Comparison Charts* can also give teachers a focus for looking at theme, story structure, character development, or other important features or concepts in a given work.

Levin (1993)

Figure 7.9 is an example of a Comparison Chart* that was filled in by five primary children. They first heard their teacher read *Pearl Moscowitz's Last Stand*, a story about taking political action in an urban neighborhood. The class had thoroughly enjoyed Pearl and the way new neighbors and different cultures merged on her block. They particularly liked the ways in which Pearl dealt with the electrician who came to cut down her tree. They talked about what makes people neighbors and some of the ways that neighbors can work together to protect their neighborhood. Because she wanted them to see other ways of being neighborly, and other challenges that neighbors sometimes

Mitchell (1993)

face, their teacher also read them *Uncle Jed's Barbershop*. Uncle Jed and his neighbors—mostly black sharecroppers—lived in the segregated South in the 1920s. There was much need, and Uncle Jed was always willing to help. The children were shocked by the local doctor's refusal to treat Uncle Jed's niece, Sarah Jean, and had many questions about the "whites only" policy in the hospital. When their teacher told them the same had been the case even when she was a little girl, they wanted to know how old she had been when things changed. The teacher wrote *rights* on the board and talked about some of the rights people were supposed to share. This conversation carried over

Blumberg (1996)

into their library period. As a result, the librarian shared *Bloomers!* with the class. Now they had another kind of *right* to think about. Their teacher suggested that it might help to organize some of their ideas if someone would work on a Comparison Chart*.

figure 7.9

A Comparison Chart*
for Three Books

	Problem	Solution	Right	Responsibility
UNCLE JED'S BARBERSHOP	Uncle Jed wants a barbershop.	He saves and saves.	Right to work.	Work hard and save.
	Sarah Jean needs an operation.	He gives her his money.	Right to be cared for when you are sick.	Take care of people when you can.
	Uncle Jed lost all his money.	He saves and saves and finally gets his barbershop. His dream came true.	Right to have your money safe in a bank.	Help people who *really* need it.
PEARL MOSCOWITZ'S LAST STAND	The city wants to cut down the last gingko tree on Pearl's block.	She tries to stop him from cutting down the tree.	Right to have a say in what happens where you live.	To take care of your neighborhood.
		She chains herself to the tree until the mayor listens, and she keeps the tree and gets more trees.	Right to have a mayor listen to you.	To have good reasons.
BLOOMERS!	Women's clothes were very uncomfortable. They made it hard for women to do their work.	Women made a new kind of clothes, with pants.	Right to wear what you want.	
	Some women wanted to wear different clothes.	Some worked for other changes for women: voting and traveling.	Right to vote and be equal.	You should vote.

The teacher drew the chart on a large sheet of construction paper and discussed the categories with one group of children. These categories provided them with a focus for problem solving and discussion that centered on the three books. They talked about the three stories and noted details that were alike and different and spent some time talking about the illustrations. They noted stylistic matters; for example, that in two of the books the illustrators drew cartoonlike or stylistic figures, while in *Uncle Jed's Barbershop,* the illustrations were more realistic. They also talked about the kinds of rules that caused problems in each book. The chart thus served as a springboard for a rich and lengthy discussion about characteristics of the books. When it came time to fill in the chart, they were able to draw on each text for specific words as well as ideas about the rights and responsibilities of neighbors.

Children are also quite capable of discovering their own categories. Again, this activity provides a focus for discussion of the many elements in books or other resources. As with the other types of Graphic Organizers*, the finished chart is only a representation of some of the findings of children's study and analysis; it provides a means and a stepping-stone to writing and talking about findings with others. Therefore, charts frequently serve as a summary of a range of reading transactions children may have had in reading books. The charts are also important prewriting experiences because many of their categories are incorporated into the stories or reports that individual children write. In a third/fourth-grade classroom, for example, a group of children read four "inchling" stories—folktales that center on the tiny size of the main character. Following their reading, each child shared his or her particular story with the group. There was much discussion of themes, events, and other details as the children attempted to choose categories that would capture the features of all or most of their books and then to decide on labels for these categories. Eventually they decided on thirteen: book title, country (of the folktale's origin), magic object, wishes, sacrifices, where they (the parents) worked and what they worked for, where they went and why, size (of the tiny character), what they took (on their journey), Japanese words, whom they met on their journey, how they got the child, and characters. Once the categories were named, the children wrote the details from each book on pieces of paper and glued them on an appropriately labeled piece of chart paper. (See Figure 7.10.)

> Children become more critical readers when they develop their own categories.

figure **7.10**

A Comparison Chart*
for "Inchling" Stories

Following the completion of a Comparison Chart*, many children choose to write their own stories or to illustrate certain events in the books studied. After a study of informational texts, children may write a report on a specific animal or phenomenon that has been included on a Comparison Chart*. A third-grade class read many books on dinosaurs as part of a DISAPPEARING ACTS thematic unit. Comparison Charts* were constructed by small groups to compare dinosaur characteristics such as habitual behavior or physical features. Included in the chart was a category listing other animals that lived at the same time. Several children became interested in one of these animals, the mammoth, and did more research on it. One child wrote a report on her findings, one wrote a cartoonlike saga featuring Wild Willy Mammoth (influenced by Aliki's *Wild and Woolly Mammoths*), and another child (using ideas from Joanna Cole's *Evolution*) constructed his own plaster fossil of a mammoth. In a first-grade unit on FLIGHT, children in a small group completed a Comparison Chart* on various ducks, using the following simple categories: type of duck, looks, home, food, and habits. After they finished the chart, each child illustrated one of the ducks and wrote a brief description of it.

Children can also include categories about illustrations—how they were done (media), whether they were realistic or abstract, and the ideologies they may depict, and so on. In addition, Comparison Charts* can synthesize and organize information from a range of sources—besides books, hands-on explorations, observations, historical photographs, websites, and so forth. These charts can even be used to organize ideas via each source, making explicit any different or conflicting information or perspective and also facilitating the citing of sources.

Venn Diagrams* and Two/Three-Column Charts*

This set of Graphic Organizers* also organizes information. The Venn Diagram* is usually depicted as three overlapping circles. In the nonoverlapped space in the two outer circles, students note the differences between two animals, countries, machines, historical persons, stories on the same theme, information books on the same topic, and so forth. Then in the space in the middle—the area of circle overlap—similarities are noted. In practice, such diagrams are useful only if a few items of similarity and difference are being identified. That is, unless very large circles are used, students sometimes find it hard to write small enough to list items (especially in the middle, overlapping space for jotting down similarities).

Two other types of charts—the Two- and Three-Column Charts*—overcome this space restriction and are, therefore, easier to use to categorize different ideas or information. The Two-Column Chart*, also called a "T-Chart," is where students make various distinctions or contrasts, some of which have already been mentioned under the Inquiry Phases section. There are many possibilities: What I Know/What I Wonder; Questions/Answers; Topic/Details; Text Meanings/Picture Meanings; Major Text Ideas/Minor Text Ideas; Big Questions/Small Questions; Claim or Conclusion/Evidence; What's Interesting/What's Important; and so forth. Thus, these could be used across the curriculum and in almost all of the inquiry phases. One column could be used for pictures or other images. For example, in math, students might have one column for Calculations or a Story Problem and Pictures in the other column illustrating the number operations or details of the story problem. In science, one column could describe procedures of an experiment, with the second column illustrating the major steps. Because students are being more conscious about what should go in each column, such charts guide their understandings in inquiry. Moreover, because students tend to put down ideas in their own words or voice in these charts, the problem of plagiarism during writing up their investigations is less likely. (See the T-Chart under the Observation/Inference* section in this chapter.)

As it implies, the Three-Column Chart* asks for three distinctions or contrasts. One example was illustrated under the Literature Response Groups* section. Often students

---

Charts provide a focus or structure for further writing.

Aliki (1977); Cole (1987)

Allen (2000); Tierney & Readance (2000)

Bromley et al. (1995); Daniels & Zemelman (2004)

Harvey (1998); Harvey & Goudvis (2000); Tierney & Readance (2000)

who, in previous instruction, have been required only to provide literal summaries of text have difficulty understanding what is meant by "response." Thus, a Three-Column Chart* having columns such as Facts/Questions/Response or Topic/Details/Response helps students to integrate information but also offers a personal response. Another way such a chart might be utilized would be for students to expand the Claim or Conclusion/Evidence T-Chart listed previously by adding a Resource column where students would record the relevant book or source they used in their inquiries. Or students might have one column that expresses a written Response, a second that includes one or two significant or important Quotes, and a third that depicts a Picture/Symbol.

Teachers could provide a few examples of how these latter two types of charts might be used in the classroom in Focus Lessons* and then be open for students to create new ones that seem relevant and useful in their ongoing endeavors. Teachers might keep a list of possibilities and then add ones that students have developed for reference by the class.

Literacy Activities and Experiences

Reading Activities and Experiences

This section describes various activities or experiences related to reading. It is important to recall that although reading is the focus here, in an integrated language classroom reading is integrated with writing, speaking, and listening, and it occurs for many purposes across the curriculum. In addition, because most texts are multimodal, including both written messages and images, how images might be incorporated into literacy experiences is addressed.

Reading Aloud*

Reading Aloud* to children is a necessary component in integrated language classrooms. Most teachers have times when they read to the whole class; they may also read aloud to small groups during the day. Whole-class read-alouds contribute to classroom community, all class participants sharing certain texts together as a common experience. Reading Aloud* should occur at all grades, even in the departmentalized middle school grades. In the latter case, teachers may only read aloud on certain days of a week or put aside so many minutes to read. Older struggling readers especially need to hear the linguistic patterns and rhythms of different genres and author styles that the read-aloud activity offers.

Books should be selected according to children's interests and developmental background and also to stretch their imagination, extend and spark new interests, foster an awareness of various genres, and develop an appreciation of fine writing and illustration. Teachers who want help in selecting quality literature can turn to their librarian for advice or to award lists such as the Newbery and Caldecott winners and honor books. *Booklist* and *The Horn Book* (see Chapter 3) only review books that they recommend for children and star those they judge to be outstanding. Three other professional journals—*Language Arts, Social Education,* and *Science Teacher*—publish a yearly list of books that are named as outstanding in the fields of language arts, social studies, and science.

Enthusiasm for the selected book, story, poem, and so on is the first ingredient of good Reading Aloud*. Teachers should always read the text ahead of time so that they are aware of its content and so that their reading is smooth and fluent. A teacher's reading delivery depends on the text being read and that teacher's own style. For example, some teachers are good at doing character voices, sound effects, and physical gestures but children can also be enthralled by the quiet warmth of a gentler voice.

Reading Aloud* really matters!

Calkins (2001); Duke & Bennett-Armistead (2003); Fisher & Medvic (2003); Hahn (2002); Tunnell & Jacobs (1989)

See also Huck & Kiefer (2004)

Reading Aloud* seems to work best when children are gathered on a rug or special place close to the teacher. Reading picture books with the book at shoulder level, pages facing the children at their eye level, gives them plenty of time to look at the illustrations and enables them to enter the visual as well as the verbal world of the book. Nonfiction books that include pictures or other visual images—diagrams, graphs, and so forth—should also be shared in a similar way.

Books or other texts can be introduced in various ways: by a brief discussion about the author or illustrator; by asking children to predict what the story or text is about by examining the cover and interpreting the title; by linking the topic, theme, author, or illustrator to other books children may know; and so forth. With chapter books, teachers can have children discuss the progress of the book so far and consider what is likely to occur next.

Hahn (2002)

Teachers may also plan for places in the text to stop during reading (using small Post-it Notes as reminders) to encourage children's comments or questions about what has been read or to foster predictions about what is yet to be read. It is not a good idea to ask too many questions, and the kinds of questions used should be those that help children make their own discoveries. (See the discourse excerpts in Chapter 2.) Providing spaces for students' initiations of their own comments or questions promotes collaborative dialogic response and inquiry. These spaces for student response makes the Reading-Aloud routine a culturally responsive one—they can contribute their own "ways with words" and cultural perspectives. Students should feel comfortable about initiating discussion, and this practice might have to be more explicitly encouraged if students are only familiar with teacher-controlled IRE discourse patterns during read-aloud sessions.

See Pappas & Zecker (2001a, 2001b) for examples of urban teachers creating collaborative read-alouds.

Heath (1983); Ladson-Billings (1994); Moll (1992); Nieto (2000)

Questions to make children aware of the craft of writing should also be considered. Questions can be posed to get children to recognize the power of particular words or phrases used by the author—how they sound, how they help paint a picture, and how they ask and answer certain questions about the author. We want children to appreciate authors' choices so that they become reflective of their own choices in their writing. Many children like to sketch and/or write in their Sketchbook Journals* during the read-aloud time.

Although most read-alouds should be collaborative—where both student and teacher voices can be heard—these occasions also provide scaffolding of reading/viewing processes. That is, sometimes teachers might read texts as "think-alouds." Here they read and then talk aloud to students of their ongoing transactions with text—their interpretations or questions. These thinking-aloud strategies would also incorporate how they make sense of the images and how these meanings are connected to those expressed in the text. All genres should be shared in this way, especially those that students may be using in their inquiry projects, because different genres having different types of images would invoke different transactions. (See Chapter 6 for a review of the range of transactions possible.) Excerpts from longer texts may be used for this purpose.

Daniels & Zemelman (2004)

See Wilhelm (2001) for a repertoire of think-aloud strategies.

After they have finished reading, children may want to discuss the book by relating ideas in the text to their own experiences or to other texts. Sometimes, depending on the book, it is useful to give children time to think and ponder about ideas in the text and then to go back and reread particular passages either at the end of a Reading Aloud* session or later in the day. It is important to note, however, that not all texts have to be discussed to be enjoyed, understood, or appreciated. It is also a good idea to frequently read whole texts aloud more than once; often it is during the second or third reading of a book that the most sensitive responses are brought to the surface. This practice also encourages favorites, making certain books "friends" for life.

Holdaway (1979)

Retellings*

Bauer (1993); Tierney & Readance (2000)

The most important aspect to keep in mind in using Retellings* in the classroom is authenticity. Retelling a story or nonfictional text should have purpose, otherwise it is just a mindless, literal summary to people who already know the text. However, when students use Retellings* to share the major ideas in a set of books on a theme that have been read by members in a Literature Response Group* (that is, where each student reads his or her book on a theme), then students have reasons for providing the "gist" of each book they are studying. Another example might be when different small groups have investigated a separate community animal (ants, bees, gorillas, whales, etc.—see the example under Semantic Maps*) and create jigsaw groups, with each group having a representative from each small group, to identify what similarities might exist among all of the community animals.

Harvey (1998); Harvey & Goudvis (2000)

Retellings* can also be a means to "publish" the findings of inquiries. Students who have been studying various inventors or important people in a particular historical period, and so forth, may use Retellings* as panel members or news reporters to share the ideas they have gleaned from their inquiries. In doing so, students are considering the *role* they are playing, the *audience* to whom they are speaking, the *format* or genre they are using, and the *topic* they are covering. This entails purposeful synthesizing for authentic purposes.

See Daniels & Zemelman (2004) for more retelling experiences for older elementary and middle school students.

Storytelling is also a type of Retellings* and an alternative to Reading Aloud*. An art form that needs to be valued and perpetuated, storytelling by teachers provides opportunities for more intimate rapport with children because no book separates the teacher and the audience. It isn't necessary to memorize stories to be a good storyteller, but careful planning is essential. The teacher needs to be familiar with the plot, the characters, and the "flavor" of the book's language. If certain chants or refrains are repeated in the text, those should be memorized. Stories such as *The Magic Porridge Pot* and *The Teeny Tiny Woman* are good for younger children. The use of simple props or visual aids (e.g., a flannel board or puppets) can help teachers recall the story's key elements, and it encourages children to want to retell and reenact their own versions of the story. Bryan's West Indian story *The Cat's Purr* is a favorite of middle elementary children (seven- to nine-year-olds). Even older fifth through eighth graders, who might be reading short stories in anthologies or books such as *Seedfolks,* in which each chapter describes a particular person from a different cultural background who contributes or is somehow involved in a community garden, also enjoy hearing a story told. As teachers demonstrate such a skill, students can also take their turns in providing a storytelling. We know of a second-grade classroom that has one day a week where students run the Reading Aloud* session. They can either read a book to the class or may provide a storytelling of a favorite book. Whole-school storytelling festivals also support such experiences.

Galdone (1976, 1984)

Bryan (1985)

Fleischman (1997)

Sustained Silent Reading (SSR)*

Sustained Silent Reading (SSR)*, sometimes also called USSR (Uninterrupted Sustained Silent Reading) or DEAR (Drop Everything And Read), is simply periods of quiet time set aside during the day when children read books of their own choosing. Usually, an SSR* period is initially ten minutes or so and then gradually lengthened. In many upper-elementary classes, forty-five-minute or longer periods may occur. In some schools, everyone (adults and visitors included) picks up a book and reads. The rationale for SSR* is to demonstrate to children that adults who are important to them also enjoy reading. Thus, SSR* fosters fluency by giving children opportunities to practice reading while it also encourages the joy of reading.

Beers (2003); Tierney & Readance (2000)

SSR* for younger elementary children may involve looking at the pages and softly telling (or "pretend reading") their own versions of books or quietly reading aloud as they read to themselves. The emphasis should always be on the enjoyment of reading. A wide variety of reading materials of varied reading levels and interests are essential. In the beginning, especially for children who are unfamiliar with SSR* time, teachers may have to guide children to books of interest or remind them to think ahead about what they will be reading during SSR* so that they don't spend a lot of time just finding

SSR* fosters the enjoyment of reading.

something to read. A timer of some sort can also be used in the beginning to mark the end of the SSR* period and to congratulate children on their capability to sustain a certain number of minutes of reading.

Beers (2003)

For upper grade and middle school classrooms that have departmentalized organizations and have classes that are only forty-five to fifty minutes long, it is easy to "skip" SSR*. However, finding even ten to fifteen minutes a day or several days (that students can count on) is important for all students, but especially to struggling readers who might have less opportunities or inclinations to read. However, as they see their peers engaged in books and rumors spread about particular "good" books, they also get "hooked."

Sometimes teachers might have two SSR* periods—one where students can read anything and one where they read anything that is related to the unit theme. In some urban schools we know, where students stand in line to use the restrooms, teachers bring a crate of books along and students choose a book to read while they wait their turn. Thus, teachers can be quite creative in finding time for SSR*.

Buddy Reading*

Buddy Reading* is also sometimes called Partner Reading.

Calkins (2001)

Many teachers implement Buddy Reading* as an alternative to SSR*. Buddy Reading* acknowledges the social nature of reading by having children pair up, each with a book of their own choosing, to read to their partner. Children take turns reading different books or pages of the same book. The books can be of any genre and buddies may read all of the text or just excerpts. Moreover, "reading" the pictures should also be part of the experience—see the Introduction Chapter where kindergarten buddies explored the pictures in pop-up books.

See Mossip (1985) for an example of Buddy Reading* by children of different ages.

Samway, Whang, & Pippitt (1995)

Buddies do not have to be at the same reading level because they are selecting their own material. Buddy Reading* can occur within one classroom or children from different grade levels can read together. When older elementary children, who might be reluctant or less able readers, are paired with younger children, they have good reasons to practice the books they are to share. Fluency and self-confidence as readers are fostered. Older children also frequently enjoy experiences of Retellings* where partners tell each other a recent or favorite book. Making and sharing Big Books* with younger children is another feature that can be incorporated in a Buddy Reading* program.

Book Talks*

Bauer (1993); Calkins (2001); Huck & Kiefer (2004)

Book Talks* are great ways to publicize good books. Frequently teachers schedule Book Talk* time right after SSR*. It is important, however, for teachers to model or demonstrate this activity for children, perhaps as they highlight books that will be part of a thematic unit. The first few pages can be read or an amusing or exciting part recounted. Assuming the role of one of the characters is another Book Talk* technique. Excerpts from several novels or dust jacket summaries can be offered. Special objects that are important elements of stories (a pebble in *Sylvester and the Magic Pebble,* an old key in *The Secret Garden,* or a peach pit in *James and the Giant Peach)* can serve as foci for Book Talks*.

Steig (1979); Burnett (1962); Dahl (1961)

Book Talks* can be about books from a wide range of genres.

Duke & Bennett-Armstead (2003)

Aliki (1988)

Cole (1986)

Freedman (1987)

Book Talks* should not be limited to fiction. Mentioning all the experts involved in finding and digging up dinosaurs—paleontologists, geologists, draftsmen, workers, photographers, and specialists—and what they do may be a selling point for Aliki's *Digging up Dinosaurs.* Or showing the page where the magic school bus rises into the clouds in Cole's *The Magic School Bus at the Waterworks* may draw children to read and find out about water facts. Sharing some of the photographs in Freedman's *Lincoln: A Photobiography* or relating some of the things about Lincoln in the book that were interesting to the teacher may be ways this book might be "sold." Children quickly pick up on these techniques and develop their own ways of "selling" books. It is hard to resist when a friend says, "This is the best book I ever read!" or "This was so interesting, I couldn't put it down!"

Frequently, teachers do short Book Talks* in preparation to students choosing books for Literature Response Books* where small groups of children read and discuss a book. Often these books may be around a theme—see the "outsiders" books talked about in the Introduction Chapter. The teacher does a brief Book Talk* for each book so students know what books are available.

Samway & Whang (1996)

*Literature Response Groups**

Literature Response Groups* (often called Literature Circles or Book Clubs) are opportunities for a small group to discuss books in depth with one another. At times teachers will ask children to self-select into discussion groups based on books to be read as an exploration of a theme. Frequently, however, these groups are organized and run by the children themselves because they have all read the same book and want to talk about it. Or they may be reading books on a common topic or from a common genre or tackling similar problems in projects in a thematic unit. They may post an announcement on the Message Board* asking for interested participants. Many teachers set some time aside in integrated work time on certain days for such group interactions so that they themselves can periodically sit in on the discussions. When a teacher joins in as a member of a Literature Response Group*, the teacher works hard at being a participant, not as someone who asks all the questions or directs and controls the discussion.

The way the teacher handles discussion at Reading Aloud* sessions provides a framework that children can adopt in their own Literature Response Groups*. In the beginning of the year, teachers can sit in on the Literature Response Groups* more frequently and model ways to phrase questions or comments about texts so that children get ideas about the kinds of transactions possible. Some teachers begin with roles for the members of groups (e.g., Connector, Questioner, Passage Master, Vocabulary Enricher, Illustrator, and so forth). Although those who suggest using them argue that they should be employed only temporarily, we have found that most of the time such roles do not contribute to good discussion. That is, students go around the group just contributing what they were supposed to contribute, but no real conversations occurs. Instead, helping students to prepare their own responses ahead of time and supporting them in the kinds of "rules" of discussion that will facilitate good discussion (e.g., being respectful to others' ideas, not hogging the conversation, piggybacking on others' ideas, etc.) often results in successful talk. For those students who may be new to Literature Response Groups*, having the whole class set up the rules and responsibilities ahead of time and having a series of debriefings on how things went, including the content and the process of the group discussions, are useful.

Thus, children should be encouraged to develop their own questions for Literature Response Groups*. Most teachers ask children to come to Literature Response Groups* prepared, with their Journals* (a particular response Journal* just for this discussion group routine) or Sketchbook Journals* in hand. They have used these Journals*—writings and drawings—to muse about personal reactions, to wonder about events, themes, and ideas in a book, or to note favorite passages and descriptions. Chambers suggests that in discussions responses to books often fall into three categories: Readers share enthusiasms, puzzles or difficulties, and connections or patterns. These "three sharings" could be used as a framework for journal writing and for beginning discussions. Many teachers encourage children to mark important places in their books with stick-on notes as they read. These flags mark passages that they want to return to later to think about more carefully. This may have been a place in the book that was particularly moving or exciting or a place where they got confused. These flags might also mark places where they noticed something special about the author's writing or where they had questions about the author's perspective or point of view.

Literature Response Groups*, Literature Circles, and Book Clubs bring children together to talk about books.

See Daniels (2002); Daniels & Zemelman (2004); Hill et al. (1995); Raphael et al. (2002); Samway & Whang (1996); and Short & Pierce (1998) for descriptions of book discussion groups.

Teachers can demonstrate ways in which readers talk about books during read-aloud time.

Be careful about roles.

Sketchbook Journals* and Book Response Journals* are a source for discussion questions.

Chambers (1996)

Focus Lessons* can help prepare children to conduct their own discussions.

Unsworth (2001); Wilhelm (2004)

Harvey (1998)

Questions in Literature Response Groups* often center on the craft of writing fiction or information books.

Calkins (2001); Carroll (2004); Samway & Whang (1996)

Gauch (1975)

Teachers can conduct Focus Lessons* on what that preparation for response groups might consist of. They can suggest that children first ask themselves personal, experiential questions about the book at hand: What stands out for me? What do I feel about the ideas in this book? What are my reactions? What's my favorite part? Other questions children might also want to consider are those that connect ideas in the text under discussion with prior experiences or similar ideas in other texts: What did this book make me think of? And the teacher would want to emphasize that these questions can be asked of illustrations as well. Other questions or responses—descriptive and analytic, interpretive and elaborative, evaluative and self-evaluative—can be illustrated by having children brainstorm ways they could relate to individual texts. (See Chapter 6 for a review of reader transactions.) Often students' early efforts in response are summarizing the text—this is usually due to prior instructional practice that emphasized summary or literal questions/answers and not response. Thus, teachers might share student examples (with their permission or with no name attached) along with examples of a range of response possibilities. Creating Three-Column Charts* that ask for "facts," "questions," and "response" for a while may help such readers differentiate response from summary (or facts). Using drawings or symbols for reactions to text also facilitates response.

In these responses, comments, or explanations, the author's craft and ideologies should be specifically addressed. Suggestions for questions to consider can be provided: What questions would you ask if the author were here? What sections of the text are effective in relating the setting of the story or in explaining a particular concept or process in an information book? What underlying values does the author (and illustrator) seem to have about what he or she is writing? Were the characters believable? What did you like about the author's style? What questions is the author answering in this book on snakes, tunnels, Lincoln, velocity, immigrants, or whatever? Are there questions that the author didn't answer or points of view that the author did not consider?

Literature Response Groups* can also begin by having children do dramatization or writing. The teacher can ask members of the group to take the role of the towns-people in Gauch's *Thunder at Gettysburg*, maybe as they met at a public meeting, at the beginning of the book, or after the Rebel soldiers came to town but before the Union troops arrived. Then children can be asked to have another public meeting after the battle, with discussion revolving around people's changing views about the "victories" of war, and the author's view of war and how it is communicated in the text. Children's writing responses—perhaps regarding what Tillie, the main protagonist in *Thunder at Gettysburg*, could have written in a letter to her cousin about her experiences during the battle and what she saw of death and destruction—can also be a focus of discussion in a Literature Response Group*.

Discussion in some Literature Response Groups* may result in constructing a collage, Comparison Chart*, or some other kind of Graphic Organizer*. These visuals give children a focus for sharing their understandings and responses with other class members. Ideas from the discussion may also spark a range of writing as well as lead children to read or reread other books on the same topic, by the same author, or in the same genre.

Reading Conferences*

Because children in integrated language classrooms for the most part choose their own reading materials, reading is truly individualized. Consequently, many teachers have individual conferences with children to talk about reading. (Other teachers have many shorter, less formal conferences when they see children reading in the classroom, followed by more general conferences where reading is addressed along with other learning.)

The two primary purposes of Reading Conferences* are to assess and to guide: to assess children's strategies in reading; to understand their range of reading transactions and purposes; to ascertain their abilities to read critically; to determine children's reading needs and interests and their attitudes of reading in general; and to suggest other books, genres, or topics to consider.

Reading Conferences* are usually organized into four parts: sharing, questioning, oral reading, and encouraging and guiding. Most teachers keep a particular notebook or journal in which to make notes and record pertinent information gained in the conferences. They prepare for a conference by going over this and any other information they have observed about the children's reading, so that they know what questions to ask.

Reading Conferences* have four parts.

See also Butler & Turbill (1984), Hepler (1991), and Hornsby & Sukarna (1988) for other ideas for Reading Conferences*.

SHARING

First, the children share responses about past or present reading materials. They may begin by summarizing briefly what they have written in their Sketchbook* or response Journals*, and then focus more on one or two texts. How and why the texts are being read can be pursued, and any information about a related Book Extension*, activity, or project in which the book is involved can be discussed.

QUESTIONING

The teacher asks one or two searching questions about one of the books or texts the children have read. These questions can concern the theme of the book or the author's style in describing a character or setting, or they may help to explain a concept or process. They may also address one or two of the students' drawings or visual images and ask about what meanings they depict and how these meanings might be related to the written meanings. Teachers may not have read all the books their children are reading, so some teachers take turns addressing a text they know about in one conference and then asking about an unfamiliar text in the next conference. This enables teachers to acquire useful information about the children's awareness of audience.

ORAL READING

The teacher listens to children's reading of a short section of the text that has been chosen for sharing. Teachers usually allow children to select the part they will read aloud, but sometimes teachers may ask them to read a part discussed during sharing or questioning. The teacher notes the child's miscues (see Chapter 8)—how the child is integrating cueing systems, self-correcting, and expressing the language of the text. If relevant, the teacher might note if the student might refer to an illustration and/or how he or she reads the minor text (labels, captions, etc.) near images. (Some teachers tape this part of the conference as well as record their impressions of children's reading strategies.)

ENCOURAGING AND GUIDING

The teacher discusses future plans in reading. Suggestions about the selection of other books written by the same author and with the same theme or topic are made. If children are limiting their reading to one or two genres, teachers may "nudge" them to try books in other genres. Possible ideas for Book Extensions* may also be offered.

Teachers can have a Reading Conference* with children once a week or once every two weeks. As a result of the data acquired in Reading Conferences*, teachers may organize a follow-up conference with a small number of children to foster some specific reading strategies. For example, if children seem to overly rely on graphophonemic cues in their own oral reading, the teacher may develop CLOZE* or other activities to get them to use syntactic and semantic cues as well. Or if after the set of conferences with children, teachers realize that many children demonstrate such an overreliance (perhaps as the result of instruction in the previous year), they may set up a series of Focus Lessons* to encourage children to use more meaning-driven reading strategies.

Reading Conferences* can be conducted with students in any elementary grade, even with kindergartners and young first graders who may not as yet be reading from print. In these cases, children can be asked to reenact a book by approximating the text ("pretend reading") or retelling it or by having them "read" a message they have dictated (see Chapter 8). Children show amazing progress in a very short period when they are treated as independent readers, and Reading Conferences* are important ways to demonstrate and emphasize this independence to them.

Big Books*

Holdaway (1979)

Big Books* are simply oversized books containing texts written (and illustrated) on large pieces of paper or cardboard with print big enough for a group of children to see. Big Books* were developed by Holdaway so that children in the classroom could interact with meaningful texts much in the same way that preschoolers interacted with them in book-sharing experiences at home with their parents and other important literate adults. The teacher points, frequently using the handle of a wooden spoon or a ruler, to the words when reading the text in the Big Book*. Then, in rereading the text, children are encouraged to join in. Later, the Big Book* is placed somewhere in the classroom so that children can role play reading the book. The original, small version of the text is available for children to practice on. Through these book-sharing and other literacy experiences, children learn to read—from many approximations to more competent, accurate renderings—in a self-monitoring, self-correcting manner.

Holdaway (1979); McKenzie (1977); Pappas & Brown (1989)

Commercially made Big Books* are available, but these are usually very expensive and sometimes not good-quality literature but just large versions of basal passages. For these reasons, and because teachers want to use books having to do with a particular thematic unit, teachers usually make (with the help of their children) their own Big Books*. Sometimes the books are made ahead of time by the teacher, a colleague, or parent. Teachers can make simplified drawings or trace pictures enlarged by an overhead projector. Teachers frequently discover that they have many friends or parents who are "closet" artists and enjoy illustrating Big Books*.

Children learn a lot when they are involved in illustrating Big Books*.

Many teachers put in the text only and have children illustrate the books. For example, they share the text with the whole class first, and then a small group of children of varying abilities do the illustrations. The book can be constructed with small metal binders or shower hooks so that individual pages can be worked on separately. Valuable discussion and rereading occur as children decide who will illustrate each page and how. Children can explore many types of media in these illustrations. The teacher usually needs to remind kindergartners and many first graders to draw "big." Children should also be encouraged to avoid drawing pencil drafts first, for rarely do their resulting illustrations retain the detail of the drafts. After the illustration is completed, children in the group practice the book and read it to the whole class or to children in another class. Large pieces of Plexiglas of several sizes to match varying sizes of books and with holes on the side for the binder rings make excellent book covers that stand up without an easel and are easy for young children to handle. Children's paper covers naturally adhere to the Plexiglas covers due to static electricity, so the expense of supplying sturdier paper book covers is avoided. (Large tablets from art supply stores can also be used to make Big Books*.)

Plexiglas makes great Big Book* covers.

Making Big Books* with children

Some teachers go through the whole process of making Big Books* in the presence of a small group of children. Using paper or cardboard strips, the teacher writes the words of the text, having children refer to one or more copies of the book to check that mistakes are not made. As the teacher writes the words, he or she talks about the sequence of the message, mentions the characters and other aspects of the book, and refers to spellings and the use of some feature of punctuation (e.g., how quotation marks indicate the words people say). When the whole text is written, both teacher and children read the strips, which are placed on the floor or taped on the board with masking tape. Children pick pages to illustrate, then the group assembles the book by matching strips with illustrations and gluing them on larger pieces of paper.

Besides following words with a pointer—which facilitates children's understanding of one-to-one word correspondences and of the directionality of print—other aspects of written language can be facilitated through the use of Big Books*. Cardboard masks (cardboard frames with holes the width of a line of print and a movable sliding strip) can be made to focus on certain properties of certain phrases or words, thus making children aware of repetitive refrains or to examine various spelling patterns or graphophonemic relationships. With the use of Post-it Notes, CLOZE* applications can also be made by covering particular words or parts of words to facilitate children's use of surrounding cotext to figure out or predict individual words.

Cunningham et al. (2004); Tierney & Readance (2000)

Clay (1979)

Holdaway (1979)

See Fisher (1991) for ideas for using masks with Big Books*.

Patterned books (books that contain rhyme, rhythm, or repetition of certain language patterns) make good Big Books*, but other fictional books and books of informational genres should be considered. For example, children also enjoy Big Book* versions of information books such as *Tunnels, Big City Port,* and *Squirrels.* Teachers can also make their own Big Book* collections of rhymes, poems, recipes, or songs. Big Books* foster children's beginning sight vocabulary quickly, but when children are exposed to a range of genres through Big Books*, a lot more about the registers of written language is fostered. Children, with the help of their teachers and usually in a small group, can write their own Big Books*, perhaps to publish the findings of a project or an in-depth study on some topic in the thematic unit.

Gibbons (1984); Maestro & Del Vecchio (1983); Wildsmith (1974)

Teachers typically use Big Books* of existing literature through the second grade. However, older children may want to make them for use in lower-grade classrooms or to use with younger children in a Buddy Reading* program.

CLOZE*

A CLOZE* passage is a short excerpt—usually several paragraphs—of text in which certain words are deleted. This passage is shared with children in a problem-solving, guided reading lesson. The deletions in an otherwise complete flow of language can be provided in different ways. Usually, one word out of fifteen is deleted, but gaps can occur more frequently if the text still seems meaningful in that way. All the blanks in a CLOZE* can be uniform, or the blanks can resemble the length of the actual word. Some of the letters for the deleted words can be provided, or certain kinds of words can be deleted (e.g., pronouns, adverbs, and adjectives).

In Cloze Passages* words are systematically deleted to encourage problem solving.

Children apply a variety of strategies in a meaningful context.

The CLOZE* passage can be put on a large piece of paper and taped on the board or on a transparency so the group can brainstorm while they try to fill in the blanks. Children can also work on their own copy individually, with a partner, or within a small group. If the beginning of a text is not chosen as the CLOZE* passage, it is important to read the text up to that excerpt. In filling in the blanks, children are encouraged to predict what makes sense. An important aspect of the procedure is for children to justify or tell why their response fits and is meaningful; teachers should accept any reasonable response. In this way, children become sensitive to the linguistic constraints operating on the context—they develop word-attack skills and inferential reasoning. Confirming and self-correcting strategies are induced when children debate as to what the most appropriate response is for a gap. Such strategies can be especially critical for children who believe that reading is merely accurately decoding each word of the text.

Fisher (1991, 1995); Cunningham et al. (2004); Routman (1988); Weaver (2002)

It is also useful to have children engage in CLOZE* activities with passages from different genres so that they can become aware of the different vocabulary and language patterns realized in them.

Tierney & Readance (2000)

Say Something*

Say Something* activities have been designed by Harste and his colleagues to help children develop a more functional and social view of reading. Partners read the same

Beers (2003); Daniels & Zemelman (2004); Harste et al. (1996)

See Borasi & Siegel (2000) for Say Something* examples in math classrooms.

selection, either aloud or silently. Both read the first several paragraphs, then stop to "say something" to their partner about what they have read. Then the second person says something about what was read. The Say Something* can consist of a range of transactions: responding to something that was just read, predicting what might happen next, or sharing experiences related to the ideas of the text at hand (see Chapter 6 for the types of transactions possible). Then the partners repeat the process: They read the next several paragraphs and take turns "saying something" to each other.

When most partners have finished reading, the teacher sets up a group discussion, perhaps by constructing a Semantic Map*. A central topic is placed in the middle of a large piece of paper or transparency, and children are asked to offer ideas that the author expressed. These ideas are webbed off the central topic. As children contribute, they are asked to explain and justify how and why their responses are relevant concepts and ideas and how and why these ideas relate and interrelate.

Coding Text*

Daniels & Zemelman (2004); Harvey (1998); Harvey & Goudvis (2000)

As adults we often highlight, underline, and make marginal notes on texts we read. Because many texts in the classroom or obtained from the library have to be shared during the year (and subsequent years), students have little opportunities to use these strategies to make sense of text. Coding Text* offers ways for students to help readers to monitor their comprehension and recall what they have read. Using copies of articles from magazines or newspapers or materials downloaded from websites, students can code texts for understanding. (Some schools provide students with two paperback books per term that are theirs to keep, in which they can write in as they like.) Teachers might provide Focus Lessons* to demonstrate its use: for example, an asterisk for interesting, a question mark for a question or an aspect to explore, a "C" for confused, an "I" for important, and so forth. Students can use these or create their own codes for their own specific purposes and for different genres. For example, students might include a code to mark an "interesting fact" or "learned something" in nonfictional texts, and "I wonder why this happened" or "events that remind me of an experience that I know" for fiction. Besides writing directly on texts as described previously, it also possible to place codes on small Post-it Notes. In sum, such activities promote active reading and help students really think about what they are reading.

Writing Activities and Experiences

The activities and experiences we now discuss have to do with writing, but it is important to emphasize again that writing (like reading) is rarely a separate activity in integrated language classrooms. As discussed earlier, substantial contributions have been made about how to implement in the classroom a process-conference approach to writing, as researchers and educators have termed current views of writing. However, this approach frequently includes a "writing workshop," a certain period set aside each day, during which children write. In an integrated language classroom, writing experiences—prewriting, drafting, revising, editing, and publishing—happen all day across the curriculum. Children take notes during a scientific observation, jot down their responses to a book they may be reading, write questions or comments during their study of some primary materials to prepare for a small-group discussion, compose an invitation asking parents or another class to come to a play they have written, or write a thank-you note to a guest speaker who visited their class. The "formal" writing workshops suggested by Graves, Calkins, and Atwell, among others, are, therefore, not usually implemented as such, but certain important features of these workshops are incorporated by teachers in the writing experiences for children.

Atwell (1998); Booth (2001); Calkins (1994); Carroll (2004); Graves (1983); Fletcher & Portalupi (2001)

Instead of a special time, teachers frequently designate a special place—a table or corner of the room—for drafting or peer conferencing, where children share their rough drafts to get feedback. Teachers may then drop in for informal conferences with children, while also checking in with children working elsewhere at other projects. Many teachers routinely set aside some time, perhaps a portion of the integrated work time, to have more formal individual Content Conferences*. Another separate place for Editing Conferences*, where children can receive editing help from peers or the teacher, may also be established. Within such a framework, specific properties of writing workshops and other writing activities and experiences of the process-conference writing approach are discussed later in more detail.

Journals*

Journals* can be used in the classroom in many ways. Varying kinds of journals serve varying purposes. We have already discussed response Journals* under Literature Response Groups*, in which children write their responses, comments, and questions (and drawings) about the texts they are reading. Other kinds of journals have also been mentioned in this book (e.g., the math story problem Journals* described in Chapter 5). The specific type of journal depends on the needs of the class.

Fulwiler (1980, 1982)

Some teachers have children use private, diarylike journals, in which children record their personal feelings, with the agreement that their responses are confidential and, therefore, are not read or responded to by the teacher or peers. However, most of the time, despite their personal nature, Journals* are communications that can be shared. Two types are covered here: Dialogue Journals* and Sketchbook Journals*. Differences between the two kinds of Journals* exist, but they are all similar in that they provide for informal writing experiences that allow for personal growth and reflection. (Sometimes teachers use only one Journal* that has sections—one for response for Literature Response Groups*, one for Math, one for Social Studies and Science, and one for Inquiry Projects.)

Journals* promote personal expression and reflection.

DIALOGUE JOURNALS*

The rationale for Dialogue Journals* is that they provide a means for children to share with the teacher, privately and without any worry about evaluation, by writing their reactions, questions, and concerns about any aspect of their experiences in and out of school. In this way, the teacher gets to know more about what each child is doing and thinking. Teachers also use Dialogue Journals* to demonstrate the communicative function of writing to children. This is especially important for those who, because of previous instruction, link writing only with evaluation. Dialogue Journals* encourage spontaneity in writing, which in turn fosters self-confidence and writing fluency.

See also Tierney & Readence (2000) for a discussion of Dialogue Journals*.

Keep the following in mind when implementing Dialogue Journals* in the classroom:

Guidelines for using Dialogue Journals*

1. Use a separate tablet or spiral notebook for each child. Many teachers make journals simply by stapling some paper together, perhaps using a construction paper cover that children decorate themselves. Have children date each entry. Have a special place in the classroom where the journals are stored so that children know where to get and return their journals for response.
2. Set up a schedule for the children to write in their journals. Many teachers have children write every day; others follow a Monday, Wednesday, or Friday routine. Some teachers also discuss with children the times in the daily schedule that may be good for writing in their journals (e.g., on arrival, after lunch, or after physical education).
3. Encourage children to write about anything they want. Many teachers have a whole-class session in the beginning of the year to brainstorm possible topics for

journals. It is important to assure those children who aren't sure that they have anything to write on some particular days that they can write exactly that: "I can't think of anything to write." Sooner or later children (even the most reluctant ones) write in their journals because they see their peers writing and getting responses from the teacher.

4. Assure children that they can use invented spelling and that their entries can be as long or short as they want. If teachers make a big deal about quantity, children are frequently reluctant to write until they have "enough" to say. In the early grades, children should be told that they can make pictures if they don't have anything to write. It may be necessary to get kindergarten and first-grade children (who may be prephonemic, early phonemic, or letter-name spellers—see Chapter 8) to read their entries to the teacher and then have the teacher write down their responses (while saying the message aloud) in front of the child.

5. Respond to children's entries frequently; otherwise, children are likely to see writing in their journal as a drudgery rather than a dialogue.

6. Respond to the content of the message the child has communicated. What is wanted are two-way communications, so teachers should try not to contrive their responses to present conventional forms or grammatical structures.

Evaluations or judgmental responses should also be avoided. For those children who frequently state that they have nothing to write, the teacher can respond, "I'm sorry you can't think of something right now, but I'm sure you will think of something soon." Including a message about something they have observed about the child, followed by a specific question, sometimes breaks the ice. If children then write in their journals, don't congratulate them; simply respond to what they have communicated. If young children have drawn a picture, respond by commenting on the content of the illustration. (Young children also may need help in reading the teacher's responses.) Sometimes adding a question regarding their drawings leads children to try to write back.

In sum, Dialogue Journals* can have many good effects. Teachers get to understand their children better and children's writing fluency is fostered. Teachers' responses provide meaningful resources of the conventions of written language and even help many children in reading, especially in the early grades. Most important, children see themselves as writers, and they begin to feel that they can write for other purposes in the classroom.

SKETCHBOOK JOURNALS*

We emphasize the multimodal nature of meaning-making in this book. The use of Sketchbook Journals* provides a way for students to write down their responses to texts they are reading and information they are acquiring in various inquiry projects, *as well as* to depict these responses and ideas through art and use a variety of visual images or designs. "Sketchbooks" have a long history as a means to use drawings to collect ideas and personal recordings of events. Adding written thoughts provides more avenues to communicating ideas and feelings, developing ideas, exploring and experimenting with ideas, applying ideas, and planning and making sense of the wonders and realities of the world.

As was discussed in Chapters 1 and 6 and mentioned throughout this book, art or drawing is not a "fun activity" here. It is a powerful way to depict meanings, to express thoughts, ideas, and feelings across the curriculum. Besides pictures, diagrams, graphs, cross sections, maps, tables, and graphic designs all count as possibilities to include in Sketchbook Journals*.

Many teachers make their own Sketchbook Journals* by including lined and unlined paper. Others have students (especially older students) buy binders that include both types of paper. Another idea is to use notebooks that have pages

Efland (2002); Goldberg (1997); Moline (1996); Sedgwick (2002); Wilhelm (2004)

Robinson (1995)

See Moline (1996) for great examples of how children can use visual information across the curriculum.

with blank tops and lines beneath. At any rate, the use of images works better on blank, unlined paper.

We have given many examples of how Sketchbook Journals* might be used in the classrooms throughout the book. Some of these are using them to respond to books, to document ideas in hands-on explorations or experiments, to organize information gathered in various inquiry projects, to record and illustrate data, to document and exhibit important ideas over time, and so forth. As students use both text and images in these journals, they look closely and critically at sources, and they learn how to see the ways in which authors and illustrators express meanings differently and to understand how to connect ideas expressed in each mode.

Moline (1996); Unsworth (2001)

Group-Composed Writing*

Group-Composed Writing* is a means for children to share the process of writing and to negotiate the form of various types of writing. Group-Composed Writing* can be done in two ways: (1) Teacher-Led Group-Composed Writing*, in which the teacher does the transcribing and leads the composition process; and (2) Peer-Collaborated Group-Composed Writing*, in which children contribute portions or sections of a larger piece and do the transcribing themselves. In both versions, children are supported in the writing process because they share the process and learn from one another about their composing strategies.

McKenzie (1985); Short & Harste (1996)

TEACHER-LED GROUP-COMPOSED WRITING*

Teacher-Led Group-Composed Writing* works well with younger children because the teacher takes over some of the mechanical aspects so that children can concentrate on the content. The idea applies to children of any age because it enables the teacher to demonstrate the thinking process involved in getting ideas into print and to make explicit the kinds of choices writers face—choices of voice, purpose, and form, as well as the medium aspects involved in creating a finished piece of writing.

Teachers demonstrate the writing process.

Medium aspects of written language can also be referred to in Teacher-Led Group-Composed Writing*.

Group writing can be initiated by the teacher or children. Once children have collaborated in a Group-Composed Writing* activity, they are quick to suggest their own ideas. Perhaps the teacher has just finished a particularly delightful story and has seen several children reworking or reenacting versions of the story in their art or play. Using a large sheet of chart paper or an overhead transparency, the teacher may ask for volunteers to help write a group version of the story: How should we begin our story? Children are encouraged to draw on the ideas depicted in their drawings or play routines and to use their own experiences with stories in general to write a new version. As the teacher writes their suggestions, he or she talks about what is happening in the transcribing process, mentioning the need for spaces between words, the use of capitalization and punctuation, and spelling. As the story evolves, parts are reread every so often and questions are posed: How does that sound so far? Is there anything we can change to make it better (clearer, more exciting, more interesting)? As children make suggestions for changes, parts can be crossed out or written in, even cut and pasted in if necessary to demonstrate that first-draft writing is often messy but dynamic.

Revising strategies are illustrated.

After children have agreed on a final version, it can be published—by simply rewriting it on a new piece of paper or by turning it into a Big Book* that children illustrate. In the following excerpt, kindergartners used the pattern in Martin's *Brown Bear, Brown Bear, What Do You See?* to write their own version using characters from *Goldilocks and the Three Bears* and other books they had been reading. (For example: Papa Bear, Papa Bear, what do you see?/I see Mama Bear looking at me./Mama Bear, Mama Bear, what do you see?/I see Paddington looking at me./And so forth. . . .) Each child then illustrated one of the bear characters, and their paintings were hung next to the appropriate verse on a large bulletin board display. Another example is when urban first-grade children created a new version of Collier's *Uptown*. In this book each

Martin (1983)

Collier (2000)

page begins with "Uptown is . . . " (e.g., "a row of brownstones" or "weekend shopping on 125th Street") with an elaborated sentence or two to explain this first sentence. Children created their "uptown" book that reflected the various places and events occurring in their city.

Group-Composed Writing* is useful with children at any age. With older children, a group-writing session may center on more advanced understandings of style and form. For example, several children may have decided to create a class newspaper, but their first front-page news seems like a fictional story. By sharing the task of writing one of the newspaper accounts with the children, the teacher can help them use a reporter's voice and present information in a more newslike format. They could also be shown how reading helps writing by looking at some real newspaper samples to get a sense of this style of writing and the ways it differs from other genres (in terms of form and ideology). Or as students in the LANDSCAPES thematic unit begin to write up their findings on Rome and Greece that they have decided to publish in the various genres they have noticed in Langley and de Souza's *The Roman News* and Powell and Steele's *The Greek News*, the teacher works with a small group who is having difficulties in writing the advertisements they have started. Because students expect to illustrate some of these advertisements, the teacher sketches the ideas they have for them also, discussing how they might be placed with their written text.

Langley & de Souza (1996); Powell & Steele (1996)

Harste et al. (1996); Short & Harste (1996)

PEER-COLLABORATED GROUP-COMPOSED WRITING*

In Peer-Collaborated Group-Composed Writing*, children do their own transcribing. It is especially useful for less proficient writers who may be overwhelmed by writing a whole book or piece on their own. Children can contribute a "chapter" in an "All About" book (on, e.g., rocks, tunnels, dinosaurs, or bears), collaborate on a fairy tale in which each writer composes an episode that tells how a particular character uses up one wish, or write a biography of a famous person in which each member concentrates on a certain period of the person's life. In Peer-Collaborated Group-Composed Writing*, the teacher's role is one of helping in the coordination of the project and supporting the decision making of the group.

*Authors' Folders**

See also Atwell (1998), Calkins (1994), Short & Harste (1996), and Fletcher & Portalupi (2001) for other ideas on Authors' Folders*.

Authors' Folders* are those in which children keep their ongoing current writing. Frequently, the folders are kept in the back of Journals*, of which they are a part. Two other folders for each child are usually kept: one in which children keep copies of final drafts that they have revised, edited, and published (children don't revise, edit, and publish everything they write); and one in which they collect other miscellaneous writings (abandoned partial drafts, prewriting notes, etc.). Many teachers staple or tape blank paper or forms on each of the four sides of the folder. Although not always noted below, drafts of children's images that accompany their writing are also included.

The organization of an Author's Folder*

OUTSIDE FRONT

The Topics Sheet is where children can jot down ideas or topics for future pieces that emerge as they read, engage in various projects, or interact with other children in the classroom.

INSIDE FRONT

The Writing Log is where children provide some information to indicate the status of their pieces. They enter the date in the "Date" column, and in the large column titled "Status" (for younger children, it may be called "What I Did Today"), they note the draft or images they are working on, the piece or image they are revising, any prewriting activity they have done, and the piece they have had a peer conference on (and with whom). By reviewing this log, teachers can quickly monitor what's happening in writing for individual children. They can see if a child may be bogged down on a piece and needs help. They can note when children will be ready for more formal Writing Conferences*.

INSIDE BACK
The Evaluation Form includes a "date" column and two other columns, titled "Message Ideas" and "Medium Ideas." (For younger children, these columns can be called "Meaning Ideas" and "Editing Ideas.") Some teachers call the latter column "Spelling/Punctuation/Etc." Observations about what children have learned are written either by the children or the teacher under the appropriate column heading. Comments about children's new strategies for forming the content or meanings in their writing or images are noted under "Message Ideas," and new growth regarding their use of medium aspects of written language and various conventions of images are recorded under "Medium Ideas." This information is gathered by the teacher in everyday informal observations and interactions with children (these informal observations can be jotted down on Post-it Notes or self-adhesive mailing strips and placed on the evaluation form) and in more formal Writing Conferences*. This evaluation sheet provides both a means for monitoring children's writing and a self-evaluation tool in that children are expected to review it when they revise and edit a piece.

See Chapters 6 and 8 for more information on the Message/Medium aspects of language and characteristics of images.

OUTSIDE BACK
The Published Writing Form is where children list their published pieces. Children frequently refer to the Published Writing Form when they write an "About the Author/Illustrator" section for a book they are to publish.

Authors' Folders* are stored in a special place for easy access by both teacher and children. Most teachers go over approximately six folders each night so that they review a child's work at least once a week. Obviously, they can review more folders of younger children who usually write shorter pieces. The folders are important, for they are a means of documenting growth over time and provide an important measure of accountability.

Authors' Folders* provide sources of evaluation and accountability.

Writing Conferences*

Like reading, children's writing is individualized in an integrated language classroom. Children have had different prior writing experiences, know different things about the registers of written language, and choose to write on different topics and genres. Therefore, as for reading, many teachers have separate individual conferences with children about their writing. And, just like reading, other teachers have many more short, less formal conferences with children as they see them writing in the classroom. They then have more general conferences with children when writing is addressed along with all their other learning.

See also Atwell (1998), Calkins (1994), Short & Harste (1996), and Fletcher & Portalupi (2001) for other ideas on Writing Conferences*.

Two major types of Writing Conferences* are covered here: Content Conferences* and Editing Conferences*. Teachers usually address content or the message aspects of children's writing separately from the medium aspects (spelling, punctuation, etc.). Peer conferencing is an important part of the process–conference approach, so this topic is included in the discussion that follows. Again, reference to images that might be integrated in multimodal texts is also included.

Message aspects of language and images are addressed in Content Conferences*, medium aspects of language and images in Editing Conferences*.

CONTENT CONFERENCES*

Teacher–Student Conferences. The major purposes of conferences are to assess and guide. Teachers have roving Content Conferences* all the time when they interact with children who are engaged in the process of writing or drawing, either at the designated writing table or elsewhere in the classroom. They may have jotted down information during these interactions, perhaps on Post-it Notes or self-adhesive mailing strips.

Roving Content Conferences*

More formal Content Conferences*

Children prepare before having a conference with the teacher.

Steps in conducting a Content Conference*

A review of the message aspects of texts discussed in Chapter 6 and of the message questions illustrated in Chapter 8 is important for conducting successful Content Conferences*.

See Glasswell et al. (2003) for tips on having productive conferences.

(These might have been put on the Evaluation Form in the child's Author's Folder* or on sheets in his or her learning portfolio—see Chapter 9.) In the more formal Content Conferences*, teachers will have read the child's text and examined any sketches they might have included. These are usually scheduled on the basis of a sign-up sheet on which children indicate their readiness for a Content Conference*. Children will be expected to have already read their text "to the wall" so they can catch omitted words or awkward wordings themselves. They also may have had a peer conference with another classmate and revised their piece on the basis of that feedback. They will also be expected to have revised their text according to any relevant comments on the Evaluation Form in their Author's Folder*.

In the Content Conference*, the teacher focuses on the content of the text or the way a child has organized the meanings or message of the text. (See Chapter 6, especially Table 6.4, and Chapter 8, particularly the message and image analyses and the section on kid-watching writing.) First, it is best to comment on something positive about the writing (or images)—what the child knows and has done well. A teacher may say how much information about turtles there is in the child's text or remark on some writing strategy: "I felt I was right there because of the way you described that place in the beginning of your story" or "That was an interesting way to conclude your text." Or for images, "You have quite a few details depicted" or "I felt that your drawing of the character really showed those emotions you talk about in the text." Then the teacher asks one or two questions in a way that allows the children to retain ownership of their writing and begin to solve their own problems. Teachers try to assist children with genre or form problems and address difficulties regarding missing (or excessive) information, sequencing, cohesiveness, and so on. They try to respond to children's text as an inquisitive reader: "Tell me more about X" or "I'm not sure that I understand Y." For images, "Do you think you have the accurate proportions for the parts of that animal?" or "This is a historical picture piece, right? Do you think your pictures reflect the appropriate clothing for the time?" Teachers' final comments or questions concentrate on what the writer/illustrator plans to do with the text and images as the result of the conference; they help the writer in the process of revision by asking, "What do you think you'll do next?"

At the end of the Content Conference*, teachers and children go over what should be written under the "Status" section of the Writing Log and under the "Message Ideas" section of the Evaluation Form in the Author's Folder*; usually what was discussed regarding the message aspects of the text (and images) or what the child has decided to work on in revising text.

Teachers have Content Conferences* with young elementary children (kindergartners and first graders) as well, but they are very careful not to dampen the children's spirits by insisting on too much revision too soon. Teachers must show young children delight and excitement with their early writing efforts so that the children see themselves as writers and continue to be motivated to write. However, many young children enjoy Content Conferences* because they like the special attention their writing gets. They also like completing the forms in the Author's Folder*.

Children respond to one another's messages during conferences.

Procedures for peer conferences

Peer Content Conferences.   Children share their writing informally all the time in an integrated language classroom, but peer content conferences are occasions to obtain more focused feedback on a finished (or partial) draft from one or two classmates. Many teachers designate certain places in the classroom for peer content conferences: a corner, a supply closet, or the hall outside the classroom.

Children internalize ways of acting in peer conferences through their participation in individual conferences with the teacher. Teachers also go over guidelines about how peer conferences are to be conducted. A peer conference usually consists of three parts. First, the writer reads the text aloud; older children can read silently. Visual images that are included with the written text may also be addressed. Then the listener/reader makes some positive comment about it (e.g., a part that was particularly exciting, interesting, or clear). Finally, the conference partner points out the place or places that could be improved. All comments to the writer must include a reason; a remark such as "It's good" is not sufficient. After the peer conference, writers have to decide what feedback, if any, to consider in revision. Children are asked to summarize these remarks on their "Status" section of the Writing Log in their Authors' Folders*. Some teachers also develop a special Peer Conference Sheet with places to jot down both kinds of feedback—positive and "needs help on"—as well as what the writer was looking for in the conference and what next steps he or she is planning regarding the text. Teachers can then monitor whether children are routinely dismissing useful feedback and can address this problem in their conferences with them.

EDITING CONFERENCES*

Teacher-Led Editing Conferences.   After children have decided on the content of their draft of their writing and images (if relevant) and done all the revision they want to do, they focus on the medium aspects of their text (and image) by editing. Teachers deal with editing in varying ways. Most teachers expect children to address editing matters themselves before a teacher-led conference. Some set up a special place—an editing table or corner supplied with a dictionary and thesaurus, colored pens or pencils, and perhaps specially developed checklists—where children do their editing. Children use a pen or pencil in a different color from that of the text and go over their text, concentrating especially on the issues in the "Medium Ideas" section of the Evaluation Form in their Author's Folder*. They correct spelling and punctuation, delete words or phrases, and insert others for better transitions or clarity.

When the writers have finished editing, they sign up for a conference with the teacher or indicate in some other way that their text is ready for teacher review. The teacher goes over the text with a pen of a third color, changing only the medium aspects, not the content. With respect to any pictures children may have included, most teachers do not write on their images but jot down notes on Post-it Notes near the feature they want to comment on—for example, whether the color is the best one to use, or whether an object should be on the left-hand side in an image rather on the right, and so on. (See Chapter 6 for possible items that might be addressed.)

Some teachers do this editing alone and then set up an Editing Conference* with the child; some do it with the children, explaining their changes. In either case, usually only one issue is emphasized. At the end of the conference, the children record that issue under "Medium Ideas" on the Evaluation Form in the Author's Folder*.

As in Content Conferences*, teachers must be very careful in dealing with editing matters with emergent writers and illustrators. Many teachers wait until the end of kindergarten or the beginning of first grade to talk with children about medium aspects. Because the children lack knowledge of many of the conventions of writing (and images), teachers want to encourage them to write using approximations. Of course, teachers do edit the children's work when some of their texts are published (e.g., typed texts that children illustrate and make into books). Children's attempts to read these corrected texts as they illustrate them is one of the best ways to foster reading development.

Peer-Led Editing Conferences.   Many teachers do not edit everything children publish but establish peer teams to play certain editing roles. Peer editing is especially useful in dealing with work that will be published through Displays*, charts, and so on in the classroom, and editorial boards can review classroom newspapers or literary magazines. The teacher and children together can decide what editing procedures will be followed in special class projects.

Teacher-led editing conferences

Peer-led editing conferences

Publishing Experiences*

Publishing is a way of sharing.

In Chapter 6, we emphasized that publishing has to do with sharing. For this reason, publishing can include much more than the publishing of final drafts; any of the writing experiences discussed in Chapter 6 can be published. In addition, as we have emphasized throughout the book, most texts are multimodal—besides the language message of texts, there are also images that are published. In this chapter, however, four aspects of publishing are covered in more detail: Dummy Books and Text-Image Templates*, Displays*, Bookmaking*, and the Author's Chair*.

DUMMY BOOKS AND TEXT-IMAGE TEMPLATES*

Johnson (1997); Kiefer (1995); Shulivitz (1985)

See Stephens (1995) for a picture-book that illustrates how an author/illustrator uses a Dummy Book* in creating a storybook.

An important aspect of publishing involves how to display the writing and images of their texts. Authors and illustrators create storyboards—or Dummy Books*, as we call them, because these multimodal products could be of any genre—to figure out how to position written text and visual designs. Many decisions during the revising and editing processes have already been made to determine what meanings are to be expressed via each mode and in major versus minor text (the labels, captions, keys, etc.). Now it is time to organize these ideas for sharing. Figuring how many pages (including the half title page, the total title page, copyright/dedication page, about the author/illustrator page, etc.) are to be used and how headings (and subheadings) and size, font, and boldness of print are to be employed, and so forth, are facets of this process. In addition, getting a sense of the flow or sequence of segments of text and order of illustrations is a critical feature of creating Dummy Books*. Versions of Dummy Books* are also employed for brochures, multipage leaflets, or perhaps PowerPoint presentations.

See Moline (1996) for examples of Text-Image Templates*.

When a text is to be published in a nonbook format—perhaps on a poster or chart to be placed in a class museum or other display that might accompany various objects that may have been created as part of inquiries (dioramas, time lines, student-produced Jackdaw* materials, experiment apparatus, and so forth)—then "one page" or a series of separate "pages" of Text-Image Templates* are employed. Using newsprint or other inexpensive paper the size of the poster or chart to be used in publishing, a mock-up model or prototype is created to show how to juxtapose the text/image elements. Some of the same features listed earlier for Dummy Books* are also relevant here. Students draw boxes on the Text-Image Template* to organize the information in the various text/image elements. Making their own decisions on how to handle layout problems helps students to understand how to deal with those they encounter as readers or viewers.

DISPLAYS*

Displays* should be aesthetically pleasing.

Careful display or presentation of projects helps children develop a sense of accomplishment and pride in a job well done as well as a sensitivity to the effects of their work on others. Displays* can include anything and everything: posters, charts, maps, puppets, games, dioramas, and the like.

Children are encouraged to mat finished artwork and writing, thinking about spacing and visual qualities in mounting their work. Mats or borders can be made by gluing the finished work to a larger sheet of construction paper. The mats can vary to include freeform shapes and multicolored backgrounds. A combination of these ideas can be used in mounting several works, thereby adding visual interest or unity to the finished product, as shown in Figure 7.11.

Teachers have several roles in displaying. They provide the materials, demonstrate and suggest some of the possibilities, and support and coordinate children's decision making. Many teachers in traditional schools spend a lot of time and money buying commercially made pumpkins, valentines, bunnies, and so on to decorate their bulletin boards and classrooms. But do these materials reflect the children's interest or under-

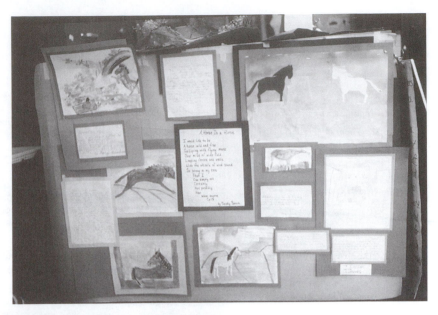

<figure>figure **7.11**
**Examples of Matted
Finished Artwork**</figure>

standings? In integrated language classrooms, they do—the Displays* of children's
products depict the work of a community of learners.

BOOKMAKING*

Publishing in book form lends writing a sense of permanence and value. Many forms
of Bookmaking* by children can be used regularly throughout the year, including
shape books (made with covers and blank paper cut out in a special shape to tie in with
a thematic unit), books with ring binding or binders, books with the edges stapled together with construction paper or wallpaper sample covers, and books made with cloth
covers (glued together with white glue or dry mount tissue).

Cloth-covered books take the most time and effort, but most teachers try to provide the opportunity for children to publish this type of book several times a year. Figure 7.12 outlines instructions for such Bookmaking*.

See Chambers (1986); Fennimore
(1992); Johnson (1992, 1993, 1997); and
Kiefer (1995) for good resources on
making books.

figure 7.12
Making Books

Materials:

Construction paper
Cardboard (cereal boxes or old file folders are
    best; cardboard boxes are not good)
Rubber cement or dry mount tissue (available from
    photographic supply stores)
Cloth, wrapping paper, or wallpaper

Directions:

1. Measure and cut sheets of construction
    paper for pages. For endpapers, choose
    2 sheets of contrasting colored construction
    paper (the same size) (Figure A).

2. Fold pages and end pages in half. Keep
    endpapers on the bottom (Figure B).

3. Sew along fold line with embroidery needles
    (Figure C).

4. Cut cardboard 1/4" to 1/2" larger than the
    pages for the cover.

5. Cut wrapping paper, cloth, or wallpaper 1" to
    2" larger than cover.

6. Cut cover cardboard in half, then trim 1/4" off
    each half.

7. Lay cover paper flat, place 2 cover boards on
    top leaving 1/2" between the top sheets to
    allow book to open and shut (Figure D).

8. a. Glue cover sheets to cover paper with
        rubber cement, or
    b. Place 2 sheets of dry mount tissue (cut to
        the same size as the cover board)
        between cover board and cover paper
        and press with dry iron set on wool.

9. Fold corners in to form triangles, Glue to
    cover board (Figure E).

10. Fold edges over. Glue to cover board.

11. Place pages of book on cover, endpapers on
    bottom. Center pages on cover (Figure F).

12. Glue bottom endpaper to cover.

A.

B.

C.

D.

E.

F.

Children also enjoy experimenting with techniques for papermaking and creating decorative endpapers or cover papers. Waste paper and a kitchen blender can give a finished product that is similar to fine handmade paper. (See Figure 7.13, p. 323.) Block or potato printing or other decorative techniques add special effects to endpapers or covers. (See Figure 7.14, p. 323.)

In Bookmaking*, children are encouraged to include all aspects of a book, such as dedication and title page. The inclusion of an "About the Author" page lets children tell some personal information about themselves as authors: their families, pets, hobbies, interests, and other books they have written. Children search for and read dust covers of real books for the kinds of ideas to include. Having opportunities to write such blurbs about themselves frequently motivates some reluctant writers.

figure **7.13**

HANDMADE PAPER

Materials:

Large container
Scrap paper (old newspaper, computer paper)
1/4 cup bleach
Toweling
Wooden frame covered with nylon or wire screen (small mesh)
Kitchen blender
2 pieces of wooden board masonite
Weights

Directions:

1. Tear paper into tiny pieces and add to container full of water.
   (Bleach will make paper whiter.)
2. Soak overnight.
3. Add a little water to the blender. Set blender to liquefy. Drop in soaked paper
   a little at a time. (Short pulses on the blender may be more effective.)
4. Pour mixture over screen, distributing it evenly. Let water drain off.
5. Roll pulp onto towel and press with another towel or sponge to remove water.
6. Place pulp between two boards and put weights on top.
7. Let dry.

figure **7.14**

DECORATIVE PAPERS

Chalk Dust Endpapers

Materials:

Oblong pan of water
Construction paper (The paper should have a somewhat absorbent rough texture.)
Pastel chalk (Large single sticks, available in art supply stores, provide the richest color and
   the greatest amount of chalk dust.)

Directions:

1. Using a kitchen knife, scrape the chalk over the pan of water in random spots. A second
   or third color can be added.
2. Place a sheet of paper gently on the surface of the water, tapping it lightly to remove any
   air bubbles.
3. Remove the paper carefully and let it dry. When dry, the chalk dust will be bound to the
   paper in a delicate attractive design.
4. Repeat the process on the reverse side for the sheet of endpaper that is not glued to the
   cover board.

Bookmaking is an art that extends back through the centuries and warrants special attention at some point in the elementary school years. The study of bookmaking can include a visit to a local printing plant or a small independent press where type is set by hand and pictures are printed from metal etchings or wood blocks. These small print shops sometimes make their own paper, using old rags and handmade molds. Local artisans familiar with oriental techniques of papermaking who use rice paper and such natural items as pressed flowers, or craftspersons familiar with making marbleized paper for endpapers and covers, may be available and willing to visit the classroom.

AUTHOR'S CHAIR*

The term *author's chair* has both specific and general meanings in publishing. In a specific sense, the author's chair is an actual chair in a classroom on which writers sit when they present their own writing to peers. In a general sense, however, the Author's Chair* represents the broad range of sharing possibilities in the classroom. It also establishes

Calkins (1994); Graves (1994); Fletcher & Portalupi (2001); Weaver (2002)

See Wolfer (2001) for an example of the use of Author's Chair* in an urban first-grade classroom.

Tierney & Readence (2000)

Many forms of sharing or publishing are possible.

It is important to modify Author's Chair* if students see it as the "hot seat."

Krogness (1995)

linkages between writers and readers (as well as viewers and illustrators, and writing and reading) because it provides opportunities for peers to ask questions about what authors/illustrators did or were trying to do. It helps authors/illustrators to understand that readers/viewers may have different interpretations and values of their work and facilitates an awareness that both readers/viewers and writers/illustrators have options or choices in the literacy process.

This general sense also means that publishing is more than the act of authors reading final drafts to the class (or possibly various visual designs). It includes the sharing of partial drafts that need feedback and suggestions; the presenting of plans or Semantic Maps* to be explored by a small group; giving a play or Puppet Show*; demonstrating a game; and the showing of artifacts such as dioramas, topographical maps, or papier-mâché tunnels or animals.

Sometimes children may see the Author's Chair* as being on the "hot seat." This usually occurs when they have had few experiences in the writing-process approach or when they have poor attitudes about themselves as writers. A modification can be instituted where the sharing is not done by a sole author but is more of a communal affair. A small group of children may meet with the teacher to celebrate drafts and images. They can also share good starts in drafts and places in their texts where their writing is going well; in addition, they can talk about the difficulties or struggles they are having in their writing and get suggestions that might help. Similarly, they may offer images they have created and ask for guidance on them and how they might relate to the linguistic message. Thus, in all versions of the Author's Chair*, the context should be a supportive one and one in which all students are eager to participate.

Developing a Repertoire of Literacy Strategies

See Fisher (1991, 1995); Holdaway (1979); and Routman (1988) for similar lists of strategies.

Allington (1994); Cunningham (2005)

Babbitt (1975)
Colman (1995)

It is important to remember that authentic experiences with reading and writing such as those suggested previously provide the best means for the development of literacy and learning. Within this context teachers should use techniques to help children develop strategies that concentrate on meaning at the same time they develop children's understanding of the underlying structures of written language. These techniques should include teacher modeling with direct explanations and demonstrations of the ways that readers seek out meaning. For example, the teacher might make use of the overhead projector to demonstrate how to make inferences about the character of the stranger in a passage from *Tuck Everlasting*. Or he or she might use a selection from an information book like *Rosie the Riveter* to show how she skims material to find out about women's employment opportunities just prior to World War II.

Rather than overemphasize word accuracy (especially at the early stages), teachers' guidance should foster good methods for predicting that will get children to make an educated guess using all available information—from the print (physical layout and medium aspects, etc.), the message or register and genre of the text, or their experiences. When readers get "stuck," the following teacher prompts or suggestions help children develop their own strategies:

Rerun. Remind the child to start the sentence again when he or she stops mid-sentence. ("Try it again.") Starting again enables children to gain a refreshed feeling of how the message is structured.

Consider sense and structure. Ask the child if what has just been read made sense. ("Does that make sense? Does that sound right?")

Read on. Tell the child to skip the word by substituting "blank," and read on to the end of the sentence ("Now, what do you think that word is?")

Predict. Encourage the child to make a good guess. ("What do you think it could be?")

Substitute. Tell the child to put in another word that fits or that means the same. ("Can you use something that means the same here?")

Picture. Ask the child to imagine what's going on. ("Can you picture what's happening?")

Refer to picture. Ask the child to refer to the pictures or images for ideas of what the word might be. ("Can the pictures help you decide what this word might be?")

Use a placeholder. Ask the child to put in a "stand-in" for the same word recurring in text. This is especially useful for proper names of persons and places. ("Can you decide on the same 'stand-in' for this word?")

Identify. Ask the child to find that word on a previous page or paragraph. ("Where else did you see that word?")

Compare. Ask the child if it looks like a more familiar word. ("Does this word look like some word that you know?")

Inspect. Ask the child to take a careful look at the word, keeping the meaning of the text in mind. ("Could it be . . . ? What would you expect to see at the beginning of . . . ? What would you expect to see at the end of . . . ?")

No matter what prompt or suggestion teachers use in supporting children's reading, it is important that they give children time to self-monitor and self-correct. If teachers swoop in with their prompts too soon, children will not have opportunities to apply their own strategies or to self-correct, and the self-regulating behavior that characterizes fluent, effective reading will not be developed. It is also important for teachers to help children be aware of their strategies. When teachers ask questions such as "How did you know?" or "Why did you think it was . . . ?" children become more conscious of the metalinguistic and metacognitive strategies they are using. They are more likely to use them on their own and to gain independence in reading.

Metalinguistic and metacognitive awarenesses are fostered.

Understandings about the underlying structures and conventions of written language will emerge as children engage with meaningful texts. Then, as teachers take time to observe children reading and writing, they can begin to make decisions about providing Focus Lessons* on strategies and conventions when (and if) children need more explicit instruction. In the following sections we provide some background and make suggestions for experiences that further support children's growing facility and fluency in reading and writing.

Teaching Phonics and Spelling in Context*

English is an alphabetic writing system in which written symbols (graphemes) represent spoken sounds (phonemes). The English spelling system has many irregularities because of the number of cultures that have contributed to the language. (Spanish, in contrast, is much more consistent in its sound/symbol relationships.) While there seems to be a correlation between ability to read and a knowledge of letter/sound relationships, there is no research to tell us whether the knowledge of letter/sound relationships is necessary to learn to read or whether letter/sound relationships *follow* from children's interactions and experiments with written language. Children instructed in intensive phonics and spelling programs may initially show reading gains, but in most studies the advantage of phonics is gone by the sixth grade. More importantly, these intensive, decontextualized programs take time away from real reading and writing. For children who receive intensive phonics instruction apart from meaningful reading and writing experiences, reading comprehension often suffers in the later grades—they become word callers. Similarly, when teachers concentrate lessons on

See Adams (1990), Strickland & Cullinan (1990), and Wilde (1992, 1997) for several views on phonics instruction.

See Dahl et al. (2001) for a range of strategies for teaching phonics/spelling in context.

Hillocks (1986); Weaver (1996)

spelling and grammatical rules at the expense of meaningful composition, children fail to improve in their ability to make meaning through written language.

Research does indicate that in order to benefit from formal phonics instruction children must be phonemically aware; that is, they must be aware that spoken language consists of a series of sounds. Furthermore, research also shows that those children who *are* phonemically aware (have experience in word play, nursery rhymes, nursery songs, etc.) don't need much formal instruction in phonics.

Cunningham & Cunningham (1992); Yopp (1992)

Research findings strongly suggest that giving children experience with books and encouraging them to experiment with invented spelling supports their ability to distinguish letter/sound relationships and to segment words into sounds. Thus, we can reassure teachers that by creating rich and meaningful learning and literacy activities centered around real books they are providing children with the experiences they will need to become strategic lifelong readers. This includes children who come to school speaking any of the many variations of English or who have acquired English as a second language.

Children develop concepts about sound–symbol relationships as they listen to stories and play with language and poetry.

Goodman (1993); Wilde (1992, 1997)

Within this context, teachers become careful observers of children and can determine which children may need more direct instruction in phonics and when they are ready for it. For example, in a first-grade classroom the children and the teacher were reading Maurice Sendak's *Alligators All Around: An Alphabet*. On each page, the children chimed in with their own words that began with that letter. "P—PUSHING PEOPLE" read the teacher, and the children chimed in with "Peter Pan, Pinocchio, peanut butter, Popeye, penguin." When one child volunteered the word "bat," the teacher replied "Pat, bat. Bat is a B word." Later she asked that the child to do a word sort with all the words he could find that began with the letters P and B. This is a much sounder approach than giving all children the same instruction at the same time whether they need it and whether they will benefit from it. Here, we suggest activities on which this focused instruction could center.

Sendak (1962)

Barry (2001); Pappas et al. (2001)

Routman (1996)

1. Encourage children's natural inclination to play with language. Collect and share favorite nursery rhymes and playground jingles from around the world and display them around the classroom. Counting-out rhymes such as "Hacker packer soda cracker, Hacker packer too. Hacker packer soda cracker, Out goes you" invite further manipulation of sounds when children make up their own verses. Word games also focus attention on sounds in words. Teachers might pronounce the individual sounds of a word and ask children to guess the word, for example, "I'm thinking of fruits we eat, a—pp—le." Or they can help children draw out the sounds of words that they want to spell. The first grader who writes, "A kobra coda cil you. It is a kida saka that is vary poans."(A cobra could kill you. It is a kind of snake that is very poisonous) is very much aware of the segments of sound in spoken language.

See Yopp (1992) for suggestions for language games.

2. Read books that focus attention on language. Stories and poems with repetitive language draw children's attention to features of words, especially when they are involved in Reader's Theater* or Choral Reading*. Alphabet books and books like *Roar and More* or *Small Green Snake,* in which printed words are a prominent feature of the visual art, also encourage children's exploration of letter/sound relationships.

Kuskin (1990); Gray (1994)

3. Keep Focus Lessons* simple within the context of meaningful text. Teaching all the letter sound correspondences in English would involve learning some 211 rules. Many of these *do not* have a high degree of consistency. The advice is to keep phonics simple and to teach consistent patterns when children seem ready for them. By simple we mean teaching initial and final consonants, consonant clusters, consonant digraphs, short vowels in a CVC pattern, long vowels with markers (silent partners), *-ed* spelling of past tense, and consonant doubling when adding an ending to a CVC word. These patterns are best learned within the context of real reading and writing. When they read their own writing or use Big Books* such as *The Little Red Hen* or *Mrs. Wishy Washy,* for example, children have many opportunities to find, identify, and use consonant and vowel patterns or word endings.

Barton (1993); Cowley (1981)

Adams (1990); Routman (1996)

4. Teach high-frequency word patterns. The teaching of rhyming phonograms (families of words) or the manipulating of onsets (initial consonant sounds) and rimes (e.g., *-ack, -eat, -ill, -ock, -ing*) is recommended. For example, if a teacher notices that several children are having trouble with the word *fill* she might ask them to list all the words they can think of that end in *-ill*. Their chart could be hung on the wall and added to as they find more words that fit the pattern. Children would then be expected to use these words correctly in their writing. Books such as Charlotte Pomerantz's *If I Had a Paka* and *Here Comes Henny* or favorite poems such as David McCord's "The Pickety Fence," could be transferred to large chart paper with blanks left for onsets or rimes: "The p_ _ _ety fence, the p_ _ _ety fence. Give it a l_ _ _ it's the p_ _ _ety fence. . . ." Children who are familiar with the refrains could then write in the proper letters on the charts.

Pomerantz (1993); Pomerantz (1994)
McCord (1986)

5. Encourage children to study words. Semantic Maps* or word walls can become a center for word studies relating to thematic units. Children of all ages can be encouraged to categorize words according to various phonetic and meaning-based patterns. Young children might sort pictures or word cards into categories of long and short *e*. Older children might group words that are derived from a common base word (e.g., *lumen, luminous, luminescent, luminescence, luminiferous, luminosity, illuminate*).

See Bear et al. (1996), Cunningham (2005), and Waggstaff (1997–1998) for additional ideas for word study.

Teaching Grammar in Context*

Traditionally, teaching grammar has usually meant identifying parts of speech (nouns, verbs, adjectives, adverbs, etc.) and their function in sentences, types of sentences (questions, commands, declarative statements), and so forth. Teacher-led lessons on grammar "rules" (e.g., "a sentence must have a subject and predicate [a noun and a verb]" or "never start a sentence with 'and' ") are covered, followed by students completing workbook pages on the grammatical concepts. Rarely do these lessons have any relevance to students' current understandings or difficulties in crafting their own sentences in writing texts. As a result, students often find this "formal" study of grammar very boring. Moreover, because its attention is solely at the sentence level instead of the text and genre level, it frequently leads to even more misunderstandings than help. Research has demonstrated over and over that teaching formal grammar systematically and in isolation does not lead to improvement in students' writing; that is, teaching grammar this way just doesn't transfer.

See Weaver (1996) for a recent review of this research.

Grammar, or what we call "lexicogrammar" (which focuses on both vocabulary and linguistic constructions—see Chapter 6), is very complex. We best teach it not by emphasizing "rules" but by helping children see the typical—and atypical—linguistic patterns that are found in various genres. We best teach it in context, that is, by using literature and children's own writing examples in Focus Lessons* and in writing conferences. Chapter 6 illustrates how linguistic patterns are expressed in various typical and "fuzzy" texts (ones that include linguistic features from more than one genre), and Chapter 8 shows how an analysis of students' writing could enable a teacher to address grammatical issues in conference. Next we suggest other possibilities. Although we often refer to books that are usually for younger readers, they could still be used in Focus Lessons* for older elementary and middle school children. Of course, taking excerpts from other texts written for older elementary students could also be employed.

The term *lexicogrammar* emphasizes that the wordings chosen in linguistic structures are important in identifying genres.

Carroll (2004); Krashen (1993); Weaver (1996)

SHOW HOW A PARTICULAR TEXT FEATURE IS REALIZED IN DIFFERENT GENRES

Use several books that can show how different text features work in different genres—how actions work, how time is expressed differently, or how texts begin and end in various genres.

Explore the same text feature in different genres.

As was illustrated in Chapter 6, the element of description could be examined by showing excerpts from books of different genres. You can point out the many relational processes or verbs in *Squirrels* and *The Ladybug* (e.g., "[A squirrel] *is* a furry, small animal . . ."; "The ladybug *has* two pairs of wings") that are used in description in most informational books.

Then these could be contrasted with mental verbs (verbs of cognition, affection, and perception) that express the human intentions, reactions, and motivations that are typically found in fiction. Thus, "Owl . . . *liked* to work all night and sleep all day" in

The Owl and the Woodpecker shows how this verb of affection is intermingled with the description of that character's habitual action in the beginning of the story. Similarly, in the novel, *Child of the Owl*, when Casey goes to live with her grandmother, Paw-Paw, in Chinatown, the description of that place is interspersed with her reactions to it. "But it was the people there that got me. I don't think I'd ever seen so many Chinese in my life before this." All mental processes are used: affection ("got"), cognition ("think"), and perception ("seen"). Another feature you could highlight is how the informational texts use verbs that are in the present tense, whereas in the fictional ones, verbs are in the past tense (except for dialogue or in asides given by the narrator). In *A Desert Scrap-*

book, a fuzzy book, Virginia Wright-Frierson includes her personal observations and feelings ("I try to remember some of the patterns I have seen in the desert," "I love to come outside right after a rain has freshened the air . . .") along with the typical descriptions of the Sonoran desert. And, although her illustrations are in watercolor, they are scientifically accurate, unlike the more "abstract" illustrations in *Squirrels* by Wildsmith, even

though his language is typically informational. Another contrast could be how the description of another desert is achieved through poetic language in *Mojave*. Finally, you can point to the short, emotionally laden descriptions realized through short phrases that are usually found in advertisements and catalogues because the "authors" of these texts hope to entice readers to become consumers of products. (See Chapter 6 for more details on the element of description in various genres.)

Thus, by using different texts, teachers can encourage students to become detectives of how authors/illustrators use language and pictures to express their ideas and their values. Teachers can help students to better understand what people do with language through written texts and how that language is structured for use in different genres.

HAVE WHOLE-CLASS GENRE STUDIES

For each thematic unit, pick one genre that everyone writes. In the unit WHO IS A HERO?, it might be biography; in IT'S NOT FAIR, it might be persuasive essays; in a CHANGES unit, it might be historical fiction; and in DISAPPEARING ACTS, it might be informational reports on animals on the endangered species list. Students would immerse themselves in reading good examples of the genre. Teachers would conduct various Focus Lessons* on the common generic patterns, as well as on students' writing efforts. In this way, children can make more explicit to themselves some of the complexity of the lexicogrammatical structures that characterize particular genres.

COMPARE AND CONTRAST THE TEXTUAL FEATURES AND FORMAT OF A SINGLE GENRE OR TOPIC

This is similar to whole-class genre study, but here the inquiry may not lead to writing texts (at least immediately) but carefully studying examples of several books of a particular genre created by different authors and illustrators. They also may include fuzzy examples in the corpus of study. Usually the inquiry is a small-group Student-Directed Inquiry* project where findings might be depicted in a Comparison Chart*.

One such inquiry might be studying biographies, using Adler's *A Picture Book of Frederick Douglass*, Stanley's *The Last Princess: The Story of Princess Ka'iulani of Hawai'i*, and Matthaei and Grutman's *The Ledgerbook of Thomas Blue Eagle*. Besides creating categories that would capture similarities and differences of the lives of the persons involved, specific features of the language, the illustrations, and the format of the books can be examined. For example, the book on Thomas Blue Eagle is actually a fictional, autobiographical account of the life events of a Sioux boy and his imaginary drawings (by the illustrator Cvijanovic) while attending a school in the East to learn about the world of the white man. This book is written in the first person, whereas the other two books are written in the third person. Each book has distinctive format features. The book on Frederick Douglass includes an extra page at the end that lists important dates and extra information about Douglass in an "Author's Note." The book on the Last Princess shows a map of the Hawaiian Islands in the beginning of the book with information about the Hawaiian language and a bibliography at the end. The book on Thomas Blue Eagle is published as a ledgerbook with red and blue lines, and it must be turned around to be read; from the top pages then to the bottom ones, instead of reading the typical left- then to right-hand pages. No authors or illustrators are listed on the title page. However, information on them is found at the end of the book, along with a glossary and information about pictographs and the actual Carlisle Indian School the fictitious Thomas Blue Eagle attended.

See Duke & Bennett-Armistead (2003) and Duthie (1996) for similar explorations of nonfiction books in the primary classroom.

A similar inquiry might be conducted on a particular topic. Students examine the content *and* how differently authors and illustrators may format that content. For example, books about the honeybee can be used. More typical informational books can be analyzed—*The Honey Makers* by Gibbons; *The Bee* by Crewe; *How Do Bees Make Honey?* by Claybourne; *Questions and Answers about Bees* by Reigot (which uses a question-and-answer format as the title suggests); and *The Life and Times of the Honeybee* by Micucci (which has various sections that include discussions about the different colors and flavors of honey, a depiction of a hive throughout the twelve months of the year, other products using honey, and so forth). The content, language, and the format of these books can also be contrasted with the fuzzy book, *The Magic School Bus: Inside a Beehive*, by author Cole and illustrator Degan. Children may also look at the poem "Honeybees," which can be found in Fleischman's *Joyful Noise: Poems for Two Voices*. In this poem a worker bee and the queen banter back and forth. Children may also want to try to find stories having honeybees to add to their analysis.

Gibbons (1997); Crewe (1997); Clayborne (1994); Reigot (1995); Micucci (1995)

Cole (1996)

Fleischman (1988)

WRITE TWO GENRES FROM THE SAME STUDENT-DIRECTED INQUIRY* PROJECT DATA

As students are involved in various individual Student-Directed Inquiry* Projects in a subtheme or topic of a particular thematic unit, they can report on their findings in two genres. For example, in the DISAPPEARING ACTS theme, they could write a typical informational text on a particular endangered animal. They could then use the same data, the same Semantic Map* they created to organize their questions and answers about that animal in their research, to also write a story or a poem.

Writing two genres from the same data on a topic

Calkins (1994)

Younger children might be given two different inquiry Journals*. In the first they note down the interesting "facts" they have learned about a particular animal—bears or cats or pigs—from reading and hearing informational texts read to them. In the second they jot down the crazy, funny, sad, or happy actions or conflicts that specific animal characters may have experienced in the fictional books the students read in their inquiry. Drawing from each Journal*, they would write an informational book and a story.

EXPLORE THE DISTINCTIVE DIALECTS IN BOOKS

In a multicultural curriculum, specific dialects should be examined explicitly to help students gain an appreciation of various ethnic and community dialects. The African-American vernacular dialect is illustrated in William's *Working Cotton* where a day in the field of young girl and her migrant family is described ("We gets us to the fields early, before it's even light. Sometimes I still be sleep. It be cold, cold, cold"). The Appalachian dialect in storytelling ("Poppyseed's a-telling stories tonight . . .") is depicted

Examine and appreciate dialect differences.

Williams (1992)

Haley (1986)
Altman (1993)

Soto (1995)

Examining students' own and others' language patterns enables them to examine attitudes toward dialects and be more comfortable using the "Language of Wider Communication"—the various genres that traditionally have indicated greater status in society.

Conference on College Composition and Communication (1998); Gee (1996); Weaver (1996)

Common grammatical concepts

Waddell (1992)

Cushman (1994)

Base (1986)

Carlson (1997)

Heller (1989)

Teaching grammar usually involves focusing on punctuation.

Raschka (1993)
Lobel (1981)

Fox (1989)

in Haley's version of *Jack and the Bean Tree.* Another migrant story is told in Altman's *Amelia's Road,* where Spanish words are included in the English ones ("Los caminos, the roads, were long and cheerless."). The street talk of the barrio can be found in Soto's *Chato's Kitchen* ("'No problema, homeboy,' Chato said to himself . . ."). Discussions about the features found in the books and how they contribute to the meanings and feelings expressed in them helps students realize why the language is appropriate in these fictional genres. Thus, they may begin to reexamine their own dialects with new eyes and ears and write a story or poem incorporating them. They will also begin to understand that these personal, community, and ethnic dialects are not likely to be expressed in their informational reports or other genres.

USE CHILDREN'S LITERATURE TO TEACH COMMON GRAMMATICAL CONCEPTS

The concept of a sentence can be taught by providing examples from texts written by a range of authors in various genres and talking with children about how and why they think these sentences are constructed. Ask students to create a tentative definition of a sentence and have them examine their own texts of different genres to see how well the definition applies. Make problematic the common rule that sentences must have a subject and a predicate (noun and verb) by using books that have counterexamples. For example, such sentences can be found in Waddell's award-winning picture book, *Owl Babies* ("A big branch for Sarah, a small branch for Percy, and an old piece of ivy for Bill"). Similarly, many occur as entries in Cushman's Newbery Honor novel *Catherine, Called Birdy,* because this book is written as the fictional diary of a young English woman in the year 1290 (e.g., "14TH DAY OF SEPTEMBER Tangled my spinning again. Corpus bones, what a torture").

Parts of speech can be taught through books. For example, an alphabet book, *Animalia,* by Graeme Base contains sentences like "An armored armadillo avoiding an angry alligator" for the letter A and "Diabolical dragons daintily devouring delicious delicacies" for D. Here there are opportunities to identify nouns, adjectives, and adverbs and what appear to be verbs (*avoiding* and *devouring*) in a delightful way. In these structures, the adjectives precede the nouns, but in *ABC I Like Me!* by Nancy Carlson they are found in a different kind of construction (e.g., "I am Awesome, Brave, and Cheerful"). The adjectives follow the relational verb *am,* similar to the ones we see so frequently in informational texts. Ruth Heller's *Many Luscious Lollipops: A Book about Adjectives* and other books in this series (on adverbs, nouns, and verbs) can also be used to teach these concepts.

Frequently, teaching grammar requires giving attention to punctuation. Reading Raschka's *Yo! Yes?,* which consists of a dialogue between two boys, helps make the use of punctuation become more explicit. How to use commas to punctuate a series of terms can be illustrated in Lobel's *On Market Street.* Here the terms are the one-word items bought on a market street ("I bought . . . apples, books . . . yarns, zippers.") In Mem Fox's *Shoes from Grandpa,* the terms are much longer, as each family member offers to buy some kind of clothes or accessory to go with the new shoes that Jessie has gotten for her birthday from her Grandpa. In a cumulative manner, each idea is repeated throughout the book, and commas are used to mark the series (e.g., "And her mom said, 'I'll buy you a skirt that won't show the dirt, to go with the socks from the local shops, to go with the shoes from Grandpa' "). Quotation marks could be illustrated with this book as well.

Thus, the idea is not to place that much emphasis on the grammatical terminology or definitions per se, but to help children develop an understanding of the function of punctuation and common grammatical concepts. Teachers might make mention of them again in an incidental way during their conversations with children—"See how you might use more adjectives to modify these nouns you are using"—as these concepts seem to be relevant in their writing.

BASE FOCUS LESSONS* AND INDIVIDUAL EDITING CONFERENCES* ON THE ANALYSIS OF STUDENTS' WRITING

Base your instruction on your own observations of what your students are doing in their writing. Figure out—with the child—what genre he or she is attempting, and have your suggestions and feedback address both the message and medium aspects of his or her texts (see Chapter 8 for examples). In Focus Lessons* use texts written by students, with their permission, or your own that reflect particular lexicogrammatical issues or any problems that might have arisen.

Avoid the very popular, commercially produced Daily Oral Language (DOL) Program for teaching punctuation, capitalization, usage, and so on. In this program, a teacher writes two sentences that need "correcting" on the board each day, and then invites students to orally provide the necessary corrections. Or students may copy them, correct them, and then discuss them orally as a group. These sentences are isolated sentences, not text or genre based. Moreover, too often the errors that the program sentences may be illustrating are not ones your students are making most frequently. Thus, although it seems that only a small amount of time might be used daily on the program, it is usually wasted time if the areas of errors are not related to students' actual difficulties.

Children's own writing as the context for instruction

Create your own Focus Lessons* based on your observation of students' current understandings of grammar.

Summary

Teach grammar in context. Help students see the typical patterns of various genres and appreciate the complexity of language and how it is used for various social purposes. Most linguistic knowledge is learned incidentally and informally through actual use. You can help children of diverse ethnolinguistic backgrounds learn about their own grammatical structures as well as those of others by making sure that your thematic units are filled with multicultural books from a range of genres. They can also see the connected nature of reading and writing—the fact that the life of a writer is the life of a reader. However, some of these understandings can be made explicit through Focus Lessons* and conferences with students. With your help, students can see themselves as language detectives and approach grammar as an interesting and exciting area of inquiry.

Make the teaching and learning of grammar exciting!

Extending Literacy Strategies

Sketch to Stretch*

Sketch to Stretch* activities help children understand that meanings can be communicated through a system other than language. Through drawing, children can transform or extend meanings expressed through language, construct new meanings, or discover insights that language alone cannot afford. Because Sketch to Stretch* activities encourage individual responses, they also help children to understand and value variations in interpretations.

Many teachers suggest Sketch to Stretch* activities as possible responses or extensions to books that children have read or heard. For example, children can sketch what the book (or selection or text) meant to them and then share them with class members. Students can make sketches on what are called "one-pagers" to prepare for discussion in Literature Response Groups*. A one-pager consists of (1) a drawing of a visual representation of ideas that each reader thinks are significant in a text; (2) one or two quotes from the text; and (3) an interpretative statement or comment (or short paragraph) that explains connections and questions that the reader has developed from the reading. Sketches or one-pagers can be used when reading the same text. Or they might be created for sets of texts that might be on the same topic or theme and, thus,

Beers (2003); Daniels & Zemelman (2004); Short & Harste (1996); Tierney & Readance (2000)

Livdahl et al. (1995)

One-pagers can be kept in Sketchbook Journals*.

may serve as a useful first step in creating Comparison Charts*. Or they might be used as part of the writing feedback that students receive in peer Content Conferences*.

Children may also be given a large piece of paper folded into four or more sections and asked to draw a picture of what happened in the beginning of the story in the first section, then what happened at the end of the story in the last section, and then what happened in the middle of the story in the other sections. Children may also include short sentences or captions in each section to correspond to their drawings. These can then be shared, used for storytelling, or as storyboards to support various Drama Experiences*.

See Wilhelm (2004) for more ideas on tableaux and other Sketch to Stretch* activities.

A type of Sketch to Stretch* possibility is creating a tableau (a French term for a scene that captures a significant moment) for major aspects of text. For narrative texts, the idea is to create one or a series of tableaux to portray story events, relationships, or thematic meanings in the whole text or excerpts of text. Often short summaries of these events also may be incorporated with the pictures. For nonfictional texts, idea tableaux may be created that depict major ideas or concepts (again, perhaps also including written text) in a text or excerpts of text.

Sketch to Stretch* activities are possible across the curriculum.

Thus, Sketch to Stretch* activities can be used across the curriculum. With non-fictional information books or topics, children may draw a picture of, say, a squirrel (perhaps also labeling its known characteristics) or a picture of what squirrels do (again including short descriptions of what they think squirrels' habits are). They may then read or listen to *Squirrels* by Wildsmith and *The Squirrel* by Lane, then create new squirrel sketches, adding, elaborating, and changing their initial drawings to reflect new information gained from these books. Such sketching activities can be used by the class as a whole to begin a new thematic unit or by a small group to depict the initial understandings of a particular topic. Children may try to sketch what they think could happen in a process in a particular science experiment and then check their ideas by actually doing the experiment. They may illustrate the process as a way of publishing their observations of the experiment. Also recall the example of fourth graders who were investigating the geographic concept of desert in Chapter 5. They began by drawing what they imagined a desert to look like. Remember how children made their own math books, using illustrations to depict their own understandings of mathematical concepts and procedures. In sum, Sketch to Stretch* activities can complement, extend, and deepen ideas, meanings, and concepts across the curriculum.

Wildsmith (1974); Lane (1981)

Graphing*

In Chapter 5, Graphing* was suggested as a major way by which children could incorporate mathematical understandings in thematic units. There are three major kinds of graphs: real, picture, and symbolic. Real graphs are especially important at the lower grades because they enable children to compare groups of real objects and provide the foundation of all other Graphing* activities. For example, a kindergarten teacher and his students created a real graph to compare and classify their shoes by considering a variety of attributes—laces or Velcro closings, right or left shoes, tennis shoes or other kinds, and colors. Once categories had been decided on, the teacher created a large grid on the floor with masking tape on which children placed the shoes according to category. Many real graphs are possible using manipulative objects in the classroom: seeds, coins, and buttons; snack items (cookies, crackers, pieces of vegetables, etc.); or blocks. Grids can be made on the floor or a table. Smaller grids can be made out of varying sizes of paper or cardboard or with any number of rows or categories.

Real graphs

Picture graphs are also appropriate at the lower elementary grades. A picture graph uses pictures or models to stand for real things. Once the kindergartners had classified their shoes on the real graph, their teacher helped them create a picture graph. The children counted and labeled each category on the real graph, then made smaller picture graphs using cutout construction paper shoes to stand for the shoes on the real graph. The possibilities for picture graphs are unlimited.

Picture graphs

Symbolic graphs, which are the most abstract level of graphs, use symbols to represent real things. The kindergartners could have constructed a symbolic graph by using an X instead of the cutout paper shoe. Symbolic graphs can be extended to represent increasingly more complex patterns and relationships and incorporate increasingly more mathematical operations. Bar graphs can be created as a result of a survey of the type of fruit children prefer or the kinds of vehicles found in the school parking lot over a week. Figure 7.15 shows how children place small paper rectangles on the graph to indicate preference in fruit. Figure 7.16 not only depicts kinds of vehicles but also involves more complex computation.

Graphs can plot frequency patterns, patterns of averages, percentages, and so on over time—for example, the number of vehicles observed over the different days of the

figure 7.15

figure 7.16

figure 7.17

Number of different vehicles found in the parking lot last week (March 6-10)

Key: Sedans ————
Station wagons – – – – –
Trucks • • • • • • •
Other ⌇⌇⌇⌇⌇⌇⌇⌇

week. Figure 7.17 illustrates such a graph. Graphs are frequently included as images in science (e.g., to display variables in experiments) and social studies texts (to depict economic trends or characteristics of countries). Thus, students need to both learn to read and interpret them and to be able to construct one themselves. Graphs and the mathematics involved with them are best understood as "real data" being gathered as part of student investigations.

In sum, a range of graphs can be incorporated into the classroom across the curriculum. For example, students studying various animal communities in the CREATING COMMUNITIES thematic unit used ideas from *Tiger Math* (a book about a real tiger, T. J., that tells of his life mostly as a cub). For each animal community (bees, ants, gorillas, etc.), a group created a circle graph, or pie graph, that showed where various bees, ants, gorillas, and so on could be found in either the United States or around the world. Other possibilities for graphing (bar graphs, line graphs, etc.) also emerged as their inquiries developed. Thus, planned graphs are considered as part of planning the WEB of a thematic unit (as was this case); others can emerge spontaneously while children are engaged in activities or projects related to the theme (which was this case, as well).

Book Extensions*

Young children learn by acting on their world, transforming it through play, art, drama, music, and language into something uniquely personal. Children can also enter into the world of the book and through these same avenues, remake and reshape their ex-

See Baratta-Lorton (1995), Lehrer & Schauble (2002), Moline (1996), and Nagda & Bickel (2000) for good discussions and examples of Graphing*.

Nagda & Bickel (2000)

periences with literature, making books memorable. It is through these transformations that the deepest response to books is possible.

Chapter 3 discussed ways to plan activities that would allow children to interact with the characters of books in the same ways they interact with people and events in real life. Activities such as these do not make workbooks out of children's literature. Instead, they represent experiences children are likely to have as language users in the real world. Children then transfer these possibilities to the world of the book. Most are designed to lead children back into the book, to refer to it for information, or to think more deeply about character motivation, themes, and ideas. Other activities can go beyond the book to help children compare and synthesize information, experiences, and ideas.

A range of Book Extensions*—for example, Semantic Maps*, Comparison Charts*, and Sketch to Stretch* activities—has already been covered in this chapter, and many others have been mentioned and illustrated in other chapters. Three kinds of Book Extensions* suitable for fictional literature—Plot Profiles*, Character Sociograms*, and Character Portraits*—are described in more detail in the following sections. Many others are possible. Figure 7.18 summarizes these possibilities.

Huck & Kiefer (2004); Johnson & Louis (1987)

PLOT PROFILES*

When children read and respond to literature, they become more informed about the structure of stories, recognizing certain clues to the kind of story they have begun (i.e., "Once upon a time" signals make-believe, whereas "It was a dark and stormy night" hints at mystery) and attending to the way in which a story rises to its climax or drops off into an ending that leaves the reader wishing for more. In integrated language classrooms, children are also authors. They write in a number of genres and so attend to literary elements from an author's as well as a reader's perspective. There are many ways to help children think about the elements of a piece of writing. Plot Profiles* are one way of calling attention to the way in which an author structures a story around a plot. Plot Profiles* also involve children in using time lines and rating scales and in plotting a graph, all of which can be used across the curriculum.

Huck & Kiefer (2004)

figure 7.18

Source: Huck & Kiefer, with Hepler & Hickman (2004)

Johnson & Louis (1987)

Plot Profiles* can be constructed with children of various ages. In working with younger children, however, the story should be fairly simple and have a strong, clear plot line. Folk- and fairytales work particularly well because the plot line tends to be clear and uncluttered. The children take a story such as *Goldilocks and the Three Bears* and begin an incident summary. The teacher records the children's suggestions as follows:

1. Mama Bear makes the porridge.
2. The porridge is too hot.
3. The three Bears go for a walk to let the porridge cool.
4. Goldilocks wanders into the Bears' house.
5. She tries the chairs.
6. She tries the porridge.
7. She tries the beds.
8. Goldilocks falls asleep.
9. The Bears come home.
10. They find the broken chair.
11. They find the empty porridge bowl.
12. They find Goldilocks.
13. Goldilocks leaps from the bed and runs away.

The teacher then shows children a time and excitement chart such as the one in Figure 7.19. The horizontal axis represents time, with number 1 being the first incident (Mama Bear makes porridge) and number 13 being the last (Goldilocks runs away). Beginning with the most exciting point (perhaps number 12, the discovery of Goldilocks), the children plot where that incident would fall in terms of time and excitement. Next, they plot the least exciting part (perhaps number 1, Mama Bear making porridge), then all the points in between. After the chart is plotted, the points are connected showing the rhythm of the story's plot.

Discussion should be encouraged throughout the plotting procedure so that the plot represents some sort of consensus. When children try this technique on other stories, they may also want to make Plot Profiles* individually or in small groups. The profiles can be the basis of some interesting discussions when children explain why they made the decisions that led to differences between charts for the same stories.

Plot Profiles* for children reading more complex books can also be an interesting way to describe plot twists visually. A mystery, for instance, can have a number of rather sharp peaks as the author leads the reader from one clue to the next. These profiles can also be quite long. Sometimes a broader definition of "incident" is required to make

See Bromley et al. (1995) for a version of Plot Profiles* called plot diagrams.

figure **7.19**

Time and Excitement Chart

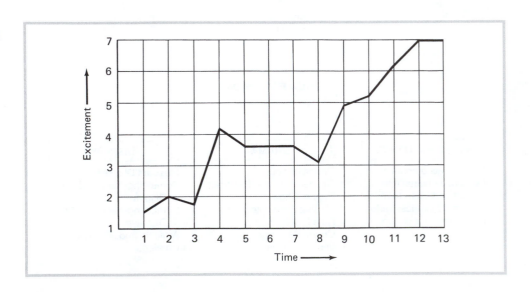

the profile less cumbersome. A child plotting Yolen's *The Devil's Arithmetic* may deal with the entire first chapter, up to the point of opening the door into the past, as one incident. Entry into the past may be a second, shorter incident, and then the period from entry until the wedding trip may be a third.

Illustrated Plot Profiles* can also be created on mural paper. At each point on the chart, an illustration represents the story incident. Children work in pairs to create the illustrations, selecting the medium that best exemplifies the incident being pictured. A sixth grader illustrating an incident in the poem "The Highwayman" decided that the scene where the highwayman is shot "like a dog on the highway" needed special attention. On a piece of black construction paper, he used white chalk to sketch in the moonlit highway, with trees picked out of the darkness and shadowy figures standing over the body of the highwayman. The highwayman was all in white except for the scarlet color at his throat where his life bled away across the dark road. The mural that resulted from this and other pictures, including collages and simple line drawings, was a dramatic illustration of the student's emotional response to this piece of literature.

CHARACTER SOCIOGRAMS*

In responding to a book she had just finished reading, one child described the power of the story this way: "It sees through the eyes of this person." In a sense, Character Sociograms* are a way of representing the reader's understanding of what he or she saw through the eyes of a literary character. More than that, however, the sociograms are an opportunity to think and talk about the relationships between characters in stories and to think about the way in which the reader is drawn into these relationships.

It is not easy to clearly describe the processes involved in creating Character Sociograms*. It may be useful to think of a sociogram as a character WEB, similar to the thematic WEBs we have already talked about. The main character, then, is thought of as the center of the sociogram, just as the theme is the center of a WEB. The other characters in the story are arranged around the central character. Arrows connect the characters and show the direction and distance of the relationships. Figure 7.20 shows such a Character Sociogram* for Viorst's *Alexander and the Terrible, Horrible, No Good, Very Bad Day.*

*Margin references:*
Yolen (1988)

Noyes (1983)

Levstik (1986)

Viorst (1972)

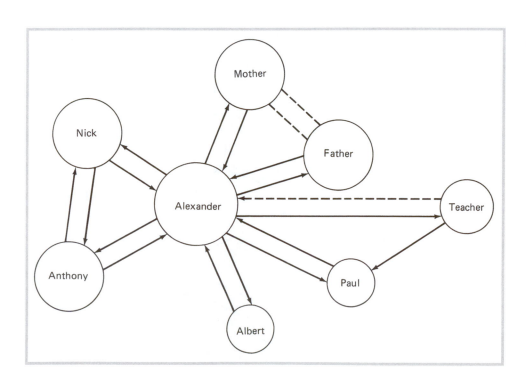

figure 7.20

Character Sociogram* for *Alexander and the Terrible, Horrible, No Good, Very Bad Day*

Some teachers have found that the initial steps in putting together a sociogram can be done by using movable objects and an overhead projector. For instance, the teacher sets out an array of small objects that can be used to represent each character in the story. Children identify an object with a character (this is an interesting part of the process, too!), and the teacher places each object on a transparency in relation to the main character. Pencils can be used as arrows and moved as discussion takes place.

Once the idea of the sociogram is generally understood, students work in pairs with either objects or paper shapes (circles, squares, etc.) and arrange their sociograms so that they can write brief statements on the connecting arrows. Figure 7.21 depicts an elaborated Character Sociogram* of the relationships in Viorst's book.

Johnson & Louis (1987)

As with most other activities described in this book, there is no single way to do a sociogram. Their power lies in the quality of the thinking and conversing children do as they construct them. The following guidelines are helpful:

Place the central character or characters at the center of the diagram.

Let the distance between characters reflect the perceived psychological distance between them.

Let the size of the shape representing a character vary with the importance or the power of the character.

Show the direction of a relationship by an arrow and its nature by a label.

Represent substantiated relationships with a solid line and inferred relationships with a broken line (a nice opportunity to discuss inferences).

Circle active characters with a solid line.

Circle significant absent characters with a broken line.

Place the characters who support the main character on one side of a dividing line and antagonistic characters on the other.

When Character Sociograms* are tried, teachers and children alike invent new conventions for dealing with new relationships. No single sociogram can ever entirely represent the relationships in a story, and no single interpretation of those relationships is

figure 7.21

An Elaborated Character Sociogram* for *Alexander and the Terrible, Horrible, No Good, Very Bad Day*

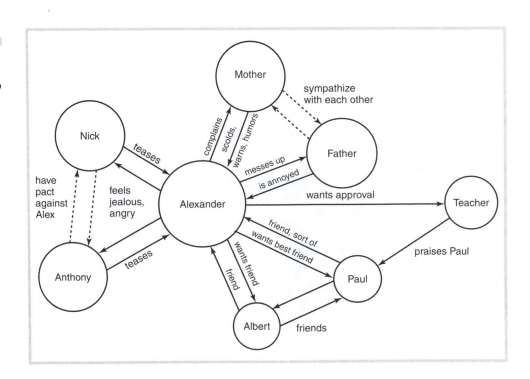

necessary or possible. Instead, sociograms are successful to the degree that they involve children in thinking carefully about their reading and support their judgments. (See the earlier section on Observation and Inference* for further discussion.)

CHARACTER PORTRAITS*

Character Portraits* are large or life-size portraits of a character in a book. Students outline the body, adding details of a character based on descriptions in the book. Also, "inner" characteristics might be depicted, as well as important objects and activities that are significantly related to the character. Dialogue bubbles are incorporated so that characters can "speak" to the audience to tell about themselves. In this way, the character can explain his or her history, feelings, details about the plot, and so forth. Character Portraits* can be done individually or in small groups.

Johnson (1997); Wilhelm (2004)

Small Charater Portraits* depict only the faces of characters—sort of small miniatures—that are drawn on the blank sides of index cards. On the lined sides, students would make some short connections of characters to their own lives or provide other significant responses related to these characters. Students create these cards and periodically share them with classmates, perhaps in Book Talks*. The cards become a documentation of the numerous texts they have read over the course of the year.

*Drama Experiences**

Creative dramatics, like the other arts, is a way of knowing. Drama can provide a rich vein of experiences that helps children to find out about themselves and others. Such insights can shape and cement children's social growth and lead to a spirit of cooperation and trust within the classroom community. Drama also allows children from a variety of cultural backgrounds to develop communicative competence by taking on many additional registers through the characters they choose to become.

Heathcote & Bolton (1995); McCaslin (1996); Siks (1977)

See Goldberg (1997) for drama ideas across the curriculum.

Way (1967)

Creative dramatics exists on a continuum from interpretive to improvisational activities, but it is not the memorization of someone else's script performed before an audience. The true value of all forms of drama lies in the process, not the product (or production). Teachers play important roles in providing and suggesting opportunities for Drama Experiences* and in supporting the aspects of this process of drama. They offer ideas, situations, and problems to pursue in drama, and they encourage individual children to participate. Most of the time children share forms of drama with others, but they can just as well create imaginary worlds for no audience but themselves. Thus, any sets, props, or costumes should be kept simple. A drama corner could contain such general costumes as hats, old coats, cloaks, and paper bags that can serve many costume functions. A prop such as a yardstick can function as a sword, a scepter, or a magic wand. Several types of Drama Experiences* are discussed in the following pages.

O'Neill & Lambert (1982)

Process is emphasized in creative dramatics.

IMPROVISATION*

Improvisation*, one of the more difficult but rewarding types of drama, gives children a problem and asks them to solve it. Children can take situations from real life (past, present, or future) or rework situations they find in literature. They assume character roles and interact to solve problems confronting them as these characters. Negotiation between the participants occurs as a drama unfolds, and the finding of joint solutions is a dynamic process. The children create new situations rather than reenact previous scenarios, yet they rely on their own experience and judgment to orchestrate these make-believe worlds.

Daniels & Zemelman (2004); O'Neill (1985); Wilhelm (1997)

Improvisation from a Book.*   In *The Green Book*, Pattie and her family are forced to leave Earth to find a new home on another planet. They can take only a change of clothes, one or two small personal items, and one book. In a small group, children

Walsh (1982)

discuss what book they will take and explain their choices. A list of books that everyone agrees are important for survival on a new planet emerges.

Improvisation* from the Past. As a wagon train heads west to California in the 1800s, many disasters befall the travelers. Winter is fast approaching, and the wagons must make it through the mountains before the winter blizzards hit. The sick and starving are slowing the group down. Children assume the roles of the settlers, both sick and healthy, and find a solution.

Improvisation* for the Future. A group of children becomes part of a community that values peace and has forbidden anyone to own or use weapons. A terrible warlike people are menacing the community's borders and threaten to destroy the family. Children search for possible solutions.

TELEVISION NEWS BROADCASTS AND TALK SHOWS*

Babbitt (1975)

Reading Rainbow is seen on Public Broadcasting System stations.

Television provides children with models for presenting information, conducting interviews, reviewing, and editorializing. Children may assume roles of favorite news broadcasters to present the classroom news, to interview historical characters, or to report on the latest information from a thematic unit. They may also give book reviews, like the children on PBS's *Reading Rainbow.* Sixth graders who had read *Tuck Everlasting* developed an Oprah Winfrey–like host who interviewed Tuck, Ma, Jesse, Miles, Winnie, and the Man in the Yellow Suit about their experiences. Class members took on the role of studio audience and asked their own questions. The children who played each of these characters had to recall events that took place in the book as they answered questions. They also had to immerse themselves in their character's personality to make the discussion more believable.

PUPPET SHOWS*

Batchelder & Comer (1956); Champlin & Renfro (1985); Lynch-Watson (1980)

Carle (1969)

Puppetry is an ancient type of drama and is still enjoyed around the world in many forms. Puppet Shows* give children a comfortable vehicle for personal expression and for writing scripts or improvising stories or other scenarios. Finger puppets, shadow puppets, and puppets made of socks, gloves, sticks, or even abstract shapes allow children to focus on the drama itself rather than on the manipulation of complex forms such as marionettes. Thus, although upper-elementary children may construct and use complicated puppets, most of the puppets younger children make or use should be kept simple. One first-grade teacher made a caterpillar out of an old brown sock and glued felt eyes to the top, then pulled it over her hand and had it "eat" through all the items of food in *The Very Hungry Caterpillar.* When she came to the part of the book where the caterpillar spins a cocoon, she pulled the bottom of the sock up over the caterpillar's head, then pulled the sock off entirely to reveal a felt "big, beautiful butterfly," which was wrapped around her hand and made to "fly away." The children were delighted and, of course, wanted to make their own caterpillars and read the story.

Older elementary and middle school students can create more elaborate puppets and Puppet Shows*. They might make puppets that portray important scenes in novels. They may also branch into nonfictional texts or topics. They might, for example, create puppets to depict various biological processes (changing of caterpillar to butterfly), or various phenomena (changing states of matter in the water cycle). In these latter cases, the Puppet Shows* serve as documentaries.

CHORAL READING*

See Beers (2003), Tierney & Readence (2000), and Wilner (1977) for more information on Choral Reading*.

Choral Reading* is an excellent way to share poetry and link it to musical performances. Poems are selected by the teacher or children. As a poem is read, everyone thinks about its mood and meaning to decide on ways to "orchestrate" its reading. The poem can be copied on an overhead transparency or a large piece of chart paper to identify the lines or refrains that are best suited to a single voice or small group interpretation and the lines that can be read by a larger group of voices. Directions such as fast/slow, loud/soft, or high/low can be incorporated, and sound effects or physical gestures can be added.

Reading materials other than poems can also be considered. Rhymes, patterned books, epics, or other books with lusciously lyrical or rhythmically sensitive language can be tried through Choral Reading*.

READER'S THEATER*

Reader's Theater* is an interpretive reading activity that allows us to relive the radio broadcasts of past or present. Unlike plays that require costumes, movement, and stage sets, Reader's Theater* is mostly auditory although it is frequently complemented by facial expressions and a few gestures. It is, therefore, well suited to tape recording for later playback at listening posts. When different groups try the same passage (or the same group attempts repeated readings), children develop the notion of multiple interpretations. They come to see that reading is an active and open process of constructing meaning, not the accurate pronunciation of words. Because Reader's Theater* usually incorporates a practice before presentation, less proficient readers are able to be successful in oral reading.

> Reader's Theater* provides an opportunity for oral reading. Attention is aurally focused.
>
> Tierney & Readance (2000)
>
> Sloyer (1982)

A short story or a part of a book that has an exciting plot, compelling characters, and language that calls for visual images should be selected for Reader's Theater*. Some information books, such as Aliki's *A Medieval Feast* and Cole's *The Magic School Bus and the Electric Field Trip*, are also possible choices. Long descriptive passages or narration do not always work well and may need to be deleted or summarized; the "he saids" and "she saids" and other less essential passages can be omitted. A narrator and character roles are assigned, an introduction is prepared, and after careful rehearsal, the "play" is presented. Although commercial scripts are available, children can write their own scripts or work with photocopies of passages on which they can make changes and highlight individual parts.

> Aliki (1983); Cole (1997)

STORY THEATER*

Like Reader's Theater*, Story Theater* involves children in interpreting written material. However, now a visual element is added. For younger children, the teacher frequently reads a story and has children pantomime the action as it unfolds. An alternative is to let several children read character dialogue and narrative while another group interprets the readings through pantomime, each child acting a particular character role. Written scripts or texts are not used, so pantomimists must listen carefully to the readers and interpret action and feelings nonverbally. Criteria for choosing material for Story Theater* are similar to those for Reader's Theater*, but now an element of character action is necessary. If a scene has characters sitting in chairs and talking, it might work well as Reader's Theater* but not as Story Theater*. Although most teachers choose stories for Story Theater*, other nonstory genres can also be used. Children can pantomime information books written by Gibbons—*The Post Office Book: Mail and How It Moves* and *Department Store*—that describe the movement of mail and the activities occurring at a department store on a typical day. Children also enjoy acting out a description of a chemical reaction, a plant's growth, or a frog's or caterpillar's metamorphosis.

> Moffett & Wagner (1992)
>
> - Story Theater* provides an opportunity for movement interpretation.
> - Some information books can also be used in Story Theater*.
>
> Gibbons (1982, 1984)

*Status of the Class**

Status of the Class* is a procedure developed by Atwell to keep track of students' daily status regarding writing. Each day the teacher quickly calls on each student to find out where he or she is in writing, and what the student is going to write about. Using a form that simply lists the names of the children down the left side with the rest of the paper separated into five columns, one column for each day of the week, the teacher

> Status of the Class* was initially used to keep track of students' status in writing.
>
> Atwell (1998)

notes what students will be doing. Besides the title of the piece, simple abbreviations are used to document the process: *PW* for prewriting activities (perhaps listing questions, making an outline or Semantic Map* to organize thoughts or ideas before attempting an initial draft); *D1, D2,* and so on for written drafts; *VD1, VD2,* and so on for visual image drafts; *PC* for peer conferencing (perhaps including the names of the peers with whom the student will conference); *SE* for self-editing, where a student goes through the last draft before publication; and *P* for publishing (the writing or typing of the final draft, along with any illustrations to be done). Content or Editing Conferences* to be scheduled with the teacher also might be determined and coded on the form. (See Chapter 6 as well as "Writing Activities and Experiences" in the present chapter for more details regarding writing.)

The Status of the Class* procedure offers a way for teachers to track students' work so they can be most responsive to them. They can best decide how and when to share their expertise. Status of the Class* also provides accountability by helping teachers and students who are working at different stages on many different pieces not to get lost in the cracks. For example, if a student has been working for several days on some aspect of the writing process, perhaps prewriting or self-editing, the teacher knows that it will be important to talk to the student that day to see what problems he or she might have and how to help. Documentation gives a teacher grounds for a heart-to-heart talk about problems in using time during writing workshop, such as playing or off-task behavior, so that the teacher can help students become more responsible.

Some teachers modify the Status of the Class* to fit the needs of their children and the way in which they organize their work. Older elementary students may use their planning Journals* to track their work. While children are at work, the teacher can check the journals, which are kept open on the students' desks, and then fill in their Status of the Class* form. Many teachers find that it saves class time to do it this way, especially if the class is large. By tracking their own work, the students have more opportunities to develop responsibility, commitment, and control in their writing and other work.

The idea of Status of the Class* can be extended and modified for monitoring other areas.

The idea of the Status of the Class* procedure has also been modified by many teachers for use in other areas of the curriculum. For example, a similar form can be devised to keep track of students' reading. Here the book or books students are reading are noted with abbreviations to indicate which page or chapter students are on in their reading and other relevant information. Initials such as *PR* (personal reading), *IR* (reading related to a particular student inquiry), or *RLRG* (reading that is part of a Literature Response Group*) might be used. Book Extensions* that students are engaged in could also be noted with initials: *CC* (Comparison Chart*) or *STS* (Sketch to Stretch*).

Status of the Class* procedures or checks are also especially useful in monitoring individual or small-group Student-Directed Inquiries*. Resources at hand or in need, problems students have resolved or still have, and facets of the project that have been accomplished or are still in progress can be documented by such a form so that teachers can keep track of the process and progress of inquiry projects.

Message Board*

See Boyd (1985) for a good classroom example of the use of a Message Board*.

The Message Board* is usually a bulletin board where the teacher and children exchange messages. The board fosters functional communication by helping children learn the range of purposes that literacy serves. Also, because both the teacher and children use the Message Board*, it encourages a sense of community. The Message Board* is usually placed near the door so communications can't be missed. Paper and envelopes, writing implements, and thumbtacks are available nearby to facilitate its use. In the beginning of the year, the teacher introduces the Message Board* by putting a welcoming note on it, along with a short set of directions for using it: that it can be used for certain times, that it can be used for personal or general messages, that all exchanges must include the names of receivers and senders, and that messages can be sealed in an envelope.

A range of teacher–children communications is possible on the Message Board*: Children may leave notes for the teacher regarding decisions they have made, or a small group may indicate that it is now ready to share the findings of its project. The teacher may suggest a book that a particular child may find useful for study or provide permission for a group of students to survey the third-graders on Tuesday on an issue related to some work they are doing in a thematic unit.

See Short & Harste (1996) for another discussion of Message Boards*.

Most of the time, however, children use the Message Board* to communicate with one another. They leave a new math story problem they have written and challenge others to solve it, they announce the creation of a particular Literature Response Group*, or they ask their classmates to help locate a book they had been using for a report they are writing. They can also write more personal messages addressed to particular children in the class.

Even though the class may also use Internet blogs (see Chapter 1) or other ways to interact with each other, having a Message Board* still offers a useful means for ongoing, quick communication.

Focus Lessons*

The idea of Focus Lessons* (frequently called mini-lessons) was developed by Calkins to teach various aspects of the writing process. In integrated language classrooms, however, Focus Lessons* are much more broadly thought of; they can deal with any topic in the curriculum, not writing only.

Calkins (1994); Routman (1996)

A Focus Lesson* is a short meeting—usually five to twenty minutes—with the whole class (or a small group), during which the teacher addresses an issue that has arisen. While teachers observe children engaged in activities in various projects they have taken on, they focus on the needs of the children rather than an artificial scope and sequence of skills. They note problems or difficulties children may be having, or they recognize children's current understandings or strategies that they can build on or extend.

Focus-Lessons* grow out of needs of children, not an artificial scope and sequence of skills.

Focus Lessons* are specific occasions in which teachers share their knowledge or expertise by providing explicit instruction. Focus Lessons* usually deal with three major issues: presenting procedural information, demonstrating techniques and strategies, and teaching specific operations and conventions. Focus Lessons* have been illustrated throughout this book, although they may not always have been labeled as such. The following examples summarize and clarify the range of possibilities.

PRESENTING PROCEDURAL INFORMATION

As one could expect, Focus Lessons* on procedures occur most frequently in the beginning of the year or at the beginning of a thematic unit. They are the ways through which teachers communicate what they expect from children and what children can expect from them. The lessons can cover the way each day will be structured and the activities that are available. They may include some of the choices for children in a particular thematic unit, how to keep a Sketchbook Journal*, or how to complete the forms in the Authors' Folders*. Focus Lessons* can cover the rules for using the Message Board*, explain how to set up a particular scientific experiment, or tell how to use Jackdaws*.

Focus-Lessons* address various procedural concerns.

DEMONSTRATING TECHNIQUES AND STRATEGIES

Focus Lessons* also involve teacher modeling and demonstrations. Frequently, children don't revise because they don't know how to actually manipulate the page, use carets and arrows, delete information, or add information when there's no room between the lines or in the margins. Thus, using a composition of their own or a text written in a Group-Composed Writing* activity, teachers illustrate revision techniques. Focus

Focus-Lessons* are opportunities for teacher demonstrations.

Lessons* can consist of various brainstorming sessions to help children consider topics for their writing, problems they may want to pursue in individual or small-group projects, and ways to go about tackling these questions in their inquiries. Focus Lessons* can demonstrate how to construct Semantic Maps* or Comparison Charts*, or how to do Character Portraits*, Character Sociograms*, Book Talks*, or various Sketch to Stretch* activities. They can examine or compare certain authors' styles (and ideologies) or the structure or organization of a particular written genre, or they can evaluate ways several authors have dealt with the same topics or information.

Sometimes a Focus Lesson* may be embedded in a typical routine such as Reading Aloud*. For example, teachers may use either a part of or a whole session reading aloud and "thinking aloud" of how they are transacting the ideas of text and the images—how they link or follow ideas being offered by authors and illustrators, how they pose questions or make predictions as they read, how they connect ideas expressed by the text and depicted in images, and so forth. In doing so, teachers demonstrate the covert thinking that they use to make sense of text. Periodic think-alouds may be employed for different genres so students become aware of the different types of thinking and questioning that are involved in different purposes of communication. For struggling readers, such modeling may be crucial for them to see how reading is an active, constructive process.

TEACHING SPECIFIC OPERATIONS AND CONVENTIONS

Focus Lessons* can deal with teaching specific conventions and skills. They can cover ways to use the cotext to figure out or identify a word when reading (see strategies described under Teaching Phonics and Spelling in Context*). They can include how to structure a business letter and how to use quotation marks or other kinds of punctuation. Focus Lessons* can show how to write up scientific observations, how to do certain mathematical operations or computations for a graph, or how to label and design a graph.

In sum, Focus Lessons* offer help and instruction on many diverse issues. It is important to know that they are rarely on procedures, techniques/strategies, or specific conventions only. Many Focus Lessons* include aspects of all three. Teachers plan certain Focus Lessons* ahead of time because they know the areas in which most children need guidance and support. However, many Focus Lessons* cannot be preplanned because they result from careful observations. They are conducted in a more spontaneous fashion because they address the needs of specific children in specific circumstances. Teachers usually keep track of their Focus Lessons* so that they know when they covered a topic and evaluate the ways in which the ideas were taken up by students. After further observation, they might tackle the same topic from another angle to see if a new approach might be more useful for children. Some teachers keep their notes or transparencies they used for Focus Lessons* in a special folder or binder that is available for students to refer to at a later date—which is especially helpful for students who were absent for a particular Focus Lesson*.

Conclusions

The activities and experiences described in this chapter are only suggestions. Teachers will make choices and draw on these strategies depending on the children with whom they work and the circumstances in which they find themselves. The activities presented here are based on teaching practices that we have seen in a variety of settings; other teachers who want to try them are free to modify or reshape them to meet their needs. They might serve as areas of teacher inquiry—see Guidelines for Teacher Inquiry at the end of the book.

Beers (2003); Daniels & Zemelman (2004); Tierney & Readance (2000)

See Wilhelm (2001) for a range of think-aloud strategies.

Focus Lessons* deal with specific conventions, strategies, and so on.

Focus Lessons* can be preplanned, or they can occur spontaneously.

References

Adams, M. J. (1990). *Beginning to read: Thinking and learning about print.* Cambridge, MA: MIT Press.

Abruscato, J. (2004). *Teaching children science: Discovery methods for the elementary and middle grades.* Boston: Pearson Education.

Alberti, D., Davitt, R. J., Ferguson, T. A., & Repass, S. O. (1974). *Teachers' guide for ice cubes: Melting rates of ice.* New York: McGraw-Hill.

Allen, J. (2000). *Yellow brick roads: Shared and guided paths to independent reading 4–12.* Portland, ME: Stenhouse.

Allington, R. L. (1994). The schools we have. The schools we need. *The Reading Teacher, 48,* 14–29.

Atwell, N. (1998). *In the middle: New understandings about writing, reading, and learning.* Portsmouth, NH: Boynton/Cook.

Baratta-Lorton, M. (1995). *Mathematics their way.* Menlo Park, CA: Addison-Wesley.

Barry, A. (2001). Now I know my ABC's, plus a whole lot more! Using alphabet books with first graders. In C. C. Pappas & L. B. Zecker (Eds.), *Teacher inquiries in literacy teaching-learning: Learning to collaborate in elementary urban classrooms* (pp. 59–78). Mahwah, NJ: Lawrence Erlbaum.

Barton, K. C. (2001). A picture's worth: Analyzing historical pictures in the elementary grades. *Social Education 65,* 278–283.

Barton, K. C., & Levstik, L. S. (2004). *Teaching history for the common good.* Mahwah, NJ: Lawrence Erlbaum.

Batchelder, M., & Comer, V. L. (1956). *Puppets and plays: A creative approach.* New York: Harper & Row.

Bauer, C. F. (1993). *New handbook for storytellers.* Chicago: American Library Association.

Bear, D. R., Invernizzi, M., Templeton, S., & Johnston, F. (1996). *Words their way: Word study for phonics, vocabulary and spelling instruction.* Columbus, OH: Merrill/Prentice Hall.

Beers, K. (2003). *When kids can't read, what teachers can do: A guide for teachers 6–12.* Portsmouth, NH: Heinemann.

Booth, D. (2001). *Reading and writing in the middle years.* Portland, ME: Stenhouse.

Borasi, R., & Siegel, M. (2000). *Reading counts: Expanding the role of reading mathematics classrooms.* New York: Teachers College Press.

Boyd, R. (1985). The message board: Language comes alive. In J. M. Newman (Ed.), *Whole language: Theory in use* (pp. 91–98). Portsmouth, NH: Heinemann.

Brandt, R. S. (1991). *Readings from Educational Leadership: Co-operative learning and the collaborative school.* Alexandria, VA: ASCD.

Bromley, K., Irwin-De Vitis, L., & Modlo, M. (1995). *Graphic organizers: Visual strategies of active learning.* New York: Scholastic.

Bryan, J. (1998). K-W-W-L: Questioning the known. *The Reading Teacher, 51,* 618–620.

Butler, A., & Turbill, J. (1984). *Towards a reading-writing classroom.* Rozelle, Australia: Primary English Teaching Association.

Byrnes, D. A. (1988). Children and prejudice. *Social Education, 52,* 267–271.

Calkins, L. M. (1994). *The art of teaching writing.* Portsmouth, NH: Heinemann.

Calkins, L. M. (2001). *The art of teaching reading.* New York: Longman.

Carroll, P. S. (2004). *Integrated literacy instruction in the middle grades: Channeling young adolescents' spontaneous overflow of energy.* Boston: Pearson Education.

Chambers, A. (1986). *The practical guide to marbleizing paper.* New York: Thames & Hudson.

Chambers, A. (1996). *Tell me: Children, reading and talk.* York, ME: Stenhouse.

Champlin, C., & Renfro, N. (1985). *Storytelling with puppets.* Chicago: American Library Association.

Clay, M. (1979). *Reading: The patterning of complex behavior.* Portsmouth, NH: Heinemann.

Cohen, E. G. (1994). *Designing groupwork: Strategies for the heterogeneous classroom.* New York: Teachers College Press.

Cohen, E. G. (1998). Making cooperative learning equitable. *Educational Leadership, 56,* 18–21.

Cohen, E. G., Lotan, R. A., Whitcomb, J. A., Balderrama, M. V., Cossey, R., & Swansom, P. E. (1994). Complex instruction: Higher order thinking in heterogeneous classrooms. In S. Sharan (Ed.), *Handbook of cooperative learning methods* (pp. 82–96). Westport, CT: Greenwillow Press.

Conference on College Composition and Communication. (1988). *The national policy* (position statement). Urbana, IL: National Council of Teachers of English.

Cope, B., & Kalantzis, M. (Eds.). (2000). *Multiliteracies: Literacy learning and the design of social futures.* London: Routledge.

Cunningham, P. M. (2005). *Phonics they use: Words for reading and writing.* Boston: Pearson Education.

Cunningham, P. E., & Cunningham, J. W. (1992). Making words: Enhancing the invented spelling-decoding connections. *The Reading Teacher, 46,* 106–115.

Cunningham, P. M., Moore, S. A., Cunningham, J. W., & Moore, D. W. (2004). *Reading and writing in elementary classrooms: Research based K–4 instruction.* Boston: Pearson Education.

Dahl, K. L., Scharer, P., Lawson, L. L., & Grogan, P. R. (2001). *Rethinking phonics: Making the best teaching decisions.* Portsmouth, NH: Heinemann.

Dalton, J. (1985). *Adventures in thinking: Creative thinking and co-operative talk in small groups.* South Melbourne, Australia: Nelson (Distributed by Heinemann, Portsmouth, NH).

Daniels, H. (2002). *Literature circles: Voice and choice in book clubs and reading groups.* Portland, ME: Stenhouse.

Daniels, H., & Zemelman, S. (2004). *Subjects matter: Every teacher's guide to content-area reading.* Portsmouth, NH: Heinemann.

de Boo, M. (1999). *Enquiring children: Challenging teaching.* Buckingham, England: Open University Press.

Delpit, L. (1995). *Other people's children: Cultural conflict in the classroom.* New York: The New Press.

Duke, N. K., & Bennett-Armistead, V. S. (2003). *Reading and writing informational text in the primary grades: Research-based practices.* New York: Scholastic.

Duthie, C. (1996). *True stories: Nonfiction literacy in the primary classroom.* York, ME: Stenhouse.

Efland, A. D. (2002). *Art and cognition: Integrating the visual arts in the curriculum.* New York: Teachers College Press.

Ellis, A. (1986). *Teaching and learning elementary social studies.* Boston: Allyn & Bacon.

Fennimore, F. (1992). *The art of the handmade book.* Chicago: Chicago Review Press.

Fisher, B. (1991). *Joyful learning: A whole language kindergarten.* Portsmouth, NH: Heinemann.

Fisher, B. (1995). *Thinking and learning together: Curriculum and community in a primary classroom.* Portsmouth, NH: Heinemann.

Fisher, B., & Medvic, E. F. (2003). *For reading out loud.* Portsmouth, NH: Heinemann.

Fletcher, R., & Portalupi, J. (2001). *Writing workshop: The essential guide.* Portsmouth, NH: Heinemann.

Fried, R. L. (2001). *The passionate teacher: A practical guide.* Boston: Beacon Press.

Fulwiler, T. (1980). Journals across the disciplines. *English Journal, 69,* 14–22.

Fulwiler, T. (1982). Writing: An act of cognition. In C. W. Griffin (Ed.), *New directions for teaching and learning: No. 12. Teaching writing in all disciplines* (pp. 15–26). San Francisco: Jossey-Bass.

Gee, J. P. (1996). *Social linguistics and literacies: Ideology in discourses.* London: Taylor & Francis.

Gerwin, D., & Zevin, J. (2003). *Teaching U.S. history as mystery.* Portsmouth, NH: Heinemann.

Glasswell, K., Parr, J. M., & McNaughton, S. (2003). Four ways to work against yourself when conferencing with struggling writers. *Language Arts, 80,* 291–308.

Goldberg, M. (1997). *Arts and learning: An integrated approach to teaching and learning in multicultural and multilingual settings.* New York: Longman.

Good, T. L., & Brophy, J. E. (1999). *Looking into classrooms.* New York: HarperCollins.

Goodman, K. (1993). *Phonics phacts.* Portsmouth, NH: Heinemann.

Graves, D. H. (1983). *Writing: Teachers and children at work.* Portsmouth, NH: Heinemann.

Graves, D. H. (1994). *A fresh look at writing.* Portsmouth, NH: Heinemann.

Hahn, M. E. (2002). *Reconsidering read-aloud.* Portland, ME: Stenhouse.

Harste, J. C., Short, K. G., & Burke, C. (1996). *Creating classrooms for authors and inquirers.* Portsmouth, NH: Heinemann.

Harvey, S. (1998). *Nonfiction matters: Reading, writing, and research in grades 3–8.* Portland, ME: Stenhouse.

Harvey, S., & Goudvis, A. (2000). *Strategies that work: Teaching comprehension to enhance understanding.* Portland, ME: Stenhouse.

Heath, S. B. (1983). *Ways with words: Language, life, and work in communities and classrooms.* Cambridge: Cambridge University Press.

Heathcote, D., & Bolton, G. (1995). *Drama for learning: Dorothy Heathcote's mantle of the expert approach to education.* Portsmouth, NH: Heinemann.

Hendrick, J. (Ed.). (1997). *First steps tioward teaching the Reggio way.* Upper Saddle River, NJ: Prentice-Hall.

Hepler, S. (1991). Talking our way to literacy in the classroom community. *The New Advocate, 4,* 179–191.

Hill, B. C., Johnson, N. J., & Noe, K. L. S. (1995). *Literature circles and response.* Norwood, MA: Christopher-Gordon.

Hill, S., & Hill, T. (1990). *The collaborative classroom: A guide to co-operative learning.* Portsmouth, NH: Heinemann.

Hillocks, G. (1986). *Research on written composition: New directions for teaching.* Urbana, IL: ERIC Clearinghouse on Reading and Communication Skills.

Holdaway, D. (1979). *The foundations of literacy.* Sydney, Australia: Ashton Scholastic.

Hollins, E. R. (1996). *Culture in school learning: Revealing the deep meaning.* Mahwah, NJ: Lawrence Erlbaum.

Hornsby, D., & Sukarna, D. (1988). *Read-on: A conference approach to reading.* Portsmouth, NH: Heinemann.

Huck, C. S., & Kiefer, B. Z., with Hepler, S., & Hickman, J. (2004). *Children's literature in the elementary school.* Boston: McGraw-Hill.

Hyde, A. A., & Bizar, M. (1989). *Thinking in context: Teaching cognitive processes across the elementary curriculum.* White Plains, NY: Longman.

Jackdaw. Grossman Publishers in association with Jackdaw Pub., Ltd., London, England.

Johnson, P. (1992). *A book of one's own.* Portsmouth, NH: Heinemann.

Johnson, P. (1993). *Literacy through the book arts.* Portsmouth, NH: Heinemann.

Johnson, P. (1997). *Picture and words together: Children illustrating and writing their own books.* Portsmouth, NH: Heinemann.

Johnson, T. D., & Louis, D. R. (1987). *Literacy through literature.* Portsmouth, NH: Heinemann.

Kiefer, B. (1995). *The potential of picturebooks: From visual literacy to aesthetic understanding.* Englewood Cliffs, NJ: Prentice Hall.

Kirshner, D., & Whitson, J. A. (Eds.). (1997). *Situated cognition: Social, semiotic, and psychological perspectives.* Mahwah, NJ: Lawrence Erlbaum.

Krashen, S. (1993). *The power of reading: Insights from research.* Englewood, CO: Libraries Unlimited.

Kress, G., Jewitt, C., Ogborn, J., & Tsatsarelis, C. (2001). *Multimodal teaching and learning: The rhetorics of the science classroom.* London: Continuum.

Krogness, M. M. (1995). *Just teach me, Mrs. K.* Portsmouth, NH: Heinemann.

Ladson-Billings, G. (1994). *The dreamkeepers: Successful teachers of African-American children.* San Francisco: Jossey-Bass.

Lave, J., & Wenger, W. (1991). *Situated learning: Legitimate peripheral participation.* New York: Cambridge University Press.

Lee, C. D., & Smagorinsky, P. (Eds.). (2000). *Vygotskian perspectives on literacy research: Constructing meaning through collaborative inquiry.* Cambridge: Cambridge University Press.

Lehrer, R., & Schauble, L. (Eds.). (2002). *Investigation in real data in the classroom: Exploring children's understanding of math and science.* New York: Teachers College Press.

Lensmire, T. J. (1994). *When children write: Critical revisions of the writing workshop.* New York: Teachers College Press.

Lensmire, T. J. (2000). *Powerful writing: Responsible teaching.* New York: Teachers College Press.

Levstik, L. S. (1986). The relationship between historical response and narrative in a sixth-grade classroom. *Theory and Research in Social Education, 14,* 1–15.

Levstik, L. S., & Barton, K. C. (2001). *Doing history: Investigating with children in elementary and middle schools.* Mahwah, NJ: Erlbaum.

Livdahl, B. S., Smart, K., Wallman, J., Herbert, T. K., Geiger, D. K., & Anderson, J. L. (1995). *Stories from response-centered classrooms: Speaking, questioning, and theorizing from the center of the action.* New York: Teachers College Press.

Lynch-Watson, J. (1980). *The shadow puppet book.* New York: Sterling.

McCaslin, N. (1996). *Creative drama in the classroom.* White Plains, NY: Longman.

McKenzie, M. (1977). The beginnings of literacy. *Theory Into Practice, 16,* 315–324.

McKenzie, M. (1985). Shared writing: Apprenticeship in writing. *Language Matters, 1,* 1–5.

Moffett, J., & Wagner, B. J. (1992). *Student centered language arts, K–12.* Portsmouth, NH: Boynton/Cook.

Moline, S. (1996). *I see what you mean: Children at work with visual information.* York, ME: Stenhouse.

Moll, L. (1992). Literacy research in community and classrooms. In R. Beach, J. L. Green, M. L. Kamil, & T. Shanahan (Eds.), *Multidisciplinary perspectives on literacy research* (pp. 211–244). Urbana, IL: National Conference on Research in English.

Mossip, J. (1985). It makes you feel needed: Students as teachers. In J. M. Newman (Ed.), *Whole language: Theory in use* (pp. 131–136). Portsmouth, NH: Heinemann.

Newmann, F., Sescada, W. G., & Wehlage, G. G. (1995). *A guide to authentic instruction and assessment: Vision, standards and scoring.* Madison: Wisconsin Center for Education Research.

Nieto, S. (2000). *Affirming diversity: The sociopolitical context of multicultural education.* White Plains, NY: Longman.

O'Neill, C. (1985). Imagined worlds in theatre and drama. *Theory Into Practice, 24,* 158–165.

O'Neill, C., & Lambert, A. (1982). *Drama structures: A practical handbook for teachers.* Portsmouth, NH: Heinemann.

Ogle, D. (1986). K-W-L: A teaching model that develops active reading of expository text. *The Reading Teacher, 39,* 564–570.

Pappas, C. C., & Brown, E. (1989). Using turns at story "reading" as scaffolding for learning. *Theory Into Practice, 28,* 105–113.

Pappas, C. C., Hart, S., Escobar, & Barry, A. (2001). Fostering first-graders' phonemic awareness and much more: Using ABC books in the reading-aloud curriculum genre. In C. C. Pappas & L. B. Zecker (Eds.), *Transforming literacy curriculum genres: Working with teacher researchers in urban classrooms* (pp. 103–126). Mahwah, NJ: Lawrence Erlbaum.

Pappas, C. C., & Zecker, L. B. (Eds.). (2001a). *Teacher inquiries in literacy teaching-learning: Learning to collaborate in elementary urban classrooms.* Mahwah, NJ: Lawrence Erlbaum.

Pappas, C. C., & Zecker, L. B. (Eds.). (2001b). *Transforming literacy curriculum genres: Working with teacher researchers in urban classrooms.* Mahwah, NJ: Lawrence Erlbaum.

Pierce, K. M., & Gilles, C. J. (Eds.). (1993). *Cycles of meaning: Exploring the potential of talk in learning communities.* Portsmouth, NH: Heinemann.

Radencich, M. C., & McKay, L. J. (1995). *Flexible grouping for literacy in the elementary grades.* Boston: Allyn & Bacon.

Raphael, T., Pardo, L. S., & Highfield, K. (2002). *Book Club: A literature-based curriculum.* Lawrence, MA: Small Planet Communications.

Reddy, M., Jacobs, P., McCrohon, C., & Herrenkohl, L. R. (1998). *Creating scientific communities in the elementary schools.* Portsmouth, NH: Heinemann.

Revel-Wood, M. (1988). Invitations to read, to write, to learn. In J. C. Harste & K. G. Short (Eds.), *Creating classrooms for authors: The reading-writing connection* (pp.169–179). Portsmouth, NH: Heinemann.

Robinson, G. (1995). *Sketch-books: Explore and store.* Portsmouth, NH: Heinemann

Rogoff, B. (1990). *Apprenticeship in thinking: Cognitive development in social context.* New York: Oxford University Press.

Routman, R. (1988). *Transitions: From literature to literacy.* Portsmouth, NH: Heinemann.

Routman, R. (1996). *Literacy at the crossroads: Crucial talk about reading, writing and other teaching dilemmas.* Portsmouth, NH: Heinemann.

Samway, K. D., & Whang, G. (1996). *Literature study circles in a multicultural classroom.* York, ME: Stenhouse.

Samway, K. D., Whang, G., & Pippitt, M. (1995). *Buddy reading: Cross-age tutoring in a multicultural school.* Portsmouth, NH: Heinemann.

Saul, W., Reardon, J., Pearce, C., Dieckman, C., & Neutze, C. (2002). *Science workshop: Reading, writing, and thinking like a scientist.* Portsmouth, NH: Heinemann.

Schaps, E., & Solomon, D. (1991). Schools and classroom as caring communities. In R. Brandt (Ed.), Readings from *Educational Leadership: Cooperative learning and the collaborative school* (pp. 61–63). Alexandria, VA: ASCD.

Schulivitz, U. (1985). *Writing with pictures: How to write and illustrate children's books.* New York: Watson-Guptill.

Sedgwick, F. (2002). *Enabling children's learning through drawing.* London: David Fulton.

Sharan, Y., & Sharan, S. (1992). *Expanding cooperative learning through group investigation.* New York: Teachers College Press.

Short, K. G., & Harste, J. C. (1996). *Creating classrooms for authors and inquirers.* Portsmouth, NH: Heinemann.

Short, K. G., & Pierce, K. M. (Eds.). (1998). *Talking about books: Literature discussion groups in K–8 classrooms.* Portsmouth, NH: Heinemann.

Siks, G. B. (1977). *Drama with children.* New York: Harper & Row.

Sloyer, S. (1982). *Readers' Theatre: Story dramatization in the classroom.* Urbana, IL: National Council of Teachers of English.

Sonnenschein, F. M. (1988). Countering prejudiced beliefs and behaviors: The role of the social studies professional. *Social Education, 52,* 262–266.

Stone, L. (1986). International and multicultural education. In V. Atwood (Ed.), *Elementary social studies: Research as a guide to practice* (pp. 34–54). Washington, DC: National Council for the Social Studies.

Strickland, D., & Cullinan, B. (1990). Afterword. In Adams, M. J. *Beginning to read: Thinking and learning about print* (pp. 425–434). Cambridge, MA: MIT Press.

Takaki, R. (1993). *A different mirror: A history of multicultural America*. Boston: Little, Brown.

Tierney, R. J., & Readence, J. E. (2000). *Reading strategies and practices: A compendium*. Boston: Allyn & Bacon.

Tunnell, M. O., & Jacobs, J. (1989). Using "real" books: Research findings on literature-based reading in instruction. *The Reading Teacher, 42,* 470–477.

Unsworth, L. (2001). *Teaching multiliteracies across the curriculum: Changing contexts of text and image in classroom practice.* Buckingham, England: Open University Press.

Vygotsky, L. (1978). *Mind in society: The development of higher psychological processes.* Cambridge, MA: Harvard University Press.

Waggstaff, J. M. (1997–1998). Building practical knowledge of letter–sound correspondences: A beginner's word wall and beyond. *The Reading Teacher, 51,* 298–306.

Watson, M., in collaboration with Ecken, L. (2003). *Learning to trust: Transforming difficult elementary classrooms through developmental discipline.* San Francisco: Jossey-Bass.

Way, B. (1967). *Development through drama.* Atlantic Highlands, NJ: Humanities Press.

Weaver, C. (1996). *Teaching grammar in context.* Portsmouth, NH: Boynton/Cook.

Weaver, C. (2002). *Reading process and practice.* Portsmouth, NH; Heinemann.

Weber, L. (1989). Teachers using historical fiction. In J. Hickman & B. Cullinan (Eds.), *Weaving Charlotte's web: Children's literature in the elementary classroom* (pp. 147–156). Needham Heights, MA: Christopher-Gordon.

Wells, G. (1999). *Dialogic inquiry: Toward a sociocultural practice and theory of education.* Cambridge: Cambridge University Press.

Wells, G. (2001a). The case for dialogic inquiry. In G. Wells (Ed.), *Action, talk, and text: Learning and teaching through inquiry* (pp. 171–200). New York: Teachers College Press.

Wells, G. (Ed.). (2001b). *Action, talk, and text: Learning and teaching through inquiry.* New York: Teachers College Press.

Wertsch, J. V. (1985). *Vygotsky and the social formation of mind.* Cambridge: Cambridge University Press.

Wertsch, J. V. (1998). *Mind as action.* New York: Oxford University Press.

Whitin, P., & Whitin, D. (1997). *Inquiry at the window: Pursuing the wonders of learners.* Portsmouth, NH: Heinemann.

Wilde, S. (1992). *You kan red this!: Spelling and punctuation for whole language classrooms, K–6.* Portsmouth NH: Heinemann.

Wilde, S. (1997). *What's a schwa sound anyway? A holistic guide to phonetics, phonics, and spelling.* Portsmouth, NH: Heinemann.

Wilhelm, J. D. (1997). *You gotta BE the book.* New York: Teachers College Press.

Wilhelm, J. D. (2001). *Improving comprehension with think-aloud strategies.* New York: Scholastic.

Wilhelm, J. D. (2004). *Reading is seeing: Learning to visualize scenes, characters, ideas, and text worlds to improve comprehension and reflective reading.* New York: Scholastic.

Wilner, I. (1977). *The poetry troupe: An anthology of poems to read aloud.* New York: Scribners.

Wilson, A. (1987). Cross-cultural experiential learning for teachers. *Theory Into Practice, 26,* 519–527.

Wolfer, P. (2001). My jounrey to create a writing workshop for first graders. In C. C. Pappas & L. B. Zecker (Eds.). *Teacher inquiries in literacy teaching-learning: Learning to collaborate in elmentary urban classrooms* (pp. 79–95). Mahwah, NJ: Lawrence Erlbaum.

Wood, D. (1998). *How children think and learn: The social contexts of cognitive development.* Malden, MA: Blackwell.

Wood, K. D., & Dickinson, T. S. (Eds.). (2000). *Promoting literacy in grades 4–9: A handbook for teachers and administrators.* Boston: Allyn & Bacon.

Yopp, H. K. (1992). Developing phonemic awareness in young children. *The Reading Teacher, 48,* 538–542.

Young, K. A. (1994). *Constructing buildings, bridges, and minds: Building an integrated curriculum through social studies.* Portsmouth, NH: Heinemann.

Children's Literature

ABC I Like Me! by N. Carlson. Viking, 1997.

Alexander and the Terrible, Horrible, No Good, Very Bad Day by J. Viorst. Illustrated by R. Cruz. Atheneum, 1972.

Alligators All Around: An Alphabet by M. Sendak. HarperCollins, 1962.

Amelia's Road by L. J. Altman. Illustrated by E. O. Sanchez. Lee & Low Books, 1993.

Animalia by G. Base. Henry N. Abrams, 1986.

The Bee by S. Crewe. Raintree Steck-Vaughn, 1997.

Big City Port by B. Maestro & E. DelVecchio. Illustrated by G. Maestro. Scholastic, 1983.

Bloomers! by R. Blumberg. Aladdin, 1996.

Brown Bear, Brown Bear, What Do You See? by B. Martin, Jr. Illustrated by E. Carle. Holt, 1983.

The Cabin Faced West by J. Fritz. Coward, McCann, 1958.

Catherine, Called Birdy by K. Cushman. HarperTrophy, 1994.

The Cat's Purr by A. Bryan. Atheneum, 1985.

Chato's Kitchen by G. Soto. Illustrated by S. Guevara. G. P. Putman, 1995.

Child of the Owl by L. Yep. HarperTrophy, 1977.

Christmas in the Big House, Christmas in the Quarters by S. McKissack & F. L. McKissack. Illustrated by J. Thompson. Scholastic, 1994.

Department Store by G. Gibbons. Harper & Row, 1984.

A Desert Scrapbook: Dawn to Dusk in the Sonoran Desert by V. Wright-Frierson. Simon & Schuster, 1996.

The Devil's Arithmetic by J. Yolen. Viking Kestrel, 1988.

Digging up Dinosaurs by Aliki. Crowell, 1988.

Dr. Xargle's Book or Earthlets by J. Willis. Illustrated by R. Ross. Andersen Press, 2002.

Evolution by J. Cole. Illustrated by Aliki. Crowell, 1987.

From Pictures to Words: A Book about Making a Book by J. Stephens. Holiday House, 1995.

A Girl Called Boy by B. Hurmence. Clarion, 1982.

The Greek News by A. Powell & P. Steele. Candlestick Press, 1996.

The Green Book by J. P. Walsh. Farrar, Straus, & Giroux, 1982.

Harlem by W. D. Myers. Illustrated by C. Myers. Scholastic Press, 1997.

Here Comes Henny by C. Pomerantz. Illustrated by N. W. Parker. Greenwillow, 1994.

The Highwayman by A. Noyes. Illustrated by C. Mikolaycak. Lothrop, 1983.

The Honey Makers by G. Gibbons. Morrow Junior Books, 1997.

How Do Bees Make Honey? by A. Claybourne. Illustrated by S. Allington & A. Spenceley. Usborne Publishing, 1994.

If I Had a Paka: Poems in Eleven Languages by C. Pomerantz. Illustrated by N. Tafuri. Greenwillow, 1993.

In Their Own Words by M. Meltzer. Crowell, 1977.

Jack and the Bean Tree by G. E. Halley. Crown, 1986.

James and the Giant Peach by R. Dahl. Knopf, 1961.

Johnny Tremain by E. Forbes. Houghton Mifflin, 1943.

Joyful Noise: Poems for Two Voices by P. Fleischman. Illustrated by E. Beddows. HarperTrophy, 1988.

The Ladybug and Other Insects by First Discovery Books. Translated from the French by C. Cramer. (American edition by L. Goldsen.) Scholastic, 1991.

The Last Princess: The Story of Princess Ka'iulani of Hawai'i by F. Stanley. Illustrated by D. Stanley. Macmillan, 1994.

The Ledgerbook of Thomas Blue Eagle by G. Mattaei & J. Grutman. Illustrated by A. Cvijonvic. Lickie Publishing, 1994.

The Life and Times of the Honeybee by C. Micucci, Houghton Mifflin, 1996.

Lincoln: A Photobiography by R. Freedman. Clarion, 1987.

The Little Red Hen by B. Barton. HarperCollins, 1993.

The Magic Porridge Pot by P. Galdone. Houghton Mifflin, 1976.

The Magic School Bus and the Electric Field Trip by J. Cole. Illustrated by B. Degen. Scholastic, 1997.

The Magic School Bus at the Waterworks by J. Cole. Illustrated by B. Degen. Scholastic, 1986.

The Magic School Bus inside a Beehive by J. Cole. Illustrated by B. Degen. Scholastic, 1996.

Many Luscious Lollipops: A Book about Adjectives by R. Heller. G. P. Putman, 1989.

A Medieval Feast by Aliki. Crowell, 1983.

Mojave by D. Siebert. Illustrated by W. Minor. Thomas Y. Crowell, 1988.

Mrs. Wishy Washy by J. Cowley. Illustrated by E. Fuller. Wright Group, 1981.

My Brother Sam Is Dead by J. Collier & L. Collier. Four Winds, 1974.

On Market Street by A. Lobel. Illustrated by A. Lobel. Greenwillow, 1981.

The Owl and the Woodpecker by B. Wildsmith. Oxford University Press, 1971.

Owl Babies by M. Waddell. Illustrated by P. Benson. Candlewick Press, 1992.

Pearl Moscowitz's Last Stand by A. A. Levin. Tambourine, 1993.

People by P. Spier. Doubleday, 1980.

"The Pickety Fence" by D. McCord in *One at a Time* by D. McCord. Little, Brown, 1986.

A Picture Book of Frederick Douglass by D. A. Adler. Illustrated by S. Byrd. Holiday House, 1993.

Pioneer Women: Voices from the Kansas Frontier by J. L. Stratton. Simon & Schuster, 1981.

The Post Office Book: Mail and How It Moves by G. Gibbons. Harper & Row, 1982.

Questions and Answers about Bees by B. P. Reigot. Illustrated by K. Hendrickson. Scholastic, 1995.

Roar and More by K. Kuskin. HarperCollins, 1990.

The Roman News by Langley, A., & de Souza, P. Candlewick Press, 1996.

Rosie the Riveter by P. Colman. Crown, 1995.

The Secret Garden by F. H. Burnett. Lippincott, 1962.

Seedfolks by P. Fleischman. Illustrated by J. Pedersen. Harper Collins, 1997

Shoes from Grandpa by M. Fox. Illustrated by P. Mullins. Orchard Books, 1989.

Small Green Snake by L. M. Gray, Illustrated by H. Meade. Orchard, 1994.

The Squirrel by M. Lane. Illustrated by K. Lilly. Dial, 1981.

Squirrels by B. Wildsmith. Oxford University Press, 1974.

Sylvester and the Magic Pebble by W. Steig. Windmill, 1979.

The Teeny Tiny Woman by P. Galdone. Clarion, 1984.

Thunder at Gettysburg by P. L. Gauch. Illustrated by S. Gammell. Coward, McCann & Geoghegan, 1975.

Tiger Math: Learning to Graph from a Baby Tiger by A. W. Nagda & C. Bickel. Henry Holt, 2000.

Tin Lizzie by P. Spier. Doubleday, 1978.

To Be a Slave by J. Lester. Dial, 1968.

Tuck Everlasting by N. Babbitt. Farrar, Straus, & Giroux, 1975.

Tunnels by G. Gibbons. Holiday House, 1984.

The Very Hungry Caterpillar by E. Carle. Philomel, 1969.

Uncle Jed's Barbershop by M. K. Mitchell. Illustrated by J. Ransome. Simon & Schuster, 1993.

Uptown by B. Collier. Henry Holt, 2000.

Wild and Woolly Mammoths by Aliki. Crowell, 1977.

Winnie the Pooh by A. A. Milne. Illustrated by E. Shepard. Dutton, 1988 (1926).

Wizard of Earthsea by U. LeGuin. Parnassus, 1968.

Women's Diaries of the Westward Journey by L. Schlissel. Schocken, 1982.

Working Cotton by S. A. Williams. Illustrated by C. Byard. Harcourt Brace Jovanovich, 1992.

Yo! Yes? by C. Rascha. Orchard Books, 1993.

chapter

8

Learning Kid-Watching Procedures and Techniques

T his chapter describes certain procedures and techniques to help you become a good kid watcher. Teachers in integrated language classrooms have certain views regarding learners (and learning), language, and knowledge (see Chapters 1 and 2). They believe that children's language and concepts (knowledge) are related to the kinds of experiences they have in a range of contexts. Consequently, most traditional ways to assess or evaluate children's development or learning are rarely useful. For example, completed ditto sheets, besides not being examples of meaningful use of language, are frequently misleading because they cannot capture the *process* of what children are actually doing or learning. "Wrong" answers can reflect children's intelligent thinking or reasonable hypotheses, whereas "right" answers can be based on misunderstandings or misconceptions. There is no way for the teacher to know which is the case because these materials offer little reliable information for making appropriate teaching decisions.

Integrated language teachers need alternative means for assessment and evaluation of children's ways with words: how they learn to use a variety of language registers in a variety of contexts and apply what they know in a range of activities and projects. Teachers need assessment and evaluation strategies that are developmentally and culturally appropriate for gaining information about what children say (and/or write and draw) and do so that they can understand how the children's schemas are being modified in various domains. This information is necessary to guide, extend, and support children's learning—to become an effective teacher. It is also critical for documenting teaching effectiveness; it provides a means for accountability. (See Chapter 9.)

This kid-watching chapter is organized into two major sections. The first section covers schemes for assessing and evaluating children's strategies and understandings in reading, writing (and drawing), and producing certain oral language "compositions" (e.g., dictations and retellings). We call these kid-watching procedures *literacy assessments*. The second section describes several *general observation schemes* for gathering information about how language and concepts are developed across the curriculum. Both sets of observation systems may initially seem formal because they are new and unfamiliar. However, with practice, these kid-watching procedures or techniques become internalized by teachers so that they can use them to evaluate children's learning and language *informally* while children are actively engaged in a range of meaningful activities in the classroom. Classroom routines (indicated by an asterisk, *), which support and use techniques that follow, are described in Chapter 7.

Literacy Assessments

Three kinds of literacy procedures are covered: (1) those that focus on reading and writing (Modified Miscue Analysis and Writing schemes, which also include the use of

---

The assessment of products without regard to process is usually unreliable.

Au (1993); Barrentine (1999); Gredler & Johnson (2004); Weaver (2002)

visual images produced with writing); (2) those that evaluate the literacy understandings of emergent learners (Concepts about Print, Approximations to Text, and Dictations); and (3) those that evaluate children's retellings of a text.

Modified Miscue Analysis (MMA)

Miscue analysis was originally developed by Ken Goodman to provide a window on the reading process. A *miscue* is defined as a deviation or difference between a reader's production and the text when the reader is reading aloud. Miscue analysis is based on two major assumptions: (1) Miscues are not random but have a variety of causes. Miscues are the result of readers' *constructions* of the linguistic message based on readers' present oral language development, their knowledge of the topic of the reading passage, their purpose for reading, and their familiarity with the register or genre of the text. Because reading is a constructive process, *everybody* makes miscues when they read aloud. (2) Miscues reflect how readers are actually using the reading process. Besides pragmatic cues (e.g., reasons or purposes for reading), reading is the integration of three major cues: *graphic cues* (some people term these *graphophonemic cues*), which deal with the set of relationships between sounds and the written forms that represent them; *syntactic cues*, which deal with interrelationships of words, sentences, and paragraphs; and *semantic cues*, which deal with the meaning of a text.

There are many variations of miscue analysis. We present a Modified Miscue Analysis (MMA) that classroom teachers have found easy to use. Briefly, the MMA is a procedure by which a child's miscues (made while reading aloud) are qualitatively and quantitatively assessed to gain insights into the child's reading strategies. Part of the procedure is to ask the child to retell the text subsequent to the oral reading.

Beers (2003); Carroll (2004); Goodman (1973, 1997); Goodman, Watson, & Burke (1987); Weaver (2002)

Miscues are constructions.

Miscues reflect the reading process in action.

The MMA taps readers' strategies.

Selection of Material

It is best to use a piece of literature (not a basal passage) that is entirely new to the student but that incorporates concepts and situations that the reader can comprehend. It can be a story, an informational piece, a magazine article, or a chapter of a book—anything that can be read in ten to fifteen minutes. It is important that the student read an entire selection even if only a portion of the miscues are later coded and analyzed. The selection must be difficult or challenging enough for the student that miscues will be made, but not so difficult that the reader will not feel comfortable reading it. (If you do not know the child well—for example, at the beginning of a school year—a useful way to determine appropriate material is to bring several selections to the MMA session and ask the child to read silently a little of each. Ask the child, after he or she reads some of each text if it seemed easy or hard to read. Don't use a text the child says is "easy" or "hard"; instead choose the text that the child describes as "sort of easy and sort of hard.") A selection must generate a minimum of twenty-five miscues to be used. A sample of fewer will be a less reliable indicator of the child's reading behavior.

Taping the Oral Reading and Retelling

The child reads from the printed text while the teacher marks on a specially prepared copy of the selection, called the MMA worksheet. The whole session is tape-recorded. The worksheet should retain the physical characteristics of the book from which the student reads. It should be an exact line-for-line copy, with sufficient space between the lines of the text so that all miscues can be clearly noted. However, many teachers use a clear photocopy of the text to save the time involved in typing a separate worksheet.

The taping should take place in a quiet atmosphere without distractions. (Frequently, teachers set up a small corner of the room where they can have conferences with individual students or small groups. This is an ideal place to do this part of the

MMA.) Students are told (1) that they are being asked to read because the teacher wants to understand how they read something they have never read or seen before; (2) that they are to read the entire text aloud and that they will be asked to retell and talk about it at the end; and (3) that they cannot be given any help during the reading. Consequently, if they come to a word that they don't know, they should do their best, as they would normally do while reading.

After the reading, students are simply asked to retell the text in their own words. If the retelling is a sparse one, the reader can be asked about a favorite or interesting part. (It is quite normal for a reader to give only a brief retelling here because the reader knows that the teacher knows the text. When retellings are short in this situation, it is important not to jump to the conclusion that the reader does not comprehend the text.) Follow-up questions can be prepared ahead of time as well (constructed perhaps to correspond to the types of transactions listed in Chapter 6) to complement the retelling, and more extemporaneous questions may be asked as appropriate.

Marking the MMA Worksheet

There are four categories of miscues.

While the reader is reading, the teacher identifies miscues and marks them on the MMA Worksheet according to the system described in Figure 8.1. Thus, the first decision to be made when a miscue occurs is what kind of deviation it represents. There are four kinds of miscues: substitutions, omissions, insertions, and reversals. These are mutually exclusive categories, and the teacher must decide *which one* more accurately categorizes each deviation. *Substitutions* involve replacing other words for those in the text. *Omissions* occur when words are dropped by the reader. There are two possibilities regarding omissions: Some omissions are fluent in that they are made without hesitation; others occur only after readers hesitate and inspect the text. Young children (e.g.,

---

figure **8.1**

Instructions for Marking the MMA Worksheet

1. *SUBSTITUTIONS:* Write the substitutions above the appropriate part of the text.
   Example: He ran down the street. [road]

2. *OMISSIONS:* Circle the *word(s)* left out. (If a reader reads "sing" for "singing," treat it as a substitution, not an omission of "ing.") Two types are possible:
   (a) *Omission without inspection (w/o I):* Just circle the omission. These are "fluent" omissions.

   Example: John drank his milk, (too.) Then he left the table.

   (b) *Omission with inspection (I):* Circle the omission and place an "I" next to it. These are omissions where the reader hesitates and inspects a word in the text, and then omits it.
   Example: He (usually) walked home alone. [I]

3. *INSERTIONS:* Place an insertion sign (carat) at the point it occurs, and then write the insertion above the line.

   Example: The hat blew ^ into the tree. [up]

4. *REVERSALS:* Use the commonly used symbol (⁀).

   Example: "Hit the ball," yelled Pete.

   ATTEMPTS AT CORRECTION:
   (a) *Attempted and Successful:* Mark (C) next to the miscue. Write each unsuccessful attempt above the word.
   Example: He watched the ships in the harbor. [shops (C)]

   (b) *Attempted but Unsuccessful:* Mark UC next to the miscue. Write each unsuccessful attempt above the word.
   Example: Tommy never heard that noise before. [hurt (uc) / hard]

   (c) *Changed Something Already Read Correctly* (rare): Mark AC next to the miscue. Write the change above the word.
   Example: The hat blew into the tree. [flew (ac)]

kindergartners and first graders) frequently make a lot of the second type; therefore, marking it may provide useful information regarding their reading development. For older elementary readers, this distinction may not be necessary. *Insertions* are words spoken by the reader that are not in the text. Finally, *reversals* occur when wordings are reversed during the reading. Figure 8.1 explains how these four types of miscues are marked and noted on the worksheet (i.e., the copy of the text that is read).

Reader *attempts to self-correct miscues* are also identified and marked on the worksheet. (Nothing is noted on the worksheet if the reader does not try corrections.) Attempts can be successful or unsuccessful and are noted accordingly. These notations are explained and illustrated on the bottom of Figure 8.1.

There are four other considerations to keep in mind in identifying miscues, as follows:

Miscues that are repeated throughout the text are coded the first time if the miscue is exactly the same each time (e.g., *Steve* for *Sven* miscued more than once). However, different miscues for the same word are each coded at their first occurrence (e.g., *Steve* for *Sven*, then *Seven* for *Sven*).

A related series of miscues can be coded as one miscue (e.g., *At first he saw* for *I first saw*). This can occur with a phrase or a clause.

Nonsense word substitutions are coded as miscues, but incomplete attempts are not (e.g., *glod* for *glad* is a miscue, but *gla-* then *glad* for *glad* is not).

Slight dialectal differences (e.g., *pin* for *pen*) are not usually coded as miscues. Judgments of acceptability should depend on what is acceptable in that dialect.

See Goodman (1993) and Wilde (1997) on the issue of dialect and reading.

Summary

Some teachers who have had a lot of experience in doing MMAs mark the worksheet as children read. Others (even those who are experienced) mark the worksheet later because they find it distracting to the reader to mark during the reading. Novices can also do the latter. Novices also find it useful simply to indicate by checks—with a pencil—places on the worksheet where there are deviations or possible miscues when they first hear the tape of the child's reading; they then listen to the tape a second time to mark the miscues with the appropriate designations.

Figure 8.2 (see p. 354) shows the first eleven miscues made by a nine-year-old boy, Mike, while reading the beginning of Wilder's *Farmer Boy*. Most of his miscues are substitutions, but examples of the other three types of miscues (an omission, two insertions, and a reversal) are also present. In Mike's dialect, *bar* for *bare* is a miscue, but in some regional dialects, *bar* would be an acceptable pronunciation of *bare* and would not be considered a miscue. Note that *Elissa* for *Eliza* is counted as a miscue the first time, but the subsequent same renditions of the name are not.

Wilder (1953)

Completing the MMA Coding Sheet

After the miscues have been noted and numbered on the worksheet, they are transferred to the MMA Coding Sheet. For each miscue, certain judgments are made. Unlike errors, which are treated in an all-or-nothing fashion, miscues represent the predictions, confirmations, and disconfirmations of readers; thus, miscues must be examined qualitatively. Some miscues represent good, effective reading strategies, others may not. Figure 8.3 (p. 355) gives instructions for completing the MMA Coding Sheet shown in Figure 8.4 (p. 356).

On the coding sheet, each miscue is evaluated with respect to its acceptability—whether it is grammatically reasonable and makes sense. Substitution miscues are also judged by their graphic similarity to the text, and a reader's attempts to correct are examined. Finally, each uncorrected miscue is evaluated to see if it resulted in significantly changing the meaning of the author's message. Figure 8.5 illustrates how Mike's miscues would be transferred onto the coding sheet.

Davenport & Lauritzen (2002); Johnston (1997)

figure 8.2

Mike's Reading of "School Days," a Chapter in *Farmer Boy*

"School Days"

0101   It was January in northern New York State,

0102   sixty–seven years ago. Snow lay very deep every–

0103   where. It loaded the bare limbs of oak and maples
            ① bar ©   ② maple

0104   beeches, it bent the green boughs of cedars
            ③ went over ④ boughts ⑤

0105   and spruces down into the drifts. Billows of snow

0106   covered the fields and the stone fences.

0107   Down a long road through the woods a little

0108   boy trudged to school, with his big brother Roy–

0109   al and his two sisters, Eliza Jane and Alice. Royal
            ⑥ sister © Elissa ⑦

0110   was thirteen years old, Eliza was twelve, and
            Elissa Jane ⑧

0111   Alice was ten. Almanzo was the youngest of all,

            –

0201   and this was his first going–to–school, because

0202   he was not quite nine years old.

0203   He had to walk fast to keep up with the oth–
            had
0204   ers, and he had to carry the dinner–pail.
            had had uc ⑨

0205   "Royal ought to carry it," he said. "He's big–

0206   ger than I be."
                               ⑩ ©
0207   Royal strode ahead, big and manly in boots, and

0208   Eliza Jane said:

0209   "No Manzo. It's your turn to carry it now,

0210   because you're the littlest."

0211   Eliza Jane was bossy. She always knew what

0212   was best to do; and she made Almanzo and Alice

0213   do it.

Notice that *maple* (for *maples*) and *sister* (for *sisters*) are treated as substitutions, not as omissions of the plural morpheme *s*. All but one of Mike's miscues are marked as being syntactically and semantically acceptable. *Boughts* for *boughs* is an interesting miscue. It is marked with a "?" under Column 9 because many teachers would mark this miscue as being syntactically acceptable in that it retains the plural morpheme. However, because *boughts* is a nonsense word, it cannot be semantically acceptable (hence, no check in Column 10) and the "meaning change" Column 13 is also checked. (In fact, a good rule of thumb is that when nonsense words are given, they are usually not semantically acceptable and they are likely to represent meaning changes.)

It is important to emphasize that although teachers try to be careful in doing MMAs to indicate what they think a reader's strategies are in the process of reading

figure **8.3**

How to Complete the MMA Coding Sheet

Column

1   *NO. (1–25).* The number of the miscue from the worksheet.

2   *TEXT.* Write the correct word or phrase that was miscued.

3   *READER.* Write the precise miscue that the reader made. If the reader makes more than one attempt at a word or phrase, code the *first* attempt.

4   *SUBS. (SUBSTITUTION).* Check (✓) if the miscue is a substitution.

5   GRAPHIC SIMILAR. (GRAPHIC SIMILARITY). Coded only for substitutions. Check (✓) if the miscue is similar. A miscue is considered graphically similar to the text if:

(1) both the first and last letters of the miscue match the first and last letters of the word(s) of the text, *OR*

(2) either the first letter *or* the last letter *and* a majority of the remaining letters of the miscue match the letters and their position in the text.

6   *OMISSIONS w/o I* (without Inspection). Check (✓) if the reader maintains reading and fluency, reacting as if the word was not there.

7   *OMISSIONS w I* (with Inspection). Check (✓) if the reader obviously spends some time studying the word before omitting it.

8   *OTHER.* Check (✓) if the miscue is other than a substitution or an omission, namely, an insertion or a reversal.

9   *SYNTAC. ACCEPT. (SYNTACTIC ACCEPTABILITY).* Check (✓) if the miscue is syntactically acceptable. A miscue is considered semantically acceptable when the resulting sentence is acceptable according to its syntax (i.e., acceptable part of speech, acceptable word order, etc.) regardless of its meaning. Also, in evaluating the acceptability of a miscue, you must consider previous and subsequent miscues in the sentence (final attempts, successful or unsuccessful).

10   *SEMAN. ACCEPT. (SEMANTIC ACCEPTABILITY).* Check (✓) if the miscue is semantically acceptable. A miscue is considered semantically acceptable when the resulting sentence is acceptable according to its meaning (i.e., it makes sense) regardless of its syntax. However, because meaning and syntax are so closely related, it is unlikely that many syntactically unacceptable sentences will retain an acceptable meaning. Again, in evaluating the acceptability of a miscue, you must consider previous and subsequent miscues in the sentence (final attempts, successful or unsuccessful). Also, consider how the reader is making sense of previous text through the miscues.

11   *CORRECT.(ION): ATT. (ATTEMPTED).* Check (✓) if the reader made any attempt to correct.

12   *CORRECT.(ION): SUCC. (SUCCESSFUL).* Check (✓) if the reader's attempt to correct was successful.

13   *MEANING CHANGE.* Check (✓) if the miscue represents a *significantly* different meaning from that intended in the text *and* if the miscue was not successfully corrected.

TOTAL   Number of checks in each column on the coding sheet.

aloud, they are necessarily involved in interpretation. That is, deciding whether Mike was self-correcting a miscue or just figuring out a word (e.g., *bar* for *bare*), or deciding whether the miscue for *boughs* should be spelled *boughts* instead of *bots* are both instances of interpretation. Moreover, determinations as to whether particular miscues affect significant meaning changes of a text's message are sometimes hard ones to make. Two general principles frequently help teachers in their interpretations in doing MMAs: (1) Consider the whole pattern of a reader's miscues when making decisions on particular miscues. For example, the teacher decided to spell the miscue *boughts* (and not *bots*) for *boughs* because Mike seemed to be sensitive to the graphic information of words in most of his substitution miscues (that is, all of his substitutions were graphically similar to the words in the text; all had checks in Column 5 in Figure 8.5).

Col. 1	2	3	4	5	6	7	8	9	10	11	12	13
No.	Text	Reader	Subs.	Graphic Similar.	Omissions w/o I	w I	Other	Syntac. Accept.	Seman. Accept.	Correct. Att.	Succ.	Meaning Change
1												
2												
3												
4												
5												
· · ·												
25												
TOTALS												

figure **8.4**

MMA Coding Sheet

Col. 1	2	3	4	5	6	7	8	9	10	11	12	13
No.	Text	Reader	Subs.	Graphic Similar.	Omissions w/o I	w I	Other	Syntac. Accept.	Seman. Accept.	Correct. Att.	Succ.	Meaning Change
1	bare	bar	✓	✓				✓	✓	✓	✓	
2	maples	maple	✓	✓				✓	✓			
3	bent	went	✓	✓				✓	✓			
4	——	over					✓	✓	✓			
5	boughs	boughts	✓	✓				?				✓
6	sisters	sister	✓	✓				✓	✓	✓	✓	
7	Eliza	Elissa	✓	✓				✓	✓			
8	——	Jane					✓	✓	✓			
9	he had	had had	✓	✓				✓	✓	✓		
10	in	——			✓			✓	✓	✓	✓	
11	best to do	to do best					✓	✓	✓			
· · ·												
25												
TOTALS												

figure **8.5**

MMA Coding Sheet for Mike

(2) Try to be consistent and be true to your own criteria for making decisions about miscues. Talking with others about their explanations for why miscues are marked helps teachers, and especially those new to MMAs, cause their own criteria to be more explicit to them, thereby making these judgments easier.

Analyzing the Oral Reading Miscues

Using the data on the coding sheet, five major questions about oral reading miscues can be considered. Answers to these questions tell how a child is using the cuing systems. The result is quantitative data—percentages that reflect certain reading strategies. Figure 8.6 lists these questions and explains how to compute the percentages on the basis of counts taken from the coding sheet.

Remember, *no* percentage resulting from your computations on Figure 8.6 can be more than 100 percent. If you end up with something higher than 100 percent, you have incorrectly counted the miscues on the coding sheet. A common mistake for computing Question 1A on Figure 8.6 (and, thus, ending up with a percentage over 100) is to take the totals of Columns 5, 9, and 10 on the bottom of the coding sheet. Instead, use a ruler so you can look at each miscue line one at a time to determine if there is a check in each of these three columns. If there are three checks, one for each of these columns for a particular miscue, then count it. If one or more of the columns do not have a check, then don't include it in your count. Thus, six of the seven substitutions Mike made have the three checks—see MMA Coding Sheet for Mike in Figure 8.5— and would be figured in the calculation in Question 1A on Figure 8.6.

> If a percentage is over 100, you have not "read" the MMA Coding Sheet correctly.

What Do These Percentages Mean?

These percentages (and the data on retelling to be described in the following section) provide useful information about readers' strategies.

---

1. The first question deals with *substitutions only* and has three parts:
   A. To what extent is the reader integrating all cueing systems (i.e., graphic, syntactic, and semantic) when making substitutions?

   $$\frac{\text{Number of miscues having a check in Cols. 5 \& 9 \& 10}}{\text{Total number of substitutions (Col. 4)}} \times 100 = \underline{\qquad}$$

   B. To what extent is the reader using syntactic/semantic information only in making substitutions?

   $$\frac{\text{Number of miscues having a check in Col. 4, no check in Col. 5, but a check in Cols. 9 \& 10}}{\text{Total number of substitutions (Col. 4)}} \times 100 = \underline{\qquad}$$

   C. To what extent is the reader using graphic information only in making substitutions?

   $$\frac{\text{Number of miscues having a check in Col. 5, and no check in Cols. 9 \& 10}}{\text{Total number of substitutions (Col. 4)}} \times 100 = \underline{\qquad}$$

2. To what extent are the miscues syntactically and semantically acceptable?

   $$\frac{\text{Number of miscues having a check in Cols. 9 \& 10}}{\text{Total number of miscues (25)}} \times 100 = \underline{\qquad}$$

3. To what extent is the reader successful in the corrections he or she attempts?

   $$\frac{\text{Total number of Col. 12 (succ. corr.)}}{\text{Total number of Col. 11 (att. corr.)}} \times 100 = \underline{\qquad}$$

4. To what extent does the reader leave meaning changes?

   $$\frac{\text{Total number of Col. 13}}{\text{Total number of miscues (25)}} \times 100 = \underline{\qquad}$$

5. To what extent is the reader stopping and inspecting text before it is omitted?

   $$\frac{\text{Total number in Col. 7 (w I)}}{\text{Total of Cols. 6 \& 7}} \times 100 = \underline{\qquad}$$

figure 8.6

Questions Regarding Patterns of Miscues

Questions 1A, 1B, and 1C, regarding substitutions, tell us whether a reader is integrating all three cuing systems or overrelying on one or two of them. Consider first 1A: What percentage level would you expect from a hypothetical fluent reader? You would expect it to be high because effective reading integrates all sources of language cues—graphic, syntactical, and semantic. And you would expect that a hypothetical fluent reader's percentages of 1B and 1C to be low and about the same. Such a reader would not rely on one cue (e.g., graphics or letter–sound relationships) over the others (syntactic and semantic cues).

Consequently, by contrasting percentages of such a hypothetical reader with those of a particular reader, a teacher can decide on appropriate instruction. For example, if a child such as Mike has percentages in 1A, 1B, and 1C similar to our hypothetical fluent reader, it would indicate that the child is integrating all three cuing systems effectively. However, if a child has a low percentage in 1A and 1B but a relatively high percentage in 1C, it would suggest that the child is focusing too much on graphics or letter–sound relationships and is missing meaning altogether, especially if the percentage in Question 4 is high. The teacher might then conduct some CLOZE* Focus Lessons* to help the child consider using more of the context in identifying words, or other lessons that emphasize meaning over the accurate decoding of words (e.g., Say Something* and Reader's Theater* activities).

Question 2 looks at the acceptability of all the miscues, not just substitutions. It tells whether the reading sounds like language and makes sense. Again, Mike's percentage (computations not included) is high, indicating that his reading is meaning driven. A low percentage for Question 2 indicates that the reader is not reading with meaning. Lessons (similar to those suggested earlier) can be created to give the reader that focus.

Question 3 gets at self-correction, an important feature of effective reading. Mike had a high percentage here. However, if a low percentage occurs here, lessons can be constructed to help the reader be more successful in correcting miscues. Or a teacher may note that the reader does not self-correct very much in general (even though there is a high percentage of meaning change) and may provide activities to motivate the reader to reread texts or self-evaluate initial responses in reading.

Question 4 involves significant meaning changes. Mike had a low percentage on this question, but if the percentage here is high for a particular reader, then again the teacher would try to get the child to focus more on meaning. For example, perhaps the teacher might include him or her in small Literature Response Groups* in which members share their interpretations of a book or text. Or the teacher might provide other experiences that require the reader to reevaluate and justify miscues (e.g., students in third grade and higher can usually profit from taping their own reading and then identifying and self-evaluating miscues).

Question 5 provides useful information for evaluating the reading progress of children who are in transition from emergent reading to more independent reading. Children in this stage do a lot of inspecting of text because they are beginning to integrate graphics with syntactical and semantic cuing systems. The results in this question can, therefore, document this development. The teacher can skip this last question for older elementary readers such as Mike.

Miscue patterns can provide important information for the teacher in two ways: in deciding on specific instructional activities to meet the needs of the reader, and in documenting a reader's strategies over time. Doing MMAs on children's reading of a variety of genres provides even more useful information for instruction and accountability. Once teachers have done one or two MMAs, they know how to "listen" for miscues and can take anecdotal records without *taping* children's reading.

By contrasting your percentages with those of a hypothetical fluent reader, you can get a sense of your reader's strategies.

Analyzing the Retelling

The retelling and discussion subsequent to the oral reading provide more information about the child's understanding of the text. Four general questions can be asked about this part of the MMA to complement the oral reading data analyzed in the preceding section:

1. What was the nature of the reader's retelling? Did the retelling include essential information expressed in the text? Did the reader adequately understand the major ideas, or the gist, of the message expressed in the text?
2. If the reader provided a sparse retelling (remember, it is normal to produce a brief response in such a social situation—i.e., when both the teacher and the reader know the text) and was asked to recount a favorite or interesting portion, did any aspects of this account indicate comprehension?
3. How did the reader respond to any questions asked about the selection?
4. Compare individual miscues when the reader had meaning changes (see Column 13 on the MMA Coding Sheet, Figure 8.3) with the retelling (and other) responses. Were there cases when the reader left a meaning change miscue yet seemed to understand the author's message in subsequent responses? That is, are there miscues that might not have been overtly correct but might have been self-corrected in the reader's mind?

Summary

Miscue analysis must seem very complicated from the foregoing description, and indeed it is *complicated* until it is tried a few times formally by examining the miscues and retellings of real readers. However, it is only through doing MMAs that teachers can know how to observe by listening to the strategies and interpretations children use in oral reading in more informal contexts. They can document conversations they have about students' miscues in the course of a busy classroom day, taking down notes about miscue patterns as children are engaged in reading aloud a section of a book in Literature Response Groups* or during Buddy Reading*, for example. Inherent in using this kid-watching technique is a new appreciation on the part of the teacher of the constructive nature of reading. Teachers learn to wait or be more patient and not intervene too soon or too much when children do not read the actual words of the text with absolute accuracy. They learn that a reader may put in a reasonable substitution or may self-correct when something does not make sense. Thus, through these informal MMAs, teachers can collect useful ongoing information to document children's progress in reading, and they can decide what instruction or intervention is appropriate to support and extend children's present understandings and efforts. They may also conduct what is called "retrospective miscue analysis"—which is especially appropriate for the upper elementary grades. They have a series of short conferences with students on selected miscues to help them be more aware of their strategies. Such initial talks involve miscues that indicate students' strategies that supported their construction of meaning; then later, the conversations cover miscues that interrupted meaning. (See the "Reading Activities and Experiences" section in Chapter 7 for more information regarding informal reading assessments.)

> See Davenport & Lauritzen (2002) for how to do "over the shoulder" miscue analysis.

> Flurkey & Goodman (2002); Goodman (1999)

Writing

The view of writing described in Chapter 6 is sometimes termed a *process-conference approach*. It emphasizes the process of writing in which writers engage, and it uses teacher (and peer) conferences to evaluate and support this process. Teacher interactions and conferences occur while children are engaged in any of the types of writing experiences (prewriting, drafting, revising, editing, and publishing) described in Chapter 6. Here, however, we focus on conferences in which the teacher confers with children on drafts that children plan to revise or edit. An analysis scheme for evaluating children's writing is presented, and on the basis of that analysis, suggestions for ways teachers can conduct conferences to support revising and editing are covered.

> Atwell (1998); Calkins (1986, 1991, 1994); Carroll (2004); Graves (1983); Moore et al. (2003)

This assessment assumes that the teacher has obtained a draft written by a child on a topic the child has chosen. If observation during the drafting process is also possible, the teacher can jot down notes about the ways children do the following:

Use space (how they start to write, the direction of writing, and whether they leave spaces between "words"), punctuation, capitalization, and paragraphing.

Form letters and words.

Correct or change what they write.

Comment on what they write.

If pictures or other images are also drawn or used, use visual designs and what they change and what they comment on.

It may be necessary for young children who use invented spellings—construct approximations on the basis of what they have learned about the orthographic system—to read their text right after they have finished so that it can be deciphered by the teacher (although experienced teachers, who have had lots of practice "cracking the code" of a range of young writers, usually can figure out these invented spelling patterns without having children read them). In integrated language classrooms, approximations are encouraged, so teachers need to know the general developmental changes in spelling. Figure 8.7 outlines general characteristics of these changes. We will go into these more when writing samples are reviewed.

Kress (2000); Temple, Nathan, Temple, & Burris (1993); Wilde (1992, 1997)

Analyzing a Writing Sample

In analyzing a draft, consider both message, or content, aspects—which includes the content of visual images (pictures, diagrams, tables, maps, and so forth), and the interrelations between the verbal and visual content—and medium aspects (see Table 6.4 for more information on these aspects). Teachers usually have separate conferences regarding these two aspects of children's writing. That is, they have Content Conferences* with children to deal with the message of a text (and of images), and they have Editing Conferences* to address medium issues after children have revised their text. Chapter 7 discusses ways to implement these conferences in the classroom, but here we concentrate on the analysis scheme and review the types of questions teachers may ask by considering several writing samples from a range of elementary-age children. We will, thus, be treating message and medium concerns together.

Content Conferences* deal with message aspects of a writer's text, Editing Conferences* with medium aspects.

The analysis of children's writing consists of asking questions about the message and medium aspects of their texts. See Figure 8.8 for a list of these questions.

Facilitating the Revising and Editing of a Writing Sample

On the basis of this analysis, teachers then decide how to conference with children about their texts. As you may have noted, an important distinction is made between helping children learn to *edit* and to *revise* their writing. Editing involves medium changes, things that an editor, teacher, or someone else can change: spelling, punctuation, noun and verb agreement, for example. Most instruction and feedback in writing have traditionally emphasized editing. In the process-conference approach, these editing aspects are considered, but they are done differently.

Revising, on the other hand, has to do with changes of the message of a text—which includes the major text, the visual images, and the minor text (e.g., labels, captions, keys) related to these images. Only writers/illustrators can revise, because only they know what they are intending to express. Although little instruction or feedback is given in the revision of writing in most traditional classrooms, it is the most important for it will help children be better writers/illustrators. Facilitating revising helps children become readers of their own writing by sensitizing them to the requirements of other readers/viewers of their writing/visual images, so that their writing is com-

The reader–writer/illustrator contract is emphasized.

figure **8.7**

Developmental Changes
in Spelling

Prephonemic Spelling

Characteristics: Prephonemic spellers know a lot about language; they know how letters are formed and that they somehow represent language. However, they string letters (mostly consonants) together in an unsystematic fashion because they have not as yet discovered the phonetic principle, that is, that letters represent the speech sounds, or phonemes, in words. Prephonemic spellers usually have not as yet learned to read.
Examples: BMKGTO (candy) MBRRDRGC (cat)

Early Phonemic Spelling

Characteristics: Early phonemic spellers have discovered the phonetic principle and attempt to represent phonemes in words with letters—they have begun to figure out how spelling works. Although they try to represent letters for sounds they hear in words, their products are sparse. That is, they usually just put down letters for only one or two sounds (and then may finish with random letters). This is because they usually do not have a stable concept of what a word is, so they can't keep words "in their minds" long enough to match sounds of words with letters. Early phonemic spellers are usually not reading as yet.
Examples: P (piano) N (engine)

Letter-Name Spelling

Characteristics: Letter-name spellers are able to break down a word into its phonemes and represent them with letters, but they work on a rule of one-to-one correspondence—one sound is represented by one letter. They are called letter-name spellers because they frequently use the sounds of the *names* of letters to stand for respective phonemes in words. Letter-name spelling is in many ways the most complex set of spelling approximations and is therefore the most challenging system for teachers to decipher. The examples below reflect some of the major rules children rely on in letter-name spelling. Letter-name spellers are often not readers, but they have a stable concept of word and are beginning to develop a slight vocabulary. When they begin to read, they will read conventional spelling but will write words in letter-name spelling (which sometimes leads to confusion when they try to read their own writing).
Examples: HARE (cherry). A good example of the use of letter-names and the one-to-one rule. Thus, consonant digraphs (e.g., *ch, sh, th, ph*) are represented by only one letter.
LAP (lamp) YET (went) Nasals (*n, m*) are dropped near medial vowels.
SOPR (supper) LETL (little). When vowels occur in syllables that are unstressed, they are said to be "reduced." In these cases, only the consonant (*R* and *L*, respectively) is provided by the child.
BAT (bet) PAT (pet) (front middle); FEH (fish) HEM (him) (front high), etc.
Lax, or "short," vowels are represented by letter-name vowels that have the same tongue positions when produced. That is, the tongue's position is in the front middle part of the mouth when the lax *e* in *bet* and the tense *a* in *bait* are made.

Transitional Spelling

Characteristics: Transitional spellers have gone beyond the one-to-one correspondence between sounds and letters. They have learned many features of conventional spelling; they include many conventional spellings—but these understandings are employed uncertainly or overextended. Transitional spelling *looks like* English and is easy to read. Frequently, transitional spellers may have all the correct letters of a word but not in the right order. Transitional spellers are readers.
Examples: NIHGT (night) DAER (dear). Correct letters but in the wrong order.
PUTT (put) DINNIGE (dining). Overextension of "double" consonants and "silent *e*" vowel pattern.

Derivational Spelling

Characteristics: Derivational spelling is very similar to transitional spelling. Derivational spellers rely on the *morphophonemic* nature of the English spelling system. That is, through their spellings, they demonstrate their awareness that the spelling of a particular word reflects, or is derived from, a "core" meaning.
Examples: EXPLAI NATION (explanation) JUDGEMENT (judgment). Spellings reflect the meaning of *explain* and *judge*, respectively.

Conventional Spelling

Characteristics: Correct spellings are used.

prehensible. Also, this is the area in which they can examine the underlying ideology of their texts and images—how their meanings might reflect certain values or biases they hold. (See Chapters 1 and 6 for a longer discussion on ideology.)

The following general guidelines are useful in conferences:

1. Have children read their writing first and note any spontaneous changes they make. (Have them read any minor text (labels, captions, keys) as well, if these are included.)

2. Point out any changes children make in reading their texts aloud that they did not note on their actual text.

figure **8.8**

Analysis Scheme
for a Writing
Sample

Use the following questions to evaluate children's texts:

Message Questions

1. What genre is the child attempting to write? How successful is the child? Are there certain beginnings, endings, and sequences used to indicate a certain genre?
2. Is the text complete according to the genre the child is attempting? If complete, is it sparse, or are relevant details and elaborations included?
3. Does the child use an interesting vocabulary? Is it appropriate to the genre attempted? Does the child use cohesive ties to knit the text together? Does the child use any words that are unclear or ambiguous (e.g., pronouns with uncertain antecedents)?
4. Are there any gaps of information or "missing links" in the text? Does the child order information to make sense?
5. Does the child appear to have audience or reader "sense"?
6. What ideologies or values (subtle or overt) are being expressed?

Visual-Image Questions

1. Does the child use appropriate visual images for the genre written?
2. Is there a good interrelationship between meanings expressed in the written message and visual images?
3. Are meanings depicted in visual images explained well in the minor text (captions, labels, keys, etc.)? Are meanings expressed in the minor text accurately depicted in visual images?
4. Are details in the visual images accurate or appropriate (e.g., that participants are depicted reflecting correct colors, correct features, and characteristic activities in nonfictional texts, or appropriate colors, features, or activities in fictional texts; that maps or diagrams are drawn in correct proportion and specificity; that graphs are clear as to what relational factors are being portrayed)?
5. Does the child appear to have an audience or viewer "sense"?
6. What ideologies or values (subtle or overt) are being expressed in the images? Are they similar to or different from those being expressed in the written message?

Medium Questions

1. Does the child show knowledge of the directionality principles of the writing system? How about the spacing principle? Layout features? Paragraphing?
2. Does the child show a stable concept of letter/word/sentence?
3. How does the child use punctuation, capitalization, and so on?
4. What does the child know about the orthographic (spelling) system? At what developmental level do you think the child is? (Give examples.)
5. How does the child control various grammatical structures (e.g., noun and verb agreement, parallel construction, and the like)?

3. Address only one or two message issues (which may include information about the content of a picture or another visual design) and only one medium concern in each conference.
4. Be positive and show interest in what children are trying to express.
5. Start by responding to a strength or positive feature of the text.
6. Don't tell children what to do, but use questions to support them in finding their own answers.
7. Leave the pencil in children's hands. All changes or additions to the writing should be left under children's control and ownership.
8. When asking a question, be sure that children are given time to respond. Have a long "wait time."
9. Try to make your questions and responses as specific as possible.
10. End each conference by asking children what they will do next.

To get an idea of the kinds of specific questions teachers may ask, we'll consider the writing samples of grade K–8 children. For each child, we'll have a "conference," in which we pretend we're the teacher. Remember that we are addressing *both* message and medium aspects of students' writing here—typically these are dealt with by *separate* conferences.

Amber, Megan, and Mike: Kindergartners

We have to be careful in our conferences with such young writers as kindergartners Amber, Megan, and Mike to encourage them to see themselves as writers, to use their own approximations for conventional forms. If we stress revising or editing too much or too soon, we can give them the message that we do not value their efforts.

Amber's and Megan's texts were the result of a MONSTERS unit, and Mike's was a sign he wrote as the result of a classroom accident.

Amber's text (Figure 8.9) is short and is about the Cookie Monster of *Sesame Street* fame.

> Revising and editing concerns in very young emergent writers must be addressed with great caution.

> Amber

MESSAGE ANALYSIS

The most prevalent issue in very young writers' texts involves trying to understand what genre they are attempting to tackle. (See Message Question 1, Figure 8.8.) This is partly because their texts are usually short; there isn't much information on which to base a reliable decision. This seems to be the case for Amber's text. What form is she trying? Is it a personal narrative? A story? And how does the last line fit with the rest of the text? Thus, a teacher might first ask a question to address this genre issue: "Amber, is this a pretend story about Cookie Monster, or are you writing about your actually seeing Cookie Monster?" Any subsequent questions would then depend on how Amber answers. If she says that it was a make-believe story, then the teacher may ask what Cookie Monster is going to do in the story and, perhaps, if Genna is going to do something with Cookie Monster. In contrast, if Amber indicates that her text is a personal narrative, then questions about what Cookie Monster did when she saw him would be appropriate. Frequently, revisions for young children like Amber are *talking* more about their texts. The teacher may not expect Amber actually to rewrite her text but may invite Amber to add those things she has related to her text, realizing that Amber may or may not be able to do so at this time. Amber has not included any pictures with her text; thus, the teacher might suggest how she might add them. "Amber, I notice you don't have your pictures yet. What kinds of pictures do you plan to use?" As Amber includes her pictures, she might add more to her written message than she verbalized in the conference.

> Revising for young children consists of them talking about their texts.

MEDIUM ANALYSIS

Most of the spellings in this text indicate that Amber is an early phonemic speller. (Her last line consists entirely of conventional spellings, but she probably has learned these

figure 8.9
Amber's Text

(Amber I saw Cookie Monster. I saw him again. I love Genna.)

words as "wholes.") "Genna" is Amber's friend; the first two letters of her text, "be," are part of Amber's name. Amber shows that she is aware of direction of print, but she does not seem to have a concept of a word (there is no spacing between words). She uses no capitalization or punctuation. At this point, the teacher would not say anything to Amber about editing. If the text is going to be published—perhaps typed up and then illustrated by Amber—then the teacher may edit it during the typing. Amber's progress in spelling will be facilitated by developing a stable concept of a word so that the teacher will engage her in many activities to facilitate this development (e.g., Dictations, discussed later in the chapter, Group-Composed Writing*, and Big Books*) as well as provide many other opportunities for her to write.

Megan

Figure 8.10 is Megan's text on dinosaurs in the form of a small, stapled, four-page booklet.

MESSAGE ANALYSIS

It is not clear from Megan's short text that includes illustrations what genre she is attempting. Is it an information book about dinosaurs? An attempt to write a story? The major issue to resolve is to help Megan decide which is the case. The teacher can begin by asking if this is a pretend story about dinosaurs or if it is an information book (notice that she uses present-tense verbs). If Megan says it is a story, then the teacher can ask her more about what exciting things the dinosaurs are doing or how they got to be friends. If Megan says it is an information book, then the teacher can get Megan to tell what else she has learned about dinosaurs that she could add to her book. Again,

figure **8.10**

Megan's Text

the teacher's expectations consist of encouraging only. Most revisions involve talking about revisions rather than actually more writing or rewriting. The teacher may suggest that Megan unstaple her booklet and add pages—with pictures—which could be Megan's revision.

MEDIUM ANALYSIS

Although there is not much to work on in her short text, Megan does have a better grasp of the medium aspects of written language than Amber. She has a better sense of space and seems to know what a word is. Megan is a letter-name speller, although her text indicates that she may be more advanced than that. She incorrectly copied the word *dinosaurs* from a big display in the classroom, and her peers helped with *friends* (also incorrect) and *lovers*. Thus, the teacher would not do anything regarding editing.

Mike's text arose as the result of a classroom accident. The children were studying guppies and other fish, and the water tank was placed on a low shelf. One day a child lost her balance and accidentally sat down in the tank. At evaluation time at the end of the day, Mike argued that something should be done about the water tank so no one else would fall in it. The teacher asked him if he wanted to make a sign to put next to the tank. With her help, he wrote, "Dont pus," and then he finished it on his own. (See Figure 8.11.)

Mike

MESSAGE ANALYSIS

There is no doubt about Mike's genre. Notice how he has incorporated the grammatical structures appropriate to signs: "Don't push . . . ," "Be careful," "Read this. . .". It is an amusing sign, of course, as very few signs include the admonition to read it. The teacher did not suggest that Mike change the last line, because Mike was the youngest of several siblings and he was reluctant to use invented spelling at all because he was afraid he might be wrong. This was an important breakthrough for Mike, and the teacher merely confirmed and shared his delight of accomplishment. They published it by hanging it on the wall near the tank, and the teacher and the children frequently reread it as a reminder. The teacher did not consider that Mike add pictures because the type of sign he created would not likely have illustrations incorporated.

DONT PUSI Me ONe
NaⱱⱱYTRTr

BK⊘   KRF

ReDⱱSⱢSN

(Don't push anyone in the water tank. Be careful! Read this sign!)

figure **8.11**
Mike's Text

MEDIUM ANALYSIS

Mike has some early phonemic inclinations (his spelling for *careful*, perhaps), but he is mostly a letter-name speller with respect to this text. He relies on letter names to spell *any* ("N E") and the beginning of *water* ("Y"). It's not clear whether he has a stable concept of a word; sometimes he has spaces between words and sometimes he runs his words together, as in the last line. The teacher does no editing because she doesn't want to risk harming his new confidence.

Annie and Robbie: First Graders

First graders Annie and Robbie are attempting to write stories. (See Figures 8.12 and 8.13.)

MESSAGE ANALYSES

Drawing is an important prewriting experience for Annie. She frequently draws (with lots of colors, which are lost in copying) on each page of her draft first, then writes what is going on in her picture. This is a complete but bare-bones story. Annie's story deals with everyday experiences—eating, going to bed, waking up, and getting dressed—but also incorporates the "fantastic" feature of having a snowman come back to life (perhaps influenced by "Frosty the Snowman" TV specials; she wrote her story in January of her first-grade year). The teacher would probably address this latter aspect of her text because it is not clear. For example, the teacher may ask, "I'm not sure about this part of your story. Did the girl's crying on the snowman *cause* him to come back to life? Tell me more about this." The teacher, thus, gives Annie an opportunity to clarify the reader's confusion and elaborate on her story to make it more comprehensible and credible.

Annie

figure **8.12**

Annie's Text

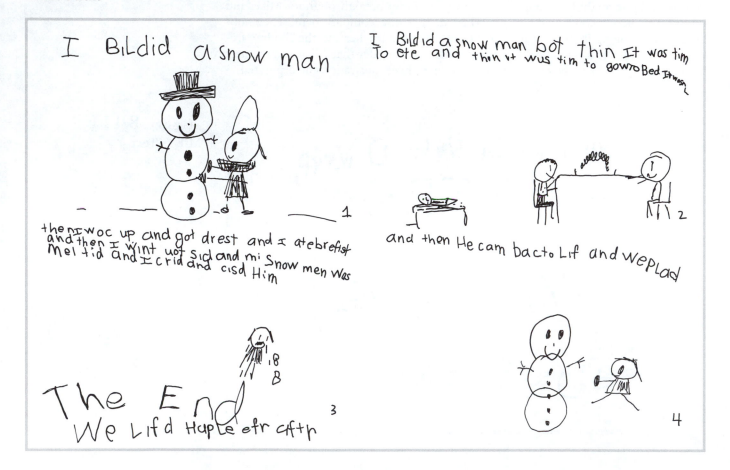

figure **8.13**
Robbie's Text

Robbie is also attempting a story, but it seems to lack certain essential parts. Like Annie, Robbie is using information about everyday experiences. He includes what he knows about parents' having favorite chairs and about visiting by including dialogue with the frog's sister. However, we don't know what has happened that has caused the frog to go to his mom's house and live alone no longer, or how the fact that the frog liked to jump a lot is related to the storyline. Consequently, the teacher would address questions to these facets of the story: "Why is the frog living alone and now deciding to go back home? Does the fact that the frog jumps a lot have anything to do with his decision?" By thinking about the teacher's reaction to his story, Robbie can begin to think of ways to revise his text to fill in pertinent details, thereby clarifying his intentions. Although Robbie has added a small frog near his written "forg," he has not added other illustrations. Thus, the teacher might suggest creating a dummy book that includes pictures so he can see how his already written story might be illustrated, and then add pages, with pictures, to cover the parts he might add in response to the teacher's questions.

MEDIUM ANALYSES

Both texts reflect letter-name and transitional spellings, but Annie seems to be more of a letter-name speller, whereas Robbie appears to be more of a transitional one. Words like "cam" (came), "bac" (back), and especially those words that incorporate the *ed* past-tense morpheme—"drest" (dressed), "meltid" (melted), and "pla" (played)—follow letter-name rules. However, Annie does have some spellings that reflect more transitional understandings: "ete" (eat), "gow" (go).

Robbie also uses letter-name spellings for *ed* words—"pakt" (packed), "jumt" (jumped), and "ansrd" (answered)—but he does include the conventional spelling of the morpheme in "kocked" (knocked) and "liked." Many of his words have all the correct letters, but they are in the wrong order, and there is evidence that he has gone beyond the letter-name one-to-one rule—"whrer" (where) and "cheir" (chair).

The teacher could address some spelling issues for each child: Both of them spelled a high-frequency word inconsistently. Annie spelled *then* conventionally and as "thin," and Robbie spelled *said* correctly once at the end of the story, but all the other times he used "siad." The teacher could point out the errors in an Editing Conference* or help Robbie understand the function of quotation marks without which it is hard to follow the dialogue. By having him mark those places (with his two index fingers) where someone is saying something, Robbie will begin to understand the role of quotation marks in a meaningful way.

Katy and Russell: Second Graders

Katy

Katy's text (Figure 8.14) was some writing done as part of an ANIMALS—LARGE AND SMALL unit in which children described their pets. (Children without pets described those they would like to have.)

MESSAGE ANALYSIS

Katy doesn't really give much description of her hamster, focusing mostly on an event in the hamster's life when he broke his leg. Two facets could be addressed. First, Katy goes on about how cute her hamster is yet doesn't tell why she feels that way. Thus, in conference the teacher could say, "You talk a lot about how cute your hamster is, but you don't tell why. What can you add here to explain why it is so cute?" The second feature that could be discussed with Katy is the confusion involved in calling the veterinarian: "Katy, I'm not clear about when your mom called the vet when your hamster was hurt. Is it important to include this telephone call, and what does this part—'Mom said no. I said ok.'—mean?" Thus, the teacher's questions are posed both to help Katy elaborate by giving reasons for her statements about her hamster and to get her to think more about the relevance and clarity of part of her text. Since Katy hasn't included pictures, the teacher might encourage her to do so. "You know, you might add your pictures as you work on these ideas. Making the pictures might help you sort them out. And, as you make your picture of Peewee, it will give you a picture of him in your mind—what he looks like, what he does—that can help you explain why Peewee is so cute."

MEDIUM ANALYSIS

Katy is in between being a transitional speller (she has many conventional spellings, plus spellings like "plese" [please]) and a letter-name speller ("crase" [crazy], "win" [when], "abot" [about], "pikt" [picked]). She has a better control of punctuation than most of the children we have met so far, but the teacher could address the role of quotation marks in the place where Annie asks her mom to call the vet. Of course, if Annie decides that the whole conversation about telephoning the vet is not necessary, then something else could be picked for Katy's attention—maybe the spelling of *when*, as that is a frequent word and would have a big payoff in editing in future pieces.

Russell

Russell's text (Figure 8.15) appears to be a story about the adventure of a little fish.

MESSAGE ANALYSIS

Russell has a very elaborate Placement (see Chapter 6). In fact, it is more than half of his text. It is almost as if he spent so much energy on this first part that he had little left to include the other essential parts of his story. Thus, Russell's conference should try to help him sustain this good beginning. The teacher's comments could be: "Russell, I really liked the beginning of your story because I could really picture what the little goldfish was like, and I can sort of figure out the end where the fish ends up in the jail and her parents help her get out. But I don't understand the middle part—what is 'zone a'? I think your readers will want to know more about this part of the fish's adventure. This is the really exciting part, isn't it?" The teacher tries to point out how an important part of the story may be missing or not clear and encourages Russell to revise by mentioning that this is the part that readers will likely find most exciting. Then

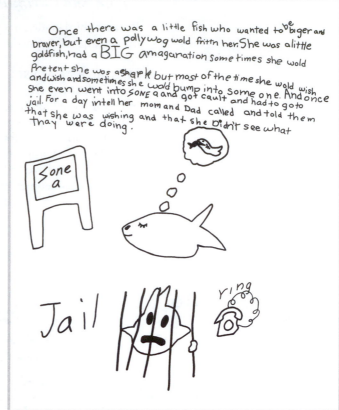

figure 8.14
Katy's Text

figure 8.15
Russell's Text

the teacher would have him talk more about what he might add, and this discussion will make his enacting this revision process on his text much easier. Russell has added pictures but they are all on the bottom of the page. However, these seem to be in the same sequence as actions he has included in his writing. The teacher would try to build on these images to help on the writing revisions. "I notice how your pictures go with lots of what you say in your writing, so as you revise, you might see how each picture goes with what you have and what new pictures you'll need to go with what you have and what you add. Use a pencil and circle what part would be on page 1, page 2, and so forth, so you'll be able to better spot which picture goes with which part. For example, your first page might be your first sentence and maybe you could have a picture of how the little fish is frightened by a tiny pollywog. What do you think?" Thus, giving Russell a first step, the teacher shows how he can see how his pictures can help him in revising his written text.

MEDIUM ANALYSIS

Russell has mostly transitional (and conventional) spellings. Spellings like "cault" (caught), "intell" (until), and "thay" (they) show that he has gone beyond the one-to-one rule of letter-name spellers. He seems to have reasonably good control of the use of commas, but he is inconsistent in his use of periods. Because he does demonstrate that he has some sense of a sentence, the teacher may extend his understanding by reading through Russell's text, pausing only when periods are there and getting him to hear how it sounds that way. Then the teacher could have Russell go through the story again (with the teacher's help), reconsidering his use of periods.

Bryan and Carla: Third and Fourth Graders

Bryan

Bryan, a third grader, has been studying kangaroos and has written a report (Figure 8.16) on what he has learned.

MESSAGE ANALYSIS

Bryan's text is a typical example of the information book genre. He does a good job in relating the typical behavior of kangaroos, where they live, and so on and is consistent in using the present tense of this genre. What Bryan seems to need help on is the organization of his information. Teacher comments could direct his attention to this issue: "You certainly have some useful information here, but I was somewhat confused about how you have ordered it. There seem to be three major subtopics here—do you agree? But sometimes you have mixed up this information, and that makes it not so clear." The teacher could then help Bryan identify these three subtopics: where kangaroos live (in Australia and where there is green grass and water), how they protect themselves, and how they give birth. The teacher demonstrates the technique by using a Semantic Map* to help him organize his data, which might provide him with a frame-

figure **8.16**

Bryan's Text

Kangaroos live in Allstrailya. They are born alive. They fight for thier companyons. They use thier feet for fighting. Thier feet have sharp clows. Thier feet could tear open thier componento skin. When they fight they put thier heads back to pretect thier eyes. Kangaroos can jump very high. They use thier strengh to jump fast enouge to get away from prediters like the coyote, and the wolf. Theese animals eat meat. Kangaroos live where the gras is greene and on the lands where water is. Becaos They eat grass. They give live birth. The babies stay in a pouch for abaut 6 mounths in a row when geting bigger their mothers pouch gets to littel and her musels have to loosen up for her babey to get out. The babby gets bigger and its on its own. Meanwile the mother gives birth to a nouther Kangaroo and this repeats twice.

work on which to revise. No illustrations are included as yet, so the teacher might talk about what kinds of pictures are appropriate in such a report and whether minor text might be added. "I think a few pictures might be good for your book. Maybe you should add one for each topic. Remember you want these pictures to be realistic ones— do you have books that can give you ideas? And you might add captions on these pictures, which would give an opportunity to add some more details that you don't have in what you have right now." The teacher may then have Bryan talk more about what he already knows that he could add in pictures and captions, or they may together look at some of the books he has used to get ideas.

MEDIUM ANALYSIS

Bryan is a typical transitional speller. For example, look at his overextension of the terminal *e* in "greene" (green) and "enouge" (enough) and his understanding of vowel digraphs in "Allstrailya" (Australia) and "anouther" (another). However, in editing, the teacher would probably address the concept of paragraphs with him. Because Bryan is working on three major points about kangaroos, this is a good time for the teacher to show him how to use paragraphs to signal this organization of his information. He will get the idea of paragraphs more easily because in his writing it can be tied so nicely to function.

Figure 8.17 is the text written by Carla, a fourth grader, at the beginning of the year. As part of a HOUSES unit, Carla and some of her classmates had recently taken a tour through a house bus. Carla and her small group decided to come up with different versions of alternative housing and describe them to their classmates.

Carla

MESSAGE AND MEDIUM ANALYSES

Carla had told the teacher that she was having trouble describing her ideas on alternative housing in a poem. Both the message and medium aspects of Carla's text are being discussed together, because the structure or form of her poem and its physical layout were integrally linked. Both Carla and the teacher looked at a variety of poems, commenting on the possibilities. Then the teacher asked Carla to see if she could structure her individual sentences (find a pattern in her text that she could follow) and group her sentences as if they were sort of stanzas. Carla thought that she liked her first two sentences: "The first one sort of tells what my dream house is." She also liked the pattern she had in the second sentence: "for a light I would . . . when it's nighttime I would. . . ." Carla noted that her third sentence began okay ("And for a special thing . . .") but that she wasn't consistent with the verb (she used *I'll* instead of *I would*). The teacher helped her go through several more sentences and then let her attempt a revision of the others on her own. The teacher suggested that the places where

---

MY DREAM HOUSE

I would like to live in a floating house on the beach. For a light I would cut some squares on the roof and when it's night time I would pin some square cloths on top of my roof windows and turn on my lamps. And for a special thing I'll cut a square on the floor in my bedroom and put a square glass between the cut wood and look at the fish before I go to bed. As for water, I'd open my back door and scoop up water from my pail and clean the water in my Water Cleaner machine that I invented. As for keeping my food cold I have two big Ice boxes. And for cooking food I have a electric stove. As for furniture there nailed to the ground. To keep me company I have a big television and some books to read. An when I need more food I climb into my little boat witch is tighten to my Boat House. An when I'm board of the same place I'm at, I have a Big motor in the end of my house and can go iney where I want.

THE END

figure **8.17**
Carla's Text

The teacher helped Carla consider her own values expressed in her text.

she wrote about water and food and so on could go together in a different stanza from the first set of sentences. The teacher also entered into a conversation with Carla about how her underlying values might be tied to the items she has included in her house. Although Carla is writing about a "dream" house, she could think more about unacknowledged ideologies she might be expressing. Carla was given the job of evaluating the rest of her poem in light of that consideration. Thus, besides the ideological issue, grammatical structure and genre format were both incorporated into this conference. Another topic that was covered at the end of the conference is the use of illustrations. All of the alternative housing texts are to be bound into a large class book, usually each text taking one page. The illustrations are to go in the margins around the writing, so the teacher would ask Carla about her plans about these as well. "Have you thought what illustrations you will add and where you should place them in the big book?" Carla stated that she had only thought about them just a little because she was still having trouble in sorting out the written part. "But I think most of my pictures will have the objects I mention or how the house is built, you know, the roof windows. I'll definitely have me in a couple of the pictures, too, lying in bed, maybe getting water, and then leaving off to visit another place at the end." The teacher nodded approval with these ideas and suggested that she sketch them out ahead of time so she'll know what size they will need to be to fit on the big-book pages.

David and Eileen: Fifth and Sixth Graders

David and Eileen are students in a fifth/sixth-grade classroom. Their texts were the result of a HEROES unit. Both wrote a biography of two heroes they had studied. These texts are quite long, so only excerpts can be provided here. Both texts were second drafts, as both David and Eileen had already had conferences with their teacher on their first drafts.

David

David, a fifth grader, wrote on Amelia Earhart. (See Figure 8.18.)

MESSAGE ANALYSIS

David starts his text by describing the search for Amelia Earhart when she disappeared, and then he uses the flashback technique to talk about her life before then. The excerpt includes the first part of his text and the last few paragraphs. David attempted a sort of fictionalized biography. In relating the episode about the small girl on the sled, he was attempting to show the type of woman Earhart was: one who "thrived on excitement." Thus, he tried to provide a "story" about the girl/woman Earhart, based on the facts he discovered about her. Sometimes he was not consistent in his efforts to do this, and most of the teacher's initial conference addressed this issue. His second draft was much better, but he still had difficulty in expressing the transitions between the different episodes he chose to highlight. He chose times in Earhart's life that appeared to be significant in her decision to become a pilot, and the teacher helped him figure out how to express the chronological events so that they were coherent, not just a listing of isolated events. The teacher also asked David if he thought he might elaborate on the "speculation" about what happened to Earhart at the end of his text, that is, whether a discussion of the various hypotheses about her disappearance might be a useful addition. The teacher and David also talked about whether he wanted to talk about how people might have treated the young girl or adult Earhart's desire for excitement. At the end, David initiated talk about the photographs he planned to include. "I found some good pictures on the Internet and a couple of books, so I plan to add one or two for each section."

The teacher addressed ideologies/values around gender in the text.

MEDIUM ANALYSIS

Both David and Eileen helped each other with peer editing, so this second draft was very polished already. David was, for the most part, a conventional speller and had a good control of conventional grammar and punctuation. The teacher pointed out that there were two instances where David did not use commas appropriately regarding appositives, so he noted them for his final draft.

figure **8.18**
David's Text

AMELIA EARHART

8:45 A.M. Amelia Earhart's voice came over the microphone giving her position. Little did she know that this would be her last message. Somewhere around tiny Howland Island her plane would disappear.

A giant search party consisting of the battleship Itasca, four destroyers, a minesweeper and an aircraft carrier and all its planes began to embark on a sixteen day search . . . . .

A small girl on a boy's sled came whistling down an icy slope, her hair flying behind her. At the end of the slope the junk man and his old horse and buggy were slowly plowing through the snow. If she kept going on her present course she would surely collide with him! She held tight and hoped. She couldn't yell because the junk man was deaf, and the horse had blinders.

Closer and closer she came! She held her breath! She shot like a bullet right underneath the horse's belly, and out through the other side without a scratch!

Another time Amelia tried to build a contraption somewhat like a roller coaster. She fell off, almost breaking her leg, and rubbed her chin raw. To her this was fun.

She thrived on excitement.

- •
- •
- •
- •

March 17, 1937: the beginning of a journey from which she and her navigator, Fred Noonan would never return.

They had made many previous stops. Now, they were heading toward Howland Island.

Their plane was circling around Howland Island. They should have landed two hours ago. Then her last message was heard.

There is much speculation on what happened at 8:45 that day.

Eileen's text was titled "Thurber Years." Figure 8.19 is an excerpt of the first part of her text (which consisted of five chapters). Eileen is a sixth grader.

MESSAGE ANALYSIS

Eileen's text on James Thurber, a second draft, represented a more typical biography in one sense, but it was unusual in that she attempted to relate Thurber's life by "cloning" his style of writing. Her initial conference mostly addressed the difficulties she had in being consistent in doing this. This second conference reexamined places in which revisions had been made and where Eileen had rethought others. The teacher asked Eileen to consider places in which Eileen tells what she is doing in reporting on Thurber's life. Eileen begins her second chapter with: "Now I'm going to tell you about his Ohio life." The teacher asked, "Now, have you included this sentence because you think Thurber would have written it this way as part of his style or because you think this is appropriate for a biography?" The teacher attempted to help Eileen decide to distinguish style versus genre issues. In her first conference with Eileen, the teacher had asked Eileen if she planned to include her own illustrations or photographs. So, in this second conference, she also asked about the visual images. Eileen answered, "I've decided to do my own illustrations. My mom told me that there had been a TV show based on Thurber's work years ago, and there were sort of animated cartoons used. I'm going to try to create cartoonish illustrations, one at the beginning of each chapter. I

> Thurber Years
>
>
> CHAPTER ONE
>
> In Which We Meet James
>
>
>   <u>Thurber Country</u>, <u>The Thurber Album</u>, <u>Lanterns and Lances</u>, <u>These and More</u>.
> Sound familiar? It should. Many has been the person who has recited these titles
> "Who are they by?" asks the naive child. This is where I come in. I feel that it
> is about time that someone else wrote about him, instead of him
> doing all of the writing. "But who is he?" you ask. I reply with "I think that
> everyone should be acquainted with James Thurber and his works." In this
> biography, I will be telling why. Also, I will tell some of his escapades during
> his career life.
>   "What other books did he write?" you could probably be wondering. Well, you
> asked for it. <u>Is Sex Necessary</u>, <u>The Seal in the Bedroom</u>, <u>Arms and Diversions</u>, and
> <u>Let Your Mind Alone,</u> are all of his works. "Are they good?" you might ask. I'll
> be contented to leave that to you.

figure 8.19

Eileen's Text

can't draw that well, but I think I can make a cartoon that would go with a major thing I talk about in each chapter."

MEDIUM ANALYSIS
Eileen is also a conventional speller and has control of conventional grammar and punctuation. However, as with David, the teacher addressed a punctuation issue in the Editing Conference*. Eileen did not always put commas or periods within the quotation marks when she listed stories written by Thurber, so the teacher pointed out how to do this.

Luis and Latisha: Seventh and Eighth Graders

Luis

Luis, a seventh grader, has been involved in inquiries about rocks and minerals as part of a LANDSCAPES unit. Students are doing different, small experiments on this topic and are making displays to show the results of these explorations. Luis's text covers his procedures and a summary on making sedimentary layers that will end up on a small poster, with a jar where he has tried to create layers to illustrate the process of forming sedimentary rocks (see Figure 8.20).

MESSAGE ANALYSIS
For the most part, Luis has used the conventional language that scientists use to describe a process and the two steps of the procedures he followed to create sedimentary layers. Except for the "I put" in the second sentence of step one, he has appropriately used procedural language ("collect," "fill," "shake"). He has present-tense verbs, general nouns to designate classes (e.g., "rocks," "layers"), and the general "you." He has also used mostly technical terms—except for the "the stuff"—and the text is nicely ordered—except perhaps for his second sentence. As Luis waited for his teacher to read

figure **8.20**
Luis's Text

How to Make Sedimentary Layers
by Luis

Sedimentary rocks are made over many years. You can understand the proces by making your own sedimentary layers. They ocur because weather and erosion break down rocks into small peces and then wind and water carry the rocks peas to rivers, lakes or other bodies of water. The peces —called sediment — build up over millions of years as layers and form sedimentary rocks.

1. Collect some gravel, two kinds of sand (corse and fine) and a little bit of dirt. I put a few tablespoons of each into a jar. Then fill the jar halfway with water and put the lid on. Shake the jar to make all the stuff is mixed together.

2. Leave the jar with the stuff overnight. You will see that the stuff has formed layers. The fine sand is on top and the gravel that is heavy is on the bottom. See the jar in the display.

If you buried the stuff it would turn into sedimentary rock after a few million years.

the text, he himself noted the "I" and crossed it out and made "Put" the first word of the sentence. The teacher addressed the two other areas. "Good job, Luis. I think this is a good summary of the sedimentary process and your experiment. I have two things for you to think about though. I felt that your second sentence kind of breaks the flow of your ideas. I think you should keep that sentence but where do you think it might go?" Luis quickly read through the text and decided that it might go right before his two steps. "I agree, because it sort of previews how other scientists could follow the procedures to make the layers. Now, I want you to look at how many times you have used 'the stuff.' You have lots of good technical terms in your text, but you need one for 'stuff.' What could you put in there instead?" Luis considered "materials" at first and then decided on "mixture" because he used "mixed" at the end of step one. The teacher agreed that "mixture" was a good word for the second step and the last sentence of the text but thought that Luis might use "materials" in step one because it might sound odd to have "mixed" and "mixture" in the same sentence, to which Luis agreed.

MEDIUM ANALYSIS

Luis used mostly conventional spellings, but he has some that result from his being a bilingual Spanish–English learner. Because Spanish is mostly a one-sound-one-letter language, second-language learners like Luis still rely on this Spanish spelling pattern when they write in English ("proces" for "process"; "ocur" for "occur"; "peces" for "pieces"). Luis will be typing his final draft on the computer, so the teacher does not identify the particular words, but tells him to note them when he does his second draft. "Luis, good job on the spelling, but there are some words that you are still having trouble with. Be sure you note those when the spell-checker underlines them in red and put your draft spellings and the correct spellings in your spelling book, okay?" The class has been working on commas in series, which occur a lot in nonfictional writing. The teacher has spotted a couple of times where Luis omitted the last comma before the "and" or "or" where the series contained three items (for example, see his ". . . to rivers, lakes or other bodies of water"). The teacher has him find one during the conference and then encourages him to find any others and fix them himself.

Latisha

Latisha is in eighth grade. Her text is the beginning of her report on "Creature Partners and Helpers." As part of a MAKING CONNECTIONS unit that middle school teachers had created, students were studying various animal and creature relationships in science class. Latisha was part of a group that focused on parasites and partners. Latisha decided to study and write on those creatures that benefit each other. Others in her group were studying the parasites and other creature relationships where mutualism did not occur. This is her first draft and she has asked her science teacher for the conference because she wanted some initial guidance about content, format, and illustrations. (See Figure 8.21.)

MESSAGE ANALYSIS

Because Latisha requested the conference with the teacher, she began by explaining how she was planning to organize the book on creature symbiosis. What she has so far is about antelopes and koalas and their partner microorganisms and then the relationship between the honeyguide bird and ratels. "So, let me tell you what I plan to include for the rest of the book and then tell me what you think." Latisha explained that after that she was going to write about how badgers and coyotes hunt and help each other. "Up till now, each creature benefits, but I am thinking of adding a group where the relationship is commensalism—one creature benefits, but the other doesn't. But it doesn't suffer either—it is sort of not affected at all. That's why I'm calling the book 'Creature Partners and Helpers.'" Her teacher thought this sounded like a good plan and then asked whether she expected to do any more research. "I noticed that you have a particular microorganism—the cillates—when you discuss the antelopes, but you don't specify the type when you talk about the koalas. Do you know if it is the same microorganisms or different ones?" Latisha said that she was definitely doing more research, but she wanted to write the structure of the book with what she had so far so that it would be easier to fill in later. "I didn't notice that about the microorganisms— I'll recheck that in my sources now and then I'll be sure to look it up in other stuff. Jerome, Kate, Lisa, and I plan to go the websites tomorrow, so I'll do that then." The teacher noted that her pictures are just sketched in now. "That was a good idea, trying to see how the pictures work with the text. Will you be using captions?" Latisha explained that the pictures are only a very rough draft right now and was hoping to see if she could find any cross sections or cutaways of an animal like an antelope that would have the microorganisms inside it. "If not, I'll just have a picture of an antelope eating grass. The koala might have a baby eating the green soup. I think I'll have captions for all of the pictures. I might find more details in my research that I can put in the captions and in the major text, too." Latisha left the conference feeling that she was on the right path in her inquiry and her writing.

MEDIUM ANALYSIS

Although Latisha's text was a rough draft, the teacher noted that she had good sentence structure for the genre she was writing and her spelling was conventional. How-

Lots of creatures have close relationships with different types of creatures. This relationship is called symbiosis. When the creatures have relationships where both creatures benefit, it is called mutualism. (This is different from a parasite-host relationship, where one creature benefits at the expense of another.)

Relationships of Mutualism

Some animals have microorganisms as partners, where both benefit. Antelopes eat grass that is made of a tough fibrous material called cellulose. It has to be broken down so that the nutrients can be absorbed into the blood of the animals. Their partners are very small single-cell creatures called cillates that help in the breakdown of the cellulose material for the antelopes to be able to get the energy from the grass they eat. In return, the antelopes' guts provide food and a safe, warm home for these microorganisms.

Koalas have a similar relationship with microorganisms. Koalas eat only eucalyptus leaves, which cannot be digested without them. Also, these microorganisms help deal with the poisons on the leaves. Baby koalas are born without these microorganisms, so they have to get them from the mother. A mother squirts a green soup of partially broken-down leaves from her rear end, which the baby then eats. Then the baby has the partners that help it to use the leaves that it eats.

Other Team Partners

Honeyguide birds' food is bee wax and larvae. They can find bee hives, but cannot on their own break through the bees' hive. So, when they find one, they signal to a ratel (also called a honey badger) by making a churring call and flashing their white wing feathers. The ratel follows the honeyguide bird to the hive and opens it with its strong claws. The ratel eats its fill and then the bird eats the leftovers.

figure **8.21**
Latisha's Text

ever, the teacher brought up two things that Latisha might keep an eye on. "I noticed when I briefly scanned throughout your text that you might be using 'then' a lot. We have talked about that before—that it is so easy to use 'and' and 'then.' Sometimes, you can't avoid it, but you might—in your final draft—go over those specially and see if you could connect ideas in a different way. For example, see the last two sentences about the koalas—how could you rewrite them so you don't have two 'thens' in a row? Also, check the third sentence about the honeyguide bird and ratel. You might make the first part of the sentence be 'when a bird finds one, it signals to a ratel' so it is all singular not plural in the first part, and singular in the second part of the sentence." Latisha circled the places with her pencil and told the teacher that she'd keep these points in mind.

Summary

In conferences, teachers address message and medium issues of individual writers. As part of message analysis, they also give feedback about the relationship between any pictures or visual design that may be included. The foregoing examples describe the kinds of problems children tackle in their developmental writing and the ways teachers can support and extend their efforts through their questions and comments in conferences. Writing Conferences* also are discussed in Chapter 7.

See Glasswell, Parr, & McNaughton (2003) for vulnerabilities in and tips for conferencing.

Kid-Watching Procedures for Emergent Learners

Before children are able to read in a conventional sense, that is, before they have acquired a sight word vocabulary or are able to figure out and use the graphic or graphophonemic cues in written language, they can engage in experiences that demonstrate their present literate understandings. Some of these were covered in the preceding section when children's invented spellings and other principles and concepts of writing were discussed. This section examines four other literacy activities involving emergent learners. When teachers know kid-watching techniques such as these, they are able to document and support the early stages of reading and writing more effectively. The first scheme involves examining what young children know about the medium aspects of written language as they help the teacher read a book. The second evaluates children's repeated reenactments of a book. The third focuses on teachers' observations while taking down children's dictations. The fourth is the retelling assessment, which can be used for emergent learners, but is also appropriate for older students. Although these assessment schemes may at first seem difficult to use, teachers soon internalize them and begin using them informally in other classroom routines.

Concepts about Print Assessment

Clay (1979a, 2001)

The Concepts about Print (CAP) assessment was developed by Clay to find out what young children already know about medium aspects of written language (e.g., directional principles; concepts of first, last, word, and letter; and punctuation). Clay's two

Clay (1972, 1979b)

little books (*Sand* and *Stones*), created for teachers to share with children, contain various alterations. A picture is inverted, lines of print are reversed and upside down, and words or letters are switched around. Teachers read the book as if the book were normal, and as they do, they ask children to help them: "How should I put the book down to read it?" "Where should I start to read?" "Which way should I go?" "What's this for (pointing to a comma, period, etc.)?" "Show me the first part I should read on this page." Thus, this book-sharing experience represents an inquiry situation for children to show what they already know about the concepts and conventions of the medium aspects before they can read conventionally from print.

Many teachers use *Sand* in the beginning of the year and *Stones* at the end (or vice versa) to assess and document children's understandings. Others, following the format of these books, design and write their own books.

Another alternative is to apply the ideas in *Sand* and *Stones* in a regular book, which is what we illustrate here. Keep the following features in mind when choosing a book:

1. Select a book in which some pages have print on both the left and right pages.
2. Select a book that has several types of punctuation.
3. Select a book that has one page with only one line of print (that is a complete sentence).
4. Select a book that has one page with three lines of print.

Rockwell (1984)

Figure 8.22 covers the instructions for sharing *Our Garage Sale* by Rockwell.

Not all the concepts are included in Clay's books (they have twenty-four items, whereas the example in *Our Garage Sale* has only nineteen), mostly because in a real book there are no inverted pages and print. It is useful to develop a CAP Scoring Sheet to administer the assessment. Figure 8.23 (p. 381) has been developed for that purpose and illustrates how Amanda, a kindergartner, responded.

The first column indicates the page of the book involved, the second column lists the concept or principle involved, and the third column lists the items. The large column notes the behavior of the child that leads to a point for each item. The information in parentheses is a reminder for the teacher who administers the assessment. The

Before starting, thoroughly familiarize yourself with this test. Paginate the book (pencil in numbers in the corners of each page). Use instructions similar to the ones suggested below. Use the CAP scoring sheet (see Figure 8.23) to remind yourself of these instructions and to score the child's responses.

Begin by saying to the child: "I'm going to read you this book, but I want you to help me." (Note: You will read the whole text but will ask questions on only some of the pages.)

COVER

Item 1 Test: For orientation of book. Pass the book to the child holding the book vertically by the outside edge, spine toward the child.
Say: "Show me the front of this book."
Score: 1 point for each correct repsonse.

GO TO. . .
Pages 2/3
Item 2 Test: A left page is read before a right page.
Say: "Where do I start reading?"
Score: 1 point for left page indication.

GO TO. . .
Page 8
Item 3 Test: Capital and lowercase correspondence.
Say: "Find a little letter like this." Point to the capital "S" and demonstrate by pointing to "Ss" if the child does not succeed. Then say, "Find a little letter like this." Point to capital "W" and "O" in turn.
Score: 1 point if *both* "Ww" and "Oo" are located.
Test: Three types of punctuation.
Read the text.
Say: "What's this for?"
Item 4 Point to the period or trace it with a pencil.
Score: 1 point for a functional definition (e.g., "It tells you that it's done, or to stop).
Item 5 Point to the comma or trace it with a pencil.
Score: 1 point for an acceptable functional definition.
Item 6 Point to the quotation marks or trace with a pencil.
Score: 1 point for an acceptable functional definition.

GO TO. . .
Page 12 Test: For directional rules.
Item 7 Say: "Show me where to start."
Score: 1 point for top left.
Item 8 Say: "Which way do I go?"
Score: 1 point for left to right.
Item 9 Say: "Where do I go after that?"
Score: 1 point for return sweep to left.
(Score items 7–9 if all movements are demonstrated in one response.)
Item 10 Test: Word-by-word pointing on one page.
Say: "Point to the words while I read." (Read slowly but fluently.)
Score: 1 point for exact matching.

(continued)

last column reflects the score for each item. You will see that the teacher jotted down some extra information on some of Amanda's responses. Item 16 has children indicate the first and last letters of a word on the line of print found on page 18: "It didn't rain on Saturday." Amanda indicated these correctly by revealing the *I* (of *It*) and the *y* (of *Saturday*), but the fact that she showed only the beginning and end of the sentence indicates that she may be just beginning to understand the concepts of first and last. The

figure **8.22**

Continued

Pages 14/15

Item 11   Test: Word-by-word pointing on left and right pages.

             Say: "Point to the words while I read." (Read slowly, but fluently.)

             Score: 1 point for exact matching.

Pages 16/17

Item 12   Test: A left page is read before a right page. (This incorporates features of Item 2 and Items 7–9. However, here the lines of print on each page in this book are placed in the same place on the page, so it would be easy for the child to indicate to read the rest of the first line on page 16 and then to the first line of page 17, then to the second line of page 16, etc.)

             Say: "Where do I start reading?"

                      "Which way do I go?"

                      "Where do I go after that?"

             Score: 1 point for left page indication.

GO TO. . .

Page 20

Item 13   Test: Concept of first and last applied to text.

             Say: "Show me the first part to read on this page."

                      "Show me the last part on this page."

              Score: 1 point if *both* are correctly indicated.

Read the rest of the book. Then go back to:

Page 18   Have two small index cards (3 x 5) that the child can hold and slide easily over the line of text to cover words and letters. To start, lay the cards on the page but leave all print exposed.

Item 14   Test: Letter concept.

             Say: "This page says, 'It didn't rain on Saturday.' I want you to push the cards across the page like this until all you can see is one letter." (Demonstrate the movement of the cards, but do not do the exercise.)

                      "Now show me two letters."

              Score: 1 point if *both* are correct.

Item 15   Test: Word concept.

             Say: "Show me just one word."

                      "Now show me two words."

              Score: 1 point if *both* are correct.

Item 16   Test: First and last letter concepts.

             Say: "Show me the first letter of a word."

                      "Show me the last letter of a word."

              Score: 1 point if *both* are correct.

Item 17   Test: Capital letter concept.

              Say: "Show me a capital letter."

              Score: 1 point if letter is correctly located.

Back

Item 18   Test: Back of book.

             Say: "Show me the back of the book."

              Score: 1 point for correct response.

Top/Bottom

Item 19   Test: Top and bottom of book.

             Say: "Show me the top and the bottom of the book."

              Score: 1 point for correct responses.

---

teacher will note in subsequent observations whether she indicates first and last letters in the same word, which will suggest greater control of these concepts.

Thus, the CAP assessment gives a score, but more importantly it pinpoints those concepts that individual children already have and those that need to be fostered.

Child: _____ Date: _____ Score: _____

Concepts About Print Test for: OUR GARAGE SALE (by Anne Rockwell)
(Keep book jacket on book)

Page	Concept/Prin.	Item	Child's behavior for giving points (Remainder for admin.)	Score
cover	front	1	Indicates front of book (Show me the front of the book)	/
2/3	left page	2	Indicates that lft. page precedes rt. (Where do I start)	/
8	capital/lowercase	3	Locates two capital & lowercase letter pairs (Ww & Oo)	/
	punctuation	4	Indicates meaning of period (What's this for)	—
		5	Indicates meaning of comma (What's this for)	—
		6	Indicates meaning of quotation marks (What're these for)	—
12	direction	7	Points at top left page (Show me where to start)	/
		8	Indicates left to right (Which way do I go)	/
		9	Indicates return sweep to left (Where do I go next)	/
	one-to-one same pg.	10	Word-by-word pointing/matching (Point while I read) *almost*	—
14/15	one-to-one lft. to rt. pg.	11	Word-by-word pointing/matching (Point while I read) *almost*	—
16/17	all lft. pg.	12	Indicates all of lft. pg. read before rt. (Where do I, etc.)	/
20	first/last text	13	Indicates first & last of text (Show me the first/last)	/
GO BACK 18	letter/word	14	Locates one and two letters (Show me one/two letter(s))	/
C A R D S		15	Locates one and two words (Show me one/two word(s))	—
	first/last ltr. of word	16	Locates first & last letter of word (Show me first/last) *ends*	/
	capital ltr.	17	Locates a capital letter (Show me a capital letter) *Saturday d*	—
back	back	18	Indicates the back of book (Show me the back of book)	/
top/bottom	tp./bottom	19	Indicates the top & bottom of book (Show me tp./btm. of bk.)	/

figure 8.23
CAP Scoring Sheet

Amanda, for example, knows orientational features of books, directional rules, and concepts of first and last. However, she does not have a stable concept of word—she could not locate one and two words (item 15) or indicate word-by-word pointing (items 10 and 11)—nor does she seem to know the functions of punctuation. Thus, the teacher will need to provide experiences to help her develop these concepts. Involving Amanda in Big Book* and Group-Composed Writing* activities and providing many opportunities for her to write her own texts will foster these concepts and extend Amanda's present understandings about written language.

Approximations to Text Assessment

The Approximations to Text (ATT) assessment is also appropriate for emergent learners. It is based on research, as well as the observations of many parents and preschool teachers, that indicates that after young children are read to, they spontaneously "re-enact" or role play "reading" on their own. As adults continue to share these books, children repeatedly "pretend read" their favorite texts, getting closer and closer to the actual wordings until they have learned them by heart. In the process, children develop an awareness of the nature of registers of written language. Their acquisition of "book language" is a gradual, constructive process. Subsequently, they begin to integrate the

Holdaway (1979); McKenzie (1977); Pappas (1993); Pappas & Brown (1989)

graphic cuing system with what they know about the syntactic/semantic or lexico-grammatical patterns of the message. Thus, ATT attempts to tap the reading process for children who cannot be evaluated through an MMA assessment.

The procedure consists of reading an unfamiliar book to a child three times, usually on consecutive days, and on each occasion inviting the child to take his or her turn to "read" or "pretend read" it. Each reading is audiotaped and then transcribed.

The teacher then compares the child's approximations to those of the book and to the ways the child's texts change across the three times. Analyses usually focus on the following four major areas:

1. *Children expand and elaborate on the message of the book across the three readings.* Children may initially give a bare-bones rendition of the text, but as they hear the text being read again and have opportunities to take their turns to read it again, they begin to fill in and add more of the author's message.
2. *Children acquire certain vocabulary used in the book.* They may provide a synonym or make up a word for certain vocabulary in early readings, but in subsequent readings they may incorporate the actual wordings of the author.
3. *Children incorporate the author's grammatical structures.* Written language uses various kinds of grammatical constructions (more use of relative clauses, passive voice, etc.) that are not as typical in oral language, so children frequently create their own versions of these structures and then gradually begin to include structures similar to those of the author in subsequent readings.
4. *Children's elaborations based on the illustrations change across the readings.* In early readings, children rely on the illustrations of a book to construct and sustain the message, but these elaborations usually drop out or are somehow incorporated or expressed more in terms of the linguistic message in later readings.

Figure 8.24 shows an ATT Analysis Sheet, which can be used to document these four types of approximations.

Teachers respond to any child-initiated question about a book's message, pictures, or print during an ATT session. At the bottom of the form (Figure 8.24), the teacher might jot down interesting questions or comments the child might have had.

Children's questions, such as "What's this word?" or "Is this word _____?" are answered unless the child asks about every other word. If it is clear—after a page or so—that the child is unwilling to follow the "pretend route," then the teacher may consider

figure **8.24**

ATT Analysis Sheet

Child's Name: _____ Date: _____ Book: _____	Reading #1	Reading #2	Reading #3
Important message ideas and details included			
Strategies in learning vocabulary			
Strategies in learning grammatical constructions			
Changes in elaborations based on illustrations			
Interesting questions, comments made			

an alternative procedure that consists of reading page by page, the teacher reading one page, then the child "reading" that page. The fact that some children are reluctant to "pretend read" is normal. It indicates that these children have acquired a lot about the graphic or medium aspects of written language and are more motivated to tackle the print realization of the message. An MMA scheme could be applied to the children's readings in these cases instead of the form illustrated in Figure 8.24.

Once learned, the ATT procedure helps teachers to appreciate children's constructive process of reading at the very early stages and to be aware of the kind of strategies children employ in learning "book language." Thus, it encourages teachers to provide opportunities in the classroom for children to reenact or "pretend read" books from a range of genres through Big Books*, Book Talks*, Buddy Reading*, and the like.

> See Pappas (1993) for examples of repeated pretend reading of stories and information books, and Collier (2003) for examples of pretend reading in an urban classroom.

Dictation Assessment

Dictation and retelling (described in the next section) are oral compositions. Although teachers are constantly encouraging children to write on their own, dictation experiences are also useful in fostering the composing process because they give children opportunities to concentrate more on creating their message. This leaves the scribing work to the teacher, who takes on the mechanical task of writing and the concerns about spelling and punctuation. Therefore, dictations provide important information about a child's potential in the composition process that is not available when only their own writings are considered. Figure 8.25, which provides examples of two stories composed around the same time (mid-October) by a first grader, illustrates this fact. Janet's dictation, which is on the top, is much more complex than her written story, which is on the bottom. (Other genres can also be dictated, e.g., poems, informational texts, and so forth.)

> Genishi & Dyson (1984); Temple, Nathan, Temple, & Burris (1993); Tierney & Readance (2000)

Dictation experiences provide a means to assess both the product and the process of children's composing. By means of the message criteria discussed earlier (see Figure 8.8), the dictation text as product can be evaluated. However, other information about children's participation in the process can also be assessed. What is the delivery style of the

---

figure 8.25

Janet's Dictation and Written Texts

DICTATION:

Once upon a time there was a little boy. And he was trying to go to sleep, but he heard a noise in the closet. So he sat up in bed. He opened the door of the closet and he looked in. There was a monster. And so he says, "Are you a scary monster?" And the monster said, "No." And so he says, "Will you play with me?" The monster says, "Of course." And so the boy called in his sister, and he said, "Here, I have a friend. He is a monster." The little girl said, "You do?" because she liked monsters. So the little boy said, "Yes." And so he asked the monster to play games with them. The monster won every game. And in London Bridges they couldn't fit their arms around him. In Hide-and-Go-Seek he had two heads so he could tell where they were going. Then the little boy asked him, "Why were you in the closest?" He said because he was looking for candy. The little girl said, "Well, I have some candy." The monster said, "You do?" And the little girl said, "Yes." And so she got him a piece, and he ate it up. But then he said, "Yuk!" He didn't like peppermint. And so he said, "Well, now I have to hunt in the closet for more candy." And so he did. And the little boy woke up and he found out that it was all a dream.

WRITING: (Note: spelling and punctuation have been corrected.)

Once there was a girl and a boy.
The girl said, "Let's play!"
So they played and played.
They turned and turned.
They got dizzy.
They stopped.
The room went around.

child's dictation? Does the child dictate the message at a pace that is easy for the teacher to take down? Or does the child seem to be unaware of constraints on the writing process, rattling on and on so that the teacher has to stop the child repeatedly to keep up? Does the child pay attention to what the teacher is scribing by seeming to read along? Does the child comment on or take notice of spelling or punctuation? Does the child initiate any repairs (or revisions) of the message during the dictation process? Figure 8.26 summarizes the kinds of behaviors that can be assessed during dictation, based on the context in which a particular dictation occurred. (Janet's dictation came about because children were creating a classroom story anthology.) At the bottom of the Dictation Assessment Sheet are instructional ideas based on the dictation activity. Having children create a series of pictures to go with their dictation would provide further information—that is, in the ways in which they could create pictures that relate to the ideas communicated in a story, poem, or informational text.

A more formal dictation assessment (usually audiotaped) has teachers keep their interactions with children to a minimum. Other than stopping children when unable to keep up with their dictation, teachers avoid commenting on or drawing the children's attention to message or medium aspects of the text being composed in order to have a clearer view of the children's understanding. Then, on the basis of the data gained in these formal contexts, teachers know what to focus on when they interact with children in subsequent dictations. They also know what other activities may be appropriate.

There are many reasons to use dictation in the early elementary grades. (Certain versions of dictation can be used with older elementary-age children, such as Group-Composed Writing* activities.) Children's sight vocabulary is fostered through dictation; children are very successful in identifying words when they are *theirs*. Moreover, many demonstrations of medium aspects of written language—directionality, spacing,

figure **8.26**

Dictation Assessment Sheet

Questions	Analysis/Observations
How well does the child control the genre being attempted? Are there certain beginnings, endings, or sequences present to indicate a certain genre?	
Is the text complete? Are details or elaborations included?	
Interesting vocabulary used? Use of cohesive ties? Ambiguous terms?	
Any missing information? Is information ordered to make sense?	
Interesting repairs used?	
Attention to transcription of medium aspects of text?	
Delivery pace or dictating style?	

Child: _____ Date: _____

INSTRUCTIONAL IDEAS:

spelling, use of punctuation, and so on—are available for children during the dictation process. Teachers can also demonstrate the revising and editing processes during dictation. Finally, once teachers have experience in assessing dictations formally, they know how to evaluate them informally. As Figure 8.26 shows, teachers can document the contexts in which dictations arise and note instructional ideas to foster and extend children's present efforts. Dictations can be important sources of evaluation and accountability, as explained in Chapter 9.

Retelling Assessment

Like dictation, retelling is a type of oral composition in which children retell or reconstruct someone else's message, not their own. However, while dictations are usually used in the early primary grades, retellings can occur at any grade level. Retelling assessment procedures consist of either reading to children or having them read, then inviting them to retell it to someone who does not know it (usually other children in the class who haven't heard or read the text). The fact that children retell the text to naive listeners is a critical factor because it provides a social context that requires children to produce a complete linguistic message. The assessment, thus, addresses children's strategies to provide such a text. Such retellings are very different from those in the MMA assessment, where the listener has knowledge of the text being read.

Retellings are audiotaped and then transcribed formally. After the reading, most teachers have the children go through it again by letting them see the pictures (if the text is illustrated) or by discussing or commenting on any questions children might have beforehand. Because reading is a construction of meaning, retellings are viewed as "new" versions of the author's message. Retellings may be organized in ways that are different from the published text and may reflect interpretations different from those of the teacher. Figure 8.27 shows a Retelling Analysis Sheet, which could be used to document retellings from such a perspective.

In the first column, the teacher considers whether the essentials of the text have been included in the retelling and notes any significant information that seems missing. The second and third columns provide places to document the interesting elaborations and substitutions children may have used. In the last column, the teacher jots down any places where children may have been unclear, used ambiguous pronouns, or otherwise made the retelling incoherent. Thus, the analysis sheet can assess children's comprehension of a particular text and at the same time document the constructive nature of retelling by capturing various learners' "ways with words" or second-language approximations in the retelling process. As an oral composition, the retelling provides a means to evaluate children's strategies in creating and organizing a text for others.

When retelling analysis becomes second nature, teachers can evaluate children's retellings in more informal contexts, such as when they retell a story using props (flannel

Brown & Cambourne (1987); Tierney & Readance (2000); Weaver (2002)

Pappas & Pettegrew (1987)

Retellings are constructions of an author's message.

Cazden (2001); Freeman & Freeman (2001); Heath (1983); Kemp (1987); Lindfors (1999); Michaels (1981); Nieto (2000); Reyes & Halcon (2001)

Child's Name: _____		Date: _____	
Was the child provided the "essential" information? Is there anything significant missing?	Has the child included interesting elaborations (extra information not expressed in the text)?	Has the child provided substitutions of wording that represent similar ideas or meanings?	Are there aspects that are unclear? Is it clear as to who is doing/going; what is being discussed, etc.?

figure **8.27**
Retelling Analysis Sheet

board characters), retell sections of a text in a Literature Response Group*, or share texts in Buddy Reading*.

General Observation Schemes

The schemes discussed in the preceding section focused specifically on certain literacy events, but teachers also need the means to evaluate how children are using language and developing concepts as they interact with others in a variety of activities across the curriculum. In the integrated language perspective, skills or strategies cannot be discerned in isolation from the culture or settings in which they appear. Valid kid-watching procedures and evaluation must include observation and documentation of children's understandings as they emerge in the natural and familiar settings of the classroom. We need to see how children are constructing concepts in particular domains, how they become experts in various topics, and how their learning develops over time in different patterns for different children. Because development is socially influenced, we need to discover how children act with partners and peers in small-group and whole-class interactions. Finally, we need to be able to find out how each child approaches, initiates, and sustains his or her work and inquiry. To meet these needs, three types of observation schemes or approaches are covered: target-child (or target-children) observation, roving anecdotal observation, and other miscellaneous observation ideas.

Target-Child(ren) Observation

Sylva, Roy, & Painter (1980)

The first observation approach is a modification of the kid-watching ideas developed by Bruner and his colleagues to document young children's sustained attention in activities in preschool playgroups and nursery schools. This scheme involves selecting a target child on whom to do repeated ten-minute observations. Teachers decide on a few children to follow each day, and using a recording sheet, they take notes on what these children do and say. See Figure 8.28 for an example of the Target-Child(ren) Observation Sheet.

At the top of the form, the teacher writes the name of the child, the date, and time of the observation. The procedure consists of making several ten-minute observations at different times of the day to capture a variety of experiences and interactions. The first half-minute of each minute is spent observing; the last half-minute is spent summarizing the child's activities and language (jotted down under the headings "Activity Record" and "Language Record," respectively). As Figure 8.28 shows, information about the context, activity, or task and any participants involved with the target child is also included on this form. At the bottom of the form, the teacher notes any instructional ideas that may come to mind and reminders for subsequent intervention. Teachers try to be unobtrusive during the observations, and most teachers use a signal system (e.g., wearing a certain hat or scarf) so that children know not to interrupt the teacher while the observations are occurring.

Describe, don't interpret yet.

It is important to write down *what the child does* in the "Activity Record" column, not an interpretation of the behavior or what can be concluded about the child on the basis of what has been seen. Relevant information about materials or objects is also incorporated in the "Activity Record" column. Under the "Language Record" column, everything that the child says and what other children say to the child is noted. It is frequently impossible to write the exact words spoken, but the gist of comments can be recorded. Abbreviations can be used, as most teachers initially find it difficult to record observations. However, with practice the observations become second nature.

Part of observation is documenting how children sustain their attention in an activity or project, so after the writing is done, the record is reviewed for coherent themes in the child's behavior, that is, a continued stream of activity during which the child seems to be following a thread. The theme may be based on the materials the child is using or

Name(s):		Date and Time Observed:	
ACTIVITY RECORD	LANGUAGE RECORD	CONTEXT/TASK	OTHER PARTICIPANTS
1			
2			
3			
4			
5			
. . .			
10			
Instructional Ideas:			

figure **8.28**

Target Child(ren) Observation Sheet

Source: Sylva, Roy, & Painter, 1980

the children he or she is participating with, but it does not coincide with a shift of activity per se. A child—let's call him Joey—may finish reading a particular book and go over to the writing center for some paper and markers, glance over the book again as he chats with a peer about some of the illustrations, and then begin a Sketch to Stretch* activity. Joey tells his friend that he's going to finish the drawing later this afternoon, but before he joins everyone in a whole-class sharing session, Joey notes in his Sketchbook Journal* his ideas for the drawing so he doesn't forget them. Although the foregoing is only a summary of the child's behavior (i.e., it doesn't include the details of a real observation record), it illustrates the fact that a particular theme can integrate several activities and places over a brief period of time. Themes are noted on the observation sheet by drawing double lines to indicate where one theme ends and another begins.

The same form can be used to record observations of small-group activities. For example, when small groups are established to work on special projects in a thematic unit, teachers can document the course of their inquiries. Instead of one child, a target group of children is the focus. Afterward, teachers record relevant instructional ideas that could be helpful to support the group work, perhaps noting a question to ask the group, or a book or other resource to suggest.

Roving Anecdotal Observation

Roving anecdotal observation has many features of target-child(ren) observation but differs in focus. In the target-children observation scheme, teachers avoid interacting with children to concentrate on the ten-minute observations. In roving anecdotal observation, however, teachers move about the room to visit children as they engage in individual and small-group activities during integrated work time. Thus, teachers gather briefer, more specific "spot" information about children's particular strengths, needs, strategies, and interests in the natural social life of the classroom. There is a range of experiences to be recorded, so each observation must be focused to provide or generate appropriate instructional strategies. Categories of interesting behavior that such observations could concentrate on include, but are not limited to, the following:

Interactions with Peers

Strategies for joining and departing groups

Responses to initiations from others

Negotiation strategies

Examples of abilities to take the perspective of others

Instances of leadership or responsibility

Examples of peer support, empathy

Cooperation strategies

Examples of turn-taking abilities

Strategies and Processes

Process of problem solving with people

Process of problem solving with objects or materials

Creative use of resources to tackle problems

Strategies for accomplishing tasks

Unusual use of objects or materials beyond conventional roles

Unusual combination of objects, resources, or materials

Representational and imaginary object use

Oral Language Samples

Interesting quotations

Sophisticated vocabulary

Unusual working definitions of words

Examples of explanations and descriptions

Examples of metalinguistic awareness (using language as an object)

Instances of register or code switching

Comments indicating awareness or examination of ideologies or values

Literacy Samples

Use of books as a resource to help solve problems

Strategies used in reading aloud

Strategies used in various writing experiences (prewriting, drafting, revising, editing, publishing)

Creative Book Extensions*

Spontaneous use of reading and writing

Unusual or interesting use of reading and/or writing in projects

Visual Design Samples

Use of illustrations or other images to make sense of texts

Strategies in using and relating major and minor text (captions, labels, keys, etc.)

Use of pictures or other visual designs to represent ideas

Strategies for finding and relating information in different communication modes

Use of minor text (labels, captions, etc.) to explain meanings in visual images

Miscellaneous

Examples of sustained attention and focusing

Self-correction strategies

Examples of reflective behavior

Examples of autonomous or self-management behavior

Examples of interesting working styles

More possibilities will become apparent as you learn more about specific curricular content (Chapter 5) and about how to implement a variety of activities and experiences in thematic units (Chapters 5 and 7). Some teachers write their observations on index cards. We like Post-it Notes because the teacher can easily transfer these notes to a separate page for each child (which can, in turn, be placed in the child's learning portfolio—see Chapter 9) at a later time. These sheets can then be easily copied to share with parents, who enjoy reading these "snapshots" of their child in the classroom.

Keep in mind the following guidelines while writing anecdotal observations:

Include the child's name (underlined), date, and perhaps where the child was observed, if relevant.

Try to confine one piece of anecdotal information to one Post-it page.

Try to confine information to *one* child's reactions or responses. If other children are involved, write additional notes for the other participants.

Confine comments to what is being observed that particular day; don't refer to behavior on previous days.

Include a description of problem-solving processes.

Teachers who are just beginning to write anecdotal observations sometimes find the last point the most difficult. However, it is critical that these notes include *how* a child accomplishes a task, rather than record *that* a child has done something. Figure 8.29 contrasts notes that provide helpful information with those that do not. As these

Describing the *process* of what the child is doing is emphasized.

Less Helpful / Informative	More Helpful / Informative
9/7 Susan in the construction area counted up to 18.	9/7 Susan in construction area using inch cubes. Spontaneously sorted cubes by color, then regrouped them and systematically counted each w/one to one correspondence until she reached 18. Then her counting became random, losing one-to-one & skipping over several cubes.

2/19 Pedro & Janet argued over a hand magnifier in science center. Pedro did not respond to Janet's repeated requests to have a turn or offer any substitutions in the center. Janet's frustration peaked and tried to grab the magnifier, and in the struggle knocked down one of the jars on the table. Janet left and Pedro picked up broken glass. Refused to verbalize the problem when I intervened.

Less Helpful / Informative	
2/19 Pedro & Janet had a huge argument in the science center. Fought over materials that they both wanted. Something broke & Janet left.	

2/19 Janet & Pedro argued over a hand magnifier in science center. Janet repeatedly asked, "When do I have a turn to use it? I need to use this one now." After 5 attempts w/same strategy, Janet attempted to grab magnifier in Pedro's hand. Pedro knocked down one of the jars when he tried to avoid Janet's grabbing. Janet left + told me that she tried to "ask for the magnifier "nicely" but Pedro was "too selfish."

Less Helpful / Informative	More Helpful / Informative
3/24 Christina helped Larry revise his book on rabbits.	3/24 Christina helped Larry figure out how to add new information on rabbits he has found for his draft. She first explained carats, but Larry said he didn't have room to just write it over the lines of his text. Then she took strips of paper on shelf & told him to staple them on the side. He began to write his info on the strips. Christina said, "I use spider legs all the time."
5/4 John read a part of his book in response group. He sometimes read haltingly but others didn't seem to notice and asked good questions. John answered them quite well.	5/4 John read a page (p26) from Fritz's Shh! We're Writing the Constitution. He paused four times, twice to re-run & twice to self-correct semantically unacceptable miscues. Others asked why he liked this part of the book. (It related the behavior of delegates during deliberation). John responded that it sounded just like the Senate Hearings he hears on TV. He wondered how laws get enacted when some go on & on & others pay no attention to what people say.

figure **8.29**

examples illustrate, the more helpful, informative notes capture the process and strategies that children actually employed, not just a statement that something occurred or that a task was accomplished.

The advantage of roving anecdotal observation is that teachers can easily interact with children while they are observing. Thus, if teachers ask a question or make a comment about children's behavior or activities, they are able to document the responses to suggestions or input. Children can also be encouraged to contribute their own observation notes when they think they have done something interesting that may have been missed by the teacher.

Miscellaneous Observation Ideas

Teachers can modify the ideas that we have discussed to come up with their own kid-watching systems of observation, such as schemes for particular purposes or checklists of various kinds. By using the same list several times over the year, teachers can document children's progress toward certain goals. Teachers can also construct checklists for certain types of activities that occur during the ongoing flow of the classroom. Checklists are timesavers and can provide useful information, but they cannot provide an adequate picture of progress unless they are complemented by more detailed observations, such as those described earlier in this chapter.

Almy & Genishi (1979)

Vignettes are also useful for assessing progress. A vignette is an account of a particularly meaningful event of a child's classroom life that represents a significant milestone—or "aha" phenomenon—for a certain child. Vignettes are similar to roving anecdotal observations and perhaps rely on them; however, vignettes are more detailed and are usually written up later by the teacher. Many teachers like to include at least one vignette per thematic unit or grading period to share with parents and to become part of the child's learning portfolio.

Specific observation sheets can be created to capture what is going on at a particular center and to document the kinds of hypotheses children are generating, the language they use to talk about what they see, and so forth. Figure 8.30 illustrates such an observation form for a classroom study of snails.

Using this form (a clean copy for each day), the teacher observes what is happening at the snail study center. In the first few days of the study, most of the teacher's notes probably center on questions 1 to 5, but as children's questions become better articulated, observations for questions 6 to 8 are filled in. By reviewing these forms during the course of the study, the teacher is able to document who was involved, the process by which children found their answers, what they produced as the result of their study, and how they relied on one another and written resources to support their inquiries. Older elementary and middle school children can create their own forms to document their work in centers or in a particular inquiry project.

Conclusions

We want children to continuously encounter novel and interesting problems. We want to encourage them to hypothesize and seek comprehension of their problems on the basis of what they presently know. We want them to use their interactions with others in the classroom community as sources for learning. Consequently, we need kid-watching techniques that are in-process assessments that let us evaluate what children are understanding about content as they are actually experiencing it. The kid-watching schemes presented in this chapter do this. The first set of procedures focused on ways to examine children's strategies in a range of literacy assessments; the last set provided more general schemes to capture the content and process of their ongoing experiences in individual and small-group activities and projects.

Evaluation in context

The approaches described here are not an exhaustive list but are offered as ways to learn how to become a kid watcher and acquire (and internalize) new ways of observing

Snail Study Center	Children involved:	Date:
① What are some of the hypotheses (or questions) Cs construct about snails?		
② What conclusions (or answers) about the snails do Cs come to?		
③ What are examples of Cs' using their "own language" to find out about snails?		
④ How does their language reflect their own feelings about snails?		
⑤ What are examples of joint action + cooperation in the learning process?		
⑥ How did books support Cs inquiries on snails?		
⑦ What writing resulted regarding Cs' study of snails?		
⑧ What other activities resulted from snails study (e.g. drawing, math, constructing, etc.)		

figure 8.30
Specific Observation Sheet

children's strategies as they go about using language and developing concepts or constructing their knowledge. In other chapters, we go into various curricular content in more detail. These chapters include examples of ways to integrate the disciplines into thematic units (Chapters 4 and 5), and they cover a variety of experiences and activities for putting an integrated language theory into action (Chapter 7). Thus, other kid-watching procedures and ideas emerge. Other issues related to kid watching and evaluation are addressed in Chapter 9. See also teacher researchers' descriptive and reflective writing and other observational ideas found in "Guidelines for Teacher Inquiry" at the end of the book.

References

Almy, M., & Genishi, C. (1979). *Ways of studying children.* New York: Teachers College Press.

Atwell, N. (1998). *In the middle: New understandings about writing, reading, and learning with adolescents.* Portsmouth, NH: Boynton/Cook.

Au, K. H. (1993). *Literacy instruction in multicultural settings.* Fort Worth, TX: Harcourt Brace Jovanovich.

Barrentine, S. J. (Ed.). (1999). *Reading assessment.* Newark, DE: International Reading Association.

Beers, K. (2003). *When kids can't read, what teachers can do: A guide for teachers 6–12.* Portsmouth, NH: Heinemann.

Brown, H., & Cambourne, B. (1987). *Read and retell: A strategy for the whole-language/natural learning classroom.* Portsmouth, NH: Heinemann.

Calkins, L. M. (1986). *The art of teaching writing.* Portsmouth, NH: Heinemann.

Calkins, L. M. (1994). *The art of teaching writing.* Portsmouth, NH: Heinemann.

Calkins, L. M., with Harwayne, S. (1991). *Living between the lines.* Portsmouth, NH: Heinemann.

Carroll, P. S. (2004). *Integrated literacy instruction in the middle grades: Challenging young adolescents' spontaneous overflow of energy.* Boston: Pearson Education.

Cazden, C. B. (2001). *Classroom discourse: The learning of teaching and learning.* Portsmouth, NH: Heinemann.

Clay, M. (1972). *Sand—The concepts about print test.* Portsmouth, NH: Heinemann.

Clay, M. (1979a). *The early detection of reading difficulties: A diagnostic survey with recovery procedures.* Portsmouth, NH: Heinemann.

Clay, M. (1979b). *Stones—The concepts about print test.* Portsmouth, NH: Heinemann.

Clay, M. (2001). *An observation survey of early literacy achievement.* Auckland, New Zealand: Heinemann.

Collier, D. (2003). Pretend readings for everybody in kindergarten—even the boys! In C. C. Pappas & L. B. Zecker (Eds.)., *Teacher inquiries in literacy teaching-learning: Learning to collaborate in elementary urban classrooms* (pp. 37–57). Mahwah, NJ: Lawrrence Erlbaum.

Davenport, M. R., & Lauritzen, C. (2002). Inviting reflection on reading through over the shoulder miscue analysis. *Language Arts, 80,* 109–118.

Flurkey, A., & Goodman, Y. M. (2000). Andrew, stuck in words: A retrospective miscue analysis case study in revaluing. In L. Denti & P. Cousin (Eds.), *New ways of looking at learning disabilities* (pp. 129–150). Denver, CO: Love.

Freeman, D. E., & Freeman, Y. S. (2001). *Between worlds: Access to second language acquisition.* Portsmouth, NH: Heinemann.

Genishi, C., & Dyson, D. H. (1984). *Language assessment in the early years.* Norwood, NJ: Ablex.

Glasswell, K., Parr, J. M., & McNaughton, S. (2003). Four ways to work against yourself when conferencing with struggling writers. *Language Arts, 80,* 291–298.

Goodman, K. S. (1973). Miscues: Windows on the reading process. In K. S. Goodman (Ed.), *Miscue analysis: Applications to reading instruction* (pp. 3–14). Urbana, IL: ERIC Clearinghouse on Reading and Communication Skills.

Goodman, K. S. (1993). *Phonics phacts.* Portsmouth, NH: Heinemann.

Goodman, K. S. (1997). Putting theory and research in the context of history. *Language Arts, 74,* 595–609.

Goodman, K. S., Goodman, Y. M., & Hood, W. J. (1989). *The whole language evaluation book.* Portsmouth, NH: Heinemann.

Goodman, Y. M. (1999). Revaluing readers while readers revalue themselves: Retrospective miscue analysis. In S. J. Barrentine (Ed.), *Reading assessment* (pp. 140–151). Newark, DE: International Reading Association.

Goodman, Y. M., Watson, D. J., & Burke, C. L. (1987). *Reading miscue inventory: Alternative procedures.* New York: Richard C. Owen.

Graves, D. (1983). *Writing: Teachers and children at work.* Portsmouth, NH: Heinemann.

Gredler, M. E., & Johnson, R. L. (2004). *Assessment in the classroom.* Boston: Pearson Education.

Heath, S. B. (1983). *Ways with words: Language, life, and work in communities and classrooms.* Cambridge: Cambridge University Press.

Holdaway, D. (1979). *The foundations of literacy.* Sydney, Australia: Ashton Scholastic.

Johnston, P. H. (1997). *Knowing literacy: Constructive literacy assessment.* York, ME: Stenhouse.

Kemp, M. (1987). *Watching children read and write: Observational records for children with special needs.* Portsmouth, NH: Heinemann.

Kress, G. (2000). *Early spelling: Between convention and creativity.* London: Routledge.

Lindfors, J. W. (1999). *Children's inquiry: Using language to make sense of the world.* New York: Teachers College Press.

McKenzie, M. (1977). The beginnings of literacy. *Theory Into Practice, 16,* 315–324.

Michaels, S. (1981). "Sharing time": Children's narrative styles and differential access to literacy. *Language in Society, 10,* 423–442.

Moore, D. W., Moore, S. A., Cunningham, P. M., & Cunningham, J. W. (2003). *Developing readers and writers in the content areas K–12.* Boston: Pearson Education.

Nieto, S. (2000). *Affirming diversity: The sociopolitical context of multicultural education.* New York: Longman.

Pappas, C. C. (1993). Is narrative "primary"? Some insights from kindergarteners' pretend readings of stories and information books. *Journal of Reading Behavior, 25,* 97–129.

Pappas, C. C., & Brown, E. (1989). Using turns at story "reading" as scaffolding for learning. *Theory Into Practice, 28,* 105–113.

Pappas, C. C., & Pettegrew, B. S. (1991). Learning to tell: Aspects of developing communicative competence in young children's story retellings. *Curriculum Inquiry, 21,* 439–454.

Reyes, M. de la Luz., & Halcon, J. J. (Eds.). (2001). The *best for our children: Critical perspectives in literacy for Latino students.* New York: Teachers College Press.

Sylva, K., Roy, C., & Painter, M. (1980). *Childwatching at playgroup and nursery school.* Ypsilanti, MI: The High/Scope Press.

Temple, C., Nathan, R., Temple, F., & Burris, N. A. (1993). *The beginnings of writing.* Boston: Allyn & Bacon.

Tierney, R. J., & Readance, J. E. (2000). *Reading strategies and practices: A compendium.* Boston: Allyn & Bacon.

Weaver, C. (2002). *Reading process and practice.* Portsmouth, NJ: Heinemann.

Wilde, S. (1992). *You kan red this! Spelling and punctuation for classrooms, K–6.* Portsmouth, NH: Heinemann.

Wilde, S. (1997). *What's a schwa sound anyway? A holistic guide to phonetics, phonics, and spelling.* Portsmouth, NH: Heinemann.

Children's Literature

Farmer Boy by L. I. Wilder. Illustrated by G. Williams. Harper & Row, 1953.

Our Garage Sale by A. Rockwell. Illustrated by H. Rockwell. Greenwillow, 1984.

Evaluation and Accountability

Imagine that, after completing the detergent-testing project described in Chapter 5, students took a test in which they filled in the blanks, listed formulas and matched results with products, defined terms, and ticked off a variety of true and false items. Although such an evaluation can tap some of what children learn, it also exaggerates the importance of specific bits of information and undercuts attention to the processes of science and the context within which information is important. As an assessment tool, this type of test ignores a wide range of significant learning activities and is incongruent with purposes and procedures in an integrated language classroom.

Yet teachers in integrated language classrooms are just as accountable for the evaluation of pupil learning as their peers in more traditional classrooms. They, too, must find ways to evaluate and assess that are congruent with their educational purposes. They must become "constructive evaluators," able both to establish a context where children engage in a variety of learning activities and to recognize students' development in that classroom context. We have emphasized the ongoing interplay or reciprocal relationship of teachers' assessment of children's learning and teachers' decisions in instruction throughout this book. Assessment here is performance-based—it captures both the processes and the products of learning—while it documents worthwhile, valued inquiries, and learning outcomes. A critical feature of this kind of assessment involves students' self-evaluation of their learning. An integrated language classroom, then, requires evaluation and assessment that can reflect how *all* children learn and think in context, how they connect what they have learned in various content domains, how they progress over time, and how they grow in their ability to self-evaluate.

The following four interrelated characteristics and challenges of assessment are important in developing such constructive evaluation techniques:

Comprehensive, Balanced, and Systematic Assessment. You want to have a broad picture of students' learning in various contexts, activities, and projects. Moreover, you want to be able to capture both the end products of student investigations—writing, art, reports, and presentations—and the processes or paths by which students produced a particular artifact. That is, student attempts, approximations, and risk taking are all important instances of their meaning making in action that need to be documented. Thus, authentic and valid assessment is systematic and multifaceted, not a single method or piece of information.

Assessment for Teaching. The major reason for assessment is to provide you with information to help you make informed decisions about your instruction and better understand your students' learning so that you can meet their needs. You want practical means to gather and record information that are part of everyday classroom activities. You want assessment that has both formative and summative

See Darling-Hammond & Falk (1997); Falk (2000); Hillocks (2002); Kuhn (2000); Shepherd (2000); Swope & Miner (2000); and Valencia & Buly (2004) for other discussions of the necessity for rethinking assessment and evaluation in education.

See Johnston (1997) for further discussion of "constructive evaluators."

Gredler & Johnson (2004); Johnston (1997); Routman (1991); Wexler-Sherman et al. (1988); Wolf (1988)

A performance-based evaluation is an authentic way to assess both process and product of learning.

Au et al. (1990); Goodwin (1997)

See King (1991) for a similar set of characteristics.

Assessment has both formative and summative characteristics.

characteristics. Assessment is formative in that it is used to help the teacher plan the kinds of topics, resources, activities, and organization children will need as they engage in thematic units. It helps you determine the Focus Lessons*, conferences, and other interactions you have with your students. Assessment is summative in that you can use it to construct a history of learners' development. It enables you to interpret children's achievement and progress.

Assessment for Students. You want assessment that can help your students be self-monitoring, self-regulating, and independent in their learning. Such self-evaluation is an integral component of ownership in learning. As they learn, children need feedback so that they can evaluate their work and use it for their own purposes. Thus, you want children to know what is expected of them and what they have achieved, and to have some ideas about what is needed for future progress and achievement.

Assessment for Parents and Caregivers. You want to communicate with parents, caregivers, and other stakeholders about students' learning. Few parents have experienced the student-directed, collaborative approach to learning found in integrated language classrooms. They want to know what their children are doing and what things you believe are the indicators of progress. They want to know what their children have achieved and what they find difficult. Providing parents with detailed information about their children and finding ways to seek further information from them help parents be partners in students' progress and achievement.

Evaluation is collaborative.

King (1994); Harp (1994); Valencia & Buly (2004)

In sum, meaningful and useful evaluation is thoughtful, ongoing, and multi-dimensional, and it takes place in authentic contexts. Because a teacher's style of teaching in an integrated language classroom is a collaborative one, evaluation is also collaborative. This type of performance-based assessment and evaluation has a functional orientation for it is an integral part of the ongoing processes of teaching and learning. It is developmentally and culturally responsive evaluation.

Major Methods of Evaluation

Daly (1989); Reardon (1994); Routman (1991); Salinger & Chittenden (1994); Lipson & Wixson (2003)

There are several major interrelated ways integrated language teachers assess and evaluate students' learning. Many are informal, but some teachers make more formal ones, too. In any case, assessment methods and techniques are tied to everyday classroom experiences, activities, and projects.

Ongoing Observations and Periodic Documentations

Evaluation is continuous and covers all aspects of an integrated language classroom.

Himley (2000); Tierney & Readance (2000)

In integrated language classrooms, teachers collaborate with children by supporting their choices of inquiries. As children pursue their investigations, teachers move around the room, interacting with individuals or small groups to find out what the children are doing and how the teachers can support their efforts. Teachers are continually evaluating and teaching; these acts are reciprocal processes. Evaluation is seen as part of a social interaction in which the teacher comes to understand the task or situation from the child's point of view, and the child is strengthened in self-evaluation. As a result, the teacher is better able to describe children through their strengths, and to put children in situations that encourage success. In Chapter 8, we discussed ways by which these reciprocal processes of evaluation and teaching can be made more explicit. Through roving anecdotal or periodic target-child observations, teachers know what kinds of experiences or resources certain children need now, when a particular Focus

Lesson* is necessary, how to evaluate children's strategies in tackling a problem, and whether a particular child needs to be encouraged to try something new.

Teachers can also keep journals of classroom events, perhaps one for each thematic unit studied during the year. These accounts review and highlight significant experiences or patterns occurring in the classroom. The journals include the teachers' own observation sheets developed to examine small-group inquiries (like the one quickly drawn up to document what was happening in the snails study described in Chapter 8). Journals can be complemented by incorporating concepts learned in a thematic unit, snapshots of the growth of a Semantic Map* or the artifacts constructed by children in the course of a unit, and a review of the various Sketch to Stretch* constructions children have used, modified, or written on their own during a unit. Such a journal helps teachers remember and reflect on how children participate in the culture or learning community of the classroom.

Teachers keep journals, too.

Fu & Lamme (2002); Hull (1988)

Keep "before" and "after" data.

Student/Teacher Conferences

Another part of ongoing evaluation is having one-on-one conversations with children. Reading and Writing Conferences* were discussed in Chapters 6, 7, and 8, but brief conferences need not be limited to literacy activities. Because literacy is integrated across the curriculum in this perspective, discussions always include specific content or a curricular domain or domains. But conferences can be planned to focus on a particular mathematical or scientific problem or a certain issue in social studies, for example, and not concentrate on reading or writing per se. Conferences provide an opportunity for joint assessment of student work, as teachers and children discuss student progress toward learning goals.

One-on-one conversations with children are important evaluative tools.

Teachers can have small-group conferences as well. Periodic documentation of the dynamics of group interactions when children collaborate to investigate a common topic is essential in this perspective that emphasizes the social, contextual influences in learning. Tape-recording or listening in on peer conferences (e.g., during Literature Response Groups*) provides still another way to document and evaluate learning and language in the classroom. Children can also take turns being "reporters" whose job is to summarize the discussion and decisions of a peer conference to share with the teacher.

Document group interactions, especially during collaborative investigations.

Student Self-Evaluation

A critical aspect of evaluation in an integrated language classroom is children's self-evaluation. This feature is usually incorporated into a child's learning portfolio, but it is such a critical factor in this perspective that we discuss it as a separate section. Self-evaluation can be seen as an extension of children's Sketchbook Journals*, in which children jot down and illustrate they ways they organize (and reorganize) their own ideas. Thus, Sketchbook Journals* are ways to make children's thinking more explicit. Self-evaluation is similar; children pause to consider what they have learned and what has been important from their own perspectives.

Self-evaluation encourages student reflection.

Hart (1994); Lenski et al. (1996); Mabry (1999); Tierney & Readance (2000)

As indicated later, an important time for children to explicitly self-evaluate their learning is at the end of a thematic unit, when they select the work to be included in their learning portfolios. As they choose some particular writing, they explain why they thought it was their best work or why it represented significant work on a particular project. Children can also be encouraged to review their Journals* periodically (perhaps at the end of a thematic unit) and write a summary of what stood out for them. Or they can include an evaluation as part of any big project (see the "Reflecting Phase" in Student-Directed Inquiry Projects* discussed in Chapter 7). Even younger elementary children can evaluate their own work. The teacher can take notes as children tell what was the best thing they have done or where they have done their hardest work. What children may think is significant in their learning may not be what teachers or parents or others deem valuable. Self-evaluation, therefore, is an important factor because it gives children opportunities to reflect on their learning, thereby helping them to be independent, autonomous, and confident learners.

Tests and Exams

Whether to give tests and exams is both an administrative and a teacher decision. Many schools adopting an integrated language perspective do not use tests because they believe that the children's work produced in various thematic units is sufficient and provides more valid indicators of children's achievements and progress.

Hyde & Bizar (1989); Hart (1994)

Others who have an integrated language perspective do not use teacher-made tests in the traditional sense. They conceive of tests in ways that make them more congruent with their instructional goals, rethinking the standard fill-in-the-blank and multiple-choice formats. For example, rather than have children give the answers to a list of math problems, teachers may ask them to analyze the problems they find the most difficult. These responses require that children identify the kind of problem and describe their approach to it. These analyses require the use of correct vocabulary, pattern recognition, and some knowledge of how to proceed. Another possibility is to have children identify five problems according to kind and then give a brief analysis of the approach to each, with no actual problem solving.

Social studies and science use laboratory-like tests.

Particularly in science and social studies, such tests have the flavor of "laboratory" assignments. They test for inquiry, one of the skills traditional tests fail to evaluate but that is critical in an integrated language perspective. It may seem difficult to construct a test that reflects inquiry skills, but it is possible. Observation and Inference*, two of the basic inquiry skills, can be tested by setting up a situation in which children are asked to observe carefully and then to make supported inferences. A test of these skills in science can include a demonstration in which children observe as the teacher places two cubes in a clear liquid. One cube floats; the other sinks to the bottom. Students are then required to list three observations and make two inferences that can be supported by their observations. Their responses are evaluated in terms of the accuracy of their observations (i.e., that they are not inferences), and the degree to which their inferences are supported by their observations.

A test in social studies can use a political cartoon relevant to the students' recent studies. The children are asked to interpret the symbols used in the cartoon to infer the cartoonist's "message." Their response is evaluated in terms of the way in which they draw on their recent study to interpret the cartoon and on the supportability of their inferences.

See also Abruscato (2004); Ellis (1997); Hyde & Bizar (1989); Levstik & Barton (2001); and Maxim (1987) for further discussion of evaluation in science and social studies.

Another inquiry skill concerns children's ability to select and evaluate data. A test item following a unit on EXPLORATIONS can involve presenting children with a problem such as the following:

> You are considering inviting Mr. Erickson to speak to your class on early European explorations of the Americas. Which statements make Mr. Erickson most qualified to speak to your class? Explain your choices.
>
> A. He is related to Leif Erickson.
> B. He has written a book on the settlement of Greenland.
> C. He conducted some of the first research on Viking settlements in Newfoundland.
> D. He is director of the Viking museum in Oslo, Norway.

To answer this question, students need to know something about the Viking explorations in North America, but they also need to be able to explain why some of Mr. Erickson's qualifications are better than others for the stated purpose. The question is embedded in both content and process, and it evaluates children's ability to make connections between the methods of study and the content studied.

Communicating data is also an important skill in inquiry, and it can be evaluated on a written test, especially if the test is open book or note. This kind of test is, to some extent, individualized. The teacher must know what questions and content children have been grappling with and then give them an opportunity to write about that. The children who found different interpretations of a historic figure, for instance, can be asked to use their notes to write an argument for accepting one interpretation over another. Another child may be asked to compare the way the textbook interprets an event in history with the way in which that event was interpreted in a piece of historical fiction.

Other possibilities are questions that ask children to construct a hypothesis to explain an observation in science or to select the most important thing they learned during a unit and then to write a statement justifying their choice. One primary teacher uses a film on the first Thanksgiving as a test of her third graders' ability to compare and contrast sources after a study based on the MATCH unit "The Indians Who Met the Pilgrims" (see Chapter 4). The film is quite short, offers a number of contrasts to the MATCH unit, and contains several inaccuracies that have been pointed out in other contexts. The test includes, among other things, having children identify three ways in which the film supports what they have learned and three ways it contradicts what they have learned. Kresse (1979)

Another primary teacher uses a "Can you spot the errors?" format for some of his testing in social studies. He constructs pictures that include errors that children's studies should enable them to identify. After a study based on Turner's *Dakota Dugout*, he presents children with a picture of a prairie home and family. He asks students to draw first a red circle around anything in the picture that would not have been there during the time of *Dakota Dugout* and then a blue circle around anything they think would not be there today. The children are, thus, required to use specific skills with a content they have been studying. The teacher does not assume that the children will know everything from the period, but he does know what the children have been studying and wants to evaluate the way in which they have been making sense of the time aspects of their study. Turner (1986)
Thornton & Vukelich (1988)

A teacher could do a similar thing in science by drawing a series of pictures showing, say, plant growth under various conditions. The children circle the picture that ends a sequence (i.e., a plant bending in the direction of the sun after a series of pictures of a bean plant on a windowsill, or a long, white stem on a plant grown with little light). Some teachers give children a series of pictures representing a process they have observed to paste in order on their test paper. A similar format can be used in math. Teachers can use data children have been collecting in a unit and construct several problems and possible solutions. Children would be asked to identify those aspects of the approach that are correct and incorrect by circling them with different colored pens.

Children can also be asked to put what they have learned to more public use. Following a study of immigration patterns in North America, one teacher presented students with a problem that was very real in the local community and emblematic of larger issues for immigrants across the country:

> Given what you have learned about Americans' and Central and South Americans' images of each other and of the problems these stereotypes can cause, what suggestions would you give to the mayor to help your neighbors better understand the Central and South Americans who are moving into this community? To help the Central and South Americans better understand your community?
>
> As a class, we will be sending our suggestions to the mayor, so be as specific and practical as possible. Provide evidence of stereotyping and information on more accurate images. Remember that these are things we think the mayor should really do to prevent stereotyping and help people from different cultures better understand each other.

Make sure criteria for an assessment task are clear to children.

Note that the criteria for the task are made clear (identify stereotypes, identify characteristics of each culture that are more accurate, and suggest ways in which city government can alleviate some of the problems of cultural misconceptions) and provide a basis for the teacher's assessment and student self-evaluation.

Most tests in an integrated language classroom are not timed to test the speed of children's thinking. Instead, children are given time to think carefully about their answers and to go back and review their responses. Most tests also require students to develop ideas in writing and to justify or elaborate on responses. Many of these tests give students an opportunity to rehearse, refine, and revise and to communicate in a distinctive "voice" or style while solving the problem at hand. This helps students to better judge the effectiveness of their work and decisions. Such tests are also closer to the way in which adults operate when they are working and more congruent with the way in which the children have been working throughout the thematic units described in Chapters 3 and 4.

Hart (1994); Johnston (1997); Wiggins (1989)

Parent and Caregiver Input

Parental involvement is a significant factor in student success, and more and more schools are inviting parents and guardians to take an active role in the assessment process. Parents and guardians often feel frustrated in interpreting reports of students' progress and in supporting their children's intellectual development. Teachers, too, often feel that it would be helpful if they knew more about students' lives outside the classroom. Parental participation in assessment can help reduce some of the misconceptions and misinterpretations made by teachers and parents and provide positive ways in which both can interact with children. There is no single best way to organize parental assessment procedures; rather, there is a continuum of efforts schools have made to better involve parents in this important aspect of their children's lives:

Fredericks & Rasinski (1990); Fried (2001); Lenski et al. (1996); Popham (1999)

Record Parent/Caregiver Expectations. Ask parents and caregivers what kind of progress they would like to see for their child, then record parents' responses and refer to them on a regular basis. This can be most easily done early in the school year and then referred to throughout the rest of the year.

Keep a Read-at-Home Log. Ask children to read to someone outside of the school setting, such as a relative, neighbor, or babysitter. Children can read books, newspapers, or magazines. Whatever the child decides to read, the listener makes an entry in the child's reading log. The entries can range from a comment on strengths in the child's reading (the ease or difficulty of the selected reading) to suggestions for other things the child might like to read. An at-home observation guide that parents can fill out between reporting periods can also accompany the read-at-home log.

Use Homework/Project Assessment. Parents can also do periodic homework reviews. A simple questionnaire can be sent to parents along with an explanation of an assignment or project with which the child is involved. Parents are asked to evaluate the assignment in terms of its level of difficulty, how well the child understood the assignment, and the appropriateness of the assignment. This provides not only feedback on the parents' response to the assignment but also an opportunity for parents to discuss the assignment with their child and make suggestions so that the teacher might be able to improve the assignment.

Invite In-School Observations. Invite parents to come to the classroom and do structured observations. (See Figure 9.1.) These observations provide a framework for a conference between parents and caregivers and teachers. Introduce the observation/conference forms early in the year and provide samples of entries other parents have made. Following such focused observation, parents have a clearer picture of both the classroom situation and their child's performance.

PARENT OBSERVATION GUIDE

Date: _____

Welcome to our classroom. While you are visiting, you might like to observe and make notes on some or all of the following:

When I watched my child as she/he was working, I expected to see:

_____
_____
_____
_____
_____

When I watched my child in the classroom, I was surprised to see:

_____
_____
_____

When I watched my child in the classroom, I was pleased to see:

_____
_____
_____

During my visit I wondered about:

_____
_____
_____

---

figure **9.1**

Managing Authentic, Performance-Based Assessment

The Why, What, How, and When of Assessment

Although it is critical to have comprehensive assessment (review the four features listed in the beginning of the chapter) so that you have a full picture of growing learners, teachers can easily be overwhelmed—feel drowned—by too much detail. Thus, you have to be selective in your assessing, documenting, and data gathering. It is very easy to say that you need to observe all the time, but in practice you are going to have to make some choices. These decisions are easier if you keep in mind the *why, what, how,* and *when* of assessment.

Fried (2001); Hart (1994); Turnbill (1989); Tierney & Readance (2000)

> *Why?* The whys are tied to your beliefs and theories of how children develop language and learn in general—they are related to the principles of the integrated language perspective discussed in Chapter 1. For example, some of the general whys you would want to consider as you plan assessment techniques—encouraging risk taking and approximation; promoting collaborative, noncompetitive learning; and fostering self-evaluation and self-monitoring—are drawn from these principles. Other whys include those you had in mind in planning particular thematic units. (See Chapter 4.) Two of the performances Caitlin Cooper planned to assess in DIGGING UP THE PAST were students' progress in learning problem-solving techniques in various domains and their appropriate and accurate use of content in problem solving. As a result, she planned opportunities for students to write

about process and content during small-group work related to different domains. In collaboration with her students, she established criteria for evaluating their work and provided regular opportunities for peer and teacher feedback about their progress. Dehea Munioz (JOURNEYS) was also interested in children's use of appropriate and accurate content, but she wanted to evaluate student progress in selecting and using genres appropriate for different audiences as well as different domains. Thus, one of her assessments was planned around a museum exhibit where students interpreted their studies in a variety of ways for particular audiences. As you look through the other prototypes in Chapter 4 you will see how assessment is tied to the particular agendas that concern the content of a thematic unit or a teacher's inquiry.

What, How, and When? These are frequently best thought of together. Sketching out a grid of possibilities is a useful way to begin. Such a plan can help your assessment be comprehensive and systematic and at the same time keep it manageable. See Figure 9.2 for the way one fifth-grade teacher began.

> A grid of possibilities can help organize assessment.

Janet listed under her "what" column six major categories that she wanted to assess or know about. Overall reading and writing development were the two top categories. Then came the understandings that were promoted by various inquiry projects in which different curricular areas were integrated and emphasized. The fourth category had to do with learning portfolios and the fifth category with the teacher inquiry she planned to do during the thematic unit. Her last category was "other," a place to include any miscellaneous assessment that didn't really fit well under the other categories. Janet's "how" section was divided into two columns—informal, ongoing assessment and more formal assessment. The "how" section encompassed her "when" considerations, too. Note that the informal, ongoing assessment column usually focused more on process; the more formal assessment column listed many of the "products" that were assessed. She typed this form with these categories ahead of time but jotted down the details by hand. These handwritten notes provided specifics and changed over the course of a unit (and from unit to unit). Janet often added ideas that emerged as she and her students negotiated how project findings were to be determined. Sometimes she dropped a technique if she thought it was too cumbersome or was not really getting at what she wanted to know.

> Assessment data overlap.

As you review Figure 9.2, two features are important to note. The first is that much of Janet's assessment "data" overlap. For example, during writing workshop, where student writing was emphasized, students were usually working on texts having to do with their individual and small-group collaborative inquiries, thus their writing during this workshop frequently included a curricular (usually an *integrated* curricular) focus. Another feature to notice is that she tried to note who had the main responsibility—student or teacher—for keeping the records of assessment. This latter feature, of course, not only helped to keep her students intimately involved in self-monitoring and self-evaluating their own learning, but it also helped her realize that she didn't have to, nor could she, collect all the records she wanted or needed for students' evaluation.

> Teachers and students share responsibility for record keeping.

Some other things are useful to take note of in Figure 9.2. Janet took anecdotal records throughout the day on Post-it Notes (see Chapter 8). At the end of each day, she put them on sheets in a loose-leaf binder that had pages for each child. She also used three Status of the Class* versions to keep track of what her students were doing in reading and writing and in their inquiry projects. Janet also had more "formal" Reading and Writing Conferences* with students. The reading conferences included assessing a short sample of students' oral reading and, through discussion with them, noting their comprehension and interpretations. The writing conferences included focused interactions with students regarding content and editing issues. Students kept daily planning journals where they noted what they hoped to work on or accomplish each day. They also used two other journals: Dialogue Journals* and Sketchbook Journals*. (These were put in one notebook for each thematic unit during the year with a

> Status of the Class* reports keep track of student projects and progress.

EVALUATION POSSIBILITIES		
What do I want to assess?	*How* am I going to assess?	
	Informal, ongoing assessment	More formal assessment
Reading development overall	(T) Anecdotal notes; (T) Status of Class R. Checks; (S) Daily planning journals; (S) Sketchbook journals; (T) Status of Class project checks	(T) Conferences; (S) Literature response journals; (T) Comparison charts; (S) Various artifacts/extensions
Writing development overall	(T) Anecdotal notes; (T) Status of class W Checks; (S) Daily planning journals; (S) Sketchbook journals; (T) Status of Class project checks; (S) writing drafts	(T) Content & editing conferences; (S) Published texts; (S) Various artifacts
Inquiry projects (individual/group)	(T) Anecdotal notes; (S) Daily planning journals; (S) Project proposals; (T) Status of class project checks; (S) Daily project evaluations; (S) Rough drafts on findings	(S) "Published" project findings; (TS) Inquiry project evaluation
Portfolio	(S) Friday portfolio review	(S) Final Portfolio evaluation + summary
My inquiry	My own journal; Student lit. response journals	Analysis of ongoing data and audiotaping of student-led lit. response groups

Other
  Written comm
  w/students
  Math
	(S) Dialogue journals
	
	(S) Math talk journals
		(S) Excerpts from dialogue journals
		
		(S) Math story problems, (S) Math solvers

figure 9.2

section of the notebook for each journal. Another journal, called math talk journal, was a separate journal as noted later.)

Janet had students develop proposals for their inquiry projects. Figure 9.3 provides an example of the simple form she developed to help students organize their proposals. Their daily evaluations of these projects and Janet's Status of the Class* records helped assess the progress of these research activities, while the final project findings and a separate evaluation by students and Janet represented more formal records.

Students develop inquiry proposals.

MY INQUIRY PROPOSAL

My question for investigation is:

_____

_____

_____

The materials I will need are:

_____

_____

_____

I may need help with:

_____

_____

_____

Plan   Accomplishment   Date

I plan to share my results by: _____

We agree to the above plan: _____

_____   _____
Student signature & date   Teacher signature & date

_____
Parent signature & date

figure 9.3

Weekly portfolio review provides on-going assessment.

Dialogue Journals* provide ongoing conversation.

Janet also used learning portfolios (to be discussed in more depth later), one for each grading term, generally corresponding to a particular thematic unit. At the end of the unit, students collected their best work and evaluated their learning for that period. Janet had found, however, that this process was too important to wait until the end of the unit, so her students had what they called Friday portfolio folders where they went through their best work for the week to share with their parents over the weekend. These Friday folders provided important ongoing assessment.

For each thematic unit, Janet chose an inquiry for herself to conduct. During the term represented in Figure 9.2, she set aside time in the schedule for students to have student-led Literature Response Groups*. She kept her own journal to study how this new addition to her curriculum was working throughout the unit—evaluating problems and successes that might occur, considering how she might need to scaffold or intervene to support groups, reviewing students' Book Response Journals*, and analyzing audiotapes of groups' literature discussions. (See Chapter 4 and "Guidelines for Teacher Inquiry" for more information on teacher research.)

Under "Other" Janet included Dialogue Journals* that students kept and to which Janet responded. The Dialogue Journals* enabled students and teacher to have ongoing conversations about anything in their lives. These were not usually part of evaluation, but sometimes students chose excerpts from them for their learning portfolios, so she kept them in mind for a potential source of assessment. She also added math to the "Other" column. Although she tried to integrate math throughout the curriculum, Janet also had a special time to focus on math understandings. Last term (and unit), she had incorporated a math talk journal, which she studied in her own inquiry, to foster the idea that math is a different way to symbolize meanings—a different "language" or "talk." Thus, ongoing assessment involved students' work in this journal. More formal ways of assessment were the story problems students wrote for homework and "math solvers," which were their weekly "tests" on math. (See Chapter 5 for more details on math.)

As you can see, for performance-based assessment to be manageable in the classroom, teachers like Janet have to make choices. They have to keep in mind *why* they are assessing and constantly check it with the *what, how,* and *when* of assessment. Having an overall plan developed at the beginning of a thematic unit—as Figure 9.2 illustrates—helps teachers realize the possibilities and make decisions that they can deal with in practice.

An overall plan helps teachers make decisions about assessment.

Storing Record-Keeping Data in Assessment

Another integral aspect of managing performance-based assessment is figuring out how to store the records of learning that are created. Because ongoing evaluation is so important, these record-keeping data in the classroom have to be organized so that they can be easily accessible to both students and teacher alike. Thinking ahead about ways to store assessment data in the physical space available in a classroom requires selection and decision making on the part of the teacher. Some ways to do this were mentioned earlier and throughout the book, but four categories of means of storage are summarized here:

Records have to be organized.

INDEX CARDS, POST-IT NOTES, LABELS
These are usually used to record periodic observational, anecdotal information gathered by teachers. They can be stored in index boxes or folders or attached to pages in the teacher's notebook or journal.

NOTEBOOKS
These can be used by both students and teacher alike to keep records. They can serve as various journals. Separate notebooks of different colors can distinguish the different journals that students might keep, or one larger notebook that has several sections, each used for a particular journal, might be used. Binder notebooks are also useful because teachers can easily set up and add pages for individual students. Notebooks can also store a particular unit's or term's records and then be placed in a more permanent folder after the unit is completed. New paper can then be added for the next unit. Students can make their own notebooks, too, by stapling or otherwise attaching some paper together with construction paper of different colors, again to note the types of journals being used (these usually work for one unit because of durability problems). Pocket folders that include paper can also be used as notebooks for journals. Usually, student notebooks or journals are stored in students' desks or cubbies, except when they are placed in a designated place for teacher response.

FILE FOLDERS
Various folders can be used to store students' ongoing writing drafts, reading logs, and so forth. Teachers can also store their record-keeping data for each child in separate folders; these might serve as the source of the teacher's contributions to ongoing documentation of students' portfolio folders. Many teachers have students keep things they are presently working on in their folders in their desks and finished work in other folders. If finished work is being displayed in the classroom or is of a size or nature that cannot be put in a folder, students (or teachers) include a short description (or even a photograph) of it as a reminder. Sturdier file folders with expandable bases can keep more permanent work done for a particular thematic unit or grading term.

BINS, BOXES, ETC.

Folders and journals that students use periodically can be placed in colorful bins or decorated boxes. Some schools also have classroom file cabinets or closets in which records, especially the more permanent ones from previous term or unit work, can be stored.

Learning Portfolios

See Tierney et al. (1991); Tierney & Readance (2000); and Valencia (1998) for more detailed discussions of literacy portfolios.

See Cohen (1969); Cole & Scribner (1974); Dyson (1987); Goodwin (1997); Heath (1983); and Jervis (1996) for discussion of children's various "ways with words" and working styles as they relate to assessment and evaluation.

Gitomer (1988); Himley (2000); Valencia & Buly (2004); Wexler-Sherman et al. (1988)

Planning portfolios can be a collaborative effort between teacher and student.

Make sure students understand the portfolio system.

An important part of assessment and evaluation from an integrated language perspective is keeping individual archives, or portfolios, on children. Some schools even keep portfolios of children's work over their years of attendance. Children's abilities and strategies are developed in meaningful, familiar contexts, and their expertise and talents grow gradually and in different patterns. Thus, gathering an extensive collection of their work and other information provides a profile that documents children's learning. The portfolio approach has long been evident in the area of the visual arts and is now suggested for reading and writing. Because reading and writing are integrated across the curriculum from an integrated language perspective, portfolios must be conceived of even more broadly as *learning* portfolios.

Anything can be included in students' learning portfolios: children's notes from their Sketchbook Journals*, anecdotal or target-child observations, snapshots of artifacts children have constructed in the course of thematic units—topographical maps, dioramas, Comparison Charts*, Sketch to Stretch* productions, published texts in various genres, abandoned drafts, Semantic Maps*, MMA summaries (or ATT or CAP assessments), Evaluation Forms from Authors' Folders*, interviews, child-made Jackdaw* materials, graphs, and so on. Most teachers collaborate with children to decide what should be included in the portfolios, choosing what they think is indicative of children's best efforts and asking children to choose the work they feel best represents their work in a thematic unit or what reflects the most difficult tasks they accomplished, or something that they may not be satisfied with, along with comments about why they think so. Teachers respect their choices but also suggest other possibilities they think might be indicative of children's best efforts. Although it is important for teachers to find ways to contribute and have a role in students' portfolios, it is critical to keep most of the control and ownership of them in the hands of the students.

It is critical to start the portfolio system in the beginning of the school year so that students will realize that there is a *process* to evaluation and take an active role in their own learning and evaluation. Giving students an overview of the system facilitates their control, organization, and responsibility in evaluation. This overview, perhaps in terms of a Focus Lesson*, should cover (1) the purpose of portfolios, (2) where work will be kept, (3) who determines the content in portfolios, (4) any records related to the content in the portfolios that the students are going to be responsible for, and (5) the evaluation of the portfolios (e.g., how they will be used for grading).

As Janet's evaluation system illustrated, many teachers do not wait until the end of a term or unit but make portfolio assessment an ongoing process. Friday is a good day for student self-evaluation for several reasons: A week is a nice period for students to focus on in reflecting on what they have learned; it gives students a good opportunity to consider and plan what they might need to work on and try to accomplish in the week or weeks ahead; and it provides the weekend for students to share their work with parents or caregivers so that these important persons can have input on what should be included in students' portfolios.

Because self-evaluation is an essential ingredient in learning portfolios, why a student has chosen certain items in his or her portfolio is a critical facet of the process. Many teachers have students attach a short sheet of paper or index card to each item,

figure **9.4**

PORTFOLIO SUMMARY FOR _____ Date _____

THEMATIC UNIT_____

List and number the items you are including in your learning portfolio.
(Be sure that you include your index card describing why you chose each item.)

What are the major things you had hoped you would learn during the thematic unit?

What are some of the major things you <u>did</u> learn? Which item or items in the portfolio show or reflect what you have learned:

    In reading?

    In writing?

    In math?

    In social studies?

    In science?

    In art, music, or drama?

What would you like to find out about and learn as a result of what you learned in this thematic unit?

on which students provide self-evaluation comments—why they chose it and what and how it documents what they have learned. Initially providing students with a list of possible "starters" helps them consider a range of reasons for including items in their portfolios—that an item is "something I am proud of because . . . ," "an example of my best because . . . ," "important to me because . . . ," or "my first time doing this."

Besides these rationales, a summary sheet for the portfolio is usually also included. Figure 9.4 shows the items on such a summary form. (Note that this form would be much larger than depicted here so students would have more room to write.)

Students list all of the items in their portfolios and then list the major things they have felt they have learned in various curricular areas. At the end, students are asked what has emerged as important things to pursue as a result of their learning in the thematic unit. This information can be valuable for parents in supporting students' learning at home, and it provides teachers with good ideas for planning the next thematic unit.

Some teachers do not use a summary sheet but have children do their own summaries by creating a booklet describing the content of their portfolios and what they have learned during the course of the thematic unit.

Conclusions

Assessment and evaluation must be consistent with principles of the integrated language perspective. Evaluation should interrelate process and content. It should also focus not on children's weaknesses but on those features of their behavior that demonstrate understanding and progress. Children are given many opportunities to monitor their own work, to revise and to evaluate it, and to work with the teacher and peers to steadily improve it. Children review their work with a partner or the teacher, and questions are

Evaluation should interrelate process and content.

Practice produces higher-quality self-analysis by students.

Teachers become researchers when they document children's progress.

See Johnston (1987a, 1987b), Valencia & Buly (2004); Wolf & Wolf (2002); and Wollman-Bonilla (2004) for more arguments for teachers as evaluators, and Cochran-Smith & Lytle (1993) and Hubbard & Power (2003) regarding information on teachers as researchers.

raised about it before a grade is attached. With practice, the children learn to be more self-analytical about the quality of their work. Because it is the children who have to do the learning, it makes sense first to teach them to be self-evaluative, and then to evaluate their progress toward that goal. Thus, evaluation should provide insights into children's evolving personal restructuring of knowledge—what they know, how they have come to know it, and what significance it has for them as members of the classroom community and the broader culture outside the classroom.

This view of evaluation puts the teacher in a different role. Teachers are researchers in that they conduct their own inquiries about the language and learning constructed by children in their classrooms. They are also reflective and self-analytical in that they document their own classroom practices and examine and reexamine their results and influences on children's learning. Thus, teachers are in a better position to document and interpret a wide range of student performance and can, therefore, provide a more accurate picture of children's learning and achievement than so-called objective tests or other instruments that attempt to assess children's understandings in "decontextualized" situations. (See "Guidelines for Teacher Inquiry" at the end of this book for more information on teacher research.)

References

Abruscato, J. (2004). *Teaching children science: Discovery methods for the elementary and middle grades.* Boston: Pearson Education.

Au, K. H., Scheu, J. A., Kawakami, A. J., & Herman, P. A. (1990). Assessment and accountability in a whole literacy curriculum. *The Reading Teacher, 43,* 574–575.

Cochran-Smith, M., & Lytle, S. L. (1993). *Inside/Outside: Teacher research and knowledge.* New York: Teachers College Press.

Cohen, R. (1969). Conceptual styles, culture conflict, and nonverbal tests of intelligence. *American Anthropologist, 71,* 828–857.

Cole, M., & Scribner, S. (1974). *Culture and thought: A psychological introduction.* New York: Wiley.

Daly, E. (Ed). (1989). *Monitoring children's language development: Holistic assessment in the classroom.* Portsmouth, NH: Heinemann.

Darling-Hammond, L., & Falk, B. (1997). Using standards and assessments to support student learning. *Phi Delta Kappan, 79,* 190–199.

Dyson, A. H. (1987). Individual differences in beginning composing. *Written Communication, 4,* 411–442.

Ellis, A. (1997). *Teaching and learning elementary social studies.* Boston: Allyn & Bacon.

Falk, B. (2000). *The heart of the matter: Using standards and assessment to learn.* Portsmouth, NH: Heinemann.

Fredericks, A. D., & Rasinski, T. V. (1990). Involving parents in the assessment process. *The Reading Teacher, 44,* 346–349.

Fried, R. J. (2001). *The passionate teacher: A practical guide.* Boston: Beacon Press.

Fu, D., & Lamme, L. L. (2002). Assessment through conversation. *Language Arts, 79,* 241–350.

Gitomer, D. H. (1988, April). *Assessing artistic learning using domain projects.* Paper presented at the annual meeting of the American Educational Research Association, New Orleans, LA.

Goodwin, A. L. (Ed.). (1997). *Assessment for equity and inclusion: Embracing all our children.* New York: Routledge.

Gredler, M. E., & Johnson, R. L. (2004). *Assessment in the literacy classroom.* Boston: Pearson Education.

Harp, B. (1994). Principles of assessment and evaluation in whole language classrooms. In B. Harp (Ed.), *Assessment and evaluation in whole language programs* (pp. 37–52). Norwood, MA: Christopher-Gordon.

Hart, D. (1994). *Authentic assessment: A handbook for educators.* New York: Addison-Wesley.

Heath, S. B. (1983). *Ways with words: Language, life and work in communities and classrooms.* Cambridge: Cambridge University Press.

Hillocks, G. (2002). *The "testing trap": How state writing assessments control learning.* New York: Teachers College Press.

Himley, M, with Carini, P. (Eds.). (2000). *From another angle: Children's strengths and school standards.* New York: Teachers College Press.

Hubbard, R. S., & Power, B. M. (2003). *The art of classroom inquiry: A handbook for teacher researchers.* Portsmouth, NH: Heinemann.

Hull, O. (1988). Evaluation: The conventions of writing. In K. Goodman, Y. Goodman, & W. J. Hood (Eds.), *The whole language evaluation book* (pp. 77–83). Portsmouth, NH: Heinemann.

Hyde, A., & Bizar, M. (1989). *Thinking in context: Teaching cognitive processes across the elementary school curriculum.* White Plains, NY: Longman.

Jervis, K. (1996). *Eyes on the child: Three portfolio stories.* New York: Teachers College Press.

Johnston, P. (1987a). Teachers as evaluation experts. *The Reading Teacher, 40,* 744–748.

Johnston, P. (1987b). Assessing the process, and the process of assessment, in the language arts. In J. R. Squire (Ed.), *The dynamics of language learning: Research in reading and English* (pp. 335–357). Urbana, IL: ERIC Clearinghouse on Reading and Communication Skills.

Johnston, P. (1997). *Knowing literacy: Constructive literacy assessment*. York, ME: Stenhouse.

King, D. (1991). *Literacy assessment in practice*. South Australia: Education Department of South Australia.

King, D. (1994). Assessment and evaluation in bilingual and multicultural classrooms. In B. Harp (Ed.), *Assessment and evaluation in whole language programs* (pp. 37–52). Norwood, MA: Christopher-Gordon.

Kresse, F. H. (1979). *The Indians who met the Pilgrims, A MATCH unit. Materials and activities for teachers and children*. Boston: American Science and Engineering.

Kuhn, A. (2000). *The case against standardized testing*. Portsmouth, NH: Heinemann.

Lenski, S. D., Riss, M., & Flickinger, G. (1996). Honoring student self-evaluation in the classroom community. *Primary Voices, K–6, 4(2)*, 24–32.

Levstik, L. S., & Barton, K. C. (2001). *Doing history: Investigating with children in elementary and middle schools*. Mahwah, NJ: Erlbaum.

Lipson, M. Y., & Wixson, K. K. (2003). *Assessment and instruction of reading and writing difficulty: An interactive approach*. Boston: Allyn & Bacon.

Mabry, L. (1999). *Portfolio plus: A critical guide to alternative assessment*. Thousand Oaks, CA: Corwin.

Maxim, G. W. (1987). *Social studies and the elementary school child*. Columbus, OH: Merrill.

Popham, W. J. (1999). *Testing! Testing! What every parent should know about school tests*. Boston: Allyn & Bacon.

Reardon, S. J. (1994). A collage of assessment and evaluation from primary classrooms. In B. Harp (Ed.), *Assessment and evaluation in whole language programs* (pp. 37–52). Norwood, MA: Christopher-Gordon.

Routman, R. (1991). *Invitations: Changing as teachers and learners, K–12*. Portsmouth, NH: Heinemann.

Salinger, T., & Chittenden, E. (1994). Focus on research: Analysis of an early literacy portfolio: Consequences for instruction. *The Reading Teacher, 71*, 446–452.

Shepherd, L. (2000). The role of assessments in a learning culture. *Educational Researcher, 29*, 4–14.

Swope, K, & Miner, B. (Eds.). (2000). *Failing our kids: Why the testing craze won't fix our schools*. Milwaukee, WI: Rethinking Schools.

Thornton, S. J., & Vukelich, R. (1988). Effects of children's understanding of time concepts on historical understanding. *Theory and Research in Social Education, 15*, 69–82.

Tierney, R. J., Carter, M. A., & Desai, L. E. (1991). *Portfolio assessment in the reading-writing classroom*. Norwood, MA: Christopher-Gordon.

Tierney, R. J., & Readance, J. E. (2000). *Reading strategies and practices: A compendium*. Boston: Allyn & Bacon.

Turnbill, J. (1989). Evaluation in a whole language classroom: The what, the why, the how, the when. In E. Daly (Ed.), *Monitoring children's language development: Holistic assessment in the classroom* (pp. 17–21). Portsmouth, NH: Heinemann.

Valencia, S. W. (1998). *Literacy portfolios in action*. Fort Worth, TX: Harcourt Brace.

Valencia, S. W., & Buly, M. R. (2004). Behind test scores: What struggling readers *really* need. *The Reading Teacher, 57*, 520–531.

Wexler-Sherman, C., Gardner, H., & Feldman, D. H. (1988). A pluralistic view of early assessment: The project spectrum approach. *Theory Into Practice, 27*, 77–83.

Wiggins, G. (1989). A true test: Toward authentic and equitable forms of assessment. *Phi Delta Kappan, 70*, 703–713.

Wolf, D. P. (1988). Opening up assessment. *Educational Leadership, 45(4)*, 24–29.

Wolf, S. A., & Wolf, K. P. (2002). Teaching *true* and *to* the test in writing. *Language Arts, 79*, 229–240.

Wollman-Bonilla, J. E. (2004). Principled teaching to(wards) the test? Persuasive writing in two classrooms. *Language Arts, 81*, 502–511.

 ## Children's Literature

Dakota Dugout by A. Turner. Illustrated by R. Himler. Houghton Mifflin, 1986.

chapter

10

Developing an Antiracist, Multicultural Community

W̶e discover how we fit together . . . my piece of the puzzle is not like anyone else's . . . my face holds the history of my people and the feelings of my heart.

Teaching Tolerance, Fall 1993, p. 1

An integrated language perspective classroom is grounded in the development of a learning community that is fundamentally democratic and inclusive. The learning community is consciously antiracist, drawing all students into full citizenship in the classroom and a multiracial/multicultural democracy and interdependent world. Multicultural and cross-cultural education must be at the heart of an integrated language curriculum, not just a marginal note slipped in during holidays or Black History Month. Culturally relevant teaching is a day-by-day enterprise. This means, as one teacher noted, having "antennas out" as you work with children, select resources and activities, put up displays, and so forth. As you think about the ways in which differences and commonalties are represented in your classroom and plan for an inclusive, integrated curriculum, consider the following:

> Does the classroom reflect sensitivity to and celebration of the cultural diversity of the students? Of the broader communities to which they belong? This means paying attention to the images displayed in your classroom—on the walls, in literature, in films and videos, as well as in the guests who work with your students. Images that affirm the cultures of diverse students can help build an antiracist community. (See the JOURNEYS and ROOTS prototypes in Chapter 4.)

> Modify the structure of learning activities. There is evidence that different cultural environments encourage different patterns and preferred styles of learning. Varying the types of activities (e.g., incorporating activities that involve movement and multisensory or multimodal experiences) can help to keep children engaged and support their learning of the different ways that meanings are expressed. As you read through the prototypes in Chapter 4, you can see that teachers are "choreographing" their days so that task structures are varied and concepts are presented in multiple ways.

> Organize heterogeneous cooperative groups that require multiple abilities. A variety of abilities are required in daily life, and should be required in the classroom. Group tasks should be *explicitly* organized so that students know that while no one person has all the abilities necessary for success, collectively they do. For instance, a teacher may explain that an upcoming task will require figuring out how something works, drawing a diagram, and constructing a new use for the system under investigation.

> Assign competence to all students. Too often race, class, gender, or ethnicity are related to status hierarchies in the classroom. Children's ideas of who is compe-

Margin notes

The learning community is inclusive.

Multicultural learning is central, not marginal.

Banks (2003a, 2003b); Bernard (1993); Ladson-Billings (1994); Mizell et al. (1993); Nieto (2000); Perry & Fraser (1993)

Richards (1993)

Celebrate and affirm cultural diversity.

Gay (1991); Cohen et al. (1994)

Vary structures of activities.

Cohen (1994, 1998); Cohen et al. (1994); Watson (2003)

Group tasks should involve multiple abilities.

Cazden (2001); Cohen (1994, 1998); Cohen et al. (1994); Watson (2003) tent or incompetent can be difficult to dislodge. As a result, teachers must work to change those expectations by assigning competence *publicly*. This means that the teacher specifies what a child does well that is relevant to a task at hand. This works best when used in conjunction with multiple ability tasks where a group *needs* particular skills and abilities. Thus, a teacher may call attention to a child's ability to organize information in visual forms, or to analyze problems logically. This assignment of competence is reinforced as students demonstrate their skills and abilities in the context of group work.

All students need to be seen as competent; teachers must publicly assign competence to low-status children.

Provide a wide variety of cultural examples and situations to illustrate major concepts and inquiries. These connect children to the topic of study and help provide models of real-world possibilities. Such examples should be carefully selected to avoid stereotyping. They should be comparable to examples taken from the "macroculture."

Provide many different cultural examples.

Banks (2003a, 2003b); Gay (1991)

Take on a critical literacy stance that engages students to examine carefully the underlying stereotypes, ideologies, and privilege and power that are depicted in texts and images and other modes of the communication landscape. This requires that you, yourself, reflect on your own beliefs about literacy, curriculum materials that might be used, and the processes that might be used and promoted in your school. All decisions in teaching are inherently political (see more at the end of the chapter), even more so in the present historical time, where new mandates seem to be issued daily. "Testing and the right answers" contradict the importance of examining conflicting perspectives that do not always lead to neat and tidy conclusions about big issues of life.

Cadiero-Kaplan (2002); Lewison et al. (2002)

In the end, however, one of the most crucial aspects of developing a multicultural, antiracist classroom is developing a core of shared values and social relationships. These values include peaceful conflict resolution, respect for individual differences, and a concern for social justice. They are built into everything we do in the classroom, from content to process, from classroom discourse to playground games. Whether we are intentional or accidental in our attention to diversity, we nonetheless build an environment that speaks to children of their place in the classroom and the world. A basic step in developing an integrated language classroom is to become intentional in our efforts to honor diversity rather than perpetuate inequities. Particularly in the current political climate, teachers must think carefully about how they will organize and explain the kind of instruction that supports the development of antiracist and multicultural school communities.

Build core values.

Allen (1999); Jennings (2002)

Redesign the Physical Environment

Room arrangement signals teacher intention and expectations regarding the flow of talk and activity in the classroom. Straight rows facing the front of the room make cooperative student efforts more difficult and encourage children to direct activity toward the teacher rather than toward their peers. The teacher easily slips into the position of dispenser of information and sole arbiter of talk, and the traditional IRE-like classroom discourse pattern prevails. (See Chapter 2 for more on this type of classroom discourse.) Here a transmission-oriented model of education gets reinforced rather than a collaborative one. Think instead about some ways in which physical changes in the classroom environment foster peer interactions.

Goodman (1986); Routman (1988)

Cazden (2001); Wells (1999, 2001); Wells & Chang-Wells (1992); Young (1992)

Exchange desks for tables, or rearrange desks into table groupings. This organizes children for group work by shifting their focus toward sharing materials, spreading out projects, and cooperating with peers. Children need not be assigned a particular seat; rather, shifting groups and activities dictates seating.

Arrange for personal space. Teachers often make "cubbies" for children's personal supplies and books by covering ice cream drums with contact paper and labeling each container with a child's name. This allows each child to have a place in the classroom that no one else may use, and it decreases problems with territoriality when seating patterns change. A child whose supplies are kept in a desk that also doubles as part of a group work table may become upset when someone else handles his or her materials. If supplies are kept in a personal cubbie away from the work area, such upsets are less likely to occur.

If keeping individual desks seems necessary, use tables or some desks as centers where children can work on projects. This also refocuses attention toward peer interactions.

Establish a gathering or sharing area. As children become engaged in interesting and meaningful activities, they need to have a gathering place in the classroom separate from their work areas. A gathering place helps reorient children when the teacher needs to focus the attention of the whole class on a single event or activity. Children may gather to hear literature, talk over matters of group concern, observe a demonstration in science, or share the results of a group project in social studies. Some teachers set off an area with a rug and cushions on the floor. Others use a bookcase to separate this area from other work spaces. One teacher simply marks off a semicircle with masking tape, and her kindergartners bring "sit-upons" when they gather in this area.

Get rid of teacher-made and commercial room decorations. Let the classroom reflect children's work.

Display children's work aesthetically. When children see all the varieties of their work respected and beautifully displayed, they tend to treat their work as being worthy of respect. Simply trimming and mounting poems, pictures, and other work and inviting children to write captions can make very pleasing displays. Displays of student work also broaden the audience with whom children share their work.

Confront the Basics

Goodman (1986); Kress (2000, 2003); Hillocks (2002); Routman (1991)

One of the basic transitions from traditional to integrated language classrooms is rethinking the way in which the use of the various modes of the communication landscape are learned. Teachers must rethink the way in which basals, workbooks, and tests are used. If basal programs have been the focus of the reading program, there are several ways to move children toward more integrated approaches to reading.

Reorganize the way in which time is allocated in the reading program. Spend time each day sharing literature with students and letting children read material of their own choice (SSR*). The element of choice is crucial in developing lifelong readers. It is also important that children have the opportunity to read many books at a comfortable level so that they begin to perceive themselves as successful readers. Be careful not to emphasize the use of so-called "leveled" books—many of these texts consist of contrived language and, therefore, are not good examples of written language, nor do they provide high-quality illustrations. Moving away from basals means moving away from the feeling that it is always "better" to read "harder" books. Most people read for a variety of purposes, rarely because they want to prove to someone else that they are "good" readers. Providing both choice and guidance is characteristic of integrated language classrooms.

Choice and guidance are crucial features of an integrated setting.

Think of the basal as an anthology, not as a reading program, and use it accordingly. Carefully review the literature in the basal. Select texts that are good literature in their own right rather than adapted or abridged versions of stories that are much better in their original form. Try forming critique groups to read and discuss these selections, and talk about these texts in the ways suggested elsewhere in this book. Use Reader's Theater* instead of round-robin reading. Let the basal become one of many sources of literature, and provide opportunities for the same kinds of extensions suggested for use with trade books. Especially look for more nonfictional texts to include because most basals emphasize fictional selections. If some of the basal selections are not good literature, label them as such and work with the children to rewrite a passage to make a story or an informational text more interesting. Try Group-Composed Writing* to improve such selections. This activity not only encourages careful reading by children but also acknowledges their right to read good literature and make quality judgments on what they read.

Eliminate ability groups. Set up Buddy Reading*, pairing weaker readers with stronger ones, or older readers with younger ones. Look through the teacher's guide for additional reading selections, and collect other books that expand and complement the basal selection. Buddies can then read and discuss worthwhile basal stories while also sharing a variety of other literature. Including a range of multicultural literature is especially critical. Search out trade books or stories to contrast with, or complement, a basal selection. After children have read the basal story, organize Literature Response Circles* to read and discuss related literature. Select students or let them self-select so that a lively discussion will ensue. A sixth-grade class reading a basal selection on Jason and the Argonauts divided into groups that included analysis and comparison of other versions of the legend, a film of an excavation in Greece that appeared to confirm the historicity of another Greek legend that students then read, and a study of books of Greek mythology to learn more about some of the mythological characters Jason encountered. Consider sharing Powell and Steele's *The Greek News* to further pique interest in other topics and to show various genres to communicate information about them.

Stop assigning workbook pages. Have children work on Book Extensions*, including the creation of Semantic Maps* and Sketch to Stretch* activities. Literature Response Circles* can work on extensions that can be shared to provide a backdrop for discussions of language use or literary interpretation. Recall, for example, the children involved in activities with Big Books* or CLOZE* activities described in Chapter 7. The children were applying skills listed in the scope and sequence of any basal program, but they were applying them in context rather than in isolation. They were using background knowledge, conventions of print, letter, and sound relationships, word endings, letter clusters, sight vocabulary, and both meaning and graphic cues. They were also searching for meaning, confirming predictions, and self-correcting their ideas as they explored both written texts and visual images. In another instance, children working on a Comparison Chart* of Asian folktales compared stories, read for details, made inferences, sequenced events, identified cause and effect, and analyzed story structure.

Generate thematic units from good basal passages. Most basal series include stories with particular themes (e.g., growing up, friendship, or mythology). Review the basal series to see how units may develop from the passages in the readers and incorporate books and activities from other content areas as you would in any thematic unit. Linking topics across the curriculum at this point may simply mean covering the units in content area texts out of the usual order.

Reduce the amount of time children spend in basal readers and increase the time spent reading literature of their choice as well as literature related to theme studies. Confine work in the basals to one day and use the rest of the week for integrated language work. If the school system requires that children complete the basal, send it home to be read and discussed with parents, or encourage its use as independent reading. During the time formerly allocated for reading groups, hold individual conferences and sit in on Literature Response Groups*.

Critique groups foster good book talk.

Chambers (1985)

See Huck & Kiefer (2004) for an excellent source for multicultural literature.

Organize Reading Buddies* and Literature Response Groups*.

Powell & Steele (1996)

Apply reading skills in context.

Increase children's opportunities to write connected discourse. Instead of filling in the blanks in workbooks, have children write in Journals*, Sketchbook Journals*, and the like.

Have children write on topics they have chosen, instead of those you have assigned so that they begin to see themselves as authors. Providing them with ways to share their writing with others in peer conferences and in the Author's Chair* gives them real audiences for their writing.

Apply writing and illustration skills in context, too.

Atwell (1998); Calkins (1994)

Try teaching writing skills in the context of children's writing rather than through separate, isolated grammar, spelling, or punctuation lessons and worksheets. Short Focus Lessons* and individual conferences with children are more meaningful ways for teachers to address writing issues and concerns. Children usually internalize and remember these written language conventions more readily when they are part of their ongoing written communication experiences. In the same way, teach about how visual images are created to depict information and how they work in different genres.

Wells (1999, 2001); Wells & Chang-Wells (1992)

Make reading and writing integral components of Student-Directed Inquiries*. When children work on such activities, they have real reasons to read, and they have more to share both orally and in writing. In the No More Litter example in Chapter 5, many of the children in the second-grade class had already experienced school failures. Several were identified as having reading problems, some were receiving special education services, and a few had been detained several times in their short school careers. Most were reluctant readers and writers, yet they were excited about the prospect of working on a real problem in their community and were soon reading and writing extensively.

Set aside time when children share their work with one another—both work in progress and completed work.

Display children's original work rather than completed workbook pages, ditto sheets, or "100%" papers.

Moulin (1988); Tierney et al. (1991); Tierney & Readance (2000)

Send samples of work home so that parents have a sense of what their children are involved in learning.

Look to the Content Areas

The transition to an integrated language classroom is made across the curriculum, not only in the areas of reading and language arts. In traditional curriculums, reading, language arts, and mathematics have had the lion's share of the elementary day. Social studies and science have had little or no instruction, being generally relegated to the end of the day or interrupted and dismissed for assemblies, announcements, and so forth. While this is nothing to celebrate, it does mean that you are probably freer to experiment and take risks in these two areas than in any other part of the curriculum. The content in these areas also lends itself especially well to the development of thematic units, and most educators are more familiar with them, so they are a good place to begin making the transition to thematic units.

Goodlad (1984); Stodolsky (1988)

Gamberg et al. (1988); Pappas et al. (2003); Wells (1999, 2001); Wells & Chang-Wells (1992)

Content areas provide in-depth study and natural language use.

Begin with a mini-unit. (A mini-unit covers material in at least two content areas and can be extended through a wide variety of literature.) Perhaps the science text has a unit on the water cycle. A mini-unit on water could begin with science concepts, including information about areas of the world and how they are affected by rainfall patterns or water sources, then expand to include other cycles in nature.

Content textbooks can give you ideas for units.

Review your district's curriculum objectives or standards in the content areas for potential themes. One sixth-grade teacher, who had initially thought he would try a mini-unit, ended up planning a much larger thematic unit when he realized how

District objectives or standards also can be a useful source for units.

easily many of the district's objectives had to do with CHANGES. Several of the objectives in science (e.g., compare the interrelationships between living organisms and their adaptations to an environment; state basic properties of solids, liquids, and gases; describe the process of inheritance and transmission of physical traits from generation to generation; interpret physiological activities that help organisms to survive) and in social studies (e.g., describe how civilizations develop technology to meet their needs; outline the social, economic, and governmental conditions that lead to various political revolutions; trace the changing role of communism in the twentieth century) could be turned into interesting, worthwhile subthemes. Moreover, he was able to include related topics that were part of the CHANGES motif by having his predominantly Mexican-American students document and study their own family and community changes in both Mexico and the United States as well as the kinds of biological, social, and emotional changes they were going through as part of adolescence. He was also able to track down wonderful children's literature from a range of genres to support students' various inquiries.

Plan activities to fit the structure or time constraints required by your school or system. In most cases, this is simply a matter of presenting integrated activities in a more linear fashion and knowing that although the state may have minimum time requirements for language arts or social studies, you will be teaching some language arts during the period set aside for social studies and some social studies during language arts time. One school calls this approach to the development of an integrated language curriculum "toe dipping" and has found it useful in introducing teachers to new ways of organizing instruction.

Learn how to present integrated activities to show how they meet state and local standards.

Organize the second half of the day—generally, the social studies and science portion of the curriculum—into long-term thematic units. Using some of the suggestions in this book, select topics that will have sustaining power for a four- to six-week period (or longer), and that integrate social studies and science. Although portions of this theme may be integrated into other parts of the day, afternoons can be devoted to the kind of thematic study characteristic of an integrated perspective. As teachers gain confidence in children's ability to work this way, and as they recognize that real learning is occurring, they broaden the types of inquiries children engage in. They begin to look for places where curricular areas overlap. If the third-grade science curriculum calls for a study of living systems and the social studies curriculum includes a unit on communities, why not combine these topics into a thematic unit? Set aside time in the afternoon for theme studies and make both science and social studies textbooks available, along with many trade books for student study.

Use textbooks as one of many sources in your room. Sometimes, teachers assume that an integrated language classroom does not use textbooks. Textbooks are often used, not as the class authority and arbiter of scope and sequence but as resources in the same way that trade books are used. This is particularly true as teachers make the transition from textbook-based to integrated language classrooms. One of the toe-dipping teachers began a thematic unit by using two conflicting textbook descriptions of the settlement of Jamestown and the role of Pocahontas. Which did students think might be correct? How could they check to find out? Soon students were checking a variety of other sources, including Fritz's biography of Pocahontas, high school and college textbooks, material from Jamestown Historic Park, and a local historian. Their final assignment was to rewrite their textbook description of Pocahontas and the settlement of Jamestown. The students were engaged in an interesting inquiry into a historical topic and a careful, critical reading of their textbook. Although they did not integrate many other aspects of the curriculum into their inquiry, they did use a variety of language, from discussion to oral reports and debates, and from taking notes to organizing those notes into a written form. The assignment did not require reorganizing the entire class or the curriculum, but it did allow the teacher to test the waters and see what happened when children

Textbooks are one of many resources available to children.

Fritz (1983)

worked in an atmosphere of independent and small-group inquiry. It also allowed the children to see the textbook as one of many available sources rather than the single most important authority on a subject. This may seem a slight shift, but it is profoundly important in helping children become more independent thinkers.

Implement and Share Your Own Teacher Research

Taking new steps toward an integrated language perspective frequently involves "learning to teach against the grain." It isn't just trying out new methods but taking to heart (and mind) the principles about learners, language, and knowledge upon which the perspective rests. Transmission-oriented teaching has deep roots, so it is likely that most of your educational experiences have been of that kind. Consequently, changing to a more collaborative approach that has teachers sharing power with their students is not easily pulled off. Reflective inquiry initiated and directed by students requires that teachers also have a reflective stance to their own teaching. Thus, teacher research—the systematic, intentional inquiry by teachers about their own school and classroom work—is a critical facet of the integrated language approach.

So far in this chapter (as well as throughout the whole book), we have covered many ideas or areas in which to toe-dip, or start to change your curriculum and teaching practices toward an integrated language perspective. These suggestions or possibilities can serve as initial topics for your own teacher research. Although most teaching could be seen as some kind of implicit inquiry, the notion of teacher research emphasizes explicitness and deliberateness of intention to study some aspect of teaching and learning. See "Guidelines for Teacher Inquiry" at the end of the book for tips to use for launching teacher inquiries.

Teaching can be a very lonely activity, especially if one is swimming against the mainstream. Therefore, it helps to build understanding among peers. One way to accomplish this is to share students' work with the rest of the school. Hang displays in the hall or invite other classes to some performance aspects of your children's work. Think about the ways in which you can elicit recognition of your children's work by both your colleagues and school administrators. The children in the No More Litter example in Chapter 5 shared their videotape with other classes and the PTA. As a result, others recognized the quality of the children's work and encouraged their continued efforts. This can establish a climate in which the innovative teacher is viewed as a good and hardworking, if rather different, teacher. Such an attitude will make further changes less controversial and may even encourage a few peers to join in making changes.

Obviously sharing the results of your teacher research and your students' work helps validate your new steps in implementing an integrated language perspective. When colleagues see your openness and willingness to experiment and hear how you have approached resolving your questions about teaching and learning, they are often eager to hear what you have to say. They will appreciate the particulars and, consequently, may be willing to try out something new, especially if they have you as a resource.

Increasingly more teachers are also publishing their teacher inquiries in public ways for wider audiences—in school, district, or community newsletters as well as professional journals, books, and other publications. These writings provide another avenue to share your results.

Invite Parents to Participate

Do not stop at the schoolhouse door. Parents have a vested interest in quality education for their children, and there is strong evidence that high levels of parental in-

---

Shifts toward independent thinking are crucial.

Cochran-Smith (1991)

Wells (1994, 1999, 2001); Wells & Chang-Wells (1992); Young (1992)

Collaborative teaching where power is shared with students is hard work—it is action research for social change.

Cochran-Smith & Lytle (1993); Pappas & Zecker (2001a, 2001b)

Let your first "steps" be topics for teacher research.

See GUIDELINES FOR TEACHER INQUIRY for more ideas on teacher research.

Cochran-Smith & Lytle (1993); Hubbard & Power (2003)

- *Help to establish a climate supportive of innovation.*
- *Sharing the details from teacher research is usually appreciated by colleagues.*

Moulin (1988); Routman (1991, 1996)

volvement are related to positive student attitudes and achievement. Too often, parents' information about what is going on in a classroom is based on student reports and community gossip. This can create problems for a teacher trying to make changes that alter the kind of information going home to parents. Some teachers have reported that parents complained when fewer dittos came home because the parents felt that their children must not be "covering" as much material. It makes sense to create advocates rather than enemies by involving parents in your program at a variety of levels. Friday portfolios (see Chapter 9), where students bring home and share with parents the week's important work, can provide the kind of specific information parents want and need about these new ideas. Another way to communicate ongoing students' work with parents is through weekly reviews. Here students briefly list some of the things they had done each week, three things they had learned, skills they worked on, what they had been reading, what they were proud of, and what they plan to work on the following week. At the end is a place for teacher comments, as well as family comments. Meeting with parents at open house or sending out letters or newsletters explaining what is going on in your class can help counter parental resistance. Remember, most parents know only transmission-oriented curriculum teaching and learning. Thus, these letters, for example, can explain Literature Response Circles* where students are encouraged to read a book of choice in a thematic unit and talk about their responses to it with a small group of their peers; the writing process you have implemented in which students write drafts that might have areas that are unclear and might be filled with grammatical errors or misspellings but will be addressed later during the revising and editing of texts; your explanation that invented spelling is not something that children do instead of learning to spell, but instead is the avenue they take to learning to spell that has the advantage of students writing all the time. In addition, sharing the results of your teacher research with parents can be an invaluable way to help parents understand the collaborative approach of an integrated language perspective.

In any event, involve parents as supporters, service givers, and facilitators. Develop a cadre of parents who collect materials from scrap lumber to computer software, donate time to help put on a play, or organize a culminating activity for a unit. Provide parents with positive access to the school and opportunities to observe classroom activity. They want their children to feel good about school, excited about learning, and confident about themselves. An integrated language approach is often vigorously supported by parents once they understand its foundations and see its effects. Parents can be powerful advocates for teachers when they can speak on the basis of observation. (See Chapter 9 for more specific ideas on how teachers can support parents' classroom observations.)

Parents can be learners. Those with younger children may especially want specific help in fostering their children's education. Some schools and classrooms have successfully organized discussion sessions where parents and teachers get together to talk about ways the home and school environments can support each other. The communication networks thus built between parents and teachers minimize misunderstandings. The teacher can show parents samples of student work and explain activities so that parents understand what is happening in the classroom and can offer constructive feedback based on their knowledge of their children. Local experts on language learning, children's literature, and child development can also be invited to parent meetings to provide additional background.

Parents have talents that can be valuable learning resources and encourage support for new programming. Some teachers ask parents ahead of time for ideas or topics that might be incorporated into the theme of the next unit. Others use parent volunteers on a weekly basis to work with children in individual or small-group situations, such as advising a special project that could use some expert assistance, sharing literature, or helping children organize their thoughts into writing. Parents work as partners with the teacher to develop a sound educational program for their children. (Examples of this partnership are given in the prototypes in Chapter 4.)

Routman (1996)

See Fisher (1995), Rief (1992), Routman (1996), and Wilde (1992) for examples of letters to parents.

Sharing teacher research with parents is critical to gaining support for an integrated language approach.

Work with Administrators

Teachers may be unaware of or confused by the plethora of guidelines and regulations for teaching and learning that exist at both local and state levels. School communities have their own share of myths about what is "required":

Myth 1.   Teachers have to cover every unit of every textbook in the order in which they are written.

Myth 2.   Teachers have to use the lesson plans in the textbooks.

Myth 3.   Teachers have to use workbooks.

Myth 4.   Children have to read every story and cover every lesson in every textbook.

Myth 5.   Teachers teach reading for only one period a day.

Such regulations are neither good teaching practice nor mandated in most districts. When confronted by such myths, do not accept them without checking things out.

Honig (1988); Stedman (1989)

Talk with the principal or the district subject coordinators to find out what is required, what is encouraged, and what is open to change in your state or district.

Become familiar with the state curriculum guides and state laws governing curriculum. Many teachers have been surprised to find that state and local guidelines are very much in harmony with practices recommended for integrated language classrooms. If necessary, point out to the administration how the integrated language program matches state and local guidelines.

In some schools, it is possible for a teacher to share plans and explain their theoretical and research bases with administrators. Generally, teachers must be prepared to show how they will cover required skills and content in the context of the thematic unit approach. In schools where administrators are more willing to believe successful practice than plans and theory, inviting them in to see student activities or the products of student projects is more likely to garner their support.

Invite the Community in and Take Children into the Community

One of the most threatening aspects of an integrated language perspective is the feeling that the teacher must know so much and be able to draw on a vast array of resources beyond the confines of the textbook. When teachers make the transition to an integrated perspective, they quickly learn that they cannot be the source of all knowledge. They begin to shift their role from information giver to fellow constructor of meaning. To be most effective in this role, teachers need to think about the community resources waiting to be tapped.

Teachers cannot be the only source of knowledge in the classroom. The surrounding community is a rich resource.

Invite community people into the classroom. Begin with the students' parents and guardians. A kindergarten teacher invites parents or guardians individually to spend some time describing to students that adult's occupation or hobby. One full-time homemaker came to class with an apron stuffed full of symbols of all her jobs: a model car for her role as chauffeur, a tiny iron for her job as laundress, and so forth. Another parent who enjoyed woodworking taught children to make birdhouses. A grandfather taught the children dances popular in his youth.

The community has a vested interest in schooling.

Community officials are often willing to come and talk to school children, as are people involved in business, service, arts, and recreational areas. When children in one school became interested in machinery, a local factory worker helped children build models of various kinds of machines. A local artist came and taught puppetry.

Inviting all sorts of people into the life of the classroom lessens the teacher's and children's isolation, lifts some of the burden teachers often feel in trying to be experts in everything, and models new ways of learning.

Take children into the community as much as possible. Try to lessen the barrier between school and the world by taking children to see people in nonschool environments. This visibility introduces the teacher and the class program to the community and builds a support group. These expeditions need not require schoolbus trips or expensive transportation arrangements. There are plenty of things to study in the immediate environment of most schools. Within a more urban community, students can use public transportation. A fourth-grade teacher arranged a bus trip to an art museum that was exhibiting African masks. As part of the class's study, students researched bus schedules, fares, distances, and transportation times in addition to developing charts of symbols and techniques used in making masks of different regions of Africa. They developed a trip book that contained necessary information for planning the trip and recording information about the uses of masks in various cultures.

Prepare your class for community contact. Well-prepared and well-behaved children are welcome in the community and are a pleasure to visit. Most people enjoy sharing their interest and respond well to children who have done some preparation before a visit. Work with children to establish ground rules for conduct and data gathering. Successful field trips and visits from community members reinforce new patterns of student responsibility for their own learning.

> Lessen the barriers between school and the "real" world.

> Prepare children for responsible participation in the community.

Find a Friend

Change is not always welcomed. If a teacher is going to be a change agent in a school, some people will resent such activity and will work to encourage a return to tradition. It is easier to resist these pressures if the teacher finds a companion who shares a similar perspective. Sometimes even a "critical mass" of two can provide enough strength to make a difference, especially if both teachers are at the same grade level. In any case, it is good to have someone not only to share and plan with but also to commiserate with when things don't go as well as hoped. It is also good to have someone with whom to share your teacher research, maybe even developing joint inquiries. Good teaching is hard work. Finding someone who supports your efforts toward being a first-rate teacher can help you withstand pressures toward mediocrity.

> Cochran-Smith (1991); Hubbard & Power (1999); Pappas & Zecker (2001a, 2001b)

> Even two can be a critical mass for change in a school.

Get Involved!

To continue teaching, teachers must continue learning. Most states require some form of continuing education, but that is not the only way to grow as a teacher. Teachers also need to grow in experiences outside the classroom. A number of professional organizations offer scholarships and other incentives that enable teachers to participate in a variety of special programs and travel for educational purposes. These programs provide opportunities to meet teachers from around the country (and sometimes, the world), to form a support group for innovative teaching, and to enrich the learning of your students. Some of the organizations that support this type of growth include the National Council of Teachers of English, the National Council for the Social Studies, the International Reading Association, the National Science Teachers Association, and the National Council of Teachers of Mathematics. These organizations and their local and state affiliates welcome teacher participation and leadership. Many teachers develop their own community or district networks through which to share teacher research, find out about new books or other resources, and discuss classroom practice. Individual enthusiasm coupled with continued education recharges intellectual batteries so that teaching remains a stimulating and mind-expanding activity.

Become Associated with a University or College

As teachers move toward a more integrated model, they sometimes take advantage of the resources in nearby colleges and universities.

Collaborative efforts between college and university faculty and classroom teachers can be rewarding to all participants, so enlist the help of a sympathetic faculty member. You can get some expert assistance without the threat of administrative evaluation, and the university representative has an opportunity to observe and participate in an important "laboratory" setting. In fact, collaborative inquiry between university-based and school-based teacher researchers is becoming more prevalent, so many university professors are eager to consider the educational issues or questions you want to study together.

Let administrators know about these collaborations. An advocate from the university or college can sometimes encourage administrators to grant a classroom teacher a bit more leeway than might otherwise be allowed. The university person can also document the class's progress, provide feedback, and serve as a resource person.

Make presentations at professional conferences. Collaborative efforts can result in presentations that put teachers in contact with like-minded colleagues and extend the needed support network.

See Miller (1990), Pappas & Zecker (2001a, 2001b), Valencia (1998), Weaver (1998), and Wells (2001) for examples of collaborative school–university work.

Incorporate Evaluation and Assessment Strategies

The performance-based procedures for evaluation discussed in Chapter 9 are appearing in a multitude of school settings. As more holistic measures of evaluation that may be relatively simple to implement are becoming acceptable even in settings where letter or number grades must be assigned for the report card, teachers can begin incorporating assessments that are more compatible with an integrated language perspective.

Keep good records. The kid-watching techniques discussed in Chapters 8 and 9 require good record keeping. They help teachers plan, of course, but they also help explain to parents and administrators what children are learning and doing. In a sense, good record keeping helps validate good teacher intuition—that sense of how children are doing and where they are ready to go next that comes from careful observation, good practice, and professional judgment.

Keep plenty of records. Especially in schools where single grades or standardized tests are the major means by which children's learning is measured and reported, it is important to accumulate other data as evidence of the kind of thinking and learning that more fully represent the progress of an individual child. One simple way to do this is to keep a learning portfolio that is periodically shared with parents. A child's story or poem, picture, or project can speak volumes about the kind of learning that is going on.

Parents can also better understand the kind of documentation represented in a portfolio than the statistical interpretations required to make sense out of stan-

Portfolios provide understandable feedback to parents.

dardized measures. Even percentage scores on a teacher-made test do not tell a parent as much as a book their child has created during a thematic unit.

Teach children how to take tests. If standardized tests are used with children in integrated language classrooms, help prepare them for the format in which it will be given. Place a few practice sentences on the board periodically to accustom them to the test format. Practice working within time constraints, as young children often lack experience with timed tests. Always try to be "true" to your beliefs about how children learn as you also teach the genre of the tests. In most cases, however, children in integrated language classrooms do as well or better on standardized tests than those in more traditional classrooms.

Reardon (1990); Wolf & Wolf (2002)

Tunnell & Jacobs (1989)

Involve children in self-evaluation. Start by inviting them to put together their own portfolio of work. Initially, it helps to provide some guidelines about what types of work to include. Suggest that children include samples of the writing that they found the most interesting, that they enjoyed doing the most, or that they found the most difficult. They may include an outline of the work they have been involved in over a particular period and provide samples of things representative of that work. Children may also include samples that represent something brand new that they have learned, or an example of something they had trouble with but think they are beginning to understand or have mastered.

Gamberg et al. (1988); Lenski et al. (1996); Tierney & Readance (2000)

Discuss evaluation with students. Some teachers provide check sheets for children to fill out that cover a child's activities for a particular period. The teacher fills out a similar sheet, and both meet to go over their evaluations. The child has an opportunity to provide feedback to the teacher, and the teacher can discuss areas of strength as well as areas of concern. In this way, even if the teacher must assign a number or letter grade, the child has a better understanding of where that grade came from and has an opportunity to provide evidence the teacher may not have considered. Thus, evaluation is collaborative, too.

Be patient. Good evaluative and assessment skills take time to acquire. They require continuous practice and careful reflection. Teachers have to be as patient with their own unfolding abilities as they are with children.

Become Politically Savvy

As indicated previously, the present political climate requires that you become politically astute. Mandates about how to teach and how to test or assess are not neutral. They may or may not be useful guidelines for supporting students' learning. They often restrict teachers' ability to made decisions in their own classrooms for their own students as individuals who have unique talents and needs. Thus, it is important to learn to resist such mandates, but you cannot be successful in these efforts unless you are knowledgeable about the issues and arguments for and against these mandates. Look for books and articles that help you—and your colleagues—to form arguments against what you think are unsound mandates and to provide alternatives that are more in line with your beliefs about teaching that supports all children's learning.

See Meyer (2002) for understanding and resisting isolated phonics instruction; Hillocks (2002) for examining how state writing assessments control learning; and Garan (2002) and Smith (2003) for exploring the problems with recent reports on "scientific" reading instruction.

Conclusions

An integrated language perspective is accessible to many kinds of teachers in many kinds of situations. It is not a lockstep model but a belief about children and learning. No teacher enters the classroom with a perfect system in place; good teachers spend their entire careers building on decisions made as they confront the realities of life in classrooms.

Teachers share responsibility for building children's futures.

Britton (1981)

This book has emphasized the importance of choices and ownership for teachers and children. Teachers generally make their choices because they care about children. Teaching requires careful thinking about the future we want for children. The debate over that future and the ways to reach it have always been with us. We argue over whether it is enough to teach children to read and write or to achieve high scores on college entrance exams, or if there is some "cultural literacy" that will enable a diverse society to function as a democracy. We debate the impact of education on children's economic futures and on the political and economic future of our world. James Britton has said that "we want children, as a result of our teaching to *understand*, to be wise as well as well informed, able to solve fresh problems rather than have learnt the answers to old ones; indeed not only able to answer questions but also able to ask them" (p. 81). Choosing to teach from an integrated language perspective provides a context in which such goals are possible. Making the transition to that perspective can be an exciting and challenging experience.

References

Allen, J. (Ed.). (1999). *Class actions: Teaching for social justice in elementary and middle schools.* New York: Teachers College Press.

Banks, J. A. (2003a). *Teaching strategies for ethnic studies.* Boston: Allyn & Bacon.

Banks, J. A. (2003b). Teaching literacy for social justice and global citizenship. *Language Arts, 81,* 18–19.

Bernard, B. A. (1993). "If it's November, it must be Indians": Challenging Thanksgiving stereotypes. *Teaching Tolerance, 2 (2),* 54–56.

Britton, J. (1981). Talking to learn. In D. Barnes, J. Britton, & H. Rosen (Eds.), *Language, the learner and the school* (pp. 81–115). New York: Penguin.

Cadiero-Kaplan, K. (2002). Literacy ideologies: Critically engaging the language arts curriculum. *Language Arts, 79,* 372–381.

Calkins, L. (1994). *The art of teaching writing.* Portsmouth, NH: Heinemann.

Cazden, C. (2001). *Classroom discourse: The language of teaching and learning.* Portsmouth, NH: Heinemann.

Chambers, A. (1985). *Booktalk: Occasional writing on literature and children.* New York: Harper & Row.

Cochran-Smith, M. (1991). Learning to teach against the grain. *Harvard Educational Review, 61,* 279–310.

Cochran-Smith, M., & Lytle, S. L. (1993). *Inside/Outside: Teacher research and knowledge.* New York: Teachers College Press.

Cohen, E. G. (1994). *Designing groupwork: Strategies for the heterogeneous classroom.* New York: Teachers College Press.

Cohen, E. G. (1998). Making cooperative learning equitable. *Educational Leadership, 56,* 18–21.

Cohen, E. G., Lotan, R. A., Whitcomb, J. A., Balderrama, M. V., Cossey, R., & Swansom, P. E. (1994). Complex instruction: Higher order thinking in heterogeneous classrooms. In S. Sharan (Ed.), *Handbook of cooperative learning methods* (pp. 82–96). Westport, CT: Greenwillow Press.

Fisher, B. (1995). *Thinking and learning together: Curriculum and community in a primary classroom.* Portsmouth, NH: Heinemann.

Gamberg, R., Kwak, W., Hutchings, M., & Altheim, J. (1988). *Learning and loving it: Theme studies in the classroom.* Portsmouth, NH: Heinemann.

Garan, E. M. (2002). *Resisting reading mandates: How to triumph with the truth.* Portsmouth, NH: Heinemann.

Gay, G. (1991). Culturally diverse students and social studies. In J. Shaver (Ed.), *Handbook of research on social studies teaching and learning* (pp. 144–156). New York: Macmillan.

Goodlad, J. (1984). *A place called school.* New York: McGraw-Hill.

Goodman, K. (1986). *What's whole about whole language?* Portsmouth, NH: Heinemann.

Hillocks, G. (2002). *The testing trap: How state writing assessments control learning.* New York: Teachers College Press.

Honig, B. (1988). The California reading initiative. *The New Advocate, 1(4),* 135–140.

Hubbard, R. S., & Power, B. M. (1999). *Living the questions: A guide for teacher researchers.* York, ME: Stenhouse.

Hubbard, R. S., & Power, B. M. (2003). *The art of classroom inquiry: A handbook for teacher-researchers.* Portsmouth, NH: Heinemann.

Huck, C. S., & Kiefer, B., with Hepler, S., Hickman, J. (2004). *Children's literature in the elementary school.* Boston: McGraw-Hill.

Jennings, I. B., with O'Keefe, T. (2002). Parents and children inquiring together: Written conversations about social justice. *Language Arts, 79,* 404–414.

Kress, G. (2000). Multimodality. In B. Cope & M. Kalantzis (Eds.), *Multiliteracies: Literacy learning and the design of social futures* (pp. 182–202). London: Rutledge.

Kress, G. (2003). *Literacy in the new media age.* London: Rutledge.

Ladson-Billings, G. (1994). *The dreamkeepers: Successful teachers of African-American children.* San Francisco: Jossey-Bass.

Lenski, S. D., Riss, M., & Flickinger, G. (1996). Honoring student self-evaluation in the classroom community. *Primary Voices, K–6, 4(2),* 24–32.

Lewison, M., Flint, A. S., & Sluys, K. V. (2002). Taking on critical literacy: The journey of newcomers and novices. *Language Arts, 79,* 382–392.

Meyer, R. J. (2002). *Phonics exposed: Understanding and resisting systemic direct intense phonics instruction.* Mahwah, NJ: Lawrence Erlbaum.

Miller, J. (1990). *Creating spaces and finding voices: Teachers collaborating for empowerment.* Albany: State University of New York Press.

Mizell, L., Benett, S., Bowman, B., & Morin, L. (1993). Different ways of seeing: Teaching in an anti-racist school. In T. Perry & J. W. Fraser (Eds.), *Freedom's plow: Teaching in the multicultural classroom* (pp. 27–46). New York: Routledge.

Moulin, N. (1988, April). *Effect of parent involvement in classroom activities on parents' and children's attitude toward school.* Paper presented at the annual meeting of the American Educational Research Association, New Orleans, LA.

Nieto, S. (2000). *Affirming diversity: The sociopolitical context of multicultural education.* New York: Longman.

Pappas, C. C., Varelas, M., Barry, A., & Rife, A. (2003). Dialogic inquiry around information texts: The role of intertextuality in constructing scientific understandings in urban primary classrooms. *Linguistics and Education, 13(4),* 435–482.

Pappas, C. C., & Zecker, L. B. (Eds.). (2001a). *Teacher inquiries in literacy teaching-learning: Learning to collaborate in elementary urban classrooms.* Mahwah, NJ: Lawrence Erlbaum.

Pappas, C. C., & Zecker, L. B. (Eds.). (2001b). *Working with teacher researchers in urban classrooms: Transforming literacy curriculum genres.* Mahwah, NJ: Lawrence Erlbaum.

Perry, T., & Fraser, J. W. (1993). Reconstructing schools as multiracial/multicultural democracies: Toward a theoretical perspective. In T. Perry & J. W. Fraser (Eds.), *Freedom's plow: Teaching in the multicultural classroom* (pp. 3–24). New York: Routledge.

Reardon, S. J. (1990). Putting reading tests in their place. *The New Advocate, 3,* 29–37.

Richards, J. J. (1993). Classroom tapestry: A practitioner's perspective on multicultural education. In T. Perry & J. W. Fraser (Eds.), *Freedom's plow: Teaching in the multicultural classroom* (pp. 47–63). New York: Routledge.

Rief, L. (1992). *Seeking diversity: Language arts with adolescents.* Portsmouth, NH: Heinemann.

Routman, R. (1988). *Transitions: From literature to literacy.* Portsmouth, NH: Heinemann.

Routman, R. (1991). *Invitations: Changing as teachers and learners, K–12.* Portsmouth, NH: Heinemann.

Routman, R. (1996). *Literacy at the crossroads: Crucial talk about reading, writing, and other teaching dilemmas.* Portsmouth, NH: Heinemann.

Smith, F. (2003). *Unspeakable acts, unnatural practices: Flaws and fallacies in "scientific" reading instruction.* Portsmouth, NH: Heinemann.

Staff. (1993). People puzzle. *Teaching Tolerance,* Fall, p. 1.

Stedman, L. C. (1987). It's time we changed the effective schools formula. *Phi Delta Kappan, 63,* 216–224.

Stodolsky, S. S. (1988). *The subject matters: Classroom activity in math and social studies.* Chicago: University of Chicago Press.

Tierney, R. J., Carter, M. A., & Desai, L. E. (1991). *Portfolio assessment in the reading-writing classroom.* Norwood, MA: Christopher-Gordon.

Tierney, R. J., & Readence, J. E. (2000). *Reading strategies and practices: A compendium.* Boston: Allyn & Bacon.

Tunnell, M. O., & Jacobs, J. S. (1989). Using "real books": Research findings on literature-based reading instruction. *The Reading Teacher, 42,* 470–477.

Valencia, S. W. (1998). *Literacy portfolios in action.* Fort Worth, TX: Harcourt Brace.

Watson, M., in collaboration with Ecken, L. (2003). *Learning to trust: Transforming difficult elementary classrooms through Developmental Discipline.* San Francisco, CA: Jossey-Bass.

Weaver, C. (Ed.). (1998). *Lessons to share on teaching grammar in context.* Portsmouth, NH: Boynton/Cook.

Wells, G. (1994). *Changing schools from within: Creating communities of inquiry.* Toronto: OISE Press. (Distributed by Portsmouth, NH: Heinemann.)

Wells, G. (1999). *Dialogic inquiry: Toward a sociocultural practice and theory of education.* Cambridge: Cambridge University Press.

Wells, G. (Ed.). (2001). *Action, talk, and text: Learning and teaching through inquiry.* New York: Teachers College Press.

Wells, G., & Chang-Wells, G. L. (1992). *Constructing knowledge together: Classrooms as centers of inquiry and literacy.* Portsmouth, NH: Heinemann.

Wertsch, J. V. (1985). *Vygotsky and the social formation of mind.* Cambridge: Cambridge University Press

Wilde, S. (1992). *You kan red this! Spelling and punctuation for whole classrooms, K–6.* Portsmouth, NH: Heinemann.

Wolf, S. A., & Wolf, K. P. (2002). Teaching *true* and *to* the test in writing. *Language Arts, 79,* 229–240.

Young, R. (1992). *Critical theory and classroom talk.* Clevedon, England: Multilingual Matters.

Children's Literature

The Double Life of Pocahontas by J. Fritz. Illustrated by E. Young. Putnam, 1983.

The Greek News by A. Powell & P. Steele. Candlestick Press, 1996.

Guidelines for Teacher Inquiry

Cochran-Smith & Lytle (1993)

Teacher inquiry is related to Student-Directed Inquiry*.

Teacher inquiry fosters the idea of teacher-as-learner.

Teacher inquiry enables teachers to examine ideologies.

Bartolome (1994); Cummins (1994); Edelsky (1994); Graves (2001); Gutierrez, Rymes, & Larson (1995); Pappas (1999)

We have argued throughout the book that teacher research—*the systematic, intentional inquiry by teachers* about their own school and classroom work—is a critical feature of the integrated language perspective. It goes along with our emphasis on student-directed inquiry where students tackle various dimensions of the essential questions of particular thematic units, do in-depth studies on them, then report their findings to the rest of the classroom participants (or even beyond to a school or community audience). Here students are seen as knowers *and* teachers, and classroom teachers become learners. Teacher inquiry facilitates this move from teacher-as-information-transmitter to teacher-as-learner by encouraging teachers to take on a reflective stance toward teaching and learning. As they explicitly research their own practice and their students' learning, teachers become knowers—professionals who gain and generate knowledge about their own practice. (See the inquiry phases discussed in Chapter 7 for the kinds of inquiry phases that teacher researchers also engage in.)

There is an important social activist agenda to teacher research as well. As we have argued throughout the book, developing multicultural curriculum that explores our underlying biases, values, and ideologies means that our pedagogy must always be critically examined. Teachers' local inquiries in their classrooms may be important sites of resistance regarding the broader power relations in the society at large. As we argued in the Introduction, teacher inquiry enables teachers to speak out as professionals.

Teacher Inquiry as Cycles of Action Research

In their inquiries, students' understanding stems from their purposeful action. It is cumulatively constructed as they bring their current knowledge or schemas to new contexts, projects, and information to make sense of them. Once again there are parallels to teacher inquiry; namely, teachers engage in spirals of observation, reflection, and action for the purpose of developing their own understanding and improving their practice. Wells outlines the four major activities of this action research:

Wells (1994)

Four components of action research

- *Observing* to make systematic observations of particular, relevant aspects of classroom life to determine what is actually happening.
- *Interpreting* these observations by reflecting on why things are happening as they are. For both those things that are working well and those that are not in the situation, they attempt to discover the factors that seem to be responsible.
- *Planning change* by constructing hypotheses for what changes might bring an improvement for the unsatisfactory aspects of the current situation. They con-

sider how one or more of these changes might be undertaken and plan how to implement it.

- *Acting out* the planned change.

Integrally related to these components of action research is the teachers' personal theory. This is the core of teacher inquiry—how a teacher's interpretative framework informs and is informed by the cycles of action research. By adopting the stance of reflectiveness, teacher researchers make the connections between theory and practice more explicit. Their theories are grounded by their practice and vice versa, and they are able to develop a more conscious understanding of the underlying basis of their actions.

Similar to student-directed inquiry, two other important activities support teacher inquiry. First, reading about other work—both theoretical and practical—related to the inquiry topic is useful in that it can inform various facets of the action research. Second, having informal, collaborative talk with interested others at every stage of the process is critical for sustaining and extending teacher researchers' efforts.

Whether you are a student teacher researcher (STR) or an already practicing teacher researcher (TR), any inquiry begins with *your own questions* about teaching and learning. Thus, we talk about questions first. Then we cover several other general topics that are involved in doing inquiry: the role of research journals and other methods of data collection; strategies for data analysis; and tips for publishing teacher inquiry. Subsequently, we suggest possible ways that student teachers might be engaged in teacher inquiry during their various fieldwork experiences, including student teaching.

A teacher's own personal, interpretative theory is at the center of teacher inquiry.

Cochran-Smith & Lytle (1993); Hobson (1996); Wells (1994, 2001)

Reading on the topic of inquiry and having conversations with others support teacher inquiry.

Altrichter et al. (1993); Wells (1994, 2001); Zeichner & Liston (1996)

Inquiries begin with questions.

Raising Questions about Teaching–Learning

Some teachers start out with a clear, formulated question, or at least a general question, "What's going on here?" or "What's the problem here?" However, many start with a very diffuse or vague interest in some aspect of the curriculum or content of a thematic unit, or curiosity about how trying out new or modified practice might lead to better learning outcomes for students, or a particular feature of student behavior that they have noted as interesting or problematic. Frequently, it is only through careful observation of the first cycle of the action research process that specific questions evolve.

Teaching–learning is a relationship, a reciprocal, dynamic connection that cannot be separated. This relationship also always involves *content*—the essential questions, important concepts, and worthwhile multicultural curriculum we have discussed throughout the book. Nevertheless, we have found that a useful way to begin to think about inquiry questions is to consider whether they focus mostly on the "teaching" side of the relationship, or whether they are directed more toward students' learning. That is, if you are interested in trying out how you might create Literature Response Groups* in your classroom—where students read the same book and then discuss it with peers in small groups—your questions would likely be concerned with questions on teaching. What books should I select for them? How can I set up a system where students could have choices? How do I help students learn their roles and responsibilities in their discussions? But notice that even though your emphasis is on questions about teaching, you cannot avoid issues of student learning. In fact, students' reactions or learning outcomes to what you implement will be your data to help you decide on the next steps you make or what teaching strategies you might need to change or revise. Indeed, a question about students' learning—How can I facilitate their authentic responses to texts?—might have been the underlying impetus for your inquiry in the first place.

However, if you had kept that question in the foreground, you probably would have generated other questions stemming from it that would be more clearly related to students' learning. What kinds of responses do students develop in small-group discussions? In what ways do peer discussions enable them to evoke both personal and critical responses to texts? How are students' responses different depending on the

See Arhar et al. (2001); Altrichter et al. (1993); Fischer (1996); and Hubbard & Power (1999, 2003) for more discussion on finding and framing inquiry questions.

Decide which "side" of the teaching–learning relationship your inquiry emphasizes.

figure **G.1**

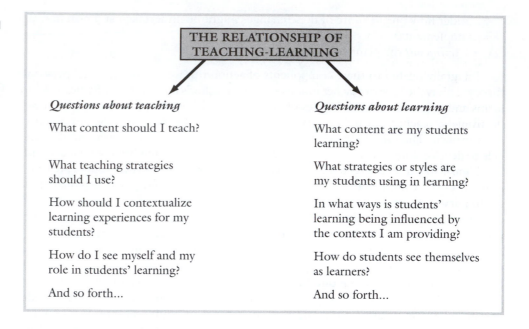

THE RELATIONSHIP OF
TEACHING-LEARNING

Questions about teaching

What content should I teach?

What teaching strategies
should I use?

How should I contextualize
learning experiences for my
students?

How do I see myself and my
role in students' learning?

And so forth...

Questions about learning

What content are my students
learning?

What strategies or styles are
my students using in learning?

In what ways is students'
learning being influenced by
the contexts I am providing?

How do students see themselves
as learners?

And so forth...

genre they are reading? Once again, although these questions rest more on the "learning" side of the relationship, the teaching influence cannot be denied. Students might begin with just retelling parts of text rather than responding to it, or they might offer only personal ones, when you had hoped that critical responses would be developed as well. Thus, you might have to create a series of Focus Lessons* to help students see the potential range of response that might be possible, or model ways of evoking critical responses during your teacher-led Reading Aloud* sessions with them.

Thus, it is impossible to separate teaching from learning; teaching influences learning and learning affects teaching. But in terms of raising questions, it usually helps to be more aware of *where* the underlying intent of your inquiry lies. Making this distinction—see Figure G.1—aids your being clearer in your own mind as to what questions you are generating, especially in the beginning of an inquiry. Whether your inquiry questions draw on either side or both sides, the process enables you to be more conscious of their source. This helps you create an initial framework for research, even though your questions are likely to become modified or even be replaced with new ones.

The Role of Research Journals in Teacher Inquiry

Research journals or diaries are a major means of record keeping in teacher research.

Altrichter et al. (1993); Hobson (1996); Hubbard & Power (2003)

An integral aspect of any inquiry is record keeping. Most teacher researchers keep a small journal to record their observations and reflections for each inquiry. However, specifying ahead of time exactly when you plan to write in the journal during your daily schedule or everyday life leads to success in keeping journals. Many TRs take at least fifteen to twenty minutes at the end of the school day as a good time for journal writing, then think of other times, such as at the beginning of writing workshop or when students are writing in their own Journals*. Other teachers, because of after-school meetings or other commitments, schedule their journal time at home, after dinner, or before going to bed.

Frequently, or at least in the beginning of fieldwork, STRs have many opportunities for observation as they attempt to understand how mentor teachers and students interact in the classroom. As they take on more teaching responsibilities, however, they meet the same challenges as teachers in finding the right spots of the day to do journal writing. Thus, a first step in teacher inquiry is to determine the times that are best for you. (See below for more on the *when* of doing journal writing.)

The format of your journal is a personal choice, but there are three features that all journals should include.

1. You want to include *both* descriptive writing and reflective writing. The *descriptive writing* is the reporting of your observation in the action research cycle. Learning to be descriptive in recording what you have observed is hard to do in the beginning, but it gets easier and faster with practice. You want details here—see the ideas provided under "General Observation Schemes" in Chapter 8. You want these descriptions to be useful at the time you wrote them, as well as later when you review, reread, and reexamine them. The *reflective writing* is the standing back, mulling over, searching for connections and possible meanings, considering various hypotheses or potential plans for action. Most TRs and STRs find ways to differentiate these two types of writing. For example, they make their journals have "double entries." That is, they have the right-hand pages of their journal be the place where they write down descriptive accounts, and the left-hand facing pages where they write down their reflections on those experiences. Or they might buy notebooks or paper (called "project planner" paper) that has a large margin. Another strategy—especially good for those who may want to take just brief notes on Post-it Notes, index cards, or large address labels, and then write up these observations in more detail on the computer—is to use brackets to distinguish the reflections from descriptions.

2. You want to be sure to note down the actions you take as part of your inquiry, with a short rationale for why you have undertaken this course of action. This documentation gives you an *instructional trail* of the various paths you have taken and helps you plan future action as you make sense of the themes or patterns that emerge in your inquiry.

3. And, along with this instructional trail, you want also to document a *data trail*—the data resources you are going to use to gather data on these instructional activities or routines. Moreover, although it might seem obvious—but sometimes is easily forgotten—all of your journal entries should be dated. You want to have a record of when you observed something relevant in your inquiry or when you took action to implement a change.

More on Journals and Other Ways to Collect Data

Just as format is a personal choice, so is the actual journal you can use. Some TRs and STRs like $8\frac{1}{2} \times 11$ pages they can place in a binder. Pages can be removed, rearranged, and are large enough to tape or staple other notes, photographs, or other relevant information. Others prefer a smaller 6×9 notebook that can be easily slipped into a purse, book bag, or satchel. As already noted, there are lots of other ways to gather information for your inquiry that complement and extend the journal. Post-it Notes, index cards, or large address labels are good for recording data for individual or group case studies. Audiotaping and videotaping are also useful means to gain information. However, although these ways for collecting data might seem easier, they will usually require that you do ongoing review and analysis. (Transcribing might be postponed to a later date, but taking notes on the tape recordings is almost always essential and is generally manageable.) Finally, of course, a lot of your documentation will also be your normal record keeping of students' work—the process and product of their reading, writing, and inquiries—as well as their record keeping of their own learning. See Chapters 4, 7, 8, and 9 for a range of other possibilities.

PREPARING FOR OBSERVATION

Another important issue regarding inquiry is deciding five questions of observation (who, what, when, how, and why). You can't observe everything all the time, so it is important to prepare for observation. Of course, your initial questions may help you

---

Include descriptive and reflective writing.

Altrichter et al. (1993); Hobson (1996)

Descriptive and reflective writing is sometimes called "raw" notes and "cooked" notes.

Hubbard & Power (2003)

Power (1996, 1999)

Document the steps of your instructional trail.

Document your data trail.

The physical size along with other characteristics of your research journal is a personal choice.

Hobson (1996)

Preparation for observation is critical.

Arhar et al. (2001); Altrichter et al. (1993)

Five questions about
observation

Who?

What?

When?

How?

Why?

with direction—see also Figure G.1 on the teaching–learning relationship. However, the following may also be helpful:

Who are you going to observe? Are you going to observe all students (for short times during a certain period), or several students or groups?

What are you going to observe? Are you going to observe a certain sequence of events in a particular routine, a student's behavior, or a certain aspect of your own behavior?

When will you do the observation and how long is it likely to take? Deciding the times when you will make your observations beforehand enables you to devote your energies to them and makes the inquiry manageable. Will it be during a particular time of the classroom day when a certain activity or routine occurs, such as during writing workshop, teacher-led Reading Aloud*, or Buddy Reading*? Or perhaps the focus might be on a particular child or group that requires that you note and record information during several times or even at specific intervals of the whole day. How long will you observe—for a thematic unit, a grading term, or the whole year?

How are you going to observe? Besides your observations (and the notes on these observations), this usually involves the the kinds of data sources you will use. Will you use audio or video recorders? Will you gather student work as data artifacts, and so forth?

Why are you doing the observation? What assumptions or expectations are you bringing to the observation? You want to strive for objectivity in observation, but your pre-judgments cannot be avoided. Thus, if you clarify ahead of time what your theories or preconceived ideas are about the context you are about to observe, you can more easily deal with them when you do your reflective writing. Your reasons for observation are also related to potential contributions of certain activities for supporting student learning.

Many TRs, such as Janet in Chapter 9, lay out the inquiry data possibilities along with their plans for the kinds of evaluative information they desire during a thematic unit so that they can envision what their inquiry will really involve and better decide what they can actually accomplish. This might lead to their cutting down on what they had initially considered or the amount of data they will gather by limiting the times, students, or groups they will concentrate on. Similarly, STRs will need to identify exactly when they think they will focus in on some aspect of teaching–learning so they can incorporate these inquiry facets in their planning of their lessons or activities. If not, they may be overwhelmed by the whole process.

What are the particulars on the ways in which you will actually to do the observation? Are you going to take "in-the-midst" notes, perhaps while you sit back but near students who are having literature discussions? Or, will you take "after-the-fact" notes that are fleshed out later in your journal using the brief fragments you jotted down while you are actually interacting with students? Will you need Post-it Notes or index cards, or a form you developed for the observation? Or will you briefly note the contextual features of an activity or routine that will be audiotaped or videotaped, and make your more detailed notes when you review the tapes at the end of the day? (See how teachers of prototypes in Chapter 4 indicated the certain times and ways of inquiry.)

"In-the-midst" versus "after-the-fact" notes

Power (1996, 1999)

Strategies for Analyzing Your Journal Entries and Other Data

Take a problem-solving stance to data analysis.

Data analysis is a way of "seeing and then seeing again." It involves re-viewing to bring order, structure, and meaning to your data. Analyzing data is frequently a difficult part of the inquiry process so it is useful to view it as a puzzle that you can approach with playfulness and risk taking. Remember that you are attempting to answer *your own questions,* so there are no correct answers here. It is these efforts that will lead you to the deep "seeing" of the underlying patterns that might be lurking under the surface. Going back to your initial inquiry questions—how they might have been modified, or how new ones have evolved—may all guide your first steps of analysis.

Although it can be said that all teacher inquiry is ongoing, there is a time in an inquiry where there is a feeling of closure or a sense that it is "done." Perhaps it is the end of a particular thematic unit, such as the ones that have been illustrated in Chapter 4. Or for STRs it might be the end of your fieldwork in a certain university quarter or semester. Or maybe there is a place where some classroom routine, for example, some way of doing Literature Response Groups*, seems to be going well for you and your students, at least for this year. Thus, it is at the end of this period that a major part of the data analysis usually occurs.

However, we recommend that you do early cycles of analysis and do not postpone everything to the end. Of course, for every cycle of action research, data analysis has been employed in some sense. We are here referring to the more *overt* sitting back to see where you are so far. Two major approaches can be used in an ongoing fashion— developing categories and coding data, and making data summaries—and can help you both monitor and evaluate your inquiry and keep you from being completely overwhelmed by the whole process.

> Ongoing cycles of data analysis are recommended.
>
> Arhar et al. (2001); Altrichter et al. (1993)

Developing Categories and Coding Data

At regular intervals of your inquiry, it is useful to try to identify emerging themes and patterns. Read through your journal. See if you can find similar issues or topics being covered. Create tentative categories to capture the patterns you are noting. List on a separate sheet these categories by giving each of them a short name or phrase that makes sense to you, along with an abbreviated code. Then write in the code next to your notes with a pencil. (You might also want to number instances of the same code.) You want to use a pencil in this initial coding because, as your inquiry progresses, you may further differentiate or collapse categories, or change your categories altogether, and the crossing out of ink-written codes usually makes a mess of your data notes.

> Try to identify emerging themes and patterns in your data and give them particular codes.

Sometimes "counting" these categories can provide useful information about the status or shape of your inquiry so far. For example, perhaps your inquiry had to do with your understanding students' literature responses. Because you note that only some types are being made by your students, you might realize that it is time for a Focus Lesson* to help students consider other possible responses. If your inquiry is more related to your own teaching strategies, then the patterns of your interactions with students— say, in content conferences over their writing—might lead you to take stock and try another approach in talking to them.

> An initial, tentative "count" of instances of particular categories sometimes helps to make instructional decisions.

Making Data Summaries

Data summaries should be no more than two pages long. They might address the following questions:

> Make your data summaries short.
>
> Altrichter et al. (1993)

1. What are the contexts in which the data were collected? What methods of collection (and why?) were used? Thus, these questions may be similar to the questions you posed for yourself in preparing for observation. However, these might have changed so it is important to reiterate them in your summaries.
2. What are the most important, surprising, and informative "facts" in the data?
3. In what ways do the data give rise to new questions, points of view, ideas, or suggestions?
4. In what ways do the data suggest your next steps, in terms of further data collection, analysis, or action?

It is also frequently useful to cross-reference the relevant journal sections (or categories or codes therein—see above), other notes you might have made on your reviews on audiotapes or videotapes, or students' work, and so on next to your answers to these questions listed previously.

Tips for "Publishing" Teacher Inquiry

The major purpose of teacher inquiry is to promote teachers' development of their own explicit, principled basis for making changes to their own teaching in order to improve the learning opportunities for their students. Thus, it isn't the reporting of the findings for others per se that is so important, but the value of the experiences that the teacher researcher had in undertaking the inquiry.

The formats, or genres, of writing up teacher inquiry frequently have to do with the purposes you have for reporting or sharing your findings and the audience with whom you wish to communicate. Thus, just as student "publishing" might be seen as "sharing" and take on many forms (see Chapters 6 and 7), reporting the findings of the inquiry work of TRs and STRs can also be expressed in diverse ways. No matter how it is reported, the following ideas can be useful:

- Be sure that you explain the context of your inquiry: who the participants are, what was done, and why. This contextualization enables others to relate your account to their own experiences.
- Tell about your own theory-in-action, interpretive framework, or your stance and ideologies or values regarding your inquiry and your interpretations and conclusions.
- Don't feel that you have to report on every single data "fact" of your inquiry. Choose the major themes and patterns as they relate to your inquiry questions and be sure that you organize them, perhaps with subheadings in your presentation or text.
- Give examples and illustrations of your findings. Also, in presenting your examples, help readers understand your interpretation of these examples or why you think they are significant as evidence of the themes you found. Sometimes TRs and STRs just make examples "stand on their own" to tell the whole story. Instead they must explain to readers in the body of their report just *how* certain features of the examples are to be illustrative of their points.
- When relevant, weave the ideas of the other work you might have read that you think is related to your inquiry topic—*but* be sure that you explicate these ideas through *your voice*. Sometimes TRs and STRs fill their reports with so many quotes from others that their stance on the ideas gets muffled or even lost.
- Try to be honest in telling the difficulties and vulnerabilities that arose for you in your inquiry. Include any findings that didn't seem to fit that you might still be concerned about. Sometimes TRs' and STRs' inquiry reports sound so rosy that others reading them either do not find the account credible enough to try out the ideas and benefit from them, or if they do attempt them and end up with unsatisfactory results, they blame themselves, or worse, their students.
- Because teacher inquiry is such an ongoing enterprise, tell about new questions or ideas that you plan to pursue in future inquiries and why.

Inquiry Possibilities for Student Teacher Researchers

STRs find themselves in different contexts than TRs. They are often in a cultural context where a classroom mentor teacher and his or her students have already developed norms, some of which are very subtle and hard to recognize. Also, much of what is done in terms of their teaching usually has to be okayed or is directed by the mentor teacher and the university or college instructor. This makes many student teachers reluctant to "step on someone's toes" in *their* steps in teaching and doing inquiry.

In contrast, TRs often need to "step on their *own* toes"—that is, to make the everyday or normal classroom activities and experiences *become* strange. Frequently,

---

There is a range of formats or genres to publish or share the findings of teacher inquiry.

Arhar et al. (2001); Cochran-Smith & Lytle (1993); Stringer (2004)

Explain the context of your inquiry.

Describe your own personal theory or interpretive frame.

Share major themes and patterns.

Give illustrative examples for your findings.

Use your own voice when you relate others' work on your inquiry topic.

Include descriptions about the difficulties of the research process and any remaining concerns you have.

Tell about new questions that have emerged.

The settings for STRs and TRs are different.

teacher research isn't gathering new information about teaching and learning as much as it is reconsidering or "REsearching" information you already have. Thus, a major goal of teacher inquiry is to make your tacit, implicit assumptions and interpretative frameworks more explicit so you can examine and evaluate them.

Student teachers find *everything* strange in a fieldwork setting and they are sometimes even frightened about how they might get through a day of teaching. As a result, they are often eager to find the right methods to teach a particular content or reading or writing and may see inquiry as some "extra" activity rather than seeing it as an integral feature of teaching. However, we think inquiry for student teachers is also important for three major reasons. First, although they find a classroom initially strange, they very easily get caught up with how things are done in their fieldwork setting and try to do exactly what they see mentor teachers doing. They quickly become socialized into certain approaches without thinking about or evaluating whether or why they should be done. Second, they may take on the methods that are being stressed in the university classroom without examining how they might or might not be related to their own developing core principles or beliefs about teaching and learning. Also, they may not consider the theoretical underpinnings that inform these methods or examine what the implications might be if these methods are uncritically replicated with classroom students' whose status may be different in terms of cultural, class, gender, and linguistic background. Third, they can learn with the help of their peers, mentor teachers, and university instructors, strategies for teacher inquiry as they are becoming teachers. Many of these skills involve ways to do careful kid-watching, thereby also enabling them to acquire useful assessment techniques.

Teacher education programs at universities or colleges usually include several fieldwork or practicum experiences. Early ones may involve mostly observation, or teaching one student or a small group. Subsequently, they may begin to develop and implement various lessons with the whole class, or complete a project with students for part of the school day for several days or weeks. They then graduate to the final experience where a student teacher takes on the teaching responsibilities for several weeks (most of the quarter or semester). Thus, the teaching experiences for STRs will vary and the contexts in which they are placed for their teaching efforts will also be quite different. Here we suggest five possible ways that STRs might be engaged in inquiry, which might be chosen and modified depending on the various factors noted previously.

Having a collaborative group to share ideas throughout the inquiry process is useful for all of the possibilities. Moreover, reports or presentations of inquiries could and should be shared with a range of audience (including university classmates and instructors, mentor teachers, fieldwork setting teachers, and so forth).

Class Inquiry

Class inquiries may be useful during early field experiences. Here your particular university or college class might choose a specific topic to investigate. For example, you might study how reading, writing, or a specific content area is taught in your respective fieldwork settings. Or you may decide to collect data on how girls and boys are treated differently in the classroom in general or during certain particular content area instruction. Another inquiry might center around examining the various interactions that occur between the teacher and the students in teacher-directed versus collaborative activities (see Chapter 2) and how they result in different patterns of classroom discourse. And even another possibility might be the ways students use text and images in different content areas, or how various graphic organizers are employed in Student-Directed Inquiry*.

These inquiries would begin in broad brushstrokes, which individual STRs would narrow down, as you meet regularly to report on your data and the methods and strategies you have employed to do your descriptive and reflective writing. It is especially

Inquiry conducted by STRs is important because it enables them to better examine familiar classroom activities and interactions, explore how methods are related to their developing personal theories about teaching–learning, and develop useful kid-watching strategies.

The possibilities for inquiry by student teacher researchers will vary.

The entire university class studies the same topic in their respective field settings.

useful for those of you who are working in the same grade to meet to discuss your ongoing findings. By sharing your data, you can begin to discover common patterns found in first- or fourth-grade teaching–learning, for example, but also begin to see how different instructional routines are done in your respective settings. As these various grade-level groups report to the university class as a whole, another facet of your inquiry could be facilitated, namely, trying to tease out which classroom student behaviors in your fieldwork settings may be developmental and which may be influenced by instructional patterns.

These class inquiries may occur throughout the semester or quarter or for a specified number of weeks. Toward the end, they may also include your own inquiry of your own efforts in teaching that has to do with the topic of the class study. These action plans would be based on the themes or patterns your group had discovered so far in your findings.

Individual STR reports may be written, which would include data analysis of the respective grade-level group data as well their own individual teaching. Or each group might write up its findings that would be part of a whole-class report.

Focus Inquiry Lesson

Focus Inquiry Lessons transform the traditional lesson plans.

As you begin to have more experience in the fieldwork setting and mentor teachers begin to give you more teaching responsibilities, you may be asked to plan specific lessons for groups of students or the whole class, all of which can be occasions for inquiry. Typical lesson plans have student teachers describing their plans for the lesson ahead of time, which are frequently checked by the mentor or university instructor. These lesson plans include the purpose or rationale of the lesson, materials, and steps the STR plans to use and take in implementing the lesson. The idea of Focus Inquiry Lessons transforms these typical lesson formats to ones where you also create questions of inquiry for yourself, as well as how you might collect data during the lesson. For example, say you are thinking of reading a story picture book on a topic or theme of the current curriculum. You might have already taken journal notes on how the mentor teacher does Read-Alouds* and/or how you might have read aloud a book to students previously. That is, you may have already completed several cycles of action research on this classroom routine and are now ready to develop a new action plan based on these findings. As described previously, you may generate questions that are related on either side of the teaching–learning relationship. Perhaps this time the concern is around teaching issues because you have noticed that you, and maybe even your mentor teacher, seem to be asking all of the questions in the read-aloud sessions, thereby controlling most of the talk in the discussions. Thus, you might consider the following kinds of questions: In what ways can I encourage *students'* responses to the book? Also, in what ways can I promote more cross-discussions—where students talk to each other about what they think about the book instead of directing all of their remarks to me? You decide to try out at least three strategies: (1) pause frequently while you read the book and look to students with an expectant manner; (2) use some very open questions, such as "What do think so far?" or "Any comments?", and to promote cross-discussion specifically; (3) try to have students address their remarks to others by saying frequently, "What's your ideas on that? Could you turn around to tell [child's name] your thoughts?"

You might take very abbreviated "in-the-midst" descriptive notes on Post-it Notes during the session, which you would expand and elaborate on in your research journal afterward. (You might also audiotape the session and transcribe sections that reflect the major features of the discourse—that is, identify where your strategies were or were not successful.)

The value of Focus Inquiry Lessons is that it helps you avoid trying to teach "perfect" lessons or worry about using the "right" teaching methods. It makes you think about your own core principles that you are developing about teaching–learning.

Case Study Inquiry

As the term implies, this is an inquiry that focuses on one case, a particular student, in the fieldwork setting, which can be done at any level of your fieldwork experiences. Here you attempt to understand what the curriculum or instructional routines of the classroom might be like from the perspective of this child. You "shadow" the child's behavior in various activities, his or her reactions to them, his or her interactions with peers and the mentor and yourself (and the gym or art teacher). You might find out other background information from your mentor teacher or other teachers your case student might have had in previous years. You may also implement various kid-watching activities with him or her—for example, do a miscue analysis, take a dictation, and collect and analyze writing samples written across the curriculum (see Chapter 8 for other possibilities).

In this inquiry you are raising questions mostly about student learning, but throughout you are also reflecting on how that learning and how his or her attitudes as a learner might have been influenced by instructional techniques and strategies. Thus, this inquiry enables you to clarify and make explicit your own connections between teaching and learning.

Case study inquiry focuses on a particular child (or group) in the classroom setting.

Mini-Thematic Project Inquiry

This inquiry is a possibility usually after STRs have already have had some teaching experiences in fieldwork settings. In the university classroom, you might have worked on developing thematic units similar to the ones illustrated in Chapter 4, perhaps with a buddy or in small groups. However, you might not have implemented any of them yet. Here you attempt to collaborate and negotiate with the mentor teacher to develop a mini-thematic unit—one perhaps that would go for a three- or four-week period. A major characteristic of this small unit would be student-directed inquiry projects to teach certain curricular content that the mentor would identify as important to be taught later in the school term and toward the last few weeks of your university quarter or semester. You would develop small WEBs for the content topic, think of the essential questions that would guide the activities and inquiry invitations for classroom students, collect the books and other materials you will need, and plan and outline the specific activities and times during the school day you would implement the mini-unit project during the three-week period. In other words, you don't take on a large thematic unit, such as the ones depicted in Chapter 4, but instead only some portions or "nodes" of one. Usually these projects involve a particular subject-area focus, but include the integration of talking, reading, and writing.

Mini-thematic unit inquiries focus on classroom student-directed inquiry projects around a "node" or subtopic of a thematic unit.

As you create your WEB and plans, you begin to think about a specific aspect of your implementation for your inquiry. Because this is likely to be a big step in your teaching and orchestrating of curriculum, it is important to be selective on your inquiry topic. You will have to decide whether you want to raise questions about your own teaching strategies or whether you will focus more on students' learning (see Figure G.1). Perhaps, because the classroom students have never conducted student inquiries in social studies (maybe the mentor teacher relies on the social studies textbook), you might focus on questions around how you will scaffold their first experience in the inquiry process. Using the ideas in Chapter 7 (Organizing/Monitoring Student-Directed Inquiry Projects*), you set up the times and methods you will use to study your efforts in this area. You will have to keep track of the larger picture in order to manage the whole project, but as you begin several cycles of the action research, you may narrow its focus to how you will try to provide feedback to students in the course of their inquiries and their reactions to any Focus Lessons* you end up having as a result of what you observe. To make the inquiry even more manageable, you might decide to take *detailed notes* only on a small group of students or several case students from several groups. (Asking your mentor teacher to take notes on particular students is also a good idea.)

If you decide to have your inquiry emphasize students' learning, you might examine how students' strategies in finding the answers to their own inquiry questions as they read various children's literature books or other resources (including the textbook) you have brought in for their use have worked. Again, you might concentrate on several students' approaches to document in greater detail to understand their difficulties and successes in finding the data they need for their projects.

As you decide on the specific contexts that you will observe, and specify your inquiry questions, you will also consider how you will collect your data. Besides your research journal in which you will keep track of issues of the whole project, you might decide to fashion a Status of the Class* sheet that lists your case students. Here you will jot down in-the-midst notes of what you say to them during their research, or if you focus on students' learning, what these students employed as strategies during their research. You will also go over students' inquiry logs (see Chapter 7) as other data for your inquiry. In addition, you think that after several cycles of observation, you might be able to identify some useful categories to use for the rest of the inquiry. These categories, then, might be included on the status sheet, enabling you to make your notes more organized and easier to write down.

Thematic-Unit Inquiry during Student Teaching

Usually STRs do their last fieldwork experience during a quarter or semester of student teaching. And for a large part of this term, they are responsible for developing a curricular unit. Here then is the opportunity for you to create and implement a larger version of a thematic unit. And in many ways you might try to develop inquiries similar to the ones that are depicted in Chapter 4.

Or, drawing on the ideas described earlier, you may fashion a series of smaller inquiries—perhaps a case student (or group) inquiry, several focus inquiry lessons, and a mini-thematic unit inquiry.

Because several STRs usually meet weekly with a supervisory university or college instructor, it may be possible to have a class inquiry as well. That is, you and your fellow STRs might choose several inquiries on common topics in your respective classroom settings. For example, you could examine the classroom discourse of various settings (see the Activity 2 in Chapter 2). Or you might all try to implement some particular routine (e.g., students doing Book Talks*, peer conferencing, or math journals). Another might be analyzing students' writing of a particular genre—informational texts, realistic fiction, or historical fiction.

Summary

Teacher research represents many things. First, of course, it is an important way in which teachers make sense of, and become reflective about, teaching and learning in their classrooms and schools. Just as inquiry empowers students, it also empowers teachers to be active learners, to construct their own knowledge, and to take a more authoritative stance toward their practice. The knowledge generated by teachers is fundamentally particular, which is also its major contribution, for it is embedded in the various social contexts of everyday teaching and learning. To sustain and support teacher research, it is important to create communities of teacher inquiry. STRs usually have other students who can serve as these communities. However, for TRs, sometimes just one other teacher at a school may provide such a community. Sometimes district or local organizations of teacher researchers are available. Ways to continue to connect with university faculty may be also a possibility. In any case, getting ongoing feedback, ideas for literature sources on topics that are being investigated, insights into how to analyze and interpret data gathered, and so forth, are all areas that such inquiry communities can offer.

Margin notes:

Thematic-unit inquiries usually occur during the student teaching experience where full-fledged units are developed and implemented.

Teacher inquiry empowers teachers.

See Pappas & Zecker (2001a, 2001b) for examples for urban teacher inquiries in which power relationships with students were changed.

See two online journals for teacher research (NETWORKS website at www.oise.utoronto.ca/~ctd/networks and ACTION RESEARCH INTERNATIONAL website at http://scu.edu.au/schools/gcm.

In sum, teachers' theories reflect certain ways of knowing because they are grounded in practice. Teacher research can also be cumulative and accessible to others, thereby playing an important role in the formation of the knowledge base of teaching in the larger educational community.

 ## References

Altrichter, H., Posch, P., & Somekh, B. (1993). *Teachers investigate their work: An introduction to the methods of action research.* London: Routledge.

Arhar, J. M., Holly, M. L., & Kasten, W. C. (2001). Action research for teachers: Traveling the yellow brick road. Upper Saddle River, NJ: Merrill Prentice Hall.

Bartolome, L. I. (1994). Beyond the methods fetish: Toward a humanizing pedagogy. *Harvard Educational Review, 64,* 173–194.

Cochran-Smith, M., & Lytle, S. (1993). *Inside/Outside: Teacher research and knowledge.* New York: Teachers College Press.

Cummins, J. (1994). From coercive to collaborative relations of power in the teaching of literacy. In B. M. Ferdman, R. M. Weber, & A. G. Ramirez (Eds.), *Literacy across languages and cultures* (pp. 295–331). Albany: State University of New York Press.

Edelesky, C. (1994). Education for democracy. *Language Arts, 71,* 252–257.

Fischer, J. (1996). Open to ideas: Developing a framework for your research. In G. Burnaford, J. Fischer, & D. Hobson (Eds.), *Teachers doing research: Practical possibilities* (pp. 33–55). Mahwah, NJ: Lawrence Erlbaum.

Graves, D. (2001). Build energy with colleagues. *Language Arts, 79,* 12–19.

Gutierrez, K., Rymes, B., & Larson, J. (1995). Script, counterscript, and the underlife in the classroom: James Brown versus *Brown v. Board of Education. Harvard Educational Review, 65,* 445–471.

Hobson, D. (1996). Beginning with the self: Using autobiography and journal writing in teacher research. In G. Burnaford, J. Fischer, & D. Hobson (Eds.), *Teachers doing research: Practical possibilities* (pp. 1–17). Mahwah, NJ: Lawrence Erlbaum.

Hubbard, R. S., & Power, B. M. (1999). *Living the questions: A guide for teacher-researchers.* York, ME: Stenhouse

Hubbard, R. S., & Power, B. M. (2003). *The art of classroom inquiry: A handbook for teacher-researchers.* Portsmouth, NH: Heinemann.

Pappas, C. C. (1999). Becoming literate in the borderlands. In A. Goncu (Ed.), *Children's engagement in the world: A sociocultural perspective* (pp. 228–260). Cambridge: Cambridge University Press.

Pappas, C. C., & Zecker, L. B. (Eds.). (2001a). *Teacher inquiries in literacy teaching-learning: Learning to collaborate in elementary urban classrooms.* Mahwah, NJ: Lawrence Erlbaum.

Pappas, C. C., & Zecker, L. B. (Eds.). (2001b). *Working with teacher researchers in urban classrooms: Transforming literacy curriculum genres.* Mahwah, NJ: Lawrence Erlbaum.

Power, B. M. (1996). *Taking note: Improving your observational notetaking.* York, ME: Stenhouse.

Power, B. M. (1999). When to write: Strategies to find time for notetaking. In R. S. Hubbard & B. M. Power, *Living the questions: A guide for teacher-researchers* (pp. 105–109). York, ME: Stenhouse.

Stringer, E. (2004). *Action research in education.* Upper Saddle River, NJ: Pearson Education.

Wells, G. (1994). *Changing schools from within: Creating communities of inquiry.* Toronto, Canada: Ontario Institute for Studies in Education Press. (Distributed by Heinemann Press.)

Wells, G. (Ed.). (2001). *Action, talk, and text: Learning and teaching through inquiry.* New York: Teachers College Press.

Zeichner, K. M., & Liston, D. P. (1996). *Reflective teaching: An introduction.* Mahwah, NJ: Lawrence Erlbaum.

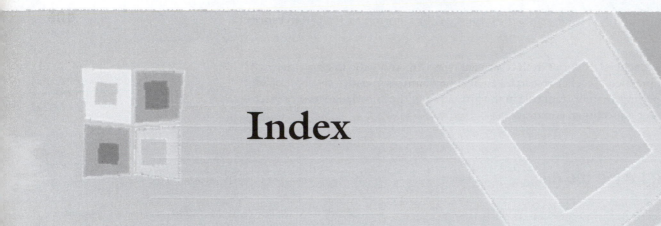

Index

Credits

Figure 1.1 & 1.2 on pp. 15 & 18 from Gordon Wells, *Learning through Interaction: The Study of Language Development*. New York: Cambridge University Press, 1981. Reprinted with permission of Cambridge University Press.

Figure 1.4 on p. 25 from Brian Wildsmith, *The Owl and the Woodpecker*. Oxford, England: Oxford University Press, 1971. Copyright © Brian Wildsmith. Reprinted by permission of Oxford University Press.

Figure 1.5 on p. 26 from Brian Wildsmith, *Squirrels*. Oxford, England: Oxford University Press, 1974. Copyright © Brian Wildsmith. Reprinted by permission of Oxford University Press.

Figure 6.1 on p. 250 from *Mouse,* text copyright © 1985 by Sara Bonnett Stein, illustration copyright © 1985 by Manuel Garcia. Reprinted by permission of Harcourt, Inc.

Figure 6.1 on p. 250 from Susan Bonners, *Panda*. Copyright © 1978 by Susan Bonners. Used by permission of Dell Books, a division of Random House, Inc.

Excerpt on p. 251 from *Mojave* by Diane Siebert. Illustrated by Wendell Minor (Crowell). Text copyright © 1988 by Diane Siebert. Illustrations copyright © 1988 by Wendell Minor. All selections by permission of HarperCollins Publishers, Inc.

Excerpt on p. 252 from *The See-through Zoo: How Glass Animals Are Made,* by Suzanne Haldane. Text and photographs copyright © 1984 by Suzanne Haldane. Reprinted by permission of Alfred A. Knopf, a division of Random House, Inc.

Table 6.3 on p. 259 from Susan L. Lytel and Morton Botel, PCRP II: *Reading, Writing and Talking across the Curriculum*. Harrisburg, PA: Pennysylvania Department of Education, 1988. Reprinted by permission of the authors.

Figure 7.4 on p. 289 from "Slave Narrative." Courtesy of the Ohio Historical Society, Columbus, Ohio.

Figure 7.5 on p. 290, photograph of a 1930s sorghum mill worked by a mule. Courtesy of the Kentucky Department for the Libraries and Archives, Frankfort, Kentucky.

Figure 8.28 on p. 387, adapted from *Childwatching at Playgroup and Nursey School*, 1980, by Kathy Sylva, Carolyn Roy, and Marjorie Painter. Reprinted by permission of Blackwell Publishers, Oxford, England.